THE AMERICANS
The National Experience

Daniel J. Boorstin has been senior historian of the Smithsonian Institution, Washington, D.C., director of the National Museum of History and Technology and Preston and Sterling Mortin Distinguished Service Professor of American History at the University of Chicago where he taught for twenty-five years. He has won many prestigious prizes for his work, including the Pulitzer Prize in 1974 for *The Democratic Experience*. He was also the Librarian of Congress from 1975 to 1987, during which period public use of the library more than doubled.

Dr Boorstin has spent a good deal of his life viewing America from the outside, first in England where he was a Rhodes scholar at Balliol College, Oxford, winning a coveted 'double-first'. More recently he has been visiting professor of American History at the University of Rome and at Kyoto University, consultant to the Social Science Research Center at the University of Puerto Rico, the first incumbent of the chair of American History at the Sorbonne, and Pitt Professor of American History and Institutions and a Fellow of Trinity College, Cambridge University, which awarded him its Litt.D. degree.

Also by Daniel J. Boorstin

Companion volumes in THE AMERICANS trilogy
The Colonial Experience (Phoenix Press)
The Democratic Experience (Phoenix Press)

Other Works
The Creators (Phoenix Press)
The Discoverers (Phoenix Press)
The Seekers (Phoenix Press)

The Mysterious Science of the Law
The Lost World of Thomas Jefferson
The Genius of American Politics
America and the Image of Europe
The Image: A Guide to Pseudo-Events in America
The Decline of Radicalism
The Sociology of the Absurd
Democracy and its Discontents
The Republic of Technology
The Exploring Spirit
The Republic of Letters
Hidden History
The Chicago History of American Civilization (Ed.; 27 volumes)
An American Primer (Ed)
American Civilization (Ed)

THE AMERICANS
The National Experience

Daniel J. Boorstin

"There is nothing like the
elbow room of a new country."
JOHN TYLER

**PHOENIX
PRESS**

5 UPPER SAINT MARTIN'S LANE
LONDON
WC2H 9EA

For Ruth

A PHOENIX PRESS PAPERBACK

First published in Great Britain
by Weidenfeld & Nicolson in 1966
This paperback edition published in 2000
by Phoenix Press,
a division of The Orion Publishing Group Ltd,
Orion House, 5 Upper St Martin's Lane,
London WC2H 9EA

A CIP catalogue record for this book
is available from the British Library.

Printed in Great Britain by
Clays Ltd, St Ives plc

ISBN 1 84212 075 1

NEW BEGINNINGS

In 1845, The Emigrants' Guide to Oregon and California *recorded Lansford W. Hastings' experience with his company of one hundred and sixty who set out overland from Independence, Missouri, on May 16, 1842:*

"Now, all was high glee, jocular hilarity, and happy anticipation, as we thus darted forward into the wild expanse, of the untrodden regions of the 'western world.' The harmony of feeling, the sameness of purpose, and the identity of interest, which here existed, seemed to indicate nothing but continued order, harmony and peace, amid all the trying scenes incident to our long and toilsome journey. But we had proceeded only a few days travel, from our native land of order and security, when the 'American character' was fully exhibited. All appeared to be determined to govern, but not to be governed. Here we were, without law, without order, and without restraint; in a state of nature, amid the confused, revolving, fragments of elementary society! Some were sad, while others were merry; and while the brave doubted, the timid trembled! Amid this confusion, it was suggested by our captain, that we 'call a halt,' and pitch our tents, for the purpose of enacting a code of laws, for the future government of the company. The suggestion was promptly complied with, when all were required to appear in their legislative capacities."

*   *   *

The nation was beginning not at one time or place, but again and again, under men's very eyes. Americans were forming new communities and reforming old communities all over the wild expanse of the western world. Within less than a century after the American Revolution—even before the Civil War—the fringe of colonial settlements, ocean-bound to their mother countries, would become a continent-nation.

CONTENTS

BOOK ONE

COMMUNITY

"America was meant to be everything. . . .
There are many soils and many climates included within the boundary line of the United
States; many *countries;* and one rule cannot be
laid down for all."

HARRIET MARTINEAU

AMERICA grew in the search for community. Between the Revolution and the Civil War the young nation flourished not in discovery but in search. It prospered not from the perfection of its
ways but from their fluidity. It lived with the constant belief that
something else or something better might turn up. A by-product
of looking for ways of living together was a new civilization, whose
strength was less an idealism than a willingness to be satisfied with
less than the ideal. Americans were glad enough to keep things
growing and moving. When before had men put so much faith in
the unexpected?

PART ONE

THE VERSATILES

New Englanders

> "I sing New England, as she lights her fire
> In every Prairie's midst. . . ."
>
> WILLIAM ELLERY CHANNING

THE American Puritans' "City upon a Hill" prospered because it was a City on the Sea. How different the story of New England, or of America, might have been if they had built their Zion in a sequestered inland place—some American Switzerland, some mountain-encircled valley! The sea helped New Englanders find resources, not in the land, but in themselves and in the whole world. The sea was the great opener of their markets and their minds.

Who could have predicted that Puritans would become Yankees? That a people noted in the Old World for stiff-necked dogmatism would on this side become exemplars of ingenuity? That an Old English sect notoriously single of purpose would become New England paragons of versatility? That Englishmen famous for keeping their eye on the path to heaven would develop an uncanny vision for new markets and a facility for shifting investments?

New Englanders proved that Americans could range the world without being uprooted, that they could cling to ancestral headquarters. The sea carried abroad hundreds of tight little shipboard communities who adventured without ever leaving New England.

New England's cosmopolitanism somehow kept her the most colonial part of the new nation. The same framework that saved 17th-century

3

American Puritans from utopianism helped their descendants fence in their shifting problems. More than most other Americans, New Englanders commanded Old World techniques. They knew how to flex Old World technicalities to seize New World opportunities.

New Englanders were the Transplanters in the first epoch of national life. What the Virginia country gentlemen had been to the English squire, what Thomas Jefferson was to Squire Western, that is what the Boston entrepreneur was to his Manchester counterpart. The contribution of New England—a stronghold of conservatism and radicalism, of genteel Brahmins and of unwashed immigrants—to the new nation was far out of proportion to her numbers or her extent. Geography, population, and ideas made her a cultural limbo between an old world that refused to die and a new world not quite born.

1

The Sea Leads Everywhere

THE SEA WAS a path direct from Old to New England, from Babylon to Zion. It was both a waterway from colony to mother country and a gulf that separated colonists from poverty, decadence, and dynastic conflict. It was a highway to the world.

The sea was impartial. It carried anything anywhere: Puritans and Bibles and theology texts to build a City upon a Hill; rum to West Africa in exchange for slaves to be carried to overwork and death in the West Indies; opium from Smyrna to China. The versatility of the sea was the versatility of New England.

The sea was empty and had no culture of its own—except that which seafarers made for themselves on shipboard. This was a blessing for New Englanders whom it enabled to go everywhere without leaving home. The earliest Puritans sailing to New England had huddled together, threatened only by God and the elements. Their new community life began at sea; the Mayflower Compact was made even before they landed. Shipboard sermons like Winthrop's "Model of Christian Charity" cemented their community while it still traveled. Unlike later companies of Americans who moved westward on the land, seaborne communities en route were not overwhelmed by sights of new plants or new animals nor threatened by savage tribes. Travelers by land saw new landscapes, they encamped, dispersed, and made homes as they went. But the very ships which brought New Englanders to their Promised Land kept them together and made them more compact, more insular, and more united when they arrived than when they had left.

5

By the early 19th century, the New Englander had learned to deal with the banian in Calcutta, the co-huang and the mandarin in China, but his peculiar talent was his inability to forget his native land. The sea captain seldom lost his nostalgia for a farm and chickens in the land of his childhood. From his "Captain's Walk" on top of the farmhouse of his ideal retirement he looked back on the wandering ocean; but the sea never became his home. When Jefferson accused the merchant of being a man without a country he spoke with the provincial voice of the Old South and he showed his ignorance of New England. Virginians seldom understood the sea-roving spirit of the New Englander, who yearned more for his native land as he wandered farther from it. Jefferson's love of Virginia was an affection for Monticello and the familiar scene of his verandah. But the attachment of Massachusetts men to their "country"—the New England patriotism of the Adamses, Perkinses, Jacksons, Cabots, and Lees—while just as profound, was more diffuse. They were attached to a spiritual and commercial headquarters.

From the earliest days in Massachusetts the wealth of the sea offset the poverty of the land. "The aboundance of Sea-Fish are almost beyond beleeuing." Francis Higginson wrote in 1630, "and sure I whould scarce haue beleeued it except I had seene it with mine owne Eyes." The first settlers found not only mackerel, cod, bass, and lobster, but also "Heering, Turbot, Sturgion, Cuskes, Haddocks, Mullets, Eeles, Crabs, Muskles and Oysters." Before the end of the 17th century, fishing was the main industry of Massachusetts Bay. The codfish was to colonial Massachusetts what tobacco had been to colonial Virginia. If the Old Dominion was founded, as its hostile critics said, "on smoke," the Puritan Commonwealth was founded on salt water. New England's fishermen, like fisherfolk in other parts of the world, had their own kind of conservatism. It once seemed only a little less difficult to convert a codfisherman into a mackerel man or a whaler, than to make an Englishman into a Frenchman or an Italian. Yet, while tobacco and the newly dominant Southern crop, cotton, put Southern roots ever deeper into the soil, the fisheries drew New England out toward the world.

The commerce of the sea demanded versatility. It called for quick decisions and the willingness to jettison unprofitable cargo. It called for sale in Buenos Aires of whatever at the moment was unusually scarce there; for the ability to pick up unexpected bargains anywhere; for changing destination from Canton to Calcutta if war threatened or storms made the passage dangerous; for sudden disposal of the ship itself if the voyage could not go on with profit. Captain and supercargo had unfettered discretion to shift investment, to convert the voyage from one purpose to another, to give up and return home—to do whatever promised most.

By 1784, when the Massachusetts House of Representatives passed a resolution "to hang up the representation of a Codfish in the room where the House sit, as a memorial of the importance of the Cod-Fishery to the welfare of the Commonwealth" (a totem which kept its place into the mid-20th century) the sacred cod had more than earned its eminence. The Revolution itself was, in a sense, a by-product of the New England fisheries. For it was to serve her fishermen that New England colonists had built their own ships and so had begun to justify English jealousy of a colonial merchant marine. The gathering place of Massachusetts rebels, Faneuil Hall, which Daniel Webster called "the cradle of American liberty," was the gift of Peter Faneuil, a Boston merchant who had prospered by carrying New England codfish to distant markets.

The peak of the New England fisheries was passed ten years before the Revolution, when New Englanders were catching more fish, and their catch was a larger part of their income than it had ever been before or would ever be again. During the era of the Revolution, New England fishing dwindled, less from the force of English laws than from the distractions and demands of war. In 1774 the little town of Chatham, for example, still had twenty-seven codfishing vessels; ten years later there were only four or five. Fishing schooners were fitted out as privateers and peace-loving fishermen became fighting seamen.

Nothing did more to make Americans independent than this very War for Independence. New fortunes, like those of George Cabot (who had been commander of a codfishing vessel by his eighteenth birthday), came now from privateering. The great world outside the British Empire, once open only to the smuggler, tempted every New England merchant. John Adams of Massachusetts, with the slogan of "fisheries or no peace," secured extensive fishing rights all over British America in the treaty of peace with Great Britain in 1783. But at the War's end, while the fisheries did revive, it was the discovery of new markets for old commodities and new commodities for old markets that stirred New England imaginations.

There are countless examples of this search: stories of men long since forgotten—so commonplace was adventure in their day—and of commodities we hardly remember. As good as any is the story of Major Samuel Shaw and the marketing of ginseng.

The first American ship to reach China arrived at Canton on August 30, 1784. In charge of the business of that voyage was Major Samuel Shaw, Boston-born veteran of the American Revolution. When a young man in his late twenties, Shaw had fought at Trenton, Princeton, and Brandywine; he had suffered with General Washington at Valley Forge; he had witnessed the mutinies of the soldiers of Pennsylvania and New Jersey; and he had heard Washington deliver his tearful farewell to his officers in December, 1783. Early the next year, Shaw like many others re-entered civil life without property and burdened with debt. When some businessmen purchased the *Empress of China,* a ship of 360 tons, and organized a venture to export ginseng to Canton, they appointed Shaw supercargo. Leaving New York harbor in early 1784, he sailed eastward to the Cape Verde Islands, enjoyed the jovial ceremony of his first crossing of the equator, saw whale and swordfish, and after six months finally reached the exotic shores of Java and Macao en route to Canton.

Until these New Englanders carried the American flag to China it had been assumed that the whole annual Chinese consumption of ginseng—a rare herb found in North America as well as China and prized by Chinese physicians as an aphrodisiac and prolonger of life—would never be more than four tons. But this first American ship alone carried ten times that amount; within another year Americans more than doubled their ginseng exports to China. The demand and the price kept up. In exchange for ginseng, American businessmen secured tea and other marketable products of China which, in turn, produced additional good profits.

At first, as Shaw explains in his journal, the Chinese could not quite understand the distinction between Englishmen and Americans. "They styled us the *New People;* and when by the map we conveyed to them an idea of the extent of our country, with its present and increasing population, they were highly pleased at the prospect of so considerable a market for the production of their own empire."

No corner of the world remained untouched by these New Englandmen. In 1784 one of George Cabot's ships carried the first American flag to St. Petersburg in Russia. From Salem, vessels traded with the west coast of Africa, brought copal for varnish from Zanzibar on Africa's east coast, and rubber and overshoes from Brazil. Boston ships carried food to starving Irishmen. They picked up sandalwood in Hawaii or otterskins in British Columbia as currency for Chinese tea. Others played "hide-and-go-seek"—finding cheap hides in South America or California to supply the new shoe factories back home. They sought out the best coffees in the Southern Hemisphere, bought Peruvian bark to make quinine against malaria, jute for gunny sacks, linseed oil for paint and ink, shellac for ships and furniture.

Nothing was too big or too small, too exotic or too commonplace for New England enterprise. Salem quickly became the world headquarters for trade in the tiny peppercorn, which in the era before refrigeration was wanted everywhere. In 1791 the United States re-exported less than 500 pounds of pepper; in 1805, it re-exported 7,500,000 pounds, which comprised nearly the whole crop of Northwest Sumatra. The immense whale, long the staple of New Bedford and Nantucket, was pursued at mortal risk on voyages lasting as long as three years all over the North Atlantic and the South Pacific.

In distant places New England became a name for the new nation. At the source of otter skins on the northwest coast of North America, "Boston" became a synonym for the whole United States. In the 1830's, prosperous native merchants on South Pacific islands thought Salem "a country by itself, and one of the richest and most important sections of the globe."

New England seafaring enterprises were a broken, shifting pattern. Before the Revolution much of this business had been outside the law; afterwards much of it was as perilous and as uncertain as the new trade routes. By contrast, the adventurousness of more ancient seafaring peoples had frozen; in the Old World the profits of the sea ran in tradition-worn channels. In early 19th-century England, for example, seaborne commerce continued to be dominated by organizations like the East India Company whose history went back to Elizabethan days. Such organizations had their own long-established practices and were regulated by time-honored government policies. It was no accident that the British East India Company commonly provided berths for unenterprising younger sons or favorite nephews of rich families. Not only in England, but elsewhere in Europe, officers at sea, like those on land, were a branch of the ruling aristocracy. It was almost unheard of for a common seaman to become first mate or captain: he had neither the education, the language, the manners, nor the "background." In New England, however, young men starting as common seamen rose to command their own vessels. A Beverly sea captain who had begun as a foremast hand on a ship out of Salem could recall that every one of that ship's crew of thirteen had risen to become master of a vessel. Since New England had no ancient trading companies nor any rigid tradition of adventure, her enterprise was controlled by upstart Cabots, Jacksons, Lees, Higginsons, and Perkinses, ingenious at finding their own markets and making their own ways. She inherited no established aristocracy from which officers were drawn nor a deep-sea proletariat from which came the "old salts" of English fiction and folklore.

2

Inventing Resources: Ice for the Indies

NEW ENGLAND DID NOT raise pepper or coffee or sugar or cotton, or any other staple crop to sell the world. The greatest resource of New England was resourcefulness. Using the sea, New England versatility made the very menaces of the landscape into articles of commerce. "New England," went the common taunt, "produces nothing but granite and ice." The supreme proof of New England ingenuity was her ability to turn her rocky soil and heavy winters to profit.

Until almost the middle of the 19th century, ice for summer cooling had been a rare luxury. The ancient Romans had brought snow down from the mountains as a curiosity. But from the beginning of history, diet had been limited by the seasons. Generally speaking, fresh fruit and vegetables were available only when just ripe, meat only as it was slaughtered, milk only as it came fresh from the cow. A recipe for a syllabub about 1800 instructed the housewife: "Sweeten a quart of cyder with double refined sugar, grate nutmeg into it, then milk your cow into your liquor." Before the days of refrigeration, milk could be preserved only in the form of butter or cheese, and meat had to be dried or salted. Everything was spiced to lend variety or to conceal the staleness.

In the 18th century, ice cream was found in Paris, in London, or in the colonies only on aristocratic tables. Occasionally on the sideboard of a great English country house one might see a water cooler which used ice. An icehouse was part of the luxurious equipment of the palace of the royal governors of Virginia at Williamsburg, of Washington's Mount Vernon, of Jefferson's Monticello, and of Monroe's Ash Lawn. Before the end of the 18th century, a few Philadelphia families had got together to maintain an icehouse and at least one rich Cambridge estate had an icehouse of its own. But there had been almost no progress in the general use of refrigeration since that winter day in 1626 when Sir Francis Bacon caught a fatal chill while experimentally burying a chicken in the snow.

Since North American summers in the same latitude were hotter than those of Europe, food spoiled here even more quickly. Putrid meat, tainted poultry, rancid cream, and sour milk were items which unfriendly European tourists in the 18th and 19th centuries especially noted in the American cuisine.

Then, quite suddenly, in the half century before the Civil War, there was a greater increase in the consumption of ice than in the whole millennium before. By 1860 the household icebox (the word had lately been invented in America) was a commonplace in growing American cities; cookbooks took it for granted. Ice cream had become a common dish, described by *Godey's Lady Book* (August, 1850) as one of the necessities of life; a party without ice cream was said to be like a break-fast without bread or a dinner without a roast. Some New York families even had ice water all summer.

The rapid growth of cities put more and more people farther from sources of fresh milk, meat, and vegetables, while the increasing number of household refrigerators enlarged the demand for ice. New Orleans, which in the late 1820's consumed less than 400 tons of ice a year, in one decade increased its consumption tenfold, in another decade twenty-fold, and before the Civil War seventyfold. Within the same period ice consumption in such northern cities as New York and Boston increased almost as spectacularly. By the late 1830's, when New England merchants suffered from high tariffs and when Boston's carrying trade between Calcutta and Europe had fallen disastrously, the new ice industry provided a staple New England export which helped save the port of Boston and incidentally revived Boston's commerce to the East and West Indies.

The "Ice Age" of American diet—with its emphasis on sanitation, nutrition, and refreshment, on the health of the body rather than the pleasures of the palate—had begun. By mid-20th century, the word "ice" in various combinations had provided more new compounds than perhaps any other word in the American language.

The man who did more than anyone else to make ice an American institution was Frederic Tudor of Boston, who came to be known as the "Ice King." An enterprising businessman cast in a New England mold, he was no Horatio Alger hero. He succeeded not by the prosaic, abstemious virtues but by a flamboyant, defiant, energetic, and sometimes reckless spirit. He was not considerate and gentle, generous and frugal, but, on the contrary, he was imperious, vain, contemptuous of competitors, and implacable to enemies. While energetic in competition, he preferred legalized monopoly. He had not risen from poverty but, like many another substantial Massachusetts merchant, amassed wealth by exploiting all opportunities, including his family connections and his social position.

Tudor came of a prominent Boston family. His father, a Harvard graduate, had studied law in the office of John Adams, had served George Washington as judge-advocate-general and then built a prosperous law practice. His three brothers graduated from Harvard, but Frederic instead began in business at thirteen. It was he who gave his brothers em-

ployment and eventually recouped the family fortunes. Despite his om-
nivorous mind and insatiable curiosity, he idealized work and the life of
action. He distrusted the idle "academic" life and worried when, visiting
his brother John's room at Harvard one day, he found it littered with
the paint brushes and canvasses of John's roommate, the romantic
painter Washington Allston.

In the winter of 1805, when Tudor was barely twenty-one, his brother
William at a gay Boston party whimsically asked why the ice on nearby
ponds was not harvested and then sold at ports in the Caribbean. Frederic took up the suggestion, as if to prove that no enterprise was too
outlandish, no commodity too commonplace, for New England commerce. He purchased a notebook, calling it his "ice house diary," and
made his first entry on August 1, 1805 in what was to be a classic record
of New England business enterprise. On the leather cover he printed
the motto: "He who gives back at the first repulse and without striking
the second blow despairs of success[,] has never been, is not, and never
will be a hero in war, love or business."

All Boston derided him as a madman when, within the year, he invested ten thousand dollars in shipping 130 tons of ice to the sweltering
island of Martinique. He then went to Martinique to promote sales by
personally showing prospective customers how to preserve and use ice.
From St. Pierre's he wrote back on March 10, 1806:

> The man who keeps the Tivoli garden insisted ice creams could not
> be made in this country and that the ice itself would all thaw before
> he could get it home! I told him I had made them here; . . . I wrote
> an order for 40 lbs. of ice, and in a pretty warm tone directed the
> man to have his cream ready and that I would come to freeze it for
> him in the morning, which I did accordingly, being determined to spare
> no pains to convince these people that they can not only have ice but
> all the luxuries arising as well here as elsewhere. The Tivoli man
> recd. for these creams the first night $300; after this he was humble
> as a mushroom. . . .

But the Martinique venture lost nearly four thousand dollars when the
whole cargo melted within six weeks.

It was fifteen years before Tudor established the ice trade as a paying
business. During all this time he struggled: to secure legal monopolies
of the trade, and exclusive rights to build icehouses in Charleston,
Havana, and in the British and French West Indies; to dominate the
New England ponds which were the source of ice; to create a demand
for ice, iced drinks, ice cream, and ice-preserved fruit, meat, and milk
in every part of the world his ships could reach. For a while, Tudor
sold chilled beverages at the same price as unchilled beverages, hoping
to encourage a taste for cold drinks. He demonstrated the use of ice in
hospitals. Wherever he managed to build an efficient storage depot, he

had a great advantage against competitors: he would sell his ice at a penny a pound till his competitor's stock had all melted at the dock and then he would raise his price to recoup his profit. "Drink, Spaniards, and be cool," he exhorted the perspiring patrons of the West Indian coffee houses, "that I, who have suffered so much in the cause, may be able to go home and keep myself warm."

Had he not conquered the technical problems, none of this would have been possible. And he doggedly devoted himself to the task of designing an efficient icehouse. Deliberately risking yellow fever in Havana to experiment on the spot, he tried every conceivable kind of insulating material—straw, wood shavings, blankets. Watch in hand, he stood outside his Havana icehouse and measured the melting water hour by hour. He recorded the effects of changes in design and of opening the icehouse doors on the rate of melting. Finally he produced an economical and efficient design for an ice depot in tropical climates. The seasonal loss from melting in icehouses of the old underground type was over sixty per cent, but in Tudor's houses it was less than eight per cent.

To secure large quantities of ice for tropical areas, Tudor had to perfect a way of harvesting ice from New England ponds so that it could be conveniently transported and preserved. The early 19th-century ice harvests had been laboriously cut by hand into pieces of miscellaneous size. When a warm winter, like that of 1818, shortened the supply from New England ponds, the captain of a Boston brig would risk ship and crew to pry fragments off a Labrador iceberg with picks and crowbars. These irregularly shaped pieces were troublesome to ship and uneconomical to store. Ship captains were ordinarily willing enough to ballast ice instead of rocks on their voyages southward, but shipowners objected because these pieces could not be tightly packed, they shifted in the hold, and their melting spoiled other cargo. It was necessary, therefore, to find a way to mass-produce uniform blocks from natural ice.

By a lucky collaboration, Tudor solved this problem. He enlisted the ingenuity of another well-born Cambridge man, Nathaniel Jarvis Wyeth, who had inherited a part of the shore of Fresh Pond, one of the best sources of ice around Cambridge. Although his father had been a Harvard graduate, Wyeth, like Tudor, passed up Harvard to go into business. Before he was thirty he was successfully running the Fresh Pond Hotel which, with its rowboats, tenpin alley, and other concessions, was an attractive summer resort for nearby cities. In 1824, Wyeth became manager of Tudor's ice company, which reaped the winter crop from Fresh Pond. Before long he invented a machine that revolutionized the harvesting of ice and without which the great New England ice industry might not have been possible.

Wyeth's solution was simple, probably suggested by the marks left by sleigh-runners on the surface of Fresh Pond in winter. His ice cutter consisted of two parallel iron runners about twenty inches apart drawn by a horse. Each runner was notched with saw teeth, making a device which cut two parallel grooves as it was pulled along. These grooves were deepened by repeating the operation; additional parallel grooves were cut by using one of the grooves as a guide. By pulling the device at right angles to the original grooves, one formed a checkerboard of squares in the ice. A few men with iron bars then pried off the cubes and floated them into a channel, quickly producing a great number of blocks of uniform dimension. At the end of the channel Wyeth provided a novel horse-drawn hoist which lifted the blocks out of the water up to a chute, which then deposited them in the icehouse on the shore of the pond.

These devices, which Wyeth had in workable form by 1825, reduced the cost of harvesting ice from thirty cents to ten cents a ton. Under the arrangement with Wyeth, Tudor controlled the use of all these devices. But these were not Wyeth's only inventions for the ice industry; he went on elaborating until, by the time of his death in 1856, its technology was almost entirely of his making. He designed a new type of ice-scraper to clean the surface of the ice before harvesting, in this way producing a still more uniform product. He discovered that sawdust could be used to prevent blocks from melting together in transit, thus keeping them neat for sale—and incidentally creating a demand for the until then useless by-product of the Maine lumber mills.

But Wyeth was no mere mechanic. During a five years leave from the ice business, after 1832, he led an overland expedition to Oregon and organized a company to exploit the Columbia River region for salmon, fur, timber, and tobacco. He thus became one of "the pioneers of the pioneers" of the Pacific Northwest. Despite a series of dramatic misadventures—lightning striking his company's ship at Valparaiso, struggles with the Rocky Mountain Fur Trading Company and the Hudson's Bay Company over the fur trade—he founded Fort Hall, a well known trading station on the Oregon and California trails. Lacking resources to establish a permanent fur-trading company of his own, he returned to Boston and re-entered the ice business for himself. He improved techniques still further. His versatile new type of ice cutter was melodramatically tested in 1844, when the Cunard steamship *Britannia* was frozen in Boston harbor; within three days he had cut a two-hundred-foot channel seven miles long to the open sea.

Despite competition from Wyeth and others, Tudor remained the Ice King. But his adventuring energies were never confined. In his early years he had traded in pimento, nutmeg, flour, sugar, tea, candles, cotton, silk, and claret. Later he dug for coal on Martha's Vineyard; he invented a siphon for pumping water from the holds of vessels; he made a new design for the hull of a ship (*The Black Swan*) and for a "double dory," supposedly an improvement over earlier fishing vessels; he operated a graphite mine; he made paper from white pine; and he experimented with the raising of cotton and tobacco at Nahant. He brought to New England the first steam locomotive, an engine of one-half horsepower which ran on the sidewalk at four miles an hour pulling a car for one passenger. He set up what was probably the first amusement park in America. And he even tried raising salt-water fish in Fresh Pond.

Tudor's miscellaneous speculations from time to time plunged him deeply into debt, even after he had put the ice trade on a profitable basis. For example, his speculations in coffee involved him to the extent of $200,000 before the end of 1834, but this drove him to redouble his efforts in the ice trade, out of which he managed to repay the coffee debt in the next fifteen years.

Tudor had now decided to ship his ice halfway around the world— to the East Indies. In May, 1833, in the most spectacular experiment of his career, Tudor sent his ship *Tuscany* with 180 tons of ice to Calcutta. To reach India from Boston the *Tuscany* had to cross the equator twice, preserving its cargo unmelted for four months. Tudor reminded his captain that ice had never been carried so far south; this was a "discovery ship." The *Tuscany* reached its destination, bringing the combined delights of a new toy and a new candy. The first shipment sold profitably, Tudor's reputation soared, and before long the ice trade flourished between Boston and the Far East. Using experience gained in the Caribbean, Tudor built a large Calcutta ice depot and encouraged Anglo-Indians to buy household refrigerators and water coolers; he tried to change their eating habits by his well-preserved shipments of apples, butter, and cheese.

Soon ice was being shipped from Boston to all parts. By 1846, sixty-five thousand tons were shipped; only ten years later more than twice that amount went in nearly four hundred different shipments to over fifty different destinations in the United States, the Caribbean, South America, the East Indies, China, the Philippines, and Australia. Ice had become a major commodity, a New England staple for the world market.

One brochure proposing a railroad to connect Fresh Pond with the docks at Charlestown asked whether ice did not contribute "as much to refreshment in the South as coal does to comfort in the North?" Others urged the importance of ice in promoting good morals. "How often do men in health drink ardent spirits as a beverage because they cannot procure good or only tepid water that ice would render palatable?" Edward Everett, American minister to England, reported receiving the thanks of a Persian prince for the New England ice which was saving the lives of patients in Persia, whose fevers were reduced by applying ice to their foreheads.

Tudor's ice industry reached not only to Persia but even to the fast-nesses of nearby Walden Pond, where it disturbed a would-be recluse named Thoreau who reported in the winter of 1846–47:

> A hundred Irishmen, with Yankee overseers, came from Cambridge every day to get out the ice. They divided it into cakes by [Wyeth's] methods too well known to require description, and these, being sledded to the shore, were rapidly hauled off on to an ice platform, and raised by grappling irons and block and tackle, worked by horses, on to a stack, as surely as so many barrels of flour, and there placed evenly side by side, and row upon row, as if they formed the solid base of an obelisk designed to pierce the clouds. They told me that in a good day they could get out a thousand tons, which was the yield of about one acre. . . . They told me that they had some in the ice-houses at Fresh Pond five years old which was as good as ever. . . . the sweltering inhabitants of Charleston and New Orleans, of Madras and Bombay and Calcutta, drink at my well. . . . The pure Walden water is mingled with the sacred water of the Ganges.

3

Inventing Resources: Granite for a New Stone Age

EARLY NEW ENGLAND FARMERS cursed the rocks that broke their ploughs, the rocks they laboriously collected along their boundaries to make fences as they cleared. The first settlers of Boston occasionally built with boulders they found strewn loose on the land, but stone in this form was not plentiful enough to become a common construction material. When houses were not built of wood, the usual materials were clay, brick, slate, cement, or red Connecticut sandstone. The great rough granite boulders made foundations and doorsteps but, even for this purpose, they soon became so scarce that the town meeting of Braintree, for example, in 1715 penalized anyone who carried a boulder away from the commons. To build King's Chapel in Boston, boulders were dug up, heated by a fire built directly on the stone, and then split by the dropping of heavy iron balls. This, the usual technique, was haphazard and expensive, and it could only be applied to boulders having a free side. In mid-18th century, German immigrants in Braintree began using gunpowder to split off large chunks of granite (hoping for the best shapes) which they then cut into smaller pieces by laboriously making a groove with a hammer having a cutting edge like that of an axe.

At the end of the 18th century an energetic governor of Massachusetts, while traveling about the state to find cheap stone for a new State Prison to be built at Charlestown, came upon a workman near Salem who used the novel method of drilling holes several inches apart and then splitting the stone in a straight line along the holes. When this improved technique for cutting granite came into general use, it halved the price of hewn granite, which now for the first time began to be in wide demand as a building material. The new Middlesex Canal, the longest in the country, from Chelmsford to Boston (employing granite for its sixteen locks), opened a convenient water passage from granite-source to port-city.

The great "Stone Age" of New England architecture, sometimes called the Greek Revival, followed. Not since the Mayans and Aztecs had North America seen so many buildings of monumental stone. In 1818 $25,000 worth of hewn granite was shipped for a church in Savannah, Georgia. And before long New England's best architects (Charles Bulfinch, Alexander Parris, Solomon Willard, Ammi Burnham Young, Gridley Bryant, and H. H. Richardson) used New England granite for homes, churches, markets, and public buildings all over the eastern and southern United States. Their work was possible only because New Englanders— by opening quarries, by inventing new ways of shaping, handling, and transporting granite, and by using their old ally, the sea—had now made stone a profitable export.

The American Revolution, in a strange and unforeseen way, was also indirectly responsible for the exploitation of Quincy granite. William (brother of Frederic) Tudor, who had first casually suggested the sale of ice in the Caribbean, is also credited with the first proposal in 1822 that a monument ("the noblest column in the world") be built on Bunker Hill to commemorate the first battlefield defense of the Republic. The design and engineering of the Bunker Hill Monument were the work of Solomon Willard, a talented jack-of-many-trades. Though coming from an old New England family, and a descendant of the famous minister, Samuel Willard, he was of the class of "self-made men" (his contemporary biographer explained) "peculiar to our own country, born with its birth—existing even before its birth as a nation—and growing with its growth, with a vigor which proves its congeniality, if not its indigenousness to the soil." As the son of a carpenter, Solomon Willard had only a common-school education and himself became a carpenter. By teaching himself the rudiments of architecture, by working hard, and by seizing his opportunities, he became a prosperous and prominent citizen. Under the direction of Charles Bulfinch, in 1818 he made the architect's model of the national capitol. In the 1820's, when American sources of coal were beginning to be exploited, he developed a hot-air system with a basement furnace and pipes leading to different rooms, which became the first widely used American system of central heating.

In 1825, Willard was chosen architect and superintendent of construction of the Bunker Hill Monument, for which he bore responsibility during nearly twenty troublesome years. The actual cost of the monument, Willard calculated, was over one hundred thousand dollars; including uncompensated services, it must have cost several times that. It had been entirely financed by voluntary contributions, but the citizens of Boston had taken twice as long to build the monument as they had to win the Revolution. At the dedication in 1843 in the presence of President John Tyler and his cabinet, Daniel Webster, who had delivered one of his most famous orations at the laying of the cornerstone 18 years before, gave the principal address. This monument, Webster commented, bore no inscription—"and it needs none, since the lessons of patriotism it is designed to commemorate, can only be inscribed upon the hearts of those who behold it."

An unexpected by-product of the building of Bunker Hill Monument was the great New England granite industry. Seeking a suitable material for the Monument, Willard had walked three hundred miles to examine different quarries until he finally discovered the granite quarry in Quincy. This was purchased in June, 1825 by Gridley Bryant, who sold it to the Bunker Hill Monument Association for $350 (still giving Bryant what was then called a "handsome profit"). From the so-called "Bunker Hill Ledge" in the Quincy quarry came the stone for the Monument. In securing this stone, Solomon Willard invented nearly every piece of machinery later used in the granite industry: lifting-jack, pulling-jack, hoist, and other devices for moving and placing large blocks of granite. Part of the construction scheme was the famous Granite Railway, planned and built by Gridley Bryant and sometimes called the first railroad in the United States. Over a primitive wooden track six inches high, covered with iron plates and resting on stone sleepers, granite blocks were hauled by horses from quarry to tidewater. It was while building this road, too, that Bryant developed his famous eight-wheel car and such other fundamental railroad devices as the switch, portable derrick, movable truck, turntable, and snowplow.

The Bunker Hill Quarry soon became a full-scale experiment in granite production. By selling granite at prime cost—only the cost of labor and materials directly used in procuring it—which was about one fourth of the going commercial price, Willard antagonized his competitors but he did widen the market. After completion of the Bunker Hill Monument, Willard could boast that the widespread use of granite as a building material was largely a result of improvements developed during its construction. "A business has grown . . . since the work commenced, and in a space of a few miles, amounting . . . to $3,000,000, which would not otherwise have been done at these quarries, and of which the work on the obelisk is but about one-thirtieth part."

In cities all along the eastern and southern seaboard, the most prominent public structures—customs houses, courthouses, markets, banks, and merchants' exchanges—were now built of granite. Willard's improved techniques of moving and placing the stone actually produced a new architectural style. Until then granite had been used mostly in small pieces for cellar walls, underpinnings, and lintels. Willard was now able to use it in large blocks, creating a monumental effect, the first example of which was, of course, the Bunker Hill Monument itself. Willard noted with satisfaction the improved construction of the granite drydocks in Charlestown and Norfolk, built soon after the commencement of the Monument. He observed a consequent improvement in "architectural taste and mechanical execution" in many buildings: in the Astor House and the Merchants' Exchange in New York, in the Tremont House, the Exchange and the Customs House in Boston, and in numerous public buildings and store-blocks elsewhere. In an age of gingerbread and gewgaws, the very intractability of granite encouraged a happy simplicity of design.

A coincidental interest in public health and landscape architecture fed a movement to replace the fetid charnel houses and the haphazard, crowded burial grounds of the colonial period with new "garden cemeteries." The leader of this movement was the versatile Boston botanist-physician Jacob Bigelow who founded Mount Auburn Cemetery in Cambridge in 1831. Its grandiose Egyptian portal, its markers and monuments for the wealthy and the famous buried there, and its neat granite curbing for its winding drives, consumed large quantities of stone from the Bunker Hill quarries. As garden cemeteries became popular, they created a large new market for Quincy granite.

With the growth of cities, the demand for a hard paving stone increased. Solomon Willard laid the first such blocks of Quincy granite in front of the Tremont House in 1840. Before the end of the century, New England was producing over sixty million granite paving blocks each year.

The influence of granite reached out—to the edge of the sea, across the sea, and among people working on the sea. When Harriet Martineau visited Massachusetts in the fall of 1835–36, she found the remote New Englanders of Cape Ann using the sea to help them harvest the granite of the land. She found them employing ox teams and sleds to embark stone for foreign parts. "Blocks of granite lay by the road-side, marked . . . prepared to order for some great building in New York, or Mobile, or New Orleans. . . . We went into a quarry, and saw an untold wealth of fissured stone. The workmen contrive to pursue their business even in the winter. When the snow is on the ground, and the process of drilling is stopped, they remove ordinary pieces out of the way, and make clear for their spring labours. They 'turn out' 250,000 dollars'-worth a-year; and the demand is perpetually on the increase."

A *tour de force* in granite was Minot's Ledge Lighthouse in Boston Harbor, completed only after eight years of planning and construction. Because of the peculiar location of the site, stones could be placed only when there was a perfectly smooth sea, a dead calm, and low spring tide. Even then nothing larger than a small sailboat could be used to carry the two-ton stones to the only point at which a boat could be brought up to the ledge. When Minot's Ledge Lighthouse first shone on November 15, 1860, it was celebrated as a prodigy of architecture and marine engineering. It was, in fact, a demonstration not only of the wonderful qualities of granite, but of the ability of New Englanders to meet the challenge of the sea. And it was not long before New England's most respectable orators had reversed the proverbial taunt. No one now could deny their boast, uttered by Charles Francis Adams, Jr., that "the three great staples of New England are ice and rocks and men."

4

Organizing the American Factory

BY THE MIDDLE of the 19th century Europeans began to notice an "American System of Manufacturing" quite different from their own. They should have called it more precisely a "New England System," for there was hardly an important manufacturing innovation in the shaping years before the Civil War that did not have its decisive trial in our Northeast.

This New England System was versatility made into a way of production. It grew not from a specialized skill at making particular things— guns or clocks or textiles or boots—but from know-how that could make anything. It was the offspring of ingenuity and lack of skill, of scarce labor and vast markets, of abundant water power and meager raw materials, of private ambition and large-scale cooperation, of commercial enterprise, corporate capital, government subsidy, and happy accident. For the first time it offered a way of planting New England's seafaring agility firmly on the land.

Transforming production by new ways of bringing together some processes and of separating others, the new factory arrangements had a revolutionary simplicity, a simplicity hidden from the custom-blinded Old World. The new combining meant simply bringing together the different processes for making a commodity under a single management and under a single roof. This was, properly speaking, the new American factory organization, which is the subject of this chapter. The second feature, a new way of separating the parts of the operation, is the subject of the next chapter.

The system, which later was to have the look of grand invention and bold discovery, began in the casual experiments of men unencumbered by century-accumulated skills and intricate social regulations. If the American Factory System was a triumph of organization and of cooperation, it was also a triumph of naiveté, for its essence was a loosening of habits and of ways of thinking. Ignorance and "backwardness" had kept Americans out of the old grooves. Important innovations were made simply because Americans did not know any better.

Nearly every feature of the American system of manufacturing, from the elements of the new textile machinery to the concept of interchangeable parts, had actually been conceived earlier by Europeans. But while a few Europeans could see the possibilities, their communities kept them powerless to give their ideas a fair trial. Too many had a stake in the older ways. Industrial progress in Europe required extraordinary courage to break the prevailing pattern; in America it required a willingness to try the obvious. American genius was less for invention or discovery than for experiment.

It was no accident that the headquarters of American seafaring adventure became the headquarters of adventure in manufacturing. Both trafficked in the raw materials of remote places; both sold to the world market. The willingness to change from one commodity to another, to invest grandly and then shift investments, to experiment with novel and outlandish products, to try new ports and test new routes—this would also be required of the new manufacturer.

The commerce of the sea had accumulated capital. And successful seafaring merchants had learned to keep a considerable proportion of their capital fluid because New England habits, climate, and landscape had discouraged the amassing of impressive manorial landed estates, or the building of luxurious mansions for descendants. Whoever heard of a New England Mount Vernon, Monticello, Montpelier, or Ashlawn? With the wealth which the Rhode Island Browns and the Massachusetts Tracys, Lees, Cabots, Higginsons, Jacksons, and Lowells had gathered from the sea, they built factories. Nathan Appleton, for example, who made his start as a seafaring merchant and later became a founder of American textile manufacturing, used to keep at least one third of his capital free for new projects and unforeseen opportunities. To this, among other practices, he attributed the success of his factory enterprises while others were failing.

Mastery of the sea, when the sea was highway to the world, meant mastery of sources of raw materials. New England's ability to bring large quantities of cotton from the South or from Egypt, of hides from Argentina or from the Pacific Northwest, enabled her to supply factories making textiles or shoes or almost anything else. And the sea led to all the customers in the world. Lowell's miles of coarse cloth and Lynn's thousands of pairs of cheap shoes would have glutted a local market, but they went profitably thousands of miles overseas to the unclad and unshod in Africa, Asia, and Latin America.

New England also possessed indirect incentives. Her lack of a rich staple crop or of abundant minerals prevented her becoming fixed in traditional ways of profiting from one or two familiar commodities. And New England businessmen handled impartially the cotton of Georgia or of Egypt or of India, the hides of South America, or the iron of England.

Even her political misfortunes pushed New England to experiment with new forms of factory organization. Jefferson's Embargo (1807–09) and the War of 1812 destroyed much of her foreign commerce and forced her to find new investments at home. It was the cities outside New England—Albany, New York, Philadelphia, Baltimore, and others—that lay near river pathways of trade with the western backcountry. Long settled areas of New York State were a barrier between Boston and the growing market on the other side. The principal New England rivers— the Connecticut, Merrimack, Kennebec, and Penobscot—ran northward. In all these ways she was badly located for shifting from foreign to domestic commerce. In New England, then, labor and capital which could no longer go to sea were tempted to other employments at home before making the great leap to the West.

The "backwardness" of the American economy and technology actually made introduction of new factory ways easier. In the highly developed economy of England, for example, the several stages of production had long been sharply defined: each had become an occupation conducted in a different place with its own business customs and plant practices. In the English production of cotton textiles, the spinner, the weaver, the dyer, and the printer each had his separate traditions and thought of himself as engaged in a distinctly separate process. There was a different market for goods at each stage. An elaborate system of exchange governed specialized traders in yarn, woven goods, and dyestuffs.

As a result many groups had vested interests in not centralizing or simplifying production. The American contrast was striking. During the colonial period, when there were already extensive manufacturing establishments in England, most crafts in America were still carried on as small family undertakings. Even at the end of the colonial period, a considerable proportion of the manufactures of the northern colonies still came from village craftsmen. Their distance from the city and from fellow craftsmen also kept them free from guilds. Americans were still without large patterns of organization.

In textiles, where the first large-scale factory of the new American type would appear, Americans had stuck with the old system of home industry. During the colonial period, the rural New England family usually spun its own yarn and made its own cloth. The only textile process commonly carried on outside the home was that of "fulling," or finishing woolen cloth, which was done by the village fuller. Most people were clothed in leather, wool, or linen; cotton cloth was still relatively expensive. American colonials who did not weave for themselves purchased woolens made in England or cottons made in Manchester or the Far East.

Before the invention of the steam engine, the principal source of power for English factories had, of course, been water. Where sources of water power had been used for centuries, the coveted rights to every millsite on a stream had long been established, pre-empted, and subdivided. Any large source had been broken down and distributed among numerous small customary users. In England, therefore, a supply of water power in one place sufficient to run the combined processes of manufacturing was virtually unobtainable in the early 19th century. The custom-bound fragmentation of power had preserved the custom-bound fragmentation of occupations. Early development of steam power at first even reinforced these tendencies. In England the invention of the steam engine and its widespread use for manufacturing before the 1820's made possible any number of small, mobile sources of power. This made it easier than ever to run a small establishment which performed only a single process in making a product.

In "underdeveloped" New England in the early 19th century, all this was different. Before the age of railroads, coal was prohibitively expensive. The steam engine was only slowly adopted for manufacturing and did not generally replace water power until the Civil War. For there were still many streams never before used for water power; their uses had not yet been legally fragmented. A firm building a factory in New England, therefore, could still purchase and control a single large source. For example, when businessmen who had established the pioneer cotton-textile factory at Waltham decided to erect another, they first "set about discovering a suitable water power." They looked for what it would have been folly to seek in England—a large new source that had never been exploited before. "Why don't they buy up the Pawtucket Canal?" Nathan Appleton, one of these businessmen, recalled a friend suggesting. "That would give them the whole power of the Merrimack, with a fall of over thirty feet." This is precisely what they did. "We perambulated the grounds, and scanned the capabilities of the place," Appleton recalled of his visit in November 1821 to the site (then occupied by less than a dozen houses, but soon to become the flourishing city of Lowell), "and the remark was made that some of us might live to see the place contain twenty thousand inhabitants."

New Englanders, then, were understandably tempted to centralize their operations in large units and to bring the several processes under a single roof. At Waltham, Massachusetts, in 1814 there appeared a factory in which all the processes of manufacturing a complex commodity were carried on by the use of power in a single establishment. Here was born the modern factory organization, which would be momentous for the whole human community within a century. It was to stir crucial changes in the relationships between capital and labor, in the nature of cities and countryside, in the position of women and of the family. Directly or indirectly, it would explain many of the distinctions between life in the mid-20th and that in the mid-18th century.

Nothing exotic or unfamiliar was produced at Waltham—simply cotton cloth. Nor were any of the processes there entirely novel. Except for a few improvements by Francis Cabot Lowell in the power loom, jobs now done inside this one large factory were precisely the same ones which before had been dispersed among separate smaller establishments. The essential novelty, as one of the factory's founders explained in his own history of the enterprise, was not the processes applied but rather their organization—"an entirely new arrangement, in order to save labor, in passing from one process to another." The processes had merely been collected and organized so that raw cotton went in one end of the factory and finished cotton cloth came out the other.

The story of this "Boston Manufacturing Company" of Waltham would be frequently repeated in the next few decades in New England. Its moving spirit was Francis Cabot Lowell, who had made his money in the importing and exporting business. A trip to England's Lancashire textile mills had awakened his imagination to the possibilities of similar manufacturing in New England, and the interruption of his seafaring enterprises by the War of 1812 gave him the leisure and the incentive to develop an American counterpart. He had the lucky assistance of Paul Moody, a self-taught inventor who later established the pioneer American factory for the making of textile machinery. Lowell's principal collaborators were his brother-in-law Patrick Tracy Jackson (grandson of a penniless Irish immigrant and son of a prosperous Boston member of the Continental Congress), who had never been to college, but who rose from supercargo on a West Indian merchantman at the age of twenty, to amass a fortune from shipping to both the Indies; and Nathan Appleton (who had been prepared for Dartmouth College but instead went into business at the age of fifteen), a talented organizer. These men were an allegory of New England enterprise.

From the world perspective what was most remarkable about the Waltham factory was less that it was actually operating by 1814 than that so obvious an innovation, a mere combination of old processes, had not occurred to somebody somewhere long before. The world's most advanced form of industrial organization now suddenly appeared in the backwaters of the New World.

European travelers were astonished by the sites of the new American factories. They were accustomed to find factories, like those in England, mired in the stench and congestion of a festering city. The New England factory sprouted on an unspoiled rural landscape. In the 1830's the visiting French economist Michel Chevalier was amazed that the great American factories were "new and fresh like an opera scene." The contrast between these and the factories of her native England struck Harriet Martineau in 1837. True enough, she said, the tourist in America would be irritated to see awesome natural scenery defaced by modern factories. But one should not forget what this meant for American workers.

> . . . to have their dwellings and their occupation fixed in spots where the hills are heaped together, and the waters leap and whirl among rocks, rather than in dull suburbs where they and their employments may not annoy the eye of the lover of the picturesque. It always gave me pleasure to see the artisans at work about such places as Glen's Falls, the Falls of the Genessee, and on the banks of some of the whirling streams in the New England valleys. I felt that they caught, or might catch, as beautiful glimpses of Nature's face as the western settler. . . . It is deplorable enough, in this view, to be a poor artisan in the heart of our English Manchester: but to be a thriving one in the most beautiful outskirts of Sheffield is, perhaps, as favourable a lot for the lover of nature as to be a labourer on any soil: and the privileges of the American artisans are like this.

Twenty years later the English traveler, Charles Weld, could still admire the happy by-product of the American backwardness in displacing water power by steam: the common prospect of "a smokeless factory town canopied by an Italian sky." American anachronism—the factory in the wilderness—helped explain not only the peculiarities of the American factory but the many other American opportunities for naive innovations in the custom-bound industrial world.

5

From Skill to Know-how:
"A Circulating Current"

THE MEN WHO made the new factory at Waltham—Francis Cabot Lowell, Nathan Appleton, and Patrick Tracy Jackson—had never before been in a textile venture, nor in any other manufacturing project. It was less their technical knowledge than their boldness, energy, enterprise, versatility, and, above all, their organizing ability that made their epochal innovations possible. In fact, their lack of strong craft traditions actually helps explain why new-style factories first appeared in New England.

During the colonial period, the center of American craftsmanship had been Philadelphia. There one found the best tailors, the best hatmakers, the best shoemakers, the best finished-metal workers, and the best cabinet makers. It was around Philadelphia that the largest number of 18th-century immigrant artisans, especially those from Germany and central Europe, had settled. The two most distinctively "American" craft products—the Pennsylvania rifle (later called the "Kentucky rifle") and the Conestoga wagon (named after Conestoga Township, in Lancaster County; later called the "covered wagon")—were actually the work of Swiss and German craftsmen who had only recently settled in Pennsylvania. In the Philadelphia area were concentrated the skilled textile-craftsmen, the spinners and weavers who turned out fine goods, elegant plaids, and hand-woven fancy designs in small shops.

These traditions of fine craftsmanship seem to have been more a hindrance than an encouragement to innovation. Just as the European industrial revolution did not come first to France, with its great artisan traditions in luxury products, but to England; so the revolutionary American factory first came not to Philadelphia but to New England.

The "American System of Manufacturing" from its very beginning was no triumph of American inventive genius. Almost all the basic inventions that mechanized textile manufacturing came from England. And they had reached America slowly. Take, for example, the machinery for spinning raw cotton into cotton thread. Fully twenty years passed after Richard Arkwright began operating his first cotton-spinning machinery in England before Americans succeeded in copying it—and that was actually a feat of smuggling!

The evidence of, American technical backwardness would be less impressive had there not been such strenuous efforts here to devise machinery similar to that used in England. State lotteries had actually been organized to collect prize money for the first inventor; the Massachusetts legislature even offered a subsidy. Despite many such incentives, American efforts failed repeatedly.

Unable to invent their own, Americans made desperate efforts to import or copy samples of English machines. But English laws forbade the export of manufacturing machinery, including models or drawings of them; even the emigration of any skilled workman who might reproduce such machinery abroad was prohibited. And New Englanders seemed to have lost that skill at smuggling which had helped build their economy in colonial days. Tench Coxe, a public-spirited Philadelphian, persuaded some London workmen to make him a set of brass models of Arkwright's patent machinery, but when the models were all crated and ready to leave England, British customs officers discovered them on the dock.

The crucial feat was finally accomplished by an adventurous young Englishman, Samuel Slater, who, at the age of fourteen, had been luckily apprenticed to Jedediah Strutt, partner of Richard Arkwright. Attracted here by American newspaper advertisements for improved cotton machinery, he was only twenty-one when he arrived in New York in 1789. Because of his knowledge of the Arkwright machinery his departure was forbidden by English law, but he left secretly, without even telling his mother. Not daring to take along plans or models, he had committed all the necessary information to his phenomenal memory. Dissatisfied with the unenterprising business methods and the meager sources of waterpower he found in New York, he accepted an invitation from Moses Brown, the Providence merchant—philanthropist after whom Brown University was named, to set up a cotton mill in Rhode Island. Brown and his son-in-law William Almy saw the opening Slater's skill gave them. They put up the initial capital and gave Slater a half interest in the business. Slater built, entirely from memory, a cotton-spinning frame of twenty-four spindles, which he put into operation. The firm of Brown & Almy prospered from the beginning.

In England itself employers could draw on the large pool of able-bodied paupers and unemployed. From crowded poorhouses they took workers who could not afford to be choosy about their employment. But in New England there were few poorhouses; laborers had more alternatives; land was plentiful, people scarce. As early as 1791, Alexander Hamilton had noted this as an obstacle to American manufacturing. Forty years later, some European travelers like the Frenchman Chevalier still expressed their surprise that American laborers were **not** forcing down wages by competing against one another for the chance to work. In America, therefore, manufacturing could secure a labor force only by attracting hands from other work or by drawing new workers into the labor market.

Such advocates of manufacturing as Alexander Hamilton had long been concerned lest the new factories disrupt American farm life by attracting away its essential labor. Hamilton himself noted that women and children were the only workers who could be spared from American farms. Brown & Almy's pioneer cotton-spinning factory at Providence, as Moses Brown himself boasted, did not at first take able-bodied men from other work. On the contrary, by drawing on a new source, it produced "near a total saving of labor to the country." The factory's first labor force consisted of seven boys and two girls, all between seven and twelve years of age. Not for long, however, could enough women and children be found to operate even this first cotton-spinning factory at Providence. Slater turned to the familiar English pattern. He attracted whole families to live in tenements or in company houses; under this "family" system every member of a family over seven years of age was employed in the factory. Such arrangements came to prevail in Rhode Island, Connecticut, and southern Massachusetts, where one began to see a factory working-class similar to that whose condition in England in 1844 Friedrich Engels painted so luridly.

In a few places appeared a more peculiarly American way of recruiting a factory work force, a way that fired the American imagination and shaped American notions of social class: perhaps America could have factories without a "factory class." Such a possibility, pure fantasy in England, seemed real enough in America because of the many alternative opportunities for employment, the well-being of the American populace, the cheapness of farming land, and the relative newness and lack of squalor of American cities.

When Francis Cabot Lowell visited England in 1810–12, he admired the Lancashire textile machinery but was horrified by the condition of the new factory class. He and his partners were determined that New England should not pay this price for industrial progress. Nathan Appleton recalled:

> The operatives in the manufacturing cities of Europe, were notoriously of the lowest character, for intelligence and morals. The question therefore arose, and was deeply considered, whether this degradation was the result of the peculiar occupation, or of other and distinct causes. We could not perceive why this peculiar description of labor should vary in its effects upon character from all other occupation.
>
> There was little demand for female labor, as household manufacture was superseded by the improvements in machinery. Here was in New

England a fund of labor, well educated and virtuous. It was not per-
ceived how a profitable employment has any tendency to deteriorate
the character. The most efficient guards were adopted in establishing
boarding houses, at the cost of the Company, under the charge of respectable women, with every provision for religious worship. Under
these circumstances, the daughters of respectable farmers were readily
induced to come into these mills for a temporary period.

This was the "Waltham" or "Lowell" system, sometimes called the
Boarding-House System. It had originated in the belief that there would
not, and should not, be a permanent factory class in New England.
The Waltham and Lowell communities became show places to support
the New England businessman's boast that his new system had "rendered our manufacturing population the wonder of the world." When
Harriet Martineau, herself the daughter of a Norwich manufacturer,
visited them in 1835, she feared that any accurate description would
tempt most of England's workers to the New World. Charles Dickens,
not known for his sympathy to anything American, toured New England
in 1842 and could not restrain his enthusiasm, describing the contrast
with the English mill towns as "between the Good and Evil, the living
light and deepest shadow."

Happy communities of well-dressed young ladies, living in spacious
houses with piazzas and green venetian blinds, spending their spare
time in churches, libraries, and lecture halls, were by no means representative of the new industrial life. Not even in America. New England,
of course, had its share of callous factory-owners who considered their
workpeople part of the machinery, but the hope of establishing factories
without a permanent factory class was widespread and vivid.

As late as 1856, Francis Cabot Lowell's nephew, John Amory Lowell,
boasted that American factory life was something new under the sun.
The factory girl, he said, was not pursuing a lifetime vocation. She was
simply spending a few years in a mill to help earn her dower or to provide for the professional education of a brother. "The business could thus
be conducted without any permanent manufacturing population. The
operatives no longer form a separate caste, pursuing a sedentary employment, from parent to child, in the heated rooms of a factory; but re-
cruited in a circulating current from the healthy and virtuous population
of the country." The ideal of a "circulating current" rather than a static
class—of men on the move rather than in the groove—grew naturally.
It flourished in this world of the undifferentiated man, where the unexpected was usual. The Old World vision of the industrious poor had
dissolved. Even more characteristic than the ideal of equality, the vagueness of social classes became an ideal in America.

In the early 19th century, labor was generally better paid in America
than in England. But the unskilled laborers profited most from their

American situation: in the 1820's, for example, they commanded a wage a third or a half higher here than in England, while the highly skilled were only slightly better off than in England, if at all. Thus the wage premium on artisan skills was much less in America than in England in the decades before the Civil War. The general labor shortage seems, as usual, to have operated most in favor of the least skilled, as did other factors: abundant land, wide geographic and social mobility, general literacy, and the lack of organized guilds. All these factors tended to reduce the social and monetary premium on the acquisition of artisan skills. Why train yourself for a task you hoped and expected soon to leave? American working men and women, already known the world over for literacy and intelligence, were not noted for specialized skills.

The purpose of the Interchangeable System, Eli Whitney himself explained, was "to substitute correct and effective operations of machinery for that skill of the artist which is acquired only by long practice and experience; a species of skill which is not possessed in this country to any considerable extent." The unheralded Know-how Revolution produced a new way, not only of making things, but of making the machines that make things. It was a simple but far-reaching change, not feasible in a Europe rich in traditions, institutions, and vested skills.

What happened in America in manufacturing was comparable to what had happened here in other fields. The scarcity of legal learning did not lead to a scarcity of laws or lawyers (we soon became the most lawyered and most legislated country in the world), but instead to a new kind of legal profession and a new concept of law; the scarcity of specialized medical learning soon led to a new kind of doctor and a new concept of medicine; and a scarcity of theological learning led to a new kind of minister and a new concept of religion. Similarly, the scarcity of craft skills set the stage for a new nearly craftless way of making things. And this prepared a new concept of material plenitude and of the use and expendability of things which would be called the American Standard of Living.

The Know-how Revolution brought an unexpected new power to make everything, and for nearly everybody! Oddly enough, the finer and more complex the machine to be manufactured, the more effective and more economical would be the new method. With a momentum of its own, this new American way of making things led people to want more and more things, in kinds and quantities never known before.

For all this New England was the center. The system would first be called the "Uniformity System" or the "Whitney System," for the key man was Eli Whitney. Though Europeans called it the "American System," it had not been invented in America nor by Whitney. Jefferson had seen it in France over a decade before, but there, when difficulties were encountered, Frenchmen preferred time-honored skills to uncertain experiments. In England too, Jeremy Bentham, his brother Samuel, and the ingenious Marc Isambard Brunel had contrived a way of mass-producing wooden pulley blocks for the navy in an effort to employ the idle hands of prisoners and dockyard workers. But in England, too, little changed for decades.

The Uniformity System was simplicity itself, yet to imagine it one again had to leave time-honored ruts. The American factory organization described in the last chapter had merely drawn together separate manufacturing processes under a single roof. Whitney's Uniformity System was more novel: it transformed the role of the worker and changed the very meaning of skill. In Europe the making of a complex machine, such as a gun or a clock, had remained wholly in the hands of a single highly skilled craftsman. The gunsmith or clockmaker himself fashioned and put together all the parts of each gun or clock. By immemorial practice, each gun or clock was a distinctive hand-crafted object, bearing the hallmark of its maker. When it needed repair it was returned to its maker or to another gunsmith or clockmaker who shaped and fitted the required piece. Nothing was more obvious than that the production of guns or clocks depended directly on the numbers of qualified gunsmiths or clockmakers.

The new Uniformity System broke down the manufacture of a gun or of any other complicated machine into the separate manufacture of each of its component pieces. Each piece could then be made independently and in large quantities, by workers who lacked the skill to make a whole machine. The numerous copies of each part would be so nearly alike that any one would serve in any machine. If one piece broke, another of its type could be substituted without shaping or fitting.

How Whitney himself came upon so simple and so revolutionary a notion, the greatest skill-saving innovation in human history, we do not know. Perhaps he had first happened on it in his search for a way of mass-producing his cotton gin. The first successful application of the idea on a large scale was in the making of muskets. The occasion was the new nation's need for firearms in the turbulent era of Europe's Napoleonic Wars. In 1798 France, under a revolutionary dictatorship, threatened war against an unprepared United States. Most of the muskets with which Americans had won their Revolution fifteen years before had been made in France or elsewhere in Europe. Since military firearms had not been manufactured in quantity in this country, the nation was, in effect, unarmed. A tightened Naturalization Act and the infamous Alien and Sedition Acts were symptoms of its hysterical insecurity.

In March of 1798, President John Adams warned that diplomacy had failed. Soon thereafter, on May 1, Eli Whitney of Connecticut wrote the Secretary of the Treasury offering his machinery, water power, and workmen (originally collected for manufacturing cotton gins) for the manufacture of muskets. Whitney signed a contract for ten thousand muskets, a fantastic number in those days, to be delivered within twenty-eight months. He was to be paid $134,000, which would have made the average cost per musket only a few dollars above that paid for imports. This was probably the first contract for mass production in the American manner.

It is significant that Whitney was inexperienced in making guns. He had probably never carefully examined the particular Charleville musket he contracted to reproduce. Had he been a skilled gunsmith, had he loved the feel and look of a beautifully crafted and ornamented piece, he might never have dared violate traditional craft standards by agreeing to mass-produce muskets by the thousands. What Whitney had to offer, he well knew, was not skill but know-how: a general organizing competence to make anything.

Whitney used up his time in perfecting his new production method. Fully twenty-eight months, the contract term for delivery of the whole ten thousand, expired without his delivering even one musket. All the while Whitney was building and equipping his new musket factory at Mill Rock outside New Haven. In January, 1801, desperate for cash and in need of moral support against influential people who were writing him off as a charlatan, he went to Washington and there gave a dramatic demonstration that proved to President John Adams, Vice-President Jefferson, and members of the cabinet that his "interchangeable system" really worked. He spread out before them the musket and a supply of its parts. Then he asked them to select any example of each part at random from its pile and to try with their own hands whether any one would fit with any other into a complete working musket lock. The proof was overwhelming. "He had invented moulds and machines for making all the pieces of his lock so exactly equal," Jefferson reported, "that take 100 locks to pieces and mingle their parts and the hundred locks may be put together as well by taking the first pieces which come to hand. . . . good locks may be put together without employing a Smith."

Now Whitney asked for another six months' grace for delivery of the first 500 muskets of his original contract and for two years beyond that to deliver the remainder. He secured everything he asked for, including another $10,000 advance, an agreement by the government to advance an additional $5000 in three months, and a further $5000 upon delivery of each 500 muskets. Although the new agreement trebled the money he received in advance and doubled the time allowed to perform his contract, Whitney was unable—by a large margin—to meet the revised terms. Not until January, 1809, ten years after the date of the first contract, did Whitney deliver the last musket of the agreed ten

thousand. He had made a profit of only $2500 on a job which con-
sumed a decade.

But Whitney had finally proved and successfully applied the basic
idea of American mass production, without which the American Standard of Living would have been inconceivable. His was a triumph of
organization. The original conception was perhaps not his own; other
New Englanders were at the same time experimenting along similar
lines. Only twenty miles away, at Middletown, Simeon North, whose
main business had been manufacturing scythes, signed his first contract with the War Department in 1799 for 500 horse pistols to be
delivered within one year. One of his later contracts (in 1813, for
20,000 pistols) provided that "The component parts of pistols are to
correspond so exactly that any limb or part of one Pistol may be fitted
to any other Pistol of the twenty thousand." Simeon's son, Selah North,
is traditionally credited with inventing the filing jig, the matching con-
cave mold which holds the metal so that any workman then necessarily
follows the required shape.

Another feature of this story is worth noting. Government subsidy
was crucial. The government's great power to invest and to wait for a
return on its investment enabled Whitney to build his factory and tool
up for mass production. This first great triumph of the American businessman was a government-sponsored and government-aided (but not
government-run) venture.

*   *   *

America was already on its way to becoming the land of human salvation and of material waste. New England versatility now shaped at
least two great and lasting tendencies in American civilization.

Machines, not men, became specialized. Where labor was scarce,
where a man was expected to turn easily from one task to another, his machines had to possess the competence he lacked. Whitney's Interchangeable System, as he himself explained, was "a plan which is unknown in
Europe & the great leading object of which is to substitute correct &
effective operations of machinery for that skill of the artist which is
acquired only by long practice & experience, a species of skill which is
not possessed in this country to any considerable extent." Specialized
machinery was required for an unspecialized people. "One of my primary objects," wrote Whitney, "is to form the tools so the tools themselves shall fashion the work and give to every part its just proportion."
American technology would be an accessory of the undifferentiated man:
the versatile, mobile American. New England had led the way.

A premium on general intelligence. In the Old World, to say a
worker was unskilled was to say he was unspecialized, which meant his
work had little value. In America, the new system of manufacturing de-

stroyed the antithesis between skilled and unskilled. Lack of artisan skill no longer prevented a man from making complex products. Old crafts became obsolete. In America, too, a "liberal"—that is, an unspecialized—education was no longer proof of gentility; it no longer showed its possessor to be liberated from the need for gainful employment. Unspecialized education was useful to all.

English observers in the mid-19th century admired the ease with which American laborers moved about the country, from one job to another. They were amazed at the general freedom from fear of unemployment, at the vagueness of social classes, at the facility of moving up from one class to another. These facts, among others, they said, explained the absence of trade unions and strikes and the willingness of American workers to try new methods. Even the skilled immigrant sooner or later found it hard to stay in his old groove. While neighboring nations in Europe had jealously guarded their techniques from one another, here individual laborers from England, France, and Germany learned from one another and freely mingled their techniques.

The New England system of manufacturing, destined to become the American system, prized generalized intelligence, literacy, adaptability, and willingness to learn. As the machinery of production became larger, more complicated, more tightly integrated, more expensive, and more rigid, working men were expected to be more alert and more teachable. Open minds were more valuable than trained hands. Technicians and industrialists from England noted a new type of workman being created in the United States. The most skilled English mechanics, they regretfully confessed, showed such "timidity resulting from traditional notions, and attachment to old systems, even among the most talented persons, that they keep considerably behind." In the American system, they said, "you do not depend on dexterity—all you want is intellect." Needing a versatile as well as intelligent populace, New Englanders now reshaped the system of education they had founded two centuries earlier to instil dogmatism and singleness of purpose. They were working a similar transformation in their attitude toward law, and through that, toward all the problems of social change.

6

A Common-Law Way of Thinking

NEW ENGLAND DEVELOPED an American System of Law as distinctive as the American System of Manufacturing. At the outbreak of the American Revolution, not a single volume of American law reports had been published; statutes were disorganized and poorly indexed. There was not one respectable specialized treatise, much less any authoritative survey. The self-educated lawyer and the lay judge were the rule. Nowhere was there an American law school. By the time of the Civil War, all this was changed. In New England, in one of the unheralded creative outbursts of modern legal history, comparable to the great age of Roman Law under the Antonines or to the Napoleonic redefinition of the Civil Law, the great outlines were drawn.

It was no accident, of course, that the dynamic center of American commerce and industry was also the center of American law. Centuries before, Plato had noticed how maritime commerce multiplies laws. In modern times, the energetic societies have been the great inventors of laws. The Romans, the French, the English, all did their best legal work during their periods of expansive, imperial enterprise. We cannot be surprised, then, that New England now became lawgiver to the new American nation.

The Puritan tradition, in its peculiar New England form, had set the stage. The pulpit, not the altar, was the focus of the congregational church, for Puritans adored the Word. Their theology, like much of the rest of their thinking, was legalistic; its "federal" theology depended on "covenant," a legal concept. Colonial New Englanders strove ingeniously to live at the same time by the Laws of God and the Laws of England. From the very beginning, from the first law establishing New England schools, Massachusetts Bay directed its citizens to read and understand the laws of their God. The frequent attacks on them for religious heterodoxy and for violations of their charter and of the laws of England had put them on their guard. Again and again they were forced to prove the legality of their acts. The American Revolution itself, led in New England as elsewhere by men who called themselves lawyers, was a vindication of legal rights.

The accomplishment of New England's lawyers, like that of her industrialists and men of business, was a work of adaptation and organization. They were imaginative importers rather than bold or original inventors. The raw materials and even the techniques of the new American legal system were not made in America. Versatility combined with colonialism to give New England her lead in preserving English legal tradition in the New World. She refurbished the old English common law for a new society now changing with unprecedented speed and, equally important, she helped prevent the introduction of a quite different legal tradition.

The years of political revolution and rapid social change in Western Europe in the first half of the 19th century saw a widespread movement there to remake laws, to replace obsolete technicality and professional monopoly. Not a few lawyers and men of letters were dazzled by the spectacular achievement of the *Code Napoléon* (1804). The strident voice of Jeremy Bentham, one of the most original and dyspeptic minds of the century, reached out to Russia and the Orient, demanding unified codes freshly designed on scientific principles. Bentham warned us "to shut our ports against the Common Law, as we would against the plague." Between 1811 and 1817, in letters to President Madison, to the State Governors, and to the American people, he generously offered to construct a complete code for the United States. Some Americans were tempted, but sensible New Englanders were not sold on so dogmatic a cure-all. "England has caught the rabies. . . ," George Bancroft exclaimed in 1827. "God preserve us from the extreme remedy of codification!"

In Massachusetts, lawyers and judges had already, between 1800 and 1823, collected and revised the laws on their books. By her Revised Statutes (prepared, 1832–34; effective, 1836), which profited from New York experience, Massachusetts managed to systematize and clarify her statute law. She did not abandon her past. What she aimed at, a contemporary reviewer observed, was simply "revision and consolidation of statutes. . . . to incorporate into the code the former decisions on the construction of the statutes revised." This was a kind of inoculation against the codifying mania. And these Revised Statutes of Massachusetts (1836) in turn provided a model which other states followed, proving that their laws too could be modernized without being entirely reconstructed.

In the era of the American Revolution, Blackstone's *Commentaries on the Laws of England* (1765–69), the first handy, readable guide to the system of the mother country and one of the earliest of the do-it-yourself books which would be so popular here, had helped unlearned Americans walk in English legal paths. But the system Blackstone described was English and not American; it was good enough for colonials emulating the metropolis, but not for a vigorous new nation needing institutions of its own.

The first successful effort to fill this need was by Nathan Dane, a Massachusetts lawyer who had graduated from Harvard College in 1778. He had twice served on commissions to revise his state's laws. His *General Abridgment and Digest of American Law* (8 vols., 1823) was the first comprehensive survey of law for the new nation. It was squarely in the great English tradition of common-law abridgments and digests which in the 18th century had helped make the myriad decided cases into a workable everyday system. The American Blackstone, as it happened, appeared not in Massachusetts, but in New York, the other great center of legal development, when Chancellor James Kent (Yale College, Class of 1781) published his *Commentaries on American Law* (4 vols., 1826–30). Kent's book became an American legal classic, going through six editions before his death and at least eight more editions afterwards. Still it was Dane who decisively shaped legal education in Massachusetts, and so gave a distinctive character to American lawyers and American law.

New England was the original habitat of the American law school. The first American law school had been founded about 1784 by Tapping Reeve at Litchfield, Connecticut, where five years later Ephraim Kirby published the first volume of American law reports. The Litchfield Law School acquired a national reputation and inaugurated a strong American tradition of formal legal training for our public men. Among its early graduates were men from every state, including Aaron Burr of New York, John C. Calhoun of South Carolina, Horace Mann of Massachusetts, George Y. Mason of Virginia, and Levi Woodbury of New Hampshire. During the early 19th century, Litchfield's annual graduating class averaged between ten and fifty-five. Before it closed its doors in 1833, it had produced over a thousand graduates, including founders of new law schools in Northampton and in Dedham, Massachusetts; in Cincinnati, Ohio; in Augusta, Georgia; and in Albany, New York. While the Litchfield Law School had proved the feasibility of American law schools, it had not set the pattern for American legal education (the normal length of its course for out-of-state students was only one year).

Even before 1829, Harvard law students were more numerous than those of Litchfield. But the decisive act in the founding of an American legal tradition occurred in that year: from money made by his *Abridgment,* Nathan Dane offered Josiah Quincy, incoming president of Harvard, the sum of $10,000 (later increased to $15,000) to establish a law professorship. One of the conditions of Dane's gift was that Joseph Story, then an associate justice of the United States Supreme Court, should be the first professor. Another condition was that the new professor should lecture on the "branches of Law and Equity, equally in force in all parts of our Federal Republic." The professor's attention was to be focused on those branches of the law "the most important and the most national, that is, . . . the same in other States of the Union as in this; making lectures on this State law useful in more States than one." This gift helped call into being an American legal system transcending the laws of the different states. Without a general American legal system, technically defined and available in books, the free commerce among our states and the industrial unity of our nation might have been impossible. Dane was more concerned for the nation than for the profession. He was less interested in training American lawyers than in creating a vital American law.

In Massachusetts, then, where, only two centuries before, New England Puritans had striven to apply the written Laws of God to the building of Zion in the wilderness, their descendants exerted a surpassing energy to elaborate and apply New English law to the building of a new nation. A dozen years earlier, in 1816, the Harvard Corporation (which had just passed from the control of clergymen to that of lawyers) had established Harvard's first law professorship. But after Joseph Story became the leading spirit at Harvard, the transformation of American legal education and the molding of an American legal system came very quickly. Within fifteen years the newborn American law had acquired its own character.

Joseph Story, who commuted from his seat on the Supreme Court in Washington to teach at the Harvard Law School, proved himself a prodigy. At the rate of about one volume a year, he produced commentaries on a wide variety of legal subjects, from the law of bailments, partnership, agency, bills of exchange, promissory notes, and equity pleading to constitutional law, conflict of laws, and equity jurisprudence. Though learned and technical, his books were not pedantic. They were bold, vigorously interpretive, broad, and constructive. Kent's readable elementary survey had proved that an American law existed; Story elaborated the tools to make it work. While his treatises did not cover every topic, they did encompass the commercial and industrial subjects that were changing most rapidly, and they included topics such as conflict of laws, constitutional law, and equity, that were peculiarly important to an expanding federal nation. Story's books were by-products of teaching, revisions of his Harvard lectures. They were to remain the basis of law-teaching all over the country and into the present century. Story had a genius for finding usable principles in the long lines of English cases and then applying them to new conditions, thus adapting the old common law to American problems. One of his most ingenious feats was to incorporate into the American common law the complex and independent English doctrines of "equity." And, by showing how these doctrines had happily embodied the wisdom of Roman law, he helped insure that the United States would live by the English common-law tradition.

The most troublesome difference between English and American law was that in England there was a single jurisdiction, a single national system of laws and courts. In the United States, each state had its own. But now the treatises of Story and others discovered in the decided cases of the different states a feasible unity. The law school, a New England invention, provided the forum for a truly national system of law. At Harvard, students from all over the country sought common principles transcending the circumstances of individual states. This search for a "national law" actually brought a national law into being. The American law school thus in the long run exerted a nationalizing influence, comparable to that which Eton and Harrow, Oxford and Cambridge long exerted on the English ruling classes.

Story's pioneering treatises did much to insure the dominance of the common law in the United States. But the common law was still essentially a judge-declared law. It hung on precedent, and not until there was in print a body of decided cases on the crucial legal questions would an American common law really be established. This too was a service of New England, and especially of Massachusetts. Within a half-century, the opinions of a series of remarkably prolific judges sitting on the Supreme Judicial Court of the Commonwealth established the independence, the adaptive vigor, and the traditionalism of American law.

The first of these was Theophilus Parsons, who became Chief Justice in 1806 and was known in his day as "The Giant of the Law." When he came to the bench, there was only one volume of printed judicial reports for Massachusetts. His opinions during his seven years filled nine volumes and were the first judicial monument of the American common law. Drawing on English precedents, English doctrines, and the unwritten Massachusetts practices of the colonial period, he produced the first broad and widely cited series of American precedents. He was a true New Englander both in his feeling for local customs and in his desire, especially in the laws of commerce, shipping, and insurance, to follow the practice of merchants. His successor as Chief Justice, Isaac Parker (first Royall Professor of Law at Harvard in 1816 and proposer of the original plan for a law school there in 1817), carried on Parsons' work.

The great lawgiving judge of the age—in many ways the founder of an American system of law—was the next Massachusetts Chief Justice, Lemuel Shaw. Measured qualitatively or quantitatively, his work had no equal. He accomplished (in his biographer Leonard Levy's phrase) the "day-by-day domestication of the English common law." During his thirty years (1830–60) as Chief Justice, he wrote a record 2200 opinions which, covering nearly every legal topic, would fill twenty volumes. Shaw's opinions are still widely cited wherever the common law lives. Few judges have shaped a great legal system so decisively and so enduringly.

On August 24, 1830, the same day that Shaw was named Chief Justice, occurred the first successful run of an American steam locomotive. Shaw's bold adaptation of the common law to the needs of railroad enterprise was only one illustration of his ready response to new needs. The first railroads posed many problems, long since forgotten, all far beyond the ken of the medieval common law. For example, all earlier "roads," whether publicly or privately constructed, were pathways on which anyone by paying a fee could move his own vehicles. The earliest railroad legislation had assumed that this was still the case and that (as Shaw later recalled) the railroad was nothing more than "an iron turnpike, upon which individuals and transportation companies were to . . . run with their own cars and carriages, paying a toll to the corporation for the use of the road only." Earlier transport businesses (waggoners, for example) picked up and delivered goods at your door. The old common law had therefore made these "common carriers" liable for any loss or damage to the goods from the moment they accepted it for transport until it was actually delivered at the door of the consignee. They were made virtually insurers, since the customer was paying for the door-to-door safe-conduct of goods. Moreover, their employees were few, the dangers of injury to them not great, and dangers could for the most part be avoided by an employee's own reasonable care.

None of these notions fitted railroads. Obviously, it was dangerous and chaotic to allow anyone who wished, to run his own cars on the track. A railroad, unlike other kinds of roads, did not need to meander across the countryside. It could best accomplish its purpose only if it took the direct route, the easiest grades. It had certain features of a natural monopoly, both in the uses to which it could be put and in the routes it required. To meet some of the new needs, Shaw introduced the expression and the important idea of "eminent domain." This American legal invention enabled the state to buy private property for a public use, which now included the use of railroads. Shaw thus recognized that, although the railroad company ran only its own cars on the line, it was actually a new kind of public highway.

With this idea he laid the foundation for the new industrial concept of a "public utility." He also legally recognized that old rules of liability, made originally for waggoners and other "common carriers," could not reasonably apply to railroads "whose line of movement and point of termination are locally fixed." Railroad companies now had to maintain stations and warehouses for the convenience of customers. While they still had to show reasonable care, they were no longer to be insurers of the goods. Shaw also expounded a "fellow-servant" rule —which relieved the employer of liability for damage which one employee suffered from another on the job—on the grounds that the employees themselves were now better situated than the employer to avoid the negligence of other employees. All these decisions helped make railroad building possible and profitable.

When Shaw had first come to the bench in 1830, Boston's trade seemed in danger of eclipse from the Erie Canal, which had recently opened a waterway from New York to the West. Railroads were a novel form of transportation with an uncertain future; when it had been proposed to build a railroad from Boston to the Hudson River, the Boston *Courier* (June 27, 1827) called it "as useless as a railroad from Boston to the Moon." In those early days, as Shaw remembered, the recently "ruinous" experience of Massachusetts private investors in turnpikes and canals made it "no easy matter to awaken anew the confidence of moneyed men in enterprises of internal improvement." Seeing the importance of railroads to the community, he was determined that obsolete laws should not stand in the way. By his understanding of the legal needs of railroads, Shaw made the common law a strong ally of industrial progress. Thus Chief Justice Shaw and his Massachusetts colleagues gave railroad law to the nation.

The great achievement of Massachusetts judges and lawyers was a way of thinking about social problems which focused on immediate, changing, and unpredictable needs, without denying the existence of principles. They did not pursue the absolute, nor expend their thinking on doctrinal quibbles. But the dynamism of New English law grew in a technical tradition. Printed matter and the written word were copiously used to describe, define, and limit each change as it was made. Change could hardly seem a menace when so sharply watched and so technically controlled.

New Englanders faced problems one at a time. "The first puff of the engine on the iron road," recalled one of Shaw's associates on the bench, "announced a revolution in the law of bailments and of common carriers." One thing at a time!—as this might have been the motto of the ancient English common law, so it could have been the motto of the new American common law. Proceeding warily and undogmatically from case to case, the common law was rich in the prudence of individual cases but poor in theoretical principles; it was adept at solving problems but inept at philosophizing about them. Underlying all were brooding omnipresences, pervading principles that could not be precisely defined.

Chief Justice Shaw in 1854 explained this way of thinking:

> The liability of carriers of goods by railroads, the grounds and precise extent and limits of their responsibility, are coming to be subjects of great interest and importance to the community. It is a new mode of transportation, in some respects like the transportation of ships, lighters and canal boats on water, and in others like that by wagons on land; but in some respects it differs from both. Though the practice is

new, the law, by which the rights and obligations of owners, consignees and of the carriers themselves, are to be governed is old and well established. It is one of the great merits and advantages of the common law, that, instead of a series of detailed practical rules, established by positive provisions, and adapted to the precise circumstances of particular cases, which would become obsolete and fail, when the practice and course of business, to which they apply, should cease or change, the common law consists of a few broad and comprehensive principles, founded on reason, natural justice, and enlightened public policy, modified and adapted to the circumstances of all the particular cases which fall within it. These general principles of equity and policy are rendered precise, specific, and adapted to practical use, by usage, which is the proof of their general fitness and common convenience, but still more by judicial exposition . . .

(*Norway Plains Co. v. Boston & Maine Railroad*, 1 Gray 263)

Only a few years later, in the era of the Civil War, this common-law approach to experience was to become a whole philosophy, or rather an American substitute for a philosophy. Its name was pragmatism. Oliver Wendell Holmes, Jr., the Shaw of the early 20th century, was an influential member of the small Boston discussion group, including Chauncey Wright, C. S. Peirce, and William James, out of which were to come the striking new statements of philosophical pragmatism. There is some reason to suspect that the pragmatic philosophy itself began simply as a way of generalizing this common-law approach.

New England was a garden of intellectual hybrids. The word "Commonwealth," like "eminent domain" and "public utility," expressed belief in the intermixture of public and private interests. A revival of the old Puritan name for Massachusetts, it was embodied in the Massachusetts Constitution of 1780 and was appropriate for Chief Justice Shaw's community. The wealth of that community, whether owned publicly or privately, was somehow held in common. Massachusetts was originally a chartered trading company: inhabitants were both citizens and stockholders. This mixed character, it was now argued, should not be forgotten. "The common good" in the preamble of the Massachusetts Constitution was a much fuzzier notion than "sovereignty," "rights," or the other currency of political theorists, and the meaning of Commonwealth would have to be defined less by logic than by experience.

7

The Improving Spirit

LITTLE NEW ENGLAND acquired a fantastic variety of institutions, of interests, and even of ways of life, and New Englanders
came more and more to see themselves as a patchwork of country
dwellers and city dwellers, farmers and factory workers, merchants and
factory owners, railroaders, canal builders and shipbuilders, old settlers
and recent immigrants (Negroes, Irish, Germans), of Congregationalists,
Catholics, Baptists, Episcopalians, Methodists, Unitarians, Universalists,
Presbyterians, and Jews. At least until mid-century, when nearly a
third of Boston's population had been born outside the United States,
growing numbers of immigrants were arriving from overseas. By almost
any standard, New England was becoming increasingly heterogeneous.

Before the Civil War, New England was also a center of emigration.
A surprisingly large number of New Englanders could be found seeking
their fortune in the mining towns of the West; many westward emigrant
companies were founded in New England. Some, like the Oregon en-
thusiast Hall Jackson Kelley, went to discover and settle the Pacific
Northwest; others were prodded by Edward Everett Hale to "Conquer
Texas before it Conquers Us" or by Eli Thayer to swell the antislavery
population of Kansas; others set up missions or trading posts in the
Sandwich Islands. In one way or another, those who stayed home were
themselves involved in the myriad interests and problems of faraway
places: by the remittances they expected or simply by the letters they
received and their affection for those who sent them. After 1830, it became ever harder for New Englanders not to see their community as a
center of change. The diversity of interests which Southerners denied,
and which their more static society had to some extent prevented, was
the very heart of New England.

A striking feature of New England public life was its abundance of
reform movements. Almost any idea for bettering the community or
some part of it soon begat a group competing in the market-place for
enthusiasm, money, and members. Every such movement attested someone's vision of a disparity between what the community was and what it
might be. In 1850, when Boston was still a city of less than 140,000,
she had already spawned scores of organizations for good causes. Southerners were right when they called New England the home of "isms,"

but they were mistaken in imagining that these weakened New England. On the contrary, the vitality of reform was the best index of a general social vitality. Seldom has such a large proportion of citizens been so alert to measure the community against its best possibilities.

At the extreme of vagueness and generality were those who called themselves "Transcendentalists." Their appeal, in their own day, came in large part from the very vastness of their aspirations. Their inflated reputation, in later generations, came from the range, sententiousness, and quotability of their literary remains. More characteristic of New England in the thirty years before the Civil War were the host of movements against specific evils; most of these were concrete and detailed in their social criticism. For example, Horace Mann of Massachusetts and Henry Barnard of Connecticut pioneered in the improvement of public schools with an approach that could hardly have been more down-to-earth. The Commissioners of Common Schools of Connecticut complained in their 1839 report that, of 40 schoolhouses in a certain county, only one had any means of ventilation, and that the average size of a school building (each housing about 30 children) was 18½ feet long, 7½ feet wide, and 7 feet high. In 1848 they reported that of the 1663 schoolhouses in the state only 873 had outhouses and 745 had no sanitary facility at all. Mann's *Common School Journal* in 1842 contrasted the "slave-ship stowage of children" with the neat buildings and "promenades" that enterprising New England farmers were commonly building for their hogs.

Josiah Quincy (mayor of Boston, 1823–28; president of Harvard, 1829–45), a pioneer in municipal reform, was said to have given his city its first thorough street cleaning in two centuries. He worked for a municipal water supply and sewage system; he fought gambling and prostitution. He also led a pamphlet war against the filth, depravity, and cruelty of New England prisons. His address to the Suffolk grand jury in 1822 was a sensational exposé of the consequences of confining young children together with hardened criminals. The Prison Discipline Society was organized in 1825, and piecemeal reform began.

The cruelties to the insane became the target of Dorothea Dix's lifelong attack. When she began teaching a Sunday-school class in the East Cambridge House of Correction in 1841, she found insane persons kept in wintry weather in an unheated room. During the next two years she made a detailed, first-hand study of the condition of the insane in the jails, almshouses, and houses of correction of the Commonwealth. In 1843 she sent to the state legislature her documented memorial, deploring "the present state of Insane Persons confined within this Commonwealth, in cages, closets, cellars, stalls, pens! Chained, naked, beaten with rods, and lashed into obedience!" As a result a bill was passed enlarging the Worcester insane asylum. She carried on her work with astonishing success elsewhere in New England, and then all over the nation.

Comparable accounts could be given of movements to relieve all kinds of underprivilege and misfortune. The Reverend Thomas H. Gallaudet, who had been trying to teach the deaf child of a fellow citizen of Hartford, was sent abroad by a group in 1815 to learn techniques for teaching the deaf. In England he found that the teaching of deaf mutes had for two generations been monopolized by a single family, who refused to give away its secrets, had already prevented schools being established in Ireland, and was now trying to extend its monopoly to America. In France, Gallaudet had greater success. He brought a French teacher back with him and established the first free American school for the deaf in Hartford in 1817. His school was remarkably effective in encouraging the education of the deaf elsewhere in the country. Gallaudet also found time to establish teachers' training schools in Connecticut, to promote the education of Negroes, to advance the higher education of women, and to work for the introduction of manual training into the curriculum.

About the same time, Dr. Samuel Gridley Howe (M.D., Harvard, 1824) set out to improve the education of the blind. Massachusetts incorporated its first school for the blind in 1829, and Howe was engaged in 1831 to organize it. After going about blindfolded in order better to understand his wards' point of view, he was able to invent new teaching techniques. By demonstrating the accomplishments of his blind students he succeeded in raising money. For forty-four years he directed the Perkins Institution for the Blind, where he trained teachers of the blind for schools everywhere. His most spectacular achievement was educating the deaf-blind child, Laura Dewey Bridgman. She entered his school just before she was eight; within a year he had put her in communication with the world and soon he had proved for the first time that the deaf-blind were not necessarily defective in intelligence. Later Laura herself occasionally taught other deaf-blind students and helped with the housework of the Perkins Institution. Charles Dickens, who visited Howe's school in Boston in 1842 and gave nearly forty pages of his brief *American Notes* to its work, was deeply moved by the charming prodigy Laura and by Howe's other deaf-blind pupil, Oliver Caswell. The philanthropic institutions of Boston, unlike many other American institutions he observed, seemed to Dickens to be models to be imitated in England.

Movements of large social reform, such as those for peace and against slavery, also found energetic supporters in New England, especially in Boston. Here too the temperance movement flourished. In 1838 Massachusetts passed a distinctive, if short-lived (repealed, 1840), temperance measure—the so-called "Fifteen-Gallon Law," which forbade the sale of less than fifteen gallons of liquor at a time, except on medical prescription. New England temperance groups distributed millions of printed appeals and secured international renown for their colorful and eloquent advocates.

*   *   *

A subtler kind of reform aimed at freeing workingmen from medieval restraints on their right to organize. It was in Boston in 1842 that the obsolete common law of conspiracy was finally revised and the American labor movement was given its charter of legality. This was accomplished by a broader and more realistic definition of the competitive economy, and by a frank acceptance of the conflict of interests. The intellectual market-place and the industrial market-place thrived together.

Before the rise of the factory system, working conditions had been determined by the job. Farm chores could not be limited to certain hours. The apprentice lived and worked with his master, and where craftsmen worked with their family, or with a few intimate helpers, it made no sense to measure the workday by a time clock. The introduction of larger units of manufacturing, closely integrated schemes of production, artificial power sources, and machinery changed much of this. It was complicated to stop and start the machinery; capital was going to waste every hour an expensive machine was not in use; processes under the same roof were tied to one another. These were all pressures toward longer hours and more concentrated and more unrelenting work. The ancient tradition of working "from sunrise to sunset," the outdoor working day, had lost its rationale. Now the regular working day varied from place to place. In some Massachusetts mills the usual working day for children was thirteen hours, excepting the Sabbath; in at least one Connecticut mill, the usual working day for adults was fifteen hours and ten minutes. The first New England agitation for shorter hours came not from factory workers but from artisans. Boston house carpenters struck for shorter hours in 1825; similar strikes followed in 1830 and 1831. Some workingmen were beginning to organize. In Philadelphia a pioneer workingmen's party had been organized in 1828, followed by one in New York the next year and by one in Massachusetts in 1834. In Boston about the same time appeared the first Trades Union in New England.

It is not surprising that employers were alarmed. Shorter hours, they warned, would "exert a very unhappy influence on our apprentices by seducing them from that course of industry and economy of time, to which we are anxious to enure them." "It will expose the Journeymen themselves to many temptations and improvident practices." The force and prestige of the ancient English common law opposed the workingmen's efforts to fight new evils. Since at least the Statute of Labourers of 1349, English law had punished collective efforts to improve wages or working conditions; as recently as 1800, Parliament had passed a new act against combinations. Reinforcing these and other specific statutes was the English common-law crime of conspiracy, which, because its boundaries were extremely hazy, became a trap for all "agitators." It served much the same purpose in the early 19th century that the labor injunction served a half century later. A combination of workingmen, the common law argued with legalistic ingenuity, might be a criminal conspiracy even though their purpose was lawful and their means not otherwise unlawful. The mere act of combining, so the argument ran, made their conduct unlawful and antisocial ("pregnant with public mischief and private injury"). Any such combination, it was said, inevitably interfered with the "natural" operations of the market, and terrorized employers and other workers. Between 1806 and 1842, there were at least a dozen cases in different states where workers were convicted of the "crime" of combination.

The case of *Commonwealth v. Hunt* had arisen in 1840 out of the irritation of Jeremiah Horne, a member of the Boston Journeymen Bootmakers' Society, which had fined him for doing extra work without pay. This fine was remitted when his employer paid him for the work, but when the union later fined him for another violation of union rules, he refused to pay the fine, even though his employer again offered to reimburse him. The union then expelled Horne and demanded that he be fired, and the union had a rule that no member could work for anyone who continued to employ a worker whose discharge the union had demanded. The employer, fearing a strike, fired Horne, who went to the district attorney with his complaint. The district attorney then drew an indictment against the Boston Journeymen Bootmakers' Society for conspiracy.

The judge of the Boston Municipal Court instructed the jury that, as a matter of law, such a combination amounted to the crime of conspiracy; their only task was to decide whether there had actually been a combining for the alleged purpose. Within twenty minutes, the jury returned a verdict of guilty against the union. The union members were defended by Robert Rantoul, Jr., a versatile reformer who had been an energetic member of the Commonwealth's first Board of Education, a temperance leader, and an opponent of capital punishment (among his other causes). He carried the union's case to the highest court in Massachusetts, where it was heard by Chief Justice Shaw. Rantoul there repeated his argument that the English common law of conspiracies was not in force in Massachusetts. It was part, he said, "of the English tyranny from which we fled."

Shaw, more flexible than Rantoul, wished both to preserve the English legal tradition and to serve the new needs of an industrial community. Instead of abandoning the common law, he reshaped it. The proper test, now stated clearly by Shaw in the epoch-making opinion he delivered in 1842, was whether the combination was "to accomplish some criminal or unlawful purpose, or to accomplish some purpose, not in itself criminal or unlawful, by criminal or unlawful means." The purpose of union members was to persuade "all those engaged in the same occupation to become members." This, he said, was not in itself unlawful.

The mere fact, Shaw added, that others might be "impoverished" by this lawful course of action did not make it unlawful. From one point of view, all bargaining in the market-place was an effort to "impoverish" others. Here Shaw declared his faith in a competitive economy and his willingness to legalize a conflict of interests within the community. The union members were, of course, "free to work for whom they please, or not to work, if they so prefer. In this state of things, we cannot perceive, that it is criminal for men to agree together to exercise their own acknowledged rights, in such a manner as best to subserve their own interests." Supposing, he said, a group of merchants sold their product so cheaply that their competitors were put out of business. This was surely no conspiracy, nor, then, was a comparable combination of workers to put whatever price or conditions they chose on their labor. Sometimes a competition which tended to impoverish others might be "highly meritorious and public spirited." "It is through competition that the best interests of trade and industry are promoted."

Shaw thus legalized trade unions. At the same time he gave new life to the common-law tradition. His opinion could not have been made or followed except in a society where change was both imagined and welcomed. Rantoul, the union lawyer (later a founder of the Illinois Central Railroad), had himself, like Shaw, long been a champion of the growing railroads. Free interchange of goods and services in a varied society full of conflicts: this alone could keep the nation prosperous and growing.

PART TWO

THE TRANSIENTS
Joiners

"It is good to be shifty in a new country."

JOHNSON J. HOOPER

"The American flies at everything. 'Go ahead
anyhow,' that is his motto. The characteristic of
his civilization must . . . be extensiveness. . . .
The American people . . . diffuses itself, its
energy, and its capital, over a whole continent."

JAMES STIRLING

IN THE heart of the continent arose a new *homo Americanus* more easily
identified by his mobility than by his habitat. He began to dominate the
scene in the years between the American Revolution and the Civil War,
and he was now shaping the new nation into a New World.

Of the new space-free man there were two types: the Transients (or
Joiners) and the Upstarts (or Boosters). Transient communities bred
Joiners by their pace and problems of movement. Upstart communities
bred Boosters by their speed of growth. The Transient communities en
route became Upstart communities when they settled.

Much of the newness of the new nation was born among these Americans moving inland from the sea. The continent, like the ocean, was a
place of wandering, unexplored and communally explorable. Traveling
the continent was like traveling the ocean. Dangers made men travel
together and stick together, forming communities as they went.

49

The American transients were something new under the sun. True enough, moving peoples—bedouins, conquistadores, crusaders, explorers, barbarian invaders—are as old as man. But where before had so many people been continually in motion over a continental landscape? Where before had migrants been equipped with tools so much more advanced than those of the aborigines? Where had so many people of their own accord taken one-way passage? Where had so many men moved to un-known, remote places, not to conquer or convert or fortify nor even to trade, but to find and make communities for themselves and their children?

New institutions grew as the Transients traveled. In order to travel, they had to make new communities. They had to devise laws quickly and enforce them swiftly, without benefit of books or lawyers. They had to leave people and things behind. Above all, they had to be willing to go ahead anyhow, forming new communities, without waiting for God or government to prepare their way.

8

On the Continent-Ocean:
Men Move in Groups

WE ALL KNOW that, when the first European settlers came across the ocean to found Jamestown, Plymouth, or Massachusetts Bay Colony, they came in groups. They came in community, depending on one another. It was with three ships that John Smith set sail for Virginia; those who disembarked with him at Jamestown on May 24, 1607, numbered 105. The crowded *Mayflower* carried, besides officers and crew, 101 passengers. The *Arbella,* in which John Winthrop came to found Massachusetts Bay Colony, was one of four ships (seven more sailed a month later); altogether six or seven hundred people arrived in the fleet. Those who crossed the water did not travel alone.

But, of all American myths, none is stronger than that of the loner moving west across the land. Without having thought much about why, we have taken for granted that, on landing, the colonial traveler no longer needed his community. The pioneering spirit, we are often told, is a synonym for "individualism." The courage to move to new places and try new things is supposed to be the same as the courage to go it alone, to focus exclusively and intensively and enterprisingly on oneself. Only so, we hear, could the threatened pioneer survive. And so, it is said, an American way was born.

True enough, the heroic individual has held the spotlight of history. Countless individual men and women kept their own records, chronicling their personal hopes and disappointments, their own acts of courage and enterprise. But groups—especially the casual, informal, readily formed and readily dissolved groups in which travelers move—keep no diaries, write no letters, compose no autobiographies. We know the names of Daniel Boone, and Lewis and Clark, and Zebulon Pike, and John Charles Frémont. But how many have heard of the Ohio Company of Associates, the Green and Jersey County Company, or the Bartleson Party?

The secrets of groups of moving Americans, more even than the other secrets of history, remain hidden from us. Clusters of people gathered for a single simple purpose (such as crossing the continent), if they did not become permanent political or financial units, remain nameless. Their chronicles had to be written, if at all, in a thousand places. Their headquarters was wherever they were, and they were ever on the move. They had no sacred archives, no trained archivists, no courthouse records or land-office files.

There was, of course, the occasional lone traveler and individual explorer. Sometimes he was the person who went there first; seldom was he the settler. It is mostly on the lecture platform, in the movies, and on television, that a lone-wolf adventurer—the Stanley or the Livingtone —is a star. In history, even the great explorer had been the man who drew others to a common purpose, in the face of unpredictable hardships. The great geographic discoveries have been accomplished less typically by individuals than by groups. On his first voyage Columbus commanded three vessels; on his second, seventeen vessels with fifteen hundred men. The genius of a Columbus, a Vasco da Gama, a La Salle, a Magellan, a De Soto, was that of the organizer. The maker and leader of a newly detached community was the man who first led other men to new, dangerously remote, places.

The continent too was an ocean. To cross the wild continent safely, one had to travel with a group. Between the American Revolution and the Civil War, those who pushed far west of the established settlements, like the Pilgrim Fathers, seldom went alone. We cannot be statistical about it. But in these years when American ways were taking shape, many, perhaps most, of the people who were the first to settle at a distance from the protected boundaries of the Atlantic seaboard, traveled in groups. Few facts were more important in shaping American institutions.

The lone adventurer was likely to be a priest, a professional explorer, a surveyor, a guide, or a hunter. Early *settlers,* those who took one-way passage and became the backbone of new Western communities, generally went together. They expressed their needs and desires in the groups they formed en route; their notions of community were in turn shaped by the group life which brought them safely to their destination. When the great-grandchildren of the Pilgrims moved farther west, they, like their ancestors, commonly moved and settled in clusters, drawn together by the perils of the unknown land. This communal experience, which would be re-enacted again and again all across the continent, had been that of the first settlements in the Ohio Valley.

An Ohio Company had been founded in 1748 by some Virginians who had sent out Christopher Gist, a professional surveyor, to explore their territory. The permanent settlements, however, were the work of a later Ohio Company of Associates, promoted by some New England veterans of the American Revolution who were trying to recoup their fortunes. Among the leaders were General Rufus Putnam and the Reverend Manassah Cutler. The versatile Cutler had already practiced law and medicine, had measured the distances of the stars, had surveyed the altitude of Mt. Washington, and had made the first systematic account of the flora of New England, when he went to New York to persuade Congress to give his company the right to take up one and one-half million Ohio acres at about eight cents an acre. The government contract was signed on October 27, 1787. Before the year's end, General Putnam was on his way west with an advance party. They set out in two units (one from Danvers, Massachusetts, the other from Hartford, Connecticut), both bound for the Ohio River. On April 2, 1788, all embarked together at Sumrill's Ferry, in Western Pennsylvania on the Youghiogheny, for the trip down the Monongohela and then down the Ohio River. On April 7, the party, forty-eight strong, landed on the east bank of the Muskingum where it joined the Ohio River, just opposite Fort Harmar. Lucky, too, that there were so many of them, for the seventy Delaware and Wyandot Indians who had come to trade furs might conceivably have had other designs on a smaller party.

These men quickly laid out their town on the compact New England model. Each settler was given a small "in-lot" within the town for a residence and an "out-lot" of eight acres for crops. On July 2, 1788, the agents and directors of the Ohio Company held their first meeting on the spot and named the town Marietta. Again following the New England example, they promptly provided a church and a school, both of which were operating before the end of July. Within a few months fifteen more families and many single men joined the town. The men in Marietta now numbered 132.

The ever-present Indian danger made such tight garrison-settlements necessary. Near this first Ohio town were Indians of the Shawnee, Delaware, Miami, and Wyandot tribes, with remnants of the Six Nations evacuated from New York. Volatile, resentful, they would swoop down without warning, killing and scalping defenseless settlers. Near Marietta one of these raids, killing eight persons, occurred in that first May of 1788. Rash pioneers, tempted to go off and settle by themselves, soon learned better. Again, on January 2, 1791, Wyandot and Delaware warriors attacked an outlying settlement up the Muskingum River, killing and burning. Other settlers in that neighborhood then built Fort Frye, a triangular palisade enclosing twenty families, ten single men, and eight or ten soldiers from Fort Harmar down the river. The whole story of the early settlement of the Ohio country was of a string of such groups —at Farmers Castle, Belpre, Columbia, Losantiville, Ft. Washington (later called Cincinnati), North Bend, Gallipolis, Manchester, and many other places.

People moving these great distances into an unknown landscape, threatened by numerous nameless dangers, banded together: not because they especially loved their neighbors or had inherited any ties to them, but because they needed one another. Westward-moving pioneers everywhere found group travel and group living normal.

Independence, Missouri, the starting point of the Santa Fe Trail and the California and Oregon Trails, was famous from the 1820's to the 1850's as a place where travel parties were put together. Here or a few miles farther west, as Josiah Gregg noted in his *Commerce of the Prairies* (1844), was "the general 'port of embarkation' for every part of the great western and northern 'prairie ocean,'" where people who had never before seen one another agreed to share daily tasks and mortal risks till they reached their destination.

The Santa Fe Trail took almost a bee-line from Independence by way of Ft. Dodge (now Dodge City) on the Arkansas River to the town of Santa Fe, then far within Mexican territory. It was used, mainly, not by emigrants but by traders. Opened by Robert McKnight and his small caravan in 1821 and defined by Captain William Becknell in 1821, it carried a thriving trade and countless passengers traveling in caravans, during the next decades. Gregg gives us a vivid account of the trail in its heyday. With a small party he left Independence, May 15, 1831, on the first of his many successful passages. "The general rendezvous at Council Grove was our immediate destination. It is usual for the traders to travel thus far in detached parties, and to assemble there for the purpose of entering into some kind of organization, for mutual security and defence during the remainder of the journey." Within a day Gregg's group joined the rear division of a caravan which consisted of thirty wagons. On May 26 they were joined by another seventeen wagons. At Council Grove they found the main body of the caravan, its effective force coming to nearly two hundred men. Not till mid-July, after about eight weeks on the road, did this caravan arrive at Santa Fe.

The caravan adventures recorded by Gregg show why it was sensible and normal to travel in groups. Against the Indians, mere numbers deterred attack and provided means of defense. "Upon encamping the wagons are formed into a 'hollow square' . . . constituting at once an enclosure (or corral) for the animals when needed, and a fortification against the Indians." Travelers who lacked such a "pen of the wagons" might find it impossible at night to control their draft animals and other cattle. The group was a protection, too, against the vicissitudes of nature. "We encountered a region of very troublesome quagmires," wrote Gregg. "On such occasions it is quite common for a wagon to sink to the hubs in mud, while the surface of the soil all around would appear perfectly dry and smooth. To extricate each other's wagons we had frequently to employ double and triple teams, with 'all hands to the wheels' in addition —often led by the proprietors themselves up to the waist in mud and water."

The constant night watch required against marauding Indians and stampeding animals made another argument against too small a party. "The usual number of watches is eight, each standing a fourth of every alternate night," Gregg recalled of his caravan in 1831. "When the party is small the number is generally reduced; while in the case of very small bands, they are sometimes compelled for safety's sake to keep one watch on duty half the night."

Or consider what might come from an accident like that recorded on the trail in the summer of 1826. A Mr. Broadus had his arm shattered by an accidental shot as he tried to draw his rifle, muzzle foremost, from a wagon. For him, the group made the difference between life and death. Dying of gangrene, he was rescued by his caravan mates:

> Their only "case of instruments" consisted of a handsaw, a butcher's knife and a large iron bolt. The teeth of the saw being considered too coarse, they went to work, and soon had a set of fine teeth filed on the back. The knife having been whetted keen, and the iron bolt laid upon the fire, they commenced the operation: and in less time than it takes to tell it, the arm was opened round to the bone, which was almost in an instant sawed off; and with the whizzing hot iron the whole stump was so effectually seared as to close the arteries completely. Bandages were now applied, and the company proceeded on their journey as though nothing had occurred. The arm commenced healing rapidly, and in a few weeks the patient was sound and well, and is perhaps still living, to bear witness to the superiority of the "hot iron" over ligatures, in "taking up" arteries.

On the emigrant trails, where there were more baggage, more women, and more children, the advantages of group travel were still more obvious. Many accounts survive of this life on the California and Oregon Trails between 1842 and the Civil War. These trails, like the Santa Fe Trail, left from Independence, Missouri, where their groups were organized; but then they followed the Platte River, past Ft. Laramie, through South Pass in the Wind River Mountains of Central Wyoming, northwestward to Ft. Hall (near the present Pocatello, Idaho), after which the two trails branched. The Oregon Trail then followed the Snake River toward Ft. Walla Walla and Ft. William (later Portland); the California

Trail turned southwest across the desert, past the present Carson, Nevada, and over the Sierras to Sutter's Fort (near the present Sacramento). From Independence to Sutter's Fort, about 2000 miles on the wagon trail, a reasonable time was five months. Travel by mule pack train instead of by wagon was, of course, possible. It even had some advantages, for packers found it easier to ford streams or go up and down rough terrain; with good luck they might arrive a month sooner than the wagons. But pack trains offered no protection against the sun and were impracticable for pregnant women, small children, the aged, and the sick. The wagon, then, was the normal vehicle for the emigrant. Although slow, cumbersome, hard to turn or to move across rivers and up and down mountains, and liable to suffer breakdown, in the long run the wagon was preferable because it protected against sun, wind, and rain, provided an ambulance by day, and served as a fortification by night. At the normal speed of two miles an hour riding was not too uncomfortable, even without springs. Able-bodied passengers got out to walk over rough places.

The wagon commonly used on the California and Oregon Trails was not the heavy six-horse vehicle designed by the Germans of Conestoga Valley in Pennsylvania but was much lighter—only half as long and a little more than half as high. It was about ten feet in length, eight and a half feet from road to top of the canvas, and when fully loaded carried a ton. Commonly drawn by a three-yoke team of six oxen, it was light enough so that, even if two oxen were lost, the wagon could still be moved.

The wagon was plainly a community vehicle: everything about it required traveling in groups. To cross deep streams or climb steep slopes the ox teams had to be doubled and the wagons managed one at a time. Many ways were found to use the group's total resources to conquer obstacles and reduce risk. For example, at the head of Goldstream Canyon where on a 250-foot slope the altitude rose 150 feet, making a 35-degree incline, the Brown Party in 1846 set up an elaborate machine to pull the wagons across the Sierra Nevada. Fifteen pairs of oxen at the top of the hill pulled a chain on a roller, which drew each wagon in turn up the hill.

Going down a steep hill was also a problem. Primitive brakes could not be relied on; there was always the danger of too much speed, of overturning the wagons or breaking the legs of the animals. For example, above Ash Hollow in the North Platte Valley was a height called Windlass Hill. Its incline was so steep that no one dared risk the tumble, and few trees were at hand to be cut and dragged for braking action. Therefore it became common practice for each company to make its own windlass from one of the wagons in order to ease the other wagons down one by one.

East of the Mississippi, large-group migration disappeared early. In

the Ohio Valley, General Anthony Wayne's victory over the Indians
at the Battle of Fallen Timbers in 1794 made it safer for an individual
or a family to travel alone and settle in isolation. Regular river transportation was established, inns along the way provided food and lodging,
roads were improved, and a mail service was begun. In the trans-
Mississippi west, large-group travel continued. For there the Indian
peril lasted at least until the defeat of Chief Sitting Bull and Chief
Crazy Horse on October 31, 1876 and the conclusion of the Nez Percé
war of the following year. The trip was still long and its natural danger
remained.

We cannot, of course, know exactly how many traveled west in the
large groups which included more than a family or two. The evidence
suggests great numbers. For example, on the "Platte Route" (a stretch
of 500 miles from Fort Kearny to Fort Laramie), the first great
emigration party, led by Colonel Stephen W. Kearny in 1845, was a
wagon train three miles long. At South Pass, Wyoming, during October
and November, 1858 (not the season of heaviest travel), a count showed
95 separate parties comprising 597 wagons and 1366 men. This great
migration across the American continent-ocean had no equal in modern
times: in the words of Bayard Taylor, the reporter sent to California by
the New York *Tribune,* it "more than equalled the great military expeditions of the Middle Ages in magnitude, peril and adventure."

The day when it became safe and normal for the lone individual or
the single family to travel into the Far West came later, with the railroads.

9

The Organizers

OUT OF THE VAST American spaces and from the need to travel in
groups came the power of the organizer. Men living beyond the jurisdiction of government, away from the places and customs of their
fathers, had to be persuaded to do their jobs. Here was a new demand
for that special combination of qualities that enabled a man to persuade
or cajole others to do their share for the group. Without the power or
tradition or prestige of an army commander, the leader of a traveling
community had to be able to get things done. He had to create an *esprit
de corps* quickly and preserve it among a miscellaneous crowd in the

face of thirst, hunger, and disease, discouragement, mortal danger, and death. A host of factors combined to give the organizer a power he had seldom before held outside of military life or civil government. In traditional, settled communities, many qualities—noble ancestry, landed property, wealth, bravery, military prowess, learning, shrewdness, or eloquence—might make a man a leader; among the transients in sparsely settled America, the leader was the persuader and the organizer.

The motley groups—"men from every class and grade of society, with a little sprinkling of the softer sex"—which formed at Independence or a few miles farther west on the trail needed leaders. The organizer created the wagon train. Sometimes a man like Col. Stephen W. Kearny plainly claimed command by virtue of his experience and military rank. Or a John Bartleson became captain because he had with him the seven or eight men needed to enlarge the party; they would not go along if their man was not on top. Often enough, however, the job was up for grabs and went to the person who combined organizing talent with an ability to win votes, for commonly the selection was democratic.

Choice of a captain, according to what Gregg called "the standing custom of these promiscuous caravans," usually came after much electioneering and "party spirit." Candidates announced themselves, sought supporters, and urged their own virtues. Then, "after a great deal of bickering and wordy warfare," the election was held, and the winner was proclaimed "Captain of the Caravan."

> The powers of this officer were undefined by any "constitutional provision," and consequently vague and uncertain: orders being only viewed as mere requests, they are often obeyed or neglected at the caprice of the subordinates. It is necessary to observe, however, that the captain is expected to direct the order of travel during the day, and to designate the camping-ground at night; with many other functions of a general character, in the exercise of which the company find it convenient to acquiesce. . . . But after this [election of the captain] comes the principal task of organizing. The proprietors are first notified by "proclamation" to furnish a list of their men and wagons. The latter are generally apportioned into four "divisions," particularly when the company is large—and ours consisted of nearly a hundred wagons, besides a dozen of dearborns and other small vehicles, and two small cannons (a four and a six pounder), each mounted upon a carriage. To each of these divisions, a "lieutenant" was appointed, whose duty it was to inspect every ravine and creek on the route, select the best crossings, and superintend what is called, in prairie parlance, the "forming" of each encampment.

The merchandise-capital of a single such caravan might be $200,000. The talents most in demand were not those of the fearless lone backwoodsman, the crack shot clad in fringed buckskin; what was needed was a shrewd and effective organizer. The transients' leader had to bring a community into being and to inspire, wheedle, bribe, or threaten its members to the performance of unfamiliar tasks on strange landscapes and against incalculable dangers. Flexibility, warmth, imagination, human breadth, and an encouraging voice were more in order than dignity, respectability, or nobility. Organizing talent was fostered, not only by group travel, but by many of the other peculiar needs and opportunities of life on a vast sparsely settled continent. Take the fur trade as an example.

The first great North American fur-trading enterprise was the Hudson's Bay Company, chartered as a monopoly by Charles II. After 1821, under the vigorous leadership of the young George Simpson, a self-made Scotsman on the American pattern, the Company attained new power and prosperity, conducting its trade through an elaborate and far-flung organization centered in London. Its main operation, strictly speaking, was fur trading rather than fur trapping, partly because of the way of life of the Indians among whom they worked. Algonquins and other northern tribes had very early acquired a taste (and then a need) for the guns, kettles, and blankets which only the European could give them, and therefore they were willing to exchange for those items the furs they themselves had gathered. But the Indians of the southern plains and lower Rockies had not been so corrupted by the white man, for the buffalo provided them a versatile raw material. Since they were less eager for the European goods, they left it to the white men to go out into these regions and trap the furs for themselves. This did not make the problem of organization any easier. On the contrary, instead of only organizing the centers to which Indians brought furs, here the white men had to organize all the activities, beginning with the actual trapping.

The chronicle of this far Western fur trade, as we can read it in the colorful pages of General Hiram Chittenden, is a story of organization and counterorganization, of companies and communications, of trading posts and backwoods towns, of loyalties and treacheries. From the outset, the transportation which made the Western fur trade feasible and profitable was a group enterprise. First came the keelboat. This vessel, which dominated the commerce of the Missouri at least till 1830 and then only slowly disappeared, was from fifty to seventy-odd feet long, and had a fifteen- to eighteen-foot beam, with a shallow draft, was sharp at both ends, and equipped with a running-board from bow to stern on either side. Especially designed for movement upstream, it was anything but a one-man operation. The usual means of propulsion was the cordelle —a long line attached to the top of the high mast, which passed through a ring fastened by a short line to the bow to help guide the boat—drawn by from twenty to forty men pulling along the shore. When the cordelle could not be used, a number of men stood on each of the running-boards, planting poles in the river-bottom and pushing as they walked toward the stern, thus propelling the boat against the current. When neither cordelle nor pole could be used, the boat was moved by oars, five or six on either side of the bow. On a long journey of a thousand miles, such a boat might at best average eighteen miles a day—every mile the product of strenuous cooperation.

Gradually the steamboat displaced the keelboat. It, too, was a cooperative enterprise, a small community in itself. In these vessels, trappers and traders went up the Missouri River from St. Louis, carrying equipment and trading-goods. Returning down the river, they carried the weary trappers and traders who had done their stint, and with them came the booty of the wilderness.

Essential, too, were the caravan and the rendezvous. Compared with river travel, travel overland required even more elaborate organization. Caravans for the Western fur trade generally formed at Independence, Missouri, where men gathered, and goods were collected and packed for the long journey by mule pack or wagon. Beyond reach of the rivers there was no other way to carry out the stuff trappers needed for their jobs and to make life tolerable in their remote stations. Caravans might move at rates of from fifteen to twenty-five miles a day, every night making camp at a place with grass, wood, and water, and organizing nightly against Indian attack. Their destination was a thousand miles or more away at the annual rendezvous. This rendezvous was as much a marvel of precise prearrangement as it was also, often, a spectacle of drunken debauch.

The rendezvous, an institution which dominated the United States fur trade for nearly two decades beginning about 1820, was a more transient, more flexible, and in many ways more complex organization than that ruling the old dominion of the Hudson's Bay Company. Up there in the North, the practice was to build durable trading posts and fortified settlements. But these were costly, difficult and dangerous to keep continuously supplied; they often irritated the Indians, and they were hard to move. William H. Ashley, versatile and enterprising St. Louis businessman, and his partner Andrew Henry organized the rendezvous system which vastly extended the range of the trappers. Their idea was simply to operate, not from fixed forts and trading posts, but at annual meeting-points.

Each year Ashley and Henry named the place, which now could be moved about yearly, with the changing fortunes of the trade. There was no year-round expense, no standing defiance of the Indians.

It was far cheaper to operate this way, but it required more organizational skill, a continuous attention to detail, an ability to shift operations and to hold the loyalty of the scores of new men for whom Ashley and Henry repeatedly advertised. The old system had required only a small permanent staff to whom the trappers brought their furs; now men were enlisted and sent out as trappers, to return at an appointed time and place. In the *Missouri Republican* of March 20, 1822, they inserted a call for "one hundred young men to ascend the Missouri to its source." During the heyday of the rendezvous system there were as many as six hundred trappers organized to scour the mountain streams of the Rockies, each returning with his booty to these annually shifting, but carefully prearranged headquarters.

The fur trade could not, of course, have flourished without the courage and staying power of these individual "Mountain Men." They knew how to survive alone in the backwoods; they knew where to find the beaver and how to elude, entice, or enlist the Indian. Hugh Glass, an early Ashley-Henry man, who acquired legendary fame, had been separated from his party in 1823 and was attacked by a grizzly bear; after being left for dead by his companions, he crawled nearly one hundred miles to Fort Kiowa, where he recuperated for a new career of personal revenge and far-flung trapping.

Such feats and those of Jim Bridger and Bill Sublette would have been fruitless and their work unprofitable without the organizer. The unsung Ulysses of these epics of the American West was the shrewd and skilful organizer, the John Jacob Astor or the William H. Ashley, who enlisted the enterprise of others to fulfil a grand and profitable vision.

Even those who fired the popular imagination by their real or imaginary exploits of marksmanship and backwoodsmanship succeeded in no small part because of their ability to persuade others to work together. Daniel Boone, for example, was notable not only because he "Cilled One Bar" but also for his skill as a leader. He had a long and active career as an organizer of men: as an agent of the Transylvania Company, when he led the first division of settlers for its new Kentucky colony in March 1775 and supervised the erection of Boonesborough; as a captain, and then as a major of militia; as a collector of sums from settlers for the purchase of land warrants; as a lieutenant-colonel of Fayette County.

With only a few exceptions, the most successful fur traders, backwoodsmen, and pathfinders of the West in the early 19th century also had political careers. The most conspicuous was John Charles Frémont, the first presidential nominee of the Republican party in 1856, who had been elected the first senator from California in 1850, and held numerous other offices. Daniel Boone, too, besides his military commands, was twice elected to the Virginia legislature and served as magistrate in the territory of Missouri. Davy Crockett, despite his reputation for shiftlessness, was elected magistrate, and served as a colonel of a militia regiment, and representative in the state legislature before his two terms in Congress. William Henry Ashley, the pioneer fur trader and founder of the rendezvous system, ran for senator and twice for governor of Missouri before his two terms in Congress. Bill Sublette filled several public offices and served as a presidential elector; he, too, ran for Congress.

The normal career for a man who had made his mark in the fur trade or in Western exploration included a term as magistrate and a go for the governorship or for Congress. The path ran from the Western trails of the fur-trading companies direct to the territorial and state and national legislatures. A successful organizer of Western expeditions was likely to have some ambition and considerable aptitude for democratic politics. The reputation of many of these men for being "loners" with a taste for the unpopulous backwoods was acquired only later, often as an embellishment by Eastern literary men and journalists who, from their city offices, cast these Westerners in picturesque roles.

*   *   *

Religion as well as politics offered at least one remarkable example of the success of the American organizer moving toward and around the West. For the Mormons had set themselves the task of discovering and cultivating the Promised Land. In many ways they obviously resembled the well-organized Puritans of early New England, who had also tried to build Zion. Like the Puritans before them, the Mormons had not the slightest doubt that they possessed the Truth by which the good society should be built; just as the Puritans called their church members "Visible Saints," so the Mormons were the Church of Jesus Christ of Latter-day Saints; like the early Puritans, the Mormons were ruled in a paternalistic, authoritarian spirit. Building their religion on the Book of Mormon, first published in 1830 from plates of gold miraculously translated by Joseph Smith of upstate New York, they were the only considerable sect until then based on a sacred book revealed in America; their Book of Mormon purported to continue the story of the Bible and of other sacred Christian writings into the New World. These Mormons were a people of extraordinary courage and fortitude and energy, but they were not regarded as acceptable neighbors, even among Westerners, who usually welcomed newcomers. Rejected in one place after another, their westward movement was a staccato series of enforced group transplantations, each more remarkable than the last as a feat of organization.

At the first headquarters in Kirtland, Ohio, Joseph Smith and his followers completed an impressive temple in 1836, but they soon became involved in land speculation, which brought them to bankruptcy. Meanwhile, a group of them had settled near Independence in Jackson County, Missouri, where their divine pretensions, their industry, thrift, and energy soon aroused jealousy, and their friendliness to the Indians stirred suspicion.

Harried from Jackson County, where their printing plant had been wrecked and their leaders tarred and feathered, they moved to neighboring Clay county, where they secured the Missouri legislature's permission to form a county of their own. "Far West," their new county seat, was built according to Joseph Smith's geometric plan: a city of twelve temples and squared city blocks, designed for an eventual population of twenty thousand. Again the Mormons prospered; again they aroused the jealous suspicions of their neighbors. The surrounding community antagonism led them to organize a self-defense group known as the "Danites" or Sons of Dan, which itself became a fertile source of anti-Mormon legends. When non-Mormons tried to prevent the Mormons from voting on election day in 1838, the Mormons fought back, and so began the first of their several civil wars. Mormon troops numbered well over a thousand. Joseph Smith, comparing himself to Mohammed, borrowed the slogan "The Alcoran or the Sword," and prophesied: "So shall it eventually be with us—'Joseph Smith or the Sword!'" But after a massacre of Mormons, Smith surrendered and was sentenced to be shot. When the commanding officer refused to carry out the order, Joseph Smith and his Saints escaped still farther westward to Quincy, Illinois. The first Mormon war had cost the Saints a million dollars and some forty lives.

In Illinois in 1839 the story began again. A new Zion would now be built at Nauvoo, again on Joseph Smith's geometric plan, only on a smaller scale. By 1842 the city counted nearly fifteen thousand. A charter from the Illinois legislature made Nauvoo a nearly independent city-state, which soon boasted a "university" and expanding visions of a roseate future. Inspired by the conviction that they were a "Peculiar People," and seizing their Western opportunity for independence, the Mormons used their organizing genius to elaborate novel elements in their theology, ritual, and institutions. These included baptism of the dead and new sealing and "endowment" ceremonies in the temple.

Plural marriage, the most notorious of their innovations, was actually practiced in Nauvoo, although publicly disavowed by Joseph Smith and other leaders. Smith received a revelation making polygamy a Church doctrine in 1843, but Church leaders consistently denied the practice until the Mormons had again moved farther west. Then, from Salt Lake City in 1852, plural marriage was announced as the doctrine, and even the duty, of Church members. The institution was subtly connected with all the rest of Mormon theology, and especially with their belief in pre-existence. If, as the Mormons asserted, countless spirits were actually wandering bodiless, impatiently awaiting some fleshly tabernacle to inhabit on this earth, then it was the duty of every man and woman to provide such tabernacles as rapidly and efficiently as possible. A woman could be saved only through marriage, and a man's reward would be the greater in afterlife the more numerous his children. Plural marriage then became a grim duty rather than a sensual pleasure. "We must gird up our loins," preached Brigham Young in Utah, "and fulfill this, just as we would any other duty."

In Nauvoo, polygamy was not yet publicly admitted as a doctrine of the Church, but there was enough else to arouse the antagonism of the neighboring Gentiles. The growing city became increasingly independent and increasingly militant: the Mormons' political power (they voted as a bloc in the Illinois legislature) seemed more and more threatening. Their ability to build a thriving city on an Illinois swamp made their neighbors fear them more than ever. It was Missouri all over again. Another splinter group had developed among the Mormons, which condemned Smith's dictatorship. When Smith used force to suppress these internal enemies, a new civil war with the outside community was under way. Joseph Smith and three other Mormon leaders were murdered in the jail at Carthage, Illinois, in June, 1844. The Illinois legislature repealed the Nauvoo charter the following year and the Mormons had to move on.

In the wintry February of 1846, Brigham Young led the Great Trek toward Utah. This brilliant example of the westward movement by groups was one of the great triumphs of organization in all American history. For the long march across Iowa, the Mormons built their own roads and bridges, and even planted crops to be harvested by those who came after them the next season. By August 2, 1847, Brigham Young was laying out the new Zion which would be Salt Lake City. Again he used Joseph Smith's geometric plan. Young's meticulous and effective organization brought party after party across the plains. One group which finally reached Utah in early October had brought 1540 Mormon emigrants in 540 wagons, with 124 horses, 9 mules, 2213 oxen, 887 cows, 358 sheep, 35 hogs, and 716 chickens. When another group of nearly twenty-five hundred arrived under Young's personal leadership a year later, they found a flourishing capital "city" and ten other settlements, already operating two gristmills and four sawmills. The Mormon epic was again about to be re-enacted—this time on a wider stage, for larger stakes, and with decisive results.

The anti-Mormon frenzy, earlier confined to their neighbors at each new settlement, now reached a new pitch and became national. And the last Mormon war was fought by Federal troops against a thriving community which had been built in less than a decade. In the unsung and inglorious Civil War of 1857–58, President Buchanan sent troops under Colonel Albert Sidney Johnson to suppress the Mormon "uprising" and restore order, liberty, and morality. Mormon leaders, after futile appeals to the Declaration of Independence and the Constitution as bulwarks of their rights, toyed with the idea of secession.

Although Brigham Young was an eminently practical man, the Mormons never were incorporated into American politics on their own terms: they failed to secure the Mormon name of Deseret, which meant so much to them; they failed to found a state that was explicitly Mormon. As a price of their incorporation, they had to compromise their doctrine. A series of Federal laws, beginning with the Morrill Act of 1862, aimed at suppressing plural marriage. Finally, in 1890 an official manifesto by President Wilford Woodruff of the Church proscribed plural marriage. Not until 1896 was Utah admitted as a State, and it remains even now a living monument to the scope that the West offered to the genius of the organizer.

10

Community Before Government

BY THE EARLY 19th century, in crowded, pre-empted Europe, "No Trespassing" signs were everywhere; control by government covered the map. America offered a sharp contrast. From the beginning, *communities* existed here before there were governments to care for public needs or to enforce public duties. This order of events was hardly possible in modern Europe; in America, it was normal.

A classic example, a prototype of the later movements of Americans, was the experience of the Pilgrims who landed at Plymouth in 1620. They were, of course, held together by a strong sense of common purpose. But since they were landing at an unexpected place, outside the jurisdiction of any government (they had intended to land in Virginia and not in New England), they were a community without government. While they were still on board the *Mayflower,* their leaders were frightened by the boasts of a few unruly passengers, who threatened to take advantage of this fact as soon as they touched land. By the Mayflower Compact they then set up a new government. The Pilgrim community thus preceded the government of Plymouth.

This order of events was repeated again and again in American history. Typical of the transients during their heyday between the Revolution and the Civil War, it helps explain many of the distinctive features of American life in the following century. As we have seen, groups moving westward organized into communities in order to conquer the great distances, to help one another drag their wagons uphill or across streams, to protect one another from Indians, and for a hundred other purposes. Knowing they were moving where jurisdiction was uncertain or nonexistent, they dared not wait for government to establish its machinery. If the services that elsewhere were performed by governments were to be performed at all, it would have to be by private initiative.

A kind of Mayflower Compact, then, was made by each group as it formed for its westward trek. By the time of the Gold Rush of 1849, it was already a well-established custom of the trail, for those venturing "through a territory where the laws of our common country do not extend their protection," to make themselves into a political body. Some groups completed their organization at their first rendezvous—say, at St. Louis or Independence. Many others waited until they had gone outside the jurisdiction of the United States. One company adopted this resolution (May 9, 1849) unanimously agreed to and signed by every member:

> . . . we the subscribers, members of the Green and Jersey Company of emigrants to California, now rendezvoused at St. Joseph; in view of the long and difficult journey before us, are satisfied that our own interests require for the purpose of safety, convenience, good feeling, and what is of the utmost importance, the prevention of unnecessary delay, the adoption of strict rules and regulations to govern us during our passage: and we do by our signatures to this resolution, pledge ourselves each to the other, that we will abide by all the rules and regulations that may be made by a vote of a majority of the company, for its regulations during our passage; that we will manfully assist and uphold any authorized officer in his exertions to strictly enforce all such rules and regulations as may be made. And further, in case any members of the company, by loss of oxen or mules, by breaking of wagon, robbery by the Indians, or in fact from any cause whatever beyond their control, are deprived of the ability to proceed with the company in the usual manner, we pledge ourselves never to desert them, but from our own resources and means to support and assist them to get through to Sutter's Fort, and in fact, we pledge ourselves to stand by each other, under any justifiable circumstance to the death.

This same group then adopted a constitution and bylaws which opened in phrases reminiscent of the Federal Constitution and which left no doubt of their intention to establish a political community. "We the members of the Green and Jersey Company of Emigrants to California, for the purpose of effectually protecting our persons and property, and as the best means of ensuring an expeditious and easy journey, do ordain and establish the following Constitution." Then followed a description of the officers (Captain, Assistant Captain, Treasurer, Secretary, and such others as might be provided by law) and their duties, and the procedure for abolishing or amending the constitution (a vote of two-thirds of the Company).

The laws of these new transient communities had certain common features. Their organization was partly military, partly civil. Officers, elected by majority vote, had a brief tenure (Captain and Assistant Captain, say, for twenty days; Treasurer and Secretary for four months) and could be removed at any time by vote of two-thirds of the Company. Crimes were described, with their mode of trial and of punishment. The bylaws of the Green and Jersey Company, for example, provided that there be a trial at the next camping place whenever a member complained to the Captain "that any of the rules or regulations had been violated, or that any of the company have violated the rules of order, right and justice, which are evident to all men." Trial by jury was the rule, juries being selected by lot from all company members except the accused, the witnesses, and the messmates of the parties. For minor offenses, the jury consisted of five persons and decided by simple majority. For murder, the jury numbered twelve and the verdict had to be unanimous; a failure of three successive juries to agree counted as acquittal. Conviction for murder meant death. For minor offenses, the jury itself prescribed the penalty. For threatening the life of another in the company, the penalty was expulsion (with supplies sufficient to reach the nearest settlement), and sentence of death if the banished person returned.

These laws were simple. Crimes were few and regulations easily understood. They could be written on five or six sheets of paper. Gambling sometimes was an offense, punished by additional guard duty. Or there might be a rule that the Sabbath be observed "as a day of rest to man and beast"—but only "when practicable and safe to the company." Laws preserved the right of friends and relatives to dine regularly in the same mess and to keep their wagons together. They prescribed the order and amount of guard duty, prohibited the carrying of loaded weapons in wagons, and specified the ways of disposing of the goods of deceased members.

There was seldom any hint of a doubt that final control on all matters rested with the majority, who had so recently made the constitution and laws, and could alter or abolish them. The majority chose all the officers and decided in each case whether an alleged crime deserved punishment. The majority constituted a kind of court of appeals: for minor offenses (not for murder), two-thirds of the whole company could set aside a jury's verdict.

Such sets of laws were used by the earliest groups who crossed the continent in wagon trains. The pioneer company of emigrants to enter California from the east overland, the so-called "Bartleson Party," which arrived (thirty-three out of the original sixty-nine) in November, 1841, after a six-months journey from Independence, Missouri, had adopted such a code on May 18, 1841, near the beginning of their journey. Nearly every one of the numerous surviving journals of overland companies records the framing of a constitution and laws "for the government of the party."

In 1849, at the time of the Gold Rush, many went by sea. These "Argonauts of '49" (as their historian O. T. Howe christens them) included over one hundred seafaring companies whose records have survived, each averaging over forty members. Every one of these companies made its own constitutions and bylaws. While their rules were generally similar to those for overland companies, they bore the traditional marks of the sea and had seafaring custom to guide them. And they bore marks of the other peculiarities of their enterprise. Most of the overland companies were organized exclusively for mutual protection on a long and dangerous journey, and for this they needed very little capital. But seafaring companies, which needed considerable capital to finance the ship, hoped to recoup the cost of transportation by the profit on the cargo. They were commercial as well as political communities. For example, when a shipboard member of the Boston and California Mining Company was convicted of theft, shortly after their ship rounded Cape Horn, he was expelled by a three-quarter vote of the stockholders and sentenced to forfeit his share of stock and the three hundred dollars he had put in.

Such do-it-yourself governments (at least those going overland) had only the most recent experience to guide them. They were not surrounded with an aura of mystery or tradition; all over the country they were formed beneath people's very eyes, and for everyday purposes. Nothing could have been more unlike the Old-World governments of sanctified vicegerents of God whose authority was rooted in antiquity, untouchable because of the "divinity that doth hedge a king."

Simple instructions for forming such governments were found in the many guides which also told emigrants how to handle the oxen, how to repair a wagon-tongue, and where were the best places to cross the rivers. For example, in Randolph B. Marcy's *Prairie Traveler, a Hand-Book for Overland Expeditions* (1859, several times reissued), which had a semi-official status, having been issued under authority of the War Department:

ORGANIZATION OF COMPANIES

After a particular route has been selected to make the journey across the plains, and the requisite number have arrived at the eastern terminus, their first business should be to organize themselves into a company and elect a commander. The company should be of sufficient magnitude to herd and guard animals, and for protection against Indians.

From fifty to seventy men, properly armed and equipped, will be enough for these purposes, and any greater number only makes the movements of the party more cumbersome and tardy. . . .

An obligation should then be drawn up and signed by all the members of the association, wherein each one should bind himself to abide in all cases by the orders and decisions of the captain, and to aid him by every means in his power in the execution of his duties; and they should also obligate themselves to aid each other, so as to make the individual interest of each member the common concern of the whole company. To ensure this, a fund should be raised for the purchase of extra animals to supply the place of those which may give out or die on the road; and if the wagon or team of a particular member should fail and have to be abandoned, the company should obligate themselves to transport his luggage, and the captain should see that he has his share of transportation equal with any other member. Thus it will be made the interest of every member of the company to watch over and protect the property of others as well as his own. . . .

The advantages of an association such as I have mentioned are manifestly numerous. The animals can be herded together and guarded by the different members of the company in rotation, thereby securing to all the opportunities of sleep and rest. Besides, this is the only way to resist depredations of the Indians, and to prevent their stampeding and driving off animals; and much more efficiency is secured in every respect, especially in crossing streams, repairing roads, etc.

It was not at all unusual for people to leave one company to join a second or a third, abandoning each when it no longer served their purpose. A man commonly stayed with his group only so long as it performed its communal function, the specific tasks for which he had joined it. Easy opportunities for such transfers were among the advantages of the established trails. It was probably more common than not for a traveler to have been in several companies before he reached his destination.

For example, James A. Pritchard, a young man of thirty-two, set out with mules, wagons, and seven companions from Petersburg, Kentucky, on April 10, 1849. They took the steamer *Cambria* up the Mississippi and arrived at St. Louis on April 13. Adding a few more to their company, they reached Independence on April 22. They made final preparations on May 3, "being all ready now to bid adieu to homes, friends, and happy Country, as it ware." By May 9 they were already "in the Indian country and there are various rumers afloat, with regard to their commiting depradations on Emegrant parties." Encountering a party from Indiana commanded by Captain Fash with seventeen wagons and sixty men, "We temporarily attached ourselves to his train untill we could make further arrangements." It took only two days for Pritchard's party to become dissatisfied with their new company. Captain Fash, with his too numerous wagons, was a slow traveler. On the second night out, seven of the eight in Pritchard's party were put on guard duty. In less than a week Pritchard's company, joined by four wagons from the Fash party, split off and proceeded on their own. But on their second night out, as Pritchard wrote in his diary, they paid the penalty for their lack of organization:

> Thursday 17th Last evening we formed our Camp regardless of shape or convenience, there being no one whos duty it was to attend to the forming the compny in proper shape. Therefore we were unable to picket our Mules so as to guard them conven[ien]tly. About 10 at night just as the Camp had become quiet, a large Mountain Woolf made his Debut and brought one of those hideous howls that will startle one from the profoundest sleep—and make him think that one of the Fiends of the infurnal regions was standing before him. And away went Picket ropes & pins, at a single dash about 40 [of] the mules were loosed. The camp was aroused, and in a sho[r]t time all but 5 Mules & one horse was recovered, all qu[i]eted. Guards were detached to go in various directions. After scowering the country round for a mile or two they returned without success. This morning several parties were sent out on horseback & about 11 AM they returned with all of the Mules and horse[s].
>
> It was now apparrant to all, that it was indispensable to have a Capt— or commander to the train—and that it must be organized with proper rules & restrictions.

Three men were nominated for captain; each of them standing apart so his supporters could form behind him. Pritchard received thirty-eight of the forty votes (one of the other candidates voted for him). He then made a few "appropriate remarks" on their past hardships, the difficulties ahead, and their duties to one another, at the close of which "one universal shout rose from the croud." "The Capt. then made a motion to have one man selected by the members of each wagon to meet at the earliest hour to draft a constitution & bylaws for the farther organization & government of the company, which motion was carried." On May 24, the constitution and bylaws were adopted.

The political problems of this company were not so easily solved. One wagon refusing to remain in its place on May 29, its members were summoned for violation of the constitution and disobedience of orders. When they remained recalcitrant, they were expelled, and this was the beginning of more serious trouble. Only a week later, the original eight Kentucky members fell into disagreement, and, having decided to separate, divided their property by an elaborate arbitration arrangement. Even after this, divisions and joinings went on, until the Pritchard remnant of the party broke up on arrival in California.

These companies were transient in every sense. Not only did the membership of each separate company ebb and flow, but if a group was too large for convenient travel (like the fifty-wagon train of "Captain" Sublette which Pritchard met), it might split. If it was too small (like Pritchard's own company after it had left Captain Fash's party) it gladly added wagons. Rarely, almost never, did the groups which had formed for the trip stay together after arrival at their destination. Since each was a community formed for a specific purpose—safe-passage across the continent—when the purpose had been fulfilled, the community fell apart. For example, of the 124 companies which left Massachusetts for California overland or by sea in 1849, not one stayed together after arrival on the west coast. Nor was this a peculiarity of Gold Rush days. Unlike the Pilgrim Fathers, who had been held together by a vision of community and a set of firm beliefs, these transient communities in the years between the Revolution and the Civil War (with only a few conspicuous exceptions, such as the Mormons) were held together almost exclusively by their personal needs. Men like the members of the "Bartleson Party" had shared mortal risks and the sight of death for six months, but on arrival in California they quickly scattered.

Out of the variety, flow, and risks of movement on and across the continent-ocean came forces which long shaped the American community, an enduring inheritance from the age of the transients.

Majority rule. Rarely in history do great numbers of people find themselves in communities which they have not only personally chosen, but have actually helped to bring into being. This happened in the transient communities of the West. In these groups majority rule was the law, not for explicit theoretical reasons but from simple convenience. Groups of men who had never met before had to assign power, to approve and revise rules, and to make vital decisions; they counted heads for lack of other ways of deciding. These transient communities were too new to have traditions, too fluid to have established social classes. In these groups there was too little wealth to give power or influence to the rich. Ancestral prestige, glory, or power could carry very little weight for the simple reason that only men's selves were known. Parents and grandparents had been left far behind; even their whereabouts, much less their wealth or power or occupation, were unknown to one's traveling companions. Majority rule was the most obvious, the simplest, and the least violent way of exercising the rule of those living and present.

Functional community. Under these circumstances chauvinism could not flourish. A community that did not do its job could not command allegiance. Governments so recently created and for such specific purposes seemed neither good nor bad in themselves; they had to be evaluated only by their performance. There was no more sanctity (and a good deal less sentimental attachment) to a company's rules than to its wagons, mules, or oxen. Each was valued for its use. The attitude toward government, therefore, in communities shaped by transients was far different from that in places where the glory of ancient battles and the dignity of anointed princes claimed a loyalty which passed all reason.

The blurred boundary between public and private. Perhaps the most important result of the transient experience was the blurring of that distinction which had meant much in European life and was already becoming the basis of European political debate in the early 19th century: the distinction between the realm of the individual and the realm of the official group—in Spenčer's later phrase "The Man versus The State"; in the parlance of political debate, "Individualism versus Collectivism," "Capitalism versus Socialism." For many reasons these distinctions would become peculiarly meaningless in America. One of the reasons was that in the beginnings of American communities the line between the private and the public was so unclear. Communities were expressly created to serve private interests, and private interests were preserved only by the express construction of effective communities.

All these momentous forces were dramatized in the transients' search for law.

11

The Natural Law of Transient Communities: Claim Clubs and Priority Rule

LONG BEFORE the Gold Rush came the Land Rush. We hear less about it because it is only another name for much of American history. A nearly empty continent provided the setting. Men who in the Old World would have hoped to acquire a ten- or twenty-acre plot after countless peasant generations, when transplanted to the New World looked forward to 160 or 320 acres or more within a few weeks or months.

But how would such lands be protected? They were in communities still without effective government. They had been so quickly acquired precisely because they were beyond the force of government. To wait for protection by the law of the distant settled East would be to lose all the advantages of being there first. Pre-emptors had to make and enforce their own law in their own way. Just as the law of the vigi-

lance associations was to be the miners' homemade law of crimes, so
western farmers and resident land-speculators would make their own
law of property. This was the law of the claim clubs.

Many of the transients' problems arose from the fact that the western
public lands open to new settlement were still technically under control
of the Federal government of the new United States, with its headquarters on the far-off eastern seaboard. Though continually changing,
Federal law offered arrangements which, at least from a great distance,
seemed to have the virtues of neatness and order.

The survey was in the foreground of eastern thinking. You could
not deal in land at a distance, they said, without an accurate definition
of what you were dealing with. As early as 1785, Federal law provided for the rectangular survey of lands into "township" units (each
6 miles square, each including 36 sections) and "section" units (each
a mile square, or 640 acres). This has remained characteristic of our
West. The simplest, most orderly, and most quickly remunerative program was to sell these large tracts to easterners with strong financial
backing. Those who had gone West and settled without proper documents were only a confusing element. And the Federal government
(beginning with the admission of Ohio, the first public-land state, in
1803) held to the policy of retaining for itself the title to all ungranted
land (except one section reserved in each township for education).
This left the Federal government in charge of that part of the land law
that most affected new settlers.

But the transients were not interested in large programs. They
stopped here or there, according to the accidents of the wagon route,
the appeal of rumor, or the appearance of the land. They did not wait
for the land to be surveyed or for government to precede them. They
could not have secured the legal documents for their tracts before they
left because, more often than not, they did not know where they were
going. Nor did they stay put. They went hoping for the best, and their
hopes carried them from place to place. However neat and orderly
might be the Federal plans and laws, the transients' pattern of settlement was anything but neat, for nearly all westward American movement in the 19th century was a Land Rush. While the disorder of the
Gold Rush was to be confined to certain places, the disorder of the
Land Rush covered the continent. Settlers were far more interested
in the qualities of the land than in the technicalities of the law. They
set up the ridgepoles of their houses and planted their crops, without
waiting for advice of counsel.

In the crucial early period of western settlement, therefore, many,
if not most, of the first arrivals were "squatters." Were they land "owners" in the strict legal sense? The answer depended on rapidly changing
technicalities about which the first settlers cared little and knew even

less. The settlement of the West, like so many of the other central events of American history, occurred in an atmosphere of pregnant legal ambiguity.

Surveys commonly lagged behind settlement; and so, too, behind the new communities. The transients had no more patience with a bureaucracy that could not assign them their lands than the miners would feel for a government that could not punish criminals. In Illinois, for example, before the end of 1828, about two-thirds of the population were "squatters"—settlers on land that still technically belonged to the United States government. This very word "squatter," in England and in the populous eastern seaboard states, had a taint of fraud. There a squatter was a person who settled on land already legally belonging to someone else, in order to acquire title by occupancy or to profit from some technical defect in the title of the original owner. But not here. The Western "squatter" was usually the actual first settler, the pre-emptor, the man who had got there first.

Only gradually did the Federal laws begin to take account of these facts of life and of the needs of the transients. Thomas Hart Benton, during his thirty years (1821–51) as senator from the new state of Missouri, championed the interests of the settlers. Leading his Western colleagues, he successfully argued against a fixed minimum price for all Western land and urged that price be graded according to actual quality. Most important, he secured changes in the laws to protect those settlers who had cultivated land on public domain without prior formalities. The law was slowly changed to save the pre-emptors.

From the point of view of the settlers, these changes were unconscionably slow, embedded as they were in complicated statutes with many other provisions and qualifications. A temporary measure in 1830 (improved and made permanent in 1841) was the first to give the settler some of the substantial legal protection he wanted against nonresident purchasers. Now a settler had the first bid on a tract up to 160 acres at the minimum price, but acreage beyond that generally went up for auction. Federal laws never managed to keep pace with the demands of these settlers on the spot, not even when the Homestead Act of 1862 enabled a settler (after five years of continuous residence and payment of nominal registration fees) to secure Federal title to 160 acres free of any other charge. By that time much of the best land had been taken up, and a Western style of life established.

Just as naturally as miners would later form Vigilance Committees against murderers and road agents, the earlier farm settlers organized to protect their land. Since there were no courts of law, they formed "Claim Clubs" (sometimes called "associations" or "unions"). Scores of such organizations sprang up in the areas of rapid Western settlement. For example, near Elkhorn Creek, Wisconsin, forty families had settled in a grove surrounded by land which had been surveyed into townships but not yet into sections, and therefore was technically not yet on the market. A Methodist circuit rider, passing there in 1835, reported:

> They had, in the absence of all other law, met & made a law for themselves. They have surveyed the township & assertained that section 16, the school section, was within the grove, & they staked it off & appointed commissioners to take care of it, preserve the timber &c. so as to make it valuable as possible when the township should be regularly settled according to law. They had also meted & bounded every mans wood land, allowing each family 40 acres of timber, & as much Prairie as he pleased to take up. Timber being the great disideratim of the country, they would not allow any one man to monopolise. . . . there was an understanding in the country, equivalent to a law of the land, that the settlers should sustain each other against the speculator, & no settler should bid on anothers land.
>
> If a speculator should bid on a settlers farm, he was knocked down & dragged out of the [land] office, & if the striker was prosecuted & fined, the settlers paid the expense by common consent among themselves. But before a fine could be assessed, the case must come before a jury, which of course must be selected from among the settlers. And it was understood that no jury would find a verdict of guilty against a settler, in such a case, because it was considered a case of self defence. . . . These things being understood no speculator dare bid on a settlers land, & as no settler would bid on his neighbor, each man gets his land at congress price, $1.25 pr. acre.

But while Vigilance Committees would be formed only against occasional dangers, "Claim Clubs" were needed constantly and from the very beginning. Without the clubs, new-settled farmers on land not yet officially surveyed could have no assurance that the land was theirs, that they could profit from their improvements, or even that they could reap the crops they had sown. Such clubs sprang up "as readily as did the sunflowers" (we are told) "wherever the prairie sod was broken" —in Illinois, Wisconsin, Iowa, Minnesota, Nebraska, and everywhere the transients settled. Organization often began with a mass meeting of the local settlers, who formed a committee to draft a constitution and bylaws and then elected officers. Each club had its established procedure for choosing juries to settle disputes, usually providing a salary for their president and their marshal, when on judicial duty. They kept a register of land titles and in many ways acted like a regular United States government land office. In some places they became the whole government, punishing all crimes against person or property. Their activities, strictly speaking, were "outside the law," but it was these clubs alone that first brought law and order.

Membership in the Clubs, as in other transient communities, was easily and quickly acquired. Sometimes a president at a mass meeting of settlers would rule that anyone could vote and be considered a legal resident who could point to the smoke of his own chimney. A typical Club constitution provided that "all persons who have resided within the limits of the county for Two months shall be recognized and considered as citizens of the County." Despite the troublesome vagueness of boundaries, the crudity of surveys, and the fluidity of membership, rules were simple, widely understood, and rigorously enforced. Every member was entitled to the protection of his fellows, but the Club had no patience with legal technicalities. "We consider the laws," resolved the Green County Claim Society in Wisconsin (1845), "like other human institutions, necessarily imperfect, but that it is no excuse for any person who takes advantage of those imperfections to degrade and oppress his fellow man."

Whatever its other faults, "Claim Club" law was usually enforced promptly and effectively. For example, the historian of the Claim Association of Johnson County, Iowa, could find no more than two cases of "claim-jumping" in defiance of the Association's rules. In one case a whipping brought the offender quickly to recognize these rules as the supreme law of the community. The other case, in November, 1839, concerned a man named Crawford who had "jumped" a claim about a mile north of Iowa City. According to Association rules, that claim rightfully belonged to William Sturgis (a member of the Association's judicial committee). Crawford, who had taken possession of the claim, still refused to give it up after a request by the Association. The Marshal of the Association then notified all members to meet at Asaph Allen's tavern in Iowa City at 10 A.M. sharp on November 7. Sixty strong men appeared at the appointed hour. They marched in a body to Crawford's cabin, where he was inside finishing it off. Once again they asked him to abandon his claim; Sturgis even offered to pay him for his labor spent on the premises. Again Crawford refused. "Without a moment's delay," a member of the Association reported, "the men ascended the corners of the house, and in fifteen minutes there was not a vestige of it left standing. Mr. Crawford was left in amazement, with axe in his hand, in the center of the vacant space once occupied by his cabin. Some of the parties suggested that the Iowa River was not far away; but milder counsels prevailed, and the company dispersed." Crawford and Sturgis again conferred, and then Sturgis announced that the matter had been adjusted to his full satisfaction, and the company dispersed. Crawford later tried to bring some of the Claim Association party before a court for punishment. But since it was almost impossible to find a judge, lawyer, or juror in Iowa who was not himself a claimholder, Crawford never succeeded. Never again was it necessary to call out members of the Association for such a purpose.

By the time federal land offices finally were opened under the Pre-emption Act of September 4, 1841, enterprising transients and specula-tors had become devilishly clever at satisfying the letter of the law. The transients had flourished under their Club Law, the spontaneous product of their communities, which disdained technicality in favor of substantial justice. They made a mockery of technicality in those federal land offices where form was often respected more than substance.

Under the rules of most such offices, a man could not pre-empt unless he had a house at least twelve feet square. But a squatter might swear that his house was "twelve by fourteen," when actually the only build-ing on his claim—one he had whittled out with a penknife—was twelve by fourteen *inches*. To be a "house" for pre-emption purposes, a struc-ture was required by some offices to have a glass window. Travelers re-ported their puzzlement at finding, in some little windowless slab cabin, a window-sash hanging inside upon a nail. Having seen similar frames hanging in other cabins, one visitor asked the owner what it was for. "To pre-empt with," came the reply. "How?" "Why, don't you understand? To enable my witness to swear that there is a window in my house!"

Sometimes the same cabin was moved from claim to claim, until half a dozen different claimants had pre-empted their separate parcels with it. A reporter in Nebraska in the late 1850's described a little frame house built for this purpose on wheels, and drawn by oxen. Let out at five dollars a day, it enabled a pre-emptor to swear that he had a bona fide residence on his claim. It was said that scores of claims had been proved up and pre-empted with this house.

No woman could pre-empt under the law unless she was a widow or "head of a family." Ambitious pioneer maidens who could not satisfy the spirit of the law were clever at satisfying its letter in order to secure their 160 acres of pre-emption land. Stories were told of babies hired out to serve such female claimants, much as the movable house served the men. The young lady would borrow a child, sign papers of adoption, swear she was head of a family, and pre-empt her claim. Afterwards she would annul the adoption papers, returning the child to its parents with an appropriate gift.

For most of the early age of Western settlement—from the first decades of the 19th century at least until the Civil War—"Club Law" was the law of the transient West. It had its faults, but they were not the faults of bureaucracy, technicality, or legalism. Club Law, like Vigilante Law, meant popular justice, quick remedies, lay procedures, and rule of thumb. It was a do-it-yourself law: the vigilantism of new landowners beyond the force of established governments.

Claim Clubs were not always agencies of democracy. Nor did they always protect the honest settler against the scheming speculator. Al-though Club Law was often the shield of the simple homesteader before

Federal Law took control, it was also a tool and a weapon of the speculator-on-the-spot. Claim Clubs acted not only to protect a squatter's title to land he lived on and was cultivating, but also to help the same squatter defend unoccupied second and third tracts against the claim of later arrivals.

Claim Clubs (sometimes called "Actual Settlers' Associations" or "Squatters' Clubs") might more precisely have been called "First-Arrival Clubs." They protected the first settlers in their right to speculate as well as in their right to cultivate. The *non*-resident who had made much money speculating in western land was, according to the Madison *Argus* (October 22, 1850), "a rare bird, more rare by far than a successful gold hunter." Unimproved absentee-owned land was exploited directly and indirectly. Sometimes it was simply seized, and the title held "by Claim Club." Sometimes the residents voted expensive local improvements, such as roads and schoolhouses, affixing their heavy costs as a tax burden on the lands held by absentees. In some places this became an avowed policy, in order to force sale by speculating absentee owners to actual residents (or at least to local speculators). There was no lack of speculators in western farm land, but the speculators who had the support of Claim Clubs were the men on the spot.

*   *   *

Claim Clubs and their Claim-Club Law expressed a distinctive spirit, an enduring legacy to the new nation. They stood for the *priority* principle, which simply meant the superior claim of those who arrived first. It also meant the superiority of the rules of the community which existed before the formal government. The priority principle itself made men hurry on. It made them insist that early arrival was no mere fact of history or biography, but a virtue for which riches were not too great a reward. The Johnny-come-lately, the laggard, the sluggard, the slow starter, the slow mover—these were weak men who had to take the leavings. The priority principle was at first, of course, an expression of the emptiness and newness of America. It was first applied in the laws of land, but it would be applied in turn in each race for the continental treasure: for gold, for water, for grass, and for oil.

The Gold Rushers later experienced many of the same problems as had the Land Rushers. For mining camps, too, were beyond the range of effective federal government. Similarities between the law of the farmer's claim clubs and the later claim law of the miners probably stemmed as much from the similarity of their problems as from remembrance of earlier solutions. First-arriving miners, like pioneer farmers, did not wait for government to be established from either the state or the national capital. Finding themselves a mining community long before there was an effective federal, territorial, or state law of mines, they simply made their own laws:

> Whereas, This district is deficient in mining laws and regulations, and disputes have arisen: therefore, we, the miners of ——— district, in convention assembled, do pledge ourselves to abide by the following laws.

As early as 1851, the California legislature declared that, in mining claims, such local "customs, usages or regulations, when not in conflict with the constitution and laws of this state, shall govern." By 1866 there were over five hundred self-organized mining districts in California, two hundred in Nevada, one hundred each in Arizona, Idaho, and Oregon; and there were perhaps fifty each in Montana, New Mexico, and Colorado. The total came to over eleven hundred. These self-governing, self-legislating units made rules which varied in detail. But they shared the basic belief that the community of men-on-the-spot could and should make and enforce their own rules. A committee of United States Senators who had examined these laws summarized their conclusions in 1866 with an appropriate senatorial elegance:

> By this great system established by the people in their primary capacities, and evidencing by the highest possible testimony the peculiar genius of the American people for founding empire and order, popular sovereignty is displayed in one of its grandest aspects, and simply invites us, not to destroy, but to put upon it the stamp of national power and unquestioned authority.

When Congress, then, passed its first important Mining Act on July 26, 1866, it simply recognized "the force of local mining-customs, or rules of miners wherever not conflicting with the laws of the United States."

These local systems of claim-club mining law all agreed on the principle of priority. "The rules and regulations of the miners . . . ," reported the Senate Committee which shaped the new federal act, "form the basis of the present admirable system arising out of necessity; they become the means adopted by the people themselves for establishing just protection to all. . . . The local courts, beginning with California, recognize those rules, the central idea of which is *priority of possession*." This meant that discovery and prior appropriation of mineral property was everywhere considered the proper source of title. Gold prizes, like land prizes, went to the first arrivals.

Some peculiarities in applying the principle did, of course, grow out of the mining operation. In the beginning, at least, the continued use of a mining claim was essential for continued legal possession. Henry George (among others) found it easy to romanticize this mining-camp law: "No one might take more than he could reasonably use, or hold for a longer time than he continued to use it. . . . no one was allowed to forestall or lock up natural resources." The fact was that there was simply no way of protecting a man's possession of a mining claim that he was not working. As soon as an apparatus of protection was developed, mineral claims became one more form of property to be bought and sold.

The priority principle was also applied to water. Beyond the hundredth meridian, where land was most plentiful, water was scarce. Yet without water land could not be used for farm or pasture, nor could gold be washed from its ore. Here again the American principle of priority transformed the law. In England, a humid country with much rainfall and many small streams, the common law had long established the principle of "riparian" rights (equal water rights for all owners of the banks of a stream). Each owner had equal rights to the use of the flowing stream, regardless of whether his land was up- or downstream, or when he first took possession of his land. The effect in England of certain technical distinctions between "natural" and "extraordinary" uses was generally to confine the upstream owner to uses that did not diminish the flow of the stream. This protected all the owners of land along the stream. All retained their right to the water for ordinary and customary uses; there was no question of priority.

In the American West, this was changed. While there were considerable variations (and changes in the common law were generally most extreme where water was most scarce: in the states from Idaho and Montana down to Arizona and New Mexico), English law was drastically modified in nearly all the Land Rush territories. In place of the common-law doctrine of equal rights among all stream-bed owners, Westerners applied the principle of priority. In its extreme form, the Western doctrine held that the first person to reach the stream and appropriate the water could draw out as much as he could use. He could draw it off in ditches or flumes to help him work distant placer mines or to irrigate lands far from the stream—even though he drained the stream dry. Here the principle of priority plainly crowded out the principle of equality. This new rule, wherever embodied in local custom, was made Federal law by an act of 1866. Some historians (Walter Prescott Webb, for example) have argued that this change in water law grew primarily out of the peculiar need for irrigation to cultivate the arid regions of the West. This does not, however, itself explain why the Western water law was given its novel form. To understand this we must see it in the whole American perspective, where everything conspired toward the priority rule.

The principle of pre-emption, of rewarding the man who got there first, lasted at least until the end of the century. The whole system of distribution which had dominated the transient West was dramatized on that April day in 1889 when nearly one hundred thousand men and women—on foot, on horseback, in wagons, and with pushcarts— lined up on the border of Indian Territory, waiting for the starting guns to be fired by army officers. Within a few hours the 1,920,000 acres of the Oklahoma District had been taken. Few knew why they had picked this plot or that. None knew what they were missing by not settling here or there. None could imagine the black gold still undiscovered thousands of feet below the surface. But they rushed to secure the parcel most to their taste . . . or the best parcel left by the faster travelers before them.

12

The Natural Law of Transient Communities: Vigilantism and Majority Rule

THE VIGILANTISM of the transients grew in communities that were yet without government. It arose, at first, not to circumvent courts, but to provide them; not because the machinery of government had become complicated, but because there was no machinery at all; not to neutralize institutions already there, but to fill a vacuum. Their vigilantism was quite obviously distinct from the legal traditionalism, technicality, and professionalism developing in these same years in England. Less obviously, it was also distinct from the "Lynch Law" of the South, for the unwritten law which ruled the South was a way of enforcing the established customs of a long settled community.

One of the more widely read handbooks of western travel, Lansford W. Hastings' *Emigrants' Guide to Oregon and California* (1845), in the passage already quoted at the opening of this volume, recounted to prospective travelers what had happened in Hastings' own company of one hundred and sixty (including eighty armed men), who had gone overland to Oregon after leaving Independence on May 16, 1842. "But we had proceeded only a few days travel, from our native land of order and security, when the 'American character' was fully exhibited. All appeared to be determined to govern, but not to be governed. Here we were without law, without order, and without restraint; in a state of nature, amid the confused, revolving fragments of elementary society!" "Amid this confusion," Hastings explained, "it was suggested by our captain, that we 'call a halt,' and pitch our tents, for the purpose of enacting a code of laws, for the future government of the company. The suggestion was promptly complied with, when all were required to appear in their legislative capacities." A member of the party, who had stated his intention to steal an Indian horse, had actually secured a rope and had gone out to do the job. On the plains, an act of this kind might, of course, have serious consequences for the whole party. The "legislative" body, which was the whole company, then, instead of making a general code, set about · deciding whether this man had already violated their law. There were speeches of prosecution and of defense. For the accused the decisive argument was that merely to talk of taking an Indian horse was "neither *malum in se,* nor *malum prohibitum.* It was not criminal in itself, for in itself it was nothing, as he had *done* nothing. It was not criminal because prohibited, for in our infant state of society, we had no prohibitory code." Acquittal was almost unanimous.

The party continued to wonder whether they should have a code. Finally, by an overwhelming majority, they adopted their committee's report "that, in its opinion, no code of laws was requisite, other than the moral code, enacted by the Creator of the universe, and which is found recorded in the breast of every man." Still, Hastings reports, "there appeared to be a strong determination on the part of some, to do something in the way of legislating." And, having already decided that it was unnecessary to legislate on fundamentals, they enacted a decree against all dogs, which required "the immediate and the indiscriminate extermination of the whole canine race, old and young, male and female, wherever they might be found, within our jurisdiction." When a few dogs were legally executed, the opposition hardened. Some dog owners threatened to kill anyone who killed their dogs, and the anti-dog party armed for battle. At that point the captain convened the company again "in its legislative capacity" and the dog decree, by nearly unanimous vote, was repealed. "This," recalls Hastings, "was our first and last effort at legislation."

In the mining camps of the 1840's and '50's we see this quest for law on a larger scale. They were communities of transients temporarily in one place; they, too, were usually remote from established centers of government, far from courts and legislatures. In describing the quest for law in the mining camps, we have the unique advantage of two vivid accounts by men raised in the transient West. In them the hero is no ripsnorting gun-toter, ten feet high. The leading role is played by each whole community, desperately reaching for its group conscience. Josiah Royce, the American philosopher, whose family had made the trek across the continent in '49, and Charles Howard Shinn, who became one of the leading conservationists of his day, were in a sense collaborators. They were both intrigued by how order came to the West, and they exchanged information and ideas. Both for Shinn in his *Mining Camps: A Study of Frontier Government* (1884) and for Royce in his *California* (1886) the story of the camps was the saga of communities in quest of law.

"Nowhere," remarked Royce, "and at no time are social duties in the end more painful or more exacting than in the tumultuous days of new countries; just as it is harder to work for months on a Vigilance Committee than once in a lifetime to sit on a legal jury in a quiet town." On the other hand the very ease with which a town government could be formed on paper sometimes "lulled to sleep the political conscience of the ordinary man, and from the outset gave too much self-confidence to the community." Miners believed that law was somehow self-discovered and self-enforcing. At the same time, their rudimentary society taught them, willy-nilly, the compelling intimacy and pervasiveness of law, the inescapable need for community. "Never did the journeying pillar, of cloud by day and of fire by night, teach to the legendary wanderers in the desert more unmistakably by signs and wonders the eternal law, than did the fortunes of these early Californians display to them, through the very accidents of daily life, the majesty of the same law of order and of loyalty to society. In the air, as it were, the invisible divine net of social duties hung, and descending, enmeshed irresistibly all these gay and careless fortune-hunters even while they boasted of their freedom."

The very techniques of gold mining increasingly emphasized co-operation and group loyalty, for the miner's equipment was at first the simple pan, soon the cradle, and then the sluice: each more complex and requiring more co-operation than its predecessor. Panning for gold was a one-man operation. But the cradle (or gold-rocker), an apparatus on rockers six or eight feet long, had to be agitated to wash out the gold-bearing earth; this usually required at least four men. Sluicing used an elaborate series of troughs and ditches to carry the gold-bearing currents through boxes where the gold could settle, and thus required several men for the co-operative labor of construction, maintenance, and operation of immovable equipment. Evolution through these stages, like everything else in a mining camp, went rapidly. By 1850, the sluice was widely used, and had already reinforced the collaborative spirit. It was in these communities, too, that the idea of partnership, later to be sentimentalized in western fiction, developed. The first use of the slang "pardner," which meant far more than a commercial colleague, probably comes from these mining camps and from around 1850. By the time of the advance of mining from California into the Rocky Mountain area after 1858 the "lone prospector" was no more than a myth. Prospecting had become a group enterprise.

Many features of their life led miners to prefer speedy justice to legal nicety. In the new-found mines, of all places in the world, time was money. In the early Gold Rush, a man's time was easily worth from $16 to $100 a day. Spanish mining laws had ordered all cases involving mines to be decided "without delay," for a few hours might separate the lucky from the unlucky. Another reason for speed was that the mining-camp officials appointed to try a particular case usually served without pay; they were therefore doubly eager to make each trial brief. In criminal cases, too, there were special reasons for speed. Seldom were there jails and rarely any paid officials to guard the accused. Trial and punishment therefore had to be speedy. In one case of a cold-blooded murder, where there were a dozen witnesses, the trial was held and the prisoner hanged within an hour of the crime. Banishment, whipping, or death became the most popular forms of punishment, because (unlike imprisonment) they required no expensive establishment and could be accomplished without delay. In an "instantly fluctuating" population, your man might not be here tomorrow; you too might have decided to move on. To help you at all, the law had to act now.

The law was invisible precisely because it was pervasive. Miners sometimes thought they had no law at all. "We needed no law," wrote an old pioneer of the mining camps, "until the lawyers came." Never did a people feel less ruled by alien technicalities, but this was only a symptom of the special kind of law they had developed and by which they were ruled. Their law was spontaneous and unself-conscious, the unreflective rules of the whole community.

The anachronism of their situation also made it easy for them to imagine they had no law. Here too (as in the colonial era), American experience produced a regression to earlier, less differentiated ways of life. Medieval Englishmen in the formative era of the common law had also thought law could not be imposed; their law was nothing but customs "to which the mind of man runneth not to the contrary." The American transients, too, were wary of complex rules and self-conscious legislation. Not the antiquity, but the very novelty, of their community made them suspicious of all elaborate, explicit, and recently concocted rules. Though they came from places where "law" was an attenuated, technical apparatus, in their new communities they could not imagine that any esoteric customs should deserve forcible respect. Among the transients, in the mining camp, the law was everybody's— to understand, to defend, to enforce.

Like other Americans before and since, like the founders of claim clubs, they were an intensely communal community before they had a well-organized effective government. A pioneer of Nevada County, California, recalled that "there was very little law, but a large amount of good order; no churches but a great deal of religion; no politics, but a large number of politicians; no offices, and strange to say for my countrymen, no office-seekers." While some of their accounts were idealized, or colored by the ancient prejudice against lawyers, we have good reason to believe that their life was at least as orderly, and perhaps a good deal more so, than life in settled eastern communities. Unguarded property was generally safe. In most mining camps a washbasinful of gold dust could be left on a table in an open tent while the owners were far out of sight working their claims. Though there were no police, provisions and tools were seldom stolen. Theft, murder, and all kinds of violence were rare.

Whatever the explanation, in the beginning the California mining camps in the canyons of the Sierra Nevada were remarkable for the spontaneity, localism, and independence with which they developed their laws. At first, of course, the miners were living outside (or against) the laws of Mexico, and not yet within the laws of any of the United States. The *de facto* Governors of California had problems enough without trying to govern the miners against their will.

An occasional remnant of Spanish colonial rule was the *alcalde,* or judge of first instance. It was an alcalde who heard disputes during the unsettled days of 1849, in a little schoolroom on the plaza of San Francisco. In civil cases he listened to the arguments, made his decision, and fixed a fee for his services, to be paid by the parties. Theoretically it was possible to appeal from his decision to the Governor at Monterey, but this almost never happened. Occasional complaints of the irregularity of the alcalde's jurisdiction attest that the judicial institutions of these spontaneous communities were (according to disgruntled parties) "neither Mexican nor American." More often than not, "alcalde" was simply a name to dignify an entirely local official who had little knowledge of any law, Mexican or American. Occasionally his office would be ornamented with an odd volume of the laws of Iowa, Illinois, Missouri, or South Carolina, or with some French, Spanish, German, or English lawbook. Half-remembered shreds of these far-off jurisdictions were patched with common sense and conscience.

What is most remarkable is how little the miscellaneous citizenry of the transient mining camps relied on outside authorities. Their law and order did not depend on the force or dignity of established governments elsewhere. Individual mining camps devised their own rules about the size, staking, and defense of mining claims; about the definition and punishment of crimes; and about all the business of government. Explicit rules like these were usually devised just as most of the rest of the government business was conducted, by a full meeting of the miners of the district. Their informal assembly was at the same time legislature, judiciary, and executive. Qualifications for membership were extremely vague; anyone present, even boys fifteen years old, could vote.

Since there was no pre-existing machinery of government, every new piece of machinery was created for a specific purpose. With the exception of the occasional vaguely empowered alcalde, the community inherited no officials, no administrative apparatus. Government activities came into being at random. Officers were not elected until needed. Once the need seemed past, the officers lost their powers.

Officials made no decisions which could not be quickly and effectively enforced. One '49er recalled:

> Crime was rare, for punishment was certain. I was present one afternoon, just outside the city limits, and saw with painful satisfaction, as I now remember, Charley Williams whack three of our fellow-citizens over the bare back, twenty-one to forty strokes, for stealing a neighbor's money. The multitude of disinterested spectators had conducted the court. My recollection is that there were no attorneys' fees or court-charges. I think I never saw justice administered with so little loss of time or at less expense. There was no more stealing in Nevada City until society became more settled and better regulated.

The "mining court" (only another name for the assembly in open council of all who swung a pick or held a claim), just as it voted punishment for theft or murder, also decided the ownership and boundaries of claims. It did not try to collect debts or to settle other minor personal disputes. The early Western mining court lacked permanent officials (except for the occasional alcalde) and lacked written laws. It kept no records. Anyone could call it into session. Those who doubted the urgency of a meeting would simply stay away.

The power of these miscellaneous miners to organize themselves was impressive. For example, there was the case of the miners of Jackson Creek Camp, Rogue River Valley (later in the state of Oregon) who deposed Alcalde Rogers. He had been elected by a few early miners before the town had boomed. A miner named Sprenger, who had been crippled in an accident, was brazenly ejected from his rightful claim by his partner Sim, who accomplished his purpose by bribing Rogers to render a "legal" decision. Rogers repeatedly refused to reconsider the case or to refer it to a jury, much less to resign as alcalde. On an autumn day in 1852, long celebrated in the lore of the southern Oregon mines, over a thousand miners (each of whom might have made from five to fifty dollars had he stayed at work that day) left picks and cradles and sluices to assemble in the main camp. From their open-air meeting they sent a committee, offering Rogers one last chance to retry the case of Sim v. Sprenger. When the committee reported back that Rogers had again refused, they formed then and there into a court of appeal. They at once elected a fellow miner, Hayden, as appellate judge. With some formality, including the impaneling of a jury, the swearing and hearing of witnesses, and argument by counsel, the case was retried. Threats of mob violence against Sim and Rogers were suppressed. In accordance with their appellate decision, Sprenger was reinstated in his partnership share and Rogers was deposed as alcalde. The good sense of a majority had thwarted both corruption and violence. Although the spontaneous will of a crowd of villagers was often capable of the worst excesses—of the kind fictionally recounted in *The Ox-Bow Incident*—Sim v. Sprenger and scores of similar cases showed the vigilantism of the transients at its best.

The mining camps that lacked laws were thus by no means lawless, but the very simplicity of their government apparatus sometimes made it easier for lawless elements to seize what government there was. Miners then also used vigilantism to set their meager government back on the right track. To do this required great tact and courage as well as considerable organizing ability.

One of the most dramatic and best recorded achievements of vigilantism occurred near the town of Bannack in the newly settled mining districts in the Territory of Idaho (now in Montana). Luckily, the events were reported in detail by an Oxford-educated Englishman, "Professor" Thomas J. Dimsdale, in a series of articles collected as *Vigilantes of Montana* (1866), which was the first book published in the Territory. The chief villain of the story was Henry Plummer, who had first arrived in the gold country in 1852, when, still in his teens, he had settled at Nevada City in the high California sierras. Before arriving in Bannack in the fall of 1862, Plummer had frequented several mining camps, had run bakeries and professional gambling establishments, and had organized a band of "road agents," highwaymen who preyed on the traffic moving in and out of the camps. In Lewiston, Plummer was reputed to be a substantial merchant on July 28, 1862, when gold (the first within the present state of Montana) was discovered at Grasshopper Creek on the eastern slope of the mountains. That site quickly became the town of Bannack. In October, 1862, bandits who had robbed a pack train of fourteen pounds of gold were hanged in Lewiston. Then Plummer, taking the hint, moved on to Bannack where he had organized a new band of road agents by April, 1863. By devices unexplained, Plummer managed to get himself elected sheriff. Two days afterward, on May 24, 1863, another placer deposit of gold which later proved to be one of the greatest in the world was discovered, this time at Alder Gulch eighty miles east of Bannack. Within three weeks another new town, "Virginia City," had been formed there. It was decided that there should be a single sheriff for all the camps east of the Bitter Root mountains and Plummer received the job.

By the summer of 1863, Henry Plummer's well-organized "road agents" were plundering the gold shipped out of these rich new-found placer deposits of western Montana. As their secret captain he found it less profitable to mine the streams than to mine the miners. Rattlesnake Ranch was their headquarters, hideout, arsenal, and resting place. In front of it stood a signpost for practicing marksmanship. Plummer, who could draw and discharge five loads from his pistol in three seconds, had the reputation of being the quickest shot in the mountains. The gang also used ranches of innocent people whose "life would not have been worth fifteen minutes' purchase if the possessor had been foolish enough even to hint at his knowledge of their doings." A conservative estimate based on bodies actually discovered and confessions made was that they had murdered at least 102 people, besides those whose remains were never found or whose fate was never definitely established.

Plummer had the great advantage of operating under cover of his office as Sheriff. He had appointed three of his road agents—Jack Gallagher, Buck Stinson, and Ned Ray—as his Deputy Sheriffs. There remained one honest deputy named Dillingham, whom Plummer's men murdered in cold blood by pistol shots fired "so closely together that eyesight was a surer evidence of the number of shots discharged than hearing."

The honest citizenry then began to organize. The whole body of miners met to try these murderers of Dillingham. Presiding was "Judge" G. G. Bissell, a medical doctor, assisted by two other local practitioners of his profession. E. R. Cutler, a blacksmith, was public prosecutor. All the citizens acted as jurors. "The jury box was Alder Gulch, and . . . the throne of Justice was a wagon, drawn up at the foot of what is now Wallace Street." The open-air trial was completed by noon of the second day when the community voted their verdict of guilty. Then, in a last-moment surge of soft-heartedness (stirred by the few women present), Plummer's men were let off.

But the community had been aroused. This was the beginning of the end for Plummer and his crew. More outrages by the road agents went unpunished until one day the mangled, bloodstained body of young Nicholas Tbalt, an orphan of German immigrants, who had been murdered for his money and his mules, was accidentally found in the brush in Stinkingwater Valley. The murderer, it soon appeared, was George Ives, one of Plummer's chief lieutenants. The trial and punishment of George Ives was the first great victory of the Vigilantes of Montana, "under the shadow of whose wide-spreading branches," Professor Dimsdale wrote in 1866, "the citizens of Montana can lie down and sleep in peace." Three or four citizens of Nevada City quickly raised a company of twenty-five which captured Ives and his two confederates, "Long John" Franck and George Hilderman, whose gastronomic feats at Bannack had made him "The American Pie-Eater." In Nevada City (just "outside the jurisdiction" of Plummer and his Deputy Sheriffs), under the bright sun of a mild autumnal morning on October 19, 1863, fifteen hundred men gathered in the streets to do their part in the trial of George Ives.

After some disagreement it was finally decided that the whole body of citizens, rather than a small jury, should render the verdict. But they would be guided by a representative group of twenty-four acting as advisory jury. Since the accused had already several times shown their determination to escape and the trial was being held out of doors, Ives and his two confederates were bound with a light logging-chain secured by padlocks. The actual trial began in late afternoon and lasted till nightfall. On the morning of October 21, the miners managing the prosecution announced that the trial must close by 3 P.M. that day—which must have pleased those who had already given two days to the trial at their own expense.

The trial itself had familiar elements. Ives tried to establish an alibi by the testimony of a man called Honest Whiskey Joe. The lawyers (imported for the occasion) made their usual shows of brow-beating and technical insolence. The defense attorney attempted to discredit the prosecutor by the fact that he was from Oberlin College. The evidence was extended to prove that Ives had on numerous other occasions been a robber and a killer. When the case had been heard and the advisory jury (23 to 1) reported "Guilty," the assembled populace then passed a motion to adopt the report. Not over one hundred of the fifteen hundred present voted against the verdict. The prosecutor at once proposed "That George Ives be forthwith hung by the neck until he is dead." The motion carried. Within fifty-eight minutes, Ives was led to a scaffold quickly improvised on the frame of an unfinished house ten yards from where he had sat during the trial. Till the last minute begging for mercy, on the very scaffold he tried to put the blame on one of his confederates. Of Ives' two accomplices, Hilderman was banished forever from Montana, while Long John, who had turned state's evidence, was allowed to remain free in the Territory.

The moral of this trial was not lost on the miners of Montana. "Four days had been expended by at least fifteen hundred men," recorded Colonel Sanders, who had conducted the prosecution, "out of deference to the forms of American institutions, and when the prosecutions were finished . . . a number of people began to inquire whether each tragedy required so much attention, and how much time would be left to pursue the ordinary vocations if this deference was to be continued, and speculations as to forming a vigilance committee grew in coherence and strength. We had our confidence strengthened by the splendid fidelity of the miners of Alder Gulch . . . and on the evening of the next day, I think it was, the nucleus of a Vigilance Committee was formed, thereafter to grow to large proportions and to determine that in the heady struggle between order and crime, order should win the final mastery."

Five men met in Virginia City and four in Bannack to organize the Vigilantes. In Virginia City they gathered in the back room of a store, where lights were extinguished while the group standing in a circle in the darkness with hands uplifted swore: "We, the undersigned, uniting ourselves together for the laudable purpose of arresting thieves and murderers and recovering stolen property, do pledge ourselves on our sacred honor, each to all others, and solemnly swear that we will reveal no secrets, violate no laws of right, and never desert each other, or our standard of justice, so help us God."

Men "who had anything to lose" supported the Vigilantes. Within a few weeks, the road agents and Plummer himself were rounded up and hanged. The reign of terror in Alder Gulch, Virginia City, and Bannack was at an end. Plummer's commission as United States Marshal for the Territory (which he had applied for during his heyday) arrived after he had been hanged.

13

Leaving Things Behind

BEHIND THEM the transients left their past, with most of its accumulated inequalities. How could a community visit the fathers' sins on the sons, if the fathers themselves were unknown?

In the old New England village, the burial ground attached to the church, prominently located near the common, displayed family names on circumstantial epitaphs. It was quite otherwise among communities on the move. For burial "according to the custom of the Prairies" was hasty. The object was to conceal, and not to mark. According to Gregg, a funeral on the Santa Fe Trail was usually summary and unceremonial. "The corpse, with no other shroud than its own clothes, and only a blanket for a coffin, is consigned to the earth. The grave is then usually filled up with stones or poles, as a safe-guard against the voracious wolves of the prairies." Travelers recall the care of their moving companies to camouflage these burial sites. Their herds were milled back and forth and wagons driven across the grave to hide telltale clues, which might have led Indians to dig up the body.

Men on the move thus found community with their ancestors quickly displaced by new-found community with their latest companions.

In the moving companies, and especially in the transient mining camps, family names were overshadowed by given names, even more by vivid nicknames. These were certainly not inherited but were given on the spot, identifying a man by his personal characteristics, his stature, his occupation, an exploit, a gesture, a feature, a quirk of body, voice, or appetite. In the Western camps, names like "Honest Whiskey Joe," "The American Pie-Eater," or "Truthful James" described people cut off from their family past, whose very nomenclature was of their own making.

In settled communities, inherited possessions (like an inherited name) distinguished a man by advantages he had not himself earned. Land was by far the most important of these, in Europe at least, for land was indestructible and descended from generation to generation in the same family by changeless rules. Not until the end of the Middle Ages did English law allow these rigid ancient rules of descent to be altered by wills. Obviously, men on the move could not carry their land with them. Anyway, in new-settled transient communities, land, stripped of ancestral associations, had become a mere commodity. Its value was its price, and its price fluctuated with the market. "Settle and sell, settle and sell," was common Western doctrine.

The first axiom for any westward-moving traveler was to travel light. If he did not start that way, the trip would discipline him to it. The diary of James Abbey, a buoyant young man who left New Albany, Indiana, for California in April, 1849, recorded the property toll of the trip across the desert, as his party approached the Sierra Nevadas:

> August 2nd.—Started out by four o'clock this morning; at six stopped to cook our breakfast and lighten our wagons by throwing away the heavier portion of our clothing and such other articles as we can best spare. We pushed on to-day with as much speed as possible, determined, if possible, to get through the desert, but our cattle gave such evident signs of exhaustion that we were compelled to stop. Being completely out of water, myself, Rowley, and Woodfill bought two gallons from a trader (who had brought it along on speculation), for which we paid the very reasonable price of one dollar per gallon. The desert through which we are passing is strewed with dead cattle, mules, and horses. I counted in a distance of fifteen miles 350 dead horses, 280 oxen, and 120 mules; and hundreds of others are left behind, being unable to keep up. Such is travelling through the desert. . . . A tanyard or slaughterhouse is a flower garden in comparison. A train from Missouri have, to-day, shot twenty oxen. Vast amounts of valuable property have been abandoned and thrown away in this desert—leather trunks, clothing, wagons, etc., to the value of at least a hundred thousand dollars, in about twenty miles. I have counted in the last ten miles 362 wagons, which in the States cost about $120 each. The cause of so many wagons being abandoned is to endeavor to save the animals

and reach the end of the journey as soon as possible by packing through; the loss of personal goods is a matter of small importance comparatively.

The opening chapter of Randolph B. Marcy's semi-official guide warned, from his quarter-century of experience, that supplies "should be put up in the most secure, compact, and portable shape." Space and weight had to be conserved for food, water, shelter, ammunition, and tools. It was important, he said, to carry an extra wrought-iron camp kettle, and an awl with a plentiful supply of buckskins for repairing shoes, harnesses, saddles, and bridles. But items which elsewhere marked off the rich from the poor—elegant clothes, heavily carved furniture, or silver service—plainly had to be left behind.

The most interesting of the items commonly left behind was, of course, women. The mining camps were notoriously masculine. In the spring of 1849, the women in all San Francisco were said to number only fifteen. Tough, bearded, weather-bronzed miners would stand in the streets for hours to have the sight of a child at play. Every camp had its quota of prostitutes, who prospered in a market of short supply, but men would travel miles to welcome "the first real lady in camp." One New England youth of seventeen rode thirty-five miles, after a week's hard work on his father's claim, just to glimpse a miner's wife recently arrived in the neighborhood. "Because," he said, "I wanted to see a home-like lady; and, father, do you know, she sewed a button on for me, and told me not to gamble and not to drink. It sounded just like mother."

The scarcity of women lowered sexual morality, and certainly made life rougher, but it was not entirely without advantages, for when women came later, along with their morality they brought inequality. As early as 1839 (and despite the recent financial panic), the "elegant and polished" ladies of Chicago were paying $500 for a ball dress. But elsewhere in the West, among the transients, where there were fewer women, ostentation was more difficult. The making of social distinctions was woman's work. " 'Putting on style,' " wrote one reporter from the Montana mining camps ". . . is the detestation of everybody. . . . It is neither forgotten nor forgiven and kills a man like a bullet." People in communities on the move inevitably seemed more equal than men and women otherwise—not because of a creed, but because of their way of life.

The successful transient had learned to remain loose and unrooted. Wagon trains settled each night in a new place. The Western landscape, from the very beginning, bore silent witness to this willingness to move on for a fresh start. Elsewhere, to abandon a town was a momentous step, compelled by catastrophe, by sudden social revolution, or by the decay of centuries. The nine cities of Troy, each built on the ruins of its predecessor, were accumulated over millennia, from the Stone Age till Roman times. Pompeii was buried by volcanic eruption. The English "deserted villages" lamented by Oliver Goldsmith in the 18th century were signs of an awakening economy with vast changes: an enclosure movement, an industrial revolution, an urban migration. The Old World thus had its ghost towns, but more often than not they were buried and men built on the rubble of their ancestors' disappointed hopes.

In America the archaeology of fast-moving men on a nearly empty continent was spread plain and thin on the surface. Its peculiar product was the abandoned place (the "ghost town") rather than the buried place. Its characteristic relics were things left by choice before they were used up. Because here space was so much more plentiful than time, the American past was displayed across the landscape.

No complete catalogue of these abandoned places can ever be made. Even a sample reminds us of the American archaeology of space, the tracks the transients left behind. In Iowa, for example, a list prepared in 1930 of towns, villages, and post offices that had been abandoned since Iowa became a territory in 1838 counted 2205. This did not include towns or villages absorbed by others, nor places which had simply changed their names, nor those laid out but never built up. These were actually abandoned places, where people once had lived, received mail, built their houses and their hopes, before moving on. A comparable list for Kansas of "extinct geographical locations" (places settled and abandoned there between 1852 and 1912) exceeds twenty-five hundred. These are only clues, but they recall how experimental were these American communities.

The new American who had left family and property in the Old World dared not be overwhelmed by regret. Westward-moving settlers found more need, more temptation, and more opportunity to move on. But even from the beginning on the eastern seaboard, the uncertain American situation had encouraged transient ways. Jamestown, the first "permanent" English settlement in America, was also one of the first American ghost towns. Founded in 1607, site of the first legislative assembly in America in 1619, it was actually the capital of Virginia until 1698. After its partial destruction by Nathaniel Bacon in his rebellion of 1676, it declined. The capital was then removed to Williamsburg in 1699. By 1722 a visitor to Jamestown reported "nothing but abundance of Brick Rubbish, and three or four good inhabited Houses."

We forget how mobile have been our state capitals—even those of the oldest states along the Atlantic. Washington, D.C., was by no means our first tailor-made capital city. By 1812, eight of the original thirteen states had a different capital city from that at the date of the Declaration of Independence, some thirty-five years before. In several cases the newly named capital, still nonexistent as a town, was conjured up specifically for the purpose. New Hampshire's capital had moved from Portsmouth to Concord (1808); New York's from New York City to Albany (1797); Pennsylvania's from Philadelphia to Harrisburg (1812); New Jersey's from Princeton to Trenton (1790); Delaware's from Newcastle to Dover (1777); North Carolina's from New Bern to Hillsboro and several other places before finally settling in Raleigh (1794); South Carolina's from Charleston to Columbia (1786); Virginia's from Williamsburg to Richmond (1779). These moves were signs of the rapid movement of the American population and the constant pressure to relocate the political headquarters nearer the center of settlements.

In the new Western territories and states, capitals were no less mobile. Take Ohio, for example. The first permanent settlement there—the first site of civil government under the Northwest Ordinance of 1787—was at Marietta, where the forty-seven men of General Rufus Putnam's New England band disembarked from the "Ohio Mayflower" on April 7, 1788. But the first general assembly on September 16, 1799, after the Ohio country had fulfilled the prerequisites of the Ordinance (5000 free male inhabitants of full age), met at Cincinnati. Congress, however, fixed the Ohio territorial capital at Chillicothe, where the second session met on November 3, 1800. Then the assembly voted to remove the government from Chillicothe back to Cincinnati in 1801. Under the new State Constitution of 1802, the capital again was to be at Chillicothe. But numerous other places still claimed the honor. An Act of 1810 then required that the capital be relocated at some place "not . . . more than forty miles from . . . the common centre of the state, to be ascertained by Mansfield's map thereof." Many towns, and many still uninhabited localities, were proposed and considered. In 1812 it was decided to remove the capital to the east "High Bank" of the Scioto River, opposite Franklinton, on the site of a future town to be named Columbus.

Indiana, too, had a migratory capital. Vincennes, its oldest town, was a territorial capital (1800–1813), but demand for a more central location caused removal to a now forgotten place called Corydon, which had been the site of the constitutional convention of 1816. Corydon, suddenly equipped for its new dignity, soon possessed a grand new hotel (only a mile from the capitol), "built for the ages," with solid stone walls eighteen inches thick. But by 1825 Corydon's day of glory had already passed, for in that year the capital was moved to Indianapolis (which had been settled only in 1820).

Illinois Territory, organized in 1809, for its first capital named Kaskaskia; but the capital was removed to Vandalia in 1820 and then (with the persuasion of young Abe Lincoln) to Springfield in 1837. A similar story could be told for most of the Western states. Here was one more sign that Americans viewed their governments functionally. When one headquarters no longer served, or another could serve better, it was time to move on.

Dominated by our picture of the Gold Rusher of '49, we have supposed that most transients knew what they were going for, even if they did not know where to find it. When we look more closely, following the fortunes of individual men and communities, we discover that they were often vague and unsure of purpose: enterprising perhaps, ambitious perhaps, but ever uncertain where their enterprise and ambition should be invested.

We are misled if we think of a westward moving line of settlement advancing like the front ranks of an army, or even if we think of the whole expansive adventure of the 19th century as a "Westward" movement. These were not men moving ever *toward* the west, but men ever moving *in* the west. The churning, casual, vagrant, circular motion around and around was as characteristic of the American experience as the movement in a single direction. Other peoples had followed expeditions toward a definite place or a vivid ideal, in crusades, invasions, or migrations. But the Americans were a new kind of Bedouin. More than almost anything else, they valued the freedom to move, hoping in their very movement to discover what they were looking for. Americans thus valued opportunity, or the chance to seek it, more than purpose.

Transient communities, then, moved about for many reasons— and sometimes apparently for no reasons; prodded by dullness of opportunity where they were, false guesses, exhausted mines, misplaced optimisms, drought, Indian attack, fire, railroad tracks that never arrived, or restlessness and exaggerated hopes. Many "extinct geographical locations" were relics of played-out resources. When Charles Howard Shinn revisited Gold Rush sites in the 1870's and '80's he eloquently reported the New World archaeology:

> Even today the smallest of these decaying camps is worth patient study. In the hollows, grown over with blossoming vines, are acres upon acres of bowlders and debris, moved, sifted, and piled up by the hands of pioneers; on the hill's sunny slope are grass-covered mounds where some of them rest after their passionate toil, their fierce and feverish wrestle with hard-hearted fortune. Once this was Red Dog Camp, or Mad Mule Gulch, or Murderer's Bar: now it is only a nameless canyon, the counterpart of hundreds of others scattered over a region five hundred miles long by fifty miles wide, each one of them all once full to the brim and overflowing with noisy, beating, rushing, roaring, masculine life. Go down and talk with those ghostly inhabitants of the ancient camp, and they will set your blood tingling with tales of the past. Twenty years, thirty years, ago? Why, it is centuries!

Agricultural communities, too, moved on. These men, who had come in less haste, moved away more gradually: from what we might now (on the analogy of the mining camps) call the farming camps. In America, and especially in the West, men expected more than a bare living and, when their struggle became too hard or their hopes were stultified, they were ready to look elsewhere.

Of the many species of American ghost towns, the quickly settled, quickly abandoned mining community still remains the most spectacular. Because the miners left their buildings and many of their furnishings behind, it has not been too difficult to refurbish towns like Central City or Aspen in Colorado. The motorist through the West sees many ghost towns pass before his very eyes: streets, lined with decaying buildings, "many a melancholy deserted village, the monument of blighted hopes." The shell has remained while the spirit has fled.

Thousands of ghost towns (like those counted in Iowa or Kansas) of quite another sort, not mining relics, were common all over the West. These were towns which gradually declined; sometimes they completely disappeared. But often they remained partially inhabited, surviving only as crossroad settlements or small villages, and the relics of their population, needing the scarce lumber, dismantled the vacant buildings which now served no purpose, except as firetraps and breeding grounds for mice and insects. The motorist through these towns today sees few signs of former prosperity. Even the shell no longer remains. The West is full of such ghost towns, which are really more ghostly than their mining counterparts, for here both body and spirit have departed.

The story of almost any one of these ghosts is a chronicle of complex frustrations and interlocking hopes. Some of these towns, within a few years of their founding, had become, in the classic language of the Jayhawkers, "too dead to skin." But sometimes, too, the dead towns were skinned and, as men moved their hopes, they actually carried their buildings with them. For example, when the town of Nininger, Minnesota, went into its decline, much of the town was physically dismantled and moved to a more promising place. Its sawmill, built in 1857, was dismantled and the machinery sold in 1860. The Handyside House, a building accommodating fifty guests, was taken to the neighboring and more prosperous Hastings. Its competitor, the Clinton House, was also transplanted. Nininger's Tremont Hall was purchased by the Masonic Lodge of nearby Cottage Grove, who took it there. This town, where there had been nothing at all in 1855, claimed a population of five hundred by the summer of 1837 and one thousand by 1858. By the time of the eighth Federal census in 1860, the population had declined to 469; by 1869, none of the original buildings remained. The village had disappeared.

The removal of buildings became commonplace. The little lumber town of Newport, Wisconsin, once favorably located with high hopes near the Delles, at the head of navigation of the Wisconsin River, began to decline when the railroad ran up the east bank of the river, passing it by. The last log from Newport went down the river in 1880, but long before that the town was virtually abandoned. Newport's local historian reported that, soon after the disappointment about the railroad, "there was a procession of buildings moving like prehistoric monsters across the landscape."

Whether or not the transients brought their buildings with them, they always brought along their hopes. These survived any number of transplantings. Could the transients themselves have made a living if they had stayed on in the exhausted mining camp, the drought-stricken farm, the lumber town forgotten by the railroad? Looking at people on other continents, we cannot confidently say that they could not have survived. But survival would not satisfy them; they aimed at prosperity. It was enough to make them move if they saw they were not likely to prosper. The mobility of the transients thus measured their determination to keep their expectations unblighted. They had come quickly and recently, and they could leave in just as short order.

14

Getting There First

THE NEED TO MOVE speedily over long distances shaped the highways and vehicles in which transients moved over the West. More than that, it developed a technology of haste. There were always the rewards that others might grab if you were not there before them. And there were long perilous stretches where desert sun, lack of water, deep snow, or hostile Indians made every prudent man move quickly to shorten dangers. Perhaps America really was the land of the future, but for the transients it seemed to be the land of now-or-never.

Americans built wagons, steamboats, and railroads not with an eye to the next generation, or the next decade, or even the next year. Craftsmen kept their eyes unashamedly on the present. It was most important to arrive there first, or, if not first, then as soon as possible. It was haste that decisively shaped the technology of American travel.

Every kind of vehicle that carried the transients around the West showed the importance of light construction, speed, and freedom of movement. Westward travelers, when they did not abandon vehicles altogether to straddle the backs of horses or mules, chose wagons different from those familiar in the east. Elegant Concord coaches and heavy Conestoga wagons were not for them. Instead, they rode the light "prairie wagons"—"smaller in size, frailer in build, without a door, with very bad springs, and with canvas blinds for windows." Built for manoeuverability and speed, they skimmed across the prairies, but were sometimes abandoned at the foot of the Sierras; often they were sold en route or disposed of piecemeal, for their valuable wheels or axles or lumber. They were seldom expected to outlast the journey.

The story of western transportation in this heyday of the transients between the Revolution and the Civil War is everywhere a story of speed. The broad Mississippi, which, measured from the headwaters of the Missouri, extended some four thousand miles, and whose navigable branches reached within eight hundred miles of the Pacific, was a natural superhighway. And western steamboat life was a racing life. Prosaic, practical, and commercial needs had first stirred the western passion for getting there first, but before long the passion acquired its own momentum. What had begun as crude necessity ended in dangerous, delightful diversion. The racing of steamboats on the Mississippi, the grand theme of Mark Twain's early experience, became, like horse-racing, a sport pursued for its own sake. But unlike horse-racing, which was aristocratic and individualist, steamboat racing was a popular and communal competition.

As early as 1787, John Fitch had made the first vessel moved by the power of steam on the waters of the United States. Within twenty years, Robert Fulton's *Clermont,* propelled by steam, made the trip from New York to Albany in thirty-two hours. By 1838, when David Stevenson, an English engineer, came to observe the extraordinary feats attributed to American steamboats, he found them navigating the Hudson River and Long Island Sound at a speed far surpassing that of any European steamer. The spirit of western steamboat travel about 1840 was summarized by the knowledgeable Baron de Gerstner, who was an eyewitness to its excesses:

> The Americans are, as is known, the most enterprising people in the world, who justly say of themselves, *"We go always ahead."* The Democrats here never like to remain behind one another: on the contrary, each wants to get ahead of the rest. When two steamboats happen to get alongside each other, the passengers will encourage the captains to run a race, which the latter agree to. The boilers intended for a pressure of only 100 pounds per square inch, are by the accelerated generation of steam, exposed to a pressure of 150, and even 200 pounds, and this goes sometimes so far, that the trials end with an explosion. Seldom they have here, as they do in Europe, fixed in the boiler a plate of a composition which melts at a certain degree of heat,

and the fire becomes extinguished by the water. The races are the causes
of most of the explosions, and yet they are still constantly taking place.
The life of an American is, indeed, only a constant *racing*, and why
should he fear it so much on board the steamboats?

In the West, economy of construction and speed had long governed
the design of river boats. Before the age of steam, most downstream
transportation there was by flatboats of varying shapes and sizes, from
twenty to one hundred feet in length and between twelve and twenty
feet wide. They were of the simplest (and often, too, of the shoddiest)
construction, made sometimes of timbers barely watertight enough
for a single voyage. When they had served their purpose, they were
commonly set adrift or taken apart by the emigrants to serve for shelter
or for fuel. In New Orleans, the demand for sawed timber for sidewalks and houses provided a thriving market for these broken-down
flatboats.

By the 1820's, when steamboats were common on western waters,
they were mostly powered by engines built in the West (Pittsburgh,
Cincinnati, or Louisville), and of a distinctive western design, specially
suited to western needs. The first steam engines in practical use in
England and America were of "low-pressure" design. This was the
type first developed by Watt, then manufactured by the firm of Boulton
and Watt, and long the standard industrial engine. Steam was accumulated in a large, double-acting vertical cylinder, but the steam reached
only a few pounds of pressure per square inch. Exhaust steam went
from the cylinder to a condenser where a jet of cold water, by con-
densing the steam, created a partial vacuum. This vacuum then allowed
the pressure of the atmosphere to drive the piston. A cylinder of large
diameter was obviously required to produce sufficient power for any
practical purpose. It was low-pressure engines of this type that were
first introduced into this country by Fulton. He imported such a Boulton
and Watt engine from England to run the *Clermont*. But this type
of engine was expensive and complicated, requiring many precision-
fitted moving parts for both cylinder and condenser.

The engine that became standard on western steamboats was of a
different and novel design. It was the work primarily of an unsung
hero of American industrial progress, Oliver Evans (1755–1819).
The self-educated son of a Delaware farmer, Evans early became
obsessed by the possibilities of mechanized production and steam
power. Ridicule and the lack of public support prevented his developing a workable steam carriage of his own design, but as early as 1802
in his mill he was using a stationary steam engine of "high-pressure" design. Engines of this type were not unknown; before Evans they were
generally considered impractical and dangerous. With an Englishman,
Richard Trevithick, who was working independently, Evans shares credit

for having first made a high-pressure engine feasible for general use.

This engine was far simpler. In its cylinder, steam was accumulated to a much higher pressure—at first from forty to sixty pounds per square inch, by 1840 to as much as one hundred pounds. It did not require a condenser, for the expanding steam drove the piston directly. The cylinder too was much smaller in diameter than that required for low-pressure engines of the same power. Exploiting these obvious advantages, Evans soon developed an engine which, by comparison with low-pressure engines, was compact, cheap and easy to make, operate, and maintain. In 1805, under his interesting title of *The Abortion of the Young Steam Engineer's Guide: Containing an Investigation of the Principles, Construction and Powers of Steam Engines,* Evans provided a do-it-yourself manual with which any skilled mechanic could make and run a high-pressure engine.

Within a decade the high-pressure engine, the new type, had become standard on western waters. Proving peculiarly well suited to western river navigation, it lasted out the steamboat age. Critics ignorant of western conditions often attacked it as wasteful and dangerous. But men who really knew the Ohio, the Missouri, and the Mississippi insisted, with good reason, that it was the only engine for them. In shallow western rivers the weight of vessel and engine was important; a heavy engine added to the problems of navigation. The high-pressure engine, compared to the low-pressure engine, was far lighter in proportion to horsepower, and, with less than half as many moving parts, was much easier and cheaper to repair. Besides, the low-pressure engine did not have the flexibility and reserve power required by the varying currents, the seasonal fluctuations, and the sudden obstructions of fast-moving waters in narrow, twisting channels. The main advantages of low-pressure engines were safe operation and economy of fuel consumption, neither of which meant much in the West. For a long time wood was cheap along the rivers and when the woodlands receded, cheap coal had become available. Even the thirty per cent difference in fuel consumption thus did not count heavily.

Western travelers, determined to get there first, willingly ran substantial risks to travel by fast high-pressure engines. When an American sailing vessel normally lasted twenty years and a whaler might stay in service sixty years, the life expectancy of a western steamboat was brief. The contrast with eastern steamboats was also striking. In 1860, for example, when the average age of steamboats actually inspected in New York was nearly nine years, in Pittsburgh it was slightly over two years.

Western steamboats showed an appalling accident record. A voyage on the Mississippi, it was often said, was far more dangerous than a passage across the ocean. There were no official figures before 1852, but we can estimate that of all steamboats built before mid-century, about thirty per cent were lost in accidents. In steamboat accidents noted on western rivers before mid-century, about one-third of the property damage, about one-half of the fatalities, and about two-thirds of the total casualties resulted from explosions. Flying wreckage, floods of steam, and scalding water killed and maimed people by the hundreds. A general demand for speed, a premium on the "hot and fast engineer" who could squeeze the last spurt of power from a decrepit boiler, had a great deal to do with this shocking accident rate. Land-rushers, gold-rushers, town-speculators, merchants, and nondescript hasty emigrants wanted to "go ahead anyhow." "Talk about *Northern* steamers," the fireman of a Mississippi steamboat sneered to an eastern traveler in 1844, "it don't need no spunk to navigate them waters. You haint bust a biler for five years. But I tell you, stranger, it takes a man to ride one of these half alligator boats, head on a snag, high pressure, valve sodered down, 600 souls on board & in danger of going to the devil."

Steamboatmen meeting in Cincinnati in 1838 to consider the causes of accidents, admitted that incompetence and carelessness were often to blame. But they concluded:

> . . . the public have, themselves, contributed in no inconsiderable degree, to increase the evil, not only by newspaper puffs, but by the constant desire which a large portion of those who travel on steamboats, manifest to "go on the fastest" and even to urge an increase of speed. Is it wonderful then that under such circumstances some commanders should be induced to force their boats beyond the bounds of safety, when great patronage and applause are the rewards for the risk incurred? This morbid appetite among travelers for "going ahead" is probably one of the greatest causes of the evils. . . .

Steamboat explosions, while not unique to the West, were a characteristically western phenomenon. Apocryphal stories abounded; how passengers who had not yet paid their fare were sent to the after part of the vessel, where, as assets, they would be least in danger from explosion; how Irishmen were preferred to slaves as firemen, because their deaths brought no financial loss to the management. Unembroidered reality was terrifying enough. In the twenty-five years before mid-century, there were at least one hundred and fifty major explosions on steamboats on western rivers, in which altogether no less than fourteen hundred people were killed. Disaster followed disaster. One of the most notorious was the explosion of the *Moselle* on April 25, 1838. It had been made a "brag" boat by the efforts of its Captain Perrin, who had broken speed records by feeding its fires with resin, by stopping only hastily at landings, and by holding all steam instead of allowing any to waste at the safety valve. At least 150 of its 280 passengers were lost by scalding water, by drowning or panic. The horrendous climax of Mark Twain's adventures on the Mississippi was the explosion of the steamboat *Pennsylvania* in mid-July, 1858, with a loss of over one hundred and fifty lives.

The same passion for speed that had made western travelers risk fire and brimstone to get there first by steamboat—and that induced Pony Express riders to risk life and limb—also explained the early displacement of the steamboat by the railroad. Railroads attracted the steamboat passenger traffic by covering distances in two or three days that had taken the steamboat a week. The American railroads, too, were to be distinctive in purpose, quality, and design.

Steamboats followed routes laid out by nature, but railroads (although never free to ignore natural contours, and inevitably guided by them) *were* the routes themselves. The railroads in the American West had the power to make a path of settlement. Perceptive Europeans noted this unique potency. "To make a railway where population exists is one thing," observed a British railway engineer in 1851, "but to make one in order to call forth a population is another." As the Scotsman, James Stirling, traveling here in 1856–57, noted:

> There seems a natural, pre-ordained fitness between the railway and the prairie; for the prairie is as eminently suited to the formation of railways, as railways are essential to the development of prairies. For hundreds of miles you have only to raise the turf, and lay your sleepers; for hundreds of miles you need neither grading nor bridging; no engineering; hardly any surveying. In one long, unwavering line your iron road passes over the level plain. And that plain, remember, costs nothing; or at most a dollar and a quarter per acre. The artificial hindrances are still fewer than the natural ones. There are no cities to be circumvented, or bridged over, at enormous cost; no gentlemen's seats whose "amenity" is to be preserved. . . . But again: the prairies absolutely make their own railways without cost to any one. The development of the country by means of a railway is such, that what was yesterday waste land is to-day a valuable district. There is thus action and reaction: the railway improves the land; the improvement pays for the railway. . . . there is nothing in history to compare with this seven-league progress of civilization. For the first time in the world we see a highly-civilized people quietly spreading itself over a vast untenanted solitude, and at one wave of its wand converting the wilderness into a cultivated and fruitful region.

The very race to cover and possess these vast untenanted solitudes itself decisively shaped American railroads. It stimulated a technology of haste, which was also a technology of progress. Beautifully symbolized in the railroads, it was later to be expressed in many other departments of American life. Railroad lines were themselves pre-emptors;

they received substantial prizes for first arrival. The great example, of course, was the first transcontinental railroad. Under the Pacific Railroad Act (July 1, 1862) the Central Pacific was to build eastward from California to the Nevada line, where it was to join tracks with the Union Pacific. But by 1866 lobbyists from the Central Pacific, in the pre-empting California spirit of the Land Rush and the Gold Rush, had persuaded Congress to amend the Act. The new Act allowed each company to build its line as far as it could—until it reached the tracks coming from the opposite direction. This created a valuable, and characteristically American, opportunity. Each additional mile constructed brought its builders large Federal loans (between $16,000 and $48,000, depending on the terrain), plus grants of a 400-foot right of way and ten alternate sections of land. The first American transcontinental railroad was thus transformed from an engineering project into a race in which construction practices of the competing companies became a national scandal.

Similar incentives on a smaller scale hastened construction elsewhere. First roads often received monopoly advantages, like those of the Camden & Amboy Railroad in New Jersey, or the exclusive right to cross Indian Territory granted in advance to the first railroad to reach its border.

It is not surprising, then, that American railroads were constructed in the quickest way, and with little regard to safety, comfort, or durability. This meant single track (with sidings for passing) instead of double. It meant steeper grades and sharper curves, for there was not time to level down inclines, to cut tunnels, or to build up embankments. Americans experimented freely (sometimes recklessly) with cheaper and quicker ways of laying track: with narrow gauges, with wooden trestleworks in place of earthen or stone embankments, with unballasted roadbeds, and with every conceivable kind of substitute material or short cut.

Flimsy construction and fast speeds over poorly graded, sharp-curving, unfenced track on rough terrain caused numerous accidents. By mid-century, American railroad wrecks, especially in the West, were as frequent and as notorious as steamboat explosions had been a decade or two earlier. In 1842 Charles Dickens, who was not easily shocked, found his first ride in an American train of the Boston & Lowell line a terrifying experience. Generally foreigners touring the United States by rail were appalled by the frequency of accidents and still more amazed that Americans should accept them as routine. An Englishman, Charles Richard Weld, recorded his experiences in 1855 on a train out of Cumberland, West Virginia, bound for Washington, D.C. Since the train was late leaving Cumberland they would have to speed, the conductor explained, to make up time.

The line after leaving Cumberland follows the windings of the Potomac, describing sharp curves. Round these the engine darted with rocket-like impetuosity, the car in which we were seated swaying in a manner rendering it necessary to hold on. A more significant hint of the impending catastrophe was given by the fall of a ponderous lamp glass on my head but with no worse result than inflicting a smart blow. Presently another glass was jerked out of its socket and precipitated into the lap of a lady; the oscillations of the car meanwhile increasing in violence.

Affairs now assumed a serious aspect and I felt certain we were on the eve of a smash. This was the opinion of a gentleman who had the care of two ladies, for he proceeded with a coolness deserving a better cause to instruct us how to place ourselves, laying great stress on the importance of sitting diagonally in order not to receive the shock directly on the knees. We were also advised to hold the backs of the seats before us. He strengthened his advice by assuring us that he was experienced in railway accidents and added that as there was far less danger in the middle than in the end car it would be prudent to change our seats at the next station.

As we expected, an accident did occur, the results of which, had we retained our seats in the last car, would have been in all probability most serious. In vain was the conductor urged to slacken the excessive speed. With blind if not wilful recklessness it was maintained and at length, when about six miles from the station where we changed our places, a terrific crash and a series of dislocatory heavings and collisions, terminating in deathlike silence and the overthrow of the car which we occupied, gave certain evidence that we had gone off the line.

When Weld crawled from the wreckage he saw that all cars except half the middle car, and the engine, had been smashed. Wheels had been whirled over the landscape. Rails were either wholly wrenched from their sleepers or rolled into snakeheads. Weld's terror turned to indignation when he found none of his fellow passengers willing to join him in complaining of the recklessness of the conductor. On the contrary, most of them praised the conductor's efforts to arrive on time.

Accidents often recurred in the same place. Alfred Bunn, an English theatrical manager traveling here in 1851, reported in amazement that a friend of his who had failed to unload a parcel from a train at the depot near his house was unperturbed, because he knew the train usually had an accident a mile farther on. Sure enough it did, and he unloaded his parcel then.

An accident rate which was shocking by comparison with that of European railroads, became, like our automobile accident rate in the 20th century, a widely recognized feature of American life. By mid-19th century, a national chorus protested these railroad casualties, but hasty, cheap construction and an obsession with speed made all the proposed remedies useless.

Still, the American determination to get there first, to build quickly and cheaply, and to travel fast, was not entirely without advantages. It helps explain many of the peculiar virtues then already visible in American technology.

Take, for example, how the bumpy, curving American roadbeds stimulated improvements in locomotive design. Michel Chevalier, the observant Frenchman sent here in 1834 to inspect American public works, noted that a rise of 50 feet to the mile (double the maximum established by French engineers) did not frighten the Americans. The French Board of Public Works had fixed the minimum radius for their curves at 2700 feet. But some of the curves on the Baltimore & Ohio had a radius as small as 400 feet, and curves of 1000-foot radius were quite normal. English engineers had even doubted that locomotive steam engines could be used at all on curved rails; few of them imagined that locomotives could ever be driven safely and at high speeds on curves of such short radius.

English doubts were confirmed when locomotives, brought across the ocean at great expense, proved unable to negotiate the meandering American roadbeds. The most famous of these imports was the *Stourbridge Lion,* the first working steam-powered locomotive (as distinguished from experimental engines) to run on American rails. It was intended for hauling Pennsylvania coal from Carbondale to Honesdale on a track which crossed the Lackawaxen Creek on a light trestle. But the track was unsafe for the *Stourbridge Lion,* which weighed seven tons (twice that specified in the contract). After a demonstration run in 1829, the famous locomotive was left on a siding to disintegrate; some of its parts were preserved as museum pieces in the National Museum in Washington. The qualities for which the *Stourbridge Lion* and other English-built locomotives brought here before mid-century were peculiarly admired—their solidity, rigidity, and heavy construction —were precisely what made them unsuitable for American rails.

Locomotives, then, would have to be specially designed for the American roads. They would have to be light and flexible, able to run on steep grades, sharp curves, and light wooden trestles. American designers proved equal to their task. Very early they produced a distinctively American locomotive, shaped less by the finesse of American technology (which did not exist) than by the flimsiness, haste, and economy of American road construction; by the scarcity of capital in general and of crucial raw materials (such as iron) in particular; by a varied landscape, where distances were great and speed was an obsession.

At first minor modifications were tried, but novel American problems required drastic changes. These came very soon. An American engineering pioneer, John Bloomfield Jervis, without European experience to misguide him, faced American problems afresh and made the first radical advance in locomotive design. He built a low-swiveling "bogie" truck of four small wheels to support the forward end of the locomotive, and then put the large heavy drive wheels (first two, later four) behind. His *Brother Jonathan* (sometimes called the *Experiment*), made in 1832, incorporated this feature. It was one of the first locomotives to have six wheels. *Brother Jonathan* in its day was the fastest locomotive in the world, capable of sixty to eighty miles an hour. All the essentials of advanced American locomotive design were presently fixed when the *Mercury* (1842) combined an extremely flexible truck suspension of Jervis' type with an improvement of Joseph Harrison's equalized drive-wheel arrangement to reduce road shock, on a remarkably light frame. The *Mercury,* carrying passenger cars at a speed of sixty miles an hour, traveled 37,000 miles in one year (1844)—the greatest mileage run by any engine till then.

Small technical changes added up to large distinctions between English and American design. English locomotives were solid, stable, heavy, and well made. Marvels of strength and precision, they were generally rigid and unadaptable. By comparison, American locomotives, a popular writer noted in 1879, seemed a "crazy affair, as loose-jointed as a basket." "The framework is light and open, and yet strong. . . . The engine is . . . hung upon the fulcrums of a system of levers, balanced equally in every direction. Let the road follow its own wayward will, be low here and high there . . . the basket-like flexibility of the frame and its supports . . . adjusts the engine to its road at every instant of its journey." Such lightness, simplicity, and flexibility would continue to distinguish much of American industrial design.

*　　*　　*

The technology of haste expressed a special attitude to time—to the present and the future and the relation between them. Perhaps America *was* the land of the future, but Americans seldom thought of themselves as building for the future. More precisely, American technology was a technology of the present, shaped by haste, by scarcity of craftsmanship, of capital, and of raw materials, and by a firm expectation of rapid change in the technology itself.

In striking contrast to all this, British railroad builders consciously built for the future. But they became prisoners of their rigid expectations. "We have deemed the inventions of railways," explained Edward Watkin, the English railroad builder who visited the United States in mid-century, "a final improvement in the means of locomotion, and we have, therefore, constructed our works to last 'for ever' of bricks and mortar. We have made our rails strong enough for any possible weight of engine; our drainage capacious enough to remove any conceivable flood . . . our bridges firm enough for many times the weight than can ever come upon them."

Americans built for the present. Worried primarily over how to make a little capital go a long way (figuratively and literally), they could not think much about durability. It was more important to get there first and fast than to build a line to serve your grandchildren. "In the construction of railways," an American witness testified before the British Parliamentary Committee on the Export of Machinery in 1841, "economy and speedy completion are the points which have been specially considered. It is the general opinion that it is better to extend the system of railways as far as possible at once, and be satisfied in the first instance with that quality of construction which present circumstances admit of, rather than to postpone the execution of work so immediately beneficial to the country."

By building rapidly and flimsily, Americans refused hostages to the future. They affirmed their faith that, in America, everything would change—including, of course, the techniques of railroad building. For them, railroads were by no means "a final improvement in the means of locomotion." The British confidence in the future, and in its resemblance to the present, made it hard for Britishers even to imagine obsolescence. But belief in obsolescence became an article of American faith.

15

The Democracy of Haste

THE AMERICAN OPPORTUNITY to travel was a great equalizer. Mushrooming systems of transportation here (as Chevalier noted in 1835) tended "to reduce the distance not only between different places, but between different classes. Where the rich and the great travel only with a pompous retinue, while the poor man, who goes to the next village, drags himself singly along in mud and sand, over rocks and through thickets, the word equality is a mockery and a falsehood, and aristocracy stares you in the face." In India, China, the Middle East, or Spanish America, Chevalier remarked, it mattered little what name was given to the government; the peasant or the laborer would never convince himself he was the equal of the soldier, the brahmin, the mandarin, the pasha, or the nobleman whose retinue ran him over or covered him with mud. Their processions filled him with awe, and he kneeled while they passed. In Great Britain, by contrast, despite inequalities of wealth and birth, "the mechanic and the labourer, who can go to the office and get a ticket for the railroad cars, if they have a few shillings in their pockets, and who have the right, if they will pay for it, of sitting in the same vehicle, on the same seat with the baronet or the peer and duke, feel their dignity as men, and touch, as it were, the fact that there is not an impassable gulf between them and the nobility." But in America, Chevalier and many others agreed, the equalizing effects of free and frequent travel were even more noticeable.

Here, where distances were far greater than in England and where common people traveled more, steam locomotion confined more people closely, in large groups, and for longer periods. All this helped erase the genteel distinctions of social class. Economy of construction, pressures to build vehicles quickly, and willingness of travelers to put up with discomforts in order to get there fast, also pushed people together more closely and more indiscriminately. In their present anxiety to arrive someplace in a hurry, passengers forgot, ignored, or abandoned the distinctions of other places and other times.

The aristocratic Philadelphian, Samuel Breck, journeying from Boston to Providence on a hot July day in 1835, recorded his dismay when more and more people were packed into his passenger car. "Two poor fellows, not much in the habit of making their toilet, squeezed me into a corner, while the hot sun drew from their garments a villainous compound of smells made up of salt, fish, tar and molasses." Then there were introduced twelve "bouncing factory girls," who promptly made themselves at home sucking lemons and eating green apples. The large social consequences of crowded, speedy American vehicles (whether steamboat or railroad car) oppressed him:

> The rich and the poor, the educated and the ignorant, the polite and the vulgar, all herd together in this modern improvement in travelling. The consequence is a complete amalgamation. Master and servant sleep heads and points on the cabin floor of the steamer, feed at the same table, sit in each other's laps, as it were, in the cars; and all this for the sake of doing very uncomfortably in two days what would be done delightfully in eight or ten. . . . Talk of ladies on a steamboat or in a railroad car! There are none. I never feel like a gentleman there, and I cannot perceive a semblance of gentility in any one who makes part of the travelling mob. When I see women whom, in their drawing-rooms or elsewhere, I have been accustomed to respect and treat with every suitable deference,—when I see them, I say, elbowing their way through a crowd of dirty emigrants or low-bred homespun fellows in petticoats or breeches in our country, in order to reach a table spread for a hundred or more, I lose sight of their

pretensions to gentility and view them as belonging to the plebeian herd. To restore herself to her caste, let a lady move in select company at five miles an hour, and take her meals in comfort at a good inn, where she may dine decently. . . . The old-fashioned way of five or six miles with liberty to . . . be master of one's movements, . . . is the mode to which I cling, and which will be adopted again by the generations of after times.

Foreigners like Dickens remarked with surprise that American trains, in contrast to those of England and elsewhere, had no first- or second- or third-class carriages. Sometimes, however, (especially in the South) there were separate carriages for men and women and for Negroes; occasionally also there were special cars for emigrants or for troops. The main distinction between the men's and the women's cars, Dickens pointed out, was that in the men's cars everybody smoked and in the women's nobody did. The prevalence of tobacco chewing gave women some of their strongest arguments for separate facilities. But specialized cars were wasteful and (with a few conspicuous exceptions) were gradually discontinued.

Not only the absence of "class" cars but the general design of American passenger cars was quite distinctive. The difference which still strikes any American who travels by rail in England or on the continent of Europe was there almost from the beginning. At first, here as abroad, every passenger car was divided into several quite separate closed compartments (each holding six or eight people) in which passengers were confined for the duration of the journey. But this design expressed a traditional and conservative technology: the earliest double-truck cars, double or triple the length of a horse-drawn carriage, had been made simply by putting together on one carrying-frame the bodies of several old-fashioned carriages. This explained why, at first, entrance doors were along the sides instead of at either end. But trains here soon adopted a more radical design. Now American passengers were seated in long box-like cars, entered from either end, and without dividing compartments. European passenger cars retained the partitions and the small compartments inherited from the old horse-drawn carriage. In Europe, until recently, it was only on some third-class passenger cars that one found the open, uncompartmented design which has long distinguished the American passenger car. In these open interiors, passengers (except in the occasional lady's car) led a free and easy life. They made themselves comfortable by removing their shoes or outer garments. They ate, drank, and conversed indiscriminately with fellow passengers.

Upper-class European travelers were embarrassed. The naturally gregarious Americans, they said, were inquisitive, pushing, and always eager to be into somebody else's business. The vast western distances strained the good nature of the squeamish or privacy-loving. The passenger trains confined dozens of all classes together for days on end. The Viscountess Avonmore in 1874 recorded her discomfort at traveling with "thirty or forty human beings . . . boxed up together for seven days and nights, crammed close to each other all day, sleeping on shelves at night and in the same atmosphere." Everybody was obliged to retire and arise at the same hour, for all beds had to go up and come down together. She saw one of her plebeian fellow passengers each morning take from her pocket a set of false teeth which, she insisted on explaining to the Viscountess, she did not sleep in because they were so expensive and she hated to use them up. The lavatory of the car was at the entrance and could not be made private either from within or without. "You cannot even tuck up your hair or roll up your sleeves," the Viscountess complained, "but some gentleman or conductor is sure to pounce upon you and remark, 'Very refreshing to get a good wash.' " On this train the friendly, community spirit was further fostered by a daily morning newspaper, the *Great Pacific Line Gazette,* printed on board.

Americans, it was said, could not endure privacy or solitude; they were so restless, they could not sit still even for a short train journey. Foreigners noted also the distinctive American design by which a fidgety passenger could wander through the train, passing out the door at the end of his car and crossing the open platform into the next. Americans thought nothing of the risk of being crushed between cars or being jolted off the train. Despite stern warnings (one company painted a gravestone on each door), Americans moved obsessively about, mingling with the passengers of one car after another. Americans, too, had a strange desire to keep going till they reached the last car, where they stood silently admiring the receding view.

Speedy travel, in the days before dining cars, did not allow leisurely meals or the time-consuming upper-class elegancies of "dining." In the early 19th century, the American penchant for the "quick lunch" was already widely noted. The irritable British naval officer, Captain Frederick Marryat, complained in 1839 that the requirement to eat in haste made American railroad travel especially fatiguing. "The cars stop, all the doors are thrown open, and out rush all, the passengers like boys out of school, and crowd round the tables to solace themselves with pies, patties, cakes, hard-boiled eggs, hams, custards and a variety of railroad luxuries too numerous to mention. The bell rings for departure, in they all hurry with their hands and mouths full, and off they go again until the next stopping-place induces them to relieve the monotony of the journey by masticating without being hungry."

An American technology of quick feeding developed very early. The "lunch-counter," offering both rapid service and enough discomfort to discourage the customer from lingering over his meal, was an American

invention of this era, a by-product of the haste of railroad travel. The
first recorded uses of the American expression "lunch-counter" are
found within a decade of the Civil War. The New York *Times* (June
10, 1857) with an eastern sensitivity complained that it was a shameful
abuse of words to use "Refreshment Saloons" to describe the places for
eating and drinking at railroad stations.

> There could not be a more inappropriate designation for such abomi-
> nations of desolation. Directors of railroads appear to have an idea that
> travelers are destitute of stomach; that eating and drinking are not at
> all necessary to human beings bound on long journeys, and that nothing
> more is required than to put them through their misery in as brief a
> time as possible. It is expected that three or four hundred men, women
> and children . . . shall rush out helter-skelter into a dismal, long room
> and dispatch a supper, breakfast or dinner in fifteen minutes.

The weary traveler was awakened in the morning by the conductor's
shout, "Pogramville—fifteen minutes for breakfast!" With no time or
facilities for washing, he barely had time to rush out for a hasty grab at
whatever food came within his reach before hurrying back to his seat.
By the end of his journey, he was certain to have "laid the foundation
for a fit of dyspepsia, which may lead to a disease of the lungs or a
fever." On few roads in the whole country were comfortable meals or
decent washing facilities to be found.

It was not until 1863 that George Pullman put into service his first
dining car open to all passengers. But within a few years the Pullman
Company found the business unprofitable and withdrew from this
restaurant business; ever since, the dining car has been a problem for
American railroads. The commonest way of eating en route was at station restaurants or lunch counters. Fred Harvey's restaurant chain developed after 1876 to serve the western railroads, and the attractive
Harvey Girls became famous—along with their motto, "Slice the ham
thinner."

An English traveler in the West in 1878 noted how quick service
and crude facilities made all customers equal.

> Thirty miles beyond Julesburg on the Union Pacific Railroad we came
> to Sidney, an eating-station and therefore a place of importance. We
> stopped half an hour to hurry out and get breakfast. . . . We were all
> served alike; everyone was given the same as his neighbor. Knives and
> forks were lamentably scarce, as usual. One knife and fork to each to
> last through the whole meal is the order of the day out here. . . . All
> ate as if for their very lives and the result was that we were all through
> together a quarter of an hour before it was time to start. For this and
> for every meal, except two, along the route of the Pacific Railroad
> from Omaha to San Francisco the charge is one dollar.

Haste and crowds not only made it difficult to preserve social distance; they tended to make the travelers themselves into "instant" communities. The priority rule again applied and again was an equalizer. Where, as on river steamers, chairs or deck space were scarce, it was a question of first come first served. With good humor people accepted the luck of the draw when they settled by lot which steamer passengers should receive sleeping berths. The crowded steamboats on Western rivers were not entirely without distinction: a wide gulf did separate "cabin" passengers from the "deck" (or steerage) passengers, who were handled like freight. But it was customary that all who traveled in the cabin should overlook differences of wealth and class to mingle equally and sociably. Class-conscious travelers from abroad were disgusted by such easy familiarity.

Steamboats on western waters, like wagon companies on the trails, were often beyond the effective jurisdiction of federal, state, or local government. These became short-lived waterborne communities. They, too, often made and enforced their law by vigilantism and majority rule. It was widely assumed that neither the captain nor any distant government, but the passengers themselves, were the proper source of law on steamboats. "At noon, every day," a notice in the cabin of the second *New Orleans* in 1817 (after listing the usual petty offenses) explained, "three persons to be chosen by a majority of the passengers shall form a court to determine on all penalties incurred and the amount collected shall be expended in wine for the whole company after dinner. For every transgression against good order and cleanliness, not already specified, such fine shall be imposed as the court in their discretion shall think fit." Seldom dared a passenger question the authority of such a court. Here, as in other western vigilante courts, procedures were brief and punishment was prompt. A murderer would be turned over to authorities at the next town, but thieves, pickpockets, and other petty offenders were summarily whipped and put ashore at whatever point (even an island or a sandbar in midstream) the steamboat was passing. One of the more terrifying examples of quick and effective justice occurred when, on a boat passing near Cincinnati in 1859, a self-appointed committee of busybody passengers became suspicious of a young man and young woman traveling together, ostensibly as cousins. On finding them occupying the same berth, the committee held the boat at the landing the next morning, escorted the young man to obtain a marriage license, and then took the couple to a minister to see them married.

The transient life thus accustomed travelers to majority rule and priority rule. A rough equality was the product of their experience.

PART THREE

THE UPSTARTS
Boosters

> " 'Dost thou know how to play the fiddle?' 'No,'
> answered Themistocles, 'but I understand the
> art of raising a little village into a great city.' "
>
> Motto on masthead of the
> *Emigrant Aid Journal*

> "Truly this is a world which has no regard for
> the established order of things, but knocks them
> sky west and crooked, and lo, the upstart hath
> the land and its fatness."
>
> Tascosa, Texas, *Pioneer*

SPEEDY growth made men and communities and cities and governments what they had never been in the Old World. A quick-grown city, founded and built by the living generation, lacked monuments from the past. It was overwhelmed by its imaginary present greatness and its debt to the future. The very existence of an Upstart city depended on the ability to attract free and vagrant people. The strength of ancient metropolises came from the inability, the unwillingness or the reticence of people to leave, but New World cities depended on new-formed loyalties and enthusiasms, shallow-rooted, easily transplanted.

The medieval town might be judged by the thickness and strength of its walls. The heavy buttresses of Carcassonne and Bruges and Saint-Malo testified to the civic devotion and foresight of their inhabitants.

Old World cities often outgrew their walls; but Upstart towns had none. Their key idea from their beginning was less defense or preservation (for there was nothing yet to preserve) than growth. They measured themselves, not by their ability to keep out invaders, but by their power to attract immigrants. The American identification of life with progress was rooted here.

The Transients had formed their communities for safe and fast movement or for some quick purpose like gold mining. They lived here today and the next day, but if they succeeded they would be safely somewhere else next year or the year after. When the Transients settled down, they became Upstarts: they had begun to live in the day after tomorrow. They thought of their whole generation and their children, and they lived now, not in movement, but in growth. Their lives depended on their own faith—a willing suspension of disbelief—that they would live forever in this new Rome, new Athens, or new London, which would become the center of their universe, and of everybody else's.

The following chapters describe ways of thought and life which arose from how these communities grew, from how fast they grew, from their hopes and illusions, from their sense of destiny, from their reaching toward the future. Old antitheses—between personal and public prosperity, between privacy and publicity—were dissolved. The new institutions of Upstart cities reshaped life everywhere in the new nation.

16

The Businessman as an
American Institution

THE AMERICAN BUSINESSMAN—a product (and a maker) of the
upstart cities of the American West between the Revolution and the
Civil War—was not an American version of the enterprising European
city banker or merchant or manufacturer. Not an American Fugger or
Medici or Rothschild or Arkwright, he was something quite different.
His career and his ideals are an allegory of an American idea of community, for he was born and bred in the dynamic American urbanism in
the period of our greatest growth.

The changing meaning of his very name, "businessman," gives us a
clue. In 18th-century England to say someone was a "man of business"
was primarily to say he engaged in public affairs. Thus David Hume in
1752 described Pericles as "a man of business." Before the end of the
18th century the expression had begun to lose this, its once primary
meaning, and instead to describe a person engaged in mercantile transactions; it became a loose synonym for "merchant." But our now
common word "businessman" seems to have been American in origin.
It came into use around 1830 in the very period when the new Western
cities were founded and were growing most rapidly. Even a casual look
at this early American businessman, who he was, what he was doing,
and how he thought of his work, will show how inaccurate it would be
to describe him as simply a man engaged in mercantile transactions. We
might better characterize him as a peculiarly American type of community

maker and community leader. His starting belief was in the interfusing of public and private prosperity. Born of a social vagueness unknown in the Old World, he was a distinctive product of the New.

The new fast-growing city, where nothing had been before, a city with no history and unbounded hopes, was the American businessman's first natural habitat. In the period when he first appeared, his primary commodity was land and his secondary commodity transportation. This transformation of land rights and transport rights from political symbols and heirlooms into mere commodities was also an American phenomenon.

The businessman's characteristics would appear in the story of any one of the thousands who made their fortunes in the early 19th century. "I was born close by a saw-mill," boasted William B. Ogden (1805–77), "was early left an orphan, was cradled in a sugar-trough, christened in a mill-pond, graduated at a log-school-house, and at fourteen fancied I could do any thing I turned my hand to, and that nothing was impossible, and ever since, madame, I have been trying to prove it, and with some success." He was destined to be an upstart businessman on a heroic scale. Born into a leading local family in a small town in the Catskills in New York, he was actively dealing in real estate before he was fifteen. Before thirty he was elected to the New York Legislature on a program to construct the New York & Erie Railroad with State aid. He was a great booster for his State, to whose growth he called the new railroad essential. "Otherwise," he argued "the sceptre will depart from Judah. The Empire State will no longer be New York. . . . Philadelphia is your great rival, and, if New York is idle, will gather in the trade of the great west."

But Ogden's enthusiasm for New York was not immovable. In 1835, the very year when the money was appropriated for the New York & Erie Railroad, he met some Eastern investors who had formed the American Land Company. They had already shown the foresight to invest heavily in Chicago real estate. One of these was Charles Butler, a politically and philanthropically minded lawyer of Albany, who married Ogden's sister. Butler himself (once a clerk in the law office of Martin Van Buren) was an energetic promoter of real estate and railroads. A man of wide public interests, he was a founder of Hobart College and of Union Theological Seminary, and an early supporter of New York University, among his other community works. He asked Ogden to go to Chicago to manage his interests. Ogden then joined in the purchase of considerable tracts there.

William B. Ogden arrived in Chicago in June, 1835. The town census showed a population of 3265, almost all of whom had come since 1832 (when the settlement had numbered under a hundred). Quickly Ogden transferred his extravagant hopes from the Empire State to the City of Chicago. In 1837, when Chicago was incorporated, Ogden was elected its first mayor, and the city census counted 4170—an increase of almost thirty per cent in two years.

"He could not forget," one of Ogden's fellow businessmen observed, "that everything which benefitted Chicago, or built up the great West, benefitted him. Why should he?" His commodity was land, whose value rose with the population. And Chicago now grew as few cities had ever grown before. The population approximately trebled, decade after decade: from 29,963 in 1850, to 109,260 in 1860, and to 298,977 in 1870. Chicago held over half a million people in 1880 and over a million by 1890, when it was already the second city on the continent. Meanwhile, real-estate values, especially in choice locations such as those Ogden was shrewd enough to buy, rose even more spectacularly. Men like Ogden proudly recorded their business success as the best evidence of their faith in their city. "In 1844," Ogden recalled, "I purchased for $8000, what 8 years thereafter, sold for 3 millions of dollars, and these cases could be extended almost indefinitely." Property he had bought in 1845 for $15,000 only twenty years later was worth ten million dollars. Successes were so common and so sudden, it was hard to know where fact ended and where fable began. Some of this purchasing was, of course, sheer speculative mania. The Chicago *American* (April 23, 1836) boasted of a piece of city property sold for $96,700 which, in romanticized arithmetic, they said had "risen in value at the rate of *one hundred per cent per* DAY, on the original cost ever since [1830], embracing a period of *five years* and a half."

Not to boost your city showed both a lack of community spirit and a lack of business sense. "Perhaps, the most striking trait of his character," a contemporary remembered of Ogden, "was his absolute faith in Chicago. He saw in 1836, not only the Chicago of today, but in the future the great City of the continent. From that early day, his faith never wavered. Come good times—come bad times—come prosperity or adversity—Chicago booming, or Chicago in ashes, its great future was to him a fixed fact." Quite naturally Ogden became a leader in community affairs, and within a few years Chicagoans called him their "representative man."

There was hardly a public improvement in which he did not play a leading role. He built the first drawbridge across the Chicago river, laid out and opened many miles of streets in the north and west parts of the city, promoted the Illinois and Michigan Canal and advocated laws for its construction and enlargement, projected and built thousands of miles of railroads serving Chicago, and did a great deal to develop Chicago's water supply, sewage system, and parks. More than a hundred miles of streets and hundreds of bridges were built at the private expense of Ogden and his real-estate clients. He helped introduce the McCormick reaping and mowing machines into the West, and helped build the first large factory for their manufacture. He was the first president of Rush Medical College (the first institution of its kind in Chicago), a charter member of the Chicago Historical Society, president of the Board of Trustees of the first "University of Chicago," and one of the first directors of the Merchants Loan and Trust Company (1857). He was elected to the Illinois Senate by the Republicans in 1860. He supported the Theological Seminary of the Northwest, the Academy of Sciences, and the Astronomical Society. The French historian Guizot only slightly exaggerated when he said Ogden had built and owned Chicago.

Characteristic also was Ogden's interest in improving transportation. An upstart community, a community of boosters measuring itself by its rate of growth, depended on transportation in a new way. Settled communities of the Old World—Bordeaux, Lyon, Manchester, or Birmingham—especially when, as in the early 19th century, they were fast becoming industrial towns, needed transportation to feed raw materials and labor to their factories and to take away finished products. But Chicago and the other upstart cities of the American West needed it for their very lifeblood. In the Old World a city might grow or decline, prosper or languish, depending on its transportation, among other facilities. But here, without transportation there was no city at all.

An American city had to "attract" people. The primary community service was to make it easier, cheaper, and pleasanter for people to join your community. In all this, too, William B. Ogden was a paragon, for he pioneered the railroads. One of the first to run out of Chicago was the Galena & Chicago Union Railroad, built to connect Chicago with the great Mississippi River traffic. Chicago businessmen bought a controlling interest in 1846, and tried to raise money from local citizens to complete the railroad. Ogden worked hard to obtain numerous individual subscriptions in small amounts. This, its first railroad, opened a new era in the life and expansion of Chicago. Citizens subscribed its stock "as a public duty, and not as an investment." "Railroads," one of Ogden's collaborators later boasted, "were built as public enterprises, and not as money-making speculations. They were regarded as great highways constructed by the people, either at the expense of the government or by means of private capital, to accommodate the public, and not for the especial benefit of the stockholders." In April, 1849, the first locomotive started west from Chicago on the Galena line.

Ogden took the lead in promoting many more railroads for Chicago. In 1853 he was a director of the Pittsburg, Ft. Wayne & Chicago Railroad; in 1857, president of the Chicago, St. Paul & Fond-du-Lac Railroad which later became part of the Chicago & Northwestern Railroad, of which he was also president (1859–68). A transcontinental railroad with Chicago as the great junction was, of course, his dream. In 1850 he presided over the National Railway Convention and, on the

organization of the Union Pacific Company in 1862, its first president
was William B. Ogden.

The Ogden story was re-enacted a thousand times all over America—
wherever there were upstart cities. Scenes were different, stakes smaller,
and dimensions less heroic, but the plot everywhere was much the same.
Here was a new breed: the community builder in a mushrooming city
where personal and public growth, personal and public prosperity
intermingled.

Another example was Dr. Daniel Drake (1785–1852), born in New
Jersey, and raised in Kentucky, whose family sent him when he was only
fifteen to study in the offices of a leading physician of the small town
of Ft. Washington (later called Cincinnati). Within a few years he himself became the town's most prominent practitioner. He opened a drug
store where, in 1816, he pioneered in the sale of artificial mineral
water; soon he was also running a general store. His *Picture of Cincinnati
in 1815,* with its full statistics, and its vivid account of the archaeology,
topography, climate, and promise of the city, was translated and circulated widely abroad. Drake, in his own way, was as much a booster as
Ogden; using subtler techniques of precise and calculated understate-
ment, he produced the first detailed account of an upstart city. Many
believed him when he concluded that small towns like Cincinnati were
"destined, before the termination of the present century, to attain the
rank of populous and magnificent cities." Drake had established himself
in the high noon of Cincinnati prosperity, before the Panic of 1819.

Drake's boosterism was as energetic as Ogden's. Hoping to make
Cincinnati a great medical center in 1819, he founded the Ohio Medical
College (later the Medical College of the University of Cincinnati). He
did a great deal to promote all kinds of community enterprises: the
Commercial Hospital and Lunatic Asylum, the eye infirmary, the circulating library, the teacher's college. He helped plan and develop
canals and he promoted railroads leading toward the South, which included the successful municipal line, the Cincinnati Southern Railway.

Still another example with a more western habitat was General
William Larimer (1809–75). Born and raised in Pennsylvania, he tried
many different businesses around Pittsburgh: a general store, a freight
service, horse trading, a coal company, a wholesale grocery, his father's
hotel, railroads, and banking. When he lost everything in the depression
of 1854, Larimer, quickly resolving to start afresh farther west, was
in Nebraska the very next spring. There he too became the instantaneous
booster of a town which did not yet exist. We have an intimate record
in letters he sent east. On May 23, 1855:

> I have taken two claims at La Platte, Nebraska Territory . . . and
> we are laying out a town. I am elected President of the Company, and

> secured ⅓ of the town. . . . I like this country very much indeed. . . .
> I think I can make a big raise here in a few years.

Already he claimed a good chance of being elected to Congress from
Nebraska. Within a week his optimism had risen still higher: he planned
to pay off his creditors with town lots, for he owned a thousand acres
within the proposed city.

> Now my plan is this: I intend to live in La Platte City. I intend to
> open up a large farm. I can raise hemp, corn or anything. . . . I will
> go on with the farm and if the land is ever wanted for a town it is
> ready. . . . I intend not only to farm simply but I will open a Com-
> mission House. I expect to supply the Territory with iron nails, lumber,
> etc., this will not only be profitable in itself but will be the great means
> of building up the city. If I go there I can build the city if I do not
> go only to sell lots as the city may never rise.

Larimer expected the transcontinental railroad to go through La Platte,
but this proved a miscalculation. Then, after a heavy winter, the town
suffered deep spring floods. "We were not long in coming to the conclusion that La Platte was doomed as a town site." The pattern of
western hope was all-or-nothing.

From La Platte, Larimer moved on to Omaha. There he lived in a prefabricated house that had actually been framed in Pittsburgh, knocked
down and shipped out in 1856. When Omaha, too, looked unpromising
(as it did within less than two years) he moved to Leavenworth, Kansas.
This was in 1858, just in time for him to learn of the discovery of gold
at Cherry Creek by Pike's Peak. Unwilling to wait for the better traveling
conditions of the following spring, Larimer and his son immediately made
up a party and left that fall. After a forty-seven-day trip, the Larimers
were among the first to arrive at the mouth of Cherry Creek, where they
found two dozen cabins under construction.

This, the first settlement in Colorado, was named Auraria. Larimer's
son recorded the events of November 17, 1858:

> On our very first night here, my father, without consulting anyone
> outside of our own Leavenworth Party, packed his blankets and some
> provisions, left camp and crossed the Creek to pick out a new site.
> He left instructions for us to get up the oxen and join him, as he
> believed the east side of the Creek was much the best location for a
> town and no one in the country laid claim to it, or if so had abandoned
> it and left the country. . . . When we finally reached the eastern side
> of Cherry Creek, we found him near the bank with a camp fire awaiting
> us. He had 4 cottonwood poles crossed, which he called the foundation
> of his settlement and claimed the site for a town,—for *the* town which
> has now grown into the one of which Colorado is the proudest.

This time Larimer chose well. He had located on the site of Denver.
At first there was competition between the sites on either side of

Cherry Creek. Then the stockholders combined and became a single city named Denver (in honor of the Virginian who had become Governor of the Kansas Territory) in 1860. "I am Denver City," Larimer wrote in a letter in February 1859. And his whole later career proved the extraordinary ability of the American businessmen of these upstart cities to fuse themselves and their destiny with that of their community—at least so long as the community remained prosperous or promising.

At the beginning Larimer had been put in charge of the town and made "Donating Agent," which authorized him to give two city lots to anyone who would build a cabin there measuring at least 16 by 16 feet. He promoted a good hotel and gave valuable shares to men "who were already or could be induced to become interested in the welfare of the city and might be influential in bringing a stage line into the country with Denver as its objective point." He encouraged the founding of drugstores, general stores, sawmills, and newspapers. Complaining that the town lacked the ultimate convenience, he finally helped organize a cemetery.

Examples could be multiplied. But even these three—Ogden, Drake, and Larimer—suggest the variety of opportunities, motives, and attitudes which created the new species *Businessman Americanus*. None of the characteristics of his American habitat was quite unique but their extreme American form and their American combination were.

Cities with no history. The upstart western cities were the rare examples of a dynamic urban environment where almost nothing had been pre-empted by history. Cities were proverbially the centers of institutions, where records were kept and the past was chronicled, hallowed, and enshrined. They were sites of palaces, cathedrals, libraries, archives, and great monuments of all kinds. The American upstart city, by contrast, had no past. At its beginning, it was free of vested interests, monopolies, guilds, skills, and "No Trespassing" signs. Here was the fluidity of the city—the spatial dimension of cosmopolitanism, movement, diversity, and change—but without the historical dimension. There were no ancient walls between classes, occupations, neighborhoods, and nationalities. The American upstart cities began without inherited neighborhood loyalties, without ghettos. "Everything," recalled Larimer, "was open to us."

Quick growth and high hopes. The pace of growth of the upstart cities fired imaginations. A town where nobody was ten years ago, but which today numbered thousands, might be expected to number tens or hundreds of thousands in a few decades. Mankind had required at least a million years to produce its first urban community of a million people; Chicagoans accomplished this feat in less than a century. Within a few days' wagon ride of Drake's Cincinnati, hundreds of towns were laid out, all guaranteed to have unrivalled advantages. Precisely one week after Larimer cut his four cottonwood poles on the future site of Denver, he wrote his wife back east that "we expect a second Sacramento City, at least." In 1834, H. M. Brackenridge noted, his Pittsburgh was changing so fast that anyone returning after ten years felt himself a stranger. He confidently foresaw that the settlement which had grown from village to big city in a quarter-century would very soon reach half a million. He could not be surprised that Cincinnati had grown from a forest to a city in thirteen years. He himself had hopes "of attaining, on the Ohio or Mississippi, distinction and wealth, with the same rapidity, and on the same scale, that those vast regions were expanding into greatness." The centennial history of St. Louis in 1876 called the city's site superior to that of any other in the world, and predicted that, when its railroad network was completed, it would outstrip Chicago and the eastern metropolises. "And yet, when this has been said, we have but commenced to tell of the wonders of a city destined in the future to equal London in its population, Athens in its philosophy, art and culture, Rome in its hotels, cathedrals, churches and grandeur, and to be the central commercial metropolis of a continent."

Community before government. On this landscape too it was normal to find communities before governments. Men in sudden urban proximity, bound together by specific, concrete purposes, first felt their common needs. Afterwards they called governments into being. From force of circumstance, then, government became functional. Early Chicagoans, and their upstart counterparts elsewhere, were not confronted with the problem of evading obsolete regulations or of transmuting time-honored tyrannies. They simply combined to provide their own water, their own sewage system, their own sidewalks, streets, bridges, and parks. They founded medical schools and universities and museums. Eager for these and other services, they created municipal governments and enlisted state and federal government aid. An upstart government had neither the odor of sanctity nor the odium of tyranny. It was a tool serving personal and community prosperity at the same time.

Intense and transferable loyalties. In upstart cities the loyalties of people were in inverse ratio to the antiquity of their communities, even to the point of absurdity. Older towns could point only to the facts of limited actual accomplishment, while the uncertain future was, of course, ever more promising. Ogden removed his enthusiasm from New York to Chicago; Larimer removed his from La Platte to Omaha to Leavenworth to Auraria to Denver. Men could do this in the twinkling of an eye, and without so much as a glance over the shoulder. Promise, not achievement, commanded loyalty and stirred the booster spirit. One was untrue to oneself and to the spirit of expanding America if one remained enslaved to a vision which had lost its promise. The ghost town and the booster spirit were opposite sides of the same coin.

Competition among communities. The circumstances of American life in the upstart cities of the West produced a lively competitive spirit. But the characteristic and most fertile competition was a competition among communities. We have been misled by slogans of individualism. Just as the competition among colonial seaboard cities helped diffuse American culture and kept it from becoming concentrated in a European-style metropolis, so the competition among western upstart cities helped create the booster spirit. Where there had been no cities before, where all were growing fast, there was no traditional rank among urban centers. If Lexington, Kentucky, could quickly arise by 1800 to be the most populous city of the West, if St. Louis and Cincinnati and Chicago had so suddenly arisen, might not some new Lexington displace them all? Many of each community's institutions had been founded to give it a competitive advantage. Dr. Drake's medical college helped Cincinnati keep ahead of Lexington, just as Ogden's streets and bridges and parks helped Chicago lead Cincinnati. Where individual and community prosperity were so intermingled, competition among individuals was also a competition among communities.

* * *

The emerging businessman of the upstart cities had much in common with the energetic American of an earlier generation. He was the Franklin of the West. He was the undifferentiated man of the colonial period, but in a more expansive setting. The new language of that day called him a "businessman"; the retrospective language of our century calls him the booster. He thrived on growth and expansion. His loyalties were intense, naive, optimistic, and quickly transferable.

Versatility was his hallmark. He usually had neither the advantages nor the disadvantages of specialized skills or monopolistic protection. In Dr. Drake's Cincinnati, physicians became merchants, clergymen became bankers, lawyers became manufacturers. "The young lawyer," H. M. Brackenridge shrewdly advised the Western seeker after fortune (in one of the first recorded uses of the word "businessman") "should think more of picking up his crumbs, than of flying like a balloon. He must be content to become a *business man,* and leave the rest to fortune." For success in this environment, the specialized skills—of lawyer, doctor, financier, or engineer—had a new unimportance. Rewards went to the organizer, the persuader, the discoverer of opportunities, the projector, the risk-taker, and the man able to attach himself quickly and profitably to some group until its promise was tested.

17

The Booster Press

THE RAPID GROWTH of Western cities created many an anachronism, as new communities borrowed techniques and institutions from the Old World or from the long settled cities on the eastern seaboard. One of the most distinctive, and in the long run one of the most powerful, of the novelties created by anachronism was the Western newspaper. For a city that still existed only in the imagination, the newspaper could, and did, do a job it had rarely done before. In Europe, newspapers had arisen to serve the needs, at first of a small literary or literate circle, later of a larger reading community. Similarly, the early newspapers on the Atlantic seaboard, often begun by an official "Publick Printer," were produced to satisfy the interests of the people already there. But the pioneer newspaper of the upstart city, like the western railroad, had to call into being the very population it aimed to serve. This gave it certain distinctive features which would long shape American life.

In the Old World, even into the 19th century, the press was tightly controlled by government. To allow an unauthorized person to operate a press and to produce books and newspapers seemed as dangerous as to leave firearms in the hands of the populace. Knowledge of recent events might be explosive or subversive. Along the Atlantic seaboard during the colonial period, government control over the press was more indirect than it was in Europe, but it was still quite effective. Commission as the "Publick Printer," with the incidental advantages of a postal monopoly (first used to entice qualified printers to sparsely settled colonies), remained an incentive to safe-and-sound conservatism. It was easy, too, on the seaboard, to control the import of printing presses into the only towns where it was feasible to operate them.

Movement westward changed much of this. The great spaces and the increasing dispersion of the population made it harder to control the movement of printing presses and to supervise their output. Soon after the American Revolution, as presses went west, the number and variety of American newspapers increased. In 1775, according to Isaiah Thomas, one of the leading printers of the age, there were only about fifty presses in all the colonies, and nearly all were on the seaboard; by 1783, not one important inland town lacked its own press. Like the musket, the newspaper became a weapon and a tool, to conquer the forest and to build new communities.

The first task of the printer in the upstart city was to bring into existence a community where the newspaper could survive. While the first English papers had sometimes started as literary journals and only later developed into news-sheets, the pioneer newspapers of the American West more often *began* as a new kind of advertising leaflet, and later became news-sheets. Only still later, and incidentally, did they turn to belles-lettres. They started by advertising the nonexistent town where they hoped to make a vigorous life. Seeking settlers from all over the country, they were probably our earliest media of national advertising. In the Old World, the papers satisfied a need; here, they excited a hope. As Captain Henry King (1841–1915), who had helped build pioneering newspapers in Illinois, Kansas, and Missouri, and long edited the St. Louis *Globe-Democrat,* recalled:

> For the first time the press manifested the pioneering instinct and proposed to lead and not to follow the course of progress—to become itself a part of the history of settlement and development. . . . There was room for the criticism that the scheme of starting a newspaper before there was any news to print was illogical, fantastic, preposterous. But it was not then, and has never since been, so regarded in Kansas. The novelty of it was infectious. A second paper was soon established at Kickapoo. Early in 1855 two more appeared here in Lawrence. Others followed as new towns were founded. The printing press preceded all the usual agencies of society. It did not wait for the rudimentary clutter of things to be composed and organized. The spirit of adventure thrust it forward ahead of the calaboose, the post office, the school, the church, and made it a symbol of conquest. Thus the theory of publicity was emphasized as a factor in the westward march of the American people and their institutions; and thus Kansas was signalized by a revelation that materially enlarged the scope and meaning of modern journalism.

Oddly enough, the American press was proliferating because of the very emptiness and vastness of the American West. In 1857 the Scottish traveler James Stirling observed that, although the long settled town of Macon, Georgia, had only three weekly papers and no dailies, the new town of St. Paul, Minnesota (also with about ten thousand people), already had four dailies and three weeklies. This showed, he said, that in America newspapers thrived not in proportion to the population but in proportion to the "general activity." It could not be argued, therefore, that the multiplicity of American newspapers was due (as Englishmen sometimes said) to their cheapness, nor (as Americans sometimes said) to the superior intelligence of their readers. Rather, it was a product of the general social condition of America. "A new and sparse population must make known its presence, its needs, and its purposes; and this is best done through a public newspaper. In an old and thickly-peopled country, where everybody is everybody else's next-door neighbour, and knows precisely what he buys and sells, advertisements are rather a luxury than a necessity. But in a country with perhaps five or six inhabitants to the square mile, and where, probably, one-half of the population arrived by the last steamer, it is absolutely indispensable for the new-come Yankee to announce his advent and his benevolent intention of dispensing dry-goods, of giving 'cash for wheat,' or lecturing on spiritualism, or drawing teeth. Advertising is there a necessity of existence; and by advertisements the newspaper lives."

The careers of these booster papers followed a familiar pattern, varying in detail only, as did the careers of businessmen. It was foreshadowed in the story of the very first press taken across the Alleghenies. When the first issue of the Pittsburgh *Gazette* appeared on July 29, 1786, Pittsburgh was a mere village, with a population of about three hundred, but to the eye of the booster, Pittsburgh was a great metropolis in embryo. Hugh Henry Brackenridge, pioneer lawyer and author of *Modern Chivalry* (sometimes called the first literary work of the American West) had moved to Pittsburgh and staked his future there in 1781, when it was an even smaller backwoods outpost. In 1786, to secure a press to serve the future city, he helped persuade John Scull and his partner Joseph Hall (who died soon after) to move from Philadelphia. A small press, together with type, ink, and paper were all packed across the mountains. They often had problems of supply; once at least, running short of newsprint, they used cartridge-paper borrowed from Fort Pitt. Lacking a mail route, Scull at first delivered the paper himself within the village and used chance travelers for delivery outside. The primary purpose of this paper was to attract settlers to Pittsburgh. If the community flourished, the *Gazette* would flourish with it. Before Scull's death in 1828, Pittsburgh was a thriving city of about twelve thousand, with perhaps that many more in the satellite towns nearby. Scull had become a leader of the community he helped build. He had helped secure a mail route to Pittsburgh, had become postmaster, president of the second bank established in Pittsburgh, one of the incorporators of the Western University of Pennsylvania (later the University of Pittsburgh), and a member of the first borough council.

Boosters for the still sparsely settled territory of Kentucky at this very time wanted a newspaper to serve their cause. They too were eager to attract settlers, and so justify their claim to become a state separate from Virginia. Failing to find an experienced newspaperman, they finally enlisted an enterprising youth in his twenties, who had been an Indian fighter and surveyor but who knew nothing about printing. John Bradford was his name, but he was no kin to the Massachusetts or Pennsylvania Bradfords. He was destined to become the pioneer printer and publisher of Kentucky. In late 1786, having accepted this assignment and having received a free lot in the village of Lexington, he sent his brother to Pittsburgh to learn the trade from John Scull. John Bradford's brother brought the press and type (ordered from Philadelphia) four hundred miles down the Ohio River from Pittsburgh by flatboat and then by trail to Lexington. The first number of the *Kentucke Gazette* (spelling changed to "Kentucky" in March, 1789) issued from his log-cabin printshop on April 11, 1787. Its primary aim was to create its community. At first Bradford had the advantage of being Printer to the Territory and did all the government work; he kept most of it for many years. Bradford issued the *Kentucke Almanac* (1788), first pamphlet of the West, and the Acts of the first session of the Kentucky Legislature (1792), which was the first book printed in Kentucky. He earned the nickname of "the Kentucky Franklin," by continuing his surveying, following mathematics and astronomy, helping to found Transylvania Seminary, Transylvania University, and the Lexington Library. He represented his county in the Kentucky House of Representatives, and he too became a leader of the community he had helped build.

The first newspaper northwest of the Ohio River also had a booster purpose. In the little village of Cincinnati, which could not have had a population of more than three or four hundred, William Maxwell issued the first number of his *Centinel of the North-Western Territory* from a log-cabin office on November 9, 1793. Warning of the danger of massacre and house-burning by Indians, a "Public Notice" offered a bounty of $168 for "every scalp, having the right ear appendant, for the first ten Indians" killed within the general vicinity of Cincinnati. Since "the want of regular and certain trade down the Mississippi" was stunting Cincinnati, Maxwell campaigned to open that river to American commerce, which would support the city, and, incidentally, his newspaper.

As the press moved farther west, the peculiarities of the American situation became more and more marked. The booster spirit called for an ever greater willingness to take risks. The more open, remote, and unsettled the surrounding country, the greater the opportunity to make mistakes. Hovering about every ghost town was the spirit of one or more ghost papers, relics of advertising that had failed. Again and again, ambitious migratory newspapermen aimed not at the known needs of an existing community but at the needs of some future community for which they desperately hoped. The first issue of Ignatius Donnelly's *Emigrant Aid Journal* (1856), which urged the nonpareil virtues of the city of Nininger (still to be constructed) in Minnesota, was actually published out of Philadelphia.

No wonder that, in their enthusiasm, they sometimes confused the vision and the reality, that (as one early editor put it) they "sometimes represented things that had not yet gone through the formality of taking place." "History will never tell how diligently the editors sought for facts to influence home-seekers, and how enthusiastically close they often came to bearing false witness, not against their neighbors, but in behalf of them. . . . when they feared they might be prevaricating they were at most only anticipating. The eggs were in the basket all right, and it was only a matter of waiting for them to be hatched. It was permissible to mix visions and prophecies with current and negotiable realities when it was all certain to come true." The *Green-Bay Intelligencer,* first newspaper in Wisconsin, announced in its inaugural issue of December 11, 1833, its "one principal object in view, viz. *the advancement of the country west of Lake Michigan.*" Beginning as only a biweekly, it expressed the hope that if the navigation of the Lakes was expanded by a canal between the Fox and the Wisconsin rivers, and the city grew, then it could become a weekly. It boasted that Green Bay bore to the Territory of Wisconsin (still to be created) a relation "more beneficial and necessary than that of Detroit to Michigan." "It is obviously destined to be one of the great channels of trade (Chicaugo being the other)."

Only about a hundred miles away, at the same time, similarly extravagant claims were being made for the future site of Milwaukee. On July 14, 1836, two months before the first official sale of land at Milwaukee and only ten days after Wisconsin Territory had officially come into existence, the first issue appeared of Milwaukee's first newspaper, the *Advertiser.* Its editor, Daniel H. Richards, had not come west from New York until late in 1835. He had passed by Chicago, where he had thought of buying Chicago's recently established first newspaper, the *Democrat.* A quick visit to Milwaukee persuaded him (as he himself related some years later) "that it possessed advantages superior to those then existing at Chicago, and consequently decided upon establishing a press here, although the whole population within a circuit of fifty miles, probably, did not at the time amount to two hundred." More than anyone else it was Byron Kilbourn, a real-estate promoter of this townsite on the west side of the Milwaukee River, who convinced the ambitious Richards that he should stake his future on Milwaukee. Richards' paper circulated mainly in the communities from which the future population of Kilbourn's settlement was expected to come. The Milwaukee *Advertiser,* as Richards its founder explained, was then "part and parcel of the project of building a city at this point and settling the then new Territory of Wisconsin." It was not merely a pioneer newspaper, it was itself a pioneering enterprise, committed to the task of creating the city it hoped to "advertise."

New political and legal units provided new opportunities for printers: laws and ordinances to be published, courts to be reported, legal notices, and legal documents. This was the assured work of the "Publick Printer," which in the colonial period had helped attract printers to established towns on the eastern seaboard, and it was all the more necessary to entice a qualified printer to the middle of nowhere. When James M.

Goodhue (only recently come West from New York) was editing the *Grant County Herald* at Lancaster, Wisconsin, in the early months of 1849, he was already watching developments in Minnesota. As soon as he heard that a new Territory was being established, he loaded a press on a steamboat up the Mississippi to St. Paul, the newly designated capital, hoping to become the Territorial Printer. His *Minnesota Pioneer* (he had abandoned his notion of calling it the *Epistle of St. Paul*) first appeared on April 28, 1849, and explained:

> But little more than one week ago, we landed at Saint Paul, amidst a crowd of strangers, with the first printing press that has ever rested upon the soil of Minnesota. Without subscription list or pledges of patronage, or the least personal acquaintance or even correspondence with any of the politicians of this young Territory, we trustingly launched out *The Pioneer,* depending upon the voluntary good will and patronage of the whole people of Minnesota, to extend it whatever support it may deserve. One of our cardinal principles is to *put our trust in the People, and not in princes.* . . . All our interests are henceforth identified with the prosperity of this town and the welfare of this Territory.

In the beginning he delivered the papers himself, at the same time gathering news for the next issue. Using the columns of his paper to answer questions of prospective settlers, he became the most effective advertiser of St. Paul and of Minnesota.

The thriving business of printing legal notices was itself a by-product of rapid settlement and expansion. Not only did it make newspapers profitable, in many places (in western New York, for example) the fees for legal notices alone made a country newspaper possible. Farther west, where boom-town hopes were higher and more extravagant, printing legal notices was even more remunerative. "Proving up," which was legally required of a homesteader, was the running of a final proof notice (stating that he had lived up to all government requirements) six times in the paper nearest his claim. A newspaper which charged from six to ten dollars for these notices had an indispensable source of income while the population of its town was accumulating. Also helpful were the "contest notices" stating that the filer of the "proof notice" had not lived up to the rules, and announcing that the contestant himself proposed to file a claim to the same land. Contest notices could be published anywhere in the county where the land was situated. In the Dakotas, for example, when the Big Sioux reservation was first opened to homesteaders, one enterprising printer set up thirty presses at different places to secure the proving up business. In Sully County, Dakota Territory, where nine papers were being published in those days, only two remained in the mid-20th century.

Local circumstances provided a wide variety of special opportunities and temptations for newspaper publishers. In Kansas, for example, newspapers were powerful, as well as profitable, weapons in the struggle between pro- and antislavery forces to populate the territory in the 1850's. The earliest English-language newspaper in Kansas or Nebraska was the *Kansas Weekly Herald,* which appeared on September 15, 1854, when Leavenworth consisted of four tents and there was not yet a single permanent building. The typesetter put together the first issue of the *Weekly Herald* under the shade of an elm tree. "Our selections have been made," the first issue boasted, "our editorials written, our proof read, sitting on the ground with a big shingle on our knee for a table. Think of this, ye editors, in your easy chairs and well furnished sanctums, and cease to grumble." Five months later, on February 9, 1855, the paper reported a circulation of 2970.

The New England Emigrant Aid Society, organizers of the antislavery cause, hired a Dr. George W. Brown to found the *Herald of Freedom.* Its first issue was published in the east, but on January 6, 1855, with the help of a few other recent arrivals, Brown issued his first number from a log-cabin office in Lawrence. By the next year he was said to have eight thousand subscribers. The *Herald of Freedom* was only one of several papers founded to serve the antislavery cause. On the other side, citizens of Atchison offered four hundred dollars to Dr. J. H. Stringfellow to found his *Squatter Sovereign.* In the riots of 1856, the "Border Ruffians" defended the cause of slavery by destroying the *Herald*'s office. A few months later, the *Herald* had its type molded into six-pound cannon balls for the attack on Fort Titus.

"The fact that the population of Cedar county is not now vastly larger than it is," the Cedar County, Iowa, *News-Letter* explained in its first issue (September 13, 1852), "can only be attributable to the want of a public journal, to unfold its resources, and make known its advantages to the emigrant." But the problem was circular, for publishing a newspaper without a metropolis or a populated countryside nearby was not easy. The primary problems, as one historian of the booster press put it, were "to get paper, to get news, and to get paid." Where cash was scarce, editors of pioneer papers advertised their willingness to be paid in corn, molasses, potatoes, cabbage, flour, meal, fruit, or kindling-wood. One desperate editor concluded his list by stating his willingness to accept "any other variety of produce except babies."

Despite all these difficulties, and a high mortality rate (at least six newspapers died in Nebraska alone in 1858), newspapers multiplied. All over the West they appeared in advance of their communities. This was made easier by the development of cheap portable presses, for example the "army press," a cylinder about one foot in diameter on top of a frame operated by a crank. It could be lifted by one strong man and was easily transported across the prairies. In the era of the Civil War, a paper could be started on one of these presses with a capital of $150.

Across the continent newspapers spawned, nourished mainly by enthusiasm and imagination. San Francisco, which did not have its first daily till 1850, had a dozen dailies by 1853. In mid-1859, two printers who had only just arrived raced for the distinction of publishing the first newspaper in Denver. Settlers placed bets and a committee was appointed to judge the contest. William N. Byers, a surveyor from Omaha, won the race by producing his *Rocky Mountain News* on April 23, 1859 at exactly 10:30 P.M., twenty minutes before his rival, the *Cherry Creek Pioneer*. The disappointed editor of the *Pioneer* immediately sold his equipment to Byers and went prospecting for gold. Before the end of 1860, Denver had three dailies.

The lure of gold or silver was not indispensable to attract a booster press. In Minnesota, for example, by the end of 1857 (a year before statehood), there were printing offices in over forty towns and villages, many of them publishing newspapers. In Wisconsin before 1850, about one hundred publishing enterprises had been started; all but about a dozen had published newspapers. In that year, when the census gave Wisconsin a population of 306,000 and Milwaukee, its largest city, about 20,000, the state had forty-two publications being printed in twenty-three towns. Before the end of 1867 at least four newspapers had been published in Cheyenne, a town that still had a population well under 800, in the Wyoming Territory, which altogether probably contained fewer than 9000. In 1870, seven newspapers were being published in the sparsely settled Dakota Territory.

The saga of the booster press in the making of upstart communities is symbolized in the career of Robert Thompson Van Horn, editor of the *Western Journal of Commerce,* newspaperman-builder of Kansas City. Born in Pennsylvania in 1824, he first tried his hand at schoolteaching and at law, and then edited several newspapers in Ohio and Pennsylvania. Everywhere he was a determined town promoter. "Standing around scratching heads," his newspaper in southeastern Ohio warned in 1850, "will never make Pomeroy the city nature intended it to be." Then, when the printing plant of the daily he tried to establish in Cincinnati burned down, he took a job as clerk on a river steamboat. "I am going out West, probably to Nebraska," he wrote his parents in 1854, "where I hope to retrieve my fortunes and kick up a dust generally among the natives." In St. Louis in July 1855, he met a lawyer sent by a committee of Kansas City businessmen to find an editor for their local newspaper. Van Horn took a quick trip to Kansas City, and agreed to take up the offer. He paid $250 as a first instalment on the newspaper and was to pay a second $250 a year later, but he did so well for the community that the committee waived the second instalment.

Within less than three years, Van Horn had become the voice of growing Kansas City, and especially of its businessmen. Anyone visiting Kansas City in 1858 (he wrote to an Ohio friend) would "wonder why God . . . first offered the continent to men at its eastern portals, and so long kept the great and glorious West a *Terra Incognita* to humanity. This is the masterpiece of creation and the perfection of topography." Speaking to the merchants of his city on Christmas Eve, 1857, when not a mile of railroad yet ran into the city, he boasted Kansas City's great future as a railroad center, and forecast a commercial prosperity eventually rivalling that of New York, Chicago, St. Louis, Cincinnati, and New Orleans. All this, he declared, was shaped by geography, "these great tracings of the Almighty's finger." Already there was some basis for his optimism, as the 1857 population statistics published in Van Horn's own *Western Journal of Commerce* attested. During that year, Kansas City had mushroomed from a population of barely 2000 in January, to 3224 in June, and by the end of the year to 5158.

Van Horn expressed both the strengths and weaknesses of the booster frame of mind. Enthusiasm for the future of his city stirred his admiration for the businessman but not for the politician. To him "progress" seemed far more important than "politics." Trying to avoid politics altogether, Van Horn trimmed to the shifting winds of community opinion. Boosterism dominated all his other sentiments. For example, when civil war broke out in Kansas in 1856 between pro- and antislavery forces, Van Horn was not distracted from the commercial progress of Kansas City. "We regret," he solemnly declared in his paper, "that the parties have concluded to go to war and settle their differences by bloodshed; but as they have so determined, we wish to remind them that they can buy powder and lead of our merchants at St. Louis prices, and other military supplies much cheaper." In Ohio, Van Horn had been a strong antislavery man. Now, his old friends found to their astonishment that the Kansas City atmosphere had made him a proslavery Democrat. One of his fellow boosters defended him simply by explaining that "as Jackson county was largely of that faith he was respected and influential at home, and able to accomplish more than if he had been of any other politics." By 1865, when the Republican party dominated the state and the country, Van Horn had changed his politics once again. "And again," one of his admiring contemporaries remarked, "he was on the side where he could do the most good for the town. And again the *Journal* became an 'advertising handbill for the town at the mouth of the Kaw,' as a Leavenworth paper called it. And ever since, the policy of the paper, as an advertising medium and agent for Kansas City, has been unchanged." Van Horn's weathervane politics elected him mayor, put him in the state legislature and sent him to Congress, but he remained first and foremost a booster.

"Politics," he said, was only important for what it could do for Kansas City. His great victory was the construction of the Hannibal and St.

Joseph bridge across the Missouri at Kansas City in 1869; this assured Kansas City's dominance over St. Joseph, Leavenworth, and other rivals, and made Kansas City a great railroad and meat-packing center.

* * *

From these tasks and opportunities of the booster press in the upstart cities came some enduring peculiarities of American newspapers and of their place in American life.

Great number, variety, and diffusion. By the mid-20th century the per capita consumption of newspapers was probably larger in several other countries (for example, Great Britain or Japan) than in the United States; but the United States remained a leader in the number of different papers being published in proportion to population. Of about 7200 daily newspapers published in the world in the mid-20th century, about one-quarter were published in the United States. Despite the rise of newspaper chains, despite combinations and mergers, the American newspaper remained a widely diffused local community enterprise, more so than in almost any of the other major newspaper-publishing countries of the world. In Japan, for example, nearly half the daily newspaper circulation was concentrated in two cities, Tokyo and Osaka; in England, an even larger proportion of the national press issued from London, and that proportion was constantly increasing; in France, the Paris press dominated the national scene. But in the United States, the situation was very different. Of course, certain big-city papers like the New York *Times* had great prestige, but the daily circulation of all New York City newspapers still amounted to only about ten per cent of the national total. Of the approximately 1800 dailies in the country, over 1500 were published in centers of less than one hundred thousand population; these provided about one-third of total daily circulation. This dispersion, which long remained characteristic of the American journalistic scene, had begun in the founding era of the American communities themselves. National and regional press services (though formed earlier) did not begin to assume their later prominence until the era of the Civil War; the rise of the nationally-known newspaper correspondent was largely a by-product of the War. Then these services themselves rested heavily on the staffs of community newspapers. Improvements in communication and transportation, such as the introduction of Rural Free Delivery by the Post Office in 1897, did not (despite widespread prophecy to the contrary) kill the community press. In the mid-20th century there were still, in addition to the small-town dailies already mentioned, about ten thousand so-called "country weeklies," which themselves reached about half the population of the United States. Diffusion of the press was a deep-rooted institution of the New World.

Freedom from government control and censorship. The local variety and wide dispersion of the American newspaper press made it extraordinarily difficult for any government to control or restrain it. While the history of the press in England and on the continent is a chronicle of stamp taxes, censorship, government control, and only partial and gradual liberation from them—and there the laws of libel have long inhibited free expression in print—the American newspaper press has had a degree of freedom bordering on anarchy. Elsewhere too, in countries with fewer and more centralized newspapers, circulation of newspapers outside the capitals was far more dependent on the rise of a postal system; hence papers were more easily controlled by the government's control of the post office. But who could muzzle a newspaper press that was diffused into every corner of a vast continent?

Community-centered and non-ideological emphasis. From the beginning, large numbers of American newspapers were the advance advertising agents of new communities. If they were subsidized, it was, with few exceptions, by local businessmen interested in community building, rather than by ideologues with an axe to grind. Much of what would later be miscalled "isolationism" (and stigmatized as an aggressive indifference to the world) in the diffused, small-city press might more accurately be described as community-ism: a preoccupation with the growth and prosperity of one's city. It was not that they loved the world less, but that they loved Keokuk more. Many features of American party politics—its local roots, its numerous "independent" shifting voters, its non-ideological character—can be explained only by taking into account a newspaper press inspired and dominated by boosterism. Some American newspapermen have called this preoccupation with the local community the leading characteristic, the principal novelty, and the secret strength of American journalism.

18

"Palaces of the Public"

"THE HOTEL," a Briton visiting the United States in the mid-1850's reported, "is quite a 'peculiar institution' of this country." Even the words describing travelers' accommodations had acquired a new meaning. In England a "tavern" had been a place of refreshment where one could buy food and drink, while a place of lodging was called an "inn." In America (as Noah Webster recorded), this distinction like many others disappeared. Here food and lodging were found in either an "inn" or a "tavern." By the era of the American Revolution, a new American word, "hotel," had become common for the public houses accommodating travelers and strangers. This was destined to be the name for a new institution. Borrowed from the French, in which "hotel" meant a noble house or (in the expression "hotel de ville") a city hall, here it named a new kind of community enterprise.

One conspicuous clue to this distinctiveness was architecture. When Alexander Mackay, an English barrister, traveled about this country in 1846–47, he observed that government buildings were often quite unimpressive. In New Orleans, for example, he found the public offices "neither elegant nor imposing." But the St. Charles Hotel, "with its large and elegant Corinthian portico, and the lofty swelling dome which surmounts it," was impressive. "With us [in England] hotels are regarded as purely private property, and it is seldom that, in their appearance, they stand out from the mass of private houses around them. In America they are looked upon much more in the light of public concerns, and generally assume in their exterior the character of public buildings." The American hotel was a far cry from the English inn, and not only in appearance. For here it played a much larger and more important public role.

The splendor of these "first-class" modern hotels, as the *National Intelligencer* explained (June 19, 1827), had fully earned them the name, "Palaces of the Public." Some called them "People's Palaces." Lacking a royal palace as the center of "Society," Americans created their counterpart in the community hotel. The People's Palace was a building constructed with extravagant optimism expressly to serve all who could pay the price. Even into the 20th century, hotels typically remained among the grandest buildings of all large American cities; in medium-sized and smaller cities, they often overshadowed all other structures. This has become so obvious a feature of American culture, and has been so widely transplanted to cities elsewhere in the world, that Americans have largely ignored its meaning.

From the early days of the 19th century, hotels were social centers. What more appropriate "palaces" for a migratory people? In the period of most rapid urban growth, it was not by churches or government buildings but by hotels that cities judged themselves and expected others to judge them. Hotels were usually the centers of lavish private entertainment (which, being held there, acquired a public significance) and of the most important public celebrations. The hotel lobby, like the outer rooms of a royal palace, became a loitering place, a headquarters of gossip, a vantage point for a glimpse of the great, the rich, and the powerful.

A distinctive architectural and engineering style soon developed, the first and most influential example of which was the Tremont House, opened in 1829 in Boston. David Barnum's lavish six-story City Hotel in Baltimore, completed three years earlier, already showed features of the modern American hotel: the size ("200 apartments"), the public aspect, and the expert management. But the design which for decades remained the standard for the American first-class hotel came out of New England. It was the work primarily of Isaiah Rogers (1800–1869), a self-educated architectural prodigy. The son of a shipbuilder in Massachusetts, he had the good luck to work in the architectural office of Solomon Willard—the same Willard who had developed the Quincy granite quarries, had built the Bunker Hill Monument, and (more important for present purposes) had developed the first widely used American system of central heating. At twenty-six, Rogers opened his own office and within two years had the commission for the Tremont House.

Building this new hotel for Boston had become a civic enterprise when the Boston Exchange Coffee House burned down in 1818. The lamented "Exchange Hotel," as the older building was commonly called, had been financed and operated by a group of local merchants. With about 300 rooms, banquet halls, dining rooms, and many other public facilities, it had often been called the largest building and the best hotel in the country. There David Barnum, "the Metternich of all hosts" and "the emperor of American landlords," first made his national reputation as a hotelkeeper. Its destruction by fire was a civic calamity, but the Panic of 1819 prevented immediate rebuilding. In 1825, a committee of merchants headed by William Havard Eliot obtained a charter for a hotel company and commissioned young Isaiah Rogers as architect.

This was a stroke of good luck for Rogers, for Boston, and, in the long run, for every American community destined to thrive with (and partly through) its hotels. Rogers, although he had almost no models to follow, succeeded in designing the Tremont House to give an unmistakable impression of elegance and public purpose, for which the Greek-revival orders, stylish in that day, were, of course, admirably suited. Its four-story façade of Quincy granite was dominated by a colonnaded portico and pilasters at the corners. The central, richly trimmed rotunda office, the numerous large public rooms, a lavish formal dining hall with a deeply coffered ceiling and a screen of Ionic columns at either end, all confirmed a feeling as different as possible from that of the 18th-century inn.

Rogers' elegant and convenient plan quickly became the prototype for the new-style American first-class hotel, and Rogers himself soon became the leading hotel architect in the nation. His work included many of the largest and best known hotels constructed in his lifetime: the Bangor House (1834) in Bangor, Maine; the Astor House (1836) in New York City; the Charleston Hotel (1839) in Charleston, South Carolina; the Exchange Hotel (1841) in Richmond, Virginia; the Burnet House (1850) in Cincinnati; the famous second St. Charles Hotel (1851) in New Or-

leans; the Battle House (1852) in Mobile; the second Galt House (c.
1865) in Louisville; and the six-hundred-room Maxwell House (begun
1859; completed 1869) in Nashville. The American "Palace of the Public"
was, in large part, the creation of Isaiah Rogers.

The American hotel pioneered the incorporation of mechanical equipment, comforts, and gadgets into architectural design. The future importance of plumbing, heating, ventilating, air-conditioning, and scores of
other real or supposed conveniences in American building was already
foreshadowed. Some architectural historians call the Tremont House the
first modern building. It was the first hotel—perhaps the first large building
of any kind in modern times—with extensive plumbing. Its most famous
feature was a battery of eight water-closets. Since plumbing above the
ground floor was still virtually unknown, these were all on the ground floor
at the rear of the central court and were connected by glazed corridors to
the bedroom wings, dining room, and rotunda. They were probably the
first in America, outside of a few in mansions. Bathrooms in the basement
were fitted with cold running water, which also went to the kitchen and
laundry. In Rogers' next large hotel, the Astor House in New York, one
of the most astonishing features was plumbing on the upper floors. Each
floor had its own water-closets and its own bathrooms (seventeen in all,
plus two showers), fed from a roof tank to which water had been raised
by a steam pump.

From that early day, American hotels remained testing places for the
most advanced domestic conveniences. The great amount of capital employed in hotel construction and the desire to outshine competitors for
both business and civic reasons made them laboratories and showcases of
progress in the technology of everyday life. The large transient population
of hotels provided a rare opportunity to whet public appetite for machines,
conveniences, and gadgets of all kinds. And this opportunity for large-
scale experiment and display eventually played a part in developing
an American standard of living.

One domestic convenience after another was first tried, and then first
widely used, in American hotels. For example, the first public building in
America heated by steam was the Eastern Exchange Hotel in Boston
(1846). Soon after, several leading hotels boasted steam-heat on all floors.
But central heating was generally confined to the public rooms and the
hallways of the bedroom floors, while the guest rooms themselves were
still heated by parlor stoves and fireplaces. The passenger elevator (originally called the "vertical railway") had its earliest trials and its first
general use in hotels. Holt's Hotel in New York had a steam-powered
lift, used mainly for baggage, as early as 1833. The first practical passenger elevators, installed in the old Fifth Avenue Hotel in New York in
1859, produced solid commercial benefits. Until then, rooms on the top
floors had been cheaper, but with the aid of the elevator, as one writer

facetiously suggested, a guest atop a hotel could "look down on surrounding buildings in the same manner as our most gracious English nobility look down upon the peasants beneath them."

New techniques of lighting also had their first extensive trial in hotels. A novelty of the Tremont House was gaslight in its public rooms (whale-oil lamps still lighted the guest chambers). Six years later, when the American House opened in Boston in 1835, it was gaslit throughout. The widely admired gaslighting of the public rooms of the Astor House in New York was facilitated by its own gas plant. Very soon after Thomas A. Edison announced the commercial feasibility of his incandescent lamp (on October 21, 1879), it was tried in hotels. Early in 1882 the Hotel Everett on Park Row in New York, the first hotel lit by electricity, was burning 101 incandescent lamps in its main dining room, lobby, reading room, and parlors. A few months later, the Palmer House in Chicago employed its own electrical plant for ninety-six incandescent lamps in two dining rooms.

Hotels were also among the first buildings to use electricity for communication. The "electro-magnetic annunciator" in Boston's Tremont House provided a system (as one wag put it) of "One ring for ice-water, two for bell-boy, three for porter, four for chambermaid,—and not a darned one of them will come." These push buttons, reputedly the first in America, buzzed the office, where they dropped metal disks showing room numbers. These were pleasantly silent compared to the hand bells which guests had used before. Hotels also pioneered the telephone. When New York's first telephone exchange opened in 1879, several hotels were among the few original subscribers. The first installation of room phones and a private switchboard for them (in New York's Hotel Netherland) came in 1894. Many minor comforts of American life also had their first trial in hotels. The spring bed, still unknown when the Tremont House opened in Boston, was patented in 1831 and within a dozen years it was used in the best hotels, although it was almost forty years before the invention of a machine for producing bedsprings would make the spring bed generally available.

The splendor and elegance of American hotels became a byword. Foreign visitors were quick to discover why these should be called the "Palaces" of a democratic people. "The American hotel," an overwhelmed London journalist wrote in 1861, "is to an English hotel what an elephant is to a periwinkle. . . . An American hotel is (in the chief cities) as roomy as Buckingham Palace, and is not much inferior to a palace in its internal fittings. It has ranges of drawing rooms, suites of private rooms, vast staircases and interminable layers of bedchambers." An English comedian staying at New York's lavish St. Nicholas—an Arabian Nights hodgepodge of window curtains costing $700 apiece, gold embroidered draperies costing $1000, mahogany panelling, rosewood carved furniture, sofas upholstered in Flemish tapestry, figured Turkish rugs, and deep Brussels carpets—refused to leave his shoes outside his door to be shined, for fear someone would gild them.

Appropriately enough, some of the first efforts to make the American hotel something new began with fanfare as part of the effort to create a suitable new national capital at Washington, D. C. The site chosen by President Washington in 1790 was not occupied by the Federal government until 1800, but, as early as 1793, before the city actually existed, there were plans to assure the capital city of its hotel. The Commissioners of the Federal City engaged an enterprising New Englander, Samuel Blodget, who had already invested in Washington real estate, to promote the undertaking. They emphasized the public significance of the building when they appointed the same architect, James Hoban, whom they had commissioned to design the President's House. The cornerstone was laid by Freemasons at a public ceremony on July 4, 1793. Blodget then tried to raise the construction money by a federal lottery (authorized by the Commissioners), the first prize to be ownership of the hotel itself (supposedly worth $50,000). It was to be called the Union Public Hotel (probably the first building to announce itself as a "public hotel"), but although widely touted as an important community undertaking, it never opened as a hotel. When the building was finally completed in 1810, it housed a Post Office and the Patent Office. The capital city did not have a first-class hotel until Gadsby's National Hotel was ceremoniously opened with a Washington's Birthday Ball in 1827.

In New York City, too, as early as the 1790's, leading merchants used an ingenious scheme to finance the building: in their "Tontine" Association, the interest of each subscriber increased as the number of subscribers was diminished by death, until finally the last survivor inherited the whole property. At least two New York hotels, including the famous City Hotel which dominated the scene between 1800 and 1830, were successfully constructed under schemes of this kind. In other places, Tontine Associations or still more complex arrangements were tried, allowing numerous small investors to help build an impressive hotel for the community.

Laying the cornerstone of a hotel was a public ceremony, commonly held on the Fourth of July. That was the date chosen for Boston's Tremont House in 1828, for New York's Astor House in 1834, and for many less famous hotels elsewhere. At the inaugural dinner of the Tremont House on October 16, 1829, Daniel Webster, Edward Everett, and a hundred other leading citizens honored the new institution with their toasts.

In the older cities of the eastern seaboard—in Boston, New York, Baltimore, or Charleston—hotels had public functions not yet acquired in Europe. The first American merchants' exchanges were informal meetings in hotels; many hotels, for example the Boston Exchange Hotel, were actually called "exchanges"; some secured banking privileges and issued paper currency. As late as the 1860's, the Burnet House in Cincinnati was issuing five-dollar bills authenticated by the hotel cashier and an engraved likeness of the building. In New Orleans, for example, the lobby of the St. Charles Hotel was the site of public slave auctions. In upstart cities, partly from the lack of other public buildings, hotels were the usual meeting places of civic committees, of associations of businessmen, and even, in the early days, of the city council and other government agencies.

Here, too, was the public information center, where new arrivals brought the latest word from distant places. The old-fashioned hotel register (in this country, contrary to common belief, not a legal requirement but only a business custom) provided reading matter for the general public. In the 1820's an English farmer stopping at a hotel in Zanesville, Ohio, noted the "folio register, in which travelers write their names, from whence they come, and whither they are bound, with any news which they bring with them." The place left for "remarks" gave an opportunity to write a few lines recommending one's wares, commenting on business conditions or on the state of the world. "G. Squires, wife and two babies," wrote a guest at Trenton Falls, New York, and added "No servant, owing to the hardness of the times." The next guest, who inscribed himself "G. W. Douglas and Servant" retorted, "No wife and babies, owing to the hardness of the times."

In Presidential election years, the citizens who recorded their political preferences in the hotel register made it one of the first opinion polls. "Each person entered the name of the Presidential candidate for whom he intended to vote," the English traveler J. S. Buckingham noted of the register at Ball's Hotel in Brownsville, Pennsylvania, in 1840. "Thus the column contained the entries of—Harrison against the world—Van Buren for ever—Henry Clay, the Pride of Kentucky—Little Van, the Magician —Old Tippecanoe, and no Sub-Treasury—the Farmer of North Bend— Hurrah for Jackson—Van Buren again—Log Cabin and Hard Cider— and so on, page after page. In this way some attempt is made to ascertain the strength of the parties; the best is most imperfect." Later the hotel became the headquarters of the first local telegraph office.

The "reading-room," too, was a leading attraction before the day of the public library. Boston's Tremont House, for example, collected newspapers from all over, offering their use free to hotel guests and for a small annual fee to local citizens.

Throughout the 19th century, after a city fire, the community hotel was usually among the first buildings reconstructed. When Boston's Exchange Coffee House Hotel burned in 1818, an editor demanded its rebuilding "for the honor of the town." So it was after the St. Louis fire of 1867. The Great Chicago Fire of October 8, 1871, destroyed nearly all the city's hotels, including the Palmer House, which had been open only a year and had been advertised as "the only fireproof hotel in the world"—but within six years Chicago had sixteen new first-class hotels (each containing from 200 to 800 rooms) and about 140 others. It is not surprising that when Barnum's hotel in Baltimore was involved in litigation in 1860, a Baltimore judge ruled it had to be kept open because, as a first-class hotel, it was a "public institution and a public necessity."

*   *   *

In early 19th-century America, then, the hotel had become something recognizably new. Even before the Civil War, it was being widely imitated in Europe and elsewhere. But in the upstart cities of the West, the hotel, like the newspaper, played a role that could not be imitated in the Old World. Here were booster hotels to match the booster press. In England the railroad hotels were the pioneers, but in America first-class hotels appeared even before the railroad. They were, in fact, often built for the purpose of attracting railroads, along with settlers, newspapers, merchants, customers, lawyers, doctors, salesmen, and all the other paraphernalia of metropolitan greatness. No wonder the age of upstart towns was the spawning season of hotels.

Anthony Trollope's lively chapter on "American Hotels" in his book on North America in the early 1860's went to the heart of the matter:

> The American inn differs . . . is altogether an institution apart, and a thing of itself. Hotels in America are very much larger and more numerous than in other countries. They are to be found in all towns, and I may almost say in all villages. In England and on the Continent we find them on the recognized routes of travel and in towns of commercial or social importance. On unfrequented roads and in villages there is usually some small house of public entertainment in which the unexpected traveller may obtain food and shelter, and in which the expected boon companions of the neighbourhood smoke their nightly pipes, and drink their nightly tipple. But in the States of America the first sign of an incipient settlement is an hotel five stories high, with an office, a bar, a cloak-room, three gentlemen's parlours, two ladies' parlours, a ladies' entrance, and two hundred bedrooms. . . . Whence are to come the sleepers in those two hundred bedrooms, and who is to pay for the gaudy sofas and numerous lounging chairs of the ladies' parlours? In all other countries the expectations would extend itself simply to travellers;—to travellers or to strangers sojourning in the land. But this is by no means the case as to these speculations in America. When the new hotel rises up in the wilderness, it is presumed that people will come there with the express object of inhabiting it. The hotel itself will create a population,—as the railways do. With us railways run to the towns; but in the States the towns run to the railways. It is the same thing with the hotels.

In some places in the West, the sudden gathering of people created a need for sleeping accommodations before there were even any solid buildings. At Lawrence, Kansas, for example, in the 1850's the first "hotel" was a large tent, divided by a row of boxes into two apartments (one for men, the other for women) with straw on the ground for beds. In the booming Dakota Territory, about twenty-five years later, an enterprising citizen of Aberdeen offered sleeping space in a circus tent, until he could build a sod structure to take its place. This was not what people meant when they talked about an American hotel mania.

What they did mean was hotel buildings ridiculously disproportionate to their surroundings—hotels built not to serve cities but to create them. Just as newspapers in the upstart West often began publication before the cities existed to support them and their editors wrote copy under elm trees and issued papers from log-cabins, so hotels sprang up in lonely woods or cornfields. They, too, attested somebody's hope of a metropolis. Facing the river at Memphis, Tennessee, for example, the imposing white-columned façade of the Gayoso House, advertised as a "spacious and elegant hotel" (completed in 1846, three years before Memphis was incorporated as a city, a decade before it had a railroad) stood surrounded by forest. By a kind of homeopathic magic, such a hotel was supposed to make a city grow. Somehow Memphis would become a cotton capital because it already had a public palace worthy of one.

About 1823 a group including Nicholas Biddle, President of the Bank of the United States, and Saunders Coates, editor of the Mobile *Register,* planned a city in the Northwest Territory to outstrip Detroit and St. Louis. They set about constructing Port Sheldon (a now abandoned site about twelve miles northeast of Holland, Michigan) at the mouth of Pigeon River. The first big item on their agenda was a "Large and Commodious Hotel." Ottawa House, which cost about $200,000, was completed just before the Panic of 1837. This grand structure, two stories high and 80 by 150 feet, fronted by a Grecian colonnade of six grooved pillars, was erected in what they hoped would be the heart of the imagined city. When built, it was in the heart of a black pine forest. Inside furnishings alone, "in a style not surpassed by any House in the country . . . entirely new, selected in Eastern Cities," were said to have cost $60,000. The last notation on the register of Ottawa House was March 1, 1842, barely five years after its opening. When the city failed, the hotel was dismantled. Four of its pillars were dragged away by ox-team for a mansion in Grand Rapids.

Corydon, the territorial capital of Indiana, which hoped to become a city, in 1816 (when it was hardly more than a hypothesis) already possessed a new stone hotel, with walls eighteen inches thick and great ceiling timbers. When Ignatius Donnelly set out to develop Nininger City, Minnesota, in 1856 he naturally included plans for a hotel, toward which each share-owner would subscribe one thousand dollars. "It is literally a cornfield, so I cannot have it surveyed," explained Charles Elliot Perkins, superintendent for the Burlington Railroad, who was exploring the land west of Ottumwa, Iowa, in 1866, "but yesterday a man came to arrange to put a hotel here. This is a great country for hotels."

"We shall have a good hotel here by spring," William Larimer wrote his wife in November, 1858, from the almost vacant site that was to become Denver. The building, he said, was already under construction, and a good hotelkeeper was on his way from Omaha. As early as 1835, Chicago (which just two years before had had a population of only 350) acquired its first brick hotel. The Lake House was on the north side of the river at Michigan and North Water Streets, then a fashionable residential area. This establishment, so elegant that its restaurant actually supplied napkins, offered the first printed menus in Chicago. Said to be "equal to the City Hotel of New York," it was "the pride of the city and the admiration of strangers." By the mid-1850's Chicago, which then had some sixty thousand inhabitants, was said to possess one hundred and fifty hotels.

Hotels were among the earliest transient facilities that bound the nation together. They were both creatures and creators of communities, as well as symptoms of the frenetic quest for community. Americans were already forming their habit of gathering from all corners of the nation for mixed public-private, business-pleasure purposes. Conventions were the new occasions, and hotels were distinctively American facilities making conventions possible. Within a century, the United States would be the most conventioning nation in the world. The first national nominating convention of a major party (that of the National Republican Party, which met on December 12, 1831 and named Henry Clay for President) was held in Baltimore, whose hotel was then reputed to be the best in the country. The presence in Baltimore of Barnum's City Hotel, a six-story building with two hundred apartments, helps explain why many other early national political conventions were held there.

In the longer run, too, the American hotels made other national conventions not only possible but pleasant and convivial. The growing custom of regularly assembling from afar the representatives of all kinds of groups—political, commercial, professional, learned, and avocational —then in turn supported the multiplying hotels. By mid-20th century, conventions accounted for over a third of the yearly room occupancy of all hotels in the nation; about eighteen thousand different conventions were held annually with a total attendance of about ten million persons.

In America the hotelkeeper, who was no longer the genial, deferential "host" of the 18th-century European inn, became a leading citizen. Holding a large stake in his community, he exercised power to make it prosper. As owner or manager of the local Palace of the Public, he was maker and shaper of a principal community "attraction." Travelers from abroad were surprised and mildly shocked by his high social position. Things were really topsy-turvy in a country where the innkeeper honored the guest by his company.

Foreign observers in the mid-19th century attributed the country's flourishing hotels "to the manner in which the population has been scattered over the surface of the Union in the natural course of its industrial development." They guessed that not one American in ten was residing in the town of his birth. The census of 1850 showed "outsiders" (the foreign-born and those residing outside the state where they were born) to be about one-third of the whole population. "It can be easily conceived what a network of relationship this makes all over the Union, and how much travelling to and fro this must give rise to, especially among a people in whom the domestic affections are so strong as the Americans."

Old World distinctions between "private" and "public" aspects of life tended to lose meaning. "Home," in England an intimate and emotion-laden word, in America became almost interchangeable with "house." Here was both less privacy and more publicity. Americans lived in a new realm of uncertain boundaries, in an affable, communal world which, strictly speaking, was neither public nor private: a world of first names, open doors, front porches, and front lawns, and naturally, too, of lunch counters, restaurants, and hotel lobbies.

In this new limbo, family life lost much of its old privacy. Casual acquaintances soon seemed "members of the family." The classic locale for this new American vagueness, for this dissolving of old distinctions, was the hotel. And a clue to its personal meaning was the new scheme, originated in American hotels, which from the beginning was called the "American Plan." The fee paid by hotel guests included meals and they ate together in a common dining room. This practice became established in the 1830's and '40's when Americans were churning around the West, and the upstart cities were springing up. At first British travelers called this the *table d'hôte* from the manner of serving (supposedly resembling the French). All the food was put on the table for guests to serve themselves. There was no need for a menu until later, when the system of service changed, allowing guests to choose among items to be brought them individually. "It is the invariable custom in the United States," the English traveler Thomas Hamilton complained as early as 1833, "to charge by the day or week; and travellers are thus obliged to pay for meals whether they eat them or not." The "American Plan" had become so standard here that Boston's Parker House (opened in 1855) became widely known as the first hotel in this country operated on what by contrast was called "European Plan," meaning that meals were not included in the price of the room. By the end of the 19th century, Baedeker's *United States* carefully distinguished hotels by whether they offered American or European plan.

From the outset, the new American custom indicated that Americans regarded hotels not merely as places for a night en route but as dwelling-places: "a home away from home." Travelers from abroad, impressed by the number, size, and conveniences of American hotels, were shocked by how many Americans lived in them permanently. There was no denying that, by contrast with those in Europe, American hotels contained a large number of permanent residents. "The chance travellers," Anthony Trollope remarked, "are but chance additions to these, and are not generally the main stay of the house." With his tourist's license to exaggerate, Trollope described hotel-living in the American middle classes:

> Housekeeping is not popular with young married people in America, and there are various reasons why this should be so. Men there are not fixed in their employment as they are with us. If a young Benedict cannot get along as a lawyer at Salem, perhaps he may thrive as a shoemaker at Thermopylae. Jefferson B. Johnson fails in the lumber line at Eleutheria, but hearing of an opening for a Baptist preacher at Big Mud Creek moves himself off with his wife and three children at a week's notice. Aminadab Wiggs takes an engagement as a clerk at a steam-boat office on the Pongowonga river, but he goes to his employment with an inward conviction that six months will see him earning his bread elsewhere. Under such circumstances even a large wardrobe is a nuisance, and a collection of furniture would be as appropriate as a drove of elephants. Then, again, young men and women marry without any means already collected on which to commence their life. They are content to look forward and to hope that such means will come. In so doing they are guilty of no imprudence. It is the way of the country; and, if the man be useful for anything, employment will certainly come to him. But he must live on the fruits of that employment, and can only pay his way from week to week and from day to day. And as a third reason I think I may allege that the mode of life found in these hotels is liked by the people who frequent them. It is to their taste.

Our imperfect statistics suggest that, in the first half of the 19th century, many urban Americans were living in hotels or boarding houses. This was especially true in the Western upstart cities, and more especially, too, among the middle classes, the leading citizens who set the tone of life. The English feminist, Mrs. Bodichon, remarked in the late 1850's that every large town in the United States had five or six, and in some places twenty or more, large hotels or boarding houses containing several hundred inhabitants. Most of this population, she said, consisted of families living there permanently. For example, in Chicago in 1844, of persons listed in the city directory, about one in six was living in a hotel, and about one in four was living in a boarding house or with his employer. Another obvious explanation, besides the migratory habits of young married Americans, was the preponderance of men in the population of these new-settled places and the scarcity of women to make households.

Still another peculiarly American circumstance encouraged hotel-living by the middle classes. This, a by-product of American equality and American opportunity, was the scarcity and high price of domestic servants. An Irish cook or housemaid, a British traveler of the mid-1850's observed, in America was an expensive luxury. "She insists on being mistress of the house. Native-born Americans are a degree more expensive and more domineering. Under these circumstances, it is natural that the American matron of seventeen or eighteen should seek refuge from this domestic terrorism in the gilded saloons of the St. Nicholas or St. Charles, or whatever other Saint may offer his protection for two and a half dollars a day." But, Mrs. Bodichon observed, the female character deteriorated in the idleness of hotel life. She compared the American hotel "ladies" to women she had seen in the Eastern seraglios. "The ladies of the East spend their days in adorning themselves to please one lord and master—the ladies of the West to please all the lords of creation."

Anyone who frequented hotels soon discovered how many Old World distinctions were dissolved in America. The European middle classes counted the right to be by oneself or alone with one's family or chosen friends among the amenities, a sign of civilized respectability. But a western traveler who found himself sharing his dinner table, and called upon to chat familiarly, with a miscellaneous company of common soldiers, farmers, laborers, teamsters, lawyers, doctors, ministers, bankers, judges, or generals, soon discovered that Americans considered the desire for privacy a vice akin to pride. To want to be left alone was "a species of neglect, if not offense, which is decidedly felt, though it may not be expressed. You may sin and be wicked in many ways, and in the tolerant circle of American Society receive a full and generous pardon. But this one sin can never be pardoned." Captain Basil Hall, traveling the country in 1827–28, complained that a "sitting-parlour" where one could be alone was almost unobtainable, even in the largest hotels and that to have a meal alone was a rare luxury, never secured without an extra fee, and usually not available at any price. Anthony Trollope, thirty-five years later, wistfully recalled the wonderfully private luxury of an English inn—one's tea, one's fire, and one's book. "One is in a free country . . . and yet in an American inn one can never do as one likes. A terrific gong sounds early in the morning, breaking one's sweet slumbers, and then a second gong sounding some thirty minutes later, makes you understand that you must proceed to breakfast, whether you be dressed or no.

You certainly can go on with your toilet and obtain your meal after half an hour's delay. Nobody actually scolds you for so doing, but the breakfast is, as they say in this country, 'through.' . . . They begrudge you no amount that you can eat or drink; but they begrudge you a single moment that you sit there neither eating nor drinking. This is your fate if you're too late, and therefore as a rule you are not late. In that case you form one of a long row of eaters who proceed through their work with a solid energy that is past all praise."

American hotels were a microcosm of American life. People in transient and upstart communities had to become accustomed to live and eat and talk in the presence of those they knew only casually. This was living "American Plan" in every sense of the word. "The tangible republic—the only thing palpable and agreeable that we have to show in common life, as republican"—this is what the American style of hotel-living seemed in 1844 to the popular wit N. P. Willis. "There are some republican advantages in our present system of hotels which the country is not yet ready to forgo. Tell a country lady in these times that when she comes to New York she must eat and pass the evening in a room by herself, and she would rather stay at home. The going to the Astor and dining with two hundred well dressed people, and sitting in full dress in a splendid drawing room with plenty of company—is the charm of going to the city! The theaters are nothing to that! Broadway, the shopping and the sights, are all subordinate—poor accessories to the main object of the visit." What good was a hotel, or a republic, if it was not a place where citizens "tolerably well dressed and well behaved" could rub elbows at a public table?

As hotel life became a symbol of the fluidity of dynamic America, Southerners boasted their immunity "from the bane of hotel life and the curse of boarding-houses." A hotel suited transients, of whom the Old South (luckily, they said) had few. Where men stayed put, then every citizen was a landholder with strong "home feeling." His fixed residence on the land rooted his feeling for the permanency of his country's institutions.

But if "American Plan," a way of life for migratory, enterprising people in upstart cities, was not without its vices, it also had its virtues. If it loosened family ties, at the same time it broke down caste walls. If intimacy and individuality were stifled, a sense of fellowship was invigorated. In America perhaps men were becoming affiliated in a new way.

19

The Balloon-Frame House

IN UPSTART TOWNS citizens could lounge in the fancy salons and bars of a public palace, yet might not find a bed of their own or shelter against the rain. Some "community" facilities were grand enough for a great metropolis, yet many private facilities were unworthy of a village. There were accomplished newspapermen and hotelkeepers in surprising numbers, but ordinary carpenters were hardly found at all.

Under pressure to build houses quickly and in large numbers when they had few or no skilled carpenters, the upstarts invented a new way of building which would set a pattern for decades to come. This story is another American parable of the unpredictable advantages of American crudities and American scarcities. Just as the lack of skilled gunsmiths had stirred Eli Whitney and other versatile New Englanders to find ways of making guns without gunsmiths, the lack of skilled builders in the upstart West also produced unexpected dividends. The "balloon-frame" house, which is everywhere in the 20th century, remains an unacknowledged monument to the Americans of these upstart towns. It was at bottom very simple: a common-sense way to meet the urgent housing needs of impatient migratory people.

For centuries Englishmen and others in temperate climates of Western Europe had been building their wooden houses (or houses with wooden frames) in a certain traditional manner. To insure strength and durability, the house was built on a sturdy frame of heavy timbers about a foot thick. These were held together by cutting down the end of one beam into a tongue ("tenon"), which was then fitted into a hole ("mortise") in the adjoining beam. Where there was a pull on the joint, the pieces were held by a wooden peg fitted into an auger hole through the joined timbers. This kind of construction was generally supposed to be the only proper way to build a house. It also required a great deal of skill: shaping tongues and grooves, boring auger holes, making wooden pegs, and finally fitting all these neatly together required the tools and the training of a carpenter. Even to suggest other methods was to question a whole guild.

The very rigidity of this belief led to the making of the first modern prefabricated houses. At first it seems surprising that, in the 17th century, prefabricated houses were shipped across the ocean to an America of virgin forests. But the need to prefabricate, then as now, came in large part from the scarcity of skills where the building was to be erected. As late as 1820, when pious Bostonians wanted to ease the life of missionaries in far-off Hawaii, they shipped a prefabricated house, the essential parts of which were a massive hewn frame, knocked down and ready to be reassembled with mortise, tenon, and wooden pegs. The old Mission House, carried eighteen thousand miles round the Horn, is the oldest wooden building in the islands, and still stands in downtown Honolulu.

This way of exporting houses was feasible in places reached directly by sea but, in the days before railroads, moving them overland was quite another matter. The needs of the upstart cities of the American West required an entirely different approach to the problem. And these cities saw a revolutionary change in the way of building houses. In the manner of other American innovations, this too was a way of making better products with fewer traditional skills.

It is appropriate that this great innovation should still be known by the derisive name, at first used to contrast its flimsiness with the craft-hewn heaviness of the traditional house. "Balloon-frame" is what respectable builders first called it because it was ridiculously light. The first strong wind, they said, would surely blow it away. But the construction they were ridiculing would, within decades, become conventional. Into the 20th century, this was the style that made possible the vast American housing developments; without it the quick-grown American city, the high standard of American housing, and the extensive American suburbs would be hard to imagine.

We do not know for sure who invented the balloon-frame. We do know that it appeared in Chicago in 1833 and that within twenty years it had prevailed in the American urban West. The first balloon-frame building was probably St. Mary's Church, erected under the direction of Father John M. I. St. Cyr, first priest appointed for the city. It was thirty-six feet long, twenty-four feet wide, a single story twelve feet high, covered by a low-pitched gable roof. The builder (perhaps also an inventor of this construction) was Augustine Deodat Taylor, a carpenter from Hartford who had arrived in Chicago only a month before. The church cost about $400 and was put up in about three months with the labor of three men. This was approximately half the expenditure of time and money then required for a similar building of conventional design. Early visitors to Chicago were astonished at the speed with which balloon-frame houses were built. In one week in April, 1834, seven new buildings appeared; by mid-June, there were seventy-five more. In early October, 1834, a writer noted that, although a year before there had been only fifty frame houses in the city, "now I counted them last Sunday and there was 600 and 28 and there is from 1 to 4 or 5 a day and about two hundred and 12 of them stores and groceries." The normal time between commissioning and completing a house was now one week!

What was the "balloon-frame"? The basic new idea was so simple, and today is so universally employed, that it is hard to realize it ever had to be invented. It was nothing more than the substitution of a light frame of two-by-fours held together by nails in place of the old foot-square beams joined by mortise, tenon, and pegs. The wall plates (horizontals) and studs (uprights), the floor joists, and roof rafters were all made of thin sawed timbers (2 x 4 inches, 4 x 4, 2 x 6, 2 x 8), nailed together in such a way that every strain went in the direction of the fibre of the wood (i.e. against the grain). "Basket-frame" was the name sometimes given it, because the light timbers formed a simple basketlike cage to which any desired material could be applied inside and out. Usually, light boards or clapboards covered the outside. Nothing could be simpler. Today about three-quarters of the houses in the United States are built this way.

This remarkable invention would not have been possible without the revolutionary advances in nail manufacturing which had been accomplished, mostly in New England, before 1830. The old craft of making and heading each nail by hand had been replaced by an American system of manufacturing which, by mechanizing the process, produced nails quickly and cheaply.

In more ways than one, the scarcity of skilled labor was crucial. For in Chicago (the balloon-frame until the 1870's was widely known as "Chicago construction") laborers of all kinds, and especially skilled carpenters, were scarce. If the flood of people who poured into the new city were to be housed quickly, houses had to be built in a new way.

The balloon-frame building, then, arose as a solution to peculiar problems of the American upstart city. In older settled communities, even in the United States, there was likely to be more balance between the demand and the supply. In older communities, too, those who needed housing could make shift—with friends or neighbors, in boarding houses, taverns, or barns—until their needs could be met. In the backwoods, a lean-to (like the one Lincoln's father made when he moved to Southern Indiana in 1816) could be put up in short order; with a little more time and a little help, a man could build a log house. But city people could not live in lean-tos, sod huts, or half-face camps; they had no time to build log-cabins, even if enough logs had been handy. Carpenters were not numerous enough nor well enough organized to persuade people that every house required their skills. People urgently needing shelter were slow to believe there was only one way to build; nor were they easily convinced that a simpler way was dangerously flimsy. Anyway a speed-minded and economy-minded people were willing to be satisfied with "lower" standards.

At first some Chicagoans, nostalgic for "handsome houses" of heavy timber and solid brick, lamented that so much of their new city was of the novel light construction, but gradually most of them discovered that balloon houses, which some sneeringly still called "shanties," actually were stronger and more durable than their sturdier-looking predecessors. For moisture tended to accumulate in the mortise-and-tenon joints and cause the timbers to rot. "A Balloon Frame looks light," recalled the architect-authors of *Woodward's Country Homes,* a widely used construction handbook, in 1865, "and its name was given in contempt by those old fogy mechanics who had been brought up to rob a stick of timber of all its strength and durability, by cutting it full of mortices, tenons and auger holes, and then supposing it to be stronger than a far lighter stick differently applied, and with all its capabilities unimpaired." The balloon-frame of thin pieces held together by nails, pointed out Solon Robinson, agricultural editor of the New York *Tribune,* was not only easier to put up, but actually "incalculably stronger when finished, than though it was composed of timbers ten inches square, with a thousand auger holes and a hundred days' work with the chisel and adze, making holes and pins to fit them."

Even before the invention of the balloon-frame, foreign visitors had been amazed at how Americans moved their buildings about. New England frame houses were sometimes picked up whole and transported to more convenient places, but to survive such treatment they had to be especially well joined together. Migratory Americans found the new balloon-frame much easier to take apart and put back together. A house simply nailed together was quickly taken down; its light parts could be piled compactly and conveniently transported, and the whole put together again by anyone who could handle a hammer. Three times within ten years of its erection in 1833, St. Mary's Church in Chicago, which was originally constructed on the canal near the southwest corner of State and Lake Streets, was taken down, moved away, and erected on a new site.

Americans on the move often wanted to take their houses along or ship them ahead. In Omaha, General William Larimer in 1856 lived in a balloon house that had been framed in Pittsburgh, then knocked down and shipped out by steamboat; when Omaha grew, he moved the house to another site. Making standardized, prefabricated houses, churches, and even hotels which could be ordered by mail for shipment to farmsites or cities in the West had become a thriving business by mid-century. By 1850, in New York alone some 5000 such prefabs had been made or were under contract to relieve the housing shortage in California. One concern there shipped 100 portable wooden houses to be carried on pack mules across the Isthmus of Panama, and another 175 went all the way by sea around the Horn. The San Francisco Astor House, a three-and-a-half-story hotel 180 feet long, containing ten shops and 100 rooms, was sent out that year in prefabricated parts by the same New York firm.

Within twenty years of the building of the first balloon-frame in Chicago, influential writers like Solon Robinson preached its virtues. "To lay out and frame a building [of traditional design] so that all its parts will come together," he said in 1855, "requires the skill of a master mechanic, and a host of men and a deal of hard work to lift the great sticks of timber into position. To erect a balloon-building requires about as much mechanical skill as it does to build a board fence."

20

Culture with Many Capitals: The Booster College

A CLUE TO the American optimistic confusion of present and future was the new vagueness in the words for urban centers. In England the word "city" had a precise meaning, distinguished historically and legally from words for smaller places. Even before the time of Henry VIII, a "city" was generally a cathedral town, and when Henry VIII founded new bishoprics, the boroughs where they were set up were officially christened "cities." So clear was the distinction that, in the 19th century from time to time, the rank of "city" was formally conferred on a few places (like Birmingham) that were not episcopal seats. In English nomenclature, then, below the city came the town, and below the town came the village, which was commonly defined as a collection of buildings smaller than a town, but larger than a hamlet.

In the rapidly growing American West, these distinctions of usage disappeared. Every settlement, real or imaginary, large or small, permanent or temporary, claimed the name of "city." Every place that claimed the honors of a city set about justifying itself by seeking to conjure up suitably metropolitan institutions. As early as 1747, a European settling in Burlington, New Jersey, noted that the place was called a "City" "tho' but a village of 170 houses." In America, then, "city" had to be defined either as an inhabited place larger than a town or (and this was the peculiarly American meaning) as "a grandiose or anticipatory designation for a mere hamlet or village." "In the course of the last two days," the Earl of Derby reported with amusement in 1826, "we passed several *cities*—some of them however almost invisible, and one or two litterally in the condition of Old Sarum." "It is strange that the name of city should be given to an unfinished log-house," Captain Marryat noted acidly in 1834, "but such is the case in Texas!" More than one traveler noted that every mining camp—not only those, like Virginia City and Carson City, that had taken the precaution to incorporate the word into their very name—called itself a city.

An easy way to prove that one's "city" was destined to be a great metropolis was to provide it as quickly as possible with all the metropolitan hallmarks, which included not only a newspaper and a hotel, but an institution of higher learning. The booster college illustrates how this ideal of the complete community promoted the diffuseness of American culture.

President Madison, in four annual messages, recommended founding a national university in Washington, D. C., to supplement the institutions of the separate states. A congressional committee favorably reported his proposal on December 11, 1816, and a bill was drawn in 1817. But President Monroe and others thought a constitutional amendment necessary to give this power to the Federal government, and the House of Representatives voted down the proposed amendment. The rise of the booster spirit reinforced these doubts. Dispersion of cultural resources, no longer a mere by-product of American conditions, was now increasingly the work of optimists in scores of communities.

Bizarre, from a European point of view, was the fact that, between the Revolution and the Civil War, much the larger number of new colleges was founded in the western outposts and on the fringes of settlements. Of the one-hundred-eighty-odd colleges and universities founded in these years which survived into the 20th century, well over a hundred appeared outside the original thirteen colonies. This disproportion is all the more impressive since population had remained concentrated in the longer-settled areas of the Atlantic seaboard. While in Europe a college or university would be found in an ancient center, in the United States it was more likely than not to appear in a town whose population and prosperity lay all in the future. For this feature of American higher education there were at least two explanations. One was the booster spirit which made every place consider itself an "Athens of the West"; another was the missionary spirit, which had led the denominations to reach out to the islands and the edges of settlement.

The religious denominations, which even in the colonial period had multiplied colleges and stimulated competition among them, during the early years of nationhood continued potent. Both the champions and the opponents of sectarian influence could not help agreeing that, for better or worse, the bulk of American institutions of higher learning were creatures of the denominations. Francis Wayland, the missionary-president of Brown University (1827–55), estimated that legislatures had not given them one-tenth the help they received from religious sources. Philip Lindsley, the pioneering president of the new non-denominational University of Nashville, wanted his institution to be "religious," but in 1834 he complained of the evils of sectarianism.

> A principal cause of the excessive multiplication and dwarfish dimensions of Western colleges is, no doubt, the diversity of religious denominations among us. Almost every sect will have its college, and generally one at least in each State. Of the score of colleges in Ohio, Kentucky and Tennessee, all are sectarian except two or three; and of course few of them are what they might and should be; and the greater part of them are mere impositions on the public. This is a grievous and growing evil. Why colleges should be sectarian, any more than penitentiaries or than bank, road or canal corporations, is not very obvious. Colleges àre designed for the instruction of youth in the learned languages—in polite literature—in the liberal arts and sciences—and not in the dogmatical theology of any sect or party. Why then should they be baptized with sectarian names? Are they to inculcate sectarian Greek, sectarian mathematics, sectarian logic, history, rhetoric, philosophy? Must every State be divided and subdivided into as many college associations as there are religious sects within its limits? And thus, by their mutual jealousy and distrust, effectually prevent the usefulness and prosperity of any one institution?

American Christendom (or at least American Protestantism) had already become a market-place, in which each sect tried to make its special product attractive to all possible consumers. The survival needs of sectarian colleges became potent and lasting influences toward the vague religiosity of American life. Although nearly every one of the new colleges had been founded and was governed by some single sect, yet generally speaking, their charters forbade religious tests for faculty or students. This legally imposed liberalism was reinforced by the need of each college for money and students. To make their colleges appeal to everybody, to people who believed anything or nothing, the denominations themselves became powerful breeders of "Nothingarianism," which some observers said was the truly dominant American sect. "A Nothingarian," the English geologist Charles Lyell observed on his visit here in 1845, ". . . was indifferent whether he attended a Baptist, Methodist, Presbyterian, or Congregationalist church, and was often equally inclined to contribute money liberally to any one or all of them." That denominationally founded colleges might rise above their origins was already demonstrated in such older eastern institutions as Harvard, Yale, Dartmouth, Amherst, and Williams.

Unless we recall the energy of this peculiarly American denominationalism, we cannot begin to understand why, before 1870, at least
eleven colleges were founded in Kentucky, twenty-one in Illinois, and
thirteen in Iowa. The "home-missionary" spirit was strong. For example,
in November, 1828, a group of zealous young theology students at Yale
who had been stirred by an essay, "The Call of the West," gathered
under the New Haven elms and pledged their lives to education and
preaching in the Far West, which was then Illinois. They called themselves the Illinois Association or the "Yale Band." One of them, Julian
Sturtevant, founded Illinois College at Jacksonville on January 4, 1830,
with nine students. In 1837, seven more Yale theology students formed
the "Iowa Educational Association . . . to establish upon a firm basis a
college for the future state of Iowa." This "firm basis," like that of other
western colleges, was a land-sale plan. Eastern missionary support thus
was as important in the founding of western colleges as was eastern
capital in the building of western railroads.

The liberal missionary enthusiasm of the founders sometimes became a sectarian rancor, which dissipated energies and stunted growth,
but the *odium theologicum* was not a prevalent disease in America.
Struggling colleges, as Frederick Rudolph has explained, "could not
really afford to make themselves any more unattractive than they frequently were, and for most Americans there was something unattractive
about the bickering controversies which denominations sometimes got
themselves into." Understandably enough, most of them tried to create
an "aura of nonsectarianism."

"A land of colleges," an American college promoter called us in 1851.
By 1880, President Frederick A. P. Barnard of Columbia was wondering
how England, with a population of twenty-three million, managed with
four degree-granting institutions, while the State of Ohio, with a population of only three million, supported thirty-seven. An explanation no
less important than denominationalism, but which President Barnard
must have found too obvious to mention, was the booster spirit.

No community could be complete without its college or university.
Usually the denominations gave the initial push and provided a plan,
but the whole community, regardless of sect, then built and maintained
the college. These denominationally founded colleges tended to take the
name of the town they were supposed to glorify. Few except Roman
Catholic colleges took saints' names or others with sectarian religious
overtones. Later some took the names of benefactors.

In the 1830's, observed Julian Sturtevant, one of the "Yale Band,"
this "mania for college building . . . was the combined result of the
prevalent speculation in land and the zeal for denominational aggrandise-
ment. . . . It was generally believed that one of the surest ways to
promote the growth of a young city was to make it the seat of a college."

Some, known as "real-estate" colleges, were purely commercial ventures, but it is remarkable, considering all the difficulties and the temptations, how many of these new communities managed to offer their citizens the means for a respectable higher education.

In some older eastern towns, community spirit, aided only a little by sectarianism or blatant real-estate interests, was enough to start a new institution. The founding of Lafayette College in Easton, Pennsylvania, is one such story. James Madison Porter, lawyer, canal promoter, and leading citizen-booster of Easton where he had only recently settled, saw how colleges elsewhere stimulated commerce and provided employment. He conceived the idea of a college in Easton, to be supported by the whole community. On December 24, 1824, an advertisement appeared in the Easton newspapers inviting all interested citizens to meet at half-past six the following Monday evening at the Easton Hotel on Center Square. In the large parlor which extended across the entire second floor of the building, the citizens met, took first steps toward securing a charter, selected a name, and elected thirty-nine men to an original board of trustees. This number included several promoters, a number of businessmen, lawyers, a physician, two newspapermen, and two hotelkeepers. Not one of the number had been born in Easton; only one had attended college.

Easton, which only thirty-five years before had been incorporated as a borough, in 1824 seemed to have great prospects, for it was strategically located at the junction of the Lehigh and Delaware Rivers, down which came boats carrying the first anthracite coal to Philadelphia in addition to flour and timber for Philadelphia shipbuilders. And now it found itself on the busy wagon route west from New York and New England. In a single month in 1824, there passed westward through the town 511 covered wagons carrying over 3000 emigrants. Easton seemed a city of the future. But how could so small a community find capital to found a college? The first efforts to raise money failed. In 1832, the trustees attracted the Rev. George Junkin, who had been head of the struggling Manual Labor Academy in Germantown, to be its first president. Relying mainly on student labor, Junkin managed to erect a few buildings and reawakened community interest. Early in 1833 when Easton was still a town of only about 3700 people, a money-raising campaign raised $2925. The next year the state legislature finally appropriated $8000, with the proviso that none of the money be used for teachers' salaries. On July 4, 1833, a festive procession starting at the courthouse in Center Square reached its climax in an impressive cornerstone-laying ceremony for the new College Edifice. This, the most spectacular community celebration since the founding of Easton, dramatized the importance of the college to the community and of the community to the college.

In the newer towns of the West, the importance of a thriving college for a thriving community seemed still more obvious. Take the College of Wooster, for example. The Presbyterian Synod of Ohio, climaxing twenty years' concern over the lack of a strong Presbyterian institution there, in the fall of 1865 authorized its committee to found a college at any place which made a bid of not less than $100,000. The leading citizens of Wooster, then a town of about 5000 people, quickly took up the proposal. "It will not only be an honor to the place," urged the Wooster *Republican* on October 12, "but it will so enhance the value of real estate throughout the whole vicinity and county that none will be losers by the investment. . . . An effort will be made to raise $100,000 in the county." Wooster would also become a metropolis when every local boy could stay home and attend "one of the best universities of the land." Early in December a money-raising campaign was organized and areas assigned to committees.

Every argument—from the certain increase in property values, to a decline in drunkenness as a result of the university's moralizing influence—was urged and repeated. But the booster note dominated: the College would help Wooster and environs grow and prosper; private and community prosperity were inseparable. Within three weeks the pledged total reached $75,000. By the end of March, 1866, the competing town of Mansfield had given up; only London remained in the race against Wooster. Their projected "university," one Wooster citizen wrote in the paper, had already made them the cynosure of the cultivated world:

> Wayne County has already become famous all over the country in view of what she proposes to do in this enterprise. The press, both secular and religious, has heralded the news from one city to another, and Wayne County is spoken of in Philadelphia, in New York, in Cincinnati, in Chicago, in fact from one end of the land to the other, as a noble county, as the home of an enterprising people, and as likely to be the seat of liberal learning. The eyes of the whole country are looking this way and hundreds are getting ready to come this way.

When the Ohio Synod met in Wooster on October 18, 1866, the citizens of Wooster and Wayne County offered a beautiful hilltop site (valued at $25,000) and $92,000 in cash (later increased to an even $100,000). The college was theirs, and was christened The University of Wooster. "What we desire," the Board of Trustees explained at an early meeting, "is to make Wooster the great educational center of Ohio as Oxford and Cambridge are in England and the Universities are in Germany and France."

This story was re-enacted all over the West. Locale and characters changed, but the essentials were the same: denominational initiative, upstart enterprise, booster optimism.

College histories, like town histories, were sagas of migratory hopes and quickly transferred loyalties. There were ghost colleges to match the ghost towns. A college that failed to fulfil its promise in short order was simply abandoned; or it bequeathed (or sometimes sold) its name, its meager equipment, and its deflated supporters to some more promising successor. Many a college which thrives in mid-20th century incorporates the legacy of numerous earlier, unfulfilled optimisms. The pedigree of Grinnell College, for example, must be traced back in this way. The 1837–38 session of the Wisconsin territorial assembly had chartered eighteen educational institutions, one of which it designated "The Philandrian College of the town of Denmark." This institution never came into being, but in its place there grew "Denmark Academy," chartered by the Iowa territorial legislature in 1843, to be the first incorporated educational institution in the territory. It was endowed with seventy-two town lots and fourteen "out-lots" as the gift of local people. A few years later, in June, 1846, a group dominated by Congregationalists founded Iowa College, which was located at Davenport after the people of the town fulfilled required conditions by pledging $1362 and thirteen lots. The original college plan centered around a permanent main building to cost not over $2000. When Davenport proved unpromising in 1858, the trustees sold the college property and invited proposals for a new site. At least eight towns and eight individual landowners replied. The most attractive offer was by Grinnell University, to which the trustees of the older college moved their scanty library, their few pieces of scientific apparatus, a meager nucleus of a museum, and the old safe containing the college papers and $9000.

"Grinnell University" (changed from "People's College") had been chartered only in 1856, when the town of Grinnell numbered some two hundred inhabitants. And it had been part of an elaborate plan for a temperance town, where every deed contained the provision that, if strong drink was ever sold on the lot, title would revert to the maker of the deed. The "university" along with the town flourished from the beginning, largely because of the promotional genius of Josiah Bushnell Grinnell, a zealous Congregational preacher, characterized by one of his contemporaries as "a living sunbeam, everywhere at home, and an unpaid advertising agency everywhere in the state and out of it." What came to be Grinnell College was thus the inheritor of miscellaneous hopes.

It is not surprising that the mortality rate of colleges, as of towns, was high. In the southwestern and western states, mortality, on the average, ran well over eighty per cent. Of the colleges and universities founded before the Civil War, fewer than one in five was still in operation by 1930. Before 1860 over 700 colleges had died. Mortality was, generally speaking, lowest in the old New England states. This is simply another way of saying that the upstarts were readier than others to overreach themselves.

It is another way, too, of showing the involvement of the college with the community. Since the founding of the nation, American leaders had insisted that a republican society would require a new kind of higher education. Benjamin Rush and Thomas Jefferson, among others, had had much to say (in Rush's phrase) "Of the Mode of Education Proper in a Republic." "Our republican form of government," urged even the conservative Yale Report of 1828, "renders it highly important, that great numbers should enjoy the advantage of a thorough education. On the Eastern continent, the *few* who are destined to particular departments in political life, may be educated for the purpose; while the mass of the people are left in comparative ignorance. But in this country, where offices are accessible to all who are qualified for them, superior intellectual attainments ought not to be confined to any description of persons."

The undifferentiated community, like the undifferentiated man, had to be prepared for all possibilities. An American style in higher education was thus a by-product of an American style in community building. Boosters all over the nation had strong notions of how their college should express, serve, and be governed by, their community. They enforced the diffuseness of American culture and strengthened local ties. Support of colleges by voluntary contributions from the surrounding community, which began very early, became a tradition which did not die. Congregationalists of Minnesota Territory in 1857 first announced their intention to found a college, then sent out a circular letter to churches in twenty towns inviting bids for the college. Five towns (Zumbrota, Mantorville, Cottage Grove, Lake City, and Northfield) offered land, building materials, and cash. Northfield sent in the highest bid. Money-raising meetings there reached a climax on October 10, 1865, when enthusiastic citizens actually pledged some $18,000 in one night. The telegram announcing the Conference decision to award the college to Northfield occasioned bell-ringing and general jubilation. The Congregational Conference defended their choice of Northfield by Northfield's location near the center of population of the state, and its impressive population, which already numbered about 1500. Local contributors to the Founders Fund for Northfield College, later to be Carleton College, numbered 201. Even state universities were of course tied to the interests of local communities. The University of Missouri, for example, was finally located only after a contest among six river counties. Columbia, in Boone County, won the prize in 1839 when citizens there raised $82,381 in cash and $35,540 in land. These contributions came from over nine hundred individuals, of whom nearly a hundred gave five dollars or less.

Citizens so involved in the founding of an institution assumed that they or their representatives should have a voice in its government. They would insist that the college serve them and their community. These circumstances strengthened that distinctive American way of governing institutions of higher education which had begun to take shape even in the early 18th century. Most American colleges and universities would be legally owned and ultimately controlled by a board of trustees drawn from the community. This arrangement, a legacy of colonial Yale and Princeton, had been tried long before the college mania of the early 19th century. The lack of ancient institutions, the lack of a body of learned and revered scholars, and many other peculiarly American circumstances made this form of government more natural here than either an autonomy inherited from medieval scholarly guilds or a Napoleonic control by the central government. Booster spirit and strong local support reinforced New World tendencies toward outside control of colleges and universities and toward strengthened ties to communities. In the optimistic view of Professor William S. Tyler of Amherst, addressing the Society for the Promotion of Collegiate and Theological Education at the West in 1856, the American college with its community trustees was "a magnetic chain of reciprocal influences, by which light flashes from the college to the community, and life streams back again from the community to the college, so that while the college redeems the community from the curse of ignorance, the community preserves the college from an undue tendency to monkish corruption and scholastic unprofitableness."

* * *

The distinctively American college was neither public nor private, but a *community* institution. In America it was of a piece with the community emphasis which already distinguished our civilization. Once again the distinction of "The Man versus The State," which was sharpened in European class wars of the 19th century, proved irrelevant in America. The supposed chastity of "private" institutions, and their supposed immunity from government support, which would arouse passion from time to time in the 20th century, was not founded in the tradition or history of American institutions.

Even institutions which in later times would be most proudly "private" were by no means clearly private in their origins. Harvard was, of course, founded by an act and appropriation of the General Court of Massachusetts Bay Colony, as Yale was by the legislature of Connecticut; both were supported by occasional public appropriations in their early years (Harvard received funds from the General Court on over one hundred occasions before 1789); both included the first magistrate of the colony on their governing board. In the early 19th century the funds of the state of New York were repeatedly distributed among such "private" colleges as Columbia, Hamilton, Hobart, and Union; similarly in Pennsylvania. Even federal land grants were sometimes given to "privately" controlled colleges, for example, to Miami in Ohio and Cumberland in Tennessee. Lotteries, from which the state treasury often took a cut, were commonly authorized by state legislatures to support "private" institutions. Benjamin Franklin, Printer, with his sharp eye for the profitable marriage of public and private interests, once printed eight thousand tickets for a lottery authorized by New Jersey to benefit Princeton. At the same time, early state universities were so poorly supported by public funds (too often given in non-negotiable land or buildings) that current operations commonly had to depend on private munificence.

The *Dartmouth College Case* (1819), which occasioned one of Chief Justice Marshall's most important decisions, although usually remembered as a barrier against legislative regulation of property, actually gave classic expression to an American concept of community control. The case arose from a dispute between Dartmouth's President John Wheelock and the board of trustees. Wheelock insisted on his power to run the institution virtually uncontrolled by the board, and the trustees declared their authority by dismissing him. College government became a partisan issue when, in 1816, the Republican governor of New Hampshire asserted the power of the state legislature to control the college in any way it pleased and incidentally made political capital by attacking as "aristocratic" the self-perpetuating board of trustees. When the state legislature changed the name from Dartmouth College to Dartmouth University and in other ways tightened state control, the trustees took the issue to court. After Daniel Webster's melodramatic plea for his alma mater, which brought tears to the eyes of the justices of the United States Supreme Court, the power of the trustees was finally vindicated. Public-spirited citizens could be assured that, even after receiving a state charter, they would be free to direct their institution according to their lights.

21

Competitive Communities

IN THE WINTER of 1858, the young members of the Nininger Boys Lyceum in the Minnesota boom town, which had been first settled only eighteen months before (and was destined to disappear within five years), debated the question, "Has Hastings grown more than Nininger during the past year?" Another question that season was, "Does Washington deserve more praise than Bonaparte?" The answer to one was no more doubtful than to the other.

Citizens young and old of each upstart town saw themselves racing against all others, and their competitive spirit left its mark on American life. "On paper, *all* these towns were magnificent," Albert D. Richardson reported from Kansas in 1857. "Their superbly lithographed maps adorned the walls of every place of resort. The stranger studying one of these, fancied the New Babylon surpassed only by its namesake of old. Its great parks, opera-houses, churches, universities, railway depots and steamboat landings made New York and St. Louis insignificant in comparison. . . . It was not a swindle but a mania. The speculators were quite as insane as the rest."

Everything that fed the booster spirit intensified competition among communities; this competition in turn prevented or discouraged the centralizing of activities. We have already seen how such competition led to the shifting of state capitals. Sometimes a consequence of legislative efforts to compromise was purposely to separate a state's commercial from its political headquarters. Thus the contest between Lexington and Louisville led to the naming of Frankfort as the capital of Kentucky in 1792; from the struggle among Steubenville and Cincinnati and others, came the creation of Columbus as capital of Ohio in 1812. In the new states of a growing new country, the landscape showed neither a lordly castle nor an imposing ancient cathedral to proclaim historic rights to the seat of government. The competition was open.

The creation of large new political units—territories and states—provided many new opportunities for ambitious communities. The state capital was always, of course, the biggest prize, but there were others. In the sparsely settled West, there ought to have been enough political plums to go around: county seats, state universities, agricultural colleges, prisons, land offices, institutions for the poor, the insane, the blind, and the deaf. But it was not only existing communities that had to be satisfied. The cities of the future were numberless, and each demanded its share.

The lore of the West is full of the bitter rivalries of enterprising early settlers for a government handout to their community. Contests were none the less bitter because the competing towns were often figments of imagination. Booster optimists were ready to believe that the government prize itself would give reality and prosperity to their illusions; every such state institution meant buildings to be built, people to be employed, food, clothing, and services to be bought. It meant clients for the lawyers, patients for the doctors, customers for the shops, guests for the taverns and hotels. Above all, it meant increased population with the increased land values that always came along.

Some of the better documented stories involved the railroads, for they had big money to spark a lively contest. The scramble for the location of the University of Illinois is a good example. Under the Morrill Act of 1862, the new university would receive a large grant of federal land; it would also be permanently supported by the state. Intense rivalry finally led the state legislature in January 1867 to pass an act permitting interested communities to submit bids. The promoters of four towns—Jacksonville, Bloomington, Lincoln, and Champaign—offered money, land, commodities, and then used every other kind of influence. Champaign had the advantage of the leadership of C. R. Griggs, a seasoned lobbyist and member of the state legislature. He was shrewd enough to raise a large sum, not for the official bid, but to finance the goodwill of the politicians who would award the prize. Then he toured the state to see that the money was effectively distributed, and, despite the threat of an investigation, he continued his activities after the legislature went into session.

The Illinois Central Railroad, which already ran through Champaign, was naturally interested in seeing the University there. It had there a large grant of land, much of it still unsold, it owned many town lots, and it would obviously profit from increased freight and passenger traffic. Therefore, it offered $50,000 in freight transportation as part of Champaign's bid, which altogether came to about $285,000. This bid was exceeded by those of the three other leading contenders: Lincoln offered $385,000; Bloomington, $470,000 (including $50,000 from the Chicago and Alton Railroad, which was competing with the Illinois Central); and Jacksonville, $491,000. But Griggs had put his money in the right places, preferring to line the pockets of legislators and political bosses instead of needlessly inflating the public bid. His shrewdness was rewarded on February 28, 1867, when, after much slander and contention, an act located the university at Champaign. The investment by the Illinois Central Railroad and by local boosters was speedily repaid with dividends. By 1870 Champaign-Urbana had already become the most populous town south of Chicago on the branch line, and real estate there was booming.

Since a state generally could support not more than one prison, one insane asylum, or one university, it became usual to disperse these institutions to spread the benefits. The institutions themselves often suffered, for they were not necessarily located in the most suitable places. There had to be prizes for everybody.

Happily, or unhappily, there were to be such prizes almost without number. The sparse population and the politically unorganized condition of the West actually helped make them possible. The largest political and legal subdivisions of the West were, of course, the "territory" or the "state," created and bounded by acts of the federal Congress, but the next smaller units were left to definition by the states them-selves. There was no clear, simple, or general rule and, most important, there were no automatic answers supplied by history. In England, by contrast, the smaller unit of government, the "county," had been the product of centuries; it was originally the domain of a "count." The colonies too had generally been divided into counties. In the thirteen original states, counties had already acquired a historical, even patriotic, aura by the early 19th century. But what would happen in the unsettled new territories and states of the southwest and the west? There, too, the subdivision (except in Louisiana) was to be called a "county."

The "county seat" (an Americanism, first recorded in 1803), the headquarters of each county, was where the administrative offices, the county court, the county jail, and the county records would all be located. If a town could not be a state capital, the next best thing was to be a county seat. The county's political, judicial, and administrative activities would build buildings, would attract people with money to spend, would boost town growth and insure against decay. Which town (or which hope-for-a-town) should be named the county seat? How many counties should there be? The answers to these questions were anybody's guess. In unsettled states, one unbuilt place had no better his-torical claim than another. Since the boundaries of counties were also unsettled, even geographic considerations were hard to measure. A town could hardly claim that its "central" location in a county entitled it to be the headquarters, when the extent and boundaries of the county were still undecided.

The upshot was the "County-Seat Wars." Such wars might be struggles among several places to possess the headquarters of a particular county. In that case, one or another would prevail. Or, on the other hand, they might be struggles for the creation of more counties, in order to provide several towns with something to be the headquarters of. Thus the object might be either to take a prize away from a rival, or to persuade the legislature (when there was no theoretical limit to the number of counties) to create enough prizes to go around.

Counties were absolute creatures of state legislatures. Restricted only by the state constitution, a legislature could establish, abolish, enlarge, or diminish any county. In the new states, the county usually started as a geographic rather than a population unit. An act of the state legislature or an executive proclamation would define the boundaries of a county, leaving its detailed organization to the people who happened to reside there. Of course, in describing the boundaries of counties, as in locating the state capital and other state agencies, legislators were subjected to all kinds of pressures: blackmail, bribes, threats, and even physical vio-lence. Land speculators with a fortune to gain (and their allies the town-boosters) were not easily discouraged nor were they pedantic in their arguments.

Commonly the war for the county seat took place in the newly delineated counties themselves, to whose voters state laws generally left the selection of the lucky place. Often land speculators took the lead, but town loyalty and the booster spirit made struggles passionate and even bloody.

Rarely did a new county contain a single pre-eminent town plainly meriting the seat. Usually the contest involved two or more contenders. Sometimes a proposed county contained no towns at all. In such cases, the competitive spirit had the widest possible field, since any group of speculators could enter their property in the race. Often these county-seat wars technically took place at the ballot box, but in scores of cases they were actually settled with payoffs, brickbats, and even with bullets. It was in the early decades, the organizing decades, of the new western states, that contests were most common and most bitter. And they occurred not only when a county was first created. Where historical roots were shallow, where people and towns were accustomed to transplanting, urban leadership never seemed finally settled. The loser of this year's contest might hope to win back the prize the year after next; but by then it might have to contend against a brand new town that had only just sprung into prominence.

In Iowa, for example, about two-thirds of its ninety-nine county seats were located only after a contest with neighboring towns. Thirty-nine of Indiana's ninety-two counties have had more than one county seat during their history; some have had as many as seven different seats. Most of the counties in Kansas, Nebraska, and the Dakotas were scenes of such contests. All over the Southwest and West, again and again in the 19th century, Americans at the ballot box defended their investments, their personal hopes, and their civic pride.

When the earliest counties were being organized, there were few inhabitants. "The conditions were ideal for the organization of a county," one old settler remarked, "inasmuch as there was an office for every man." At a county-seat election in 1858 in Cuming County, Nebraska, the town of Dewitt, which received only seven votes, was defeated by West Point, which received all of twelve votes. When Nebraska Center was named county seat of Buffalo County, it consisted of one dwelling, one store building, and one warehouse. In Harlan County, Nebraska, where three "towns" competed for the county seat, both Republican City and Melrose comprised only a store, a hitching-post, and a clothesline, while their competitor, Alma, was said to be marked only by a buffalo skull.

Sometimes the proposed county-seat town was a purely speculative real-estate venture. When there was no town in a proposed county, it was tempting for speculators to offer the state a tract of land on condition that the county seat be located there. In Fillmore County, Nebraska, one man personally offered to build a courthouse at a cost of $2500, and such offers were not uncommon. Speculators could buy a section of land (one mile square: 640 acres) at the total government price of $800, hoping, after it had been elevated into a county seat, to break it up into town lots. Figuring eight lots to the acre, there would be altogether 5120 lots in the town section. If these could be sold a $100 apiece, which was not an extravagant price in the East, the total return (afer spending, at most, three or four thousand dollars for surveying and other expenses) would be a tidy half million dollars.

Some speculators bought tracts in rival towns. The business-like explanation of C. J. ("Buffalo") Jones's heavy investments in six or eight county-seat contests in southwestern Kansas was that, if even only one of the towns he backed became a county seat, he would recoup all his losses and be financially independent for life.

If contests between nonexistent towns were often unscrupulous, in real towns contestants were hardly more willing to submit to an unpredictable, if fair, election. The small number of voters in many counties made attempts at a secret ballot futile. Lack of clear or strict voting qualifications added to the confusion; minors were usually allowed to vote. In a largely transient population, who could distinguish those who had come for the sole purpose of voting?

Kansas, a mid-19th-century national battleground of slavery and of other issues large and small, continued to be the scene of some of the most ingenious, as well as some of the most colorful and most corrupt, county-seat battles. In Ford precinct of Gray County in the southwestern part of the state, in the 1870's a secret organization euphemistically called the "Equalization Society" was formed of seventy-two members. Their sole object (spelled out in a constitution and bylaws!) was to sell their votes as a block to whatever county-seat aspirant bid highest. The members attested their democratic faith by agreeing that the money received was to be divided among members equally. All were bound by oath to vote for the town to whom the sale was made, and violation of the oath was punishable by death. T. H. Reeves, a manager of Cimarron's campaign, offered the Society for its votes the sum of $10,000, guaranteed by a bond supposedly signed by fifteen leading citizens of Cimarron. The Society duly cast its seventy-two votes for Cimarron, which was named the county seat. When the Society went to Cimarron for their payoff, they were told they could not be paid because the signatures on the bond were forged.

In Grant County, also in southwestern Kansas, the two contending towns were Ulysses and Appomattox. When, just before the election, it looked likely that Ulysses would win, two of the Appomattox managers entered into a secret pact with their opposite numbers from Ulysses to cover their losses. The pact provided that neither side would resort to bribery or other wrongful methods, and that the successful town company, whichever it might be, would reimburse its defeated rival for their expenses in attempting to build up their town. The defeated town would then be abandoned and all interests united in building up the town chosen as the county seat. Shortly before the polls closed, word of the pact leaked out at Appomattox. The rank and file of Appomattox boosters, thinking they had been sold out, took into custody the signers of the pact, threatened to lynch them, and finally let them go only after they promised to reimburse the campaign expenses of the populace. The people of Ulysses themselves had acquired a reputation for business-like methods, for voters there were paid off at the rate of ten dollars apiece as they cast their ballots. While this system seemed fair enough to land speculators and town boosters, it failed to meet the approval of the Kansas Supreme Court, which set aside at least one such election. In the long run, however, cash-and-carry democracy prevailed, for Ulysses remained the seat of Gray County.

The cost of county-seat wars was high, not only in money but in violence, in blood, and even in lives. At Dodge City, Kansas, crews known as "killers" were brought into town for the county-seat contests. Although it is not definitely recorded that they killed anyone, their presence seems to have influenced the result. As late as 1885 in Stevens County, Kansas, a county-seat war between Hugoton and Woodsdale involved kidnapping, assassination, bribery, the use of militia, and several criminal trials which reverberated for over a quarter of a century.

Many individual promoters, and some whole towns, were deluded or disappointed. Even if the magical mushroom growth supposed to follow the declaration of a county seat did not always appear, some inevitable advantages seemed to come with the distinction. A town that still remained small after designation as a county seat might otherwise have disappeared altogether. A growing town was likely to grow still more. These optimisms were enough to spawn counties by the hundreds. Old counties never died! But new counties were continually being born: by the fission of old counties, by the subdivision of newly settled and newly organized territories and states. These multiplied and dispersed the agencies of government, giving more and more Americans a personal interest in the diffuseness of American politics and, incidentally, of American culture. In many states of the vast unpopulous West, counties were just as small geographically as those of Massachusetts; in Indiana, for example, a county averaged only half the size of those originally formed in Connecticut. By the time of the census of 1960, the United States was subdivided into 3072 counties. Each had its own county seat, including a courthouse, a jail, and numerous administrative offices.

The counties remained an important and expensive feature of American life into the 20th century. It was often said, in justifying them, that any farmer ought to be able to drive to his county courthouse and back in his horse and buggy between sunrise and sunset. Governor "Alfalfa Bill" Murray of Oklahoma, in the early 20th century, actually argued that it was important to keep counties numerous and small in order to continue to encourage farmers to travel by horse and buggy rather than by automobile.

But by the 20th century many of the myriad counties had become a burden on state finances. Few could afford the paved highways required by motor vehicles. Shifting centers of agriculture and industry had left many county governments without sources of tax support. The rise and expansion of cities with all their own political machinery now created new problems of competition for the once dominant county governments. But who would champion county consolidation? One could not combine several small counties into a single large one without abolishing their county seats, each with its complement of courthouses, poorhouses, and jails, and all their officials. This form of political suicide has not been popular. And thousands of American counties remain: a vivid vestige of the upstart age, of extravagant hopes and driving competitive ambitions, in a word, of the booster spirit.

In scores of other ways, too numerous to mention, the booster spirit of the upstart West fostered cultural diffuseness. What Richard C. Wade has called "Urban Imperialism"—the competition of numerous, fast-growing urban centers, each seeking to explore and exploit and attach itself to an undeveloped hinterland—played much the same role in the spread of civilization and commerce over this continent, that the competitive imperialisms of European nations played in developing and industrializing remote parts of Asia, Africa, and Oceania. The desire of each town to become the terminus of a canal or a railroad often produced canals and railroads, which became life-promoting arteries all along their way. This competition bred a fantastic transportation network which, by comparison with Western Europe, gave the United States a railroad mileage far out of proportion to her population.

PART FOUR

THE ROOTED AND THE UPROOTED

Southerners, White and Black

"The difficulty is in the diversity of the races. So strongly drawn is the line between the two in consequence, and so strengthened by the force of habit and education, that it is impossible for them to exist together in the community, where their numbers are so nearly equal as in the slaveholding states, under any other relation than that which now exists."

JOHN C. CALHOUN

"I'm gwine to jine de great 'sociation,
I'm gwine to jine de great 'sociation,
Den my little soul's gwine to shine."

NEGRO SPIRITUAL

AN ISLAND—"The South"—was appearing within the southern United States in the first half of the 19th century, as more and more people there came to think themselves a separate homogeneous nation. That South was part myth and part fact. Geographically it was largely myth, for the lands below the Mason-Dixon Line contained samples of all the physiographic areas then found elsewhere in the United States, and even added some of their own. The southern Appalachians were the highest points east of the Mississippi River, and the coastal swamps

169

possessed the nation's largest areas of low-lying undrained lands. Virgin forests were found in Georgia, South Carolina, and Mississippi, but the southwestern fringes resembled the treeless Central Prairies and the semi-arid Western Plains. There were deep indented harbors like Chesapeake Bay and also the unapproachable sand-barred coasts of South Carolina. There were long fertile valleys and broad pine barrens; there was the refreshing coolness of the North Carolina, Kentucky, and Virginia mountaintops, and the stifling humidity of the Louisiana, Mississippi, and Florida jungles. The vast potential of agriculture extended from upland farm to valley plantation to swampy riceland. And there was, geographically speaking, very little to hold the South together: split by a great mountain range, it had few roads or other internal communications; nearly all the great rivers only marked the edges or led outward.

Culturally, too, the South had the elements of great variety. The remnants of French and Spanish culture in Louisiana and Florida, and the survivals of Roman Law in Louisiana were stronger, more widespread, and more durable alien elements than were then found elsewhere in the eastern United States. Most dramatic was the cultural gulf between the few gentlemen of old English stock who considered themselves the "Cavalier" heirs of a refined European aristocracy and the hundreds of thousands of unwilling illiterate immigrants from Africa, who brought strange tribal languages, and to whom the very name of Europe was unknown. The racial diversity was especially visible.

Despite all this, no other part of the nation became more conscious of its identity or more passionately asserted its homogeneity. Belief in uniformity tended to create uniformity. There were many Souths, but after about 1830 leading white Southerners could see only one. Theirs was a triumph of history over geography, of imagination over reality.

While these southern Americans believed their region unified by its homogeneity, what actually drew it together and made it conscious of itself was its deep and (according to white Southern belief) ineradicable, division—into white and black. The South's "Peculiar Institution" was in essence a way not of uniting but of bifurcating the life, the hopes, and the destiny of Southern communities. Leading Southerners persuaded themselves that only by dividing their communities into two could they make themselves one. And "The South" became the most unreal, most powerful, and most disastrous oversimplification in American history.

22

How the Planter Lost His Versatility

IN THE OLDER South, the activities and virtues of the city had been diffused into the countryside. During the whole colonial period, Virginia, though the most populous of the colonies, possessed not a single city; its capital, Williamsburg, was no more than a seasonal political center with a year-round population of only fifteen hundred. Every leading planter, because he was something of a merchant who kept shop for his neighbors and imported goods to his own docks, possessed some of the mercantile virtues. He had to know market conditions, which meant, of course, world conditions. The energetically run plantation in that cityless South had been a city in itself. So long as the ruling planter lived along the Atlantic seaboard rivers, bringing English ships with London commodities to his private docks, he had both the flexibility of the merchant and the stability of the farmer. The sea which carried away tobacco brought back books and ideas, and along with them, "a decent respect for the opinions of mankind."

By 1820, however, the slave states had seven cities, each with more than eight thousand inhabitants. They had all grown quickly; nearly half had been founded recently and for some specific purpose. Baltimore, with over sixty-two thousand people, was third in the nation, half the size of New York City. Founded by the Maryland legislature as an export center in 1729, as late as mid-18th century it had been hardly more than a village. Richmond, with over twelve thousand, had become the new capital of Virginia only in 1779; it did not have five thousand inhabitants until after 1800. Norfolk, Virginia's new seaport, was still a small settlement when it was burned by patriots to prevent its capture during the Revolution; though not incorporated as a town until 1805, it already had over eight thousand by 1820. Alexandria, which also then counted over eight thousand, had been founded only in 1749 and incorporated in 1779. Washington—with over thirteen thousand in 1820—was not the working federal capital until 1800 and had been burned in large part by British troops during the War of 1812.

Not a single large center in the South traced its history back to the mid-17th century. With the exception of Charleston and New Orleans, none of its cities had a flavor of antiquity. The South had no Boston, Philadelphia, New Haven, Newport, Providence, or New York, where urbanity, trade, and commerce had widened the vision of old families.

Measured only by speed of growth these were, of course, upstart cities. But their influence in Southern life was very different from that of their Western counterparts, which had grown *before* the surrounding country-side was thickly settled. In the West, as Josiah Strong observed in 1885, "the order is reversed—first the railroad, then the town, then the farms. Settlement is, consequently, much more rapid, and the city stamps the country, instead of the country's stamping the city. It is the cities and towns which will frame state constitutions, make laws, create public opinion, establish social usages, and fix standards of morals in the West." In the South, by contrast, cities appeared only after the countryside had fixed the region's character. The belated rise of Southern cities, then, meant not only that the urban influence was delayed. From peculiarly Southern circumstances the presence of the city had unique effects: it actually tended to make Southern leadership as a whole less cosmopolitan, more rural, and more withdrawn.

While commerce went to town, leadership stayed in the country. The commercial, mercantile, and world-looking activities of the large planters were transferred to the new urban centers, but the spirit of the Southern leader remained in his house on the plantation. When he left the State or National capital, he returned to the countryside, to his Mount Vernon, Monticello, Montpelier, Ash Lawn, or Fort Hill.

To understand how all this came about in the half-century after the Revolution, we must observe the effect of Independence and of the South's new crop on her way of living and of doing business. In colonial days, the tobacco planter had consigned his crop to a London "factor." The factor was a commission merchant or agent who sold the colonial client's crop, credited his account with cash received, and made purchases for him—anything from a set of Blackstone's *Commentaries* to a lady's bonnet, an elegant carriage, a case of wine, or a dozen pairs of shoes for slaves. He arranged the English education of a son or a daughter, furnished news, advised on the quality of books, clothing, and politicians. He even, on occasion, tried to help a lonesome bachelor-planter who offered to marry "on fifteen days sight," if the factor would ship with his other supplies, a young woman "of an honest family between twenty and twenty-five years of age; of a middle stature and well-proportioned, her face agreeable, her temper mild, her character blameless, her health good, and her constitution strong enough to bear the change of climate."

The London factors were the Englishmen to whom Virginia planters became most deeply indebted, but they were so far away that they could not possibly relieve the planter of his mercantile responsibilities on this side of the water. The Revolution, which finally cut the Virginia planter's ties to his London factor, helped create a new Southern institution: the American factor, who was destined to a profound influence on all Southern life and leadership. From an American headquarters—in Baltimore, Norfolk, Alexandria, or Richmond—the American factors did what their English predecessors had long been doing across the ocean. The American factor, near at hand and familiar with the local situation, was in a position to do even more for his client. It no longer required three months for reply to a letter. There could be conferences over a plantation dinner-table or in a Norfolk or Charleston tavern. As the factors prospered they hastened the growth of Southern cities. As the cities grew they drew to them, and to the factors themselves, more of the non-farming activities formerly in the hands of the colonial planters.

At first the factor had dealt in tobacco, the crop of the border-South of Virginia, Maryland, and Kentucky. His power increased when cotton became the great staple, as it was elsewhere in the South by about 1820. Other Southern staples—rice and sugar-cane—also came to be controlled by him. It was in cotton, which grew over a much wider area than any other Southern staple, that the factorage system was most highly developed. One of the least perishable of agricultural commodities, cotton was peculiarly well-suited to capitalistic enterprise and market speculation in an age of slow transportation, meager warehousing, rough handling, and long delays.

As King Cotton rose to power, the cotton factor became the power behind the throne. He decided where, to whom, and at what price the crop should be sold. He had much to say about what the planters bought with their money, where they bought, and at what prices. He had far greater power than had his English predecessor to insulate his client from the complicated urban world. He had the power not only to deal for the planter, but to prevent the planter from dealing for himself.

The customs of the factorage system were very simple and, despite local variants, surprisingly uniform. The factor ordinarily received a planter's whole crop. Unlike the broker, who dealt in the name of his employer, the factor acted in his own name. The goods, until sold, remained legally at the risk of the planter, but the factor was free to deal at his own discretion. A dissatisfied planter had no redress unless he could prove (as he almost never could) that the factor had been guilty of fraud or gross negligence. The factor's fee was generally two and one-half per cent of the price received for cotton sold and two and one-half per cent of the purchase price of goods bought—in addition to interest on money lent or credit advanced, and countless other such items as insurance, drayage, weighing, sampling, and storage.

Obviously the planter could have saved commissions if he himself had consigned his crop directly to New York or Liverpool, but he seldom dared do this. In 1835, an English merchant estimated that only a quarter of the cotton arriving in Liverpool was sent by planters on their own account, and this proportion probably decreased with the years. The factor, by offering many services not legally required, became ambassador plenipotentiary from the planter's cozy island to the world outside. Each year it became harder for the planter to escape: he might choose among factors, but the choice made little difference. From lack of inclination, lack of knowledge, lack of connections, and lack of time, he remained tied to the factorage system.

Even if the planter did not live far inland or over the mountains in the newer cotton country, he still could not follow those changing day-to-day conditions that made the price of cotton vary. In 1825, for example, the price in New York for top-grade upland cotton varied from fifteen cents a pound to thirty cents a pound; in 1840, from nine cents a pound to thirteen and one-half cents a pound. "We wrote you lately," a New Orleans factor informed his client in December 1844, "on the Subject of the Cotton market, and advising of the reception of 101 Bales of your Crop, which, believing there would occur no important improvement in prices during the season, we were in the act of preparing for sale this morning at the moment of the reception of the most disastrous news for the Cotton market we have yet received . . . . a heavy decline in Liverpool, holders pressing Sales, and manufacturers buying on their own terms. . . . What will be the effect upon our market after the excitement Subsides, we Cannot pretend to say. For the present we will offer none for sale." It was the factor's business to foresee the effects of international tensions, of weather conditions—even of sudden spring thaws or torrential rains which might make neighboring small rivers navigable and so glut the market.

The factor became the planter's confidant, acquainted with his tastes in food, clothing, and furnishings as well as with his business needs. He was invited to his client's plantation for the holidays; he entertained the planter in town. He might advance large sums on a casual request in a planter's letter or on the planter's word alone. This relationship, like so many others in the South, came to be governed by a code of honor, all the more rigid because not written down.

This informality and the factor's readiness to advance money on unreaped (or even unplanted) crops encouraged extravagance, or at least irresponsibility. A planter whose accounts were being kept for him by someone in town was never sure where he stood; he was always living off future prospects and found it hard to be prudent. "A disposition to contract debts is one of the vices of the Carolinians," wrote Dr. David Ramsay in his *History of South Carolina* in 1809. "When crops are anticipated by engagements founded on them before they are made, ruin is often the consequence, and much oftener since the Revolution than before." Foreign travelers, whose visits took them mostly to cities, obtained a biased view of the Southern character from disgruntled factors, who complained that the planters took advances only to be "squandered away in the luxuries of fashion, good eating and drinking, or an excursion to the northern states, where, after dashing about for a month or two with tandems, curricles, livery servants, and outriders, they frequently returned home in the stage coach, with scarcely dollars enough in their pocket to pay their expenses on the road."

Factors fed the mania for cotton, and lived off that mania. Every factor aimed to control more and more cotton. Every planter aimed to produce more cotton so that he might free himself from debt to the factor in some year which miraculously combined bumper yields and high cotton prices. To this end the planter wanted more land and more slaves. But his neighbors all had the same idea. As he produced more cotton, so did they; and the increase in the cotton crop helped keep down the price of cotton.

Still the cotton mania went on. "To sell cotton in order to buy negroes —to make more cotton to buy more negroes, 'ad infinitum,' is the aim and direct tendency of all the operations of the thorough-going planter," a Yankee traveler observed in 1835: "his whole soul is wrapped up in the pursuit. . . . Without planters there could be no cotton; without cotton no wealth. Without them Mississippi would be a wilderness, and revert to the aboriginal possessors. Annihilate them tomorrow, and this state and every southern state might be bought for a song."

Capitalism, then, grew in the South, but the capitalistic spirit did not. A rigid system confined the pursuers of profit in a prison of custom. The factors, the Southern merchants par excellence, never became Merchant Princes. They seem to have been a conservative lot, fearful lest any change might reduce their commissions. The planters were entangled in a net which kept them from any new opportunity, while it sapped their will to try new things. For the planter himself, this way of business spelled the decline of enterprise and versatility. For the Southern community as a whole, a distinctive and catastrophic effect was the separation of wealth from prestige. The factors, who dominated the commerce of the South, did not dominate politics or culture. It is hard to find a single Southern statesman in these years who had been a factor. Money accumulated in the cities, but political power and the voice of the South remained down on the plantation.

A new and unprecedented kind of uncommercial spirit grew in the rural South. It was one thing for an ancient European society, with a feudal past and a long tradition of subsistence agriculture, to look down its nose at tradesmen, merchants, and bankers. It was quite another for a society supported by large-scale capitalistic agriculture. The South denied itself when it proclaimed that Cotton was King and yet condescended toward those who dealt in cotton. The same blurring of the facts of life appeared in the Southern attitude toward the slave-trader, on whom, too, the Cotton South became increasingly reliant.

While New England and New York extolled commerce, built new merchants' exchanges as "temples of public welfare," and honored merchants as their leaders, Southern heroes were the figments of Sir Walter Scott or the caricatures of rural gentility found in the novels of John Pendleton Kennedy and Nathaniel Beverley Tucker. This was the heroic age of American commerce and industry—and the newly creative age of American communities. New Englanders knew it. They did not begrudge honor to men of wealth nor did they need to extol imaginary heroes. The South, however, wrote disparagingly of the wealthy and had few merchant-adventurers to write about at all.

* * *

The South's reliance on staple crops, which reached back to the colonial era, made belief in a static South plausible. For tobacco, rice, sugar, and cotton meant the dominance of routine. Techniques of Southern agriculture changed slowly, or not at all. So elementary a machine as the plow was adopted only gradually and only in scattered places; as late as 1856, many small farmers in South Carolina were still using the crude colonial hoe. There was little change in the cotton gin, gin house, or baling screw between 1820 and the Civil War. Slave laborers were proverbially inflexible, uninterested in new ways of doing old jobs.

An outward sign of changelessness was the South's everlasting *quiet*. When a Northerner, accustomed to city bustle, traveled through the peaceful countryside, he was tempted to think nothing was happening. Southerners warned him he was wrong. What had always been happening in the South, they now said, was not raucous change but quiet organic growth; in the soil God worked without clatter. Southern cities, also fearing fire, smoke, and noise, passed ordinances prohibiting the use of steam power. "Why are our mechanics forbid to use it in this city?" William Gregg asked in Charleston in 1844. "This power is withheld lest the smoke of an engine should disturb the delicate nerves of an agriculturist; or the noise of the mechanic's hammer should break in upon the slumber of a real estate holder, or importing merchant, while he is indulging in fanciful dreams. . . ."

The South was equally unfriendly to legal novelties. At this time New Englanders like Judge Lemuel Shaw were adapting the common law to the new needs of railroads and of laborers newly organizing for collective bargaining in cities. They were ingeniously elaborating the corporation to serve new purposes: to gather pennies from small investors, to encourage the boldness of large investors, to create legal hybrids for any enterprise. This was the age of General Incorporation Laws, which freed business-men from the need for special legislation every time they wanted to set up a company with limited liability, and provided simple procedures for creating new business entities. But Southern states generally were as slow to innovate for this as for any other purpose.

The joint-stock company—common in New England, New York, and the middle states, and used to some extent in the border states of Mary-land and Virginia—was rare in the deeper South. This device, by which Northerners collected resources from the whole community to build large factories, did not appeal to the Southern mind nor fit Southern ways of doing business. Business corporations, the creatures of lawyers, were born of small print. For Southern gentlemen debts were extremely personal. Washington, Jefferson, and countless others had strained to meet obliga-tions assumed in a chivalrous or thoughtless moment when they had countersigned a note for a friend. Any gentleman would willingly face ruin to meet his "debts of honor." How could he hide behind statute books to limit his liability for "just" debts?

About three-fourths of the manufacturing of the whole United States was carried on by joint-stock companies. But not so in the South. "If we shut the door against associated capital and place reliance upon individ-ual exertion," warned William Gregg, the pioneer of Southern cotton manufacturing, "we may talk over the matter for fifty years to come, without effecting the change in our industrial pursuits, necessary to reno-vate the fortunes of our State." Gregg circulated an eloquent pamphlet in 1845 to the South Carolina and Georgia legislatures, and after a strenuous personal campaign, he secured, by the majority of a single vote, a South Carolina act of incorporation for his cotton mill. But he failed in Georgia. And throughout the South (except in the border states of Virginia and Maryland, and in Louisiana, where the French left legal peculiarities) legislatures refused to pass General Incorporation Laws. Not until after the Civil War was the corporation a common form for Southern business.

Efforts to diversify the Southern economy were few and ineffective. In the pre-Civil War South two strong leaders struggled vainly against the myth of a changeless, homogeneous South. The first was J. D. B. DeBow, whose mother was born on the island of St. Helena and whose father came from New Jersey; though himself born in Charleston, he had vio-lated the Southern gentlemanly ideal by being a self-made man. At the Memphis Commercial Convention in 1845, and in *DeBow's Review,* as well as in his most ambitious work, *The Industrial Resources, etc., of the Southern and Western States* (1853), which sold six times as many copies in the North as in the South, he urged commerce and manufactures on the South. Yet, while DeBow favored protective tariffs, internal improvements, and government-supported railroads to help infant Southern industries, he saw these policies only within a South permanently resting on its "peculiar institution" and its staple agriculture. Even DeBow's *Industrial Resources,* which purported to lay out the South's variety, was full of crude generalization. "In the South the ports are good and safe. . . ." "At the South, children are never put out to nurse, but are brought up from their birth under the careful and jealous eye of the mother." On nearly every page we see *"the* southern planter"—his "easy grace, frank hospitality, warmth and fervor"—and *"the* slave"—his docility and personal devotion. On the first page of *DeBow's Review,* alongside the motto "Commerce is King" stood the words "Cotton is King." DeBow finally became a violent partisan of Calhoun.

William Gregg, who used dollars, as DeBow had used words, to argue for Southern diversity, was also a self-made man. After an early retirement, in 1844 he visited Northern textile mills and on his return the next year published a series of *Essays on Domestic Industry* urging the South to mill for itself. His own plant at Graniteville, South Carolina, prospered into the mid-20th century. But he too turned his sensible arguments for a diversified South into weapons of Southern chauvinism: at every point he took pains to show the special advantages of slave labor even for the cotton factory. He warned of Southern weakness against an industrialized North, and just before secession, in *DeBow's Review,* he pled with the South to prepare for defense by establishing its own manufactures. During the Civil War, his heroic efforts kept a cotton factory going to provide uniforms for Confederate soldiers.

But the champions of Southern diversity were few. They had little influence; their voices were barely heard among the cotton rows. The South's illusion of homogeneity was confirmed by the stability of her population and by her freedom from mass immigration from Europe, which incidentally made her seem more European. In few other parts of the country were leading citizens so ancestor-conscious, so interested in genealogy. Nowhere were they more concerned about quality of descent and "purity" of race.

In 1860, in the nation of thirty-one and one-half million, over a third of the total population was in the South. But, of the four million white foreign-born in the nation as a whole, over eighty-five per cent lived north of the Mason-Dixon Line. The few recent white immigrants in the South were concentrated in cities of the fringe states of Maryland, Missouri, and Louisiana; and in Texas where there had been some German immigration. Refugees from serfdom did not want to compete with slaves. Some immigrants were morally repelled by slavery. Except from Le Havre, passage was far easier to Northern ports. It is no wonder that the South had few voluntary newcomers. Good cheap farm land, free employment, and the opportunity to rise in the world were all scarcer in the South than in the expanding North and West.

Not many Southerners were sorry their region did not attract more white immigrants. In fact, they were generally inclined to lament the trickle that did come their way. Why should they welcome boatloads of intractable Irish, independent-minded Germans, or unassimilable Jews? The white workers who might have migrated southward, an editor in the 1850's warned, "are a curse instead of a blessing; they are generally a worthless, unprincipled class—enemies to our peculiar institutions." "The immigrants do not, like our ancestors, fly from religious and political persecution," the Richmond *Examiner* complained; "they come merely as animals in search of a richer and fresher pasture. . . . They will settle in large masses, and, for ages to come, will practise and inculcate a pure (or rather impure) materialism." In proposing his plan for Southern manufactures, Gregg had carefully explained that the best laborers would be the slaves and the unemployed whites already found in the South. Many Southern spokesmen traced national political ills (and the declining influence of the South) to the European immigrant influx, among other unwelcome changes.

23

Indelible Immigrants

IF THE LEADERS of commerce and culture in the South were becoming more and more different from the versatile merchants and manufacturers of New England and from the businessmen of the upstart cities, other Southern institutions too showed sharpening contrasts. Boosters used every form of persuasion and misrepresentation to attract newcomers. Out West a new city could not prosper unless it drew, from far and near, people so impressed by the chances of success that they willingly suffered hardships, even risking life itself, for the opportunity to start life anew. Once newcomers had arrived in Chicago, Cincinnati, Omaha, or Denver, the community became strong and stable by assimilating them into the community. New ways of providing quick housing, like the balloon-frame house, and the "palaces of the public" where today's arrivals mingled freely with old timers, together with other devices such as short residence requirements for voting, helped erase distinctions. Community-builders like Ogden and Drake and Larimer, and thousands of others, puzzled over how to make newcomers at home quickly so they would want to stay.

In the Southern states, however, slavery—the South's "Peculiar Institution"—fostered quite another attitude toward newcomers. While Boosters worried over how to attract and assimilate, in the half-century before the Civil War, Southerners were more and more concerned with how to extrude and separate.

Southerners who attacked immigration in the North somehow chose not to see Negroes as "immigrants." Increasingly after the 1830's Southern defenders of slavery insisted that their Negro slave population actually explained the South's soundness and homogeneity and stability. From a 20th-century perspective, this way of thinking seems odd, for although Negroes, with negligible exceptions, had not come here willingly, they had other indices of immigrants in extreme form: they came from a great distance and from an alien culture. But even after immigration figures began to be officially noted, around 1820, and the white newcomers were distinguished by place of origin, Negroes imported from the West Indies and Africa were not recorded, because the foreign slave trade was illegal. After 1850, when the federal census began to distinguish the "native" from the "foreign born" in the white population, all Negroes were still lumped together; regardless of nativity, they were statistically separated only into slave or free.

Statistics, then, which in the early 19th century became more and more precise and more public about white immigration, still concealed the facts about the Negro. American historians, adopting this Southern point of view, have never quite become accustomed to think of the Negro as an immigrant. Even the pioneer works of the leading historian of American immigration, Marcus Lee Hansen—*The Atlantic Migration, 1607–1860: A History of the Continuing Settlement of the United States* (1940) and *The Immigrant in American History* (1940)—virtually omit the Negro from that story.

Southerners did not count the Negro an immigrant primarily because they did not consider him a candidate for assimilation into their community. Only the free Negroes, whom they increasingly thought of as a dangerous element, were looked upon somewhat as immigrants were viewed elsewhere. Yet a third of the Southern population consisted of Negroes, many of whom had arrived within recent decades and whose number was augmented every year by current imports. In fact, of course, the South as a whole had a larger proportion of unassimilated arrivals from abroad than would trouble even New York or Boston until after the great influx of Irish refugees in the late 1840's and '50's. The South was a land of invisible immigrants, or rather, immigrants who had come to seem invisible precisely because Southern institutions had made their immigrant status indelible.

After the 1830's, Southerners themselves explained the South's division into two communities as the inevitable result of the distinction of race; to confuse that distinction, was, they said, "to find fault with God." In retrospect, however, the history of Negro slavery in the southern United States does not confirm their belief. Decades passed after his first arrival in the American colonies before the Negro acquired the status of a slave. A survey of the conditions of all laborers in 17th-century America shows, as Oscar and Mary F. Handlin have demonstrated, "that slavery was not there from the start, that it was not simply imitated from elsewhere, and that it was not a response to any unique qualities in the Negro himself. It emerged rather from the adjustment to American conditions of traditional European institutions."

During most of the 17th century the Virginia Negroes who were described as not "free" were not necessarily slaves. The opposite of "free" in those days was not "slave" but "unfree," and there were many gradations of unfreedom: villeinage, the involuntary servitude of delinquent debtors, the forced servitude on "publick works" of convicted vagrants and vagabonds, the labor of orphans and bastards compelled to earn their food and lodging, and the servitude for a term of years voluntarily undertaken by an indenture. In the first decades in Virginia, most of the population was thus in some sense unfree, for it owed some form of servile obligation; until about 1675, the status of the Negro was not peculiar. He shared his servile condition with many European immigrants; he became free at the end of his term of service; he sometimes became a landowner, an artisan, or a master of other unfree men. Negroes were still simply servants who happened to have come from Africa instead of England, Ireland, or Scotland. "Slave" was a loose word of contempt ("O what a rogue and peasant slave am I!" Hamlet, Act II, Scene 2) and not a term of legal jargon; the status of "slave" actually did not exist in English law.

Before the end of the 17th century, however, "slave" had begun to acquire a new and technical legal meaning in British North America, and the status had begun to be fixed on the Negro. Yet the form which the institution of slavery assumed was not an importation from the Portuguese or the Spanish, who had long known slavery through the Roman law. If details of the transformation are unclear, the result was plain enough. Until the 1660's, as the Handlins point out, there was actually no noticeable trend in British colonial legislation about the Negro. But for the English and other Christian immigrants whom Virginia and Maryland were then eager to attract as laborers, the colonies changed laws and shortened periods of servitude, thus brightening the prospects for an indentured servant to become free from renewal of his term of service. Southern colonials expected word of these reforms to get around among prospective immigrants in the British Isles and so speed "the peopling of the country." But the African, an involuntary immigrant, had not in the first place been attracted by the terms of service or the opportunity for a new life; therefore nothing was to be lost by worsening his status, while something was gained by extending the period of his forced service.

As the demand for labor increased and the cost of labor rose, Negroes were gradually reduced to chattel slavery; neither they nor their compatriots were in a position to protest. Maryland passed a law declaring that "All Negroes and other slaves shall serve Durante Vita." In 1670 Virginia enacted that "all servants not being christians" brought in by sea, were to be slaves for life, and at about the same time provided that conversion to Christianity would not emancipate a slave. At the beginning of the 18th century the African slave trade became more active: by 1708, Virginia had a Negro population of twelve thousand, one-quarter of whom had been imported within the preceding three years; the Negro population was nearly doubled within another seven years. The increase in the numbers of these strange and unwilling immigrants, who worked at forced labor, provided another reason to tighten legal control over them. A ban on miscegenation was introduced, largely to protect the owner's right to the labor of his slave and his slave's offspring; it was apparently not rooted in a notion of racial purity, because intermarriage with the Indians was not punished. By 1705, Virginia's Black Code, which legislated specially for the African immigrants, made their slave status indelible.

Even after the early 18th century, however, when the Negro in the southern British colonies had universally acquired the status of slave, it was by no means certain that he would be condemned to remain a permanently unassimilated immigrant in the New World. Thoughtful Southerners were full of doubts. Thomas Jefferson, in a familiar passage in his *Notes on Virginia* (1784), while wondering about the natural intellectual capacities of the Negro, lamented the effects of slavery on the white masters, and expressed his conviction that the institution could not be permanent. Since the assimilation of the Negro immigrants into the white population of Virginia was unthinkable, according to Jefferson, the happiest solution would be their colonization, conceivably on islands of the West Indies, or preferably in Africa—"drawing off this part of our population, most advantageously for themselves as well as for us." In 1835, when Harriet Martineau, the English traveler, made her pilgrimage to ex-president James Madison at Montpelier, his country seat, Madison, who was national president of the American Colonization Society, spoke animatedly of the evils of slavery, and of his hopes to relieve them by exporting Negroes.

Southerners were thus slow to accept Negro slavery as a permanent fixture of their society. And they were slow to abandon hope that its evils could be removed, if not by the abolition of slavery itself, then at least by removing the Negroes at public expense to some remote place where they could make their own life as free men. The fact of race, however, increasingly haunted Southerners with the suspicion that *these* immigrants were unassimilable.

While the Transients and the Upstarts were opening their minds, their hearts, and their communities to newcomers, and seeking ways of making their communities grow, Southerners were thus troubled by an opposite problem: how to separate themselves from an evil for which they knew themselves somehow responsible, but which would not have existed without the presence of these odd people from Africa. To think of the Negroes as fellow-seekers after the opportunities of the New World, who had an equal claim on its benefits, was precisely what Southerners could not do. In the eyes of Southern white leaders, the Negro remained a permanently alien element.

We can measure the depth and strength of these Southern convictions of the unassimilability of the Negro in the last great Southern effort at abolition. It had a strange beginning, and a still stranger end. The occasion was the bloodiest slave uprising in the history of the South. In Southampton County in southeastern Virginia, early on the morning of August 22, 1831, Nat Turner, aided by seven fellow slaves, killed his master and his master's family, then enlisted other Negroes, and within twenty-four hours some sixty whites had been killed, many of them women and children. Turner's "army," which probably never exceeded seventy men, was growing until it was overwhelmed by four companies of state militia with the aid of federal troops, of miscellaneous local fancy-dress military societies, and of overzealous, hard-drinking irregulars from all over. Several score Negroes, innocent and guilty, were shot down; of those brought to trial, twelve were transported out of the state, and twenty were hanged. Turner himself hid out for two months before he was captured and executed.

The South was terror-struck. "They lie down to sleep with fear," a sympathetic Northerner reported of the Virginians. "They hardly venture out on nights. A lady told me, that for weeks after the tragedy, she had quivered at every blast of wind, and every blow of the shutter. Bolts and bars were tried, but the horrid fear haunted the whole population day and night." The bloody slave insurrections not long before in Martinique, Antigua, Santiago, Carácas, and the Tortugas now seemed ominous. Reports of the great debate in the British Parliament in August, 1830, over abolition of slavery in the colonies were also disturbing.

Closer home there were additional causes for alarm. A supposed slave plot led by Denmark Vesey, a free Negro in Charleston, South Carolina, had been the occasion for executing thirty-seven Negroes there in 1822. In early 1830, copies of the *Appeal . . . to the Colored Citizens of the*

World . . . (Boston, 1829), a plea for a general uprising, by David Walker, a free-born North Carolina Negro, were found in the hands of Negroes in widely separated Southern states. The American Anti-Slavery movement seemed to be gaining momentum in various parts of the country: the peripatetic Quaker, Benjamin Lundy, had begun issuing his *Genius of Universal Emancipation* in 1821; the first issue of William Lloyd Garrison's fiery *Liberator* appeared on January 1, 1831.

In southeastern Virginia, where Nat Turner's insurrection occurred, white residents had their own special reasons to be disturbed. The census of 1830, lately published, showed that there were 81,000 more Negroes than whites in Virginia east of the Blue Ridge Mountains. Tidewater Virginians saw that this was a culminating trend: as recently as 1790, whites had outnumbered Negroes by 25,000; in 1800 the situation was already reversed, and Negroes outnumbered whites by 3000; in 1810 by 48,000; in 1820, by 65,000. Where would it all lead?

But these explanations of the alarm among the white population did not explain Nat Turner himself. While historians disagree on nearly all the facts about Turner's uprising, including the number and motives of Negro participants and the number of white and Negro victims, certain facts are clear from the statement which Turner himself made after his capture, and which appears to have been substantially true.

Most significant was a fact that baffled Southerners at the time: Nat Turner was not the slave of a cruel master. According to Turner's own account, his master had treated him well; his master's son had actually taught him to read. Turner's rebellion, then, was not against particular abuses of the Peculiar Institution (these, Southern defenders of slavery freely admitted) but against the Institution itself; not against a harsh master but against all masters. Turner was a man, as Joseph C. Robert recently puts it, "in whom came to focus the restless passions of a race condemned to enforced servitude."

Also significant was another fact, which Southerners thought evidenced Turner's atypical character—namely, that he was stirred by a religious passion. "He is a complete fanatic, or plays his part admirably," wrote Thomas R. Gray, the lawyer who was assigned to defend him. Later historians, too, have tended to minimize Turner and his uprising by dismissing him as a religious fanatic. He, like Puritan and Quaker fanatics before him, heard voices, saw visions, and looked for signs in the heavens. It was an eclipse of the sun earlier in 1831 that convinced Turner that the time for action was approaching; another solar phenomenon, when the sun turned "a peculiar greenish blue" on August 13, led him to fix the uprising for a week later. Turner, a Baptist preacher whose influence spread to neighboring plantations, had been encouraged by his mother to consider himself divinely inspired to lead his people out of bondage. He found his incentive and his strength in a religious faith. Despite accusations by Southerners and despite boasts by abolitionists themselves, there is no persuasive evidence that Northern abolitionists had any part in inciting him.

In other ways, too, Turner typified the uprooted African immigrant. His mother, a native of Africa, was the slave of Benjamin Turner; Nat, born on the Turner plantation, took the name of his owner. Before he was thirty, he had been the property of four different owners and in addition he had been hired to the master whom he killed at the time of the uprising. His father, whose name has not survived, is known to have run away when Nat was a child. It is not so remarkable, then, that the precocious slave, deprived of all other community, looked "fanatically" to his God for inspiration.

When the Virginia legislature met at Richmond in December, 1831, the bloodshed in Southampton County was less than four months in the past; few doubted that something had to be done to avoid a repetition. The familiar pattern in the South, after a threat, or a rumor of a threat of Negro uprising, was to strengthen measures of control, to restrict the movements of free Negroes, to make emancipation more difficult, and to reinforce the patrols. In this respect the Virginia legislators would run true to form, but that was not all that happened in Richmond that winter. In other respects the two-week debate, beginning on January 11, 1832, was a most unfamiliar performance. It was a novel and historic occasion, not only because it was the first and last time that the pros and cons of slavery were freely debated in a public body in the South, but because it was an allegory of the forces at work on the slavery issue in the nation as a whole. Moreover, it offered a preview of arguments for and against slavery that were to be advanced in the next three decades, and it was a turning point in Southern attitudes to the Peculiar Institution. The fact that the debate took place in Virginia, which had given the new nation four of its first five presidents, and which, together with South Carolina, was setting the style of Southern thought, gave the events added importance.

Even before this meeting of the Virginia Assembly, many proposals had been made to remove from the state the evils of slavery. They varied in detail, but they shared the simple assumption that the only way to rid the country of slavery was to rid it of Negroes. There is no record of a serious proposal among Southern whites at the time for the abolition of slavery without the subsequent removal of the freed Negroes. Disagreement over how to "solve" the race problem centered, then, on the question of how most economically, most rapidly, and most humanely to deport the black population. Those who had been brought here against their will surely would not have to be consulted before they were sent away.

In the first place, there was a general agreement (reinforced by deepening concern over how to control the increasing population of slaves and free Negroes in the South's growing cities) that all *free* Negroes should go. A considerable number of Southerners saw this as only a first step toward the desirable end of deporting all Negroes. A more moderate suggestion, proposed as insurance against insurrection, was to send away every year enough Negroes to reverse the population ratio of the races. Someone estimated that this could be accomplished by exporting, at government expense, about two thousand Negroes per year. The American Colonization Society, headed by ex-president James Madison, hoped that the Virginia legislature would seize the occasion to begin to extinguish all slavery, by colonization; Chief Justice John Marshall, president of the Society's Virginia branch, thought recent events ought to persuade Southern state legislatures to offer legal and financial inducements for all free Negroes to emigrate. The American Colonization Society chartered a ship on which it sent to Africa some two hundred Southampton Negroes, who had, however, first been given the additional inducement of a series of nocturnal whippings.

The most important local advocate of abolition was Governor John Floyd of Virginia, himself the owner of a dozen slaves; after serving twelve years in Congress, he had lately been elected by the legislature as the candidate of the state-rights partisans. "Before I leave this Government," Floyd wrote in his diary in November, 1831, "I will have contrived to have a law passed gradually abolishing slavery in this State, or at all events to begin the work by prohibiting slavery on the West side of the Blue Ridge Mts." To Governor Hamilton of South Carolina, Floyd explained his scheme: tighter control of all Negroes; expulsion of free Negroes; gradual purchase and the eventual export from Virginia of the whole Negro population.

The division of opinion in the December legislature re-enacted the East-West conflict already familiar in Virginia history; it was a microcosm of the larger conflict within the nation. The opponents of slavery came generally from west of the Blue Ridge Mountains where there were few Negroes, while the defenders came from the eastern slopes and the tidewater, the regions of large slaveowners with a great investment in Negro property. But there were some exceptions, like Thomas Jefferson Randolph (Jefferson's grandson), Thomas Marshall (son of the Chief Justice), and two leading Richmond editors, Thomas Ritchie and John Hampden Pleasants, who joined the antislavery forces.

On the central question of whether to abolish slavery, a tally of the votes of the 134 members shows a fairly even division of opinion: about sixty favored some immediate plan of abolition; about sixty (including some who agreed that slavery might be an evil, but insisted that the obstacles to its removal were insuperable) opposed any such move; and about a dozen, who held the balance of power, professed to favor eventual emancipation and wanted an immediate antislavery declaration, but were compromisers, preferring to postpone a decision rather than sharpen the issue. In the result, supporters of the status quo won, because they readily agreed on what they favored, while the antislavery people could not combine on any one program of abolition.

Before the legislative session ended, delegates had tried nearly every argument for or against slavery—in a public and widely reported debate which for good sense, eloquence, passion, and forensic freedom had seldom been equalled in America. The early meetings inspired high hopes. "It is probable, from what we hear," said an editorial in the Richmond *Enquirer* on January 7, "that the Committee on the coloured population will report some plan for getting rid of the free people of colour—But is this all that can be done? Are we forever to suffer the greatest evil, which can scourge our land, not only to remain, but to increase in its dimensions? . . . our wisest men cannot give too much of their attention to this subject—nor can they give it too soon." Some Virginians were dismayed to hear fellow Southerners lay bare, or even flaunt, the weaknesses of their society. The final vote, on January 25, defeated the motion that it was expedient to enact legislation at the present session to abolish slavery, by seventy-three to fifty-eight. And the meaning of it all was summarized a few days later by the editor of the Richmond *Constitutional Whig:*

> The enquiry and discussion then, have terminated in the following specific and implied declarations on the part of the House of Delegates: (1) That it is not expedient at this session, to legislate on abolition. (2) That the coloured population of Virginia, is a great evil. (3) That humanity and policy in the *first place,* demand the removal of the free, and those who will become free (looking to an extensive voluntary manumission). (4) That this will absorb our present means. (5) (Undeniable implication) That when public opinion is more developed; when the people have spoken more explicitly, and the *means* are better devised, that it is expedient to commence a system of abolition. The House of Delegates have gone this far, and in our opinion, it had no right to go farther.

However meager in outward effects, the debate of 1831–32 profoundly moved thought and feeling. Immediately it produced a wave of self-congratulatory optimism among those who did not see beneath the surface, or who overlooked the effects of the debate itself. Northerners, viewing Virginia as the traditional leader of Southern opinion, expected other Southern states to follow; one Yankee called the debate the most glorious act in Virginia history since the Declaration of Independence. Some Northerners used the Virginians' catalogue of the doleful effects of slavery to disprove the contentions of Southerners like Senator Robert Y. Hayne of South Carolina that the real cause of Southern distress was the protective tariff. Maryland newspapers contrasted Virginia's debate which, besides words, had produced nothing but more police regulations, with the Maryland legislature's substantial appropriation for African colonization.

The main effect of the debate, in Virginia and elsewhere in the South, was to put the proponents of slavery publicly on the defensive, to give them an occasion to speak out, and so to give new vigor to the Southern defense of slavery. In the spring legislative elections in 1832, several delegates from eastern Virginia who had spoken against slavery were defeated. Able Southern writers, no longer satisfied merely with refuting attacks on the Peculiar Institution, or merely with proving that slavery was not as inhumane as generally supposed, or that it actually had some civilizing effect on its victims, now mounted a counterattack. Their new strategy, devised partly from ancient and partly from modern notions, was to argue that slavery was a positive good. Earlier, during the Congressional debates on the Missouri Compromise in 1820, some Southerners had already defended their Institution for its peculiar virtues; and in the 1820's a supporting literature had begun to develop, including such works as Dr. Thomas Cooper's proof that the Bible did not forbid slavery and that the institution had, in one form or another, actually existed everywhere. But the bible of Virginia proslavery during the next crucial decades was to be Thomas R. Dew's *Review of the Debate in the Virginia Legislature of 1831 and 1832* (Richmond, 1832). Dew, a thirty-year-old professor at William & Mary College, within four years after publishing his *Review,* was made president of his college; he then led a phalanx of academic Virginians in defense of the Peculiar Institution.

The gist of the new proslavery orthodoxy was not the defense of slavery in the abstract, or merely as an institution that had survived since Biblical times and therefore could not be erased. The argument was now given a distinctive American twist, which not only distinguished the American proslavery dogma from its foreign predecessors, but set it in even more dramatic contrast to the community attitudes of other parts of the country. Dew put the whole problem of slavery in a peculiarly American, and Southern, context: "Can these two distinct races of people, now living together as master and servant, be ever separated? Can the black be sent back to his African home, or will the day ever arrive when he can be liberated from his thraldom, and mount upwards in the scale of civilization and rights, to an equality with the white?" The stages in his argument were simple. The simplicity again came from the common (and distinctively Southern) premise, which Dew said was laid bare during the Virginia debates: "where the subject of slavery underwent the most thorough discussion, all seemed to be perfectly agreed in the necessity of removal in case of emancipation." Dew thus seemed to withdraw the argument from the vagaries of religion, ethics, and social theory, and to plant it firmly in the world of economics and everyday affairs. He came close to making it a mere question of transportation. It was not surprising, then, that J. D. B. DeBow, one of the most statistically-minded of Southern thinkers, declared that Dew's "able essay on the institution of slavery entitles him to the lasting gratitude of the whole South."

First, Dew examined the various proposals for colonization, and concluded "that we can never expect to send off our black population, by their means." Then he needed only to remind his readers of their axiomatic agreement that "emancipation without deportation" was unthinkable, "that the slaves, in both an economical and moral point of view, are entirely unfit for a state of freedom among whites." His conclusion, then, was inescapable: slavery, whether in itself a good or an evil, was the necessary condition of Negroes in the United States. Of course, he embellished his thesis with scriptural, sociological, and biological arguments that had already been tried and found appealing, and that would become more and more familiar in the next decades. But what was most novel and most persuasive in his argument was its simplicity, its apparent hardheadedness, and its obvious factual basis. No wonder Duff Green, leading Democrat and influential editor of the *United States Telegraph,* hoping to unite Southerners, reprinted Dew's essay in a six-cent edition. John Quincy Adams, leader on the other side, said that Dew had opened a new era in American history.

Adams was correct. By putting the slavery argument in its peculiarly American context, Dew had sharpened the growing conflict between Southern attitudes and those elsewhere in America—those found among New Englanders, among the transients and the upstarts. In a land peopled by immigrants, which throve by planting and promoting new cities, by attracting new settlers, and by assimilating them into new communities, the South's Peculiar Institution stood out in ever starker contrast. The slavery problem was now declared to be an immigration problem; the "solution" on which more and more Southerners would agree was to keep these immigrants in America, but out of the large American community. Though ghettos were generally alien to America, Southerners now not only made their own American kind, but declared it essential to their peace and prosperity. In the longer perspective of American history, it was perhaps less the institution of slavery (which most other European peoples had, in one way or another, experienced and then transcended) than the notion that there could be an indelible immigrant, which plagued the South and the nation. Even after the legal institution of slavery was abolished, Southern belief that there could be indelible immigrants would live on. So long as the idea remained, "emancipation" would be largely ineffective; the premise from which Dew and his followers argued was that emancipation of the Negro was really impossible. "The slave of Italy or France could be emancipated or escape to the city," wrote Dew, "and soon all records of his former state would perish, and he would gradually sink into the mass of freemen around him. But, unfortunately, the emancipated black carries a mark which no time can erase, he forever wears the indelible symbol of his inferior condition; *the Ethiopian cannot change his skin, nor the leopard his spots.*"

24

Invisible Communities: The Negroes' Churches

THE EXPERIENCE which slavery imposed on the Negro immigrant, then, was the very opposite of that of other newcomers to America. The Negro, confined and controlled by his master's laws from the moment of his transportation to America, only gradually and under compulsion discovered where he was and what he was expected to do. He was first ruled by force and, even after he learned the ways and demands of his master, he was taught that he could not share the master's larger enterprises and higher purposes. The American experience of Community before Government: of people sharing interests and purposes before there was an effective force to compel their obedience— that was not for him.

The westward-moving companies and especially the upstart cities were dominated by a competitive and a voluntary spirit. The booster was always pretending he was where he was because he chose to be there; he preferred his community to all others on earth, and persuaded others to join his city and stay with it, not because of any legal or traditional compulsion, but because they too chose its attractive future. None of this entered the world of the slave. Involuntariness was the very essence of his life. A thing under the will of another, the slave (except as a runaway) was never a migrant, but always a movable. Even if he found himself in a new community, as he sometimes did in the southwestern borders, in Alabama, Mississippi, and Louisiana, this was not by his choice, but by the choice of his master.

Nor was this the only way in which the slave was deprived of a sense

of shared purposes, and of identity with his fellows. The manner of the
Negro's enslavement, as E. Franklin Frazier has shown, tended to destroy
his African culture and to denude him of his traditions as he was deposited in the New World. It took time for him to forget his own African
language and to learn the language of his master; African languages
were so numerous and slaves came from so many different language
groups that at first it was difficult for them to communicate even with
their fellow slaves. This, like all questions about the history of the
spoken language, is elusive and speculative. But our few clues suggest a
linguistic complexity which, in addition to everything else, sharpened
the newly arrived African's sense of isolation and loneliness. Gullah, the
dialect of a large number of Negroes of one region of coastal South
Carolina and Georgia, still has words in use which are traceable to
over twenty different West African languages. If the linguistic complica-
tions remain so great in the mid-20th century, what must they have
been before the Civil War, when large numbers of the Negro residents
had been born in Africa, and more were arriving every year? As late as
1858 (a half-century after the African slave trade became illegal), some
420 Negroes were landed in one Georgia seaport, direct from Africa.
What a Babel there must have been! Masters did not condescend to
learn the language of their slaves; and slaves, often unable to use their
mother tongue to communicate with one another, had to learn or invent
a pidgin if they were to communicate at all.

The African immigrant was a man without a family. There is little
evidence of the survival here even of the general African family structures; individual families were recklessly broken by the slave-importers.
At the same time, slavery put obstacles in the way of Negroes building
American families of their own like those of white Southerners. The
most obvious proof of this was the lack of family names among Negroes. Africans were not the only immigrants who had brought no
family names with them to America: in the 17th century, this was true
also of Swedes, Armenians, and Jews; by the 18th century, as the Handlins have observed, family names had been acquired by these other
groups—but not by Negroes.

Among the dehumanizing effects of slavery, none were deeper than
the obstruction and diversion of maternal affection. "Where such limitations were placed upon the mother's spontaneous emotional responses
to the needs of her children and where even her suckling and fondling
of them were restricted," E. Franklin Frazier observes in his classic
Negro Family in the United States (1939), "it was not unnatural that
she often showed little attachment to her offspring." Separations of
children from their mothers became commoner as the domestic slave
trade flourished in the decades immediately before the Civil War. Life
in slave quarters discouraged the sense of a separate family unit. Often

the relation of the foster-mother or "mammy" to her "white children," on whom she was expected to lavish her attention and her affections, diverted her maternal impulses. The idealized Negro mother, as Frazier notes, grew less out of stories of her sacrifice under slavery for her own children, than from the traditions of the Negro "mammy," in whom maternal love was a vicarious sentiment. The primacy of the mother in the Negro family arose out of the grim facts of slavery: the property-interests of her owner in her offspring, and the imposed tenuousness of the husband-wife relationship.

The sense of community that comes from the possession of civic rights —even more so, that based on participation in political groups, such as town meetings—was of course denied to slaves and even to free Negroes. So, too, the slave obviously lacked that feeling of a stake in society which comes from ownership of property, from economic competition, and from shared business enterprises.

The slave, in a word, was a man without a community. Even his relation to the plantation where he labored or to the master whom he often respected could be terminated without his consent; the new location of his labors was assigned to him arbitrarily. One of the many economic arguments for slavery was that the labor force could be moved about at the employer's will. Numerous events beyond the slave's control or knowledge—the bankruptcy of an owner, the liquidation of an estate on probate, the changing price of tobacco, rice, or cotton, or the whim or malice of a white owner—could uproot him from the place of his birth, from family and friends, to another place he had never chosen.

Where was the Negro to find his community? His situation was not entirely unlike that of the Pilgrims two centuries before. He might even have shared William Bradford's explanation of the religious incentive of the earlier immigrants: "Nether could they, as it were, goe up to the tope of Pisgah, to vew from this willdernes a more goodly cuntrie to feed their hops; for which way soever they turnd their eys (save upward to the heavens) they could have litle solace or content in respecte of any outward objects." It was not surprising that the Negro did not allow himself to remain isolated. Nor do we need far-fetched or technical arguments from African survivals to explain why he turned to religion.

A small compensation for the sufferings of slavery was a sharpening of the religious sentiment, which became intensely personal and naive and passionate, uncorrupted by institutions and prudential arrangements. In the Negro, as seldom before or since, the distinction which the Puritans noted between the "visible" and the "invisible" church was erased. The American Negro discovered a new variety of religious experience: he felt with special poignancy the uneasiness and loneliness and inadequacy, from which he could hope to find relief only by looking upward. These gropings survived in his spirituals:

> I've got a mother in de heaven,
>> Outshines de sun,
> I've got a father in de heaven,
>> Outshines de sun,
> I've got a sister in de heaven,
>> Outshines de sun,
> When we get to heaven, we will
>> Outshine de sun,
>> Way beyond de moon.

From these personal needs, and from his lack of other outlets, grew the vital, varied, and encompassing Negro churches.

> I'm gwine to jine de great 'sociation,
> I'm gwine to jine de great 'sociation,
> Den my little soul's gwine to shine.

These churches first arose, and acquired their special character, from the very restrictions of life under slavery. The shifting attitudes of white Southerners toward the Christianizing of the Negroes were compounded of fear and hope, of economic self-interest and missionary and humanitarian zeal. An ancient tradition that Christians could not be held as slaves had deterred the early efforts to convert the Indians and the Negroes, until, before the end of the 17th century, it was established by law that conversion would not liberate a bondsman. During the later colonial period there were sporadic efforts at converting Negroes, mostly under the auspices of missionary groups with their headquarters in London: by ministers of the Anglican Church, by emissaries of the Society for the Propagation of the Gospel in Foreign Parts, or by zealous individual Baptist and Methodist missionaries. Even after the revivalist efforts of the second "Great Awakening," relatively few Negroes had become members of formal Christian churches. When the Negro population, in places like eastern Virginia, began to outnumber the whites, the dominant question among whites was the effect of Christian religious activity on the servility of the Negro population. Did Christianity, by assuring Negroes that God had sanctioned slavery and would give them their reward hereafter, better prepare them to accept their lowly status? Or did it, on the contrary, stir them to dangerous notions of equality, and by encouraging them to meet together, provide a forum for agitators? Different denominations held different attitudes; every denomination changed its attitude from time to time; local events, rumors and fears of Negro unrest, affected them all. But the simple issue, which pervaded Southern white religious thinking from the early 19th century, was the effect of Christianity on slavery: on the mitigation of its evils, the increase of its goods, and the encouragement of Negro acquiescence.

The whole history of Christianity showed that it was a religion both of humility and of boldness, of the martyr and of the crusader, both of St. Francis and of St. Louis. In the Gospel, too, the Negro might find at one and the same time a salve for his wounds, a reason for his humility, a justification for his equality, and an incentive for his rebellion. But leading Southern churchmen had no difficulty making Christianity seem mainly a prop of slavery: they idealized Biblical slavery as a form of the Patriarchal family, and appointed themselves to teach the "Fathers" (i.e. the masters) the duties to their "Children" (i.e. the slaves) and the Children their duties to their Fathers. "Each planter in fact is a Patriarch," ran the argument, "—his position compels him to be a ruler in his household. . . . Society assumes the Hebrew form. . . . The fifth commandment becomes the foundation of Society. The state is looked to only as the ultimate head in external relations while all internal duties, such as support, education, and the relative duties of individuals, are left to domestic regulation."

By the 1820's Southern white clergymen were energetically discharging their responsibility to expound the Patriarchal system. "If, in addition to all other considerations, the translation from their country to this has been the means of their mental and religious improvement, and so of obtaining salvation, as many of themselves have joyfully and thankfully confessed," Dr. Richard Furman, president of the South Carolina Baptist State Convention, explained soon after the Denmark Vesey Plot, "—then may the just and humane master who rules his slaves and provides for them, according to Christian principles, rest satisfied, that he is not in holding them, chargeable with moral evil, nor acting in this respect, contrary to the genius of Christianity." But fear of Negro uprisings again and again led to restrictions on Negro religious activity, for Denmark Vesey had been an active Methodist, and "General" Nat Turner had been a preacher. When Governer Floyd opened the historic session of the Virginia legislature in December, 1831, he denounced Negro preachers as "channels through which the inflammatory papers and pamphlets brought here by the agents and emissaries from other states have been circulated among our slaves" and therefore demanded that the Negro preachers be outlawed.

With the growth of Northern abolitionism and the use of religious missionaries to spread their ideas among the Negroes, Southerners found a new reason to indoctrinate the slaves with their own brand of Christianity. The Rev. Charles Colcock Jones recalled, in his handbook for masters, *The Religious Instruction of Negroes* (Savannah, Georgia, 1842), that the years since 1820 had seen "the revival of religion in respect to this particular duty, throughout the Southern States." And he took pains to show that the master would not have to await the after-life for benefits from inducting his slaves into Christianity:

The pecuniary interests of masters will be advanced as a necessary consequence.

I do not mean that the introduction of the Gospel upon a plantation in and of itself puts new life and vigor into the laborers and the soil which they cultivate, and necessarily makes them more profitable to owners, than plantations where the Gospel is not introduced at all. By no means. Such a statement would be unfounded in fact. For there are owners who take no pains whatever to have their Negroes instructed; but who feed and clothe and lodge them well, and are humane and take the best care of them, and by careful, skilful and pushing management, go far beyond their religious neighbors in their incomes. But I mean, that religious instruction is no detriment, but rather a benefit: that, other things being equal, the plantation which enjoys religious instruction will do better for the interests of its owner, than it did before it enjoyed such instruction. Virtue is more profitable than vice; while this is allowed to be no discovery, no man will question its truth. . . .

The religious instruction of the Negroes *will contribute to safety.* . . . although, as a slave-holding country, we are so situated, that, so far as man can see, the hope of success on the part of our laboring class, in any attempt at revolution is forlorn, yet no enemy (if there be an enemy) should be despised, however weak, and no danger unprovided for, however apparently remote. . . .

I am a firm believer in the efficacy of *sound religious instruction,* as a means to the end desired. And reasons may be given for that belief. They are to be discovered in the *very nature and tendency of the Gospel.* Its *nature is peace,* in the broadest and fullest extent of the word. Its *tendency,* even when its transforming influence upon character is *not* realized, is to soften down and curb the passions of man; to make him more respectful of another's interests, and more solicitous of his favor; more obedient under authority, and patient under injuries; and to enhance infinitely in his estimation the value of human life. . . . The servant recognizes a superintending Providence, who disposes of men and things according to his pleasure. . . . To God, therefore, he commits the ordering of his lot, and in his station renders to all their dues, obedience to whom obedience, and honor to whom honor. He dares not wrest from the hand of God his own care and protection.

To further this good work, and also to reply to Northern accusations of Southern neglect of Negro souls, a great interdenominational meeting "On the Religious Instruction of the Negroes" was held in Charleston in May, 1845. It was an influential group representing the Episcopal, the Methodist, the Baptist, and the Presbyterian Churches, and including not only churchmen like the Rev. C. C. Jones and the Rev. William Capers, who was to be a founder of the Methodist Church South, but laymen like Senator Daniel Huger of South Carolina, and Robert Barnwell Rhett, who was to be Calhoun's successor in the Senate. The meeting, having collected reports from all over the South, confirmed the happy effect of religion on the discipline of the Negro. One correspondent reported that "even *non-professors* of religion, pay liberally for the instruction of their slaves, which is a strong evidence of its practicability and usefulness." "Indeed, we look upon the religious instruction of the negroes," the Meeting concluded, "as the GREAT DUTY, and in the truest and best sense, THE FIXED, THE SETTLED POLICY OF THE SOUTH. . . . *The work must go on.*"

And the work did go on, in many different ways, not all of which fitted proslavery plans. Many rural slaveowners followed the Rev. C. C. Jones's prescription of "The best form of Church Organization for the Negroes":

> In the free States it is judged most advisable both by whites and blacks, that the latter should have their own houses of public worship and church organizations independent of the former.
>
> *But in the slave States it is not advisable to separate the blacks from the whites.* It is best that both classes worship in the same building; that they be incorporated in the same church, under the same pastor, having access to the same ordinances, baptism and the Lord's supper, and at the same time; and that they be subject to the same care and discipline; the two classes forming one pastoral charge, one church, one congregation.
>
> Should circumstances beyond control require the Negroes to meet in a separate building and have separate preaching, yet they should be considered part and parcel of the white church. Members should be admitted and excommunicated, and ordinances administered in the presence of the united congregations.
>
> This mingling of the two classes in churches creates a greater bond of union between them, and kinder feelings; tends to increase subordination; and promotes in a higher degree the improvement of the Negroes, in piety and morality. The *reverse* is, in the general, true of *independent church organizations of the Negroes,* in the slave States.
>
> The appointment of *colored preachers* and *watchmen . . . by the white churches, and under their particular supervision,* in many districts of country has been attended with happy effects. . . .

On some plantations, the regular discipline required attendance by Negroes at the master's family prayers, where the galleries or a special section was reserved for them.

But these organized white churches did not encompass the religious life of the Southern Negro. The Negro developed a religious life of his own. Much of this life remained unrecorded because many of the independent Negro religious meetings were illegal, and most of their participants, including sometimes even the preacher, were illiterate. Still, we do know that such religious meetings were not uncommon, and that they became the nucleus, and later the whole organized form, of Negro communities.

The Negroes' religious life thrived in institutions that were often invisible to the white masters, and that are barely visible to the historian today. In the cities the Negroes' religious communities sometimes were quite visible: their names and even the names of their Negro preachers were listed in city directories. There the Negro need for community also found secular expression in the convivial life of the grog shop and the grocery store. But the fact that the myriad slave "churches" in the countryside were dispersed, ill-organized, unchronicled, and anonymous does not make them any less significant, nor should they be overshadowed by the more conventional religious organizations pioneered by Northern Negroes.

The continuous history of the organized Negro churches is usually traced to Philadelphia; there two free Negro clergymen, Richard Allen and Absalom Jones, who had been persuaded to keep their Negro followers within the local white Methodist congregation, were forced from their knees during prayer one Sunday when they refused to go to the gallery to which the Negroes were relegated. In 1787, they formed the Free African Society. Jones then seceded to form the African Protestant Episcopal Church, and Allen went on to found the powerful African Methodist Episcopal Church, which became a national organization in 1816 (he was its first bishop) and which later worked with the Underground Railroad.

In the long run, however, Negro life in America was deeply affected by the distinctive character of the dispersed and invisible religious communities of the enslaved Negro. Just as the Jew's attitude toward religion and his community was shaped by the ghetto, so was the Negro's shaped by slavery. And American Negroes were drawn into myriad religious communities.

Even where the master feared this clustering of his Negroes for religious purposes, he might be powerless to prevent it, and prudent masters often allowed their slaves this outlet. "On many plantations," Frederick Law Olmsted reported, after traveling through the Cotton Kingdom in the late 1850's, "religious exercises are almost the only habitual recreation not purely sensual, from steady dull labour, in which the negroes are permitted to indulge, and generally all other forms of mental enjoyment are discouraged. Religious exercises are rarely forbidden, and a great freedom to individual impulse and talent is allowed while engaged in them than is ever tolerated in conducting mere amusements or educational exercises. Naturally and necessarily all that part of the negro's nature which is otherwise suppressed, bursts out with an intensity and vehemence almost terrible to witness, in forms of religious worship and communion; and a 'profession' of piety which it is necessary to make before one can take a very noticeable part in the customary social exercises, is almost universal, except on plantations where the ordinary tumultuous religious meetings are discouraged, or in towns where other recreations are open to the slaves." The spirit of the sporadic religious meetings is not easy to recapture; perhaps the Negroes felt at home only when no white person was present.

Sometimes the rural slaves would wander into the neighboring town on Sundays, there to join in the Negro congregation. Frederika Bremer, the Swedish novelist, reported one such meeting outside Charleston in 1851:

> . . . in the village itself everything was still and quiet. A few Negro men and women were standing about, and they looked kind and well to do. I heard in one house a sound as of prayer and zealous exhortation. I entered, and saw the assemblage of Negroes, principally women, who were much edified and affected in listening to a Negro who was preaching to them with great fervour and great gesticulation, thumping on the table with his clenched fists. The sermon and substance of his sermon was this: "Let us do as Christ has commanded us; let us love one another. Then he will come to us on our sickbeds, on our deathbeds, and he will make us free, and we shall come to him and sit with him in glory."

The true picture of worship in the countless Negro churches is forever hidden from us, and it can never be verified by statistics. But we can see emerging a pattern of religious life, distinctively American, and growing out of the very conditions of Negro slavery.

The Negroes' invisible religious communities showed certain obvious characteristics. In the first place, of course, individual "churches" were extremely numerous, and each tended to have a small membership. Among white Protestants, the traditional, ritual, and theological distinctions that separated the sects tended at the same time to draw together individual congregations into large denominations. But recent and fluid Negro congregations with semi-literate Negro leaders were unaware of sectarian fine points. The individual slave "church," forbidden communication with others, thus tended to become a kind of denomination all its own. In the absence of a traditional theology, the preacher dominated the rites, holding the group together by his personality. The local autonomy within the Baptist churches, by contrast even with that of the Methodists, left the Negro preacher freer, and so helped account for the special appeal of the Baptists. Among Negroes themselves, preachers acquired a unique prestige. The semi-literacy of Negro preachers, maintained by the white fear of "overeducated" Negroes, tended to make them most emphatically preachers rather than teachers. Ability to orate, to sing, to dramatize—garnished by some knowledge of the Bible— was the important qualification. Negro religious meetings thus offered the talented Negro an opportunity for leadership which he found nowhere else. For the congregants, such a religious experience was not likely to be attenuated into something intellectual nor was it apt to be formalized into cold ritual; it tended to be direct, emotional, naive, and personal. And, most important, when the Negro's religious community was his own and not the white man's, it tended to encompass his whole community, to provide virtually his whole political, cultural, aesthetic, and social life: "a nation within a nation."

All these characteristics persisted after the Civil War, even after the slaves' invisible churches had fused with the neater religious institutions that had grown up, mostly among free urban Negroes. Negro churches continued to be plagued by splits and secessions, by countless self-proclaimed new sects; those concerned for the religious life of the American Negro would long complain that he was "overchurched." Many of these churches continued to suffer from an autocratic ministry: men exploiting this opportunity for male dominance in an otherwise restricted world. They continued to be emotional and revivalist. And these religious communities, precisely because they were so encompassing, provided the Negro, cast adrift after emancipation, with some framework for his cultural, political, and reformist efforts, some arena for leadership. These features became even more important when the Negro confronted new bewilderments and new exclusions in the city.

25

The Unwritten Law: How It Grew in Slavery

DURING THE VERY YEARS when a technical American legal system with its paraphernalia of law schools, printed judicial precedents, and professional textbooks was developing in New England, Southerners came more and more to live by unwritten law. Legal technicalities, the letter of the law, and the items in small print, they said, were for pettifogging Yankees. Great planters actually ran their affairs by informal understandings, gentlemen's agreements, and pledges of honor. Seldom in modern times had such large businesses been conducted with so little legal paper.

This explains why so many questions about Southern life must remain forever unanswered; their answers are gone with the wind. Paradoxically, it also reveals the rigidity of Southern life, for it helps us to understand how Southerners came to believe their way of life was changeless.

The key to the growth of unwritten law in the South is slavery. In the Southern states as a whole, Negroes comprised over one-third of the population during the years from 1790 to 1860, and nearly all of them were slaves. *Free* colored persons did not amount to as much as one-tenth of the Negro population of the region. The proportion of Negroes to white persons varied from state to state. In 1850, for example, Negroes comprised more than half the population in South Carolina and in Louisiana, but only about one-fifth in Tennessee and Kentucky. Slaveholders never comprised more than a small fraction of the white population in the South as a whole, and only a minute proportion of these held more than a few slaves each. At the opening of the Civil War less than five per cent of white Southerners owned any slaves and less than one per cent of the slaveowners held as many as one hundred slaves. Everywhere in the South, however, slavery governed the relations of whites to Negroes. Southerners were not mistaken when they said it fixed the tone of their life.

The critics of slavery, especially those in the North, saw only its arbitrariness. If any rule other than passion or self-interest governed the master in dealing with his slave, they seldom recognized it. Slavery, they said, was despotism. Its essential evil was that it left one man completely unrestrained in dealing with another. But the Southern Gentleman did not see slavery that way. In his eyes what distinguished slavery was not that it gave a Southern master unlimited power over his labor force, while a Northern master was controlled by law. Quite the contrary. Southerners tended to see the Northern employer as restrained only by the specific provisions of a written law, while they themselves were governed by subtle, all-pervading rules of "honor"—by a comprehensive unwritten law. Not the absence of law, but the presence of a different kind of law, distinguished a slave society from all others; Southern defenders of slavery argued that the superiority of their society came from this fact.

Being all-pervading, Southern law had to remain unwritten. So it avoided the crabbed literalness, the paltry technicalities of people who were always publishing and "improving" their statutes, their bills of rights, and their court decisions. Only so had the Southern Gentleman, suspicious of human courtrooms, put himself under the constant jurisdiction of his conscience and his God. "He is every inch, bold, self-reliant, conscientious; knowing his own convictions of duty, and daring to heed them," observed one of his admirers. "What that duty is, the Divine Teacher has inculcated in the well-known precept: 'Masters, give unto your servants . . . that which is just and impartial; knowing that you also have a Master in heaven.' This the Southern Gentleman delights to do. It is almost impossible for a citizen of the North to realize the strong ties which bind the Southern Gentleman to his bond-servants and vice versa."

Thus the South attained the humanity and charity, the warmth and generosity which supposedly distinguished it from Free Societies. It avoided the niggardliness of employers who paid cash to their "free" workers for every service rendered, and the churlishness of employees who expected no benefits except those written in the contract. Who could be generous where everything was bought and paid for? where all services and all benefits had to be itemized? The Yankee factory owner ruled severely, with the statute book in one hand and his account book in the other. The Southern planter ruled liberally because he himself was ruled by an inward unspoken law.

No system, Southern apologists argued, was better designed than slavery for manly self-government by the ruling class, since slavery imposed the least government interference between master and servant. They claimed for it all the obvious virtues of laissez faire. But there were a number of peculiarities of Southern slavery which left its laws even more unwritten—and hence even more rigid—than the laws of other slave societies.

The first of these was an ironic result of the freedom-loving character of English common law. This is an astonishing story of the unpredictable meanderings of the legal mind. English lawyers have long boasted of their common-law preference for freedom: a man is presumed innocent until proven guilty; his home is his castle; his personal rights are sacred; his liberty cannot be infringed except where law and constitution justify it, and where technical forms are observed. For several centuries a classic expression of this spirit had been the refusal of English law to recognize the institution of slavery. At least as early as the reign of Queen Elizabeth I, judges in denying a master's right to scourge a "slave" brought from Russia, "resolved, that England was too pure an air for slaves to breathe in." At the time of the first settlement of the American colonies, then, slavery was not known to English law. The definitive modern restatement of this principle was made by Lord Mansfield in the court of King's Bench in London in 1772, when he refused to order the return of a Negro to the man who owned him as a slave under the law of Jamaica and who had brought him to England. "The state of slavery . . . ," Mansfield declared, "is so odious, that nothing can be suffered to support it but positive law." The law of England gave no such support.

A catastrophic consequence of this freedom-loving spirit was that, when slavery grew up in the British Empire, there was no recognized body of laws covering it. This proved most unfortunate for the Negro, whom it left unprotected. The strong position of English law in favor of freedom was a blessing in England; it became a curse for the Negro in America. In the British West Indies, for example, courts reached the shocking conclusion "that the Colonies, having adopted the common law, and negro slavery having no existence in Great Britain, there could be necessarily no provision of that law in reference to it, and consequently the power of the master until limited by legislation was absolute." With only minor qualifications, this was to become the dominant legal doctrine of the Southern United States. A slave there would have fewer legal rights and would receive less protection from the letter of the law than anywhere else among civilized peoples.

Elsewhere in the New World—in the Spanish and French colonies, for example—the slave was never so barren of legal rights. Since slavery had long existed in Spain, Spanish colonists had a ready-made slave code. The compilation of laws which had been made by Alfonso the Learned, King of Castile and León in the 13th century, and which Spanish settlers brought with them, defined procedures for marriages of slaves, the circumstances under which slaves could acquire property and purchase their freedom, the regulations against brutal masters, and the modes of manumission. The slave thus had a legally protected status with numerous specific rights. His terms of employment were prescribed by law; there could be no doubt that in law he was a person.

This doctrine was reinforced by the Catholic refusal to recognize the inferiority of the Negro in the eyes of God. Efforts were made to instruct him in Christian truths, to prepare him for baptism, to insure his attendance at mass—to bring him into the Church. The Church, like the State, stood between master and slave. It was plain, then, in the Spanish colonies that the master's power over his slave could never be legally absolute. Slavery was simply another form of employment and, like all others, was controlled by ecclesiastical and civil law. The history of Spanish law had shown that slavery could be modified in one or another detail, that the slave could be given additional rights without annihilating the master's property in the labor of the slave.

In the Southern United States, however, conditions conspired to give slavery an absoluteness and legal simplicity unknown elsewhere in modern times. Southern legislatures and courts tended to reduce the slave to a rightless chattel. Southern settlers had arrived here poorly equipped to deal with an institution so novel in the world of English law. Not inheriting the necessary legal nuances, they applied one crude distinction they did possess: between persons and things. Given so simple a choice, Southern law chose to classify slaves as things. The only interesting question, it seemed, was whether slaves should be classified as real property (like land) or as personal property (like cattle or furniture). While the laws of the Southern states varied in detail, they ascribed to slaves some of the legal characteristics of both these categories.

Another historical accident contributed to the catastrophic Southern oversimplification. In the cosmopolitan world of Roman law, of which Spain was part, slavery had been the lot of many races. But in British

North America, except for the occasional enslavement of Indians, which was never an important element in the economy and which virtually disappeared in the South after the early 18th century, slavery was identified with the Negro. Now for the first time in Western history, the status of slave coincided with a difference of race.

Southerners thus came to believe that the difference of race itself justified slavery. The elaborate ancient laws, meant for a world in which war or poverty might make anyone a slave, seemed superfluous and irrelevant. "The difficulty," Calhoun explained, "is in the diversity of the races. So strongly drawn is the line between the two in consequence, and so strengthened by the force of habit and education, that it is impossible for them to exist together in the community, where their numbers are so nearly equal as in the slaveholding states, under any other relation than that which now exists." When the difference between white and Negro was the whole difference between freedom and slavery, there seemed less need than ever for the technical gradations of right which marked Roman and other laws of slavery. Despite the large number of persons of mixed blood, Southern statutes generally recognized only the Negro (presumed to be a slave) or the white man (presumed to be free). By moving their justification of slavery onto the ground of biology and racial theory, Southerners abandoned the foundations hallowed by Greek philosophy and Roman law. They thus unwittingly put their "peculiar institution" on the shiftiest of foundations.

The Anglican Church, which dominated Southern religious feeling in the colonial period, collaborated in this great simplification. Cut off from Roman antiquity and from Roman Catholic sophistication in dealing with slavery and with non-European races, English churchmen allowed religion to confirm the absoluteness of Southern slavery. Only very gradually did the Anglican Church recognize Negroes as "baptisable beings." If the slave was not a Christian, his "marriage" could not be a sacrament, and hence required no legal sanction. As fears of slave uprising grew, along with the growth of the Negro population, the Church often acquiesced in general prohibitions against instructing slaves or allowing them to assemble. To Southern slaveowners, their "peculiar institution" seemed necessarily static and brittle. The rigidity of the institution was a measure of its perfection. Any "meddling"—by which was meant any qualification of the master's rights—could mean nothing less than abolition, the confiscation of the master's property in his slave. Calhoun and his diehard followers had come to believe that slavery "involves not only our liberty, but what is greater (if to freemen anything can be), existence itself. The relation which now exists between the two races in the slave-holding States has existed for two centuries. . . . None other can be substituted." The slave relationship changed surprisingly little during its Southern heyday.

The most striking fact about the Southern slave laws is how few they were. There were only sparse regulations qualifying the slave's subordination or defining rights of slaves. The Southern colonists (except those in Louisiana who inherited the Roman law) were overwhelmed by the task of making a slave code of whole cloth; and they made only occasional regulations. There was nothing that could properly be called a comprehensive Slave Code, nothing comparable to the Spanish laws protecting slaves along with other subjects of the Empire. From time to time, at the scene of alarm, Southerners passed repressive legislation (sometimes called "codes") for temporary emergencies, but slave laws as a whole remained meager—perhaps the thinnest body of written laws by which a modern society has ever controlled its labor force and its most important property.

Hardly less striking is how few books on the laws of slavery came out of the South. Of course, after the 1830's, Southern lawyers, judges, preachers, physicians, and politicians poured out defenses of Negro slavery by the dozens. They argued that it was founded in human nature, in biology, in theology, and in the Bible, and that it was permanently protected by common law and the Federal Constitution. Yet they produced almost no treatises on the everyday law of slavery. With astonishingly few exceptions, the technical books come from the North. John Codman Hurd, author of the *Law of Freedom and Bondage in the United States* (1858; 1862), the leading treatise on the American law of slavery, was a native Bostonian educated at Columbia and Yale, who divided his active life between Boston and New York. Some Northerners, like George M. Stroud of Philadelphia and William Goodell of New York, wrote abolitionist tracts in the form of legal treatises. Others, like Jacob D. Wheeler of New York, with no reformer's axe to grind, offered valuable compilations of legal decisions. What is remarkable is that on this important subject Southern lawyers wrote so little.

This odd fact in a society that boasted of its foundations in slavery was partly explained by another (which Southerners themselves often noticed): the great disparity between the letter of the law—those few rules on the books—and the actual practice. Southern defenders of the Peculiar Institution could hardly deny that the letter of the law, found in the books, looked harsh. But the law by which the South actually lived, they recalled again and again, was not written in the books. The few Southern legal treatises themselves warned against mistaking the statutes for an accurate description of the Southern way of life. "So modified is the slavery here," cautioned Thomas R. R. Cobb of Georgia, whose *Inquiry into the Law of Negro Slavery* (1858) was the most extensive and technically the most competent of the Southern treatises, "partly by natural law, partly by express enactment, and more effectually by the influence of civilization and Christian enlightenment, that it is difficult frequently to trace to any purely legal sources many of those protecting barriers, the denial of whose existence would shock an enlightened public sense." The first "law" of slavery, as Judge John Belton O'Neall of South Carolina and other eminent Southerners insisted, "is that of kindness from the master to the slave. . . . slavery becomes a family relation, next in its attachments to that of parent and child."

The severe laws on the books, even hostile observers noted, were not rigorously or regularly enforced. Many, passed in times of fear or hysteria, were kept through inertia, only to be handy for a future emergency. Perhaps never before or since—except in modern totalitarian states—have legal rules been applied so whimsically, arbitrarily, and unpredictably. While defensive Southerners emphasized the amelioration of the slave's condition which this made possible, in fact the departures from the letter of the law often made the slave's condition worse than the law allowed.

There was no denying, however, that the disparity between statute and practice was universal. "The restrictions upon slaves are very rigorous in law," a Yankee traveler noted in 1835, "but not in fact." Southerners rightly argued that what abolitionists read in lawbooks did not give an accurate picture of what really happened in the South. We have already noted the laxity of masters in obeying laws against religious meetings by slaves. And there were many other examples. The laws establishing the "Patrol System"—a local militia for controlling the movements of slaves—were plain and strict, but, in quiet times, enforcement was lax. Judges from the bench instructed the patrols "to overlook a harmless violation, a venial transgression of the strict letter." The laws generally prohibited trading by slaves and forbade their acquiring horses, boats, firearms, or other items that could be used for escape or insurrection. But the letter was ignored to enable slaves better to serve their masters or to pursue useful occupations. Numerous statutes prohibited teaching slaves to read or write; the South Carolina laws, widely copied, as early as 1740 had imposed a fine of £100 for each offense. To combat the threat of abolitionist literature, legal penalties were actually increased and legislation multiplied. But in 1857, a hostile Scottish traveler reported that in Richmond almost every slave child was learning to read; that in Columbia, South Carolina, twenty or thirty Negroes were earning a dollar a month by teaching reading to their fellow-slaves; that Negroes were being instructed by whites in the very corridors of his hotel.

"The inability of the slave to contract," Cobb explained in his *Law of Negro Slavery*, "extends to the marriage contract, and hence there is no recognized marriage relation in law between slaves." But here too the facts were far different. In scores of ways, marriage among slaves came to be recognized. It became common to have marriage ceremonies performed by Negro or white preachers followed sometimes by a feast with gifts from the master and others.

Inevitably, then, the South idealized its unwritten law, as that which made its society possible and its institutions good. Precisely because the law was unwritten, it seemed all the less changeable. And the unwritten law did not merely govern; it tyrannized the South. Like the Quakers before them, the Southerners would not tolerate any compromises for fear all would be lost: as Quakers lived by an unwritten theology, so Southerners too lived by an unwritten civil law; both were rigid and unbending.

26

How Southern Gentlemen Became Honor-bound

THE VIRGINIAN THOMAS JEFFERSON concluded the Declaration of Independence with a climactic pledge of "our sacred Honor"—to support the constitutional rights of British America. By the 1830's Southern gentlemen had transformed their code of honor into something much more personal. Among his equals, as with his inferiors, a Southern gentleman was not to be governed by the letter of the law. It was again untrue, however, to say that he felt obedience to no law at all, for he was expected to obey an unwritten law, as punctilious as it was vague, as demanding as it was elusive. How this code came into being and how it came to command a voluntary but abject obedience is the subject of the present chapter.

Between master and slave, the unwritten law—the law of charity and of conscience—was supposed to fulfil the spirit of the written law. Among equals, however, the unwritten law, which was called the "Code of Honor," was still wider in scope and still more forceful. Southern gentlemen who obeyed the code were expected to settle serious grievances among themselves not only outside the written law, but flagrantly against it. At the core of the Code of Honor was the duel. And Southern apologists were right when they called the duel a touchstone of Southern morals, because it showed what leading Southerners were willing to risk their lives for. It helps us discover what they meant by manliness, decency, and courage.

The prevalence of duelling in the South is especially significant because the practice had been so plainly outlawed on the statute books. The printed laws of every Southern state in the early 19th century explicitly prohibited duelling, and in terms that were neither vague nor mild. North Carolina (by its act of 1802) prescribed the death penalty. In South Carolina, for example, an act of 1812 prescribed a year in prison and a fine of $2000 for all participants in a duel, including seconds; the survivor in a fatal duel was guilty of homicide. Incidental legal penalties automatically barred duellists from law, medicine, the ministry, and all public office. Some states, like Alabama, required lawyers, members of the legislature, and other officials to take an oath that they themselves had never duelled nor aided in any duel as seconds or otherwise.

But duelling had not been an old Southern institution. During the colonial period, duels had been rare everywhere in British America, including the South. All the colonies together left records of only about a dozen duels in the century and a half between the founding of Jamestown and the outbreak of the Revolution. Colonial opinion generally condemned the practice, and in those days a Virginia gentleman could ignore a challenge without losing face; challengers themselves were sometimes punished by law. The few duels that occurred usually involved military men.

Not until the American Revolution did duelling spread. Caste-conscious European officers—British, German, and French—who had come to fight a public war brought along the chivalric traditions of a private warfare that vindicated the honor of gentlemen. Young aristocrats with Rochambeau and De Grasse preferred the duel for certain disputes; Lafayette was reported to have wanted single combat against the Earl of Carlisle, whom the English had sent as their peace commissioner. Later, after the French Revolution and the fall of Bonaparte, French *emigrés* in New Orleans started what one Louisianan called "a renaissance in duelling, as in the other condiments of life."

It was between the Revolution and the Civil War that duelling had its remarkable American growth. There were duels in all parts of the country. Less than a year after he signed the Declaration of Independence, Button Gwinnett was killed in a Georgia duel (with the incidental effect of greatly inflating the price of his autographs). Most notorious was the encounter between Aaron Burr and Alexander Hamilton on July 10, 1804, on the heights of Weehawken, New Jersey, where Hamilton was killed—on the very same site where his son Philip had died in a duel less than three years before. The Burr-Hamilton duel inspired President Timothy Dwight's sermon against duelling to the students of Yale (September 9, 1804), and an anti-duelling movement gained momentum along with other reforming enthusiasms in the North. But at the same time, duelling became more firmly established than ever in the South, where it continued until well after the Civil War.

Of Southern statesmen who rose to prominence after 1790, hardly one can be mentioned who was not involved in a duel. Of course, no official record remains. For, although duels were illegal, prosecutions were extremely rare and no reliable statistics are therefore possible. The numerous encounters of which we know are a mere minimum. Andrew Jackson, Henry Clay, John Randolph of Roanoke, Jefferson Davis, Alexander Stephens, Judah P. Benjamin, W. L. Yancey, and Sam Houston—all challenged or were challenged at one time or another, and most of them more than once.

The history of the South in this age is full of duelling dramas with prominent figures in starring roles. For example: Henry Clay vs. Humphrey Marshall (January 19, 1809), and vs. John Randolph of Roanoke (April 8, 1826); James Barron vs. Commodore Stephen Decatur (March 22, 1820 at Bladensburg, Maryland), in which Decatur was killed; Thomas Hart Benton vs. Charles Lucas (September 27, 1817, at St. Louis), in which Lucas was killed; Governor William C. C. Claiborne of Louisiana vs. Daniel Clark (summer, 1807 at New Orleans); Edmund Flagg vs. the editor of the *Sentinel,* Vicksburg, Virginia (1840); Edwin Forrest, the actor, vs. James H. Caldwell (c. 1824 at New Orleans; Caldwell refused the challenge); General Nathan Bedford Forrest (who apologized and refused when challenged); Governor James Hamilton of South Carolina, who reputedly fought fourteen duels, always wounding his opponent; Roger W. Hanson of Kentucky, later a Confederate General; Congressman George McDuffie of Georgia vs. Congressman William Cumming of Georgia (c. 1822, at Washington, D. C.), vs. Congressman Thomas Metcalfe of Kentucky, and vs. Congressman Joseph Vance of Ohio (who declined); Congressman Richard D. Spaight of North Carolina vs. Congressman John Stanly of North Carolina (1802). And there were scores of others.

Memorable contests of Southern public life commonly occurred under duelling oaks. Major General (later President) Andrew Jackson met Charles Dickinson of Nashville, a handsome lawyer, sportsman, and man-about-town on May 30, 1806, just across the state line (to avoid the laws of Tennessee) in Logan County, Kentucky. In the background of this encounter loomed political rivalry (Jackson had already served as Judge of the Tennessee Court of Appeal and as Member of Congress), the honor of women, love of horses, and other paraphernalia of Southern chivalry. Jackson's dubious conduct on this occasion—he pulled the trigger a second time when it failed to fire on his first try—dogged him throughout his political life. Henry Clay's duel against Humphrey Marshall arose out of Marshall's attack on Clay's demagoguery" in supporting measures in the Kentucky legislature to protect manufactures.

Both duellists were slightly wounded, but Clay was out of the legislature for three weeks and his partisans ever afterward boasted that their hero had "fought and bled for the cause of protection when he first championed it." It was Judah P. Benjamin's challenge to Jefferson Davis for dishonorable words in debate (Davis declined the duel, giving a public apology instead) that confirmed Davis' high estimate of Benjamin's character and began their close political association.

Scattered clues suggest how widespread duelling was among Southern leaders and how readily public opinion condoned or praised the practice. In Alabama, for example, the General Assembly in 1841 passed special acts excusing thirteen named citizens from the oath disclaiming duels; similar acts passed at least two other sessions of the Alabama Assembly within the following six years. "The score of duels," a New Orleans lady recalled, "was kept like the score of marriage offers of a belle." Some individuals claimed as many as fifty. One man fought a duel against his brother-in-law; another man and his son both scheduled duels on the same day. On one Sunday in 1839, in New Orleans alone ten duels were fought. Many tombstones in the old cemetery there were inscribed, "Killed on the field of honor."

The frequency of duelling is further attested by the minuteness and profusion of customary rules. The most widely used handbook was *The Code of Honor, or Rules for the Government of Principals and Seconds in Duelling* (1838) by Governor John Lyde Wilson of South Carolina, which went through several editions, the last in 1858. Louisianans were inclined to follow the more punctilious "twenty-six commandments" of duelling by John McDonald Taylor of New Orleans. Different weapons—swords in Louisiana, pistols in Kentucky—were usual in different parts of the country. An authentic gentleman knew the etiquette: that he must cast his note of challenge "in the language of a gentleman," avoiding opprobrious epithets; that he should refuse a challenge from another who was not a gentleman; and that he should delegate proper authority to his second. Niceties of the code were widely respected. Formal arrangements for the encounter between Jackson and Dickinson in 1806 were signed by both their seconds:

> It is agreed that the distance shall be 24 feet, the parties to stand facing each other, with their pistols down perpendicularly. When they are ready the single word *fire* to be given at which they are to fire as soon as they please. Should either fire before the word is given, we pledge ourselves to shoot him down instantly. The person to give the word to be determined by lot, as also the choice of position. We mutually agree that the above regulations shall be observed in an affair of honor depending between General Andrew Jackson and Charles Dickinson, Esq.

On another occasion, when Andrew Jackson was challenged by a person he "knew not as a gentleman," he refused to accept the challenge, but he did offer to go to any "sequestered grove" and shoot it out informally, on the express understanding that this was not a gentleman's duel. Once, when James Hamilton, Jr., noted duellist and sometime Governor of South Carolina, was a second, he refused to allow his principal, Congressman George McDuffie of Georgia, to duel with Congressman Thomas Metcalfe of Kentucky, because Metcalfe had violated the code by choosing rifles.

The stylized ceremony of a proper Southern duel between two gentlemen must not be confused with the common brawl or "shooting scrape" (an Americanism first recorded in 1831), found at this time in all parts of the country. In the more recently settled western South—in Arkansas, Alabama, Mississippi, and in over-mountain Tennessee and Kentucky— as well as among the poorer classes in the older South, there was a tendency toward informality. The same statute books that forbade formal duels also often prohibited more informal affairs of honor. For example, the Alabama laws of 1837 (outlawing duels in general) specifically punished the carrying or use of that poor man's duelling sword "known as Bowie knives or Arkansas Tooth-picks." A world separated the elaborate ritual encounter between two Southern gentlemen from the sudden affray among pistol-packin' quick-on-the-trigger Westerners, but traces of the formal duel often remained in the vulgar versions. In his *Georgia Scenes* (1835), Augustus B. Longstreet recounts a fight in which the parties, having used only their bare hands and sharp teeth (removing an ear, a piece of a cheek, and a finger), finally washed off the blood, shook hands, and, like gentlemen who had just duelled, considered their dispute at an end.

What a man defended in a duel was something far more elusive than his legal rights. For the South's "fatal custom" existed less to avenge murder or to protect life, limb, or property, than to preserve a man's "good name." While duels were commonly called "affairs of honor," and the duelling ground was the "field of honor," this honor was another name for reputation. Wilson's *Code of Honor* explained that good repute was more precious than life itself. Merely by choosing to duel, one showed he esteemed the opinion of his fellow gentlemen more than life or legal rights. "The slanderous tongue of the calumniator, who, by secret whisper or artful innuendo, has sapped and undermined his reputation" —this was the great evil against which a duel was the gentleman's only proper shield. Andrew Jackson declared "the slanderer . . . worse than the murderer," and agreed that unless the slanderer could in some other way be "frowned down" by society, all attempts to suppress duelling would be vain. Only when Dickinson publicly labelled Jackson "a worthless scoundrel, poltroon and a coward," did Jackson challenge him. Almost all the duels we know arose from insulting words, spoken or written.

The duel then was a ritual in which a gentleman submitted himself to the community's good opinion, or rather to the opinion of his equals, which was commonly called the "Code of Honor." An expression of the same attitude was the tradition of military honor exemplified in the chivalrous spirit of George Washington, Andrew Jackson, and Robert E. Lee, and preserved between wars in many small Southern military academies. From this era too came the so-called "honor system" of administering examinations. At the University of Virginia in 1842, Henry St. George Tucker, who had headed Virginia's Supreme Court before becoming professor of law and chairman of the faculty, brought the custom into American life. It soon spread to other parts of the South and elsewhere.

The "honor" which lay behind all this was by no means easy to explain to outsiders, and this was one of its most characteristic features. "This honor," the Northerner Frederick Law Olmsted observed, ". . . comes to be little else than a conventional standard of feelings and action which must be habitual to entitle a man to consider himself a gentleman." It was a name for the apparent paradox that, while Southern gentlemen in the three decades before the Civil War boasted of their high-minded indifference to "public opinion" or the good opinion of the whole world, they respected nothing more than their local reputation, or the good opinion of their fellow Southern gentleman. "To those whose god is honor, disgrace alone is a sin." They explained that, while the slave of public opinion took his orders from the public press and from the clamorous voice of his mobbish inferiors, the gentleman of honor obeyed the unspoken expectations of his equals. The rules of the Code of Honor, too, being habitual, could not really be taught or learned, much less comprehended in the pages of a book: they had to be inherited, or absorbed from the atmosphere. Such a law was as different as possible from the increasingly technical and professional and written law developing in New England. It also expressed a spirit different from that in the transient or upstart communities, where the priority rule of the claim clubs was made by and for recent arrivals, or where mining-camp vigilantes tried cases in the presence of the whole assembled community.

The Southern gentleman's Code of Honor—for all the minutiae of his duelling handbooks—had to be learned at his mother's knee; it could be known only to the initiate. There were no written directions for becoming a gentleman. The South's most important laws, then, its only laws that were relentlessly enforced, had grown from the South's own soil, and its Peculiar Institution. Such mystic effluvia were not to be caught in some lawyer's book, nor were they easily described to Yankees, immigrants, or foreigners.

The mystique of honor thus implied belief in a changeless society. Southern belief in the unwritten law, expressed in the attitude to slavery,

to the duel, and in many other ways, expressed faith in the stability—
or even the immobility—of a Southern way of life. Unwritten law was
a law men could not make or change. Strangely enough, it did not even
need to be enforced, except in rare and extreme cases, for it was only
another name for the way the community actually worked. And, among
Southern gentlemen, "honor" became less an ideal toward which they
strove than an idealization of their actual conduct.

27

Metaphysical Politics

THIS SEEMING IDENTITY of things as they were with things as they
ought to be, came from a vision of a society without conflict. "Owing
to the great diversity of interests in the Free States," a Southerner observed in 1860, "their public men are not continued long enough in
service—an indispensable requisite to the thorough accomplishment of
the statesman. If there were in the North some one predominating interest,
no matter what, which would command always a popular support, it
would not be a great while before a change for the better would be
observable in her public men." Northern politics, riven by controversy,
no longer attracted "the choicest spirits," those who wished to live
"cleanly and like a gentleman." Despite the actual fragmentation of
Southern life, Southerners became increasingly reluctant to see conflicting interests, or to imagine themselves either a laboratory for new institutions or a place for founding new communities. "The Southerner
can understand nothing of all this," Olmsted observed in 1854, "he
naturally accepts the institutions, manners and customs in which he is
educated, as necessities imposed on him by Providence. He is loyal to
'Society,' and it is opposed to his fundamental idea of a gentleman to
essentially deduct from them or add to them."

In New England the sharp awareness of conflicting interests produced
a reforming effervescence. There were countless co-operative societies,
movements for tax reform and prison reform, for the salvation of sailors
and the establishment of Sunday Schools, for Temperance and the Ten-
Hour Day, against imprisonment for debt, against capital punishment,
against banks and monopolies, for free education, for abolition, for

women's rights, and for world peace—and innumerable other causes pettier or more grandiose. A single Convention of the Friends of Universal Reform in Boston in 1840 collected under one roof: feminists, abolitionists, Muggletonians, Dunkers, "Come-outers," Seventh-Day Adventists, Unitarians, and some individuals who belonged to churches of which they were the sole members. Elsewhere, too, in these years there sprouted all sorts of experimental communities: New Harmony in Indiana (1825), Brook Farm in Massachusetts (1841–46), Sylvania Phalanx in Pennsylvania (1842), the Oneida Free Love Colony in New York (1848), the Village of Modern Times on Long Island (1851), the Icarian communities in Texas (1848), Illinois (1849), Missouri (1856), and Iowa (1857), among many others.

As late as the 1830's some reforming sentiments were heard below the Potomac—for example, during the historic debate on abolition in the Virginia legislature in the winter of 1831–32. But then, as we have seen, the Southern proslavery champions elaborated their arguments, and—with the founding of the American Anti-Slavery Society in Philadelphia in 1833, with the debate at Lane Seminary at Cincinnati in 1834, and with the transformation of abolitionism into a widespread religious revival, under the messianic leadership of Theodore Dwight Weld, William Lloyd Garrison, and Wendell Phillips—Southern resistance hardened. Southerners built what Clement Eaton has called an "intellectual blockade." "The South, in view of the excitement on the general conditions of the Negroes, in the North and West, has become sensitive," wrote the Rev. Charles Colcock Jones of Riceboro, Georgia, in 1842. "We have been thrown from necessity into an attitude of self-defence, and our strength consists in our union. Hence the public mind exercises a sleepless vigilance, that it may detect, either from abroad or originating at home, any sentiments or opinions hostile to our social constitution. There is less discussion, and less freedom of discussion, than in by-gone days. What we once bore from ourselves, is with difficulty borne now. That man runs the risk of losing popular favor whose candid statements and appeals, designed to do good *at home*, are seized upon with avidity, and perverted and made matter of accusation against us *from abroad*. He has to pass between Scylla and Charybdis."

Like the clergy, the press smelled out the slightest scent of social criticism. In the proud claim of William Woods Holden (who had made his *North Carolina Standard* the most powerful newspaper in the state), the South "uniformly rejected the isms which infest Europe and the Eastern and Western States of this country." "Newspapers devoted to socialism or to social equality, nihilism, communism or to infidelity in any of its shapes or shades, could not live in the atmosphere of North Carolina." In 1836, when Angelina Grimké published an antislavery pamphlet from Philadelphia, the mayor of Charleston informed her aristocratic Charleston family that she would not be allowed to return to the city. Even polite controversial literature, like the writings of Ralph Waldo Emerson, was not widely read in the South.

Sacks of abolitionist propaganda were destroyed by local postmasters, and obstruction of the federal mails (for the sake of "public safety") became a bulwark of Southern complacency. A Kentucky lawyer, Joseph Holt, who was President Buchanan's Postmaster General, sanctioned (1859) the local ruling which barred abolitionist literature from the mails in Virginia. His brother, R. S. Holt, another patriotic Southerner, asked (October 27, 1850) whether "Southern chivalry" dared allow the importation of Northern ice to cool its mint juleps.

The extreme defender of the peculiar institution, George Fitzhugh, gave a whole chapter of his *Cannibals All!* (1857) to "The Philosophy of the Isms—showing why they abound at the North, and are unknown at the South." The disarmingly simple reason he offered was that in the North reforms were more needed, while the South, blessed by slavery, lacked the very evils against which reforms might be directed. Reform, he said, like public philanthropy, was as superfluous to the South as it was necessary to the North.

The one "ism" with some appeal in the South was the least radical of them all: prohibitionism. During the thirty-odd years before the Civil War, the temperance movement was the only "reform" that attracted even a small number of leading Southerners. Calhoun's successor in the Senate, Robert Barnwell Rhett of South Carolina, who was sometimes called "the Father of Secession," and Governor Henry H. Wise of Virginia, later a Confederate General, were prominent teetotalers and champions of prohibition. In 1839, Joseph Flournoy, a wealthy Georgia planter, toured his state with a monster prohibition petition, which mustered a respectable fifty-four votes in the Georgia legislature against the ninety-eight which defeated the bill. The Sons of Temperance in Georgia claimed an impressive membership of over 13,000 in 1851. General John Cocke of Bremo, Virginia, a well-to-do planter of old family, who dominated the Board of Visitors of the University of Virginia for thirty-three years, led the demand for nationwide prohibition, and was elected president of the American Temperance Union in 1836.

Some Southerners said that the Southern gentleman's "out-of-doors and a-horse-back mode of living" explained his "wholesome," uncritical view of his society. Crowded Northern cities, they said, were a natural habitat of agitators and wild-eyed reformers. It was not surprising then, that the lyceum movement, founded by Josiah Holbrook in Millbury, Massachusetts, in 1826 and with nearly 100 branches founded in the next two years, did not flourish in the South. Southern audiences did not welcome controversial lectures like those which the Boston Lyceum, the Franklin Institute of Philadelphia, the Cooper Union of New York, and countless other foundations elsewhere were bringing to public platforms.

The absence of substantial European immigration into the South also helped keep her free of disturbing alien ideas. In New England the imported doctrines of German transcendentalism and oriental mysticism had become the adopted parents of numerous reforming projects. In the person of Carl Schurz, German political ideas also helped form the Republican Party in the West. There were few comparable imports into the South. Francis Lieber, the liberal refugee from political persecution (1819–24) in Germany, who taught at South Carolina College, was a conspicuous exception; but he was suspect for his abolitionist sympathies and, despite a world-wide reputation, failed to secure election as president of his college. One of the South's most "European" characteristics was its tendency to import ideas not through aspiring immigrants or disillusioned revolutionaries but in the antiseptic pages of books. The fact that the principal railroads in the Upper South ran northward rather than inward from the seaports posed an obstacle to the direct importation of ideas from Europe. Since Southern imports came mainly through the North, it was not too likely that reforming ideas would be imported intact, if at all. While reformist ideas reached the North from Europe piecemeal, by the time they reached the South they were commonly bundled together in packages that included abolitionism. All reform thus acquired a Yankee taint.

Meanwhile, in the North and West, the early decades of the 19th century were an era of widening franchise and of the rise of mass political parties. In national politics the era of the "Virginia Dynasty"—of Washington, Jefferson, Madison, and Monroe—lasted only until about 1825; property qualifications for voting were then still the rule. New Jersey (1807) and Maryland (1810) had abolished property qualifications, but not until the admission of new western states (Indiana, 1816; Illinois, 1818; Alabama, 1819) did white manhood suffrage become widespread. Gradually the democratizing movement prevailed in the populous states of Connecticut (1818), Massachusetts (1821), and New York (1821), and it gained momentum with the revision of other state constitutions (1816–30). By 1830 the number of qualified voters was double what it had been a decade before. The new politics of mass appeal brought with it the national party conventions, campaign ballyhoo, city bosses, local political machines, and the elaboration of a politics of compromise.

In a homogeneous South, however, where the interests of all men of good will were supposed to be identical, the arts of compromise and of mass appeal were not so highly valued. From the colonial period, in the Virginia House of Burgesses a man could achieve political power without opposing any strong interest group: the more articulate large planters were simply representing the smaller and less articulate ones.

"They were trying to get ahead," C. S. Sydnor observed, "on parallel rather than on conflicting lines." Almost every white man was engaged in agriculture; planters differed in the scale, rather than in the nature, of their activity. The House of Burgesses deliberated more like a trade association than the legislative body of a diversified community. This set the pattern for a society that valued loyalty and honor but had little experience with compromise.

Compromise in fact came to seem equivalent to dishonor. For honor, like chastity, could not be a question of degree. After 1830, the increasing devotion of the Southern gentleman to his Code, like the colonial Quaker's devotion to self-purity and conscience, was a measure of his incomprehension of, and even his growing contempt for, the arts of politics. In words oddly reminiscent of the Quaker martyr Mary Dyer, the South Carolina editor, Benjamin F. Perry, in 1860 declared, "You are all now going to the devil and I will go with you. Honor and patriotism require me to stand by my State, right or wrong."

The absence of conflict in the Southern patriarchal society became an axiom. Whatever benefited master also benefited slave: antagonism of interests, whether between Negro and white or between merchant and planter, was a fabrication of Northern propagandists. Since there were no "special interests" worthy of respect, every honest Southern politician was by definition a statesman, speaking for the whole community. Dissent gradually acquired the name of treason, and every imputation of treason called for defense on the field of honor. Politics, an open forum in which controversies were never finally concluded, could only displace Patriotism, which was a virtue pure and simple. Serious disagreements, it was assumed, could be "settled on the field of honor," where somehow both parties would be vindicated by the Code. The Civil War would finally turn the whole land into a "field of honor." The Southern people, urged Alexander H. Stephens, future Vice-President of the Confederacy, should assert their rights "at any hazard, though there be nothing at stake but their honor." The merest "pin prick" to Southern honor, Governor Wise of Virginia declared in 1856, would justify breaking the beloved Union. From a Southern point of view, the Civil War would avenge honor rather than resolve problems.

The tribulations of Southern newspaper editors illustrate this uncompromising spirit of Southern politics. Editors who wanted to stay alive were careful not to offend. Since it was unmanly to go to court for slander, an editor had to stand ready to defend his opinions with pen in one hand and duelling pistol in the other. For example, in 1832, when Benjamin F. Perry's Greenville *Mountaineer* opposed South Carolina's Nullification Ordinance and urged compromise, he was challenged by Turner Bynum, editor of the rival Greenville *Sentinel*. Bynum was, in Perry's words, "a false hearted demagogue and a jesuitical slanderer, whose patriotism consists in egotistical declamation, and whose chivalry has been wasted in words." On the morning of August 6, 1832, their seconds measured the ground in a forested spot on an island in the Tugaloo River, and there Perry reluctantly met Bynum on the field of honor and, by killing him, settled the issue. Another example: the editor of the Baton Rouge *Gazette*, J. Hueston, once taunted the Democratic party for nominating for Congress Alcee LaBranche (one of the few men in public life in Louisiana who had never duelled), whom he described as "destitute of spirit and manhood." The upshot was a duel in which LaBranche vindicated his honor and Hueston was killed. Just before the War, the editor of the Richmond *Enquirer*, Jennings Wise, fought eight duels in less than two years.

Defenders of the South after about 1830 boasted their freedom from "public opinion" as if it were a disease. And in the three decades before the Civil War, the South preferred the literariness of the few to the literacy of the many. Colleges and military academies for sons of ruling planters flourished. In the 1850's there were more college graduates in proportion to the white population in Virginia than in Massachusetts; in 1860 both Virginia and Georgia had more "colleges" in proportion to total population than either New York or Massachusetts. But public education languished. Primary and secondary educational systems and general literacy lagged far behind. While there are no reliable statistics, we have reason to believe that illiteracy in the South was more widespread than elsewhere in the nation: the great majority of Negroes were illiterate, and so were a far larger proportion of the whites than in the North. Southern emphasis on an educated leadership was of a piece with Southern unconcern for popular instruction. "To secure true progress," George Fitzhugh explained in 1857 with his usual brilliant extremism, "we must unfetter genius, and chain down mediocrity. Liberty for the few—Slavery, in every form, for the mass!"

Between the 1830's and the Civil War, as world opinion crystallized against slavery, Southern gentlemen boasted their high-minded indifference. "A decent respect to the opinions of mankind," which to Jefferson had seemed a prop of patriotism, now seemed treason. "The Southern Gentleman . . . ," D. R. Hundley exulted in 1860, "chooses to have an honest opinion of his own, and would rather stand in the shoes of the meanest slave on his plantation, of the laziest and most ignorant gumbo whose back was ever made to bleed under the overseer's lash, than to become that *thing*—that most emasculate and miserable mockery of a man—the SLAVE OF PUBLIC OPINION. . . . Do not wonder, therefore, that the Southern Gentleman has never been, and is not now, influenced by the popular and world-wide denunciation of the 'peculiar institution.' For he is a man every inch, bold, self-reliant, conscientious; knowing his own convictions of duty, and daring to heed them."

This lack of interest in the shifting winds of opinion and in the compromises of conflicting interests also helps explain the flowering of political theory in the pre-Civil War South. Had New Englanders and New Yorkers and Illinoisans been less interested in compromise, might they too perhaps have better sharpened their distinctions? This was the Great Age of American Political Theory, and the South produced virtually the only American works of political theory to rank with those of the Old World. Was it so surprising that a people who had come to live by the changeless absolutes of unwritten law proved adept at abstracting the essences of political thought? First came John Taylor of Caroline County, Virginia. In solid, closely-reasoned works—from his *Arator* (1813) through *Inquiry into the Principles and Policy of the Government of the United States* (1814), *Construction Construed and Constitutions Vindicated* (1820), *Tyranny Unmasked* (1822), and *New Views of the Constitution* (1823)—he defended Southern agrarianism and state-rights. Then Calhoun, whose *Disquisition on Government* and *Discourse on the Constitution and Government of the United States* (both posthumously published in 1851) are the pinnacle of political speculation in America. And finally Alexander H. Stephens of Georgia, whose *Constitutional View of the Late War Between the States* (1868–70) was a masterful autopsy of Southern rights. This trilogy of political theoreticians is without match in all American history.

"Metaphysical politicians" was the phrase by which practical Northerners as early as 1839 stigmatized the Southern patriots—"in contradistinction to those whose immediate object is the increase of trade and traffic. The Northern papers advocate each only *a particular part* of a political system: one, a bank in New York; another, one in Philadelphia, &c. . . ." Southern apologists increasingly championed not specific projects nor a complex region but an abstract cause: *"The* South." What passed for politics in the South, then, was really not politics at all. Pre-War conventions of Southern representatives—even the so-called "Commercial Conventions" in Macon, in Augusta, and in Charleston, produced almost no practicable schemes. "The South," a Southerner lamented, "so far as she sought industrial advancement, was in a maze, a novice not knowing to what projects to lend strength . . . never willing to start with homely enterprises that are suggested by genuine recognition of economic needs." Her statesmen aired proposals to secure free navigation of the Amazon, to cut a canal across the Isthmus of Tehuantepec, to go adventuring in Nicaragua, to build a railroad from the Mississippi to the Pacific, or to introduce slavery into Central America. If indeed this was politics, it was hardly the kind the South most urgently needed.

BOOK TWO

NATIONALITY

"Manifest destiny iz the science ov going tew
bust, or enny other place before yu git thare."

JOSH BILLINGS

A GREAT resource of America was vagueness. American uncertainties, products of ignorance and progress, were producers of optimism and energy. Although few acknowledged it, in the era between the Revolution and the Civil War this vagueness was a source of American strength. Americans were already distinguished less by what they clearly knew or definitely believed than by their grand and fluid hopes. If other nations had been held together by common certainties, Americans were being united by a common vagueness and a common effervescence. Their first enterprise was to discover who they were, where they were, when they were, what they were capable of, and how they could expand and organize. Their America was still little more than a point of departure. The nation would long profit from having been born without ever having been conceived.

PART FIVE

THE VAGUENESS OF
THE LAND

> "But what of the 'Great American Desert,'
> which occupied so much space on the map a
> generation ago? It is *nomadic* and elusive; it
> recedes before advancing civilization like the
> Indian and buffalo which once roamed it. . . .
> Driven from the plains east of the Rocky Moun-
> tains, the 'Great American Desert' seems to
> have become a fugitive and vagabond on the
> face of the earth. It was located for a time by
> the map-makers in Utah, but being persecuted
> there, it fled to Arizona and Nevada."
>
> JOSIAH STRONG

NOTHING did more to keep the American open to outrageous novelties and happy accidents than the indefinite arena of his life. Of course
he expected the unexpected. Even so, American experience held a still
vaster stock of the unpredictable than he dared imagine. Never before
had so populous a modern nation lived in so ill-defined a territory. The
continent was only barely explored, yet settlers preceded explorers.
Their maps were few and poorly drawn. Mapped in myth, mountain
ranges, rivers, lakes, deserts, all became figments of optimism or of
desperation: an Eden or a Hell—the Great American Garden or the
Great American Desert.

During the first century of national life, Americans lived not at a
verge, but in myriad fuzzy-edged islands. Westward advances were not

a line. And American life, like the nation itself, was distinguished by its lack of clear boundaries. The continent was covered by penumbras, between the known and the unknown, between fact and myth, between present and future, between native and alien, between good and evil.

They lived on a little-known continent, but they did not know how little they knew. Yet if they had known more they might have dared less. Their enterprises were stirred by misinformation, fable, wild hopes, and unjustified certainties.

28

A Half-known Country:
Settlement Before Discovery

"DISCOVERY" OF AMERICA had only begun. One of the decisive American anachronisms, one of the odd, lucky, shaping facts about this nation, was that it had begun to flourish even before it was explored—and partly even because it had not yet been explored. This explained much of its precocity and vitality. In the New World, a nation could grow while it discovered itself.

For Americans, then, discovery and growth were synonymous from the very beginning. Old World nations knew—or thought they knew—their extent, their boundaries, their topography, and their resources. Americans expected their nation to grow as they discovered where they were and what they had to work with. If America had not remained a "dark continent" throughout nearly the whole first century of its national existence, it is doubtful whether Americans could have been so vital and so excited.

America was so fertile a repository of hopes because it was so attractive a locale for illusions. The map of America was full of blank spaces that had to be filled. Where solid facts were scarce, places were filled by myths—largely European in origin. A mere rumor that Coronado had somewhere reached the sea became the cartographic certainty that he had touched the great Western Ocean. Coronado's places wandered all over the map, dragging with them names offered by Niza and other early bewildered explorers. Quivira, in origin probably a little village of

Wichita Indians in central Kansas, became the great mysterious Empire of Quivira. Map-makers with nothing new to report were grateful for mythical place names—Quivira and Tiguex and Cibola and Tontoneac —which they moved fancifully about. "They could be used wherever a white space would otherwise evidence geographic ignorance, and since their customers would certainly never go to Quivira to ascertain the truth, they were quite safe." The wanderings of these and other mythic places are depicted in Carl I. Wheat's magnificent volumes, unparallelled Odysseys of fabled cities tossed about on the turbulent sea of imagination.

To illustrate this fertile ignorance, I will only briefly tell the story of a single cluster of these illusions. The tale of the mythical River of the American West—the "San Buenaventura"—is rich in symbolism and irony. The antiquity and grandeur of this particular illusion, and its vivid survival into mid-19th century, give it special interest. European encounters with America in the late 15th century had been, of course, largely a result of European interest in the Orient. Hope for a westward water passage to Asia dominated all else. When the North American continent was found to be an obstruction, the waterway through the continent was only more eagerly sought. As the outlines of the New World were gradually defined, the hardening lines of knowledge excluded a westward sea passage at one place after another. But the hope for a waterway did not die; it simply moved to some still blank spot on the map. This cartographic migration is one of the most pathetic stories in the history of man's wishful thinking. It was to be capped by an irony worthy of some malicious god.

Search for the seaway across the continent proceeded in both directions. In the Pacific between the 16th and the 18th century, Spanish explorers who were seeking the transcontinental passage actually reconnoitered the coast of North America to above sixty degrees north latitude. The Dominguez-Escalante Expedition of 1776, hoping to find a route from Santa Fe to the Spanish settlement at Monterey on the California coast, explored and first mapped the great Colorado Plateau. Their map hopefully depicted a single great Lake Timpanogos (a combination of the Great Salt Lake and Utah Lake) with a large, supposedly navigable river flowing westward, presumably to the Pacific Ocean. Optimistic Spanish fathers in California meanwhile elaborated the fiction of a waterway to the interior, imagining that the streams descending from the Sierras had originated in the Rockies. These rivers, they said, were probably navigable, and hence promised the long sought commercial routes between Spain and China.

All these notions were incorporated in a 1784 map of Spanish North America which, despite its faults, was the best yet. Its streams on the Pacific Coast showed how the waters from the western slopes of the Rockies north of the Colorado River flowed westward into the Pacific.

Up to 1793, Spaniards in the Pácific continued probing for the western water entrance across the continent. At the same time, Spanish explorers from Louisiana came up the valley of the Missouri reaching for the ocean. Explorers eager to magnify their discoveries, travel-writers eager to please their readers, and cartographers eager to ornament the blank places on their maps, collaborated to perpetuate the ancient respectable belief in a waterway through the continent.

Disagreement centered not on *whether,* but on *where,* the transcontinental sea passage would be found. The Scottish explorer Alexander Mackenzie, in his journal (1802) suggested the Columbia (which he mistook for the Fraser River, which actually ran far north in British Columbia) as the probable future route between Atlantic and Pacific. Thomas Jefferson himself mistakenly identified the Columbia River with the Oregon (or "River of the West," a vestige of the mythical "Sea of the West," whose reputation reached back to the time of Verrazano). He believed the passage to India would be by way of the Missouri and the Columbia. And so he hopefully instructed Meriwether Lewis in 1803: "The object of your mission is single, the direct communication from sea to sea formed by the bed of the Missouri, and perhaps the Oregon. . . ." Of course, Lewis and Clark did establish *land* communication between the Missouri and the Columbia rivers, but the Rocky Mountain passes they found were steep and they certainly found no navigable water route. As traffic increased and knowledge grew in that area, it appeared ever more plain that the longed-for sea passage must be found elsewhere.

Once again the inextinguishable hopes had to be relocated. By now there remained only two areas where geographic darkness offered attractive locales. One, of course, was the Arctic. When the ice barrier east of Greenland melted between 1815 and 1817, the English, who had not sought the passage to India there for two centuries, energetically revived their quest. The other likely area, the last large repository of geographic ignorance in the present area of the United States, was what we now call the Great Basin. This was the territory between the forty-second parallel and the Mojave River. A great deal of "evidence" suddenly seemed to point to the actual existence of the long sought transcontinental water passage in that last resort.

The first half of the 19th century thus saw what Gloria G. Cline has aptly called a "cartographic extravaganza," in which, again and again, myth nearly conquered reality. The influential maps of Alexander Von Humboldt, Zebulon Pike, and Lewis and Clark between 1810 and 1814, all documented the myth which was to last still another three decades. This is not surprising since Pike and Lewis and Clark had copied Humboldt's map; Humboldt himself had never seen the region, but had copied a still earlier map that dated back nearly forty years. Lewis and

Clark showed the coveted river starting in the Rockies and running straight through the mountains westward to the Ocean. Other enterprising mapmakers, assuming that if there was one such river passage, there must be others, drew half a dozen Rocky-Mountain-fed rivers into the Pacific. The broadest, most appealing, and longest-lived of these, first sketched by the cartographer for the Spanish expedition of 1776, was the river known as the "San Buenaventura." The prosaic daily experiences of fur traders like Ashley, Smith, Walker, and Peter Skene Ogden did little to dry up that river. Nor did the maps of Gallatin, Bonneville, and Burr, which began to fill the blank spot with an interior basin lacking any drainage to the sea. These maps were all published before 1840, but they either did not circulate or were too disheartening to be believed. "Some of the maps consulted, supposed of course to be correct," John Bidwell wrote of his preparations for his epochal 1841 overland trip to California, "showed a lake in the vicinity of where Salt Lake now is; it was represented as a long lake, three or four hundred miles in extent, narrow and with two outlets, both running into the Pacific Ocean, either apparently longer than the Mississippi River." The salty waters of the Great Salt Lake were, of course, a diabolical coincidence which made it harder than ever to doubt that this might be an inreaching arm of the great Western Ocean.

Belief that there must somewhere exist a westward waterway was widespread and respectable. Senator Thomas Hart Benton, of Missouri, argued long and loud for a sea passage to India. First he was inclined to follow Jefferson's route up the Missouri River, but he was optimist enough to send his son-in-law John C. Frémont in quest of still others. There was, of course, a wonderfully appealing symmetry to a majestic San Buenaventura River. The continent had been largely explored by water, at first along the Atlantic coast and later down the rivers of the Mississippi basin. What more providential or more appropriate than that there be similar passageways all through the West?

The last resting place of the fabled westward passage to the Orient was magnificently ironic, for now finally explorers and cartographers and visionary statesmen had desperately located their heart's desire— their San Buenaventura—in the one great area of the North American Continent that not only had no grand rivers, but actually had no outlet at all to the sea! They had put it, of all places, in the Great Basin! This place was actually a geographic monstrosity: in the heart of a well-watered continent a vast area dispersed its waters not to any of the oceans, but in some mysterious way into the very earth itself. What more suitably unpredictable ending for one of the most indomitable of American illusions?

In 1844, and not before, Frémont concluded that this supposed locale of the transatlantic waterway was not only no habitat of rivers flowing oceanward, but was actually without any exterior drainage at all. On May 23, 1844, almost precisely a year after having left Kansas, Frémont, encamped on the shores of Utah Lake, finally described the great area between the Wasatch and the Sierra Mountains (including much of Oregon, virtually all of Nevada, western Utah, and California north of the Mojave River) as a land of interior drainage, a "Great Basin" without outlets to the sea. This was not simply the removal of another blank space on the map, but a great geographic discovery in the long unveiling of North America, for it laid waste the last imaginary habitat of the mythic San Buenaventura. It was a sobering and disillusioning experience.

*　　*　　*

The tale of the San Buenaventura is only one episode in the American Decameron of men's love affairs with their illusions. In the early 19th century, North America, especially the part contiguous to the new United States, was ideally qualified to seduce explorers, cartographers, botanists, geologists, illustrators, anthropologists, and scores of other devotees of still new sciences. The New World dwelt in an enticing penumbra, neither so well lit as to stultify imagination nor so darkly unknown as to intimidate the half-courageous.

Many circumstances in the American West worked to preserve the general ignorance of the nation's geography. Colonial rivalries had not fostered publicity of such information as there was. The early Spanish explorers of North America were not eager to share their meager knowledge, which was a precious instrument of empire, as closely guarded as a nation's skilled workers or gold bullion.

The chronicles of Western exploration are therefore full of unknown first discoveries. Lives were wasted simply because the earliest discovery was not publicized. The famous South Pass in Wyoming through which California immigrants poured in mid-century had probably been discovered in 1812 by Robert Stuart in John Jacob Astor's employ, but the information had not got around. No one was sure precisely where Stuart had been. Knowledge of the Pass was not general until after Jedediah Smith's rediscovery of it in 1824, when it began to come into use by fur traders. Similarly, the honor of discovering the Great Salt Lake is much disputed. Did it belong to Jim Bridger? Early in 1825 while exploring the mouth of the Bear River on one of Ashley's fur-trapping parties (possibly headed by Bill Sublette), Bridger followed the river through its canyon, and reached the edge of the salty lake, believing it an arm of the sea. Had the trapper Étienne Provost possibly seen the Lake in the fall of 1824? If neither of these actually saw the Lake, the honor may go to Peter Skene Ogden's Snake Country Expedition of 1824–25. In that expedition's journal for May 5, 1825, Ogden recorded "a fine Plain covered with Buffalloes and thousands of Small Gulls the latter was a Strange Sight to us I presume some large body of Water near at hand at present unknown to us all." If any of this group saw the Lake, it was probably not Ogden, but one of his men. Ogden himself very likely did not see the Lake till December 26, 1828. What is remarkable is how little each of these knew of what the others had done or were doing.

One advantage of these failures of communication was that the joys of first discovery were spread among many people. In September, 1843, fifteen years after Ogden first glimpsed the Great Salt Lake, Frémont saw "the object of our anxious search—the waters of the inland sea, stretching in still and solitary grandeur far beyond the limits of our vision." "We felt pleasure also in remembering that we were the first who, in the traditional annals of the country, had visited the islands and broken with the sound of human voices, the long solitude of the place." Frémont did not know that almost twenty years before, in 1826, Jim Bridger's party of trappers had paddled around most of the lake in improvised boats of buffalo or elk hide. Perhaps this was just as well, for it left him free to enjoy his "discovery."

On his next expedition, in 1845, when Frémont and his party moved westward from the southern edge of the Great Salt Lake again they enjoyed a "first" encounter with one of the grand features of the continent. He was told no one had ever crossed the vast plains in that direction. The Indians on the spot reassured him of this; there was no water out that way. The guides on his staff, knowledgeable mountainmen like Kit Carson and Robert Walker, knew nothing of that country. Again, in retrospect, we see how ill-informed they were, for nearly twenty years earlier Jedediah Smith had actually crossed the Great Salt Desert.

The reasons for such costly failures to pool information were not far to seek. As William H. Goetzmann has explained, the fur trapper who knew rich streams and easy ways to reach them was like the man who knows a good fishing hole. He was not eager to share what he knew. Successful trappers knew their way to the most rewarding beaver streams by the easiest passes and through the greenest natural pasture; they knew the safest way to cross the desert. Their business was furs, not maps. For example, Jedediah Smith, who probably knew as much as anyone in his day about the West, sketched very few maps, and they were all lost. Jim Bridger, who guided the Stansbury expedition to the Great Salt Lake in 1850 and Captain William F. Raynolds' Yellowstone expedition of 1859, could, when requested, supply nothing better than a crude chart extemporaneously drawn with charcoal on a piece of buffalo hide.

The rendezvous system, which, as we have seen, demanded an extraordinary organizing talent, also required an intimate knowledge of the landscape. Year after year several hundred men, dispersed to remote corners of the fur trappers' West, managed to reassemble on schedule. "They did not resemble Achilles," Bernard De Voto explains, "but they were prepared to meet several hundred others on the day appointed and at the place assigned, and did not care if the geographers had moved it a full ten degrees. They went about the blank spaces of the map like men going to the barn. The Great American Desert was their back yard." They themselves had little need of maps; they carried their information in their heads. This made them personally indispensable and kept the American West long a mystery to the outside world.

Had geographers known more, or had they known less, the unfilled continent might not have been so inviting. This providential half-knownness of the American scene helps explain the energy and the passion, the obsessive singlemindedness and the fickle shiftiness, with which Americans so quickly moved their hopes from one San Buenaventura to another.

With little to go on, hopes and fears often ran to wild extremes. The mind embroidered what it had; reluctant to fill blank spaces in maps with anything so commonplace as arid plains or temperate grasslands, people seized evidence of more interesting, more colorful, more danger-ous, or more rewarding landscapes.

"I saw in my route in various places," Zebulon Pike had reported of his trip west of the ninety-fifth meridian in 1806, "tracts of many leagues where the wind had thrown up the sand in all the fanciful forms of the ocean's rolling waves and on which not a speck of vegetable matter existed." In 1819–20, Stephen H. Long of the United States Topographical Engineers traveled from an encampment at the junction of the Platte and the Missouri Rivers (now the border between Nebraska and Iowa), along the Platte to the front range of the Rockies, then south and east through Oklahoma to Fort Smith in Arkansas. "In regard to this extensive section of country," he incautiously reported, "I do not hesitate in giving the opinion, that it is almost wholly unfit for cultivation, and of course, uninhabitable by a people depending upon agriculture for their subsistence. Although tracts of fertile land considerably extensive are occasionally to be met with, yet the scarcity of wood and water, almost uniformly prevalent, will prove an insuper-able obstacle in the way of settling the country." The vast neighboring areas east of the Rockies, he said, might be well suited for buffaloes, wild goats, and other wild game but for nothing else. On his map, published in 1823, he here inscribed in large letters "Great American Desert." He thus helped create a new geographic myth, destined to be one of the most vivid and most potent myths of the first half of the 19th century.

Numerous ambiguities surrounding the meaning of "desert" com-pounded the uncertainties of the landscape. As that word gained currency to describe parts of the West, to some it meant a kind of American Sahara, to others an unpleasant place fit only for Indians, and to still others it carried a variety of other forbidding connotations. It became almost as indefinite in its meaning as in its location.

The widespread scarcity of wood and water were of course real facts which Walter Prescott Webb and others in the 20th century showed to be shaping influences of this West. But the waterless, treeless, uninhabitable desert east of the Rockies—the desert born in Long's imagination and confirmed by scores of other mapmakers, travelers, writers, and fireside taletellers—was pure myth, no more substantial than the majestic San Buenaventura. But just as the unfounded hope for a great Mississippi of the West had enticed explorers to risk their lives, incidentally discovering unexpected but very solid facts, so did belief in this Great American Desert move thousands of Americans until after the Civil War. Haunted by visions of broiling sands and blinding sun, Americans hastened westward. Imaginary perils of geography were added to the real threats from nature and the Indians, and the scarcities of wood, water, and other resources. They thus left behind the hospitable plains of the midwest on their unknowing way to more arid regions. The Great Plains became a barrier to be crossed with all possible speed, perhaps delaying settlement of the fertile midwest by several decades.

These frightening visions had other effects. Was not such a Great American Desert admirably suited to contain the Indians? In 1823, Secretary of War John C. Calhoun proposed to President Monroe that the approximately fourteen thousand Indians then in the Old Northwest (the region around the Great Lakes and between the Ohio and the Mississippi rivers) be removed to the northern part of the Desert, and that the seventy-nine thousand Indians comprising the southern tribes be removed to its southern part. Among the resulting advantages listed by Calhoun were the opening of valuable eastern lands to white settlement, the prevention of future conflict between the races, and the removal of Indians from further contagion by white men's sins and diseases. The thirty thousand dollars required to persuade the Indians, Calhoun explained, was a small price for this "permanent" solution of the Indian problem. While some professional geographers and government officials, as Francis Paul Prucha has recently shown, would not have agreed that the Indians were being removed to a "desert," such was the popular view. Calhoun's plan for a "Permanent Indian Frontier," enacted in 1825, proved less permanent than he had supposed, for the myth of the Great American Desert did not live forever. As it was gradually dispelled, white men began to wonder whether this land west of the ninety-fifth meridian might not, after all, be better than the Indians deserved.

The people who, despite everything, in the 1830's and '40's and '50's settled in large numbers west of the Mississippi in the very heart of the "Great Desert," rebelled against this slander of their chosen land. The executive committee of the Kansas Historical Society in 1860 reported how well they remembered that in their school days "the books taught us that this central plain we now occupy was a portion of the great American desert." They built a counter-myth of their own. Not merely disavowing their region's barrenness, they fabricated a new legend of its rare fertility. But the older myth gave ground only slowly. The Pacific Railway Surveys in the 1850's still drew a forbidding picture. The Union Pacific Railway Charter in 1862 was meant less to provide a link to the plains than to assure a speedy bridge across them. It was a cut through the mid-continental barrier, connecting settlers in the Mississippi Valley with those on the Pacific Coast.

The new myth, no less than the old, testified to man's indomitable will to believe. Now the settlers who moved up the valleys of the Platte and the Kansas rivers, as Henry Nash Smith eloquently recounts, replaced the myth of the Desert by the myth of the Garden. From earliest colonial times, Europeans had seen the land of the Atlantic settlements as a New-World garden long kept virgin to redress the overcultivation of the Old. It was easy to extend this myth beyond the Mississippi.

The magic by which the imagined desolation would be transmuted into an imagined Eden was hinted by Josiah Gregg in his *Commerce of the Prairies* as early as 1844. Might not the arrival of settlers itself do the job?

> Why may we not suppose that the genial influences of civilization —that extensive cultivation of the earth—might contribute to the multiplication of showers, as it certainly does of fountains? Or that the shady groves, as they advance upon the prairies, may have some effect upon the seasons? At least, many old settlers maintain that the droughts are becoming less oppressive in the West. The people of New Mexico also assure us that the rains have much increased of latter years, a phenomenon which the vulgar superstitiously attribute to the arrival of the Missouri traders. Then may we not hope that these sterile regions might yet be thus revived and fertilized, and their surface covered one day by flourishing settlements to the Rocky Mountains?

Gregg himself suggested that this great climatic change was accomplished by the very process of irrigation.

A still more appealing version of the myth was spread by newspapermen reporting the construction of the Union Pacific amid the growing populations of Kansas and Nebraska in 1866 and 1867. As more people arrived out there, they said, somehow rainfall increased. Welcome "scientific" foundation for the new mythic hopes was supplied by the widely publicized Geological and Geographical Survey of the Territories, which began work under federal auspices and under the direction of Ferdinand V. Hayden, in Nebraska in 1867. Its technical reports were remarkably popular in the West. "It is believed," Hayden publicly informed the Secretary of the Interior (1867), ". . . that the planting of ten or fifteen acres of forest-trees on each quarter-section will have a most important effect on the climate, equalizing and increasing the moisture and adding greatly to the fertility of the soil. The settlement of the country and the increase of the timber has already changed for the better the climate of that portion of Nebraska lying along the Missouri, so that within the last twelve or fourteen years the rain has gradually increased in quantity and is more equally distributed through the year. I am confident that this change will continue to extend across the dry belt to the foot of the Rocky Mountains as the settlements extend and the forest-trees are planted in proper quantities."

This appealing theory was supported by the monograph on "Agriculture in Colorado" by Hayden's entomologist and botanist, Cyrus Thomas, which recorded the scientist's "firm conviction" that increasing rainfall somehow came from settlement of the country "and that, as the population increases, the amount of moisture will increase." Respectable agronomists like Samuel Aughey, Professor of Natural Sciences at the new University of Nebraska, espoused the optimistic theory. Their collaborative efforts were happily assisted by a series of abnormally wet years after the Civil War. A slogan was coined and repeated for decades: "Rain Follows the Plough."

It is not hard to understand the booster appeal of this doctrine. The notion may originally have been borrowed from French or English scientists. But in the booming West, to deny it, even to doubt it, was to betray the community. Cattlemen who refused to believe were accused of selfishly wanting to discourage immigration so they might keep for range what might have become valuable cultivated land. Irrigation projects were opposed, not only because a large enough number of new arrivals would make irrigation superfluous, but also because talk about irrigation reduced land values by advertising the insufficiency of natural rainfall.

Soon the extravagance of this booster answer to the myth of a Great American Desert far exceeded the extravagance of the myth it was answering. Especially attractive to city-developers was the doctrine of the flamboyant William Gilpin (1813–92). A versatile soldier-explorer-editor who had accompanied Frémont on his expedition of 1843, he joined Thomas Hart Benton in promoting a central route for the transcontinental railroad and became the first territorial governor of Colorado. In three books, *The Central Gold Region* (1860), *Mission of the North American People* (1873), and *The Cosmopolitan Railway* (1890), Gilpin elaborated an appealingly simple theory of his own which he had been widely advocating in speeches and essays since about 1846.

Drawing on the German philosopher-naturalist Alexander Von Humboldt, he developed a theory of geographic determinism designed to please the most enthusiastic mid-western booster. Following Humboldt, Gilpin found the key to his prophecies in the "Isothermal Zodiac." This was an undulating belt of approximately thirty degrees (about 2300 miles wide; from about the twenty-fifth to the fifty-fifth degree) encircling the earth across the Northern Hemisphere. Through the middle of this belt ran the "axis of intensity," roughly along the fortieth degree of north latitude, where the mean annual temperature was 52° Fahrenheit. "Within this isothermal belt, and restricted to it, the column of the human family, with whom abides the sacred and inspired fire of civilization, accompanying the sun, has marched from east to west, since the birth of time. Upon this axis of intensity have been constructed the great primary cities, which have been from age to age the foci from which have radiated intellectual activity and power. . . . the Chinese, the Indian, the Persian, the Grecian, the Roman, the Spanish, the British, finally, the republican empire of the people of North America. . . . this zone belts the globe around where the continents expand and the oceans contract: it undulates with the axis of warm temperature (52 degrees of mean heat): it contains ninety-five one-hundredths of the white people of the globe, and all its civilization!"

What more obvious then, than the need for a world railroad encircling the globe along the Axis of Intensity? Hydrographic maps in Gilpin's *Central Gold Region* showed that the Great Basin of the Mississippi was "the ampitheatre of the world . . . the most magnificent dwelling marked out by God for man's abode." Compare the continents: Europe culminates in its center into the icy masses of the Alps; Asia similarly rises into the Himalayas; Africa and South America, so far as they were known at all, were "perplexed into dislocated fragments."

> In contrast, the interior of North America presents towards heaven an expanded bowl, to receive and fuse into harmony whatsoever enters within its rim. So, each of the other continents presenting a bowl reversed, scatter everything from a central apex into radiant distraction. . . . In geography the antithesis of the old world, in society we are and will be the reverse.

Each of Gilpin's cosmic generalizations resounded with booster overtones for the projects in the midwest in which Gilpin himself happened to be interested. For example, the central route (along the thirty-ninth parallel) for the transcontinental railroad. In the 1840's, Gilpin had bought land on the edge of Independence along the Missouri River. Then he had persuaded the city council to extend the town limits to include his property, which he subdivided into town lots. This land, as it happened, was at the center of Gilpin's hydrographic circles on the continent. The map which Gilpin prepared and circulated of "Centropolis" showed that the national capital by a higher geographic necessity should be moved to the very heart of Gilpintown. While promoting this particular property, he discovered another geographic law: the great emporiums of the world were located on the great rivers, and in North America these cities had to be about one hundred leagues (350 miles) apart. Luckily this was just the distance Independence and Gilpintown stood from St. Louis.

When his ambitious project for Gilpintown collapsed, Gilpin discovered happily that he had put his great central city ten miles too far east. In 1858, then, his new map of "Centropolis" located the capital at the present site of Greater Kansas City, to which Gilpin had shifted his booster loyalties. When, a dozen years later, Gilpin had moved these loyalties still farther westward to Denver, his science kept pace with his investments. Gilpin's *Notes on Colorado* (1870) announced his discovery that, because population had begun to condense itself farther west along the Axis of Intensity, Denver was now the "focal point of impregnable power in the topographical configuration of the continent." At this last locus of Gilpin's personal fortunes he found the true gateway for all transcontinental movement.

*　　*　　*

In the geographic darkness of the West, some like Gilpin managed to convince themselves and others that they had found what they wanted. That same darkness concealed many a swindler, who lured his quarry to a blank place on the map, there to find whatever he chose to plant. The hoax became a minor western institution, and figured prominently in western folklore. Mythic mines were legion; they multiplied in vast regions of half-knowledge, where weariness, desperation, and optimism prepared travelers to believe they had found Golconda. A beautiful example was the Great Diamond Hoax of 1872, commonly called the biggest western mining swindle of the 19th century.

One foggy morning early in 1872, two dishevelled prospectors, looking as if they had just returned from distant diggings, entered a bank in San Francisco and asked a bank officer to see them privately. With elaborate furtiveness, they instructed him to keep safely for them a small bag whose contents they reluctantly revealed to be diamonds. They swore him to secrecy, then disappeared. The clerk, of course, immediately communicated the secret information to the other bank officers, who in turn passed it on confidentially to a select group of the richest men in San Francisco, who at once began a search for the two mysterious prospectors. By a happy coincidence, within a few weeks

Philip Arnold and John Slack reappeared. After considerable persuasion (which included payment to them of about $600,000) they allowed themselves to be included in a new mining company, whose sole purpose was to exploit the mythic but still unlocated diamond mines. Arnold went East with some backers so that the diamonds could be examined for genuineness by Tiffany & Company of New York. Tiffany reported the diamonds to be real and an additional group of New York backers was then organized. To reassure themselves and other potential investors, they hired an impeccably honest mining-consultant to prepare an on-the-spot report of the mines. Henry Janin (who had made his reputation by condemning nearly every scheme he had been called to report on) agreed to visit and assess the diamond fields. Arnold and Slack then took Janin to the fields, the location of which by elaborate subterfuges was still kept secret. Janin returned to announce that the diamond fields were real. Before long, at least one investor had put in $660,000 and others had "invested" to the tune of $10,000,000.

Arnold and Slack, far from being the bumpkins they seemed, proved to be two of the most sophisticated swindlers of modern times. On remote mesas in northwestern Colorado, they had actually staked out a claim, and had spared no trouble or expense in salting it with small diamonds and rubies. Their protection, of course, was the vastness of the country, the remoteness of their find, and the general geographic ignorance. If they could keep the location of their diamond fields secret from the general public, allowing only a few credulous colleagues to be guided to the spot, they might pyramid their investment into a substantial fortune before they could be exposed.

The diamond fever rose from May to November of 1872. Other swindlers—or promoters—appeared all over the West, not only in San Francisco, but in Denver, Salt Lake City, and elsewhere. Exposure of the hoax might have been indefinitely delayed had not the hoaxers thoughtlessly located their diamond field in the neighborhood of the fortieth parallel. In 1867 the Congress had authorized its famous Fortieth Parallel Survey: "a geological and topographical exploration of the territory between the Rocky Mountains and the Sierra Nevada mountains, including the route or routes of the Pacific railroad." In charge was the indomitable Clarence King, whom Henry Adams idolized as "the ideal American they all wanted to be." In the summer of 1872, King and his men were still at work on their survey. When King heard about the diamond fields (of which he had so far found no trace), he was troubled. An assigned purpose of his survey was to advise Congress and the nation of the natural resources of the area; if he had actually missed something as valuable as a diamond field, his own professional reputation, and the reputation of the whole Fortieth Parallel Survey (as well as of future surveys), would be put in doubt.

By uncannily clever detective work, King and three of his fellow-surveyors pieced together the fragmentary clues incautiously dropped by the diamond promoters. These clues led to the Yampa–Green River country of northern Colorado and Utah and southern Wyoming. In the end, King's party had nothing to follow but a hint that Janin had accidentally let slip: the diamond hunters had camped at the foot of a pine-covered mountain, which in June was still covered by some snow, and to the northeast side of which no high mountains could be seen. Finally, in early November, King found the desolate place where claim notices had been posted. (It is still called Diamond Peak in Colorado.) Tracks from the notices converged on a sandstone ledge. There, near the surface, they found numerous small diamonds and rubies. King, already puzzled that gems should be found in this kind of geologic formation, noticed that the diamonds and rubies appeared only near the windswept table rock that was the heart of the claim. He also noted the curious fact that for every twelve rubies there was one diamond. His party then took out their sieves and tried the surrounding area. They found gems only in those places where the earth was already disturbed. A few were discovered inside anthills, but only where a telltale footprint had been left nearby. As a final test, King and his party dug a deep hole and sifted all the earth; they found no gems.

King was now convinced that the diamond mine was a hoax, and that he could prove it. He raced across country to the railroad for San Francisco, anxious to reach Janin and other innocent backers before rumors might give the hoaxers a chance to escape or to capitalize further on their swindle. King succeeded in persuading the investors of their deception. The hoaxers were never brought to justice but King became a hero for his courage, his scientific sleuthing, and his command of Western geography. It was ironic that, while the seven large volumes of the Fortieth Parallel Survey (1870–78) set a new scientific standard for government publications, became an international geographic classic, and led to establishment of the United States Geological Survey (1878) with King at its head, it was his lucky exposure of the Diamond Hoax that brought King public notice. The San Francisco *Chronicle* thanked "God and Clarence King" for escape from "a great financial calamity." Other newspapers, too, said that this one act had more than paid for the survey of the fortieth parallel, and proved that further surveys were desirable. Unwittingly, the hoaxers of Diamond Gulch thus promoted exploration of the continent.

*   *   *

The vagueness that inspired the extravagances of mapmakers and the wild promises of hoaxers also made Americans eager for pictures of their exotic continent. The scarcity of precise knowledge gave such knowledge as there was a peculiar appeal. In the colonial period the ungathered novelties of this new world had fostered a natural-history emphasis. The wealth of new sights in the early 19th century continued to stir naturalists to name and classify and depict what they saw. John James Audubon (1785–1851), who had spent much of his youth in Kentucky before becoming a taxidermist in Cincinnati, had early begun to draw and paint the birds of the New World in their natural setting. In 1826 he went to Britain, and with the help of a London engraver produced his elephant folios (*The Birds of America*, 1827–38) which offered over a thousand life-sized illustrations of five hundred species, in color. But such works as Audubon's were for the naturalist or the rich collector. A widespread demand for pictures of the West, and for vivid representations of the outer fringes of settlement, enabled landscape painters to flourish as never before.

Enormous panoramic paintings of the Mississippi River were among the most spectacular efforts to capture the continent's varied grandeur. The most famous of the panorama-painters was John Banvard, who was born in New York City in 1815, and who, at the age of fifteen, wandered out West where he taught himself how to paint. About 1841 he conceived his plan "to paint a picture of the beautiful scenery of the Mississippi, which should be as superior to all others, in point of *size,* as that prodigious river is superior to the streamlets of Europe—a gigantic idea!—which seems truly kindred to the illimitable forests and vast extents of his native land." "The idea of gain never entered his mind when he commenced the undertaking," wrote his anonymous biographer (probably Banvard himself), "but he was actuated by a patriotic and honorable ambition, that he should produce the largest painting in the world." To secure the sketches for his masterpiece, he spent over a year riding up and down the River in a skiff, suffering every hardship.

Banvard's completed canvas, when first exhibited at Louisville, in October, 1846, was an immediate success. The Louisville *Courier* hailed it as "the greatest and proudest work of art in the world." The "program notes" (which included a version of the Mike Fink legend, "The Last of the Boatmen . . .") were entitled: *Description of Banvard's Panorama of the Mississippi River, Painted on Three Miles of Canvas, exhibiting a View of Country 1200 Miles in Length, extending from the Mouth of the Missouri River to the City of New Orleans, being by far the Largest Picture ever executed by Man.* When Banvard took his painting on tour, he was everywhere acclaimed. "I see a panorama of the Mississippi advertised," Longfellow, who had just completed the first part of *Evangeline,* wrote in Boston in his journal. "This comes very *a propos*. The river comes to me instead of my going to the river; and as it is to flow through the pages of the poem, I look upon this as a special benediction." And after attending the artist's performance he noted: "Went to see Banvard's moving diorama of the Mississippi. One seems to be sailing down the great stream, and sees the boats and the sand-banks created with cottonwood, and the bayous by moonlight. Three miles of canvas, and a great deal of merit." After successes in New Orleans, New York, and Washington (where the Senate and House passed resolutions declaring the Panorama "a truly wonderful and magnificent production"), Banvard, armed with a letter of commendation from Edward Everett, late minister to England, to the president of the Royal Geographical Society, went on to greater triumphs abroad, where he was honored by Queen Victoria's summons to a command performance at Windsor Castle.

His method of displaying his ten-foot-high canvas was ingenious but simple. Rolled on upright revolving cylinders about twenty feet apart, the picture passed gradually before the spectators as the artist commented on his work. "Upon a platform is seated Mr. Banvard," reported the *Illustrated London News,* "who explains the localities as the picture moves, and relieves his narrative with Jonathanisms and jokes, poetry and patter, which delight his audience mightily; and a pianoforte is incidentally invoked, to relieve the narrative monotony." Since the painting was in motion and had to be viewed from a distance, it was more like stage-scenery than studio art. A press notice explained:

> You pass by, as in a rapid voyage, "temple, tower, and town"; and in an hour and a half's sitting, there is brought vividly before you all the chief incidents of savage and of civilized life, from the wigwams of the Indian and the log hut of the settler, to the lofty domes and graceful spires of the gay and crowded city. You flit by a rice swamp, catch a glimpse of a jungle, dwell for an instant on a prairie, and are lost in admiration at the varied, but ever glorious dress, in which, in the Western world, Nature delights to attire herself.

Banvard was not without competition. At least four other painters offered their own versions of "The Greatest Painting in the World," depicting the greatest river in the world. Each claimed to be the "true originator" of the idea, and boasted that his canvas was bigger, and therefore better, than the others. John Rawson Smith, Banvard's earliest rival, described his own work as "one-third longer than any other pictorial work in evidence; Four miles in Length" and "beyond all comparison, better than the smaller painting called Banvard's." The supposed measurements of all the panoramas had the truth—and the appeal—of other tall tales. The prize for actual size should probably have gone to Henry Lewis, whose "Great National Work" did measure twelve feet high and nearly 4000 feet (about three-quarters of a mile) long, and had to be seen in two evenings.

The interest of these works was more geographical than artistic: both painters and promoters advertised them as an educational and scientific experience. "In America," John Rawson Smith explained, "the country itself is ever on the change, and in another half century those who view this portrait of the Mississippi will not be able to recognize one twentieth part of its details. Where the forest now overshadows the earth, and affords shelter to the wild beasts, corn fields, orchards, towns, and villages, will give a new face to the scene, and tell of industry and enterprise, which will stimulate to new and untiring efforts." "Alligators and other creatures of the deep, of which Europeans only hear and read, are seen sporting in several places: and thus the beholder is constantly reminded that it is of no familiar scene he is the beholder." The desire of Americans for such information about the West was attested by the fact that in six weeks at Saratoga, New York, Smith's panorama earned twenty thousand dollars.

It was not only these folk painters of geographic newsreels who prospered. The mid-century was the heyday of an important and aesthetically more respectable group whom James Thomas Flexner has christened the American "Native School." As Flexner explains, they expressed widespread "communal experiences and ideals" by portraying the grandeur, the mystery, the variety, and the color of the American landscape. In the later 18th century, the great American painters— Gilbert Stuart, Benjamin West, John Trumbull, and others—produced portraits or historical or allegorical scenes, very much in the academic European tradition. But portrait-painting, somehow, was more congenial to an aristocratic society, like that of 18th-century England, or to a commercial society like that of 17th-century Holland, than to America. By the mid-19th century, some of the best American painters were still sometimes serving their apprenticeship and earning their bread and butter by doing jobs that would later fall to the photographer, but the important and distinctive work of the age was of another sort. William Cullen Bryant pointed the peculiar American challenge when he warned a painter who was about to depart for Europe:

> Fair scenes shall greet thee where thou goest—fair
> But different—everywhere the trace of men.
> Paths, homes, graves, ruins, from the lowest glen
> To where life shrinks from the fierce Alpine air.
> Gaze on them, till the tears shall dim thy sight,
> But keep that earlier, wilder image bright.

Works by living American painters—many of whom depicted "that wilder image"—had a popular appeal which was probably never exceeded. New York exhibits of such works, between 1839 and 1851, attracted an average annual attendance equal to over half the population of the city; this was, proportionately, three times as many as those who attended the Metropolitan Museum of the city a century later.

The vigor of these portrayers of the American landscape was impressive. There was the pioneering of Thomas Cole and Asher B. Durand, founders of the so-called Hudson River School, who went into the Catskill Mountains and painted precise, if romanticized, images of wild scenery direct from nature. There were the great illustrators of the West of the American Indians. Lewis and Clark had not taken an artist with them, but when Major S. H. Long crossed the Great Plains to the Rockies in 1819–20, he was accompanied by Samuel Seymour, an illustrator, whose drawings of Indian life soon excited wide interest. The greatest and most self-conscious of the recorders of the Indian was George Catlin (1796–1872), who had been raised in the Wyoming Valley of Pennsylvania among memories of some of the bloodiest Indian raids of the Revolutionary era. After attending the famous law school in Litchfield, Connecticut, and after an abortive career in law, Catlin turned to painting and made a living briefly as a portraitist; then, in Philadelphia about 1824, when he saw a delegation of Indians from the West—"in all their classic beauty with shield and helmet, tunic and manteau—tinted and tasseled off exactly for the painters' palette"— he determined (on the analogy of Charles Willson Peale's portrait gallery of Revolutionary notables) to make his own "Indian Gallery."

During the next years Catlin traveled over the West with his wife, painting and sketching "to use my art and so much of the labors of my future life as might be required in rescuing from oblivion the looks and customs of the vanishing races of native man in America." His problems were very different from those of the fashionable portrait artist who posed an aristocratic clientele, for many Indians feared they would die if he possessed their painted image. In his drawings and paintings, and in his *Letters and Notes on the Manners, Customs, and Condition of the North American Indians* (1841), he left a brilliant record of exotic features of the American landscape. Even art, however, did not escape the politics of Westward expansion, and the problems arising out of the uncertainties of the western border. In 1852, when Daniel Webster led Northern Senators to support the purchase of Catlin's "Indian Gallery" for the nation, the Southern majority voted the bill down. Southerners wanted the West for the expansion of their Peculiar Institution, and they feared Catlin's paintings would arouse sympathy for the Indians whom the Southerners and their slaves would displace.

Catlin was only one of a galaxy of painters of the Indian West; Karl Bodmer, Alfred Jacob Miller, and Charles Deas, and others who flourished before the Civil War, added vividness to the nation's uncertain western boundaries. Their work was supplemented by that of other artists who sought scenery far wilder and more forbidding than that which had enticed the Hudson River School. Albert Bierstadt, founder of a Rocky Mountain School, and Thomas Moran who did huge canvases of the Grand Canyon of the Yellowstone and the Chasm of the Colorado (bought by the Congress for ten thousand dollars apiece), and still others whose names became attached to remote western lakes and mountains and rivers, reminded Americans of how much in the land they had settled still remained to be conquered and discovered.

*   *   *

America was one of the last places where settlers would come in large numbers before the explorers, the geographers, the painters, and the professional naturalists. Already in the colonial period, this curious fact had brightened American thinking as physical and intellectual expansion became synonymous. Knowledge came naturally, and this shaped the very definition of knowledge. This was crucial too for the spirit of the new nation.

It was hard to be confined by knowledge still ungathered. On a half-known continent, it was difficult to disprove even the most extravagant visions—of sea passages to India, of a mythic garden destined for great cities, of a new Golconda. All this made the booster spirit possible and kept it alive. It also kept alive the competition between communities. What could not be disproved of a Nininger could not be disproved of a Hastings. Ignorance itself was an unacknowledged source of imagination and energy. What they didn't know couldn't stop them. Of course the actual settlers in the West were occasionally haunted by Great American Deserts which did not exist. But, more important, they were also often enticed by extravagant visions of a future which did exist, which the very extravagance of their vision helped call into existence. Discouraging facts could be discounted, or mistaken for their opposites, while booster extravagances could not be disproved. If the ignorance at the very scene was vast, it was even vaster on the eastern seaboard where many crucial decisions had to be taken.

29

Packaging a Continent

BACK ON THE eastern seaboard, men running the government of the new United States glossed over their ignorance. Few members of Congress had been in the half-known West. For them the continent— or at least the federal land, which comprised much of the future United

States—was a commodity. It had to be neatly parcelled for sale. Congressmen did not worry about how to get from here to there, or precisely where South Pass was to be found, or whether a river ran this way or that. They worried most over two other problems: first, how to make as much as possible of the West quickly salable, while spending as little as possible on costly surveying and mapping; second, how to package these parcels so that each purchaser could know precisely where his parcel was, and hence could feel assured that his title and ownership were safe. These overriding concerns, however irrelevant to the urgent problems of actual life in the West, shaped the patterns of American land ownership, land use, and land exhaustion for the following centuries.

The American anachronism of Settlement before Discovery, as we have seen, fostered the optimistic, competitive, booster spirit. It helped keep Americans mobile, hopeful, and none too well informed about the actual resources at their disposal. So, too, this anachronism of land mapped and sold before it was explored, known, or surveyed was to have effects almost as profound, and just as widespread. The crucial fact was that the United States Congress had begun to debate American land policy and to fix the pattern of sale long before they had any but the foggiest facts about the vast territories they were disposing.

Not until the creation of a Corps of Topographical Engineers by Congressional Act of July 5, 1838, was the groundwork laid for systematic surveys. Under these or related auspices some great work was eventually accomplished. But still the mapping was fragmentary and for some limited purpose: a wagon road, a railroad, or to mark the Mexican boundary. Only after the Civil War were there systematic, broadly scientific surveys of great areas.

Finally, in the later decades of the century, between 1867 and 1879, came the four great geographical and geological surveys of large areas of the West. All were under federal government auspices, and each came to be identified by the name of its leader. Ferdinand Vandeveer Hayden (1829–87), beginning in 1867, pioneered in surveying much of Colorado, Idaho, Montana, Wyoming, and Utah. Then came Clarence King's Fortieth Parallel Survey (1866–77), extending from eastern Colorado to the California line. Soon thereafter, John Wesley Powell perilously followed the course of the Colorado River (1869) and surveyed the Rocky Mountain Region (1871–78). Lieutenant George Montague Wheeler completed the last of the great surveys (1871–79) in his report on the territory west of the hundredth meridian. But three-quarters of a century before these great surveys were begun and while much of the continent was still shrouded in darkness, officials of the new United States government on the eastern seaboard had urgently required some policy for disposing of the land.

In older cultures, two aspects of land seemed most important in distinguishing it from other economic goods. First, the *qualitative uniqueness* of each parcel: location is unique; no two tracts can be in the same place. Second, the *indestructibility* of every parcel: a house can crumble, a horse can die, silver can be stolen, a gem can be lost, "one generation passeth away, and another generation cometh, but the earth endureth forever." Nowhere—not even in America—could land be quite divested of these inherent peculiarities, yet here land began to be treated almost as if it did not have these qualities.

In America the vast unoccupied space, the lack of a known history, and the scarcity of people, all helped make land something like grain or money, each unit of which could be treated like any other. Here, for example, it came to be assumed that land might simply be "used up," and that its user would then expect to move on to "newer" land. Once again, the vastness of American space tended to make space irrelevant in America. Nothing was more effective in giving land its novel place in American life than that the continent so long remained unknown and uncharted, for ignorance led those who officially dealt with land to treat it as if its units were nearly all alike.

Even before the Federal Constitution of 1787, the young nation possessed an embarrassment of landed wealth which had to be defined, organized, and governed in some way or other. As soon as the Congress accepted Virginia's cession of its lands northwest of the Ohio River on March 1, 1784, a national domain was created. By cessions from Massachusetts and Connecticut, and others extracted from the Indians, the domain quickly grew to fill out the Old Northwest. Thus, barely a year after the Treaty of Paris, which recognized American independence, had taken effect, the nation was burdened with organizing, outside the states themselves, an area about twice the size of France, an area whose geography and resources were still a dark mystery.

Discussions in the Congress over the shapes, sizes, and precise locations of possible new territories and states to be formed eventually from this area were an exercise in metaphysics, *a priorism*, and prophecy. They could not have had much to do with the actual geographic facts— with the special opportunities and dangers of the landscape, with rainfall, wind, soil, or waterways. All these were still unknown. Jefferson's reformist, geometric imagination (which had already made him champion the metric system of measurement and of money) was again awakened, and his committee proposed a plan for all the western lands which, in slightly amended form, became the Ordinance of 1784.

The geographic pattern which Jefferson proposed was the soul of neatness. Starting northward from the thirty-first parallel, each new state was to be rectangularly defined, each to include two degrees of latitude. The eastern and western boundaries were to be meridians of longitude: one passing through the Falls of the Ohio, the other through the mouth of the Great Kanawha River. This provided a kind of checkerboard. Each square would be given a synthetic name, like Polypotamia, Polisipia, Metropotamia, or Assonisipia. The true neatness of Jefferson's scheme does not appear when we superimpose it on a modern map, but on Thomas Hutchins' inaccurate map of 1778 (the one Jefferson probably relied on), it looks much better, for there Jefferson's North-South meridian running through the Falls of the Ohio strikes Lake Michigan almost precisely at its southern tip.

Jefferson's checkerboard scheme, incorporated in the Land Ordinance of 1784, never actually went into effect, largely because of the objections of James Monroe, who had himself just returned from a trip to the Northwest. Monroe reported that the land out there was "miserably poor." What he had seen around Lake Michigan and Lake Erie and along the Mississippi and Illinois Rivers was vast swamps and marshes, occasionally interspersed by "extensive plains which had not had from appearances and will not have, a single bush on them, for ages." Therefore, he said, since Jefferson's little rectangles would never do for states, fewer and larger units were required. George Washington, too, objected to the Jeffersonian scheme, which he feared would encourage a thin and widely scattered population. "Compact and progressive Seating will give strength to the Union. Sparse settlement in several new States, will have the direct contrary effect." The Northwest Ordinance of 1787, then, in a general way adopted Monroe's preference for fewer and larger states ("not less than three nor more than five"), but wisely left their precise definition to the future.

While some of the large-scale questions could be postponed, the small-scale questions could not. Congress could wait to decide the number and boundaries of the future states, but dared not wait to delimit the precise parcels to be offered for sale. Out there people were actually settling every day, making new farms and communities. They wanted to own their lands and they wanted to be sure their titles would stick. Despite its ignorance of the topographic details, which was at least as great as its ignorance of the large geographic outlines, Congress could not wait. Many pressure groups forced Congress to go into business even before it knew what it had for sale. Fortunately, Jefferson's scheme for making states by superimposing vast quadrangles on the still unknown western landscape was rejected, but his geometric scheme was applied on a smaller scale to mark off individual lots. This explains why in the 20th century the vast and varied continental United States startles the air traveler by the rectangular symmetry of its fences and roads.

More than three-quarters of the present area of continental United States is visibly subdivided in a rectilinear pattern. Roads are oriented to the principal points of the compass. The American land (smaller rectangles subdivided from squares one mile by one mile, which are in turn grouped in larger squares six miles by six miles) has thus remained one of the largest monuments to *a priorism* in all human history. And in a country which is a byword for adaptability and empiricism! Our land pattern is a relic of the young nation's need to make a commodity of its land, and hastily to map and sell it, even before it was explored or surveyed. It is one of the first examples of the peculiar importance of packaging in America.

The items to be packaged were parcels of outlying wilderness. A member of Congress in 1784 explained the two policies between which they chose:

> It has been the custom of the southern states to issue warrants from a land office. The person taking a warrant has to look for unlocated lands to cover with his warrant, of which he makes a return. In this way the good land is looked out and seized on first, and land of little value and of all shapes, left in the hands of the public. But this . . . soon rises in value, and is bought by the holders of the adjacent good lands, in their own defence. In the eastern [New England] states . . . the custom has been to sell a township by bonds [predetermined boundaries], or certain lots taken flush, good and bad together, and to pass out settlement in compact columns.

Would they extend the Southern system by which land was first settled and then surveyed? or the New England system, by which small contiguous parcels, already surveyed, were one after another gradually filled in with settlers? The Southern system was well suited for sales to individual settlers. On the other hand, the New England system rested on the practice of first vesting title to entire townships in an organized group of proprietors, through whom title was then assigned to individuals. Thus it had been well suited for communal settlement. Thomas Jefferson of Virginia and Hugh Williamson of North Carolina, first framers of the plan for the public lands, naturally inclined to the Southern system they knew. For western needs that system offered the great advantage of assuming settlement before survey.

New elements in the situation were Jefferson's special enthusiasm for the decimal system and Williamson's experience in Holland. One of Jefferson's pet projects at this time was to simplify all units of measurement; and he may have been influenced by a grand French project for a national survey from a base line. Meanwhile Williamson's education in Holland, a Roman-law country, had familiarized him with the Roman and Dutch rectangular systems of land division. Thus, for quite different reasons, both men favored imposing a neat grid pattern on all land, regardless of natural features. Their report to the Congress in 1784, modified and embodied in the Land Act of 1796, afterwards effectively dominated the vast federal domain.

The idea of marking off the landscape in neat rectangles was far from new. In 1669, even before the Lord Proprietors of Carolina had sent any colonists to the New World, their Fundamental Constitutions of Carolina provided for the survey of the entire land area of the colony into squares, each of 12,000 acres (about 4 x 4 miles). Early in the next century, Sir Robert Montgomery's scheme (1717) for the London planners of Georgia had specified geometric districts between the Altamaha and the Savannah Rivers, containing 116 squares each of precisely 640 acres (1 x 1 mile). General Henry Bouquet's plan, published in 1765, for garrisoned settlements on the upper Ohio River offered a similarly precise blueprint. "Curved lines, you know," Daniel Drake remarked in the early 19th century, "symbolize the country, straight lines the city." A checkerboard neatness governed the street pattern of Western towns like St. Louis and Cincinnati.

The scheme finally incorporated in the Act of 1796 was a New England-style modification of the Southern warrant system. Settlement was permitted before survey, but land could be purchased only in rectangular pieces. Each small rectangle (640 acres), newly christened a "section," was one mile square. These were grouped into larger rectangles ("townships") six miles square. A minimum price per acre was fixed for all land, regardless of quality. Half the townships were to be sold in single sections, half in units of eight sections each. This checkerboard pattern was imposed on nearly the whole nation outside the original colonies: rich valleys, subhumid prairies, barren deserts, rocky mountain slopes, all were sliced into squares and offered in packages of the same size.

While such a mode of sale ignored the uniqueness of each piece of land, it was "attended by the least possible expense, there being only two sides of the square to run in almost all cases." The simplicity of property lines would also presumably produce "exemption from controversy on account of bounds to the latest ages." Each parcel was identified by number in a standard numbering system. This avoided the clumsy European practice, imported to the American colonies, of describing parcels "by metes and bounds." In colonial times, a Massachusetts landowner might own a parcel legally described as "beginning at the Foot of the Gulley below his House and running three hundred and twenty Pole North Five Degrees West to Red Oak marked AB then running Eighty three Pole East to a Spruce Tree marked AB then running South three hundred and twenty Pole to a Pitch Pine marked AB then running Fifty three Poles West and by South which makes up the one hundred & thirty four Acres." Under the new grid system an owner could describe his parcel simply as "the northeast quarter of section 6 in township 39 north, range 14 east of the third principal meridian." Any settler possessing rudimentary means of measurement could now verify the bounds of his purchase.

A technical problem arose from the fact that, because the earth is spherical, its meridians converge toward the poles. Therefore, if boundary lines conformed to the true meridians, the plots could not be perfect squares. A solution already developed by 1804 was to begin surveying each large area by first laying down at a convenient arbitrary point a "principal meridian" (on a meridian of longitude), then a "base line" (a parallel of latitude) crossing at right angles. Starting at the point of intersection, the neighboring areas were marked into rectangular subdivisions in four independent quadrants. New parallels of latitude (called "standard latitudes") were run out at intervals of twenty-four miles. This meant that only every fourth township was bounded by a true parallel of latitude. Although there resulted a slight offset of boundaries at each standard parallel, this did not create a substantial problem, for redefinition of "standard latitudes" every twenty-four miles minimized the accumulation of error.

A large practical problem arose from the fact that this whole system presupposed survey prior to settlement. But advance survey of each little parcel in the extensive public domain was not feasible. Into vast areas of the West, as we have seen, settlers poured without awaiting legal formalities. The land they cultivated often spilled over from one quarter-section or section to another. They had not the foggiest idea where the lines on the checkerboard might be found, but they learned quickly enough where streams ran, or which pieces were sandy, rocky, swampy, or well drained. Many communities, through their claim clubs, made their own rules. Then later when federal surveys finally came through, forceful local precautions prevented existing property arrange-ments from being unduly disturbed.

The land itself was more varied than Jefferson and his contemporaries dared imagine. In those days even the "Far West" (then the Northwest Territory) hardly hinted the geographic gamut—from snow-capped mountains and subarctic tundra to lush subtropical forests, everglades, and deserts of sand and salt—which was to be the United States. Everywhere the rectangular land survey imposed the same grid. Everywhere it became the base for geometric arrangements of roads, fields, fences, and streets. In the long run, land use itself would be governed by the shapes and sizes of these parcels originally packaged for sale.

The founders had successfully devised a cheap way of preparing land for market. Other consequences of the system were discovered too late. The size of the normal farm unit (the basic "section" of 640 acres and its subdivisions, the 320-acre half-section and the 160-acre quarter-section) naturally enough had been determined by the familiar needs of the farmers of the humid eastern seaboard. In the East, the average annual rainfall is remarkably uniform—between about forty and sixty inches a year—and lands are naturally irrigated by a wide-spreading network of rivers and streams. In this area, there are few parcels of land as large as a half-section which lack water. But in much of the West, and especially west of the hundredth meridian, water is scarce.

John Wesley Powell pointed out this crucial difference in 1878 in his epochal *Report on the Lands of the Arid Region of the United States.* According to him, more than four-tenths of the whole continental United States (excluding Alaska) was an "Arid Region." In the vast western stretches, where mean annual rainfall was less than twenty inches, agriculture like that of the eastern seaboard was not feasible. Where possible at all, western agriculture there depended on irrigation. For this small irrigable part, the chief water sources were large streams, which could be developed only by cooperative labor or by large expenditures of capital for dams. Timber lands amounted to only about twenty per cent of the Arid Region. Most of the region was suitable only for pasturage, and, because the grass was so scanty, this land was valuable only in large quantities. Each pasturage farm needed a small tract of irrigable land watered by a small stream or spring. Pasture land too was obviously useless without water, which in these areas of scarce rainfall could be had only from streams.

Here in the Arid Region, the grid pattern became doctrinaire nonsense. A section of 640 acres was far too small to support a family raising cattle. Many such rectangles contained no water at all. According to Powell, the minimum farm-pasturage unit should have been quadrupled to 2560 acres. But the only water might be concentrated in a few sections, whose lucky owners then had power of life and death over their neighbors.

The community emphasis, Powell argued, was inescapable. Land boundaries should conform to watercourses rather than to the compass. For the very life of cattlemen, he said, would depend on their ability to share water and provide other common facilities. Settlers of the arid west would be drawn together by the character of their land, much as Puritan New Englanders two centuries earlier had been drawn together by their beliefs. "As the pasturage lands should have water fronts and irrigable tracts, and as the residences should be grouped, and as the lands cannot be economically fenced and must be kept in common," Powell observed in 1878, "local communal regulations or co-operation is necessary." Ironically, in the long run there were few stronger pressures to communal effort in the West, to vast co-operative projects of irrigation, dams, and controlled water sources, than those arising from the oversimplified land packaging of the first years of national life.

30

Government as a Service Institution

AMERICA, THEN, OFFERED a novel opportunity to "create" property owners, and no governmental power was more important than the power to give title to pieces of the New World. Power of governments over the land shaped distinctive American attitudes to government. Those who came to think that their birthright included a piece of the continent, came also to think it a task of governments to make the land accessible, to increase its value and its usefulness. And there were enough different forms and shapes and sizes of government to provide citizens continually with some political agency or other from whom they could expect such services.

"Plenty of good land," Adam Smith explained in his *Wealth of Nations* (1776), "and liberty to manage their own affairs their own way, seem to be the two great causes of prosperity of all new colonies." Smith boasted that Britain had come closer than other countries to making colonial lands widely available for cultivation and improvement. In British colonies, he said, far less than elsewhere, was land monopolized by a few large holders. But Americans still did not find British land policy free enough for their taste. The Declaration of Independence accused the King of having "endeavoured to prevent the population of these States; for that purpose obstructing the Laws of Naturalization of Foreigners; refusing to pass others to encourage their migration hither, and raising the conditions of new Appropriations of Lands." By its Proclamation of 1763, which declared the Appalachians the western boundary between their settlements and a permanent Indian reservation, the British had hemmed in the colonists. Then, by the Quebec Act of 1774, Parliament had extended the boundaries of Canada down behind the colonies to the Ohio River, including vast tracts long claimed by several colonies. But for many other reasons, too, including the wasteful ways of colonial agriculture, Americans wanted more and more land.

During and after the Revolution, lands remained the main stumbling block to a new American nation. Of the original thirteen colonies, seven claimed extensive and often overlapping western lands (several running to the Western Ocean); the rest were confined in clearly marked narrow boundaries along the seacoast. The small or hemmed-in states, led by Maryland, delayed entering a new government to persuade the others to put their unsettled western lands into a common treasury, from which they could later be parcelled out by the new central government. Maryland refused the Articles of Confederation until such concessions were made. When Virginia (1781) and Massachusetts (1785) yielded their lands, the new nation became a substantial reality. Not until 1802 did the last of the great landowning states give in. For this great "public domain," there was no close analogue in the modern history of Europe. The weak new nation, still unsure of its powers to tax or to legislate, had at its disposal a landed territory greater than all the states together and larger than any established Western European nation.

In the decades after Independence, this posed a unique challenge to government in the United States: first to the federal government and then indirectly to other units of government. How to occupy and exploit the continent itself? How to disperse landed property among the people? How to make these lands valuable and productive, and their new communities prosperous? Governments in America, from force of circumstance, then, were agencies for creating and protecting new property. Americans, from the beginning, expected their governments to help them make the most of their unprecedented opportunities. Governments here had thrust on them new tasks and new expectations of service.

The notion rooted in American patriotic pseudo-folklore that "free" land left the American a self-dependent individual hardly accords with the facts. In more settled societies like England, where the landed wealth had been appropriated by individuals long centuries before, a man received his land through the generosity of his lord, his landlord, his father, his grandfather, or his brother. The American contrast was striking. Here, though the scope for individual initiative in securing land was greater than ever before, the direct help of government was also newly important. Only a government could convert possession into ownership. No wonder, then, that in America—where everybody, or nearly everybody, hoped to become a landowner, and where government was the great landowner—everyone looked to governments for some personal benefaction. Americans expected their governments to give them clearly bounded parcels of land, to confirm their ownership, and to protect their possession against French, Spanish, or other European intruders, and against Indian marauders. They expected the government, in addition, to help make and keep their land accessible and to help increase its value. The whole American situation led them to expect more from large organized political units, the states and the federal government, than did their contemporaries in the Old World.

Take, for example, the American mode of building railroads. In England railroads, as well as most canals, were built by private funds, unaided by government. In the United States, by contrast, every form of government—federal, state, county, and municipal—gave substantial help. Why the difference? In England the large capital required for rail-road-building was available in private hands, but in the United States capital was still scarce and the corporation was only beginning to be developed. Furthermore, in England and often too on the European con-tinent, a railroad ran along established and flourishing avenues of trade. A line between London and Manchester, for example, could count on heavy traffic as soon as it was in operation. But an American railroad (as the London *Times* once observed) might run from "Nowhere-in-Particu-lar to Nowhere-at-All." The American railroad, like the booster hotel and the community newspaper of the upstart city, was often built in the hope that the railroad itself would help call into being the population by serv-ing which it would prosper.

"No new people can afford to construct their own railroads." So ran the refrain in Henry Varnum Poor's *American Railroad Journal,* which repeatedly distinguished between long-settled regions, which had ac-cumulated capital in private hands, and the American West, which still needed government aid. "A great and extensive country like this," William H. Seward of New York told the Senate in 1850, "has need of roads and canals earlier than there is an accumulation of private capital within the state to construct them." To American railroad promoters this seemed a plain fact, which justified or even required the aid of all governments. The enterprising men who secured government subsidies, grants, and loans for building canals and railroads out into risky un-settled territory should rank high among pioneer builders of the American West. They, like the fur trappers, the river boatmen, the organizers of westward-moving wagon trains, and the boosters of upstart cities had seized peculiarly American opportunities.

Among these opportunities we must count the numerousness of government units (federal, state, and local) and the lucky fact that a great public domain of unprecedented wealth and proportions was at the disposal of governments. The newness of these governments—and their lack of established traditions and of time-honored dogmas—made them readier to experiment with their wealth and their power to lend and to borrow toward any promising public purpose. Without a simple traditional concept of "national interest" or a rigid doctrine of the boundaries of public enterprise, they listened more sympathetically to all requests for aid.

During the pioneer age of railroad building, in the decades before the Civil War, Americans showed great ingenuity in devising ways for governments to help them construct their long and expensive new lines. The muckraking bias of the late 19th century has put these activities in a false perspective. Hardly a textbook of American history fails to reprint the map of "Federal Land Grants for the Construction of Railroads and Wagon Roads, 1823–71," which shows vast stretches, a sizable proportion of the area of western states, granted to railroad builders. The common innuendo is that there was something peculiarly corrupt about these proceedings, otherwise why would so much land have been given away? But railroad companies were only one class of beneficiaries of the nearly universal government assistance.

The government promotion of railroads, and of the canals before them, which Carter Goodrich has documented, is a parable of the distinctive roles of governments in America. Communities grew and population expanded as government-aided canals and railroads were built ahead of the traffic. The railroads themselves brought into being the population that used them. Whether this could have happened without the substantial government assistance is debatable, but the historical facts are clear. The westward expanders were pushing out to places they hoped to make into thriving communities. Their booster railroads universally expected help from public agencies; they were not disappointed.

Aid came from all units of government. States, counties, and cities, in varying proportions, continually helped during the 19th century. Federal aid came in great lumps when expansion met a large natural obstacle, where settlement was too sparse, or where local governments were too weak to give the needed help. First, in the great push across the Appalachians, the federal government acknowledged its responsibilities when, in 1806, Congress authorized surveys for a National Road or Turnpike (later commonly known as the Cumberland Road), eventually to run from Cumberland, Maryland, across the mountain barrier to Wheeling on the Ohio River and beyond (roughly along what later became U. S. Highway 40). This road was constructed directly by the federal government.

Then, in 1808, Albert Gallatin, Jefferson's imaginative Secretary of the Treasury, gave the Senate his remarkable Report on Roads and Canals, a comprehensive scheme he had worked out with Jefferson for a federally-aided transportation system to cover the nation, connecting the eastern rivers with the Mississippi basin. The impending war with Great Britain delayed Gallatin's projects, but nearly every one was finally accomplished over the next sixty years—by varying combinations of private, local, state, and federal resources. The second great federal push began when the empty prairies had to be crossed, and reached its climax with the conquest of the Rocky Mountains and the Sierra Nevadas. Here was no avenue along safe and settled lines of trade, but an eighteen-hundred-mile leap from the remote Missouri River to the Pacific Ocean across lands nearly unsettled. The result was the largest federal grants to railroads.

Forms of aid varied as promoters devised requests suited to their peculiar needs and to the prejudices and temptations of legislators and commissioners. Most familiar, and most important for the longer routes, was the gift of public lands by both the federal government and the states. Texas, for example, which had retained its public lands when it entered the Union in 1845, eventually made gifts to railroads amounting to over thirty-two million acres, over one-sixth of the area of the state. The land grants for railroads, like those for wagon-roads before them, were not merely for the right-of-way, but included (in the usual federal grants) alternate sections (640 acres) within a specified number of miles on either side of the road. In grants to railroad companies the minimum width of this strip was ten miles, the maximum eighty miles, ranging then from five to forty sections on either side.

Every other conceivable form of aid was given. Direct grants of money came sometimes from treasury surpluses, sometimes from public borrowing. The state of North Carolina, having exhausted its borrowing capacity in 1873, authorized counties along the line of a railroad to levy a special tax payable either in cash or in country produce. Remission of taxes and exemption from state and local taxes were another form of aid. For example, the federal government from time to time remitted duties on iron imported for rails. As early as 1787, the state of South Carolina had offered credits against duties on the importation of slaves as encouragement of improvements of the Catawba and Wateree rivers. The ingenuity of promoters and their legislative friends was inexhaustible.

By 1860, state and local governments had given for improvements in transportation (in addition to lands, materials, and special privileges) direct financial grants with a face value of over four hundred million dollars. About sixty per cent of this, Goodrich estimates, came from the seven states directly facing the Appalachian barrier. New York State spent nearly seventy million, Virginia over fifty million. Western states like Missouri and Tennessee spent amounts equally large in proportion to their population. Although local governments as a whole spent only a quarter of the total, Baltimore's expenditure was greater than that of many state governments. Portland, Louisville, and Mobile each spent more for such improvements than did their respective states.

After the failure of numerous projects in the depression years following 1837 and 1839, some states adopted legal prohibitions against state aid to internal improvements. Despite the many discouraging experiences, some programs of state aid were actually at their height during the 1850's. But by 1861 clauses against state aid were common in state constitutions. One important effect of these was to pass more responsibility for aid down to the local governments. And during the '50's the federal government, too, had returned with large-scale aid to the railroads in the form of land grants. While the particular source of government aid was frequently shifting, expectations of some form of public assistance never died.

Such a large and varied assortment of governmental units made possible a nearly unbroken pattern of government aid. When President Monroe withdrew federal support from the Cumberland Road because of a supposed lack of constitutional authority, the states stepped into the breach. When the states became cautious of financial involvement in the early 1840's the prosperous and optimistic upstart cities were ready to help. Meanwhile, by the 1850's, the federal government once again was ready to give its strong support. An alert American railroad-promoter or land-developer could nearly always find some public agency or other ready to contribute capital and share the risk of exploiting and improving the continent. In the half-century before the Civil War, American governments, despite (or perhaps because of) their overlapping, vaguely defined, and ill-organized responsibilities, delivered the expected services.

Just as the boundaries between one governmental unit and another were vague, so too were the boundaries between "public" and "private" responsibilities. The basic importance of real estate as a resource and a commodity in a newly developing country made the distinctions between one man's interest and another's hard to define. Everybody seemed to profit from growing populations and expanding, prospering communities. Another American peculiarity, as Goodrich has pointed out, was that public and private activities in promoting internal improvements were generally not considered competitive. Nor were they thought to be exclusive alternatives. Jared Sparks, a strong supporter of all such improvements, voiced a general opinion in the *North American Review* (1821) when he appealed for support "equally to individuals, corporate bodies and state legislatures." The same meetings held to urge government aid also roused enthusiasm for private contributions. Promoters of the Western Railroad went house to house in Boston "to urge upon each one, as a matter of duty, as well as of interest, to do their share to advance this great work." When an Iowa court forbade Marshalltown from giving municipal funds to a railroad, the city fathers declared a holiday, while the local band helped raise the funds by voluntary gifts. A flourishing community spirit in the upstart towns made people eager to get the job done. If not by one arm of government, then by another; if not by the government, then directly by the people.

But the booster spirit was also a competitive spirit. The rivalry that inspired the county-seat wars or the struggle for a state prison or a university, inspired an equally bitter fight for the advantages of a turnpike, canal, or railroad. As early as December, 1806, the Commissioners to lay out the National Road noted the special difficulties they faced from "the solicitude and importunities of the inhabitants of every part of the district, who severally considered their grounds entitled to preference." The Erie Canal (constructed 1817–25), by connecting Albany on the Hudson River with Buffalo on Lake Erie opened a waterway eastward from Ohio, Indiana, Michigan, Wisconsin, and Illinois, and gave a great competitive advantage to both Buffalo and New York City. "They have built the longest canal in the world," boasted a speaker at its opening, "in the least time, with the least experience, for the least money, and to the greatest public benefit." Governor De Witt Clinton had been the principal promoter, the state of New York had been the organizer and financier, and subscriptions had come almost entirely from citizens of the state, in modest amounts. Other regions and metropolises would not be left behind. Maryland and Baltimore met the challenge by two great enterprises reaching across the mountains to the Monongahela and the Ohio. On July 4, 1828, the first earth was turned for the Chesapeake and Ohio Canal and for the Baltimore and Ohio Railroad, both competing for the opportunity to help the community grow. The canal was supported mainly by the state of Maryland and the railroad by the city of Baltimore. Meanwhile complaints were heard in Virginia that too much of that state's wealth had been allowed to "pass out of her hands to enrich the coffers of her neighbors." South Carolina, urged on by its energetic Governor George McDuffie, hoped by its own project (1836) for crossing the Appalachians to make Charleston into "the New York of the South."

Each successful project spawned others supposed to benefit from its predecessor. For example, the prospering Erie Canal intensified the rivalry between Troy and Albany to be the main Hudson River junction for traffic from the West. Troy spent nearly three-quarters of a million dollars on a municipally owned railroad; Albany countered with a quarter-million grant to the Mohawk and Hudson line.

Upstart western cities battled furiously for advantages. In Ohio nearly every railroad built between 1836 and 1850 received financial support from counties or cities. Cincinnati lavished its efforts to attract metropolitan connections both eastward (through the Little Miami) and westward to St. Louis. When the census of 1860 showed the city slipping from its first rank west of the Appalachians, Cincinnati's *Daily Times* declared it was "a matter of life or death" to secure a railroad southward to meet the competition of Louisville. The provision in the Ohio state constitution against a city becoming "a stockholder" in railroads was evaded when Cincinnati built the railroad *entirely* on its own account. St. Louis, fired by the booster spirit, before 1861 had subscribed over six million dollars for railroads to make the city and county great. The county distributed its shares of railroad stock to property owners, "thus giving every taxpayer an interest in the road in proportion to the amount of his taxes" and "a voice in the election of directors and location of the road." A similar practice was followed in Iowa and elsewhere.

The railroad promoters, asking communities to bid against one another, profited by deflecting their route this way or that. Citizens of North Liberty, Iowa, in public meeting adopted a resolution (December 13, 1865), "That Johnson County donate half a million dollars rather

than this Rail Road should be made twenty miles east or west of us."
In 1869 Indiana railroad-builders were openly offering to run their line
through Covington in return for a donation of eighty thousand dollars;
otherwise, they threatened to move it in the direction of Perryville. Sometimes this competition produced bizarre results. The New York and
Oswego Midland railroad, completed in 1873, had gone zigzagging across
the state in search of municipal bonds. When larger cities like Syracuse
refused to subscribe, the line actually secured some six million dollars in
municipal aid from nearly fifty towns, mostly small. To pick up these
sums it ended up crossing the breadth of the state without passing
through a single major city.

It is no wonder that the transcontinental line, the greatest of American
railroad projects, was long delayed by local competition for places along
the route. Not until secession removed from Congress the advocates of a
southern route was it possible to begin to approach a decision on federal
aid. But a bitter struggle still continued between the advocates of a
central and those of a northern route. The route of the proposed transcontinental line, a New Mexico representative complained, would not be
acceptable "unless it starts in the corner of every man's farm and runs
through all his neighbors' plantations." The Pacific Railway Acts (1862;
1864) would have fixed the eastern terminus at Omaha and would have
been a victory for the "Iowa-Chicago interest" (supported by New
York) over the "Kansas-St. Louis interest" (supported by Cincinnati,
Baltimore, and Philadelphia). The competing pressures were too great.
Federal aid finally made the Omaha route only one out of five. What
might have been a great artery, as one critic objected, now became
nothing but a sprinkler.

31

Uncertain Boundaries

IN THE UNITED STATES, from sheer force of geography, the boundaries of national aspiration long remained unmarked and unlimited. This
political vagueness, which was one of the nation's most fertile resources,
took three forms: first, a general uncertainty about national boundaries
in the west, north, and south; second, an uncertainty about the relation
of the territory of the new nation to that of the Indian "nations" who had

been there first; and third, an uncertainty whether, and if so by what legal means and to what geographic limit, areas outside the original thirteen colonies should be annexed. The first two of these uncertainties I will describe in the present chapter, and the third I will describe in the following chapter.

In the colonial period, at least a half-dozen royal grants of American lands—by James I, Charles I, Charles II, and George II—had avoided geographic detail. They simply specified that granted land (between designated points on the coast, or between certain degrees of latitude) should run (in the language of James I's grant to Virginia, 1609) "from Sea to Sea." "Throughout the mayne Landes there," Charles I's grant (1629) to the Massachusetts Bay Company read, "from the Atlantick and Westerne Sea and Ocean on the East Parte to the South Sea on the West Parte." Of course, nobody then knew even approximately how far west was the Pacific Ocean.

Geographic misconceptions were so basic that modern maps cannot show the boundaries of the newly independent United States as understood by the negotiators (1779–83) of the Anglo-American Treaty ending the Revolution. The crucial features appear very different on our more accurate maps than on the eight-sheet 1:2,000,000-scale map (2d ed., London, 1755) by Dr. John Mitchell of Urbanna, Virginia, which they actually used. Even the Mississippi River was largely a matter of conjecture. Above the junction with the Ohio, where Mitchell's map shows the Mississippi wandering vaguely off toward the west, the distance between the southern tip of Lake Michigan and the nearest point on the river appeared more than twice as far away as it actually is. Some members of the Continental Congress, confusing the Mississippi with the Missouri River, criticized the treaty negotiators for putting the boundary too far east, a confusion common at the time, which made a difference of a third of a million square miles. For clarity, however, it made little difference which river was intended, since the upper reaches of both rivers were shrouded in fog.

The Louisiana Purchase of 1803, the first addition to the ill-defined territory of the original colonies, doubled the area of the United States and pushed the nation farther into the unknown West. The new territory stretched along virtually the whole western boundary of the nation which it covered with a still more impenetrable haze. We have often heard the Louisiana Purchase described as one of the great real-estate bargains in history. To understand our history we must remember that it was a surprise package. Much of its value came from the uncertainty of its extent and its contents.

The treaty of 1803, by which Napoleon's government ceded all Louisiana to the United States, actually did not mark clear boundaries. Its evasive language (adopted from the treaty by which France had three years earlier acquired Louisiana from Spain) ceded "the Colony or Province of Louisiana, with the same extent that it now has in the hands of Spain, and that it had when France possessed it; and such as it should be after the Treaties subsequently entered into between Spain and other States." This riddle was not unintentional. "I asked . . . what were the last bounds of the territory ceded to us," Robert R. Livingston, the American commissioner, reported of his conversation with the French Foreign Minister on May 20, 1803; "he said he did not know; we must take it as they had received it. . . . Then you mean that we shall construe it our own way? I can give you no direction; you have made a noble bargain for yourselves and I suppose you will make the most of it." Napoleon, told of the uncertain boundary, reassured his minister that if there had not already been such an uncertainty it would have been shrewd policy to put one there.

Since the 17th century, France had been claiming the Western Ocean as the boundary of her American possessions. On this or some other foundation, Jefferson himself, as he indicated in his instructions for the Lewis and Clark expedition, seems to have thought that the Louisiana Purchase probably extended to the Pacific. But the western boundary of which he thought there could be absolutely no question was "the highlands on the western side of the Mississippi, enclosing all its waters, the Missouri, of course." West of that, the boundary might be open to debate.

Such uncertainties left open many possibilities. On the southeastern boundary, for example, Chancellor Robert R. Livingston, who himself had negotiated the vague terms, happily discovered (in Henry Adams' phrase) "that France had actually bought West Florida without knowing it, and had sold it to the United States without being paid for it." And so arose the American claim to West Florida.

Except for a part of the line of the Mississippi, the whole boundary of the Purchase (which of course meant the whole western and southern boundary of the United States) was long disputed. This vagueness would dominate American foreign policy for decades, and would help entice settlers from the United States, making a western penumbra for the nation. Texas, for example, was widely assumed to have been part of the Louisiana Purchase. When, in 1819, the Adams-Onís Treaty with Spain ceded East Florida to the United States but defined the westward boundaries of the Louisiana Purchase in such a way as to exclude Texas, many like Senator Thomas Hart Benton condemned the "surrender." Vast new ambiguities were created when that treaty defined the forty-second parallel reaching to the Pacific as the southern boundary of the Purchase. These extensive uncertainties appear vividly on any map that shows the various lines seriously proposed by the Spanish or American negotiators before 1819. Even after this definition toward the

south, the northern boundary of the United States still remained unmarked, and would remain so for another quarter-century.

*   *   *

Besides all this, peculiarly troublesome legal ambiguities arose from
the presence of the Indians. Who had owned the American continent
before the Europeans arrived? How and from whom did Europeans
secure their first title to the land? Could Americans in the early 19th
century admit that the Indians still owned any of the land? When the
European settlers came in the 17th century, it seemed to many of them
that the continent was not yet clearly possessed by anybody at all. Dealing
with Indians was, of course, very different from dealing with Europeans.
The Indians did not follow the genteel European laws of war, nor did they
follow the European customs of peace and treaty-making.

How could the land be "legally" acquired? European experience offered
no precedent. And throughout the first century of our national life the
question haunted Americans. Not because Americans were especially
virtuous, but because in the competition for the continent any little
advantage was worth seizing, and even a shadow of "legality" might
seem persuasive to someone. As Indians found themselves more and
more at the mercy of their invaders, the relation between Americans and
Indians became more and more legalistic. Land titles vaguely derived
from the Indians clouded the boundaries of the new nation with still
another uncertainty.

Why did irresistible European conquerors ever bother to "buy" their
lands from the Indians? By the strict letter of English law in the 17th
century, the Crown (having "discovered" the territory) had pre-empted
North America as a protectorate; title to American lands therefore could
be secured only by grant from the Crown. The Pilgrim Fathers may or
may not have shared their first Thanksgiving with the Indians, but we
have no record of their having paid the Indians for the title to their land.
The Dutch in North America, compared to the English, had only a flimsy
"right of discovery"; unlike the Spanish, they had no donation from the
Pope. They had to find or build other legal foundations, and they therefore
began the practice of "buying" their lands from the Indians. In 1626,
Peter Minuit, in charge of the Dutch settlement on Manhattan Island, paid
the Indians sixty gulden for that twenty-thousand acre tract of woodland.
It was not as unfair a bargain as sometimes represented, for although the
dollar equivalent of the price was only about $24, in purchasing power at
the time it amounted to several thousand mid-20th century dollars. Oddly
enough, this very episode, which became a parable of white men
swindling the Indians, in its own time actually revealed an overscrupulous
Dutch conscience. The remarkable fact was not the price they paid the

Indians, but rather that the Dutch felt it necessary to pay any price at all. It was a dangerous precedent.

Thereafter, while a Dutchman could hold title to American land under Dutch law only if he also had a grant from Dutch authorities, the Dutch required the prospective owner first to have acquired some title from the Indians. When, after 1629, the patroon system of colonizing in large estates was introduced on the Hudson, each patroon was required to secure a title from the Indians before he could receive one from the Dutch authority. Not until the English had their first land disputes with the Dutch did they too begin "buying" tracts from the Indians. The English, however, still treated such "purchase" not as an essential of good legal title but simply as a matter of good conscience or appearance. Roger Williams' fanatical obsession with the rightful original title of the Indians and his insistence on their right of sale irritated the conscience of his New England contemporaries. His Rhode Island was then the one English colony in which the English charter (1644) was granted only *after* the land had been purchased (1636; 1638) from the Indians. Although the English, both in New England and elsewhere in the American colonies, continued their practice of "purchasing" the Indians' lands, they never changed their legal position that the Indian title had no standing in English law. All the Indian lands, they continued legally to assume, were a kind of public domain. The Crown alone could grant title, and to anyone it wished.

In the eyes of English law, an Indian "deed" thus remained only an indication of Indian willingness to vacate lands to which the Indians had never had any legal title in the first place. Of course, for this reason alone the Indian deed was desirable. To some conscientious New Englanders it offered an additional personal advantage of evidencing "a just and equitable as well as a legal right to the land." But, as William Christie McLeod reminds us, had it not been for the passionate moralism of Roger Williams, the complacent fiction of "purchasing" Indian land might have died with the Dutch West India Company and never have taken root in the English colonies.

The occupation of the American land thus began in a quite un-European moral-legal confusion. Until well after the Civil War, the peculiarly American problem of the relation of latecomers to the original possessors of the soil continued to haunt American consciences and fog American vision. "The anomalous relation of the Indian tribes to the government," the Commissioner of Indian Affairs complained to President Grant in 1873, ". . . requires that they be treated as sovereign powers and as wards at one and the same time." This had helped keep the national boundaries vague, and incidentally rendered all the legal and political devices of national expansion problematic.

How imperfect were the prophetic powers of Americans in the early 19th century! They could not imagine, much less predict, the speed with which citizens of the United States would fill the continent. Nor could they suspect the rapid decline of the Indian tribes. That those once terrifying, once majestic "nations" would within a century become powerless, pauperized wards, confined to a few barren tracts, was beyond the wildest imaginings of the wisest or the most malevolent statesmen of the age.

During the imperial wars with the French in the mid-18th century, the British thought the power of independent Indian tribes might be decisive. At first each British colony dealt as it pleased with its own neighboring Indians, while the more centralized French successfully used Indian tribes as military allies in their grand strategy. General Braddock, not otherwise noted for his skill in American backwoods warfare, in 1755 appointed his own Indian agents, hoping in this way finally to co-ordinate Indian policy. Thereafter the British Crown took charge of Indian affairs. The British, always adept at legal fictions, now pretended that the Indians were actually sovereign "nations" owning their own land. The Crown claimed nothing more than an exclusive option to purchase these lands if and when the Indians chose to sell.

During the founding of the new nation, it seemed possible that one of the United States might be made up exclusively of Indians. There, it was suggested, the various tribes would be combined and would live as equal members of the federal union, thus not only solving the Indian problem but strengthening the Union. The Treaty of Fort Pitt, which the American Revolutionaries negotiated with the Delawares in 1778 (ratified by Congress in 1805), expressly provided that, with the approval of Congress, friendly tribes headed by the Delawares might join the Confederacy in a state of their own. In 1785, too, the treaty between the United States and the Cherokees provided "that the Indians may have full confidence in the justice of the United States respecting their interests, they shall have the right to send a deputy of their choice, whenever they think fit, to Congress."

Within the Louisiana Purchase, many Americans envisaged a consolidated Indian state or states, in every way a part of the Union. A plan for colonizing in that territory all the Indians who could be persuaded to move from the east was considered by Jefferson. The Rev. Jedidiah Morse, author of the pioneer *American Geography* (1789), who had served as secretary of the Society for Propagating the Gospel among the Indians and Others, was commissioned by the federal government in 1819 to travel among the Indians and study their condition. After traveling in the Northwest, he proposed to the Secretary of War in 1822 that "this territory be reserved exclusively for Indians, in which to make the proposed experiment of gathering into one body as many of the scattered and other Indians as choose to settle here, to be educated, become citizens, and in due time to be admitted to all the privileges common to other territories and States in the Union." President Monroe in his last message to Congress in 1825, when Indian affairs in Georgia had reached a crisis, proposed that the eastern tribes be moved west of the Mississippi, there to be consolidated into a protectorate of the United States, which would thus extend its influence to the Pacific. Although statehood was not specifically mentioned, it was the obvious consequence of these proposals. Statehood was clearly implied by Calhoun, Monroe's Secretary of War, who had lately received Jedidiah Morse's report. The intention to set up such an Indian state or to leave the Indians themselves free to establish one was suggested from time to time until after the Civil War. As late as 1871, President Grant as a part of his Indian "peace policy" recommended establishing an area south of Kansas for "collecting most of the Indians now between the Missouri and the Pacific and south of the British possessions into one Territory or one State." This state would have been exclusively Indian.

Meanwhile, the question of Indian rights and of European ownership of lands once held by Indians had been befuddled in still other ways. The New England Puritans, for example, applying the elementary Biblical principle that man acquires title to the earth by possessing and improving it, had concluded, in John Winthrop's words, that "the Indians having only a natural right to so much land as they had or could improve . . . the rest of the country lay open to any that could and would improve it."

The numerous crudely drawn treaties with Indian tribes were overlapping and contradictory. General Anthony Wayne's Treaty of Greenville (1795) with chiefs representing the Delaware, Shawnee, Wyandot, and Miami confederacies, following their defeat at the Battle of Fallen Timbers, had divided the whole Northwest Territory between Indian lands and those open to white settlements. This line roughly separated the actual areas of Indian and of white settlements into the early 19th century. Then, within the next half-century, additional treaties and special purchases with confused boundaries were negotiated with individual tribes or fragments of tribes. It was uncertain which Indian titles had been "extinguished."

The American situation led Jefferson to suspect that "our geographical peculiarities may call for a different code of natural law to govern relations with other nations from that which the conditions of Europe have given rise to." Edward Everett later explained that the absence in America of clear, long-established *legal* boundaries like those found in Europe had inevitably given a new significance to all *natural* boundaries. One momentous practical conclusion, which Everett himself drew when he was Secretary of State, was that mere "legal" possession of colonies in America by a European country did not give it any right to interfere in this remote continent.

Conflicts with the Indians over land titles and over the actual occupation of the West lasted through most of the 19th century. After the Civil War, Indian reservations, ranges, and hunting grounds were scattered all over the western half of the nation. The policy of establishing reservations exclusively for the native peoples reached its height in 1870, when their combined area was larger than the states of California and Oregon.

In the years just after the Civil War, more Americans were in direct physical conflict with Indians than at any other time since the colonial period. Then came the climax of the policy, begun with the Louisiana Purchase, of removing Indians to the Trans-Mississippi West. That policy had banked up—against the expanding American settlements—Indians who still possessed some military power and much pride. Chief Bear Rib of the Unkpapa Sioux during a treaty discussion in 1866 at Fort Pierre (in the present South Dakota) plaintively asked:

> To whom does this land belong? I believe it belongs to me. If you ask me for a piece of land I would not give it. I cannot spare it, and I like it very much. All this country on each side of this river belongs to me. I know that from the Mississippi to this river the country all belongs to us, and that we have travelled from the Yellowstone to the Platte. All this country, as I have said, is ours, and if you, my brother, should ask me for it, I would not give it to you, for I like it and I hope you will listen to me.

The Americans did not listen.

Yet the Indians could not be ignored, for they threatened life and land in many parts of the West. As late as 1869, the United States Commissioner of Agriculture warned that the "fifty thousand hostile Indians" ranging the territory between the Missouri River and the Rocky Mountains showed "a stolidity of character and an inaccessibility to civilizing influences . . . remarkable even in this strange race of men." He exaggerated neither their number nor their hostility. Against them the United States Government had established over 110 forts manned by about 20,000 troops in that upper Missouri country alone. But demobilization after the Civil War had left too few men in the army to police the South and the Indians at the same time. In the whole West in 1870 there were probably about two hundred thousand Indians; the Indian threat was not yet a mere legend.

New residents on the vast plains of Colorado, Wyoming, and Montana petitioned Congress for help. They complained that not enough troops were defending their land, that the forts were too weak, and too far apart. In the federal offensive of 1876, Chiefs Sitting Bull and Crazy Horse were finally defeated, but this turning point came only after the annihilation of Custer and his 264 men at the Battle of the Little Big Horn. Cattlemen and other settlers continued to argue against establishment of Indian reservations, which, they said, served as government-protected fortresses into which the hostile Sioux could retire to gather strength for new raids. In 1880 half the state of South Dakota was still considered Indian land.

Before the Civil War, the western lands had become pawns in the North-South conflict over slavery. Many on each side hoped that the Indians would be a permanent dam against westward expansion by the other. The Senate Committee on Indian Affairs had reported in 1836 that "with this uninhabitable region on the west of the Indian Territory, they cannot be surrounded by white population. They are on the outside of us, and in a place which will remain on the outside." During the debate in 1837 over an Indian territory bill, Southerners proposed to block Northern expansion by giving the Indians all the land north of Missouri and west of the Missouri River up to the Rockies. Comparable Northern plans to settle the Indians in the southwest seemed to have a similar objective. Attempts to organize Nebraska were blocked by claims that treaty guarantees had reserved the country exclusively for Indians.

So long as the Indians remained strong enough to make trouble—for at least a century after the nation was born—American citizens found it in their own interest to keep Indian bounds and Indian claims vague. To confirm Indian possession of a clearly defined territory would only strengthen Indian belief in their right to perpetual possession of that territory. More often than not, Indian ownership of a particular tract was explicitly recognized only *after* the Indians had sold it to the white men. Indian willingness to sell was generally treated as the best, and often the only, proof of Indian ownership. The Indians thus remained a moving cloud conveniently obscuring vision of the national boundaries. Without these many vague and wandering "nations" at our edge, the limits of our nationality might have had to be more sharply and more rigidly defined. This was the last service of the Indian to the white man.

32

A Dubious Destiny

SELDOM IF EVER had a modern nation been so uncertain of its geographic extent, its mode of growth, and the institutions by which it would affiliate with its neighbors. How was the nation to organize its expansion? How far was the United States of *America* destined to extend?

On these, as on other important subjects, the members of the Constitutional Convention of 1787 had not agreed. Perhaps because they did not consider these questions urgent, they had not troubled to formulate clear answers. Or perhaps because they disagreed, they preferred to keep their answers vague.

The Constitution was, of course, framed by the representatives of thirteen specific states strung along the eastern seaboard. Each of these original states touched the Atlantic Ocean. The Constitution they were making was not for an inland, land-bound nation, much less for a continent-nation. In the Constitutional Convention of 1787, the debate over the passage concerning the admission of new states was narrow. By "new states," the delegates said, they meant states that might be subdivided from the original thirteen states, from the western lands they claimed, or from land ceded to the United States by the British under the Peace Treaty of 1783. If any were expecting new states to be carved out of vast new acquisitions of national territory, their thoughts were not recorded.

The actual debates in the Philadelphia Convention on August 29 and 30, 1787, showed the familiar conflict between the large states and the small states, between those with extensive western domains and those with none. In the foreground was a dangerous idea, as Gouverneur Morris put it, "the idea of dismembering the large States." The two main questions discussed were whether the new states to be carved from old territory should be expected to assume part of the existing public debt as a condition of their admission to the union, and whether consent should be required from the legislatures of the older states from which they were being carved.

There are few hints that anyone in the Convention thought the problem amounted to more than how to organize the then roughly circumscribed area of the new nation. The delegates, of course, made plain their determination not to throw the balance of national power into the unpredictable West. For on the Atlantic seaboard fears had long been widespread that indiscriminate westward expansion would diffuse the population too thinly. "If it were possible by just means to prevent emigrants to the Western Country," George Mason of Virginia told the Convention, "it might be good policy." But, he and others added, it was hard to discourage emigration, and the people who were bound to pour into the West had to be treated as equals.

The reaction of leading Americans to the Louisiana Purchase in 1803 shows how unprepared they were for the great dispersion across the Mississippi. In later years statesmen competed for the honor of foresight, but the more we learn of the actual story of the Louisiana Purchase, the more it seems the product of coincidence, misunderstanding, and good luck. Had communication between Washington and our diplomatic representatives abroad been as speedy then as it was to become later in the 19th century, the Purchase might never have been negotiated. There is little evidence that, before the Louisiana Purchase, Jefferson or anyone else seriously imagined that the United States would extend across the Mississippi. In the early 19th century, the notion of a Great American Desert on the western fringes of the nation had already acquired mythical certitude. And President Jefferson's description of Louisiana, submitted to Congress in November, 1803, while admitting the very boundaries to be obscure, said that the few settlements "were separated from each other by immense and trackless deserts." During the early years of the century, the desert barrier became more vivid, confining the national imagination and haunting settlers.

When the Treaty to purchase the Louisiana territory was brought back to the United States in midsummer, 1803, the response was less exuberance than fear—fear that since the Constitution had made no provision for national expansion into new territory, such expansion might stretch the Constitution to the breaking point; fear that indiscriminate westward expansion might dangerously diffuse the six million who were already scantily spread over an area several times that of any of the nations of western Europe. Many public men believed that the strength of a nation was measured not by its area but by the concentration of its population and the effective occupation of its territory. Some shared the views of a French geographer who in 1804 saw the great expansion of the territory of the United States as "a prolific source of present weakness and future disunion."

Nor were these fears entirely groundless. It has been estimated that between 1809 and 1829, a period of great expansion, the per capita real income in the United States fell about twenty per cent. At the time of the Louisiana Purchase some eastern businessmen had already begun to fear the westward drain of their capital resources. A quarter-century later their fears were still alive, when Secretary of the Treasury Richard Rush warned, "The manner in which the remote lands of the United States are selling and settling, whilst it may tend to increase more the population of the country, . . . does not increase capital in the same proportion. . . . the creation of capital is retarded, rather than accelerated, by the diffusion of a thin population over a great surface of soil. Anything that may serve to hold back this tendency . . . can scarcely prove otherwise than salutary."

By July, 1803, Jefferson had already sent his cabinet his proposed constitutional amendment to allow the acquisition of Louisiana and to hold the Union together by blocking the westward diffusion of population. His amendment, which specifically incorporated Louisiana into the Union, added that "the rights of occupancy in the soil and of self-government are confirmed to the Indian inhabitants as they now exist." A special constitution was to be created for the new territory north of the thirty-second parallel (virtually the entire Purchase, except for the present state of Louisiana), the whole of which was to be reserved for the Indians. The "great object," according to Jefferson, was "to prevent emigrations, excepting to a certain portion of the ceded territory."

The Congressional debate over the Louisiana Purchase beginning in October, 1803, was curious and significant. Since this was to be the first addition to the original national territory as described in the Treaty of 1783, it was the first legislative test of national thinking about expansion. And it betrayed the confusion of surviving framers of the Constitution when confronted by this momentous question. Federalists like Gouverneur Morris, who had been active in the Constitutional Convention, now reversed their usually broad view of the federal power. They insisted that the Congress could not "admit, as a new State, territory, which did not belong to the United States when the Constitution was made." In retrospect, Morris, who two decades earlier had drafted the crucial passage, now explained that he had purposely kept the language of Article IV vague. He himself had expected "that, when we should acquire Canada and Louisiana, it would be proper to govern them as provinces, and allow them no voice in our councils." But, he said, since others then had disagreed, he had preferred to avoid dispute by not bringing the question into the open.

In 1803 Jefferson's Republicans, who were noted for their strict construction of the Constitution, at first admitted that the Constitution had not clearly given Congress or the President power to expand the nation. Then Jefferson himself, in a surprising reversal of his usual position, urged Congress that it first ratify the treaty and pay the purchase money, "then appeal to the nation for an additional article to the Constitution approving and confirming an act which the nation had not previously authorized. The Constitution has made no provision for our holding foreign territory, still less for incorporating foreign nations into our Union. The Executive, in seizing the fugitive occurrence which so much advances the good of their country, have done an act beyond the Constitution. The Legislature, in casting behind them metaphysical subtleties and risking themselves like faithful servants, must ratify and pay for it, and throw themselves on their country for doing for them unauthorized what we know they would have done for themselves had they been in a situation to do it." He argued not from future grandeur but from present need. Citizens of the United States who were already settled across the mountains on the hither side of the Mississippi had to be able to ship their products down that river. The Purchase, he explained, was the only way to provide their lifeline to the world.

By the time Congress met to consider the Treaty in October, Jefferson had persuaded himself and his party that the needs of the nation were so great and so obvious that no amendment was required. His

Federalist opponents now became eloquent on the dangers of colonialism and the perils of boundlessly extending the national domain. Again and again Federalist orators warned of the dilution of the Union. If the Constitution had wisely required a full two-thirds majority for its least alteration, how dangerous (said Senator Tracy of Connecticut) to allow Congress by a bare majority to "admit new foreign States, and swallow up by it, the old partners. . . . the relative strength which this admission gives to a Southern and Western interest, is contradictory to the principles of our original Union."

Such fears were compounded when in December, 1810, it was actually proposed that one small piece of the Purchase (the Orleans Territory) be admitted to the Union as an equal state. Until then all states newly admitted to the Union had been fashioned from the territory of the United States as defined in the Peace Treaty of 1783. This issue was mixed up with the unsettled larger question of the actual boundaries of the United States. The proposed state of Louisiana would include a piece of West Florida that perhaps still belonged to Spain. But the essential question, now more sharply put, was the dilution of the original Union. "If this bill passes," Josiah Quincy of Massachusetts inveighed in the House of Representatives on January 14, 1811, "it is my deliberate opinion that it is virtually a dissolution of this Union; that it will free the States from their moral obligation; and, as it will be the right of all, so it will be the duty of some, definitely to prepare for a separation—amicably if they can, violently if they must." The majority of the House voted down the Speaker's decision that this was disorderly language, but the bill passed and Louisiana became a state in 1812.

This first step toward continental expansion increased alarmist fears that the whole Union would be changed in character, that the original partners would be overwhelmed, and that before long there would be a new nation with a new constitution. The obstinate Federalist Fisher Ames spoke for fellow New Englanders when he warned that adding the alien territory of Louisiana opened the floodgates to peoples who had no understanding of the sacred Anglo-Saxon principles on which the Union had been founded. "Otters in the wilderness," he said, were as likely to understand "as the Gallo-Hispano-Indian *omnium gatherum* of savages and adventurers." No wonder, then, that during the War of 1812, when British troops approached New Orleans, a loyal New Englander like Timothy Pickering hoped that city would fall to the British. Then the trans-Appalachian West might join the British victors, leaving a smaller but tidier United States.

If the destiny of lands adjoining the original United States was so uncertain, what of more distant America? This question was posed dramatically and unexpectedly, not on the shores of the Mississippi

but in the farthermost reaches of South America. Napoleon's invasion
of Spain in 1808 had been the occasion for revolts by Spain's South
American colonies against her antiquated colonial rule. In 1810, juntas
were set up in Buenos Aires, Bogotá, Caracas, and Santiago de Chile.
At first purporting only to hold the lands against the French for the
deposed Spanish King Ferdinand VII, they soon became full-fledged
independence movements. Jefferson in 1811 saw there another sign
that America "must have its separate system of interests, which must
not be subordinated to those of Europe." In 1822, President Monroe
and the Congress recognized the revolted colonies as independent
nations. The most significant fact, as Dexter Perkins has noted, was that
the United States undertook so momentous a step without consulting
with any European power—"on a purely American basis, and from a
purely American point of view." This itself unmistakably declared the
separation of the American from the European political sphere.

In 1823, the political future of the North American continent was
still largely a mystery. But before the end of the third decade of the
19th century, South America (already long subdivided for purposes
of Spanish and Portuguese rule) was marked off substantially into the
countries of the 20th century. North of the Isthmus of Panama, only
one tiny segment (little more than the thirteen former British colonies
and their subdivided westward extensions, all east and south of the
Mississippi River and the Great Lakes) had yet attained a national
identity which would survive into the 20th century. Mexico, as late as
1822–23, included Guatemala and other Central American states to
her south; and she stretched vaguely northward through what is now
the western United States, to our present boundary with Canada. In
the far west and northwest, an uncertain conflict was brewing among
Mexicans, British, and Russians, in which the United States was to
play a still unforeseen part. The political future of two-thirds of the
continental United States was still in doubt.

The contrast in this respect between North and South America in
that era is striking. South America was already replete with governmental organizations reaching back to the early 16th century. However
corrupt, inefficient, or tyrannic these colonial governments may have
been, they were highly organized and had quite well covered and subdivided the continent. Just as the earlier Spaniards and Portuguese had
organized their rule by using the political structure of the Indians, so
now the Latin-American revolutionaries of the early 19th century
adapted to their needs an elaborate but obsolete political, economic, and
ecclesiastical machinery. But in the vast stretches of North America
the American anachronism was being again and again re-enacted: Community before Government. In the North American West, communities
had sprung up, often far from one another, often "beyond the juris-

diction" of the United States but not unambiguously within the jurisdiction of any other government. Clusters of people bound by common
hopes, common worries, and common illusions, they were communities.
Their lack of established patterns of government added to their problems, but their freedom from obsolete local patterns of government
also had advantages. They were perhaps more free than such large
numbers of men at their stage of civilization had ever been before
—free from the need either to live within, or to rebel against, a rigid
pattern imported from far away and long ago.

National arrogance in the 20th century has led us to assume that
Latin America can do nothing better than follow the North American
pattern, and especially that of the United States. In the early 19th
century, however, there were imaginative American statesmen who could
think of no grander fulfilment of our federal republican ideal than that all
North America, following the Latin American example, should form itself
into several independent and self-governing nations.

The general belief that people from the United States would spread
over the continent did not necessarily mean that they would remain a
part of the United States. For example, since Oregon was so remote,
American statesmen long assumed that its inhabitants were destined to
govern themselves. "Free and independent Americans, unconnected
with us but by the ties of blood and interest, and employing like us
the rights of self-government"—this was how Jefferson viewed Astoria,
John Jacob Astor's post in the Pacific Northwest, and the settlements
spreading from it. During the War of 1812, Jefferson, admiring "the
germ of a great, free and independent empire on that side of our
Continent," still hoped that, even if Astoria should fall to the British,
the peace terms with the British would both recognize the Astoria
country's "independence" and recognize the United States' right to
protect Astorians from foreign interference. Jefferson propagandized
for an independent Pacific republic, and in the 1820's many leading
Americans—including Albert Gallatin, James Monroe, William H.
Crawford, Henry Clay, Thomas Hart Benton, and probably James
Madison—shared the vision.

This role of the United States as a planter of new nations had an
appeal we have long since forgotten. The northern and southern boundaries of the United States, Thomas Hart Benton of Missouri confessed
in the Senate on March 1, 1825, were still unclear. Their definition
should be left to Nature and to posterity. But he added:

> Westward, we can speak without reserve, and the ridge of the Rocky
> Mountains may be named without offence, as presenting a convenient,
> natural and everlasting boundary. Along the back of this ridge, the
> Western limit of the republic should be drawn, and the statue of the
> fabled god, Terminus, should be raised upon its highest peak, never to

be thrown down. In planting the seed of a new power on the coast of the Pacific ocean, it should be well understood that when strong enough to take care of itself, the new Government should separate from the mother Empire as the child separates from the parent at the age of manhood.

Americans had long disagreed, and would continue to disagree, over the proper location of "the fabled god, Terminus." In 1804, the novelist Charles Brockden Brown, exhilarated by the Louisiana Purchase, scorned those narrow minds who saw the United States confined by the St. Lawrence on the north and the Gulf of Mexico on the south. "We may be sure that, in no long time, it will stretch east and west from sea to sea, and from the north pole to the Isthmus of Panama." A popular Fourth-of-July toast at Waterville, Maine, in 1815 offered: "The Eagle of the United States—may she extend her wings from the Atlantic to the Pacific; and fixing her talons on the Isthmus of Darien, stretch her beak to the Northern Pole."

Until the War of 1812, however, such extravagant visions were not common. Jefferson himself, who as early as 1809 had expressed an interest (which he never abandoned) in incorporating Cuba into the Union, hoped that the War of 1812 would bring in Canada to round out "such an empire for liberty as she has never surveyed since the creation." While Monroe, who became President in 1817, was willing to confine the nation by the Rocky Mountains, his Secretary of State John Quincy Adams could not agree. In Cabinet discussion of the treaty with Spain which brought Florida into the Union in 1819, Secretary Adams expressed confidence that, before the passing of centuries, Spanish possessions on our south and all British possessions on our north would be incorporated into the United States. Our purchase of extensive Spanish possessions, he said, "rendered it still more unavoidable that the remainder of the continent should ultimately be ours. But it is very lately that we have distinctly seen this ourselves; very lately that we have avowed the pretension of extending to the South Sea; and until Europe shall find it a settled geographical element that the United States and North America are identical, any effort on our part to reason the world out of a belief that we are ambitious will have no other effect than to convince them that we add to our ambition hypocrisy." Adams therefore opposed Monroe's proposed declaration that the westernmost settlements should soon be expected to separate from the Union.

Secretary of War John C. Calhoun supported Adams. "The passion for aggrandizement was the law paramount of man in society," Calhoun insisted, and he concluded with unintended irony that "there was no example in history of the disruption of a nation from itself by voluntary separation." The insecurity of these convictions was revealed in Calhoun's own changing views. Before very long, Southern and Northern statesmen both had new reasons to fear indiscriminate expansion. To their old doubts and fears—of colonialism, of racial miscegenation, of dilution of the good old union—now were added domestic political fears in both South and North that to add new states would strengthen the other section.

The story of sentiments about expansion in the era between the American Revolution and the Civil War is thus one of confusion and vacillation, of bold hopes and timid doubts. There was hardly a statesman of the era who did not, at one time in his career, see the United States much more narrowly confined and, at another time, far more vastly extended than it would prove to be. To see the growth of the nation as the inevitable filling of obviously predestined bounds is to miss the peculiar confusion, the peculiar hope, and the peculiar promise of American thinking about the national future in that formative century. In historical perspective, then, the effort in the Civil War by one part of the Union to set itself up as an independent nation does not seem quite so mad an enterprise.

The geometric neatness of American political boundaries was still in the future. The vast Oregon country, for example, which comprised all the later states of Washington, Oregon, and Idaho, and large parts of Montana and Wyoming, was the scene of joint occupation by Americans and British for nearly thirty years after 1818. American negotiations with the British were a continuing effort to keep boundaries vague until American emigration might settle the question.

The independent Republic of Texas, recognized by the United States in 1836, remained a separate nation until its incorporation into the Union in 1845. President Sam Houston himself, during the troublesome negotiations with the United States, came to see annexation as a mixed blessing for Texas. His doubts led him as late as 1844 to authorize a joint alliance with Great Britain and France in order more firmly to establish Texas' independence. Within the United States, of course, opposition to annexation was violent. The same John Quincy Adams who, twenty-five years earlier, had insisted "that the United States and North America are identical," in 1843 led the fight against annexing Texas. Joined by a dozen other prominent Americans in a forceful address to the nation, he warned that the request for annexation did not express the true will of the people of Texas. It was, they said, a Southern imperialist conspiracy; annexation would dissolve the Union.

Hopes and uncertainties did not end at the Rio Grande. Some, like Adams, remained adamant for a tight little Union with its delicate old balance of forces. With equal enthusiasm others promoted an "All Mexico" movement. Before, during, and immediately after the War with Mexico (1846–48), a wide assortment of outspoken Americans, by no means a mere lunatic fringe, declared the United States false to her destiny if she did not extend her empire of liberty all the way down to the Isthmus of Panama. In June, 1846, when Walt Whitman heard of discontent in Yucatán, he wrote an editorial under the heading, "More Stars for the Spangled Banner," cheerfully observing that Yucatán "won't need a long coaxing to join the United States."

California, which later came to seem so integral a part of the United States, was a scene of turbulence, uncertainty, and confusion in the first half of the 19th century. Settlers from the United States had begun to colonize the San Joaquin Valley as early as 1843. By 1846 there were still only about five hundred Americans settled on the California coast, as against about ten thousand Mexicans of Spanish stock and over twenty thousand Indians. In that year a California Republic, shakily independent, was declared. But difficulties of communication between Washington and the west coast, rivalries between navy and army, continued Mexican army opposition, antagonism between sections of the great region, and the restlessness of a predominantly non-American population kept the California pot boiling. The discovery of gold at Sutter's Mill in January, 1848, had not been in anyone's plans. The Gold Rush suddenly increased the number of settlers from the United States to about one hundred thousand within two years. Even so, the political destiny of California remained obscure.

The territory of California was ceded to the United States by the Treaty of Guadalupe Hidalgo in 1848, but the admission of California to the Union in 1850 was less to fill out a clear vision of national destiny than to adjust the balance of power within the old Union. When California finally entered the Union as an equal state, it was as only one item in the miscellaneous and delicately balanced Compromise of 1850, only (in Calhoun's phrase) "another precarious counterweight in equilibrium between the sections." The national destiny was still further beclouded when Webster and others argued—from their geographic ignorance—that Congress did not need to decide whether to extend slavery into the territories in 1850, because slavery had already been somehow "excluded" by soil and climate.

In the mid-19th century, "Manifest Destiny" covered a multitude of doubts. While the notion of a divinely intended expansion of European settlers was as old as their settlement of North America, the phrase "Manifest Destiny," which became the most popular way of expressing the idea, was coined by the exuberant John L. O'Sullivan in the New York *Morning News* in December, 1845. "Manifest destiny," Josh Billings observed after the Civil War, "iz the science ov going tew bust, or enny other place before yu git thare." "Thare is such a thing az manifest destiny, but when it occurs it iz like the number ov rings on the rakoon's tale, ov no great consequense only for ornament."

Not the "manifestness" but the uncertainty of the national destiny was first the great motive and emotive power of the national life. Had the Founding Fathers been more certain, had their provision for the expansion of the national territory been less obscure, the Civil War might either have been postponed or have come much sooner. The continental extent of the nation and the means of associating or dissociating its parts—these were not settled until the Civil War resolved them in a sea of blood. The uncertain years before 1865 exacted their price in wild hopes, black despairs, and dissipated energies. When before had a nation so rent itself over conflicting mirages: the cozy old Union confined in 18th-century boundaries? or a grand new nation, as boundless as the future? The Civil War, which seemed to settle the nation's continental destiny, would provide a kind of repose in national politics. But was this not, in part at least, the rigid repose of death? Not again, until perhaps the mid-20th century, would uncertainties about the national bounds and the national destiny be so stirring.

Meanwhile, the very uncertainties which inspired and exhilarated Americans also made them feel a special need of reassurance. The more uncertain the destiny, the more necessary to declare it "manifest." This was a clue to the nation's new ways of thinking and speaking. An America which was producing men to match her mountains was also producing a new lexicon which in its own way matched the vagaries of the Congress and the landscape.

PART SIX

AMERICAN WAYS OF TALKING

"Whereas the House of Representatives, in common with the people of America, is justly proud of its admirable native tongue, and regards this most expressive and energetic language as one of the best of its birthrights. . . . Resolved, therefore . . . that the nobility and gentry of England be courteously invited to send their elder sons, and such others as may be destined to appear as public speakers in church or state, to America, for their education; that the president of the United States be requested to concert measures with the presidents and heads of our colleges and schools, for the prompt reception and gratuitous instruction of such young persons, and to furnish them, after the expiration of a term of —— years, certificates of their proficiency in the English tongue."

Resolution proposed in *The North American Review* (April, 1820)

"Instead of that multiplicity of dialect, by which mental communication and sympathy between different nations are restrained in the Old World, a continually expanding realm is opened to American intellect, by the extension of one language over so large a portion of the Continent."

EDWARD EVERETT

275

THE new riches of an American language were not found in the pages of an American Shakespeare or Milton but on the tongues of Western boatmen, town boosters, fur traders, explorers, Indian-fighters, and sodbusters. While the greatness of British English could be viewed in a library, the greatness of American English had to be heard to be appreciated. America had no powerful literary aristocracy, no single cultural capital, no London. And the new nation gave the language back to the people. No American achievement was more distinctive or less predictable.

The American millions were thinly diffused and rapidly moving. In Europe, generally speaking, a mark of the lower classes was their geographic as well as social immobility. The lowest class, the "lumpenproletariat," was rooted to the ground like a tree stump. It was mainly the upper middle class, the aristocracy, or the learned élite who traveled: on a "Grand Tour" to round out a university education, on a commercial venture, on a scholarly pilgrimage to sit at the feet of a great man, on a holiday or health trip to a noted spa, or on a religious or diplomatic mission. In America the contrast was reversed. Here was no monolithic peasant mass, no coherent aristocratic class. Here it was commonly the "aristocracy"—for example, the country-seated gentry of upstate New York and tidewater Virginia—who were the less mobile. And it was the middle and lower classes—seeking their fortunes in the wagon companies going west, in the transient mining camps, and in the upstart towns—who were on the move. They moved frequently, and moved everywhere. Even the Negroes, though they were not free to move after they arrived, had been brought here on a long involuntary journey, and added some words from faraway Africa.

Peoples who had been born into other nations and other languages were now bound together by American English in spoken community.

33

An Ungoverned Vocabulary

THE BOUNDARIES of linguistic propriety in America were as uncertain as those of geography; it was as hard to define American speech as to demark the national territory. Where the American nation was expanding fastest, on the edges of the unknown, there too was the great expansion of vocabulary. As the nation grew by communities moving "beyond the jurisdiction," the language too grew not by "legal" incorporation of new words into grammar books and dictionaries, but by the unauthorized, unnumbered, casual novelties of actual speech.

In this first era of national life, when American speech was acquiring its new vitality, many American academic students of language and American literary writers were trying to keep the language "pure." These Mrs. Grundys, the self-appointed censors of linguistic morality, never worked harder. "The preservation of the English language in its purity throughout the United States," declared John Pickering at the beginning of his *Vocabulary or Collection of Words and Phrases which have been supposed to be peculiar to the United States of America* (1816), "is an object deserving the attention of every American, who is a friend to the literature and science of his country." Pickering concluded that the language of the United States "has in so many instances departed from the English standard, that our scholars should lose no time in endeavouring to restore it to its purity, and to prevent future corruption."

The pale thread of defensive purism runs through academic writings on the American language between the Revolution and the Civil War. The learned Dr. Beck, principal of Albany (New York) Academy, in

1829, while especially admiring Pickering's proofs "that in many instances the charges of English writers are either unfair or unfounded," also pleaded for linguistic "purity." Down south in the same year, Dr. Dunglison in the *Virginia Literary Museum and Journal of Belles Lettres, Arts, Science etc.*, explained that the American language was "purer" than Pickering had supposed. According to Dunglison, if Pickering had only been better acquainted with the dialects of the English provinces, he would have realized how many of his supposed Americanisms were not American inventions at all. John Russell Bartlett prefaced his *Dictionary of Americanisms* (1848; 4th ed., 1877) by asserting that, despite English charges against Americans "of perverting our vernacular tongue, and of adding useless words to it, . . . in the belief of the author, the English language is in no part of the world spoken in greater purity by the great mass of the people than in the United States."

By 1859 the defense had reached such proportions that Dr. Alfred L. Elwyn, a Philadelphia aristocrat, could list 463 terms in his sizable *Glossary of Supposed Americanisms*.

> It has been the assumed privilege of English travelers and authors to twit us upon the supposed peculiarity and oddity in our use of words and phrases. An examination of the language of their own country has convinced us that this satire was the result of ignorance: those who made it were unacquainted with the language and early literature of their own people, and thence very naturally supposed that what they heard here was affected, coined, or barbarous. The simple truth is, that almost without exception all those words or phrases that we have been ridiculed for using, are good old English; many of them are of Anglo-Saxon origin, and nearly all to be heard at this day in England: a difference of circumstances may have altered a little their application, but still not enough to render our mode of employing them at all absurd.

In this sense, then, American English was even more "correct" than that spoken in England.

However strenuously the learned writer in the *Virginia Literary Museum* might insist that "the number of real Americanisms is small," the brash vitality of American speech burst out everywhere. John Russell Bartlett, in the century's most ambitious catalogue of American linguistic crimes (real or supposed), confessed that "our *literary* dialect" was inferior to that of England. But he still insisted that Americans generally *spoke* an English purer even than that spoken by the mass of Englishmen. Aiming at "a Vocabulary of the *colloquial* language of the United States," Bartlett included "all the perversions of language, and abuses of words into which people, in certain sections of the country, have fallen, and some of those remarkable and ludicrous forms of speech which have been adopted in the Western States." Repeatedly he explained his focus on "the colloquial or familiar language." After the Civil War (while still defending the theoretical "purity" of American spoken English), Bartlett included every slang term he could find. He rejected the suggestion that printing slang words in his dictionary would "perpetuate" their use. What preserved words, he argued, was not dictionaries, but usage. "Slang terms will remain in use only so long as they may be useful in colloquial language. . . . Slang is thus the source whence large additions are made to our language."

In vain schoolmarms labored to make their unruly pupils at least seem educated by teaching them to spell correctly, and tried to keep high and well repaired the fences of linguistic propriety. American cultural insecurity had provided a large and profitable market for Noah Webster's *American Spelling Book,* had made a fetish of "correct" spelling and had created a vast demand for Webster's *Dictionary.* But despite all this, America offered ideal conditions for vitality and flexibility and novelty in the spoken language. These were roughly the conditions most favorable to the creation of slang. "Three cultural conditions," remarks Stuart Berg Flexner in his admirable *Dictionary of American Slang* (with Harold Wentworth), "especially contribute to the creation of a large slang vocabulary: (1) hospitality to or acceptance of new objects, situations, and concepts; (2) existence of a large number of diversified subgroups; (3) democratic mingling between these sub-groups and the dominant culture." Slang is language in common informal use or in informal use by only a portion of the general public but not yet considered sufficiently dignified or formal to be accepted into standard literary usage. Since in America the boundaries of standard speech were even vaguer than elsewhere, the distinction between slang and "correct usage" was also vaguer. And the distinction became vaguer and vaguer as the American word-stock grew, as American civilization became more confident of itself.

The American language became the apotheosis of slang. Cultivated American speech was far readier to accept the slang of the humbler classes than was cultivated (or literary) British English. Walt Whitman in his *November Boughs* (1888) was one of the first to describe unashamedly—and even to boast of—this peculiarly American achievement:

> Slang, profoundly consider'd, is the lawless germinal element, below all words and sentences, and behind all poetry, and proves a certain perennial rankness and protestantism in speech. As the United States inherit by far their most precious possession—the language they talk and write—from the Old World, under and out of its feudal institutes, I will allow myself to borrow a simile even of those forms farthest removed from American democracy. Considering Language then as some mighty potentate, into the majestic audience-hall of the monarch ever enters a personage like one of Shakespere's clowns, and takes position

there, and plays a part even in the stateliest ceremonies. Such is Slang, or indirection, an attempt of common humanity to escape from bald literalism, and express itself illimitably, which in the highest walks produces poets and poems, and doubtless in pre-historic times gave the start to, and perfected, the whole immense tangle of the old mythologies. For, curious as it may appear, it is strictly the same impulse-source, the same thing. Slang, too, is the wholesome fermentation or eructation of those processes eternally active in language, by which froth and specks are thrown up, mostly to pass away; though occasionally to settle and permanently chrystallize. . . .

The science of language has large and close analogies in geological science, with its ceaseless evolution, its fossils, and its numberless submerged layers and hidden strata, the infinite go-before of the present. Or, perhaps Language is more like some vast living body, or perennial body of bodies. And slang not only brings the first feeders of it, but is afterward the start of fancy, imagination and humor, breathing into its nostrils the breath of life.

The unprecedented American literacy, by a delightful democratic paradox, thus tended to give the literary language itself a more slangy flavor. Another ancient monopoly, the monopoly of the literati, was being dissolved and its powers were being dispersed into the whole people.

Americans were likely to use a word for any purpose it served. They, like some of the great English writers (notably Shakespeare: "Uncle me no uncle."), did not heed the grammarians, who insisted that a particular word was nothing but, say, a noun. Even in the colonial period, English critics of the American vocabulary objected to the American freedom, which they called license, with the "proper" grammatical functions of particular words. David Hume had objected to Franklin's adaptation of the noun *colony* into the verb *colonize*. Franklin himself, whose model was Addison, objected to the American practice of using nouns like *notice, advocate,* and *progress* as verbs. The noun *clapboard* was used as a verb here as early as 1637; and verbs were made of the nouns *scalp* (1693) and *tomahawk* (1711). The process went on. In the early 19th century *deed* (1806), *lynch* (1835), and *portage* (1836) all became verbs. The word *interview,* in its modern journalistic sense, seems to have been used first as a noun (1869) and almost immediately afterwards as a verb (1870). The American freedom took every possible form. Adjectives, for example, became nouns, as when the old *personal* became a name for an item in a newspaper (1864). Or a verb like *dump* became a noun for the place where waste was dumped (1784). Similarly the journalistic verbs *to scoop* (to get the advantage of) and *to beat* became the nouns *scoop* (1874) and *beat* (1873).

It was not simply this new promiscuity of American usage that amplified the language. Some notion of the range and variety of "the peculiarities of the English language, as spoken in America" comes from what William C. Fowler, Professor of Rhetoric at Amherst, offered as his Classification of Americanisms (1850):

I. Words borrowed from other languages, with which the English language has come into contact in America.

1. Indian words, borrowed from the original native tribes. Here belong many geographical proper names; as, *Kennebec, Ohio, Tombigbee;* also a few appellatives; as, *sagamore, quahaug, succotash.*

2. Dutch words, derived from the first settlers in New York; as, *boss,* a master; *kruller; stoop,* the steps of a door.

3. German words, derived from the Germans in Pennsylvania; as *spuke, sauerkraut.*

4. French words, derived from the first settlers in Canada and Louisiana; as, *bayou, cache, chute, crevasse, levee.*

5. Spanish words, from the first settlers of Louisiana, Florida, and Mexico; as, *calaboose, chaparral, hacienda, rancho, ranchero.*

6. Negro words, derived from the Africans; as *buckra* [white man]. All these are foreign words.

II. Words introduced from the necessity of a new situation, in order to express new ideas.

1. Words connected with and flowing from political institutions; as, *selectman, presidential, congressional, caucus, mass-meeting, lynch-law, help* for servants.

2. Words connected with ecclesiastical institutions; as, *associational, consociational, to fellowship, to missionate.*

3. Words connected with a new country; as *lot,* a portion of land; *diggings, betterments, squatter.*

Some of these words are rejected by good American writers. They are not of such a nature as to make a new dialect.

III. The remaining peculiarities, the only ones which are truly distinctive, fall for the most part under the following heads:—

1. Old words and phrases which have become almost obsolete in England; as, *talented, offset* for set off; *back and forth* for backward and forward.

2. Old words and phrases which are now merely provincial in England; as, *hub,* now used in the midland counties; *whap,* a provincialism in Somersetshire; *to wilt,* now used in the south and west of England.

3. Nouns formed from verbs by adding the French suffix *ment;* as, *publishment* for publication; *releasement* for release; *requirement* for requisition. As the verbs here are all French, the forms of the nouns are undoubtedly ancient.

4. Forms of words which fill the gap or vacancy between two words

which are approved; as *obligate,* comp. *oblige* and *obligation; variate,* comp. *vary* and *variation.* The existence of the two extremes confirms the propriety of the mean.

5. Certain compound terms, which, in England, have a different compound; as, *bank-bill* for bank-note; *book-store* for bookseller's shop; *bottom-land* for interval land; *clapboard* for a pale; *sea-board* for sea-shore; *side-hill* for hill-side. The correctness of one compound, in such cases, does not prove the incorrectness of the other.

6. Certain colloquial phrases, apparently idiomatic, and very expressive; as *to cave in,* to give up; *to flare up,* to get excited suddenly; *to flunk out,* to retire through fear; *to fork over,* to pay over; *to hold on,* to wait; *to let on,* to mention; *to stave off,* to delay; *to take on,* to grieve.

7. Certain words used to express intensity, whether as adjectives or adverbs, which is often a matter of mere temporary fashion; as, *dreadful, mighty, plaguy, powerful.*

8. Certain verbs expressing state of mind, but partially or timidly; as, *to allot upon,* to count upon; *to calculate,* to expect or believe; *to expect,* to think or believe; *to guess,* to think or believe; *to reckon,* to think or imagine.

9. Certain adjectives, expressing not only quality, but subjective feelings in regard to it; as, *clever, grand, green, likely, smart, ugly.*

10. Certain abridged expressions; as, *stage* for stage-coach; *turnpike* for turnpike-road; *spry* for sprightly; *to conduct* for to conduct one's self. There is a tendency in most languages to such contractions.

11. Quaint or burlesque terms, whether verbs, as *to tote, to yank;* or nouns, as *humbug, loafer, muss; plunder* for baggage; *rock* for a stone.

12. Certain very low expressions, mostly political; as *slang whanger* [low, noisy talker or writer], *loco foco, hunker; to get the hang* of a thing, for to learn how to do it.

13. Ungrammatical expressions, disapproved by all; as *do don't; used to could* for could formerly; *can't come it* for can't do it; *there's no two ways about it* for it is just so.

*   *   *

Since the spoken word is, of course, gone with the wind, our first problem in chronicling the rise of a distinctively American usage of words is to find written evidence of the words actually spoken by un-literary people. We can easily enough find literary versions of the colloquial language of ordinary men, in books like Joseph G. Baldwin's *Flush Times of Alabama and Mississippi* (1853) or James Russell Lowell's *Biglow Papers* (1848; 1867), but these versions are, at best, second-hand.

We do possess one rich and peculiarly American mine of evidence: the copious records of the Lewis and Clark expedition, the most celebrated American exploration of the age. There we can watch the English language stretch and adapt itself to the landscape of the New World. The records are all the more valuable because, although copious, they were not written by educated men. The whole party of forty-five which set out from the neighborhood of St. Louis in 1804 did not include a single man of learning. Captain Meriwether Lewis, in charge, and probably the best educated of all, had received only informal and desultory schooling; he never fulfilled his ambition to attend William & Mary College or any other. Two years of experience at the White House as Jefferson's private secretary had, of course, broadened his knowledge of the world. Yet, while praising Lewis for his honesty, his powers of observation, and his familiarity with the West, Jefferson had to admit his lack of scientific knowledge. Captain William Clark had less formal education than Lewis. Many members of the party bordered on the illiterate. Not one could by any possible stretch of the imagination be called a scientist or a literary man.

Jefferson's insistence on detailed and careful journals led several besides the leaders to record what they saw. Lewis and Clark themselves kept journals, as did their four sergeants; all but one of these accounts have survived. According to tradition, at least three of the twenty-three privates kept diaries, but only one has been found. In their first published forms, many of the manuscripts had been "improved" by literary editors, but fortunately most of the actual manuscripts survived and were finally printed in their original form. The most complete journal (the last to be discovered and the only journal by one man to give an unbroken day-by-day account of the whole trip) was by one of the sergeants.

Whatever else the Lewis and Clark party thought they were accomplishing, they unwittingly garnered the linguistic wealth of a new world in their intimate record of the simultaneous processes of geographic discovery and linguistic invention. "They were truly linguistic pioneers," Elijah H. Criswell concludes from his lexicon of their journals, "as well as pioneers in the literal and material sense." It is impossible to measure their achievement by mere statistics, but nearly two thousand terms in their vocabulary were in one way or another American novelties; of these at least a thousand words appeared in these journals for the first time.

The journals were a rich treasure-house of new American usages, of American peculiarities of spelling, of distinctively American forms of a verb or a noun, of American conversions of one part of speech into another, and of American uses of a term already archaic or obsolete in England—all of which were the more authentic, because recorded without any specifically linguistic purpose. Over five hundred terms (borrowed from Indian languages more than from any other source) described new botanical or zoological phenomena. Many of the Americanisms found in these journals were not destined for wide usage, but others had already entered everyday speech or were destined to do so: bayou, bowery, butte, cache, calumet, cent, complected, hickory, hominy, illy, interpretress, jerk, killdeer, kinnikinic, maize, moccasin, moose, opossum, pawpaw, peltry, pecan, pemmican, persimmon, planter, portage, prairie, raccoon, sassafras, skunk, slew, squash, squaw, tamarack, timothy, tomahawk, tote, wampum, whippoorwill, and Yankee. Their pages are peppered with peculiarly American combinations of English words, for example: back of (adv.), back-track, basswood, black bear, grizzly bear, bluegrass, bottom-land, box alder, brown thrush, buckeye, buffalo robe, bullfrog, bull-snake, canvasback, catbird, coal-pit, copperhead, cut-off, bald eagle, gartersnake, ground hog, ground squirrel, half-breed, head-right, blue heron, honey-locust, horned lizard, huckleberry, hunting shirt, ironwood, blue jay, keel-boat, kingbird, kingfisher, buffalo lick, lodge-pole, May-apple, medicine-man, moccasin snake, mocking bird, mountain ram, mountain sheep, mule deer, muskrat, night-hawk, overall, overnight, white pine, pitch-pine, sweet potato, prairie-dog, prairie fowl, prairie lark, prairie wolf, rattlesnake, red elm, red oak, rocky mountains, running time, sage-bush, sandhill crane, sapsucker, sea-otter, service-berry, snowberry, snow-shoe, sugar maple, whistling swan, timber-land, trading-house, garden truck, tumble-bug, turkey-buzzard, black walnut, war-party, wood-duck, and yellow jacket.

Striking evidence of the American need for new expressions was the many English words which the Lewis and Clark party were now using with new meanings. These included: baggage, bar, barren, biscuit, bluff, boil (n.), brand, brush, buffalo, bug, chance, chunk, clever, corn, crabapple, cranberry, creek, crow, cuckoo, dollar, Dutch, elder, elk, elm, fix, fork, gang, gap, glade, gnat, grouse, hazel, hornet, hound, hump, knob, lick (n.), lodge, lynx, mad, make out, mammoth, meal, medicine, mink, mistletoe, notion, onion, otter, pantaloon, partridge, pattern, pelican, pheasant, plunder, police, quail, raft, rat, rattle, raven, roasting ear, robin, rock, run (n.), rush, salmon, scalp (v.), settlement, sick, sign, slash, snag (v.), snipe, some, split (n.), stage, store, stud, suit, turkey, twist, village, whip, woodsman.

We have a hint of the rapidity with which the language was growing in the thousand new *words* first appearing in these journals (including terms hitherto unrecorded in any dictionary). And we have a hint of the rapidity with which the language was still changing: very few of the place names, for example, which were invented by members of the Lewis and Clark expedition, actually survived into the period of permanent settlement.

* * *

More pervasive, and in the long run more important than the inventions of explorers or the bizarre extravagances of backwoodsmen and riverboatmen, which were celebrated by Mark Twain and others, was a general looseness, a fluidity of everyday speech. This was noted as early as 1855 by Charles Astor Bristed, a Yale graduate who went to Cambridge University, and whose essay "The English Language in America" described and defended the distinctiveness of the American language. Instead of denying that Americanisms were numerous and widespread and then deploring them (as was fashionable among the literati), he found the peculiar promise of the American language in the strange fact that Americanisms had so rapidly become widespread. "The English provincialisms," he explained, *"keep their place;* they are confined to their own particular localities, and do not encroach on the metropolitan model. The American provincialisms are most equally distributed through all classes and localities, and though some of them may not rise above a certain level of society, others are heard everywhere. The senate or the boudoir is no more sacred from their intrusions than the farm-house or the tavern." It was less the specific American deviations or any peculiarities of American literary style than the peculiarly American power and predominance of the popular (and relatively classless) spoken language that had given the English language a new flavor in America. "When it comes to *talking,*" Bristed concluded, "the most refined and best educated American, who has habitually resided in his own country, the very man who would write, on some serious topic, volumes in which no peculiarity could be detected, will, in half a dozen sentences, use at least as many words that cannot fail to strike the inexperienced Englishman who hears them for the first time."

In America, then, the flow of linguistic influence was upward. What Mencken calls the "flood of racy and unprecedented words and phrases" issuing from the main currents of American life would engulf the literati themselves. The grand invention of American English was the new power it gave a churning, miscellaneous people to make a language of their own and to make the language their own.

Verbal extravagances were, of course, numerous: nouns like *guyascutus, scalawag, shebang, shindig, slumgullion, sockdolager, spondulix,* or verbs like to *absquatulate* (to leave in a hurry), *to exfluncticate* (to overcome, beat thoroughly, or use up), *to hornswoggle, to skedaddle, to squiggle,* or adjectives like *hunkydory, rambunctious, scrumptious, slambang,* and *splendiferous.* And there were rich inventions from many individual prefixes like *ker-* (*ker-flop, ker-bim, ker-splash, ker-thump, ker-bang, ker-plunk, ker-squash, ker-swosh, ker-slap, ker-whut, ker-chunk, ker-souse, ker-slam, ker-flummux*).

But, while these oddities startled the staid English traveler, they were less significant than the new vigor of the whole vocabulary. Leaving aside self-conscious elegancies like *to doxologize* (to give glory to God as in doxology; a pulpit-pomposity) or *to funeralize* (to conduct a funeral) or the new lingo of politics, we find many expressive novelties that still flourish in the everyday speech of the 20th century. New verbs were made (by what linguists call "back-formation") from old nouns: *to resurrect* (from resurrection), *to excurt* (from excursion), *to resolute, to enthuse.* Other inventions, which shocked or dismayed purists when first uttered in that age (sometimes by western representatives on the floor of Congress) included: *to affiliate, to endorse, to collide, to jeopardize, to predicate, to itemize, to Americanize.* Even commoner American verbs arose from everyday speech: *to aggravate, to boom, to boost, to bulldoze, to coast* (on a sled), *to corner* (a market), *to crawfish, to engineer, to lynch, to splurge.* Our inheritance from that age includes such everyday adjectives as: *non-committal, highfalutin, well-posted, down-town, played-out, down-and-out, under-the-weather, on-the-fence, flat-footed, true-blue.* Or such familiar American usages as *slim* (for small, as in *slim chance*) or *plumb* (as in *plumb crazy,* a revived English archaism).

One common activity which left a rich legacy to our spoken language was the drinking of alcoholic beverages. Wentworth and Flexner observe that *drunk* is the concept with the greatest number of slang synonyms in the American language. This is due, in part, to the enrichment of our vocabulary by words from immigrant tongues; also, perhaps, to the immigrants' special need for the solace of drink. Whatever the explanation, Americans, more than others, seem to have enjoyed talking about their drinking. The basic American vocabulary of alcoholic conviviality dates from what Mencken called "the Gothic Age of American drinking as of American word-making"—the years between the Revolution and the Civil War.

In that age we already find the essentials of an American drinking vocabulary. *Bar-room* (1807) and *saloon* (1841) were Americanisms for which there appeared countless euphemisms. Ask the *bar-tender* (1855) *to set 'em up* (1851)! Do you want only a *snifter* (1848), or do you prefer a drink precisely measured by a *jigger* (1836), a *pony* (1849), or a *finger* (1856)? Ask for a *long drink* (1828), unless you prefer your whiskey *straight* (1862; the English word was *neat*). Would you like an *eggnog* (1775), a *mint-julep* (1809), or some kind of *cobbler* (1840), for example, a *sherry cobbler* (1841)? The more unfamiliar inventions of the Gothic Age include: a *horse's neck, stonefence* (or *stone-wall*), *brandy-crusta, brandy-champarelle, blue-blazer, locomotive,* or *stinkibus.* The world-famous *cocktail*—destined to become one of the most prolific American inventions, linguistic or otherwise—came not from a later effete era, but from that same Gothic Age. Its first recorded use, in the Hudson, New York, *Balance (and Columbian Repository)* on May 13, 1806, explained:

> *Cock tail,* then, is a stimulating liquor, composed of spirits of any kind, *sugar, water,* and *bitters*—it is vulgarly called *bittered sling.* . . . It is said, also, to be of great use to a democratic candidate: because, a person having swallowed a glass of it, is ready to swallow any thing else.

By 1822 someone had defined a simple Kentucky breakfast as "three cocktails and a chaw of terbacker." In his *Dictionary of Americanisms* (3d ed., 1860) John Russell Bartlett still listed simply the *cocktail*—"A stimulating beverage, made of brandy or gin, mixed with sugar and a very little water." By his fourth edition in 1877, he enumerated seven varieties: brandy, champagne, gin, Japanese, Jersey, soda, and whiskey.

The most successful and most characteristic of all Americanisms, by vote of experts and amateurs alike, dates from this period: *O.K.* Its origin remains a favorite academic battleground. Until recently the weight of evidence seemed to derive it from "Old Kinderhook," a nickname for Martin Van Buren in his presidential campaign when he was supported by Democratic *O.K.* Clubs in New York. Now, however, the better view among specialists is that it originated as an acronym of *oll korrect* (for "all correct"), but that Andrew Jackson (sometimes credited with that spelling of the phrase) had nothing to do with it. In any case, the expression surely originated in the early years of the 19th century and by mid-century had begun to acquire its present general meaning. Within three decades, *O.K.* had infected the language of England.

The first half of the 19th century was the great age of foreign borrowings into the American language, for it was the first period of widespread contacts here between settlers of British and non-British origin. From the Dutch there were only a few word-borrowings after the beginning of the 19th century (for example: *bedspread* (c. 1845); *dope* (after 1807), destined to numerous proliferating senses; and *to snoop* (1832)). But it was then that other European languages made their great contribution to American speech.

While French, through Canada, had added some words (for example, *prairie, batteau, portage,* and *rapids*) in the colonial period, not until the Louisiana Purchase did American speech borrow substantially from the French. And many of these newly-borrowed words were geographic. *Prairie,* although actually used by Americans before the Revolution, had not yet entered Webster's *American Dictionary of the English Language* in 1828, but, by the time of the Civil War, the movement of people around the *prairies* increased the need for the word. By the second half of the 19th century several score compounds (e.g. *prairie-dog, prairie-hen, prairie-squirrels, prairie-State, prairie-wolf,* etc.) were in use. Early 19th-century borrowings from the French included *butte* (1805), *chute* (1804), *coulee* (1807), *crevasse* (1813), *depot* (railroad; 1832), *picayune* (1805), *to sashay* (1836), and *shanty* (1822).

The importance of the territorial element in American culture is nowhere better illustrated than by the fact that American English probably borrowed more words from Spanish than from any other language. The Spanish language was sometimes merely a vehicle for bringing in Indian words (e.g. *coyote*), but in the first half of the 19th century it added numerous words of its own. Many of these Spanish borrowings have remained among the most distinctive and expressive words in everyday American speech, especially notable, Harold W. Bentley concludes, "for local color effects, for their richness of connotation, including humor, for picturesqueness, or for descriptive contribution of some kind." They include: *adobe* (1759), *alfalfa* (1855), *bonanza* (1844), *bronco* (1850), *buckaroo* (from Spanish vaquero; 1827, 1889), *burro* (1844), *calaboose* (through Louisiana French, 1792), *canyon* (1834), *cinch* (1859), *corral* (1829), *fiesta* (1844), *frijole* (1759), *lariat* (1832), *lasso* (1831), *loco* (1844), *mesa* (1759), *mustang* (1808), *padre* (1792), *patio* (1827), *peon* (1826), *placer* (1842), *plaza* (1836), *pronto* (1850), *ranch* (1808), *rodeo* (1844), *savvy* (from sabe, 1850), *sierra* (1759), *sombrero* (1823), *stampede* (1844), *tortilla* (1831), *to vamoose* (1847; possibly begetting *to mosey*), and *vigilante* (1865).

Word-borrowings were by no means proportionate to the numbers or the volubility of immigrants from a lending country. German, after Spanish, gave us the greatest number: at one extreme such academic expressions as *kindergarten* (1855; 1862), and at the other such informal expressions as *nix* (1855), and *ouch* (1837). To the German we also owe *to loaf* (1835), *loafer* (1840), *to bum* (1863), *bum* (noun, 1862), *bum* (adj., of poor quality, 1859), *bub* (as playful form of address, 1839), *dumb* (meaning stupid, 1825), *fresh* (in sense of impertinent, 1848) and *shyster* (1846). Some of the more obvious borrowings of German food-words are *pretzel* (c. 1824), *pumpernickel* (in Longfellow's "Hyperion," 1839), *lager* (1854), *bock beer* (1856), and *to dunk* (1867). Most of the other now familiar German borrowings in our food vocabulary (e.g. *delicatessen, sauerbraten, stein, zweiback* (now spelled *zwieback*) etc.) come from later in the century.

To the Irish, on the other hand, we can trace few linguistic innovations. A scholar in 1855 said that their only effect on the language of New York had been the widespread use of *shall* (for *will*). They contributed few new words, even during the decades after the Civil War: *speakeasy, shillelah, smithereens,* and possibly also *lallapalooza* nearly exhaust the list. Perhaps their greatest general influence was not through new words or new meanings but rather through reinforcement of certain archaic speech habits which had survived in Ireland: *ag'in* for *against, bile* for *boil, ketch* for *catch, chaw* for *chew, drownded* for *drowned, heighth* for *height, h'ist* for *hoist, jine* for *join,* and the use of the definite article as in French or German ("I had *the* measles."). The

Irish (because, Mencken suggests, an Irishman is almost incapable of saying plain *yes* or *no*) gave us some of our most vivid intensives and stretch-forms, like *yes indeedy* (1856) *yes sir-ee* (1846), and *no sir-ee* (1845). From the Irish, too, probably came *teetotal* (1834), *teetotaler* (1834), *teetotally* (1839), which soon became westernized into *tee-totaciously* (1859). In this receptive age, even the Chinese, a tiny fragment of the national population, contributed a few words of general use, for example: *chow, to kowtow,* and *to yen.*

American speech offered an unparalleled example of a living language reborn within the memory of two generations. It could not have been planned nor, once growing, could it be controlled. Literary men, self-conscious devotees of the Old World, were troubled that its growth had been unruly and unapproved by its self-appointed guardians. In the accents of the Old World, the expatriate Henry James complained in 1905:

> All the while we sleep the vast contingent of aliens whom we make welcome, and whose main contention, as I say, is that, from the moment of their arrival, they have just as much property in our speech as we have, and just as good a right to do what they choose with it —the grand right of the American being to do just what he chooses "over here" with anything and everything: all the while we sleep the unnumerable aliens are sitting up (*they* don't sleep!) to work their will on their new inheritance and prove to us that they are without any finer feeling or more conservative instinct of consideration for it, more fond, unutterable association with it, more hovering, caressing curiosity about it, than they may have on the subject of so many yards of freely figured oilcloth, from the shop, that they are preparing to lay down, for convenience, on kitchen floor or kitchen staircase.

34

Tall Talk: Half-Truth or Half-Lie?

IN SO EXPANSIVE an era, the old boundaries—between fact and wish, between the indicative and the optative, between the present and the future—no longer served. The word "tall" in England had long meant simply "high" or "lofty," and in this sense "tall talk" would have meant the opposite of "small talk." In America, the word "tall" meant not only high or lofty, but "unusual," "remarkable," or "extravagant." And these were precisely the distinctions of the American experience. No language could be American unless it was elastic enough to describe the unusual as if it were commonplace, the extravagant as if it were normal. The extravagance of the American experience and the inadequacy of the traditional language made tall talk as necessary a vehicle of the expansive age of American life as the keelboat or the covered wagon.

Tall talk described the penumbra of the familiar. It blurred the edges of fact and fiction. Discovered and established by urgent need and quick consent, tall talk was a language without inhibitions. It did not grow, it exploded from sudden popular demand for modes of speech vaguer, less clear-edged, more ambiguous than the existing language provided. It responded to the newness and uncertainties of the New World. It was the language of Community before Government: of people who first shared experiences and purposes, and only later legislated about them.

To say simply that tall talk was the language of exaggeration misses the point. It was needed because the Old World notion of exaggeration had itself become inadequate. It was an explicit popular form of what later found expression in stream-of-consciousness literature: "to depict the emotional and mental reactions of characters to external events, rather than the events themselves." Strangely like 20th-century advertising language, tall talk was the language of the neither-true-nor-false, the language of ill-defined magnificence. It is misleading, too, simply to call tall talk Western humor. It was not exclusively Western, nor was it simply humor. Its peculiar importance was in its ambiguity: was it or was it not humor?

This ambiguity was noted by Thomas Low Nichols, the physician-journalist who had been born and raised in New England, had lived and doctored in upstate New York, and in the 1850's preached free love and health fads in Ohio and the Mississippi Valley:

> The language, like the country, has a certain breadth and magnitude about it. A Western man "sleeps so sound, it would take an earthquake to wake him." He is in danger "pretty considerable much," because "somebody was down on him, like the whole Missouri on a sand-bar." He is a "gone 'coon.' " He is down on all "cussed varmints," gets into an "everlasting fix," and holds that "the longest pole knocks down the persimmons." A story "smells rather tall." "Stranger," he says, "in bar hunts I am numerous." He says a pathetic story sunk into his feelings "like a snagged boat into the Mississippi." He tells of a person "as cross as a bar with two cubs and a sore tail." He "laughs like a hyena over a dead nigger." He "walks through a fence like a falling tree through a cobweb." He "goes the whole hog." He raises "right

smart of corn" and lives where there is "a smart chance of bars." "Bust me wide open," he says, "if I didn't bulge into the creek in the twinkling of a bedpost, I was so thunderin' savagerous." . . . The southwestern man was "born in old Kaintuck, raised in Mississippi, is death on a bar, and smartly on a painter fight." He "walks the water, out hollers the thunder, drinks the Mississippi," "calculates" that he is "the genuwine article," and that those he don't like "ain't worth shucks." He tells of "a fellow so poor and thin he had to lean up agin a saplin' to cuss." He gets "as savage as a meat axe." He "splurges about," and "blows up like a steamboat.". . .

American humor consists largely of exaggeration, and of strange and quaint expressions. Much that seems droll to English readers is very seriously intended. The man who described himself as "squandering about permiscuous" had no idea that his expression was funny. When he boasted of his sister—"She slings the nastiest ankle in old Kentuck," he only intended to say that she was a good dancer. To escape rapidly, west of the Mississippi, might be "to vamose quicker'n greased lightnin' down a peeled hickory."

Some of the most colorful and quotable examples expressed a gargantuan extravagance. Read Thornton's justly famous discovery in a Florida newspaper of the 1840's:

As we were passing by the court-house, a real 'screamer from the Nob,' about six feet four in height, commenced the following tirade: —"This is *me*, and no mistake! Billy Earthquake, Esq., commonly called Little Billy, all the way from No'th Fork of Muddy Run. . . . Maybe you don't know who Little Billy is? I'll tell you. I'm a poor man, it's a fact, and smell like a wet dog; but I can't be run over. I'm the identical individual that grinned a whole menagerie out of countenance, and made the ribbed nose baboon hang down his head and blush. W-h-o-o-p! I'm the chap that towed the Broad-horn up Salt River, where the snags were so thick that the fish couldn't swim without rubbing their scales off!—fact, and if any one denies it, just let 'em make their will! Cock-a-doodle-doo! Maybe you never heard of the time fhe horse kicked me, and put both his hips out of jint— if it ain't true, cut me up for catfish bait! W-h-o-o-p! I'm the very infant that refused its milk before its eyes were open, and called out for a bottle of old Rye! W-h-o-o-p! I'm that little Cupid! Talk about grinning the bark off a tree! 'taint nothing; one squint of mine at a bull's heel would blister it. O—I'm one of your toughest sort,—live for ever, and then turn to a white oak post. I'm the ginewine article, a real double acting engine, and I can out-run, out-jump, out-swim, chaw more tobacco and spit less, and drink more whiskey and keep soberer than any man in these localities. If that don't make 'em fight (walking off in disgust) nothing will. I wish I may be kiln-dried, and split up into wooden shoe-pegs, if I believe there's a chap among 'em that's got courage enough to collar a hen!"

The *screamer* (1818) was actually only exaggerating the common voice and tone.

Not only legendary hell-roaring screamers, but even ordinary men spoke their own primitive vividness. Common or garden variety Americanisms, if not melodramatic enough to be quotable nor extravagant enough to be laughable, yet were spicily concrete. Whatever you do, it's *not my funeral* (1854). Are you willing *to face the music* (1850)? Or, on that issue do you prefer to stay *on the fence* (1828)? Beware of the man with *a chip on his shoulder* (1840; 1855), for his anger will not *peter out* (1854). He may *fly off the handle* (1825). But *keep a stiff upper lip* (1815). Try to find out if he is *in cahoots* (1829) with somebody who has the *know-how* (1857) for a *knock-down and drag-out* (1827; 1834) fight. If he has, you may be a *goner* (1847), he may *make the fur fly* (1804), and finally *knock the spots out of you* (1861). Don't let him *dodge the issue* (1846). Don't be afraid to *knuckle down to* (1864) the job yourself. Don't let him *pull the wool over your eyes* (1842). Maybe that man will yet *get religion* (1826). He better learn that he is not a *high-muck-a-muck* (1856). He is the sort of person one must *handle without gloves* (1827). Never let him *get the drop on* (1869) you. If things don't *pan out well* (1868) you may be *barking up the wrong tree* (1833). Then you may want to *pull up stakes* (1841), and go where you have a better chance *to strike it rich* (1852; 1869) and where you can afford to dress up *fit to kill* (1856). *No two ways about it* (1818), a man of *horse sense* (1832) can enjoy life without having *to do a land-office business* (1839).

The more concretely the American spoke, the more, to the ears of the Old World, he sounded like a "tall talker." One could not talk big without talking concrete. The line between the specific and the hyperbolic was anything but clear in the American experience. How could it be otherwise in the language? Fantasy often seemed tame beside the grandeur of fact. When before had the concrete and the fantastic been so hard to distinguish? Where else could tall talk be the language of calm and honest men? Where else was everyday experience so unmistakably tinged with the incredible?

Tall talk, then, was heard not only on keelboats, in wagon trains, about mining camps, and among fur traders. It resounded from the pulpit, the professor's lectern, and the halls of Congress. It reached up. Preachers and teachers and congressmen joined the crowd. Thus spoke an Oregon candidate for office in June, 1858:

> Fellow-citizens, you might as well try to dry up the Atlantic Ocean with a broomstraw, or draw this 'ere stump from under my feet with a harnessed gad-fly, as to convince me that I ain't gwine to be elected this heat. My opponent don't stand a chance; not a sniff. Why he ain't as intellectual as a common sized shad. Fellers, I'm a hull team with

two bull-dogs under the wagon and a tar-bucket, I am. If thar's anybody this side of whar the sun begins to blister the yea'th that can
wallop me, let him show himself,—I'm ready. Boys, I go in for the
American Eagle, claws, stars, stripes, and all; and may I bust my ever-
lastin' button-holes ef I don't knock down, drag out, and gouge everybody as denies me!

Tall talk was admirably suited to high-flown American political speech.
Witness Davy Crockett's "Celebrated War Speech," as recorded in one
of the Crockett Almanacs, popular between 1835 and 1856.

Fellow-Citizens and Humans:

These is times that come upon us like a whirlwind, and an airthquake:
they are come like a catamount on the full jump! We are called upon
to show our grit like a chain lightning agin a pine log, to extarminate,
mollify, and calumniate the foe like a niggar put into a holler log
and rammed down with a young sapling!

Pierce the heart of the enemy as you would a feller that spit in
your face, knocked down your wife, burnt up your houses, and called
your dog a skunk! Cram his pesky carcass full of thunder and lightning
like a stuffed sassidge and turtle him off with a red hot poker, so
that there won't be a piece of him left big enough to give a crow a
breakfast, and bite his nose off into the bargain. Split his countenance
with a live airthquake, and tarrify him with a rale Injun yell, till he
gives up all his pertensions to the clearings this side of Salt Pond, and
clears out like a streak of greased lightning chased by the crocodiles
of the Mississippi.

Hosses, I am with you! and while the stars of Uncle Sam, and the
stripes of his country wave triumphantly in the breeze, whar, whar,
whar is the craven, low-lived, chicken-bred, toad-hoppin', red-mounted,
bristle-headed mother's son of ye who will not raise the beacon light
of triumph, smouse the citadel of the aggressor, and squeeze ahead for
Liberty and Glory! Whoop! h-u-rah, hosses, come along—Crockett's
with you—show us the enemy!

While Davy never delivered this eloquence during his terms in Congress,
many there before and after him would have been proud to claim it for
their own.

The American political system—with its many representative bodies
of tireless talkers—federated, compounded, and enlivened the language.
The history of our spoken language is recorded in the proceedings of
Congress. "The chief reason why we have, and continue to have, the
various strange and odd modes of using language and of utterance," the
aristocratic Philadelphian Dr. Alfred L. Elwyn apologized in his *Glossary
of Supposed Americanisms* (1859), "is, that we have no standard for
either. The people of England have Parliament, filled with men of the
best education, to be their standard; the people of this country will

hardly look to their National Legislature for an example in the use of language or of national refinement." This was his way of saying that Congress was a grand arena for tall talk. Stirred by the greatness (real or supposed) of all issues, by the dignity of the environment, inspired by the captive audience before them and the boundless audience outside, plain Americans became flamboyant. Congressmen in session exchanged purple extravagances which they took home and dispersed into their continental constituency.

As tall talk reached high places, it did not necessarily improve. It often became pompous instead of vivid, bombastic instead of strong. The rolling, rounded periods of Congressional oratory sometimes faintly suggest an American Demosthenes or Cicero or Burke—or orators trying to play the roles. Frequently they spoke desiccated tall talk, as in this fragment of the eulogy of John C. Calhoun, spoken by Albert G. Brown of Mississippi in the House of Representatives, April 17, 1840:

> And how—how, sir, shall I speak of him—he who is justly esteemed the wonder of the world, the astonisher of mankind? Like the great Niagara, he goes dashing and sweeping on, bidding all created things give way, and bearing down, in his resistless course, all who have the temerity to oppose his onward career. He, sir, is indeed the cataract, the political Niagara of America; and, like that noblest work of nature and of nature's God, he will stand through all after time no less the wonder than the admiration of the world. His was the bright star of genius that in early life shot madly forth, and left the lesser satellites that may have dazzled in its blaze to that impenetrable darkness to which nature's stern decree has destined them; his the mighty magazine of mind, from which his country clothed herself in the armor of defence; his the broad expansive wing of genius, under which his country sought political protection; his the giant mind, the elevated spotless mien, which nations might envy, but worlds could not emulate. Such an one needs no eulogium from me, no defence from human lips. . . . The story of his virtuous fame is written in the highest vault of your political canopy, far above the reach of grovelling speculation, where it can alone be sought upon an eagle's pinions and gazed at by an eagle's eye. . . . his eulogium will be heard in the deep toned murmurs of posterity, which, like the solemn artillery of heaven, shall go rolling along the shores of time until it is ingulfed in the mighty vortex of eternity. Little minds may affect to despise him . . . be it so; insects buzz around the lion's mane, but do not arouse him from his lair. Imprecations will add but other links to the mighty chain that binds him to his countrymen; and each blast of your war trumpet will but awaken millions to his support.

During the debates on the Oregon question, as Representative Cathcart of Indiana observed, the American eagle had "so often been made to take flight, that his shadow may be said to have worn a trail across the basin of the Mississippi."

The tall story was simply an application to narrative of the special characteristics of the new American speech. It turned a piece of tall talk into a kind of narrative. And its extravagance might come from its uninhibited language, from its half-believed events, or from both. A good example is Davy Crockett's own way of explaining the Oregon Question:

> I expose the reader has heered o' them diggins out West, that are called Oregon, and how the British wants to have a joint occupacy of that 'ere clearing. It's a sort of insinewation that we can't take keer of it alone, and it puts me in mind o' the joint occupacy of me and a painter [panther] when we both found ourselves together on a branch of a tree. The place war big enough for us both, but we couldn't agree to stay there together.
>
> Thar war once a pesky Yankee pedlar that put up at my house, and had as much bear's meat and whiskey in his long guts as he could carry, but he wasn't satisfied with that, for he wanted the joint occupacy of my wife too. So when I got out of bed early in the morning, he crept along to the disputed territory and began to turn down the coverlid. My wife heered him, and made believe she war asleep, but kept one eye open. Jest as he put one leg into bed, she took a clothesline that hung close by, an' tied it round his ankle, and made him fast by one leg to the bed-post. Then she got up and opened a hive of bees on him. He danced and roared most beautiful. And I think John Bull will do the same when he gits among the Yankee bees of Oregon.

The American fantasy did not spend itself on small things; everything was imagined to be even larger than it was. The dwarfs and elves and other tiny people who fill the legends of other countries have somehow not been indigenous to American soil. The infant Davy Crockett was rocked by water power in a twelve-foot cradle made from the shell of a six-hundred-pound snapping turtle, varnished with rattlesnake oil, and covered with wildcat skins. According to the almanacs, he could "walk like an ox, run like a fox, swim like an eel, yell like an Indian, fight like a devil, spout like an earthquake, make love like a mad bull." His knife Big Butcher was the longest in all Kentucky, his dog Teazer could throw a buffalo.

35

Booster Talk: The Language of Anticipation

"THERE IS A FIGURE of rhetoric adopted by the Americans, and much used in description," wrote the English traveler Morris Birkbeck in 1817; "it simply consists of the use of the present indicative, instead of the future subjunctive; it is called anticipation. By its aid, what *may be* is contemplated as though it were in actual existence." Having been told that Pittsburgh was "the Birmingham of America," there Birkbeck "expected to have been enveloped in clouds of smoke, issuing from a thousand furnaces, and stunned with the din of ten thousand hammers." He found nothing of the kind, but only a crude western town, whose whole industry was smaller than many an individual enterprise in Britain. His disappointment might have been avoided, he said, had he been acquainted with the peculiarities of American speech.

Among these none was more distinctive than the American freedom with nouns—both common nouns and the proper names of institutions, things, places, and people—which seemed to have taken on an active, fluid aspect. Much of what struck foreign observers as bizarre in American description was a new linguistic confusion of present and future, fact and hope. This became a mannerism, or even a mode of American speech. Statements which foreigners took for lies or braggadocio, American speakers intended to be vaguely clairvoyant. The American booster often was simply speaking in the future tense, asserting what could not yet be disproved. Even in colonial times men writing about America had found it hard to confine themselves to demonstrable facts.

Now, especially in the booming West, men acquired a habit of innocent overstatement. They seldom said less than they intended. The scarcity of women, which left men in control of the language as of everything else, helped account for the prevalence of slang and hyperbole. "One marked feature of social intercourse," Professor Thomas J. Dimsdale observed of Montana mining towns in mid-century, "and (after indulgence in strong drink) the most fruitful source of quarrel and bloodshed, is the all-pervading custom of using strong language. Men will say more than they mean." To describe this American habit as simply the "glorification of the commonplace" misses something peculiarly American. As tall talk confused fact and fiction in interestingly uncertain proportions, so booster talk confused present and future.

Most obvious was the use of aspiration words for institutions. "City" replaced "town," "university" designated an institution which in Europe might have been called a "college," and "college" became a name for almost any educational effort, however meager its resources. Even grander words described institutions that hardly existed at all. The elegant "hotel" was widely applied to ramshackle, flea-bitten inns and taverns. Americans thought they were not exaggerating but only anticipating—describing things which had not quite yet "gone through the formality of taking place." These were not misrepresentations but optimistic descriptions. Before the end of the 19th century, the English journalist George Warrington Steevens had noted that the American "never builds himself a house; he builds himself a home." What in England would have been called a tavern or a public house, in America became a "saloon" (originally borrowed from the French "salon")—an Americanism in this sense, to convey a hoped-for gentility. Any auditorium for public entertainment, however crude, became the local "opera house." "Lyceum," the name of the Athenian garden where Aristotle taught, became the common American word for a program of itinerant lectures and entertainers. Even "state" acquired a new aspirational meaning. Here the word indiscriminately described any component of the Union, while in England "state" meant nothing less than the whole body politic organized for supreme civil rule and government.

Free to name as they pleased, Americans often cast their nomenclature in the mold of their hopes. For example, what was the new nation to be called? The answer was not as obvious then as it now seems. At the time of the Revolution, some, including Philip Freneau, proposed "Columbia" (after the discoverer, Columbus). And there were many outlandish suggestions (for example, a Latin ending added to a contraction of the English "freedom" making "Freedonia" or "Fredonia"). "United States of North America" was used in the first treaty with France. "The thirteen united States of America," the form used in the title of the final engrossed version of the Declaration of Independence, was more tentative. But "the United States of America" in the preamble of the Federal Constitution was anticipatory in at least three senses: It expressed hope that the new nation be *united,* that the components really be *states,* and that somehow they could be identified with the whole of *America.* Soon after the Revolution, the disadvantages of this name appeared. Most conspicuous was the fact that it yielded no precise adjective. Citizens of the new nation therefore were tempted, to the chagrin of other New World nationals, to monopolize the continental adjective, to consider citizens of the United States alone to be "American."

A surprisingly large number of the names chosen for new communities were intended to foreshadow prosperity, wealth, culture, or glory. Unless the founders were willing to be crudely explicit—like the

Kansas boosters who named their town (soon to be extinct) "Wealthy City," or those in Montana who named their town "Paradise"—they inevitably expressed their aspirations by borrowing the names of famous centers of the Old World. *Oxford,* for example, was a name frequently imported; it was used for the site of Miami University (1809) in Ohio and of the University of Mississippi (1848). *Cambridge* survives into the 20th century as the name of towns founded before the Civil War in Illinois, Maryland, Massachusetts, Minnesota, Nebraska, New York, and Ohio. Self-conscious reaching for glory appeared also in the popularity of *Athens* for new centers of learning in Alabama (Athens College, 1842), Georgia (University of Georgia, chartered 1785, established 1801), Ohio (Ohio University, 1804), and West Virginia (Concord College, 1872), and to towns which survive from the early or mid-19th century in New York, Pennsylvania, and Texas.

The lists of ghost towns show that a grand and ancient name did not, of course, assure the vitality or longevity of the namesake. For example, a partial list of ghost towns in Kansas (1859–1912) includes: Alexandria, Athens, Berlin, Calcutta, Chicago (3), Cincinnati, Cleveland, London (2), Moscow, Oxford, Paris, Pittsburgh (2), Rome (2), Sparta, St. Louis. Similar lists could be provided for other states. While the classical vogue in architecture flourished, all over the nation places multiplied which boasted the names of Carthage, Corinth, Ilion, Ithaca, Rome, Syracuse, or Troy.

In 1846, when settlers founded a town at the junction of the Ohio and Mississippi rivers in southwestern Illinois, they thought they saw a resemblance to the site of the Egyptian metropolis; they optimistically called their "city" Cairo. The atmosphere of grandeur was preserved in the neighboring new villages which in turn called themselves Karnak, Thebes, and Joppa. The area actually came to be known as "Egypt," with a distinction commonly made between Little Egypt (immediately around Cairo) and Greater Egypt. By an unexpected twist, when at the first Chicago World's Fair in 1893, the name "Little Egypt" was preempted by a famous hoochy-koochy dancer, the region was left, willy nilly, to glorify itself as "Greater Egypt," which name remained in use into the mid-20th century.

36

Names in Profusion and Confusion

IT WAS NO EASY JOB to find, or make, a name for every place in the New World. Competent guesses put the number of proper names in use in the United States in mid-20th century for different places— including geographic features like mountains, bays, rivers, streams, creeks, waterfalls, and lakes, and political and social units like counties, cities, towns, and streets—at a minimum of one million, but the figure may run to three million or more. The number of extinct and obsolete place-names themselves might come to a million. A large proportion of the place-names in current use, perhaps as many as half, were given before the end of the Civil War. The naming of the nation was a gigantic, tantalizing, and complicated task. And it was largely accomplished during the first half of the 19th century. Luckily the story has been told for us in George R. Stewart's admirable *Names on the Land* (rev. ed., 1958).

Here men discovered that place-names were not exclusively a legacy from ancestors or a fiat of sovereigns. Place-naming could not be post-poned, and it became a popular do-it-yourself job.

In the colonial period, names of new settlements were often retro-spective, looking back to England. Some town names, like Boston, Cambridge, Hartford, New London, New York, Plymouth, or Worcester, or county names, like Berkshire, Essex, Hampshire, Middlesex, Norfolk, Suffolk, or colony names like New Jersey, New Hampshire, or New York, were obviously nostalgic. In the South, places like Annapolis, Charleston, Jamestown, and Williamsburg, or Georgia, Maryland, and Virginia honored English sovereigns. A few, like Salem (from the Hebrew *shalom,* "peace") or Providence or Philadelphia, carried a plain message of their own. Some, like Pennsylvania or Baltimore, commemorated proprietors or founders. Others, like Cape Cod, Newport, or Long Island, were purely descriptive. Still others—like Massachusetts, Merrimack, Con-necticut, and Roanoke—came from the Indians.

The naming of towns was commonly supervised by a central authority —the General Court or Royal Governor—in each colony. Within any particular jurisdiction, therefore, duplications were rare. "But with the Revolution," explains George R. Stewart, "every man was as good as another to give a name. Freedom ran wild, and under the banner of democracy arose an unfortunate repetition of the more popular names.

In a period of rapid expansion towns and counties were being established every day, and each county must be split into a score of townships. The demand for names outran the supply, and the result was both monotony and confusion." During the early decades of the 19th century, when the rate of community founding was highest, Congress did not even try to regulate names. Few state legislatures intervened, and the Post Office Department exercised no effective control. This left the power to name in local hands.

Americans strained their imaginations, and they rifled Bibles, dictionaries, encyclopaedias, schoolbooks, and novels. But the freer they were to devise their own labels for hundreds of new places, the less the names meant, emotionally or geographically.

The largest single naming job was accomplished perforce by the Lewis and Clark expedition. Everywhere they looked they found unnamed places—geographic features, which, if only for convenience and future reference, they had to christen. Some places they named after an obvious physical characteristic (Crooked Falls, Diamond Island, Milk River), an incident (Council Bluffs, Colt-Killed Creek), a member of their party (Floyd's River, Reuben's Creek), one of their patrons (Jefferson's River, Madison's River), a wife or a lady-love (Fanny's Island, Judith's Creek, Martha's River), and in a dozen other less obvious or less familiar ways. It has been suggested that their naming was conscious and careful, since they were seldom repetitious and they seem to have avoided commonplace terms. Later explorers had to do the job all over again, because the inadequate maps so often left them uncertain whether the mountain or the river they were looking at was the one somebody else had named.

Western communities, especially the mining camps, acquired bizarre and vivid names, for reasons now hard to recapture. The California mining landscape was marked by such places as Stud-Horse Canyon and Dead Mule Canyon, Poker Flat, Seven-Up Ravine, Brandy Gulch and Jackass Gulch, and Hardscrabble. Some towns advertised themselves by names like Gold Hill, Rich Bar, or Ophir. Or they warned away visitors and competing prospectors by calling themselves Hungry Camp, Humbug Canyon, or Poverty Hill. Often they were merely flamboyant or whimsical, like Gomorrah, Hell-out-for-Noon City, Hen-Roost Camp, Slumgullion, One Eye, Quack Hill. Not infrequently they were profane or indecent.

Although at least twenty-seven of the state names were finally borrowed from the Indians, the "Indian" names which Whitman and others found so appealing offered no general solution to the problem of finding place-names. There were numerous Indian languages, few of which were accurately or intimately known by non-Indians. The Indians sometimes had no names for the most familiar places, which apparently seemed too conspicuous to need naming.

Nevertheless, Walt Whitman and others imagined that the Indian languages could supply a mellifluous and truly American nomenclature. "What is the fitness—what the strange charm of aboriginal names?" asked Whitman. "They all fit. Mississippi!—the word winds with the chutes—it rolls a stream three thousand miles long." Mississippi had an authentic Indian origin, but many supposedly Indian names were coined by writers like Schoolcraft or Longfellow, or were recklessly moved about the continent. An Iroquois name was transferred to Louisiana or a Cherokee name to Pennsylvania. Many were pure romantic invention. The confusion among Indian tongues was such that when one tribe borrowed a name from another which spoke a different language, it had no idea of the meaning. Thus the Hurons took the beautiful name *Susquehanna* (meaning "muddy river") from the Delawares; as Raven McDavid observes, they then transformed it into a meaningless word which appeared in French as *Andastoei* and later in English as *Conestoga*—eventually a name for a branch of the Susquehanna, for a town, for a wagon, and for a cigar! The Indians, not without a sense of humor, used language as a way of jibing at their conquerors. They were freer to play tricks because they had many names for the same place, or no name at all. Sometimes, as Mencken observes, when a stranger pressed the Indians for a name, they gave him whatever first came to mind, or the worst name that was current. Some names offered by Indians were equivalents for "Far Away," "Here," "Good morning," "That is the river," or "Go to Hell!" Often the Indian names for particular geographic features were numerous, uncertain, or unpronounceable. Thus to give a state, a city, or a region its "Indian" name was a highly speculative scientific exercise to which legislators were seldom equal.

Take the naming of Colorado, for example. In November, 1806, when Captain Zebulon Pike was exploring the southwestern part of the Louisiana Purchase, he discovered a high, snow-capped mountain, which he called Grand Peak. Through his reports of his expedition the mountain came to be widely known, and it was generally called Pike's Peak. After gold was discovered in this region in 1859, settlers there demanded to be organized into a new territory. Some suggested the territory be named after Pike; but until then, no American except Washington had been so honored. No states had been named after Franklin, Jefferson, or Jackson, all of whom were far better known. What, then, should the territory be named?

The first bill to create the territory, offered in the House of Representatives in 1859, provided for the establishment of "Colona Territory." It did not pass. The origin of this proposed name was uncertain, but it may have been formed from *Colón,* the Spanish form of *Columbus,* and thus perhaps another version of "Columbia." The Committee on Territories recommended "Jefferson," which did not appeal to the Republicans, one of whom moved to substitute "Osage." People in the proposed new territory then petitioned in vain for the name "Jefferson." But when Senator James S. Green of Missouri, chairman of the Senate Committee on Territories, offered his bill, it called for a new "Territory of Colorado." This name, known then only as that of a river far on the other side of the mountains from the famous Pike's Peak gold region, had few supporters. Newspaper reports indicated that among other names considered by the Senate Committee were *Yampa* (meaning "bear"), *Idaho* (meaning "gem of the mountains"), *San Juan, Lula* (meaning "mountain fairy"), *Arapahoe* (after the Indian tribe), and that the House Committee was actively considering "the very appropriate name" *Tahosa* (meaning "dwellers on the mountain tops"). One paper reported with satisfaction that certain "anti-barbarian names" were also being suggested, notably *Lafayette, Columbus,* and *Franklin.*

The issue was especially complicated because *Idaho,* an "Indian" name which later linguists discovered to be a fabrication, had popular support. It was recommended by the convention of the territory seeking admission, it was approved by the Committee on Territories, and a bill embodying this name was offered in 1861. Meanwhile, for some unaccountable reason, misgivings about this beautiful "Indian" word began to stir. The territorial delegate to Congress was reported to have discovered that *Idaho* did not actually mean "gem of the mountains," as some had said. Lovers of the region may have feared, in view of some meanings unwittingly accepted elsewhere through Indian words, that the name meant something unmentionable. On presentation of the bill on the Senate floor, the following exchange was heard:

> *Mr. Wilson:* I move to amend the name of the Territory by striking out "Idaho" and inserting "Colorado." I do it at the request of the delegate from that Territory, who is very anxious about it, and came to see me today to have that change made. He said that the Colorado River arose in that Territory, and there was a sort of fitness in it; but this word "Idaho" meant nothing. There was nothing in it.
>
> *Mr. Green:* The name of Idaho was put in at the instance of the delegate from the Territory.
>
> *Mr. Wilson:* He has changed his opinion.

In the ensuing confusion, some Senators thought they were changing the name of what was still referred to as "Arizona," and others objected because they had actually wished to reserve "Colorado" for that other territory. Nevertheless, the region under discussion was created as the Territory of Colorado on February 28, 1861, and was admitted as a state in 1876.

Similar musical-comedy episodes were enacted again and again. In that very session another region, then commonly known as *Washoe,* was proposed as a territory. The name did not satisfy some members of the

Committee on Territories, who offered instead the name *Nevada*. This was a shortened form of *Sierra Nevada* (Spanish for "snow-covered mountain"), but the people of the region noted (what was apparently unknown to the senators) that the mountain range of that name actually lay almost wholly in California. Moreover, the climatic implications of the name were misleading for a dry sage country. When the Constitutional Convention met out there in 1864, and the secretary proposed the constitution for "the State of Nevada," some delegates objected. They made their own counter-proposals ranging from *Washoe* (after an Indian tribe, and then a common name for the region), to *Esmeralda* (after a mining camp), *Humboldt* (after the German scientist-explorer), *Sierra Plata* ("mountain silver"), *Ore Plata* ("gold-silver"), and even *Bullion*. But *Nevada* prevailed in Congress, and so it remained.

Why *Idaho,* a name so nearly given to Colorado, had such an appeal is a mystery. Its charm must have been largely melodic, for nobody knew exactly what it meant, nor did it have a traditional geographic application. Among the various etymologies of the word *Idaho,* one is that it came from "Idahi," the Kiowa-Apache name for the Comanche Indians (who lived around Pike's Peak); another derives it from a similar Shoshonean greeting word that meant something like "good morning." Nowadays experts agree that it could not have meant "gem of the mountains" (the meaning then most commonly attributed to it), for these Indians did not have the notion of precious stones. After gold was discovered in the Snake River Valley, a region of the Shoshone Indians, a new state was proposed and one of the most frequently suggested names was again *Idaho*. The reason given for this, as George R. Stewart points out, was less that *Idaho* was a Shoshone word (which it may not have been at all), than that it was commonly found in the local newspapers. The bill affecting that region proposed by Congressman James M. Ashley of Ohio, Chairman of the House Committee on Territories, was to establish the new "Territory of Montana." This passed the House. But in the Senate there was trouble, which went roughly as follows:

> *Mr. Wilson:* I move to strike out the name of the Territory, and insert "Idaho." Montana is no name at all.
>
> *Mr. Doolittle:* I hope not. I hope there will be no amendment at all. Montana sounds just as well as Idaho.
>
> *Mr. Wilson:* It has no meaning. The other has.
>
> *Mr. Doolittle:* It has a meaning. It refers to the mountainous character of the country.

The Senators, having been again reminded that Idaho meant "gem of the mountains" and was therefore beautifully appropriate, referred the bill back to the House with the name changed from Montana to Idaho. And so it remained.

How *Montana* ever became a candidate for the name of a Territory or State is not quite clear. One story suggests it was first used as a western place-name by a Pike's Peak prospector who happened to be a college graduate and who named his town-site "Montana" (from Latin for "mountainous"). The town died, but its name was supposedly remembered by Governor James W. Denver, territorial governor of Kansas, who suggested it along with *Colorado* to Senator Stephen A. Douglas as suitable for one of the new territories. "I have that name ['Colorado']," Denver reported Douglas to have told him as they scanned a western map, "selected for one down here, but I want a name for this territory up here in the mountains." When Denver proposed "Montana," Douglas then asked his wife (who had some knowledge of Spanish) what the word meant, and she confirmed that it meant a mountainous country. Senator Douglas then decided Montana would be a good name for a Territory. From this apocryphal origin, the name presumably reached the House Committee on Territories.

Congressman Ashley of Ohio, Chairman of that Committee, also took a fancy to the name "Montana." When, in 1864, citizens of the eastern part of the Territory of Idaho requested to be formed into a territory of their own, they asked to be called Jefferson Territory, but again Republicans like Ashley would have none of that. "The name of this new Territory—Montana—strikes me as very peculiar," objected Senator Charles Sumner of Massachusetts. "I wish to ask the chairman of the committee what has suggested the name. It seems to me it must have been borrowed from some novel or other. I do not know how it originated." Senator Benjamin F. Wade of Ohio replied that he had not the slightest idea, and that he would be glad to substitute "any proper Indian name" if Senator Sumner would only suggest one. Sumner begged off, saying he did not know that country well enough. Senator Howard then volunteered that he had looked up "Montana" in his old Latin dictionary, and found it "a very classical word, pure Latin. It means a mountainous region, a mountainous country. . . . You will find that it is used by Livy and some of the other Latin historians, which is no small praise." "I do not care anything about the name," asserted Senator Wade. "If there was none in Latin or in Indian I suppose we have a right to make a name; certainly just as good a right to make it as anybody else. It is a good name enough." So the new Territory was called Montana—an ambiguous monument to the classical learning or the linguistic inventiveness of the Congress. A similar story, with only minor variations, could be told of the naming of Oklahoma, Wyoming, the Dakotas, and other states.

The railroad builders, who had to name every station along the way, faced an exhausting task. Since they came in from the outside, they knew little or nothing of local traditions. But often there was really nothing to know since the places they were naming did not yet exist.

There was nobody to help and nobody to object. The task of making up names, then, was left to some railroad official or other. For example, as George R. Stewart recounts, a vice president of the Milwaukee railroad who actually named thirty-two stations in the state of Washington later explained: he had looked for short names that were easily spelled, that were distinctive in print, in Morse code, and when spoken, that were satisfactory to the Post Office Department, and that were pleasant-sounding. By a strenuous exercise of free-association, he christened the required number of stations with a variety of names ranging from Warden ("after a heavy stockholder") to Othello ("after the play"), Ralston ("after a health food"), Horlick ("after the malted milk"), Whittier ("after the poet"), and Laconia ("on account of its location at the summit—after what I thought was Laconia in Switzerland located high up among the Alps, but in looking over the Swiss map this morning I am unable to find a place of that name there").

Another task of invention was still larger and no less urgent. Streets in all the rapidly growing towns needed names. In the multiplying cities of the Southwest and West, several different patterns were followed. Some adopted the Philadelphia system of numbered streets in one direction, named streets in the other. Others adopted a plan based on the compass, with parallel streets, some north-south, others east-west, and various schemes for symmetrical naming and numbering. Others followed New York by criss-crossing "streets" in one direction with "avenues" in the other. Still others used some plan of their own devising, or allowed whim or chaos to prevail. The system of numbering streets (and houses), which seems to have developed in New York in the later 18th century, was favored by many western town-builders. It suited booster enthusiasm, for a- system of numbered streets was readily and indefinitely expandable. A house with a number was definitely a city house; new arrivals from the farm were proud to have a number.

*   *   *

The contrast of American nomenclature to that of the Old World was never better stated than by Horatio Greenough, the New England-born sculptor, who returned from Italy in 1851:

> I was wandering, the evening of my arrival in Washington, after a nine years' absence: musing as I walked, I found myself on the banks of the Potomac. I was reflecting upon the singular contrast between the non-committal, negative nomenclature of these avenues and streets and the sagacious policy which in Europe makes every name a monument, every square enforce the creed, every bridge echo a historical fact, or record a triumph of principle. Nature in the moral world still abhors a vacuum, and I felt that A. B. C. street were temporary names —squatters, waiting till the rightful lords of the domain shall appear.

What expressed American culture was less the names themselves—a rag-bag of reminiscence, nostalgia, aspiration, hyperbole, prefabrication, invention, and whimsy—than the speed and the sudden need for naming, and the strain of the job. *A List of Post-Offices in the United States,* which first appeared separately in 1803, offered Americans their first opportunity to assess their success in christening a new world. Soon thereafter, the New York legislature, noting the inconvenience "from several of the towns in the state having the same name," arbitrarily changed the names of thirty-three places. Other states gradually followed this example. A consequence was to increase the number of synthetic, exotic, or meaningless names in the sheer effort to avoid duplication. By mid-19th century, the Post Office Department had somewhat reduced the confusion by its own campaign against duplication, and by insisting on a distinguishing additional word ("North," "New," or "Center") wherever duplications remained. Before the Civil War, changing the names of towns had become almost as common as changing personal or family names was among immigrants in the later 19th century.

Men founding new communities in raw places, accustomed to transplanting their civic loyalties, saw nothing strange in changing the name of their half-born city. In desperation, promoters sometimes thought a new name might give new life to a failing enterprise. Legislatures became accustomed to requests from residents to change their town's name. It was not unusual at a single session to approve a half-dozen changes. In addition, changes were often made locally, without appeal to any outside political body. A village of fifty-odd people settled on the east bank of the Hudson above Albany had long been known as "Vanderheyden's Ferry," after a local family, until some ambitious citizens demanded a change, and in 1789 a public meeting of the village voted to rename itself "Troy." The offended Vanderheyden family long continued to call the place "Vanderheyden, *alias* Troy." One town in New Hampshire, called "Adams" in 1800, conveniently changed to "Jackson" in 1829.

Ghost names, like ghost towns, came to characterize the American landscape. The number of extinct names of *inhabited* places alone, according to one estimate, is probably about equal to the fifty thousand still in use. While Americans ridicule the quaint and cumbersome place-names of other parts of the world, and especially of the British Isles, our own place-names are a hodgepodge beyond compare. The efforts of the Post Office Department and the Board on Geographic Names have done little to organize the chaos—an everyday reminder of the American's limited powers to organize his world. And of his peculiar opportunities for new monotonies, new confusions, and new frustrations.

37

A Declamatory Literature

THE LITERATURE OF the new nation became accessory to the spoken word. The most distinctive, most influential, and most successful forms of the new American literature were expressions in print of spoken American. An American counterpart of European belles-lettres, insofar as there was such a counterpart at all, did not appear until the American spoken language had acquired its special character. Then it, too, bore marks of the peculiarly American situation; it testified to the American rebirth of the vernacular, to American preoccupation with community, with the concrete, the relevant, the here-and-now. Much of it, at its best and most characteristic, would be the *spoken* word cast into print. It was a self-conscious, sound-conscious literature—self-conscious in the sense that it was aware of its *sound,* of its *audience,* of its effect as a stirrer primarily of common sentiments between a speaker (rather than a writer) and a listener (rather than a reader). It was a declamatory literature.

This American literature was never better described than by Dr. Daniel Drake in his "Discourse on the History, Character, and Prospects of the West" delivered at Miami University in Oxford, Ohio, in 1834. Drake, the New Jersey-born, Kentucky-raised physician was an early settler and powerful booster of Cincinnati. He knew the life of the upstart towns and shared their founding enthusiasms.

> The Literature of a young and a free people, will of course be declamatory, and such, so far as it is yet developed, is the character of our own. Deeper learning will, no doubt, abate its verbosity and intumescence; but our natural scenery, and our liberal political and social institutions, must long continue to maintain its character of floridness. And what is there in this that should excite regret in ourselves, or raise derision in others? Ought not the literature of a free people to be declamatory? Should it not exhort and animate? If cold, literal, and passionless, how could it act as the handmaid of improvement? In absolute governments all the political, social, and literary institutions, are supported by the monarch—here they are originated and sustained by public sentiment. In despotisms, it is of little use to awaken the feelings or warm the imagination of the people—here an excited state of both, is indispensable to those popular movements, by which society is to be advanced. Would you rouse men to voluntary action, on great public objects, you must make their fancy and feel-

ings glow under your presentations; you must not merely carry forward their reason, but their desires and their will; the utility and loveliness of every object must be displayed to their admiration; the temperature of the heart must be raised, and its cold selfishness melted away, as the snows which buried up the fields when acted on by an April sun; then—like the budding herb which shoots up from the soil —good and great acts of patriotism will appear. Whenever the literature of a new country loses its metaphorical and declamatory character, the institutions which depend on public sentiment will languish and decline; as the struggling boat is carried back, by the impetuous waves of the Mississippi, as soon as the propelling power relaxes. In this region, low pressure engines are found not to answer—high steam succeeds much better; and, although an orator may now and then explode and go off in vapor, the majority make more productive voyages, than could be performed under the influence of a temperate heat.

The spoken word, even in the colonial period, had a peculiarly prominent place in America. The Puritans had put the pulpit in place of the altar; their great utterances were sermons. As the nation struggled into self-consciousness, the orator—the man speaking to or for or with his community—acquired a mythic role.

In Great Britain, parliamentary government and the common law had, of course, given great prominence to forensic utterance, such as Edmund Burke's speeches on conciliation and against Warren Hastings, and Robert Emmet's plea; Victorian politics would resound to the rolling periods of Gladstone and the sharp witticisms of Disraeli. Many of Britain's leading men of letters, like Matthew Arnold and John Ruskin, were famous for their lectures. British history, too, would give a large role to the spoken word. But, in that long drama of action-packed centuries, individual utterances seemed much less crucial. In the much briefer history of the United States, Americans were glad to find words to fill the place of action.

In this first national era, the "great orations" were widely recognized as the levers of American history and the formulae of American purpose. The signposts of a national destiny that was gradually becoming visible were public speeches of one kind or another: eloquent words spoken from the pulpit, in the courtroom or the legislature, or on the lecture platform. The peculiar fitness which the age found in this genre is revealed by the fact that many of the most influential, longest remembered, and most popularly memorized of these were actually not delivered at all on their supposed occasion. Of many of the most famous and most widely quoted, we possess texts which are no more than apocryphal. Some were grossly revised and improved versions; others were the work of posthumous ghostwriters, fabrications out of whole cloth. The popular desire for forensic utterances that were credal and prophetic moved public men to be oracular, flamboyant, and magniloquent, to soar from the particular occasion to national destiny and eternal verities; and it made Americans so hungry for resounding utterances that they relived their past in counterfeit orations.

From the era of the Revolution, the ringing words were those imagined to have been heard. For example, James Otis' speech against the writs of assistance before the full bench of the superior court of Massachusetts in February, 1761, became in the first decades of the new nation, a sacred utterance. "Otis was a flame of fire!" John Adams, who had been present on the occasion, recounted in 1817, ". . . he hurried away every thing before him. American independence was then and there born; the seeds of patriots and heroes were then and there sown." But nobody knows exactly what Otis said. Although William Tudor's life of Otis (1823) offered a detailed account to a hungry public, his words were based on Adams' notes (the principal contemporary record), which were scanty and by no means verbatim. Otis' most famous utterance—"Taxation without representation is tyranny"—is not in Adams' notes at all. It does not appear until about 1820, when Adams finally expanded his notes taken a half-century before.

The composition of Otis' classic speech was the work, not of the Revolution itself, but of this later era. A prime example of posthumous ghost-writing, it was, as we shall see in a later chapter, New England's belated answer to Virginia. At the time of its concoction in the early 19th century, Virginians had begun to push their claim that American independence had been born in Patrick Henry's speeches before the Burgesses in 1765 and 1775. The earlier of these was Henry's tirade against the Stamp Act, reputedly ending, "Caesar had his Brutus—Charles the first, his Cromwell—and George the third—may profit from their example." The later speech, pleading for colonial preparedness to fight, was the supposed source of "Give me liberty, or give me death." But in fact, Henry's most famous speeches appear to have been the work almost as much of William Wirt, his 19th-century biographer, as of Henry himself. Historians still debate which, if any, of the words for which Henry has become famous were his own.

One of the most widely quoted and memorized of the "historic speeches" of the age was one of its most blatant concoctions. In his speech on Adams and Jefferson on August 2, 1826, Daniel Webster, at the height of his oratorical powers, conjured up a vision of the Continental Congress in 1776. John Hancock was presiding and delegates were debating the wisdom of an immediate and absolute declaration of independence. One speaker counseled caution. Then John Adams (as Webster imagined him) arose and uttered the oration prepared for him by Webster.

Sink or swim, live or die, survive or perish, I give my hand and my heart to this vote. It is true, indeed, that in the beginning, we aimed not at independence. But,

"There's a divinity that shapes our ends."

The injustice of England has driven us to arms; and, blinded to her own interest, she has obstinately persisted, till independence is now within our grasp. We have but to reach forth to it, and it is ours. Why then should we defer the declaration? Is any man so weak, as now to hope for a reconciliation with England, which shall leave either safety to the country and its liberties, or security to his own life and his own honor! Are not you, sir, who sit in that chair, is not he [Samuel Adams], our venerable colleague, near you, are you not both already the proscribed and predestined objects of punishment and of vengeance? Cut off from all hope of royal clemency, what are you, what can you be, while the power of England remains, but *outlaws*? . . . For myself, having twelve months ago, in this place, moved you, that George Washington be appointed commander of the forces raised, or to be raised, for the defense of American liberty; may my right hand forget her cunning, and my tongue cleave to the roof of my mouth, if I hesitate or waver in the support I give him. . . .

We shall make this a glorious, an immortal day. When we are in our graves, our children will honor it. They will celebrate it with thanksgiving, with festivity, with bonfires, and illuminations. On its annual return they will shed tears,—copious, gushing tears; not of subjection and slavery, not of agony and distress, but of exultation, of gratitude, and of joy.

Sir, before God, I believe the hour is come. My judgment approves the measure, and my whole heart is in it. All that I have, and all that I am, and all that I hope in this life, I am now ready here to stake upon it; and I leave off as I began, that, live or die, survive or perish, I am for the declaration. It is my living sentiment, and, by the blessing of God, it shall be my dying sentiment; independence *now,* and INDEPENDENCE FOREVER.

Included in McGuffey's *Eclectic Readers* as one of Webster's best works, under the heading "Supposed Speech of John Adams," it was read aloud and memorized by generations of schoolchildren.

American history began to seem a series of events connecting famous orations. In 1816 John Adams himself expressed the wish to collect the great orations, "then write the history of the last forty-five years in commentaries upon them." Less learned Americans, whose knowledge of American history was largely drawn from the samples of eloquence in McGuffey, were even more inclined to see these great orations as the dominant and creative "events" in the making of the nation.

We still find it hard to think of the national history between the Revolution and the Civil War as not having been largely enacted in great speeches. From the tradition of that age we inherit the picture of crucial issues being fought over and settled by forensic eloquence. That was, of course, the age of Calhoun, Clay, and Webster, the senatorial "triumvirate" whose rolling periods resounded throughout the nation. But was there any other country of comparable size where forensic eloquence counted for so much? Career after career was made by a mellifluous voice. The two ponderous volumes of Senator Thomas Hart Benton's *Thirty Years' View, or, A History of the Working of the American Government . . . from 1820 to 1850* (1854–56), which chronicled history through forensic battles, was a characteristic political autobiography. Oration seemed almost to displace legislation as the main form of political action. The "great speeches" of that era possessed a popular power, a historic significance, and a symbolic meaning difficult for us to understand.

In the Webster-Hayne Debates, for example, Americans saw an oratorical prefiguring of the Civil War. The occasion for that Great Debate of the generation was a resolution (December 29, 1829) by Senator Samuel A. Foot of Connecticut proposing an inquiry into the expediency of limiting the sales of public lands to those already in the market, to suspend the surveys of the public lands, and to abolish the office of Surveyor General. In the passionate view of Senator Benton of Missouri, the purpose of the resolution was "to check emigration to the new States in the West—to check the growth and settlement of these States and territories—and to deliver up large portions of them to the dominion of wild beasts." The Senate debate (January 19–27, 1830) between Daniel Webster of Massachusetts and Robert Y. Hayne of South Carolina, wandering away from Foot's resolution, expatiated upon the origin of the Constitution, the nature of the Union, and the powers of the federal government. Webster and Hayne held the center of the stage but others also tried their eloquence. The most widely quoted passage (a favorite for schoolboy orators) was Webster's peroration to his first reply to Hayne (January 27, 1830):

> When my eyes shall be turned to behold, for the last time, the sun in heaven, may I not see him shining on the broken and dishonored fragments of a once glorious Union; on States dissevered, discordant, belligerent; on a land rent with civil feuds, or drenched, it may be, in fraternal blood! Let their last feeble and lingering glance, rather, behold the gorgeous ensign of the republic, now known and honored throughout the earth, still full high advanced, its arms and trophies streaming in their original lustre, not a stripe erased or polluted, nor a single star obscured, bearing for its motto no such miserable interrogatory as, What is all this worth? Nor those other words of delusion and folly, Liberty first, and Union afterwards: but every where, spread all over in characters of living light, blazing on all its ample folds, as they float over the sea and over the land, and in every wind under the whole

heavens, that other sentiment, dear to every true American heart—
Liberty *and* Union, now and for ever, one and inseparable!

Webster's public biography is chronicled by his great speeches—his
tearful plea for his alma mater in the Dartmouth College Case (1816–
19), his histrionic discourse in commemoration of Jefferson and Adams
(1826), his two grandiose replies to Hayne (1830), his speeches at
Bunker Hill Monument (1825, 1843), and his "Seventh of March
Speech" (1850), in reply to Calhoun's "Fourth of March Speech"
attacking Clay's Compromise of 1850. And he was only one of the more
prominent among many who launched their political careers on an ocean
of words.

Abraham Lincoln's career could be similarly traced, from his early
courtroom pleas and stump speeches through his "House Divided"
speech at the Republican convention in 1858, the ensuing Lincoln-
Douglas Debates during the campaign, his Cooper Union Speech in
1860, the Gettysburg Address in 1863, and his Second Inaugural in
1865. To grasp the biblical force of Lincoln's style we must remember
that he spoke in an age of swelling periods and fustian phrases.

American life—with its federal system, its new communities, its
numerous legislatures, its several systems of courts, and its regular and
frequent elections—multiplied the need and the opportunity for public
speech. The brevity of the American tradition and the scarcity of sacred
political texts gave the Great Debates (Webster-Hayne, Lincoln-Doug-
las, etc.) a peculiar role in helping the nation publicly discover itself.
"There can be no lack of opportunity for acquiring and displaying
eloquence in this country," observed Samuel Lorenzo Knapp in his
Lectures on American Literature (1829), the first book attempting to
describe a literature distinctively American. Each of the twenty-four
states, as Knapp noted, had its own legislature, averaging over 150
members who met for two months or more each year. From the thir-
teenth century B.C. to the third century B.C., Knapp boasted, "Athens
did not produce more than fifty-four distinguished orators and rhetori-
cians. We have had many more than that number within half a century."

Whether or not we agree that Otis, Henry, Webster, and Calhoun
out-spoke Pericles and Demosthenes, we cannot deny that oratory had
become the main form of American public ritual. Some of the forensic
rituals established soon after the Revolution became so much a part
of American life that we cannot imagine that they ever had to be invented. Take, for example, the Inaugural Address of the President. The
Federal Constitution did not mention this, nor for that matter any other
inaugural ritual, although it did prescribe an oath or affirmation to be
taken by the President before assuming office. The Constitution did
require the President to "from time to time give the Congress Information of the State of the Union" and to recommend measures for their

consideration. After Jefferson, however, no President until Wilson delivered his annual message in person. There was no precise precedent
for a President's inauguration (the closest analogue perhaps was the
British monarch's "Speech from the Throne" at the opening of a new
parliament), but American Presidents, beginning with George Washington, seized the occasion of their inauguration to deliver an address.

Unlike the British analogue, the American inaugural speech was not
directed to the closed audience of the Congress, but to an open public
assembly. In the coronation of a British monarch, no part of the
elaborate ritual was an original address by the monarch himself. In
a new nation lacking inherited ritual, an original oration filled the
vacuum. The inaugural address, like the sermon in a New England
Puritan service, held the center of attention. By 1832, in fact, the adjective "inaugural" had come to be used as a noun to mean the President's inaugural address. And similar ceremonies became routine for
governors of states, heads of colleges and others. After the national
presidential nominating conventions got under way in the 1830's they,
and the popular campaigns which they sponsored, provided thousands
of new occasions for public address, from the formal acceptance speech
to the extemporaneous whistle-stop remarks.

Another American oratorical institution of this vintage is the practice of recognizing the two highest ranking students in a graduating
class by allowing them to give valedictory and salutatory orations at the
commencement ceremony. Both "valedictorian" and "salutatorian" are
words found as early as the Revolutionary era; they came into common
use with the multiplication of colleges eager to tie themselves to their
communities. The practice spread down to high schools, and later even
to grade schools.

Orations were also a form of entertainment. In new towns in which
the theater was unknown or taboo, the spellbinding stump orator was
a 19th-century American version of the bard, troubadour, or minnesinger.
Without a common religious liturgy or an ancient sentiment-laden church
to be the destination of their ceremonial processions and the focus of
their rituals, Americans found a substitute in the speaker's platform.
On a historic occasion like the Anniversary of the Boston Massacre,
sharing the orator's words was itself an act of community. Municipal
authorities and other public bodies would designate their official "orator"
for each occasion, or they created a regular office of "town orator" or
"city orator." "There are few men of consequence among us," John
Adams remarked in 1816, "who did not commence their career by an
oration on [Boston Massacre Day,] the fifth of March." James Spear
Loring's seven-hundred-page biographical work, *The Hundred Boston
Orators appointed by the Municipal Authorities and other Public Bodies,
from 1770 to 1852,* was a Who's Who of the city's public life. When the

Fourth of July, the first national holiday, appeared, its typical celebration naturally gave the center of the stage to the "Orator of the Day."

*   *   *

Education, too, became more and more declamatory as preachers dominated the new denominational colleges. Many a "professor" came without any "teaching" experience other than that of the pulpit. It was common for the college president to hold the chair of "mental and moral philosophy" and classrooms were places of exhortation. "Education," declared the catalogue of Denmark Academy, the first incorporated educational institution in the Territory of Iowa (1843), "consists in the amount of manhood, spiritual as well as intellectual, which is developed, and not in the abundance of facts with which the mind is gorged."

Even the colleges were too rooted for a rapidly moving population. Another institution was needed: a mode of education requiring no dormitories or classrooms, no library, no fixed faculty, and no rigid curriculum. Precisely this was provided by the "American Lyceum," a forensic scheme of education. The Lyceum movement when it first flourished in New England expressed a reforming spirit. Its sudden success elsewhere in the country came from its special fitness to serve the upstart towns; it was a spoken counterpart to the newspaper or how-to-do-it manual.

This American Lyceum movement was founded by Josiah Holbrook of Darby, Connecticut, who graduated from Yale College in 1810 and early mixed an interest in business with a concern for educational reform. He tried combining manual training and farmwork with book-learning in an experimental school he opened on his father's farm. Then, after attending Benjamin Silliman's science lectures at Yale (1813–17), he became an itinerant lecturer on scientific subjects. In 1826 he proposed his new idea in his article "Associations of Adults for Mutual Education," and organized "Millbury Lyceum No. 1, Branch of the American Lyceum" in Massachusetts. The purpose of the Lyceum was to enlarge educational opportunities: by improving conversation, directing amusements, establishing museums and libraries, stimulating interest in public schools, helping to educate and train teachers, and in scores of other ways.

"Lyceum," from the Greek name for the garden at Athens where Aristotle taught, suddenly became an Americanism. Holbrook could hardly have imagined the success of his movement. Within eight years, three thousand lyceums led and run by local citizens had been founded throughout the country. For example, Daniel Webster was an organizer and president of the Boston Lyceum. "The Lyceum—or the course of winter lectures in towns and villages all through the country—," *Harper's*

Magazine observed in 1858, "has now become a fixed American institution." The most important stimulus to popular education until its time, as powerful and as characteristic as the public school system itself was soon to become, the Lyceum helped found and develop the regular public schools. Not until about 1890 did the Chautauqua movement, which emphasized entertainment more than instruction, take its place.

Although the Lyceum organized many activities (vividly recounted by historian Carl Bode), the heart of its program came to be the public lecture. It was a kind of educational evangelism, with the part of the circuit-riding preacher now played by the itinerant lecturer. Here is Salem's list of topics for the Lyceum season 1838–39:

Topic	*Lecturer*
The Character, customs, costumes, etc. of the North American Indians	George Catlin
Causes of the American Revolution	Jared Sparks
The Sun	Hubbard Winslow
The Sources of National Wealth	C. H. Brewster
Common School Education	C. T. Torrey
The Capacity of the Human Mind for Culture and Improvement	Ephraim Peabody
The Honey Bee	H. K. Oliver
Popular Education	R. C. Winthrop
Geology	Prof. C. B. Adams
The Legal Rights of Women	Simon Greenleaf
Instinct	Henry Ware, Jr.
Life of Mohammed	J. H. Ward
Life and Times of Oliver Cromwell	H. W. Kinsman
Memoirs of Count Rumford	A. C. Peirson
The Practical Man	Convers Francis
The Poet of Natural History	J. L. Russell
The Progress of Democracy	John Wayland
The Discovery of America by the Northmen	A. H. Everett
The Satanic School of Literature and Its Reform	Samuel Osgood
The Education of Children	Horace Mann

The 1830's and 1840's saw a mania for lectures satisfied by other organizations as well. In Boston, for example, during the winter of 1837–38 there were twenty-six different courses of lectures, attended by about 13,000 listeners. This includes only those courses composed of at least eight lectures. All over the country—less in the Old South, but in ever-growing numbers in the Southwest and West—audiences sought men of eloquence, of presence, and of reputation, who could hold their attention. The words of those men, we must not forget, were first spoken—and spoken again and again—before they reached the printed page. The rewards and opportunities of the lecture platform helped create a declamatory literature. In America there emerged a literary man known primarily for the printed versions of his platform utterances.

Ralph Waldo Emerson, whom tradition has made the leading spokesman for American literature in the first century of national life, was by far the most popular of the "literary" lecturers and one of the most popular of all the lecturers in a much-lectured age. What makes Emerson's essays sometimes seem repetitive, cryptic, contradictory, and obscure is actually that we are trying to read what was designed in the first instance not to be *read* but to be *heard*. The primary effect which Emerson aimed at, with impressive success, was not on the eye but on the ear. To the Lyceum audience, what counted was not the word-by-word meaning of the literary composition, but the total effect of a declamatory performance. It is fitting that this literary oracle of the age should have been the foremost example of the declamatory character of American literature.

Emerson's platform appeal was undeniable, for he said something which all grades of literacy and sophistication liked to hear. Even if he did not always draw the largest audiences nor command the highest fees, he lectured all over the country and was invited back to the same platforms again and again. Emerson's lectures between 1833 and 1881, as we learn from William Charvat's study, numbered about 1500, in twenty-odd states and Canada, and in some 300 different towns. The strain of long journeys on dirty trains and bumpy roads—"the plunge into this great odious river of travellers, into these cold eddies of hotels and boarding houses"—taxed even a strong physique. The lecture season ran from November through March, when travel was most uncomfortable—and Emerson could not stand the cold. His familiar greeting to hotelkeepers was, "Can you make me red-hot?"

During most of Emerson's active life (at least until 1860), his income from books was negligible and his principal source of livelihood was lecturing. Not until about 1878 did his publishers put him on an annuity, which yielded him a minimum of $1500 a year—a sum then, of course, worth several times its present purchasing-power. His regular fee for an individual lecture usually ran from ten to seventy-five dollars, but for a full-dress series (like the seven lectures in Philadelphia in January, 1854) he might with luck exceed a thousand dollars. In the 1830's and 1840's Emerson arranged either "private" series, for which he took the financial risk by hiring the hall and selling the tickets, and then pocketing the profits; or "public" series, in which some sponsoring organization guaranteed him a flat fee. Not until the 1860's were there commercial agencies to arrange lectures on commission.

An itinerant lecturer, like a circuit-riding preacher, did not need something new for each occasion. As Emerson grew older, he tended to reuse each individual lecture more and more frequently. For example, within a year after he had composed a new series of six lectures on "American Life" in 1864, he ran through them at least seven times on his way from Boston to Milwaukee and back. The most popular of these, entitled "Social Aims," he delivered at least seventy times within five years, each time in a different town in fifteen different states, netting altogether over $4000.

Repeated delivery of a lecture was Emerson's way of testing and polishing his writing before publication. His journal for 1834, at the beginning of his lecture career, described the policy he followed for a lifetime. "When a village lyceum committee asks me to give a lecture, and I tell them I will read one I am just writing, they are pleased. Poor men, they little know how different that lecture will be when it is given in New York, or is printed. I 'try it on' on them; 'The barber learns his trade on the orphan's chin.' " It was Emerson's practice to write out his lectures and carefully to save his manuscripts. Understandably he was irritated when newspapers reported his lectures in full; when the New York *Tribune,* with a large circulation in country towns, produced a nearly verbatim account of one of his lectures, he complained, for they had spoiled it for future use.

Emerson's reputation as a writer was first made by his two series of *Essays* published in 1841 and 1844, which came mainly from four series of lectures. He had selected paragraphs from different lectures, had put them together, and revised them again. In later years his lectures as delivered were closer to their final published form. With experience, he found that a lecture, once it had been well tested on the lyceum circuit, could be printed almost without revision. For example, *Representative Men* (1850) was actually published with the subtitle: *Seven Lectures. The Conduct of Life,* published as a book in 1860, he had first begun to deliver as lectures in 1851.

Out of this peculiarly American form of audience-testing, Emerson produced an American kind of aural literature—declamatory, exploratory, and popular. Its faults of obscurity, repetition, and contradiction, like its virtues of oracular ambiguity, sonorousness, and simplicity came from its success as spoken words. The lecture situation, then, as Bode explains, "at its best provided a continuing dialogue between audience and author which was inspiring to both. As he read his first drafts to his audiences, he could see what was effective, what was not. Popular taste and literary artist met and agreed. . . . In the process an American literature developed which was not only American in the simple sense of being by Americans but also American in responding to American ideas and attitudes. This was explicitly native literature, in which native audiences had played their part."

While Emerson was the greatest of the makers of our declamatory literature, he was not unique. The Age of the Lyceum heard a host of lecture-bards who spoke their words to audiences before these were printed for readers. Many now forgotten platform spellbinders like Bayard Taylor, E. P. Whipple, Park Benjamin, and J. G. Saxe dramatized their travels or orated their verse. Even the ungregarious Thoreau seems first to have conceived in the form of a lecture much of what he wrote. He made almost nothing from his writing, but did profit from his lecturing. Melville was much less successful on the lecture circuit. Nevertheless his writing resounds with the spoken word. Many of the figures and turns of style in *Moby-Dick,* as Alan Heimert has shown, were taken directly from the political speeches and other declamatory literature of the day. The reform issues of the time, too, provided topics for the declamations of Wendell Phillips, William Lloyd Garrison, Horace Greeley, Lucy Stone, and Elizabeth Stanton.

* * *

The American religious leaders of the age, like their political and educational counterparts, were noted less for their writing than for their speech. The great names among them—Lyman Beecher, William Ellery Channing, Theodore Parker, and others—were accomplished platform performers. Big-city religion was dominated by the rhetoric of magniloquence; evangelical Protestantism, the first distinctively American religious movement of national proportions, made the spontaneous spoken word the key to the religious experience. The great leaders in the flourishing revivalism of the half-century before the Civil War awakened and aroused followers by the sound of their voices. To get their proper message we should not read but listen.

Some revivalists made a doctrine of the plainness of their language and the extemporaneousness of their speech. Many of them also made a principle of the itinerancy of the ministry; for these, a congregation at any particular time was defined by the reach of a preacher's voice. They were Samuel Lorenzo Knapp's "true orator" for whom "stone or stump will answer for a tripod, and to him the common air is full of Delphick incense." Revivalism was no American invention, but in America its popularity and its power owed much to the fact that it depended on public speech.

America had set the stage for a religious experience that was communal and public, that thrived on loquacity and on colloquial vividness. The successes of American revivalists from Lyman Beecher (1775–1863) to Billy Sunday and Billy Graham in the 20th century are impressive. A pioneer who, as much as anyone else, set the style of American evangelism was Peter Cartwright. Son of a Virginia Revolutionary soldier who was "a poor man and not so much a bad as a good-for-nothing kind of man," Cartwright was raised in Kentucky and received his exhorter's license from the Methodist Church in 1802, when he was only seventeen. He had almost no formal education. For a half-century, as itinerant preacher he traveled the backwoods circuits of Kentucky, Tennessee, Indiana, and Ohio, using his loud voice, eloquent tongue, ready wit, and strong arm to overcome skeptics and to corral souls for the Lord. He became the first American master of the revivalist camp-meeting. His preaching felled hundreds who lay on the ground till he raised them to the mourners' bench, then singing and shouting to salvation. During his later years Cartwright was twice elected to the Illinois state legislature. The only recorded defeat of his career was in 1846, when he ran for Congress against Abraham Lincoln, whom he had tried to discredit for "infidelism."

Cartwright never lost faith in his own spoken word, but was always suspicious of the school-bred, hothouse readers who tried to make learning do for religion. "There was a large concourse of people in attendance," he recorded of a meeting in Winchester, Illinois, in 1837. "The house was crowded to overflowing; our seats were temporary; no altar, no pulpit, but our meeting progressed with great interest. The members of the Church were greatly revived, many backsliders were reclaimed, and scores of weeping and praying sinners crowded our temporary altar that we had erected." A "fresh, green, live Yankee from down East" with a recent diploma, emissary of the Home Missionary Society to these cannibals of the West, stood up to say his studied piece. "The frame building we were worshiping in was not plastered, and the wind blew hard; our candles flared and gave a bad light, and our ministerial hero made a very awkward out in reading his sermon. The congregation paid a heavy penance and became restive; he balked, and hemmed, and coughed at a disgusting rate. At the end of about thirty minutes the great blessing came: he closed, to the great satisfaction of all the congregation. I rose and gave an exhortation, and had a bench prepared, to which I invited the mourners. They came in crowds; and there was a solemn power rested on the congregation." One man, weighing two hundred and thirty pounds was stirred, rose to his feet and shouted for mercy. The hothouse reader kept telling him, "Be composed; be composed." "Pray on, brother; pray on, brother," Cartwright exhorted; "there is no composure in hell or damnation." The large man seized the little Yankee and holding him in his arms jumped from bench to bench until everyone felt the power of the Living Word.

This great revivalist movement in the first half of the 19th century, sometimes called the second "Great Awakening," was among other things an uprising against Calvinistic determinism. Now each man had the power to save himself: the preacher's voice could actually rouse him to salvation. Out of these experiences came Charles Grandison Finney's *Lectures on Revivals of Religion* (1835), a practical handbook for evangelists which has never been excelled. Its first American edition sold twelve thousand copies in three months after publication. It became the basic textbook of modern revivalism, was translated and sold widely abroad. Finney was asked in 1835 to establish a theology department at Oberlin College, newly founded in Ohio; as president of Oberlin (1851–66) he spread his influence from religion into education. Another great evangelist of the day, Lyman Beecher, told his students at Lane Seminary, "Young men, pump yourselves brim full of your subject till you can't hold another drop, and then knock out the bung and let nature caper." Declamatory religion for some decades ruled the American West.

*   *   *

The broad Mississippi of declamatory literature was fed by several streams. Most powerful was the wide current of magniloquence: the memorable utterances (real or imagined) of James Otis, Patrick Henry, Daniel Webster, John C. Calhoun, and Ralph Waldo Emerson, who spoke the highfalutin language. They were self-conscious, serious, or even solemn, and they spread over the continent. Through them the American declamatory literature would endure. But there was another stream—less dignified and less moving, but no less American—a democratic, vernacular form of belles-lettres. It entertained not by self-conscious literariness, but by contrived illiteracy. Its stock in trade was not the flamboyant metaphor, the periodic sentence, the sophisticated synecdoche, but the homely anecdote, the outrageous exaggeration, the overstated dialect. This "lower" strain, no less than the "higher" strain of the newly developing American literature, exploited the *spoken* word, real or imagined.

The rhetoric of anecdote and horse sense took its clue from the magniloquence which it travestied. The pomposity and long-windedness of the one gave point to the simplicity and terseness of the other. The resounding word gave both genres their character and their appeal. One of the first examples of this form was the writings of Seba Smith. His creation was "Major Jack Downing," a rustic philosopher-adventurer from the little Maine village of Downingville. The letters of Major Downing were first published in Smith's own newspaper, the Portland *Courier* in 1830. Despite (or perhaps because of) his lack of education, his crude grammar, and his erratic spelling, Major Downing seemed always to go to the heart of the matter. Setting out as a peddler of cheeses and barrel hoops, one day he wandered into the Maine legislature, and so entered politics. Then, as an office-seeker, he went to Washington, where he became a confidant of President Andrew Jackson. Downing's political career (including a candidacy for the Senate and for the Presidential nomination) lasted until the 1850's. He offered a welcome, if obvious, contrast to other public men of his day. Downing entitled his collected letters, parodying Benton, *My Thirty Years out of the Senate* (1859).

During the height of the nullification controversy, when South Carolina was threatening to secede from the Union, Major Downing reported his conversation (January 17, 1833) with President Jackson:

> "Now," says I, "Gineral, I'll tell you jest what I think of this ere business. When I was a youngster, some of us Downingville boys used to go down to Sebago Pond every spring and hire out a month or two rafting logs across the pond. And one time I and Cousin Ephraim, and Joel, and Bill Johnson, and two or three more of us had each a whopping great log to carry across the pond. It was rather a windy day, and the waves kept the logs bobbing up and down pretty considerable bad, so we agreed to bring 'em along side-and-side and lash 'em together and drive some thole-pins in the outermost logs and row 'em over together. We went along two or three miles pretty well. But by and by Bill Johnson begun to complain. He was always an uneasy, harum-scarum sort of a chap. Always thought everybody else had an easier time than he had, and, when he was a boy, always used to be complaining that the other boys had more butter on their bread than he had. Well, Bill was rowing on the leeward side, and he begun to fret and said his side went the hardest, and he wouldn't give us any peace till one of us changed sides with him.
>
> "Well, Bill hadn't rowed but a little ways on the winward side before he began to fret again, and declared that side went harder than t'other, and he wouldn't touch to row on that side any longer. We told him he had his choice, and he shouldn't keep changing so. But he only fretted the more, and begun to get mad. At last he declared if we didn't change with him in five minutes, he'd cut the lashings and take his log and paddle off alone. And before we had hardly time to turn round, he declared the five minutes were out, and up hatchet and cut the lashings, and away went Bill on his own log, bobbing and rolling about, and dancing like a monkey, to try to keep on the upper side. The rest of us scrabbled to as well as we could, and fastened our logs together again, though we had a tough match for it, the wind blew so hard. Bill hadn't gone but a little ways before his log begun to roll more and more, and by and by in he went splash, head and ears. He came up puffing and blowing, and got hold of the log and tried to climb up on to it, but the more he tried the more the log rolled; and finding it would be gone goose with him pretty soon if he staid there, he begun to sing out like a loon for us to come and take him. We asked him which side he would row if we would take his log into the raft again. 'Oh,' says Bill, 'I'll row on either side or both sides if you want me to, if you'll only come and help me before I sink.' " . . .
>
> "And now, Gineral, this is jest what I think: if you let South Carolina cut the lashings you'll see such a log-rolling in this country as you never see yet."

The letters of Major Downing were an immediate success. They were soon reprinted in Boston, then elsewhere in New England, and before long had a national audience. The genre was widely imitated, and by so many who used Downing's own name that the original Major Jack said he had to identify himself by the scar on his left arm.

Major Downing was only one of the first of a long line in an American form of popular literature. He illustrated many features which his successors had in common: fragmentary form (lending itself to first piecemeal publication in newspapers or magazines), reliance on anecdote, affectation of semiliteracy or illiteracy (Seba Smith had actually graduated with honors from Bowdoin College, 1818), appeal to horse sense, and, above all, full exploitation of the tone and manner of the informally spoken word. Major Downing, like his most eminent successors, was omni-partisan, seeing something good and something bad on all sides. They all belonged to the party of horse sense which found more truth in a good joke than in a high principle.

Franklin's Poor Richard had been a forerunner of Downing. But Poor Richard was still tinged with colonialism: he did not dare to be a jocular illiterate. Downing's most eminent successors included Davy Crockett (who lived before Downing, but whose influential apocryphal writings first appeared between 1834 and 1836). The mid-century decades, the heyday of silver-tongued magniloquence, were also the heyday of the horse-sense anecdotalist and the crackerbox philosopher. From New England came the voice of James Russell Lowell's Hosea Biglow, whose utterances had less popular appeal when polished and published in book form (1848; 1867) than when they had originally appeared in the Boston *Courier* or the *Atlantic Monthly*. Much of Biglow's wisdom remains relevant:

> Fust come the blackbirds clatt'rin' in tall trees,
> An' settlin' things in windy Congresses,—
> Queer politicians, though, for I'll be skinned
> Ef all on 'em don't head aginst the wind.

From the South came the backwoods sharper Simon Suggs, Alabama newspaper creation (c. 1846) of Johnson J. Hooper. Few were more popular than the notorious Artemus Ward (created by Charles F. Browne) whose wise sayings began to appear in the Cleveland *Plain Dealer* in 1857 and whose fence-straddling made him a byword. "My political sentiments agree with yourn exackly. I know they do, because I never saw a man whose didn't." Josh Billings, perhaps the most famous, was invented by Henry Wheeler Shaw, who also had his start in the small newspapers. *John Billings, His Sayings* (1865) offered some of the most widely quoted aphorisms of the day. Billings' popularity was reinforced by his annual *Allminax* (1869–80). In the later 19th century, leading carriers of the tradition were the indomitable Mr. Dooley (by the Chicago newspaperman, Finley Peter Dunne; in book form, 1898–1919), and then, in the 20th century, Abe Martin and Will Rogers. The tradition was also to be continued in the comic strips of Al Capp and others.

Crackerbox philosophers were legion. What made them famous was not their "writings" but their "sayings." The cast of their mind was revealed in the sound of their talk. They were a popular literature of the spoken word.

Out of that heyday and out of that tradition came two of the most durable and most characteristic of American literary figures. Much of the special genius of Mark Twain consisted in his ability to capture the casually spoken word and to give literary form to the anecdotalism and horse sense which for others remained mere fragments. He was, of course, one of the most successful lecturers in all American history. But it was significant that Twain's important writings did not come until after the Civil War (*Roughing It,* 1872; *Tom Sawyer,* 1876; *Life on the Mississippi,* 1883; *Huckleberry Finn,* 1885) when much of the turbulence of the churning West was past. All this writing was nostalgic—a faint echo of the blustering, loud-talking, slang-slinging voices of the earlier creative age of an American language. The expansive, slippery vitality of American speech was never quite captured in extended literary form; Mark Twain's best effort came only when the language had ceased blustering and was no longer expanding so explosively.

The greatest and most durable monument to the power of the spoken word in that age is Abraham Lincoln. Although he is one of the giants of an "American" literature, virtually his whole literary fame rests on his spoken utterances. He drew together the two divergent and complementary streams of American declamatory literature. Purifying the public oration of its pomposities, its circumlocutions, and its affectations, at the same time he purified the anecdotal, horse-sense saying of its vulgarity, its crudity, its newspaper transience. No one better combined the virtues of each to create classics of declamatory literature which would long speak to a popular federal nation.

The singleness of language in America was a great new opportunity, but the opportunity could be realized only if the language remained the possession of the people themselves. Edward Everett, reputedly the most eloquent orator of the age, whose nearly forgotten two-hour oration at Gettysburg preceded Lincoln's remarks, had begun his forensic career and attracted wide attention with a Phi Beta Kappa Oration at Harvard on August 26, 1824, on "The Circumstances Favorable to the Progress of Literature in America." There he exclaimed:

In Europe, the work of international alienation, which begins in diversity of language, is consummated by diversity of race, institutions, and national prejudices. . . . While, on the other hand, throughout the vast regions included within the limits of our republic, not only the same language, but the same national government, the same laws and manners, and common ancestral associations prevail. Mankind will here exist and act in a kindred mass, such as was scarcely ever before congregated on the earth's surface.

PART SEVEN

SEARCH FOR SYMBOLS

"The American has, in fact, yet no character;
neither the clown nor the gentleman. . . ."

HUGH H. BRACKENRIDGE

AGAIN the familiar Old World sequence was disarranged; the pace
was new. A nation appeared here before there was a national spirit
of the kind which elsewhere had created nations. Everywhere, American
haste and New World self-consciousness left their mark.

National symbols and popular heroes had commonly been a by-
product of a long history—of wars and of the struggle for nationhood.
Henry V and other historical plays would not have been possible
without an already flourishing national spirit for which they became a
vehicle; Shakespeare was both a product and a maker of English nationhood. In Europe, a people that wanted to know itself, its ways of thinking, its peculiar forms of wit and beauty and virtue and vice and heroism
could look to its very own literature, the classics of its mother tongue.
But Americans found the treasures of their English mother tongue and
most of their historic past set in the Old World. Those had been accumulated long before their nation was imagined.

How, without losing those, were they to find—or make—American
heroes? How could they discover themselves in an American history?

38

Heroes or Clowns?
Comic Supermen from a Subliterature

EARLY 19TH-CENTURY America offered many obvious features of a Heroic Age—a half-known wilderness where men were threatened by untamed animals and hostile tribes—and it is not surprising that there soon appeared American counterparts of the ancient heroes. But the uncertainties of national boundaries and aspirations and language, and the unsure line between fact and hope, had their counterparts in uncertain boundaries between the heroic and the comic. Our first popular heroes came on the scene to a chorus of horse-laughs. The vehicles of national ideals were the butts of national laughter. This unfamiliar combination was a product of American peculiarities.

Precisely how European heroes of the Heroic Age—Achilles, Beowulf, Siegfried, Roland, King Arthur, and others—arose, is of course shrouded in mist. It seems likely that they first appeared in oral legend, only gradually finding their way into formal written literature. From oral legend or minstrelsy to literary epic was a long journey. The passage of centuries distilled and elevated and "purified" the heroic characters, and self-conscious chroniclers gave their subjects grandeur and dignity.

All this was different in the United States. David Crockett (1786–1836) was still alive when oral legends about him began to circulate. He was not yet dead when his exploits, real or supposed, were already embalmed in print. Through his "autobiographical" writings (probably

327

written mostly by others) and other episodic accounts, he became widely known over the continent within a decade of his death.

At least two crucial distinctions, then, mark the American making of a popular legendary hero. First, there was a fantastic chronological abridgment: from elusive oral legend to printed form required here a few years rather than centuries. Legends hastened into print before they could be purified of vulgarities and localisms. Second, the earliest printed versions were in a distinctively American form; they were not in literature but in "subliterature"—writings on popular or vulgar subjects, belly-laugh humor, slapstick and tall tales, adventures for the simple-minded. Crockett was not written down in any American counterpart of the *Historia Regum Britanniae* nor in any *Morte d'Arthur:* the Crockett anecdotes plunged headlong, in a decade, from the small world of fire-side anecdote and barroom wheeze into the great democratic world of print. Widely circulating, inexpensive publications dispersed the Crockett legends as they fell from the lips of raconteurs. They entered at once into a thriving subliterature.

In Western Europe, too, there was, of course, a subliterature of ballads, broadsides, parodies, almanacs, and other ephemeras of popular entertainment and instruction even as early as the 17th century. But literacy there was long confined to a small fraction of the upper classes. Extensive, dignified works—the Bible, prayerbooks, sermons, epics, treatises—were being printed long before literacy was widespread. Not until the 19th century had the English working classes generally learned to read. By the time there was a considerable reading audience reaching down into the populace, a vast literature of great dignity, of Shakespearean drama and Miltonic epic, had grown and taken the center of the national stage.

Not so in the United States. Here, from colonial times, literacy had been more widespread than in the mother country. The reading audience for a subliterature already existed at the nation's birth. Thus, in the first century of national life a subliterature grew and flourished at the same time that American writers were trying to give the nation its own dignified and elevated literature. In America, again, the familiar European calendar of cultural development was abridged and confused. A subliterature, which in other countries was made possible by a seeping down of literacy after the nation had established its literature, was to develop in America almost before the nation produced a literature.

Davy Crockett was the most important and, for some time, the most widely known popular candidate for national hero-worship. The vehicles which spread his fame, like everything else about him, beautifully illustrate the peculiar American situation. Crockett, the son of a Revolutionary soldier who became a tavern-keeper, was born in northeastern Tennessee in 1786. He ran away from home at the age of 13 to escape a beating, wandered about for several years, and married at the age of 18. Failing to make a go as a farmer, he joined Andrew Jackson in the Creek War of 1813–14 and served for a while as a scout. He later hired a substitute to complete his term of enlistment and moved to southern Tennessee, where he began his career of public service, first as an apponted justice of the peace, then as a colonel of militia. In 1821, Crockett was elected to the state legislature. Moving again, he settled at the extreme western edge of the state (where his nearest neighbor was seven miles away) and was quickly elected to the state legislature again from his new constituency. Then, on a dare, he ran for Congress, and, much to his own surprise, was elected. He served for three terms. When not at the state capital or in Washington, he lived the perilous life of the backwoodsman: during one nine-months period he killed 105 bears; he nearly died while floating a load of barrel-staves down the Mississippi in 1826.

He had little education and little respect for book-learning; the rules of spelling, he said, were "contrary to nature." As a judge (when he did not know the meaning of the word "judiciary") he "relied on natural-born-sense instead of law-learning." In the Tennessee legislature, Crockett had voted against Jackson for senator, and very early he began voting against Jackson's policies in Congress. This made him a welcome backwoods symbol for the anti-Jackson Whig party just being organized, but it angered his Tennessee constituents who finally refused to send him back to Congress. Crockett then left Tennessee, partly in pique and partly moved by enthusiasm for the war for Texas independence. Arriving at the Alamo in Febraury, 1836, he died a martyr's death a few weeks later in its final defense.

The exploits, real or imaginary, of Davy Crockett were quickly circulated in print: in newspapers, in almanacs, and in books. Shrouded—or rather, haloed—in a multiplex ambiguity, even their authorship is uncertain. Crockett himself may have had some hand in books about him published before 1836, and Whig journalists and others also did their own embellishing. Most of the later almanac stories are anonymous. But there is no uncertainty about the popularity and wide circulation of the printed legends of Davy Crockett. *Sketches and Eccentricities of Col. David Crockett* (1833), *An Account of Col. Crockett's Tour to the North and Down East* (1835), and Crockett's *Life of Martin Van Buren* (1835) reached a large audience. *A Narrative of the Life of David Crockett, of the State of Tennessee* (1834), which came to be called his autobiography, reached best-seller proportions. A posthumous literature, including works like *Col. Crockett's Exploits and Adventures in Texas* (1836), grew and whetted the appetite for still more legend. Then came the so-called "Crockett almanacs." The earliest, printed in Nashville in 1835, bore the title, *Davy Crockett's Almanack, of Wild*

Sports of the West, and Life in the Backwoods. Calculated for all the States in the Union. In its first issues it drew on the "autobiography" but later offered items (with the ostensible authority of the "heirs of Col. Crockett") which Crockett himself was supposed to have prepared before his death. Nashville imprints were issued until 1841, when other Crockett almanacs began to appear in New York, Philadelphia, Boston, Albany, Baltimore, Louisville, and elsewhere. At least fifty appeared before 1856. These almanacs, embellished by rough woodcuts and as crude in typography as in content, were destined to become expensive collector's items in the mid-20th century.

The Crockett almanacs, like their predecessors, contained much information and misinformation besides the "true adventures" of Davy Crockett. They included adventures of Mike Fink, Daniel Boone, Kit Carson, and of the more obscure backwoods supermen, and miscellaneous stories of plants and animals, as well as the pithy sayings, medical hints, and helpful facts of weather, astronomy, and astrology, which had long been the staples of the almanacs.

This proliferating subliterature—lowbrow printed matter, fertilized by vulgar humor and the popular imagination—was one of the first characteristically American genres. It is not surprising that the new nation should have expressed itself in a subliterature. For a turbulent, mobile, self-conscious, sanguine, and literate people, it took the place of belles-lettres. In the colonial period, the characteristic American printed matter had been not the book or the treatise but the newspaper, the pamphlet, the how-to-do-it manual, the sermon, and the letter. This new literature was designed for people who did not read books. Intended for a predominantly masculine public, it was self-consciously unliterary and ungenteel, belligerently formless and unashamedly crude.

The American people, Dickens wrote in his *American Notes* (1842), "certainly are not a humorous people, and their temperament always impressed me as being of a dull and gloomy character." Dickens was only one of the European travelers of that day who rebuked Americans for their seriousness. Mrs. Trollope, in the first edition of her *Domestic Manners of the Americans* (1832) also had asserted that Americans lacked humor; but in a revised edition (1839) she explained in a footnote that the advent of Jack Downing had disproved her claim. Such opinions were not likely to be altered by the successful American belles-lettres of the day. In the half-century before the Civil War it was characteristic that "American" writers who were most lionized and admired in Europe were those—like Washington Irving (1783–1859)—whose masters had been the politest of the polite English men of letters, Addison and Steele and Goldsmith. Much of Irving's writing was actually on English and European subjects, which he suffused with a romantic aura; much of his active life he spent abroad, absorbing the atmosphere of

England and Spain. Even his "Legend of Sleepy Hollow" and his "Rip
Van Winkle," although American in locale, were based on familiar
European sources. The English and French writers who admired him as
a pre-eminent "American" writer were admiring a slightly Americanized
version of themselves.

What escaped Dickens and other European travelers was that America
was already producing a new kind of literature, one by new kinds of
authors and for new audiences. As late as 1877, for example, George
Meredith asserted that the comic artist required "a society of cultivated
men and women." It was hard to imagine that the very "coarseness"
and "grossness" (Meredith's anathema-words), the lack of elegance and
ceremony, which seemed to explain why Americans were so "dull and
gloomy," might itself be the source for a distinctively American genre,
which was anything but humorless. The new American subliterature,
which they failed to praise, had escaped their notice—by Old World
standards, it was beneath their notice.

American humor and American popular heroes were born together.
The first popular heroes of the new nation were comic heroes and
the first popular humor of the new nation was the antics of its heroic
clowns. The comic and the heroic were mixed and combined in novel
American proportions. What were the dominant themes of these mock-
heroics? What made them comic, and what made them heroic?

The heroic themes are obvious enough and not much different from
those of other times and places. The Crockett legends, as Richard M.
Dorson has explained, repeat the familiar pattern of the Old World
heroic story: "the pre-eminence of a mighty hero whose fame in myth
has a tenuous basis in fact; single combats in which he distinguishes
himself against dread antagonists both man and beast; vows and boastings; pride of the hero in his weapons, his horse, his dog, his woman;
the remarkable birth and precocious strength of the hero; a tragic death
in which the invincible but mortal champion is treacherously or un-
naturally slain." Achilles, Beowulf, Siegfried, Roland, and King Arthur
—each in his own time and place—relived the familiar heroic role.

Crockett, too, conquered man and beast with a swaggering non-
chalance. "I told the lying sarpint to own he war chawed up," Crockett
warned the beaten Yankee, "or I would make fiddle-strings of his tripe.
So he squat low and felt mean. He sneaked off like an Injun in a clear-
ing." Crockett overcame animals by force of body and will. He killed
four wolves at the age of six; he hugged a bear to death; he killed a
rattlesnake with his teeth. "When I come home of a dark nite," Crockett
recounted of the panther he had tamed, "he'll light me up to bed with
the fire of his lookers; he brushes the hearth off every mornin with his
tail, an' o' Saturdays does all my wife's heavy work. He rakes in all
her garden seed with his claws, does all of little Buffalo Crockett's extra

screamin', wipes our feet off with his back arter we wash 'em, helps to currycomb the horses with his nails, and lets my wife hackle flax upon his teeth. If he don't, then feed me for dinner to a flock o' hungry wild-cats in winter." Crockett mastered the forces of nature. He had his own way, for example, to escape from a tornado:

> Then came a roar that would have made old Niagara sound like a kitten; the trees walked out by the roots, and danced about like injins; the houses come apart; the people screamed all sorts o' frightened-to-death-ativeness, and some of them appeared to be going up to heaven heels foremost. . . . Fortunately, a stray streak of lightnin' came passin' along, so jist as it come I grabbed it by the fork, and sprung on it. Ben follered, and held on to my hair; I greased it a leetle with a bottle of rattlesnake taller, and the way we streaked it, and left the tornado behind, was astonishin' to all natur.

Crockett's most famous natural exploit was saving the earth on the coldest day in history. First he climbed a mountain to determine the trouble. "The airth had actually friz fast on her axes, and couldn't turn round; the sun had got jammed between two cakes o' ice under the wheels, an' thar he had been shinin' an' workin' to get loose till he friz fast in his cold sweat." Crockett rescued all creation by squeezing bear-grease on the earth's axis and over the sun's face. He whistled "Push along, keep movin'!" The earth gave a grunt and began moving. "The sun walked up beautiful, salutin' me with sich a wind o' gratitude that it made me sneeze."

Not the gargantuan feat nor the fearlessness nor the bold huntsman's prowess was peculiarly American. Far more distinctive was the comic quality. All heroes are heroic; few are also clowns. What made the American popular hero heroic also made him comic. The pervasive ambiguity of American life, the vagueness which laid the continent open to adventure, which made the land a rich storehouse of the unexpected, which kept vocabulary ungoverned and the language fluid—this same vagueness suffused both the comic and the heroic. Both depended on incongruity: the incongruity of the laughable and the incongruity of the admirable. In a world full of the unexpected, where all norms were vaguely or extravagantly defined, readers of the Crockett legends were never quite certain whether to laugh or to applaud, whether what they saw and heard was wonderful, awful, or ridiculous. "May be . . . ," wrote Crockett, "you'll laugh at me, and not at my book." In a more fully explored, better known, more predictable world, they would have been more certain of the meaning of what they saw and of the reactions they should express. Crockett's boastings were not entirely distinguish-able from the honest optimism of the booster, from the blatant lies of the land-promoter, or from the common hopefulness of the transient.

Even today, when we are fascinated by the spectacle of the American superman of that age, we are seldom sure why. Are we admiring the beautiful, the grand, the big, or the ugly?

A kind of "pride in ugliness, or in the ability to depict ugliness," as Dorson has remarked, was characteristic of these Crockett stories. Old Bill Wallis, for example, was so ugly that flies would not light on his face. When, at the age of ten, he saw his reflection in a stream, he ran for his life, hollering for help at every step. "His face, generally, had the appearance of a recently healed blister spot. . . . His mouth—ruby-red—looked as if it had been very lately kicked by a roughly shod mule, after having been originally made by gouging a hole in his face with a nail grab!" Were the words in these stories really *words?* Gully-whumping, slantendicler, discomboberate, absquatulate, homogification, circumbustifikashun, flutterbation. Elegancies? Illiteracies? How much of it all was a hoax?

Some of our shrewdest students of comedy agree that detachment, a certain ability to look at oneself from the outside, is essential to the comic spirit. According to Constance Rourke, this explains why the American comic spirit did not begin to flourish until after the War of 1812 had more firmly established the American nation. Americans, feeling themselves more secure, could then look on themselves with a new detachment. A similar sense of detachment, of distance from oneself, is also required for the heroic. Distance makes both heroes and clowns. Great heroes are men from whom one feels at a great distance. Of course, this distance can be provided by the centuries. "Distance lends enchantment," if a cliché, is also an ancient and familiar theme. "Glories," said John Webster, "like glow-worms, afar off shine bright, but look'd too near have neither heat nor light."

Yet there is more than one kind of distance. In America, in this as in many other ways, space played the role of time. If Americans, in their new country, could not be separated from their national popular heroes by hundreds of years, they were in any case separated by hundreds of miles. This sense of distance was possible as it had not been in smaller, more homogeneous nations. The great and varied space provided distance for both heroic and comic perspective.

In 1840 the cultural distance between Boston, New York, or Philadelphia and the Tennessee or farther-western backwoods was probably as great as that between the England of the 12th and the England of the 6th century. And the geographic distance from Boston to the western boundary of Tennessee was greater than that between London and Algiers. The printed matter in which the legends of Crockett and other heroes of the backwoods were most widely circulated came from the remote eastern capitals.

The vastness and variety and freshness of the American landscape, of its flora and fauna, of custom and costume, nourished American subliterature and gave American subjects great promise for the comic and the heroic. This comic-heroic subliterature drew on the whole half-known, unpredictable continent. It garnered oral tales from far-away corners of the nation and retailed them to the amusement, wonder, and delight of fellow Americans who had never seen such places and could not be sure whether what they read was ridiculous or wonderful. It is only a half-truth, therefore, to speak of American humor and American heroics in this period as "regional." Individual stories were regional only in the sense that they were set among the conspicuous peculiarities of some particular region. Many of the best works of the subliterature appeared first in the New Orleans *Picayune,* the St. Louis *Reveille,* the Cincinnati *News,* or the Louisville *Courier.* Then gradually, by compilation and republication, they reached the nation. Their wider comic and heroic appeal, and their place as national legend, finally came from the fact that there was a large audience of fellow Americans remote from these scenes that was eager for entertainment and for sagas to dramatize the distinctive appeal and grandeur of their whole country. Regional distinctions themselves thus made possible a flourishing national subliterature.

Perhaps the most important vehicle of the age for collecting and disseminating the subliterature about the Southwest and the West was published in New York City. *The Spirit of the Times* was founded in 1831 by William T. Porter, a Vermont-born son of a horse-fancying family. Originally conceived as a sporting journal, Porter's magazine called itself a "Chronicle of the Turf, Agriculture, Field Sports, Literature, and the Stage." Unable to find writers or readers for a conventional turf magazine, Porter changed its character to suit the American situation. "Trammelled by circumstances, retarded by inexperience, we groped our way slowly into those Southern and Western regions of our country where the sports we advocate were more generally appreciated and more liberally encouraged." In place of professional writers, he sought and found amateurs by the dozen—lawyers, doctors, printers, planters, merchants, and men of no particular profession—who filled his magazine with racy tales and sketches. In the issue of 1839 (expanded to twelve pages) he boasted "nearly SEVEN PAGES OF ORIGINAL MATTER, from the pens of no less than *thirty-three correspondents!"* By 1856, Porter had claimed a circulation of 40,000. *The Spirit of the Times* was to be a bible of the subliterature. Like many other ephemeral publications, it gave form to scattered anonymous tales.

It was not mere tall talk when Porter boasted in *Big Bear of Arkansas* (Philadelphia, 1843) that "a new vein of literature, as original as it is inexhaustible in its source, has been opened in this country within a very few years, with the most marked success." Never before, he ex-

plained, had there been authors quite like these. The title-story in this
magazine anthology has deservedly become the classic example of the
comic-heroics of the American subliterature. The core of the marvelous
tale is *ambiguity*. Nothing about the story is unambiguous. Even the
title, *Big Bear of Arkansas,* refers ambiguously to the monster killed
in the climax or perhaps to the storyteller himself. When the monster-
bear finally dies, it remains tantalizingly unclear whether the hunter had
actually shot the bear or whether "that bar was an *unhuntable bar, and
died when his time come."* The final ambiguity arises from the fact that
the storyteller himself has fallen under the spell of his own tale. The spirit
of the story, like that of much other subliterature, is in the one word
"Prehaps!" " 'Prehaps,' said I, 'friends'—getting wrathy—'prehaps you
want to call somebody a liar.' 'Oh, no,' said they, 'we only heard such
things as being *rather common* of late, but we don't believe one word of
it; oh, no,'—and then they would ride off and laugh like so many hyenas
over a dead nigger."

On the national scene, Crockett's only serious competitor was Mike
Fink. Last of the keelboatmen, Fink (1770–1823) had three careers—
first fighting the British and the Indians, then fighting the Ohio and the
Mississippi in the days before the steamboat, and finally as a Rocky
Mountain fur trapper. The Fink stories were most popular between 1830
and 1860 when the Crockett almanacs themselves celebrated Fink's
varied exploits. Perhaps it was nostalgia that made the new age of the
noisy steamboat romanticize the heroes of an era when men pulled
against the river. Fink, like Crockett, was both hero and clown, adept
at the marvelous and the ridiculous—"a helliferocious fellow and an
almighty fine shot."

On at least one occasion, Fink bested Crockett himself at a famous
shooting match. "I've got the handsomest wife, and the fastest horse, and
the sharpest shooting iron in all Kentuck," Fink taunted Crockett, "and
if any man dare doubt it, I'll be in his hair quicker than hell could scorch
a feather." "I've nothing to say against your wife, Mike," answered
Davy, "for it cant be denied she's a shocking handsome woman, and
Mrs. Crockett's in Tennessee, and I've got no horses. Mike, I dont
exactly like to tell you you lie about what you say about your rifle, but
I'm d——d if you speak the truth and I'll prove it. Do you see that are
cat sitting on the top rail of your potato patch, about a hundred and fifty
yards off? If she ever hears agin, I'll be shot if it shant be without ears."
And so their shooting match began. It ended when Mike became "sorter
wrothy, and he sends a ball after his wife as she was going to the spring
after a gourd full of water, and nocked half her coom out of her head,
without stirring a hair, and calls out to her to stop for me to take a
blizzard at what was left on it. The angeliferous critter stood still as a
scarecrow in a cornfield, for she'd got used to Mike's tricks by long

practiss. 'No, No, Mike,' sez I, Davy Crockett's hand would be sure to shake, if his iron war pointed within a hundred miles of a shemale, and I give up beat. . . ."

There were other, lesser heroes. Some were city types like Sam Patch, the Rhode Island cotton spinner who survived a jump over Niagara Falls (1827) but died in the Genesee Falls (1829). "There's no mistake in Sam Patch," was his battlecry. He was constantly proving his favorite motto: "Some things can be done as well as others."

All these figures were dramatized by traveling companies which reached into the remote villages, where they acted on improvised stages or in the open air. The stage along with the press, as Dorson remarks, helped make these legends national by carrying native folk humor to urban audiences. Mose the Bowery b'hoy, swaggering fireman from New York—whose adventures took him to the California gold fields, to France and Arabia, and who called himself "the far-famed and world-renowned"—had first become notorious through the popular play, *A Glance at New York*, which opened in 1848. The stage-Yankee, beginning as a buffoon, gradually acquired heroic qualities, but never ceased to be a marginal character between the comic and the heroic, continually puzzling and enticing audiences by this very ambiguity. As a Louisville playbill for October 31, 1856, announcing "New York As It Is" warned:

> Mose, the far-famed and world-reknowned, presents himself at our theatre this evening. . . . No two characters have been more misunderstood than MOSE and LIZEY. This hero and heroine of humble life have been too often considered perfect rowdies and profligate outcasts, while the very reverse is the case. MOSE, it is true, is one of the fire b'hoys, full of fun, frolic and fighting, but without one vicious propensity in his nature; and LIZEY, is a good-hearted, worthy and virtuous woman, attached to MOSE with no other prominent fault than the very excusable one of striving to imitate the peculiarities of the man of her heart.

Many others admired James H. Hackett in the role of "Nimrod Wildfire" in James Kirke Paulding's *Lion of the West* (1830), a stage version of Crockett which prospered on the boards all over the country for over twenty years. Or they marvelled at Dan Marble playing *Sam Patch, or the Daring Yankee*. Of course there were others—backwoodsmen, Yankees, boatmen, according to the fashion of the day.

The American clownish heroes were supermen. They did not transcend man but exaggerated him. They were flamboyant, gargantuan, and wonderfully efficient, but they lacked grandeur. It was no accident that Americans sought heroes in a subliterature, and never found them there. The American subliterature was a natural birthplace and natural habitat not for heroes but for supermen. The American supermen, the Davy Crocketts of the subliterature, showed Americans strenuously trying to idealize themselves, to make an ideal simply by exaggerating the commonplace. It is not surprising that they did not succeed. The effort was amusing; its result was comic rather than epic.

After the Civil War, the comics and the heroics tended to separate. Crackerbox wisdom was retailed, not in the mouth of a Ring-tailed Roarer, a strong-man of gargantuan proportions, but in the homely newspaper wisdom of Josh Billings, Petroleum V. Nasby, and Artemus Ward. Professional funny men took over in the role of amateur philosophers. Sometimes, as with Abe Martin and Will Rogers in the 20th century, the rural flavor remained, but they too had become men of words and not of deeds.

39

The Mythologizing of George Washington

NEVER DID A MORE incongruous pair than Davy Crockett and George Washington live together in a national Valhalla. Idolized by the new nation, the legendary Washington was a kind of anti-Crockett. The bluster, the crudity, the vulgarity, the monstrous boosterism of Crockett and his fellow supermen of the subliterature were all qualities which Washington most conspicuously lacked. At the same time, the dignity, the reverence for God, the sober judgment, the sense of destiny, and the vision of the distant future, for all of which Washington was proverbial, were unknown to the Ring-tailed Roarers of the West. Yet both Crockett and Washington were popular heroes, and both emerged into legendary fame during the first half of the 19th century.

The legendary Washington, no less than the legendary Crockett, was a product of the anachronism and abridgment of American history. Crockett and his kind, however, had first been spawned by spontaneous generation. They began as by-products of American life rather than as artifices of an American literature. The legends of the comic supermen, which had originated in oral anecdote, never entirely lost the sound and accent of the raconteur's voice, even when frozen into their crude literary form.

There were elements of spontaneity, of course, in the Washington legend, too, but it was, for the most part, a self-conscious product. The

Crockett and Fink legends caught the spoken echoes of campfire and saloon, captured and diffused them in crudely printed almanacs, in sporting magazines, and anonymous wheezes. The Demigod Washington was to be a cumbersome figure of literary contrivance. The contrast between the Crockett subliterature (flimsy, ephemeral scraps which seldom could be dignified as "books") and the Washington literature (heavy, elegantly printed works, copiously illustrated by maps and engravings, the proud personal product of eminent statesmen and famous writers) was as striking as that between the legendary characters of the two men themselves.

Although both were peculiar products of America, only Washington became part of the national protocol. How this happened showed how different was the Washington legend from its superficially similar counterparts in the Old World. There, names like Romulus and Remus, Aeneas, Charlemagne, Boadicea, King Alfred, St. Louis, St. Joan, and the Cid, glorified the founding of their nations. Some were more mythical than others, but when the modern nations of Italy, France, England, and Spain became self-conscious, the challenge to national historians was to give these hazy figures some historical reality, to make them more plausible by clothing them in historical fact. These nations, which had attained their nationality gradually over the centuries, already possessed legendary founding heroes when they became nations. The challenging task was to historicize them.

Not so in the United States. Here a new nation sprang into being almost before it had time to acquire a history. At the outbreak of the Civil War, there were men alive who could remember the death of Washington; he was still an emphatically real historical person. The national problem was not how to make Washington historical; quite the contrary: how could he be made into a myth? The very brevity of American history made special demands, but Americans of the age proved equal to them.

A measure of their success is how much has been popularly forgotten of the true story of George Washington, especially of his later years. Few Americans remember that Washington had more than his share of enemies, that for all his life he was a controversial figure, and that during his presidency he was personally libelled with a venom aimed at few of his successors. We cannot understand how powerful were the marmo-realizing forces of the early 19th century unless we recall the acrimony, the bitter partisanship, the malicious rumor, and the unscrupulous lies which stormed about Washington during the last decade or so of his life. He had already become the arch-villain for all those who opposed the Federalists, including Jefferson and his followers, but the climax of Washington's unpopularity came with Jay's Treaty. This had been negotiated with Britain by John Jay, Washington's emissary, to resolve differences left unsettled at the end of the Revolution, or which had newly arisen since then. When the terms of the treaty were published in March, 1795, furor shook the country. Southerners objected to its provisions for payment of pre-Revolutionary debts (in large part owed by Virginians); New Englanders objected to its restrictions on United States shipping to the West Indies. Attacks on Washington, who was held responsible for the treaty, were collected by Benjamin Bache, Franklin's grandson, who printed many of them in his *Aurora* in Philadelphia, to be widely copied by such Republican papers as the New York *Argus,* the Boston *Chronicle,* the *Kentucky Herald,* and the *Carolina Gazette.*

"The American People, Sir," the *Aurora* warned, "will look to death the man who assumes the character of a usurper." "If ever a nation was debauched by a man," it added in December, 1796, "the American nation has been by Washington." "If ever there was a period for rejoicing, it is this moment," Bache announced on March 6, 1797, when Washington left office to be replaced by John Adams. "Every heart, in unison with the freedom and happiness of the people, ought to beat high in exultation, that the name of Washington ceases from this day to give a currency to political iniquity and to legalize corruption." Washington was accused of every kind of crime, including stealing from the public treasury. When the circulation of some of these papers fell off, Jefferson himself urged Republicans to support them by soliciting subscriptions; he called them the last bulwark of free speech and representative institutions. Federalists aimed their notorious Alien and Sedition Acts of 1798 (many of the leading anti-Federalist writers were European refugees) at these publications. Then Washington himself, smarting under the venomous attacks, approved the prosecutions which, on dubious evidence, he called necessary to prevent "a disunion of the States."

When Washington died on December 14, 1799, he was anything but a noncontroversial figure. Not only his judgment but his integrity had been publicly impugned. He had been taunted into condoning means of dubious constitutionality to punish his enemies and to silence their presses. But he was destined to a stature in death which he had never attained in life.

What is most remarkable is not that Washington eventually became a demigod, Father of his Country, but that the transfiguration happened so quickly. There is no better evidence of the desperate need Americans felt for a dignified and worshipful national hero than their passionate haste in elevating Washington to sainthood. Never was there a better example of the special potency of the Will to Believe in this New World. A deification which in European history might have required centuries, was accomplished here in decades.

Between Washington's death in the last month of the last year of the

18th century and the outbreak of the Civil War, his worship had acquired a full cultic apparatus. To this end many people had collaborated, but the cult could not have grown so quickly or so vigorously without the peculiar American needs and vacuums.

The Sacred Life. It was appropriate to the cultic character of the Washington legend that its first high priest and one of its leading inventors was a charlatan—an amiable and energetic charlatan, but nevertheless a charlatan. And it was appropriate to the American character of the cult that this high priest should have been a salesman, in fact a supersalesman who had thoroughly mixed religion with salesmanship. The notorious Mason Locke Weems, better known as "Parson Weems," even before Washington's death had been collecting biographical materials. Born in Maryland in 1759, the youngest of nineteen children, he was in Britain studying medicine at the time of the Revolution. In 1784 he became one of the first Americans after the War fully ordained by the Archbishop of Canterbury for the Anglican ministry in the United States. After a brief and desultory clerical career, he turned to bookselling, for which he had both passion and genius. Although he had no permanent pulpit after about 1793, he continued to exercise his ministry with gusto through the printing, writing, and especially the selling of edifying books. Weems, during the last thirty years of his life (1795–1825), traveled the country between New York and Georgia as an itinerant salesman of salvation and printed matter. Besides selling his own books, he was agent for Matthew Carey and C. P. Wayne of Philadelphia. Traveling about in a wagon which carried his wares, he was ready, depending on the circumstances, to deliver a sermon or a political oration, or play his fiddle. After he had gathered his crowd and warmed them to good humor, he would sell the books from his wagon—patent medicine for all the ills of the spirit. "Part Whitefield, part Villon," Albert J. Beveridge accurately characterized him, "a delightful mingling of evangelist and vagabond, lecturer and politician, writer and musician."

Wandering over the countryside, he became a one-man market-research enterprise. Never was a cult devised for an audience better pretested, nor a national hero more calculatedly concocted to satisfy the demand. As early as 1797, Weems pointed out to Carey a rich untapped market. "Experience has taught me that small, i.e. quarter of dollar books, on subjects calculated to *strike* the Popular Curiosity, printed in very large numbers and properly *distributed*, w^d prove an immense revenue to the prudent and industrious Undertakers. If you coud get the life of Genl. Wayne, Putnam, Green &c., Men whose courage and Abilities, whose patriotism and Exploits have won the love and admiration of the American people, printed in small volumes and with very interesting frontespieces, you w^d, without doubt, sell an immense number of them. People here think nothing of giving 1/6 (their quarter of a dollar) for anything that pleases their fancy. Let us give them something worth their money." Weems turned to the work himself, and on June 24, 1799, he wrote Carey from his home at Dumfries, Virginia, where he was to raise a family of ten children.

> I have nearly ready for the press a piece christen[d], or to be christen[d], "The Beauties of Washington." tis artfully drawn up, enliven[d] with anecdotes, and in my humble opinion, marvellously fitted, "ad captandum—gustum populi Americani! ! ! !["] What say you to printing it for me and ordering a copper plate Frontispiece of that HERO, something in this way. George Washington Esq[r]. The Guardian Angel of his Country "Go thy way old George. Die when thou wilt we shall never look upon thy like again" M. Carey inver.&[c].
>
> NB. The whole will make but four sheets and will sell like flax seed at quarter of a dollar. I cou'd make you a world of pence and popularity by it.

In October he again wrote Carey that he now had "on the Anvil and pretty well hammer'd out a piece that will sell to admiration.

THE TRUE PATRIOT

or

BEAUTIES OF WASHINGTON

Abundantly Biographical & Anecdotical
Curious & Marvellous"

Weems, therefore, was ready and waiting with his commodity when the great demand was created by the death of Washington. Less than a month after Washington's death, Weems effervesced to Carey:

> I've something to whisper in your lug. Washington, you know is gone! Millions are gaping to read something about him. I am very nearly prim[d] and cock[d] for 'em. 6 months ago I set myself to collect anecdotes of him. You know I live conveniently for that work. My plan! I give his history, sufficiently minute—I accompany him from his start, thro the French & Indian & British or Revolutionary wars, to the Presidents chair, to the throne in the hearts of 5,000,000 of People. I then go on to show that his unparrelled rise & elevation were owing to his Great Virtues. 1 His Veneration for the Diety, or Religious Principles. 2 His Patriotism. 3[d] his Magninmity. 4 his Industry. 5 his Temperance & Sobriety. 6 his Justice, &[c]. &[c]. Thus I hold up his great Virtues (as Gov[r] McKean prays) to the imitation of Our Youth. All this I have lin[d] and enliven[d] with *Anecdotes apropos interesting* and *Entertaining*. I have read it to several Gentlemen whom I thought judges, such as Presbyterian Clergymen, Classical Scholars &[c]. &[c]. and they all commend it much. it will not exceed 3 royal sheets on long primer. We may sell it with great rapidity for 25 or 37 Cents and it w[d] not cost 10. I read a part of it to one of

my Parishioners, a first rate lady, and she wish^d I w^d print it, promising to take one for each of her children (a bakers dozen). I am thinking you coud vend it admirably: as it will be the first. I can send it on, half of it, *immediately.*

Carey was too slow for Weems, who within three weeks had found other means. Four printings of this eighty-page booklet arranged by Weems himself appeared in 1800, but Weems still kept after Carey "to make this thing profitable and beneficial—Everybody will read about Washington. . . . I know you desire to do *Good* . . . We may preach through the Example and Virtues of Washington—Adams & Jefferson both will approve of our little piece.—I am in expectation of good things shortly for you. You know what I mean—Money." This happy marriage of philanthropy and avarice produced Weems's life of Washington, destined to be perhaps the most widely read, most influential book ever written about American history.

Soon after Washington's death, his nephew Bushrod Washington persuaded Chief Justice John Marshall to undertake the official life. This enterprise too was to have a shaping influence on American thinking about American history, not through its success but through its resounding failure. Weems had been employed by the publisher C. P. Wayne of Philadelphia to sell subscriptions to Marshall's monumental five volumes at $3 a volume. When the first instalment of Marshall's work finally reached subscribers in 1804, it quickly established the book as the publishing catastrophe of the age. The whole Volume One, called "Introduction," was consumed by a pedantic account of colonial history beginning with Columbus; toward the end were two casual mentions of Washington. Dull, laborious, rambling, and secondhand, the work lumbered into its third, fourth, and fifth volumes. According to John Adams, Marshall's life was not really a book at all, but rather "a Mausoleum, 100 feet square at the base and 200 feet high."

Weems, seeing a public hungry for a readable story about the National Hero, was frantic with disgust and disappointment. He repeatedly begged Carey to dispose of the Marshall venture and provide something more salable. Even before the Marshall fiasco was fully disposed of, Weems returned in earnest to do the job himself. Profiting from Marshall's mistakes, in 1806 he revised his little pamphlet to give it everything Marshall's work had lacked. Though still only eighty pages, it now had more form, more facts (invented when necessary), and contained a number of appealing new anecdotes. After Marshall's final volume appeared in 1807 and Weems was disburdened of the whole profitless business, he turned his spare energies to enlarging his pamphlet to a book of some two hundred pages ("6th edition," 1808). On the title page Weems styled himself "Formerly Rector of Mount-Vernon Parish," which added authenticity for all readers who did not know that such a parish never existed. After 1808 only minor changes and additions were made.

In substantially this form, Weems's *Life of George Washington: With Curious Anecdotes, Equally Honourable to Himself and Exemplary to His Young Countrymen* went through twenty more "editions" before Weems's death in 1825. Within a decade of its first publication, this work probably sold well over 50,000 copies (Marshall's had sold closer to 5000!), making it a best seller for its time. Still Weems, who had made the mistake of selling the copyright of his book to Carey in 1808 for a mere $1000, failed to persuade Carey to let him enlarge the work further or to issue an "elegant edition" at three or four dollars. "You have a great deal of money lying in the bones of old George," Weems wrote Carey in January, 1809, on a theme he repeated again and again, "if you will but exert yourself to extract it."

While Weems aimed to produce a book primarily for "the admiring eyes of our *children*," his book should be classified neither as juvenile nor as nonfiction but as booster literature. Others applied their booster enthusiasm and booster optimism to the future; he applied his to the past. While others were boosters for this or that part of the country, he was one of the first national boosters. Weems, like other boosters, asserted facts for which there was little or no foundation, but we must not forget that, in the contagious vagueness of American life, distinctions which elsewhere seemed sharp—between fact and wish, between history and prophecy—were hard to draw. Thus Weems began his chapter on the birth and education of his Hero:

> To this day numbers of good Christians can hardly find faith to believe that Washington was, bona fide, a *Virginian!* "What! a buck-skin!" say they with a smile, "George Washington a buckskin! pshaw! impossible! he was certainly an European: So great a man could never have been born in America."
>
> So great a man could never have been born in America!—Why that's the very *prince of reasons* why he should have been born here! Nature, we know, is fond of *harmonies;* and *paria paribus,* that is, *great things to great,* is the rule she delights to work by. Where, for example, do we look for the *whale* "the biggest born of nature?" not, I trow, in a *millpond,* but in the main ocean; *"there go the great ships,"* and there are the spoutings of whales amidst their boiling foam.
>
> By the same rule, where shall we look for Washington, the greatest among men, but in *America?* That greatest Continent, which, rising from beneath the frozen pole, stretches far and wide to the south, running almost *"whole the length of this vast terrene,"* and sustaining on her ample sides the roaring shock of half the watery globe. And equal to its size, is the furniture of this vast continent, where the Almighty has reared his cloud-capt mountains, and spread his sea-like

lakes, and poured his mighty rivers, and hurled down his thundering cataracts in a style of the *sublime,* so far superior to any thing of the kind in the other continents, that we may fairly conclude that great men and great deeds are designed for America.

This seems to be the verdict of honest analogy; and accordingly we find America the honoured cradle of Washington, who was born on Pope's creek, in Westmoreland county, Virginia, the 22d of February, 1732.

As the work begins, so it ends. The three final chapters, on the character of Washington, describe his religion, his benevolence, his industry, and his patriotism—all as the natural response of the greatest of all men to the greatest of all challenges, America.

George's father, we are told by Weems, took every chance to implant virtues in his son. When the boy was only five, his father and a cousin took him walking one fall in the apple-orchard. "Now, George, said his father, look here, my son! don't you remember when this good cousin of yours brought you that fine large apple last spring, how hardly I could prevail on you to divide with your brothers and sisters; though I promised you that if you would but do it, God Almighty would give you plenty of apples this fall. Poor George could not say a word; but hanging down his head, looked quite confused, while with his little naked toes he scratched in the soft ground. . . . George looked in silence on the wide wilderness of fruit; he marked the busy humming bees, and heard the gay notes of birds, then lifting his eyes filled with shining moisture, to his father, he softly said, 'Well, Pa, only forgive me this time; see if I ever be so stingy any more.' "

And, of course, there is the famous story of the cherry tree:

> "*I can't tell a lie, Pa; you know I can't tell a lie. I did cut it with my hatchet.*"—*Run to my arms, you dearest boy,* cried his father in transports, *run to my arms; glad am I, George, that you killed my tree; for you have paid me for it a thousand fold. Such an act of heroism in my son, is more worth than a thousand trees, though blossomed with silver, and their fruits of purest gold.*

And then the story of how George's schoolmates wept when George left them. How George hated to fight, yet performed feats of strength. How, after Braddock's defeat, a "famous Indian warrior" swore that "Washington was not born to be killed by a bullet! For, I had seventeen fair fires at him with my rifle, and after all could not bring him to the ground." How, during her pregnancy with George, his mother dreamed a dream which foretold his greatness and the history of the Revolution.

The great gap in our documentary knowledge of Washington, especially in his early life, Weems filled with materials borrowed, stolen, or invented, describing events which, from their very nature, were virtually impossible to disprove. Who could confidently assert that the cherry-tree episode had *not* occurred in the privacy of the elder Washington's household? Or that Mary Washington had *not* experienced such and such a dream? Perhaps, as Marcus Cunliffe ventures, these apocryphal anecdotes survived precisely because they did express, however crudely and inexactly, some sort of general truth about the Hero. Certainly what Weems said was what many people wanted to believe. And by these tales Weems sold his book, and through his book he sold another commodity, the Hero. Was this or wasn't this a hoax? Who could say?

Weems was only one of scores of acolytes of the Washington cult. Before Washington's death, although there were brief biographical sketches in magazines or in general works like Jedidiah Morse's *American Geography* (1789), there seems to have appeared no book-length treatment of his life. Soon after Weems's revised version of 1806, several other more or less readable lives appeared, but most of these were serious works, not directed to the juvenile audience or the unliterary public. For some years Weems had a virtual monopoly of the popular market. Then in 1829 appeared Anna C. Reed's life, written for the Sunday Schools (a newly flourishing American institution), and in the centennial year, 1832, Samuel G. Goodrich, whose literary factory produced over a hundred children's books under the pseudonym of "Peter Parley," offered a successful juvenile biography. The life of the Hero was being celebrated in many other forms—in long poems, plays, and even in *A Life of George Washington in Latin Prose* (1835) by an Ohio schoolteacher.

Meanwhile, the story of Washington's life was being retold in heavy tomes by scholars and men of letters. Perhaps there is no better evidence of the piety which the name of Washington excited than that, in the centennial year of Washington's birth (1832), there appeared a revised edition of Marshall's *Life,* only slightly condensed. It was followed by a one-volume school edition (1838). Others too turned out works that were less readable than monumental. Of these ambitious tomes, the least heavy was the two-volume life (1835) by the novelist James Kirke Paulding. Then came Jared Sparks's pious and ponderous life, which appeared as Volume One (1837) of his edition of the *Writings.* The best of these works was Washington Irving's five volumes, but he too was afflicted by the contagion of dullness. Judging from the sets of Irving which survive into the 20th century with virgin pages, these volumes also were more widely bought than read. But Washington's posthumous life had only begun.

The Sacred Writings. The Washington cult, it is important to note, flourished long before there existed any printed collection of the writings of the Hero. Nowhere could the scholar, much less the citizen, read the authentic words of Washington himself. The more widely Washington was adored, the more superfluous—and in many ways the less interesting —his own writings became.

In this cultic spirit, a third of a century after his death, the first edition of Washington's writings appeared. At an early age Jared Sparks (1789–1866) had begun to think about a collection of the Hero's writings. Sparks was a New Englander of humble birth who, after working his way through Harvard College, had by his social grace established himself among the Boston élite. He studied divinity and then filled a Unitarian pulpit in Baltimore for a few years. Returning to Boston, he took over the *North American Review,* which he built into the leading critical journal of national circulation. He was a man of many talents, with a sense for the tastes and book-buying interests of the intellectual community. It was the edition of Washington's writings that established Sparks's national reputation and led to his appointment in 1838 as McLean Professor of Ancient and Modern History at Harvard—the first professor of history (other than ecclesiastical) in a university in the United States—and then to his presidency of Harvard (1849–53).

Securing permission of the Washington family to publish the writings of their ancestor was no easy matter. George Washington's literary executor and the inheritor of Mount Vernon was his nephew, the rigid and unimaginative Bushrod Washington (Associate Justice of the Supreme Court, 1798–1829), who, in refusing Sparks (March 13, 1826) explained that he and Marshall were planning three volumes of selected letters from the Revolutionary period, to be followed later by a pre-Revolutionary selection. Six months later, Sparks, undiscouraged, tried again to persuade Bushrod Washington to give him access to the papers, adding that he would go ahead anyway, gathering copies of the papers wherever he could find them, and that, since the papers would eventually reach the public eye, Bushrod might better choose to supervise the work. Sparks would allow him to withhold whatever he thought unsuitable for publication. "If the entire works of Washington were presented to the public in a form suited to the dignity of the subject, a national interest and a national feeling would be excited, and a wide and honorable patronage might be expected." Sparks then added an argument more substantial: an offer to give Bushrod Washington half the profits of publication. In January, 1827, (after urging by John Marshall, who had been prodded by Sparks) Bushrod Washington accepted the proposal. Under the final terms, half the profits were to go to Sparks, the other half to be equally divided between Bushrod Washington and John Marshall.

Over the next several years Sparks collected manuscripts, copied official documents, and showed an energy in gathering materials which was unprecedented in American historical scholarship. He soon decided that the number of volumes should be determined by "the probable demand in the market, as well as the nature of the work." Sparks's twelve-volume edition (1834–37) included eleven volumes of selected writings and Sparks's biography of Washington (1837). Despite the large editorial expenses ($15,357.37) which had to be deducted, the net returns were sizable. In 1837, when Sparks sent the first share of profits to the heirs of Bushrod Washington and John Marshall, the total sum to be divided was $15,384.63. For twenty years Sparks was sending additional shares of the profits to the Washington and the Marshall families.

Sparks's *Life and Writings of George Washington* was greeted by loud and indiscriminate applause. Surviving members of the Washington family found it perfect and sent Sparks a cedar cane cut from the tree which shaded Washington's tomb. Sixty-three pages by Edward Everett in the *North American Review* exhausted superlatives: "Not a single trait of indiscretion is disclosed in his work." George Bancroft, still near the beginning of his career, found the work "beyond my praise for its calmness, accuracy, and intense interest of authenticity."

"You are a lucky fellow," Bancroft had written Sparks as early as 1827, "selected by a favoring Providence to conduct a good ship into the haven of immortality, and to have your own name recorded as the careful pilot." And Sparks was less the historian than the acolyte, less the discoverer of the true than the adorer of the good. Appropriately, the founder of historical scholarship in the United States was a high priest of the Washington cult. Sparks again and again went through the motions of strenuous historical research. Before his publication of the diplomatic correspondence of the Revolution (12 vols., 1829–30), of the writings of Washington, and of Franklin (10 vols., 1836–40), no substantial printed sources were available on the crucial era of American history. But for the study of modern history in American universities this was, as Samuel Eliot Morison observes, a "false dawn." Sparks, the first professor of his subject, left no disciples, and it would be nearly a half-century before American history would begin to flourish as a profession. One reason must be found in how Sparks and his contemporaries conceived the subject. The vice of Sparks's historical work was not that it was conceived in sin, but rather that it was conceived in virtue.

Sparks followed the style of his day. His biography, which prefaced the writings, was pious, pallid, and reverential. The Hero was of commanding figure, symmetrical features, indomitable courage, pure character, and perfect judgment; "his moral qualities were in perfect harmony with those of his intellect." Sparks's appendix, "Religious Opinions and Habits," was an ingenious whitewash in which Washington's failure to attend communion became an argument for his religiosity. "He may have believed it improper publicly to partake of an ordinance, which, accord-

ing to the ideas he entertained of it, imposed severe restrictions on outward conduct, and a sacred pledge to perform duties impracticable in
his situation. Such an impression would be natural to a serious mind . . .
a man of a delicate conscience and habitual reverence for religion."
There was no passage in Washington's writings, Sparks noted, which expressed doubt of the Christian revelation. In a man of such Christian
demeanor, what more conclusive proof that he was a true and tolerant
Christian?

The writings were edited in a similar spirit. In selecting a mere eleven
from what might have filled four times that many volumes, Sparks had
ample freedom to ennoble his subject. While Sparks did not actually
add passages of his own, he omitted passages at will without warning
the reader and he improved the language when it seemed unworthy of
the Hero. He explained all this in his introduction: "It would be an
act of unpardonable injustice to any author, after his death, to bring
forth compositions, and particularly letters, written with no design to
their publication, and commit them to the press without previously sub-
jecting them to a careful revision." Challenged later on his editorial
methods, Sparks argued with charming naiveté that he was really being
true to his subject because Washington himself in his old age had revised
his early letters. Wherever Sparks had the choice he preferred Washington's own later revisions (again without warning the reader) in place of
what had actually been written in the heat of the events. And Sparks
made changes on his own. Where, for example, Washington had written
of the "rascally crews" of New England privateersmen, Sparks emended
the text to read simply "the crews." Washington's reference to the "dirty
mercenary spirit" of the Connecticut troops became "the mercenary
spirit," and their "scandalous conduct" was softened to their "conduct."
"Old Put." became the more dignified "General Putnam." When Washington referred contemptuously to a small sum of money as "but a flea-
bite at present," Sparks improved it to read "totally inadequate to our
demands at this time." Sparks again and again and again changed the
words to make them worthy of his Hero.

Nearly fifteen years passed before any respectable public voice objected to Sparks's unobtrusive embellishments of Washington. In 1833,
when Sparks sent Justice Joseph Story a specimen volume, Story privately
expressed his enthusiastic approval: Sparks had "done exactly what
Washington would have desired you to do, if he were living." But
Story indicated concern lest a "cynical critic" should sometime in the
future cavil over these improvements. Not until 1851 was there so much
as a peep from any such "cynical critic," when two letters by an un-
identified writer to the New York *Post* compared Sparks's version with
another recently published version of certain letters from Washington
to Joseph Reed, his military secretary during the Revolution.

The opening gun in a major (though finally unsuccessful) attack on Sparks's editorial integrity was fired by an Englishman, who was a noble lord and an accomplished scholar. The cultic sacredness of Washington's writings was revealed in the indignation against this attack and in the solid support of the American scholarly world for Sparks's way of elevating the American Hero. In December, 1851, Lord Mahon (later Lord Stanhope), a well-known English man of letters, who had been active in the Historical Manuscripts Commission, published the sixth volume of his seven-volume *History of England from the Peace of Utrecht to the Peace of Versailles.* "Mr. Sparks," he observed in the appendix, "has printed no part of the correspondence precisely as Washington wrote it; but has greatly altered, and, as he thinks, corrected and embellished it." He accused Sparks of "tampering with the truth of history." This remark, so inconspicuously placed, might have been little noticed had it not touched so sacred a figure. The immediate reply was an eighty-page counterattack by John Gorham Palfrey, the well-known Unitarian clergyman and historian who had followed Sparks as editor of the *North American Review*, in the form of a review of Mahon's work. In a pamphlet-war that lasted nearly three years, Sparks (then President of Harvard College) defended himself and his Hero; hostilities ended in a personal truce between Lord Mahon and Sparks.

The great significance of this controversy was to reveal an orthodoxy among American scholars who competed with one another in expressions of cultic reverence. Among Sparks's supporters were Francis Parkman, William H. Prescott, Senator Charles Sumner (who hailed Sparks "triumphant"), James S. Mackee (Librarian of the State Department and official custodian of the Washington Papers, which were now owned by the government) and, most appropriately, the eminent Professor Andrews Norton, who had attained fame as a pioneer in the use of new "critical" techniques to establish the genuineness of the New Testament. The best evidence of the general satisfaction with Sparks's way of editing was that, during the half-century after the appearance of Sparks's edition, there was no other edition of the Writings.

The Sacred Remains. The struggle over the possession and proper location of the bodily remains of the Hero, if not equaling that over the Holy Grail, expressed a not dissimilar cultic spirit.

At the death of Washington, Congress unanimously adopted a joint resolution directing "That a marble monument be erected by the United States at the Capitol of the city of Washington, and that the family of General Washington be requested to permit his body to be deposited under it, and that the monument be so designed as to commemorate the great events of his military and political life." Mrs. Washington approved the plan and a year later, in December, 1800, the House passed a bill appropriating $200,000 to construct a marble mausoleum, pyramidal in shape, with a base one hundred feet square, to receive Washington's body. At that time the Capitol building still consisted of only one wing; the present rotunda and crypt below it were not yet built. There seems to have been a notion of somehow including the tomb of Washington in the Capitol complex itself. Some Southerners opposed the project, arguing that the sacred remains properly belonged where they already were, at Mount Vernon. Partly because of the division of opinion, nothing was done. A new House committee in 1830 recommended that "the remains of George Washington and Martha Washington be entombed in the same national sepulchre, that immediately over the centre of his tomb and in the grand floor of the Capitol shall be placed a marble cenotaph in the form of a well-proportioned sarcophagus. . . . Immediately above this, in the centre of the Rotunda, a full length marble equestrian statue of Washington, wrought by the best artist of the present time. . . . These memorials, little costly and ostentatious as they may appear, will better accord with the feelings of this Nation and more appropriately commemorate the pure and elevated character of our Washington than could any the most expensive or splendid monument or mausoleum." Meanwhile, as 1832, the centenary of Washington's birth, approached, sectional passions (sharpened by the South Carolina nullification movement) ran high.

After the British, who occupied the city in 1814, had burned the interior of the Capitol building, Charles Bulfinch had rebuilt the central portion (1818–29) with a crypt designed to receive Washington's body. The plan of the joint Congressional committee for the Washington centennial celebration centered around the transfer of Washington's body from Mount Vernon to the Capitol crypt. In a bitter Congressional debate during January and February of 1832, Southerners, reluctant to part with the National Relic, concocted all sorts of reasons against allowing the removal. A representative from Maine charged that the whole debate was a contest between the State of Virginia and the great United States. Henry Clay of Kentucky urged the removal because "he would himself discriminate between Washington and any man who had lived, from Adam down."

Southern representatives, foreseeing civil war and their separation from the Union, imagined the resulting indignities. "Remove the remains of our venerated Washington," warned Wiley Thompson of Georgia, "from their association with the remains of his consort and his ancestors, from Mount Vernon and from his native State, and deposit them in this capitol, and then let a severance of the Union occur, and behold! the remains of Washington on a shore foreign to his native soil." Others objected that, with the westward movement of the population, the capitol would doubtless also be moved: "Shall the remains of our Washington be left amidst the ruins of this capitol, surrounded by the desolation of this city?" "If our population is to reach to the Western Ocean," replied Joel B. Sutherland of Pennsylvania, "and the seat of Government is to be removed, when we carry away the ensigns of power from this place, we will carry with us the sacred bones of Washington." Others argued that the very presence of Washington's remains would somehow mollify and sanctify the deliberations of Congress. "No act can be done by the Government," pleaded Jonathan Hunt of Vermont, "that would have so deep and permanent a moral influence in uniting the people and cementing the Union of this confederacy, as the burial of Washington in the capitol."

The debate came to an abrupt end on February 16, when, less than a week before the proposed ceremony, John Augustine Washington, then the occupant of Mount Vernon, flatly refused to allow removal of the Hero's body. After a mysterious attempt to steal Washington's body from his tomb at Mount Vernon in the 1830's, a new tomb was completed there; it was locked, and the key was thrown into the Potomac.

The Annual Rites and a Declamatory Liturgy. In the mid-20th century, the only birthday anniversary (other than December 25) celebrated as a legal holiday by every state of the Union is February 22, the birthday of Washington. In the early 19th century, when the new nation still had almost no history, the birthday of Washington shared with the Fourth of July—the birthday of the Republic itself—the annual patriotic rites. On both these occasions, the center of interest, the usual ritual, was an oration. Repetitious, florid, pompous, bombastic, and interminable, the oration followed a pattern that was as set as if it had been prescribed by a liturgical authority. One example will do almost as well as another. Daniel Webster declared at the centennial of Washington's birth on February 22, 1832:

> Washington stands at the commencement of a new era, as well as at the head of the New World. A century from the birth of Washington has changed the world. The country of Washington has been the theatre on which a great part of the change has been wrought; and Washington himself a principal agent by which it has been accomplished. His age and his country are equally full of wonders; and of both he is the chief.

Orators said the brevity of American history was more than offset by the grandeur of a Washington. John Tyler (later President) declared at Yorktown in 1837 that the Hero was greater than Leonidas or Moses, for, conspicuously unlike Washington, the one died with his men and the other never entered the Promised Land. John Quincy Adams found combined in Washington, more than in Aeneas or King David, "the spirit of command and the spirit of meekness." "To add brightness to the sun or glory to the name of Washington," Abraham Lincoln said at Springfield on February 22, 1842, "is alike impossible. Let none attempt it. In solemn awe pronounce the name, and in its naked deathless splendor leave it shining on."

Most popular and most repeated was Edward Everett's oration, which he delivered on circuit for the Mount Vernon Association to raise funds to purchase Washington's residence as a public shrine. From 1856 to 1860, Everett traveled over the country, and by delivering the same two-hour oration some 129 times, he raised about $90,000. His oration, "The Character of Washington," immediately became a classic in the national liturgy. Starting with the young Washington—"twenty-four years of age, a model of manly strength and beauty, perfect in all the qualities and accomplishments of the gentleman and the soldier, but wise and thoughtful beyond his years, inspiring at the outset of his career that love and confidence which are usually earned only by a life of service"—Everett sketched the heroic career. In an age "first in the annals of our race for great names, great events, great reforms, and the general progress of intelligence," Washington was greatest of all. Shining above the tawdry tyrannies of Peter the Great of Russia, Frederick the Great of Prussia, and Napoleon the Great of France, was the star of Washington.

A great and venerated character like that of Washington, which commands the respect of an entire population, however divided on other questions, is not an isolated fact in History to be regarded with barren admiration, —it is a dispensation of Providence for good. It was well said by Mr. Jefferson in 1792, writing to Washington to dissuade him from declining a renomination: "North and South will hang together while they have you to hang to." Washington in the flesh is taken from us; we shall never behold him as our fathers did; but his memory remains, and I say, let us hang to his memory. Let us make a national festival and holiday of his birthday; and ever, as the 22d of February returns, let us remember, that while with these solemn and joyous rites of observance we celebrate the great anniversary, our fellow-citizens on the Hudson, on the Potomac, from the Southern plains to the Western lakes, are engaged in the same offices of gratitude and love. Nor we, nor they alone, — beyond the Ohio, beyond the Mississippi, along that stupendous trail of immigration from East to West, which, bursting into States as it moves westward, is already threading the Western prairies, swarming through the portals of the Rocky Mountains and winding down their slopes, the name and the memory of Washington on that gracious night will travel with the silver queen of heaven through sixty degrees of longitude, nor part company with her till she walks in her brightness through the golden gate of California, and passes serenely on to hold midnight court with her Australian stars. There and there only, in barbarous archipelagos, as yet untrodden by civilized man, the

name of Washington is unknown; and there, too, when they swarm
with enlightened millions, new honors shall be paid with ours to his
memory.

As sectional antagonisms sharpened, Washington's light was made to
illuminate more brightly one side or the other. For Calhoun, he became
the patron saint of Independence; for Webster and Lincoln, the patron
saint of Union.

Washington had become the Savior as well as the Father of his Country. "From the first ages of the world," Representative Benjamin C.
Howard of Maryland observed in Congress (February 13, 1832), "the
records of all time furnished only two instances of birthdays being commemorated after the death of the individual: those two were the 22d of
February and the 25th of December." "To 'Mary the Mother of Washing-
ing,' whose incomplete monument at Fredericksburg lies shamefully
neglected," said the Rev. J. N. Danforth in Virginia on July 4, 1847,
"we owe all the mighty debt due from mankind to her immortal son."

The Icon. Nothing better reveals the cultic, sacred character of Washington than the conventional appearance of his familiar portrait. Seldom
has a historic figure been cast so universally in a single mold: the
stereotype of Washington was cast by Gilbert Stuart. Many contemporary portraits of Washington were painted or sculpted between 1772
and 1799 by the best artists of the age: the Peales (Charles Willson,
James, and Rembrandt), John Trumbull, William Dunlap, Edward
Savage, Du Simitière, Houdon, Ceracchi, and others. Every known
medium was employed, not only oils and marble, but wood, ivory, wax-
reliefs, life-masks, shadow-pictures, and profile-drawings with the aid
of a mechanical pantograph called the "physionotrace." Washington became inured to long and repeated sittings. What became the classic portrait was highly idealized. Lasting popular devotion significantly fixed on
Gilbert Stuart's unfinished portrait (the "Atheneum") that was suffused
with an unworldly haze.

Gilbert Stuart, who had been born in Rhode Island, decided at the
age of twenty that the American colonies were no place for a painter.
In 1775 he went to England, where he spent five years in the studio of
another expatriate American, Benjamin West. Quickly acquiring a rich
and fashionable portrait clientele, he competed successfully with Ramsay,
Reynolds, Romney, and Gainsborough. When he returned to the United
States in about 1793, possibly to escape imprisonment for debt, his
avowed object was to recoup his fortunes by painting Washington;
Stuart hoped eventually to make "a plurality of his portraits" with which
to repay English and Irish creditors. His first painting of Washington,
done from life in 1795, brought him orders from thirty-one subscribers
for thirty-nine "copies." This was only a beginning, for no one knows

precisely how many copies of his portraits were made by Stuart or his disciples or imitators.

The peculiar appeal of the Stuart portraits may be their very stiffness, which seems a kind of idealization. In human vividness they are much inferior to the portraits by Rembrandt Peale, which never had the vogue or appeal of Stuart's. The explanation, as Rembrandt Peale himself recounts it, is quite irreverently commonplace.

> Judge Washington informed me . . . . that the day his Uncle first sat to Stuart, he had placed in his mouth a new sett of teeth, made by the elder Gardette: they were clumsily formed of Sea-horse Ivory, to imitate both teeth & Gums, and filled his mouth very uncomfortably, so as to prevent his speaking, but with difficulty; giving to his mouth the appearance of *being rinced with Water*—(these were Judge Washington's Words). At a subsequent period, Mr. Stuart himself told me that he never had painted a Man so difficult to engage in conversation, as was his custom, in order to elicit the natural expression, which can only be selected and caught in varied discourse. The teeth were at fault; and, unfortunately for Mr. Stuart, they were always again put in at each sitting, with the expectation that eventually they would become easy—but they were finally rejected. It was fortunate for me that my Study was begun *before* the new teeth were finished, and that my Sitter each time came to me with the old Sett furnished him in New York many years before.

These dental circumstances, combined with Stuart's genius for idealizing his subject, produced a portrait perfectly suited to the American's ideal of his Hero.

Not oil, but marble, seemed the most appropriate material for the character and the image of Washington. A catalogue of the sculptured icons itself fills a volume. There was the famous life-size bust by the French sculptor, Houdon, of which countless replicas were made and which has become standard. There was the bust made from life by the Italian adventurer Ceracchi, which he then repeated in colossal size. There was the statue by the celebrated Canova.

Most impressive (and controversial) of all was the work of Horatio Greenough, the New England sculptor who had been given a government commission in 1832 to make a statue of Washington for the Capitol rotunda, at a fee of $5000. After eight years' labor in his studio in Florence, Italy, Greenough produced the statue; it was ten and a half feet high and weighed twenty tons. The freight bill across the Atlantic was $7700 and the cost of removal from the Navy Yard to the Capitol rotunda was another $5000. The Capitol entrance had to be widened to admit the colossus, but, when in place, its weight was too much for the floor; it was removed outdoors to the east front. The bill to this point was $21,000. By now it had become a public scandal, not only because of its cost, but because, ironically, Greenough's very effort to deify the Hero had outraged public decency and seemed itself a kind of blasphemy.

Greenough's statue, modelled after Phidias' colossal ivory and gold Zeus for the temple at Olympia, showed Washington seated on a carved throne, naked to the waist, with drapery over his legs and sandals on his feet. Patriotic Americans were shocked that Washington, of all people, should be displayed without clothing. "Washington was too prudent, and careful of his health," wrote the New York socialite, Philip Hone, "to expose himself thus in a climate so uncertain as ours, to say nothing of the indecency of such an exposure, a subject on which he was known to be exceedingly fastidious." The same public whose committee of clergymen had approved Hiram Powers' totally naked female *Greek Slave* and had approved the nakedness of Greenough's earlier *Chanting Cherubs* "awoke," as Greenough said, "with a roar at the colossal naked-ness of Washington's manly breast." The statue remained controversial until, a half-century later, it was removed to the decent obscurity of an alcove in the Smithsonian Institution where it remains. "Did anybody ever see Washington nude?" Nathaniel Hawthorne asked in 1858. "It is inconceivable. He had no nakedness, but I imagine he was born with his clothes on, and his hair powdered, and made a stately bow on his first appearance in the world."

The public shock at this fleshly version of the Hero made it easier for the Washington Monument Association to complete its fund-raising ($87,000 by the end of 1847). This Monument appropriately enough, commemorated the Hero not in any human form, however godlike, but in a geometric obelisk of abstract perfection.

The Sacred Name. In the United States the very name of Washington has been honored uniquely. In 1791, while the Hero himself was still alive, the Commissioners for the proposed capital, although they had no legal authority to name the city, christened it the City of Washington. Despite the prevailing partisan bitterness, their choice was not effectively disputed. Washington, too, was the only person after the colonial period whose name was given to a state. "There has been but one Washington upon earth," observed a member of Congress in 1853, during the debate on the organization of Washington Territory (later to become the State of Washington), "and there is not likely to be another, and, as Providence has sent but one, for all time, let us have one State named after that one man." In mid-20th century Washington, leading all others, appeared in the name of at least 121 post offices. He was far ahead, too, in the number of counties named after him; thirty-two states have Washington counties. Of the states which have no such counties, as George Stewart remarks, six were among the smaller of the thirteen original colonies and thus already had their counties named before 1775; and most of the rest were states in the far west which were not organized until after the Civil War, when the Washington cult had declined.

*   *   *

A cult confers immortality on its acolytes as well as on its object. Davy Crockett shared his earthy American world of comic supermen not with the Hero, but with the Salesman of the Hero. In the third part of the "Autobiography" of Davy Crockett, which describes Davy's journey to Texas from his home in Weakley County, Tennessee, he recounts how in that year of 1835 (when actually the body of Parson Weems was already ten years in its grave) Weems's spirit and his evangelical salesmanship went marching on. At Little Rock, Arkansas, Crockett found a traveling puppeteer about to be attacked by a crowd because he was too drunk to put on the show they awaited. There was no one to play the fiddle, and the puppeteer's "sick wife and five hungry children" were going to suffer. The salesman-parson who had just arrived with his ramshackle wagon full of books and pamphlets for sale promptly came to the rescue. After reading from "God's Revenge against Drunkenness," a pamphlet he offered for sale from his wagon, the ghost of Weems played his fiddle, saved the show, and took up a collection for the friendless showman and his family. The immortal Parson "placed his trunk of pamphlets before him, and proceeded on his pilgrimage, the little children following him through the village with bursts of gratitude."

40

How Local Patriotism Made National Heroes

THE AMERICAN PANTHEON was filled only gradually. The galaxy of lesser demigods who, in 20th-century retrospect, seem always to have been there, did not rise above partisanship to become canonized in the national mythology until the mid-19th century or later. The character of Jefferson, for example, was long and bitterly debated. Not until 1858, when (from New York of all places!) Henry S. Randall's three-volume life gave a solid base for refuting the anti-Jefferson myths, did Jefferson begin to become a truly national hero. Benjamin Franklin was a curious case. In his own time he, too, had been a partisan figure, suspected by many in Pennsylvania who were not of his own party. Although he was a versatile and charming personality, his role in the Revolution had first been ambiguous and was never spectacular. He spent much of his public career abroad. No edition of his writings appeared in this country until 1818; Sparks's edition in ten volumes, with his usual improvements of the text, appeared in 1836–40, and Franklin's unfinished *Autobiography*, first published in a French translation, was not published complete in the United States until 1868. There was something about the character and deeds of Franklin—his mixture of the commonplace, the cosmopolitan, and the detached—which made him unsuitable as a national hero.

The first effective efforts to create national heroes to stand beside Washington did not find raw materials in such towering personalities as Franklin and Jefferson, who had become world-renowned. Instead, local patriots exploited local materials, and the first national heroes were to be the by-products of regional rivalry and provincial patriotism: the spiritual cement for a nation still unsure of itself.

The first major product was Patrick Henry. The eloquent Virginian had become something of a legend long before his death in 1799, but his last years, like Washington's, had been covered by a partisan cloud. After 1795, he moved toward the Federalist party, stood for office on their ticket, and finally became an arch-enemy of Jefferson, Madison, and many of his old Virginia friends.

Henry, after his fashion, was to have his Weems. While Weems's Washington was a human prodigy, William Wirt's Patrick Henry was a Great Virginian. Wirt, a cultivated Virginia lawyer and man of letters, had been of counsel for the prosecution in the case against Aaron Burr and he became Attorney General under President Monroe, a post he held for over a decade. About 1805 he conceived a biography of Patrick Henry; his *Sketches of the Life and Character of Patrick Henry,* which finally appeared in 1817, was dedicated "To the Young Men of Virginia." "Mr. Henry became the idol of the people of Virginia. . . . His light and heat were seen and felt throughout the continent; and he was every where regarded as the great champion of colonial liberty. The impulse thus given by Virginia, was caught by the other colonies. Her resolutions were every where adopted, with progressive variations." This was his theme, and he developed it with Weemsian style and imagination.

Unlike Weems, he had made a serious effort to gather reminiscences from people who had actually known Henry. Although he had spent a full dozen years gathering materials about his subject, this made surprisingly little difference in the product. Before he was midway in the writing he had decided to invent wherever necessary. He wrote his friend Judge Dabney Carr (August 20, 1815):

The incidents of Mr. Henry's life are extremely monotonous. It is all speaking, speaking, speaking. 'Tis true he could talk: —"Gods! how he *could* talk!" but there is no acting "the while." From the bar to the legislature, and from the legislature to the bar, his peregrinations resembled, a good deal, those of some one, I forget whom, —perhaps some of our friend Tristram's characters, "from the kitchen to the parlor, and from the parlor to the kitchen." And then, to make the matter worse, from 1763 to 1789, covering all the bloom and pride of his life, not one of his speeches lives in print, writing or memory. All that is told me is, that, on such and such an occasion, he made a distinguished speech. Now to keep saying this over, and over, and over again, without being able to give any account of what the speech was,—why, sir, what is it but a vast, open, sunburnt field without one spot of shade or verdure? My soul is weary of it. . . . I have sometimes a notion of trying the plan of Botta, who has written an account of the American war, and made speeches himself for his prominent characters, imitating, in this, the historians of Greece and Rome; but I think with Polybius, that this is making too free with the sanctity of history. Besides, Henry's eloquence was all so completely *sui generis* as to be inimitable by any other: and . . . I never saw or heard him. . . .

Again: there are some ugly trait's in H's character, and some pretty nearly as ugly blanks. He was a blank military commander, a blank governor, and a blank politician, in all those useful points which depend on composition and detail. In short, it is, verily, as hopeless a subject as man could well desire. I have dug around it, and applied all the plaister of Paris that I could command; but the figtree is still barren, and every bud upon it indicates death instead of life.

But, in the end, Wirt, like Weems, was undaunted by his meager raw material. Almost singlehanded, he beatified Patrick Henry.

Concentrating on the Revolution, Wirt gave to Henry, and through him to Virginia, the leading role. He drew the deathless scene of Henry's bold outburst during the debate in the Virginia House of Burgesses on Henry's resolutions (May 29, 1765) against the Stamp Act. "In a voice of thunder, and with the look of a god," as Wirt wrote, Henry exclaimed, "Caesar had his Brutus—Charles the first, his Cromwell—and George the third—('Treason,' cried the speaker—'treason, treason,' echoed from every part of the house.—It was one of those trying moments which is decisive of character.—Henry faltered not for an instant; but rising to a loftier attitude, and fixing on the speaker an eye of the most determined fire, he finished his sentence with the firmest emphasis) *may profit by their example. If this be treason, make the most of it.*" In the Revolutionary cause, no one was ahead of Patrick Henry. "His vision," Wirt explained, "pierced deep into futurity; and long before a whisper of independence had been heard in this land, he had looked through the whole of the approaching contest, and saw, with the eye and the rapture of a prophet, his country seated aloft among the nations of the earth." With no text to rely on and only the vague recollections of contemporaries, Wirt himself concocted what was to become the most famous utterance of the whole Revolution: Henry's "Give me liberty, or give me death!" speech, as supposedly delivered in the House of Burgesses (March 23, 1775).

Passing lightly over Henry's less attractive features, Wirt underlined his Hero's role as a great popular leader, "one of those perfect prodigies of nature, of whom very few have been produced since the foundations of the earth were laid." Compounded largely of "plaister of Paris," Wirt's Partick Henry sprang to life and still stalks the American patriotic imagination. Wirt portrayed him as "The first statesman and orator in Virginia"—a legendary Virginia. Some of the more knowledgeable or more partisan contemporaries—John Taylor of Caroline, John Randolph, and Thomas Jefferson—objected to this fustian ideal, but objections died with the men who had known Henry personally, and the legend grew.

The local patriotism was visible not only to Virginians. Wirt had made his theme plain enough to irritate the regional loyalties of others. Wirt's *Henry,* published in November, 1817, at once excited interest in New England. John Adams managed to borrow a copy and promptly wrote to Wirt that he could not help remarking, "*Erant heroes ante Agamemnona*"—there were heroes before Agamemnon. "If I could go back to the age of thirty-five, Mr. Wirt, I would endeavor to become your rival. . . . I would adopt in all its modesty, your title, 'Sketches of the Life and Writings of James Otis, of Boston' and, in imitation of your example, I would introduce portraits of a long catalogue of illustrious men, who were agents in the Revolution. . . ." Adams then offered a list: most were New Englanders, many from his home state.

> I envy none of the well-merited glories of Virginia, or any of her sages or heroes. But, Sir, I am jealous, very jealous, of the honor of Massachusetts.
>
> The resistance to the British system for subjugating the colonies, began in 1760, and in the month of February, 1761, James Otis electrified the town of Boston, the province of Massachusetts Bay, and the whole continent, more than Patrick Henry ever did in the whole course of his life. If we must have panegyric and hyperbole, I must say, that if Mr. Henry was Demosthenes and Mr. Richard Henry Lee, Cicero, James Otis was Isaiah and Ezekiel united.

This question of priority was not trivial. It troubled Adams, who was eager to have the record set right, to prevent Virginia from seizing laurels which belonged to others. Before the week was out, he wrote asking John Jay to correct Wirt's misstatement that Henry had been the original author of the Address to the People of Great Britain (July 5, 1775). He wrote to Hezekiah Niles, reminding him that it was James Otis' oration against the writs of assistance as early as February, 1761, that had "breathed into this nation the breath of life." The true beginnings of the Revolution, Adams held, were way back in 1760, in Massachusetts, and if Wirt had known more of the facts, he would have seen "that Otis, Thacher, Samuel Adams, Mayhew, Hancock, Cushing, and thousands of others were laboring for several years at the wheel before the name of Henry was heard beyond the limits of Virginia."

Adams was not alone in his pique. The *North American Review,* the country's leading literary organ and the mouthpiece of the New England literati, also took offense. In its long review, it showed how the priority Wirt claimed for Virginia really belonged to Massachusetts. Otis had resisted British tyranny and had himself been taunted by the cry of "Treason!" several years before Henry. Wirt claimed the Committees of Correspondence to have originated in the resolutions in the Virginia House of Burgesses on March 12, 1773. "The truth is," the reviewer objected, "the plan originated in Boston, more than four months before it was meditated in Virginia. It was devised by Mr. Samuel Adams and Mr. James Warren, of Plymouth, and the first Committee was appointed, on the motion of Mr. Adams, at a town meeting held November 2d, 1772." And so on.

New Englanders were not satisfied by mere defensive tactics. Within a few years they produced a series of counterblasts which in their own way would enrich the national tradition. Early in 1818, Adams' letters correcting Wirt were published in *Niles' Weekly Register*. The next year Adams collected and republished the "Novanglus" essays he had written in 1774–75, adding other items proving the priority of New England in the Revolution. Meanwhile, Adams persuaded William Tudor, son of his former law clerk, to wrote a full-length biography of James Otis.

William Tudor was well qualified to defend the honor of New England. The Boston-born (Harvard College, Class of 1796) brother of Frederic Tudor (to whom he had originally proposed the idea of the ice trade), he had served in the Massachusetts legislature, and had been the founder and first editor of the *North American Review*. His preoccupation with New England brought the magazine the nickname the *North Unamerican*. He was also a founder of the Boston Athenaeum, a promoter of the project to establish a Bunker Hill monument, and an active member of the Massachusetts Historical Society.

When Tudor's *Life of James Otis, of Massachusetts* appeared in 1823, it showed that Virginians had skilled rivals in the use of plaster of Paris for patriotic purposes. Otis' life, like Henry's, offered many difficulties to the conscientious biographer. Documentary materials were scanty, partly because near the end of his life Otis had collected and burned many of his papers and pamphlets. Although Otis' fame had come from his speeches, there were no contemporary texts; only rough notes had been taken by witnesses. Otis' public career had been brief. He first became known in 1761 and his public career was ended in 1769 when John Robinson, a commissioner of the customs whose accusations of treason he had publicly denied, hit him over the head in a Boston coffee house. Thereafter, Otis had lucid intervals but he never fully recovered his sanity. He was occasionally violent, turned to drink, and was declared *non compos mentis* by a probate court in 1771. Otis lived on until 1783 when he died, as he had said he hoped he would, by a stroke of lightning.

From such meager materials, Tudor's ingenuity produced a New England hero who was both earlier and greater than his Virginia counterpart. Tudor reconstructed Otis' speech against the writs of assistance which had been used to enforce the British government's unconstitutional efforts to collect taxes in the colonies. And there was James Otis defending the Revolutionary cause nearly four years before Patrick Henry had made his first notable utterance. In that speech, as we saw in an earlier chapter, Otis supposedly provided the slogan "Taxation without representation is tyranny." In September, 1762, Otis had composed and read to the Massachusetts legislature a bold remonstrance to the Royal Governor. "It would be of little consequence to the people," Otis asserted, "whether they were subject to George, or Lewis, the King of Great Britain, or the French king, if both were arbitrary, as both would be, if both could levy taxes without Parliament." At the reading of this passage, Timothy Paine, the member from Worcester, cried out, "Treason! Treason!" According to Tudor, this was three years before a similar scene was enacted in the Virginia House of Burgesses.

Tudor went on to recount Otis' political leadership of Massachusetts during the crucial years, his leadership in the Stamp Act Congress, his composition of the "Circular Letter" (1768) of the Massachusetts legislature calling on the colonies to unite against British taxation, his martyrdom at the hands of a British customs commissioner, and finally his death by a stroke of lightning:

> When God in anger saw the spot,
>   On earth to Otis given,
> In thunder as from Sinai's Mount
>   He snatch'd him back to Heaven.

A comparison of the reconstruction of Otis' famous speech which Adams supplied to Tudor in 1818 with Otis' published work and with Adams' fragmentary notes, taken when he actually heard the speech nearly sixty years before, shows, as Adams' grandson and editor Charles Francis Adams noted, "that Mr. Adams insensibly infused into this work much of the learning and of the breadth of views belonging to himself."

Leading New Englanders found Tudor's *Otis* much to their taste. "The best representation possible . . . of the state of feeling in New England out of which the Revolution was produced," observed George Ticknor, an influential Boston pundit. "There is nothing like it in print, . . . nor could such a book be made twenty years from hence, for then all the traditions will have perished with the old men from whose graves he has just rescued them. It takes prodigiously here, and will, I think, do much good by promoting an inquiry into the most interesting and important periods of our history." The Adams-Tudor version of Otis and of the origins of the Revolution was perpetuated in Boston's Fourth of July Orations, which were made into a book and given by a patriotic Bostonian to every school in the city, every academy in the state, and every college in the United States.

The birth of the nation was still a matter of some personal reminiscence by men whose only American loyalty, until the day before yesterday, was to their Massachusetts or to their Virginia. The expression "my country" in America had meant my colony or my state long before it meant anything else. Even in the early 19th century, to John Adams it still meant Massachusetts and to Jefferson it meant Virginia. These local loyalties—and local prejudices—were the first raw material not only of an American patriotism, but of an American history.

41

The Quest for a National Past

BEFORE THE REVOLUTION, each colony had viewed American history as the history of itself. A respectable tradition of historical writing had developed, but it was a provincial tradition, compounded of local pride, promotional ardor, and more than a touch of antiquarianism. Hardly a colony lacked a book on its founding, its deeds and delights, but there was no unifying all-American institution (except the British Empire) on which to focus the loyalty of subjects or the pens of historians.

When the Revolution came, then, the colonies still lacked an American history in both the literal and the literary sense. One of the most surprising facts about the American Revolution was that a generation of such articulate and self-conscious men should have produced so little historical writing about so dramatic an event. One explanation must be that the American was unaccustomed to treating American events as a whole and unused to writing about events taking place outside his own colony. It was a time before prompt or organized news-reporting. Even military commanders had difficulty keeping abreast of news outside the immediate neighborhood. The headquarters of the new national government were mobile; its records were scanty, poorly noted, and poorly preserved. The momentous Philadelphia Constitutional Convention of 1787, where, if any place, a sense of making history must have been present, left only a fragmentary record. If James Madison (who was not the official secretary) had not happened to be present, our information about the deliberations would have been scanty. New publishing difficulties faced the American writer: general economic conditions were often precarious, the American book market was uncertain, and the British market for American books was closed. It is not surprising, therefore, that for some decades efforts at writing and publishing national history were meager and unsuccessful.

The important studies of the American past during the first decades of the new nation were scattered, independent efforts, inspired primarily by loyalty to a state or region. In the 20th century a national point of view seems "normal," while regional, state, and local history is likely to seem interstitial, incidental, or antiquarian. But that is not how the study of our national history began. Elsewhere, in Great Britain, for example, there had been a long national history and a firm and rich national literature before county and local historical societies began their work. Not here; in the young United States the national history was first depicted not in broad panoramic strokes, but as a mosaic of local stories.

For at least a half-century after the Declaration of Independence, it was generally assumed that a history of the United States would consist of a history in turn of each of the states. The history of states and regions seemed primary; the history of the United States seemed contrived and derivative. Many years would pass before Americans would see their history the other way around.

The numerous, independent state and local historical societies were a by-product of the new nation; they originated (David D. Van Tassel has explained) as "weapons in the battle to dominate the writing of national history." The first of their kind was the Massachusetts Historical Society. The Rev. Jeremy Belknap, a Boston-born congregational minister—helped by four friends (including James Winthrop, librarian of Harvard College, and William Tudor, the scholarly father of the Tudor who was to immortalize Otis)—organized the group, which aimed "to mark the genius, delineate the manners, and trace the progress of society in the United States, and . . . to rescue the true history of this country from the ravages of time and the effects of ignorance and neglect."

"We intend," Belknap explained, "to be an *active*, not a *passive*, literary body; not to lie waiting like a bed of oysters, for the tide (of communication) to flow in upon us, but to *seek* and find, to *preserve* and *communicate*, literary intelligence, especially in the historical way." Chartered by the Commonwealth as the Massachusetts Historical Society in 1794, it received quarters in Boston's attractive new Tontine Crescent, designed by Charles Bulfinch. Here was the beginning of the historical-society movement that was destined to spread all over the young nation. The Society's efforts resulted in the most important collection of early American manuscripts outside the Library of Congress, but its heavy emphasis, from the beginning, was on New England. It did more than any other single agency to preserve the authentic colonial records, to edit, print, and diffuse them, and so to nourish a pride in the local past which has continued to distinguish New England men of letters. The first ten-volume set of its *Collections* appeared in 1809, and by mid-20th century the Society had issued over two hundred such volumes.

New York was the first to follow Massachusetts' lead. The historical society there was mainly the work of a picturesque promoter, John Pintard (recently bankrupted by losing a million dollars in a stock-promotion scheme), who "could indite a handbill that would inflame the minds of the people for any good work. . . . could call a meeting with the pen of a poet, and before the people met, he would have arranged the doings for a perfect success. He knew the weak points of every man, and he would gratify the vanity of men and get their money." Having developed a passion for preserving historical manuscripts, he began by trying to organize a historical museum under the auspices of the Tammany Society, of which he was the first Sagamore and later the Grand Sachem. But this enterprise was perverted into a commercial side-show and zoo (it was later purchased by P. T. Barnum and was the scene of some of his most successful hoaxes, including his stuffed South Sea Mermaid). Then Pintard persuaded the legislature to found the New-York Historical Society in 1804 and to appropriate twelve thousand dollars for it in 1812.

The other states soon followed. When the Historical Society of Pennsylvania appeared in 1824, a local chauvinism was obvious: membership was restricted to persons domiciled in Pennsylvania for at least ten years. Historical societies were soon founded in other New England states— Maine (1820, the very year of statehood), Rhode Island (1822), New Hampshire (1823), Connecticut (1825), Vermont (1838)—to claim their share of the laurels from Massachusetts. In the new West, a state historical society appeared within a few years of the birth of each state. Just as a hotel or a railroad might bring into being the population that required it, so a historical society would somehow conjure up a past. These appeared in rapid succession in Tennessee (1820), Ohio (1822),

Illinois (1827), Michigan (1828), Indiana (1830), Missouri (1844), and Wisconsin (1846). In the South, Virginia led the way (1831); there, Chief Justice John Marshall headed the society, which, according to one member, aimed, by an honorable competition with Massachusetts and Pennsylvania "to pluck up drowning honor by the locks." Then came North Carolina (1833), where Archibald De Bow Murphey, the pioneer social reformer, who wanted to improve the economy of the state by a great system of canals requiring federal funds, complained that by 1820 North Carolina had received from the federal government only "two miserable lighthouses." Explaining that this might be due to the state's lack of pride in itself, he proposed a history of North Carolina to raise their standing in the Union "and make our state respectable in our own eyes."

Nor was the state the smallest active unit. Parts of states (for example, East Tennessee in 1833 and Western Pennsylvania in 1834), counties (for example, Essex in 1821 and Worcester in 1825, both in Massachusetts), and cities (for example, Albany in 1828 and Marietta in 1841) also set about recording their special past and vindicating their local honor.

The semicentennial of the Declaration of Independence in 1826 invigorated anew the state societies and stirred competition among these for materials from foreign archives. And the rising sectional loyalties and antagonisms in the decade before the Civil War brought the activities of local historical societies to a climax.

The power of localism was demonstrated by the repeatedly futile efforts to found a historical society with national membership and a national point of view. In 1812, the scholarly and prosperous printer Isaiah Thomas urged the special advantages of locating such a society's headquarters where he had built the country's largest printing and publishing business, at the small inland town of Worcester, Massachusetts, "for the better preservation from the destruction so often experienced in large towns and cities by fire, as well as from the ravages of any enemy, to which seaports in particular are so much exposed in time of war." But the American Antiquarian Society did not become the center for writing the national history; as the best collection of state and local histories, it too became a citadel of the state-by-state approach to the American past.

Not until 1884 did The American Historical Association provide a national focus for the work of all historians. It was 1907 before there was a separate professional society for historians writing about the United States.

*   *   *

Some of the ablest searchers for symbols of a larger national past turned to biography. The immense popularity of Davy Crockett's "Autobiography," Weems's *George Washington,* Wirt's *Patrick Henry,* Tudor's *James Otis,* and similar works, contrasted sharply with the meager demand for books about the whole national past. Long before there was any substantial literature specifically recounting the national history, there were American biographies of every shape, size, and description. Biographers rushed in to fill the vacuum of national memory. The very recency of the age of the "Founding Fathers" provided an opportunity and a temptation to elaborate personal reminiscence, family and local piety.

Jeremy Belknap's *American Biography: or an Historical Account of those Persons who have been distinguished in America, as Adventurers, Statesmen, Philosophers, Divines, Warriors, Authors, or other Remarkable Characters. . . .* (1794; 1798), aimed to provide an American Plutarch. He and his imitators hoped to appeal to readers in "all parts of the Continent" simply by selecting heroes from all over. Another device was tried by the Sanderson brothers and their collaborators in Pennsylvania, who put together in nine volumes the *Biography of the Signers of the Declaration of Independence* (1820–27). Washington Irving evaded and transcended local patriotism in his readable three-volume life of Christopher Columbus, whom he cast in the role of the first American hero.

The most ambitious, and in the long run the most successful, effort at a biographical substitute for national history was Jared Sparks's *Library of American Biography* (1834–48), which eventually came to twenty-five volumes. He conceived the set in 1832 as "in some degree a connected history of the country . . . to illustrate the character and acts of some of the most illustrious men of the nation." Drawing his contributors from all over, Sparks offered a tactfully balanced diet of patriotic tidbits from North, South, East, and West.

Sparks was careful to deal out the honors generously to all parts of the country, and he included many figures who, either because of their minor role or their historical remoteness, were not the focus of partisan passions. One volume, for example, included the ornithologist Alexander Wilson of Pennsylvania and Captain John Smith of Virginia. Not until the project was well established and safely launched into the second series, did Sparks dare to deal with the controversial local patron saints. Then in a single volume he combined a life of the French explorer La Salle with one of Patrick Henry, following this with another which offered between the same covers James Otis of Massachusetts and James Oglethorpe of Georgia. The author of the sketch of Patrick Henry prudently fogged over the touchy question of Revolutionary priorities:

> His claim to the honor of having given the first impulse to the revolutionary movement, is a question hardly susceptible of a satis-

factory solution, since no event, prior to the battle of Lexington and the declaration of independence, was so decidedly different in character from a variety of others occurring at about the same time, as to merit, in contradistinction from them, the praise of being the first step in the progress of the revolution. It is certain, however, that, in one of the two leading colonies, during the period immediately preceding the revolution, Henry was constantly in advance of the most ardent patriots, and that he suggested and carried into effect, by his immediate personal influence, measures that were opposed as premature and violent by all the other eminent supporters of the cause of liberty. It was the good fortune of Henry to enjoy, during his lifetime, the appropriate reward of his extraordinary merits, and the almost unbounded admiration and respect of his countrymen.

Sparks's own contribution early in the series was a volume devoted to the "Life and Treason of Benedict Arnold," a subject on which patriots all over the country could heartily agree.

When Ralph Waldo Emerson, in his "History," a lecture he had given many times before it was published in his *Essays* in 1841, exclaimed that "there is properly no history, only biography," he was not merely uttering a transcendental truism. He was actually describing, while trying to justify, a vacuum in American letters: there was still very little national historical writing adequate to its subject. The republican idea of "Representative Men" never lost its appeal for Emerson. But in America there were peculiar difficulties in trying to make biographies into a popularly appealing historical literature. Where, as in Europe, the makers of history had been knights, noblemen, kings, and queens, even their private lives were glamorous. But here, as St. George Tucker warned Wirt on his life of Patrick Henry, "Our scene of action is so perfectly domestic as to afford neither novelty nor variety." No wonder, then, that John Marshall was tempted to substitute the whole career of the New World for the life of his hero, and that Weems was tempted to invent or embroider trivia.

Not until after the Civil War would a national perspective on American history begin to seem normal. Even before the end of the 18th century, however, there had been some evidence of the desire, if not the capacity, to envisage a national past. At that time nothing was more expressive of the inchoateness of national sentiment, of the pessimism about the national future (as contrasted with the future of particular states and regions), or of the strength of local patriotism, than the thin and feeble writings about the national history. For years, Americans leaned heavily on Englishmen. Accounts of the Revolution were borrowed freely from the *Annual Register,* an English Whig publication in which Edmund Burke had written a year-by-year summary of the events of the Revolutionary years. American interpretations of the Revolution (as Wesley Frank Craven has shown) for over a half-century were dominated by the vigorous book of an English Tory, George Chalmers, whose *Political Annals of the Present United Colonies* (1780) emphasized the weaknesses of British imperial policy, the long New England struggle for independence, and the importance of testing American Revolutionary claims by the evidence of recent British constitutional history.

The first published "American" effort at a full history of the Revolution was by the passionate and unreliable William Gordon, an English-born clergyman who had come to America in 1770 to join the cause of Independence. Over many years he gathered materials for a history, only to find, when he was ready to publish, that his work would be unacceptable here. Returning to England, he finally published his *History of the Rise, Progress, and Establishment of the Independence of the United States of America* (4 vols., London, 1788) but only after it had been much revised, garbled, and toned down. His work too was finally shown to be mostly plagiarized from the *Annual Register*. It was a woman, Mercy Otis Warren (sister of James Otis and friend of Abigail Adams), who wrote the first substantial and comprehensive history of the Revolution by an American hand (3 vols., 1805). Significantly, it was not an American but an Italian, Charles Botta, whose *History of the War of Independence* (first published in Italian, 1809; translated into English, 1820) became the first standard account for Americans of all parties. John Adams called Botta the best, and Jefferson predicted it would become "the common manual of our Revolutionary History."

When the Rev. Abiel Holmes (father of the Autocrat of the Breakfast Table) set out in his *American Annals* (2 vols., 1805; 2d edition, 1829) to offer a general American history from the beginning to the date of publication, he could honestly say that "while local histories of particular portions of America have been written, no attempt has been made to give even the outline of its entire history." Although ambitious in his pioneer effort to encompass all American history, the best he could offer was "annals"—year-by-year lists of events all over the continent—for he had no unifying theme.

Unfocused interest in an "American" past and vague reverence for a still inchoate national tradition were expressed in other ways. For example, in the collection, preservation, and reprinting of historical documents. The first and one of the most zealous of these collectors, Ebenezer Hazard of Philadelphia, took advantage of his travels while Surveyor-General of the Post Office (1777–82) during the Revolution, and used a government grant of one thousand dollars, to copy and collect documents. But his *Historical Collections* (2 vols., 1792–94), which dealt only with the discovery of America, the earliest colonies, and the New England Confederation, sold so few copies that they were not continued.

Still Hazard had begun to develop a national point of view later expressed on a larger scale by Peter Force, whose *Tracts* (4 vols., 1836–46) and *American Archives* (9 vols., 1837–53) are still used by historians of the Revolution. This preoccupation with written and rare printed sources of the colonial period, like the obsession with biographical narrative, absorbed energies which Americans had not yet found a way of expressing in coherent national history.

To understand the great and lasting impression made by George Bancroft, who now appeared on the scene, one must remember the situation into which he came. Citizens of this literate but new and insecure nation were seeking eagerly for signs and symbols of their nationality. American historical writing by the year 1834, when the first volume of Bancroft's work appeared, was not so much a wasteland as a clutter of undergrowth. The American who looked back across his New World past found clusters of documentary collections, patriotic biographies, and works of state and local filio-pietism. No broad path had been cut from the whole continental past to the national present.

It is not surprising, then, that when a man of prodigious industry, lively imagination, and literary genius set himself this pathfinding task, his product was the great national monument of the century. But who could have predicted that this work would come as it did? The first great national history, which dominated American reading and thinking about the national past, was the product not of a chauvinist but of a cosmopolite. For Bancroft, the American story was only a fragment of the unified story of mankind.

Born in 1800, son of the Rev. Aaron Bancroft (the first president of the American Unitarian Association, who had abridged Marshall's five-volume Washington into a single volume), George entered Harvard College at the age of thirteen and was graduated in the class of 1817, having become a favorite of Professors Andrews Norton and Edward Everett, and of President Kirkland himself. He spent a year studying divinity and then was sent abroad on a purse which Kirkland had collected from Harvard friends (seven hundred dollars a year for three years, plus one thousand dollars for a year's travel in Italy and France, to which his father added five hundred dollars). With these resources, ample for the time, young George spent four years studying and traveling on the continent and in England. He spent two years at Göttingen studying oriental languages and Biblical subjects and then studied briefly in Berlin and Heidelberg before going on to Paris and London; finally, he topped off his European journey with a tour of Switzerland and Italy.

When Bancroft returned to America in August, 1822, his broad European experience was rare among his contemporaries. Besides having acquired a speaking knowledge of modern European languages that was uncommon among American intellectuals, he had made the personal acquaintance of a galaxy which included Goethe, Alexander Von Humboldt, Cuvier, Lafayette, Gallatin (then United States Minister to France), Washington Irving, Napoleon's sister, Princess Pauline Borghese, Countess Guiccioli, and Lord Byron. His old mentor, Professor Andrews Norton, was so shocked when the promising young man whom he had sent abroad to study theology returned wearing a silken beard and foppish costume and greeted him with a kiss on each cheek, that he wrote Bancroft never to visit his home again. Despite all his later success, Bancroft never re-entered the bosom of Boston respectability. This estrangement helped thrust him out into the great world of ideas and into a world-view that revealed to him the special American destiny.

Abroad, Bancroft had come under the influence of German historians, especially of Arnold Heeren; from them he had learned both a respect for historical sources and a technique for seeking objectivity. Heeren's theory of the unity of mankind, rooted in ancient Greek and European political systems, was reinforced by Bancroft's strongly Unitarian background. When Bancroft first thought of writing history—as early as 1828—he seems to have conceived of a general history, in which the story of the United States would have been only one part. When he produced the first volume of his history in 1834, although his focus was on America, the story was still presented as only one recent crucial episode in the history of man.

Bancroft was an American missionist but not a chauvinist. The history of this nation for him revealed the role that one segment of the human race played in the dramatic progress of mankind. This grand theme was subtly revealed in the fact that, although he called his volumes a history of "the United States of America," the whole of the original work treated only the years before the history of the new nation, strictly speaking, had even begun. The first nine volumes, published at intervals over three decades (1834–66), brought the story from the earliest French and Spanish settlements in the late 15th and early 16th century down to 1776. The tenth volume dealing with 1776–82 (1874) was still subtitled "The American Revolution." Only as an afterthought did he produce his two-volume *History of the Formation of the Constitution* (1882). Thus his great pioneer "national" history described the country before it had become the nation. Yet to him this was no paradox: the very theme of American history was pre-national and international. The American mission—an ingathering of peoples to advance the search for human freedom—was never better exemplified than in the colonial era, when people were first being drawn here from the nations of the world, and had first tried to express their composite and compounded strivings. This very belief in an American mission, a

"City upon a Hill," was to be reinforced by the enduring power of Bancroft's own work.

Bancroft's theme, as he summarized it in his oration on "The Necessity, the Reality, and the Promise of the Progress of the Human Race" (1854), was universal:

> The reciprocal relation between God and humanity constitutes the UNITY of the race. The more complete recognition of that unity is the first great promise which we receive from the future. Nations have, indeed, had their separate creeds and institutions and homes. The commonwealth of mankind, as a great whole, was not to be constructed in one generation. But the different peoples are to be considered as its component parts, prepared, like so many springs and wheels, one day to be put together. . . .
>
> In this great work our country holds the noblest rank. . . . Our land is not more the recipient of the men of all countries than their ideas. Annihilate the past of any one leading nation of the world, and our destiny would have been changed. Italy and Spain, in the persons of COLUMBUS and ISABELLA, joined together for the great discovery that opened America to emigration and commerce; France contributed to its independence; the search for the origin of the language we speak carried us to India; our religion is from Palestine; of the hymns sung in our churches, some were first heard in Italy, some in the deserts of Arabia, some on the banks of the Euphrates; our arts come from Greece; our jurisprudence from Rome; our maritime code from Russia; England taught us the system of Representative Government; the noble Republic of the United Provinces bequeathed to us, in the world of thought, the great idea of the toleration of all opinions; in the world of action, the prolific principle of federal union. Our country stands, therefore, more than any other, as the realisation of the unity of the race. . . . Finally, as a consequence of the tendency of the race towards unity and universality, the organization of society must more and more conform to the principle of FREEDOM.

Bancroft hardly deviated from this theme, from the opening sentence of his first volume, which declared that "The United States of America constitute an essential portion of a great political system, embracing all the civilized nations of the earth," to the closing sentence of the twelfth volume, which noted that, in 1789, "all the friends of mankind invoked success on the unexampled endeavor to govern states and territories of imperial extent as one federal republic." Bancroft showed the tributaries of older nations flowing into the stream of American history, there to be mingled and purified before flowing out again. Though his focus was on America, his standpoint was the world. He recounted the events and contributions of the nations of Europe, he speculated on the consequences for America of events in Spain, France, or England. A less chauvinistic expression of nationalism would be hard to find.

The work was an immediate success. It was estimated that, within a year of its publication in 1834, Volume One had entered nearly a third of the homes of New England. Royalties from his *History* made Bancroft a wealthy man. Within ten years, that first volume had gone through ten "editions"; it had gone through twenty-six by 1878. And people bought and read later instalments in large numbers as they appeared.

Since his success was largely due to his ability to rise above provincial loyalties, it is not surprising that his work did not wholly satisfy the native sons of any one colony. The conservative Whiggish New Englanders did not like his Jacksonian-Democratic point of view. Loyal Virginians objected to being lumped together with Massachusetts. Bancroft suffered the proverbial disdain of aristocratic Bostonians for those who have a "merely national" reputation. His outspoken support of Jackson, Van Buren, and Polk put him almost beyond the bounds of respectability. In due course, however, Bancroft was rewarded for his party loyalty, first as Collector of the Port of Boston, then as Polk's Secretary of Navy, then as acting Secretary of War, and later as Minister to Great Britain. Until nearly the Civil War, his politics, by setting him apart from the cliquish Bostonians, qualified him for a more national view of the American past.

Long before the end of his prodigious life, Bancroft's eminence transcended party; his public posts were among the least remarkable of his distinctions. Leopold Von Ranke (somewhat to Bancroft's irritation) called his history "the best book ever written from the democratic point of view." His master Heeren called his work "truly inspired history." Never before or since has an American national historian been so widely acclaimed abroad. At home, too, his fame increased with the years. Twenty-one years after he had served as the official Congressional eulogist on Andrew Jackson's death in 1845, he delivered the Lincoln memorial speech before a joint session of Congress on February 12, 1866. It was an act of personal, not party, recognition when President Andrew Johnson appointed him Minister to Berlin in 1867, and President Grant kept him on. He was voted access to the floor of Congress. When he died in 1891, President Harrison ordered flags at half-mast as Bancroft's body returned to his native Worcester.

During Bancroft's prime, the easiest—some thought the only—way to attract wide attention as an American historian was to become an anti-Bancroft. The Whig lawyer and editor, Richard Hildreth (also from Massachusetts), made one such effort with his six volumes (1849–52), which went up to the Missouri Compromise in 1820. He tried to use Bancroft as a foil for his own strongly Federalist interpretations, his studied dispassionateness, and his emphasis on economic factors. George Tucker, a versatile man of letters who had been professor of ethics at the University of Virginia, attempted to redress Bancroft's bias on the other side in a work (4 vols., 1856–57) which defended slavery and which, with a strongly Southern point of view, carried the account up to 1841. But none escaped the overshadowing eminence of Bancroft.

Why was Bancroft's success so immediate, so widespread, and so enduring? The very weaknesses of the American national spirit in the early decades of national life, the prevalence of conflicting localisms, the vagueness and confusion about the meaning and purpose of the nation, had given a peculiar role and a peculiar opportunity to Bancroft as high priest of American nationality. For many Americans he was less historian than prophet, for he used the national past as testimony of the national mission. That mission was not preached in the accents of chauvinism or xenophobia. On the contrary, it was the mission of mankind that had revealed to him a peculiar destiny for America. In the very quest of the first Americans for their purpose, Bancroft had found a symbol of national purpose, confined not by political boundaries but only by the hopes of all mankind.

42

A Festival of National Purpose

IF THE MAKING of popular legendary heroes and the mythologizing of the Father of his Country were remarkably speedy, the making of other patriotic symbols and rituals for the new nation was slow and halting. For example, the national flag and the national anthem which would dominate patriotic occasions in the 20th century became clearly defined only after the Civil War. The first flag under which the colonists fought in the War for Independence was that raised by Washington's continental army at Somerville, Massachusetts, on January 1, 1776. This so-called "Grand Union" flag consisted of the British cross of St. George and St. Andrew on a blue field, and thirteen alternate red and white stripes; it closely resembled the flag which the East India Company had been flying in colonial ports since the early 18th century. A resolution of the Continental Congress in Philadelphia in the summer of 1777 prescribed that the flag of the United States have thirteen stripes, alternate red and white and "that the union be thirteen stars, white in a blue field, representing a new constellation," but this was so vague that all sorts of variations remained possible. There was still widespread uncertainty, even in the army, as to what the national flag really was, and when and how it should be displayed. Americans actually fought the Revolution under local banners showing a variety of devices—rattlesnakes, pine and palmetto trees, eagles, symbolic chains, anchors, and mottoes such as "Don't Tread on Me," "An Appeal to Heaven," "We are One," and "Vince aut Morire"—but not under any authentic national flag.

The standard of the United States prepared at Washington's direction was not delivered to him until March, 1783, when the fighting was over. The principal hand in designing it was probably that of Francis Hopkinson, a versatile Philadelphia judge, and a signer of the Declaration of Independence. The Betsy Ross legend can be traced to her grandson, who recounted his family tradition to the Pennsylvania Historical Society in 1870, but it has no substantial foundation in history.

After the admission of the two new states of Vermont and Kentucky, Congress in 1794 enacted that the flag should have fifteen stripes and fifteen stars, but defeated a proposal "to fix forever the Flag of the United States." Even after the number of states had further increased, this fifteen-star, fifteen-stripe flag flew over American ships in the War of 1812; such was the flag which Francis Scott Key saw. Then, in 1818, after the variety of practice was pointed out in Congress (Congress itself was flying a flag of eighteen stripes, while the New York Navy Yard's flag showed only nine), the number of stripes was fixed by law at thirteen, with the understanding that a star would be added for each new state. But variations in public practice continued. An observer on the Fourth of July, 1857, amused himself by noting "the various designs displayed on vessels, hotels, and public buildings in New York. The majority of the ships had the stars arranged in five horizontal rows of six stars each, making thirty stars in all,—thirty-one being the proper number at that date. . . . Some had one large star formed of thirty-one small stars, and this style prevailed at places of public amusement and over the hotels of New York and Jersey City. Other vessels had them in a lozenge, a diamond, or a circle. One vessel had one large star composed of smaller ones within a border of the latter; another carried the thirty-one stars in the form of an anchor. . . ."

Not until long after a flag of stars and stripes had been enacted was it officially and universally used. Beginning with General Anthony Wayne's Indian campaign of 1793, United States Army banners were generally blue, displaying a bald eagle holding the shield of the United States in the center, with a varying number of stars (for the states) in varying patterns at the top and a regimental device below. Perhaps this helps explain the origin of the "spread eagle" used to describe the oratory of Senator Thomas Hart Benton and other champions of westward expansion. (This Americanism first appears in this sense around 1858.) Only gradually were army units required to carry the Stars and Stripes: garrisons and artillery (1834), infantry (1841), engineers (1866), Marines (1876), cavalry (1887). Despite the bathos written about the flag and its meaning, its history until the Civil War expressed nothing so much as chaotic growth. Finally, an executive order of President Taft on June 24, 1912, prescribed a uniform design.

The story of the national anthem is not dissimilar. Quest for a single patriotic song was obstructed by partisan feelings: "Hail Columbia," a leading contender, written in 1798 by a prominent Federalist, Joseph Hopkinson, at first appeared to be a political rather than a national hymn. It is a familiar story how the words to "The Star-Spangled Banner" were written by Francis Scott Key, when he was aboard a British vessel on September 14, 1814, negotiating the release of another American, and witnessed the bombardment of Fort McHenry, near Baltimore. But Key's own political sentiments (there were strong anti-British overtones in his song; especially in the seldom-sung third verse which exults that "Their blood has washed out their foul footstep's pollution") doubtless delayed the adoption of his song as a hymn of patriotism. "The Star Spangled Banner" did not generally appear in school songbooks until the 1850's, and not until the 1890's did Army and Navy regulations specify that it be played on ceremonial occasions. At last, the Act of Congress of March 3, 1931, legally prescribed Key's song as the National Anthem.

In the first decades of national life, it was by no means clear what, if any, occasions should be celebrated as national holidays. In this, as in their other efforts at national self-definition, Americans were long confused and troubled by uncertainty and by competition among local and partisan loyalties. Vestiges of this confusion have remained into the later 20th century when, technically speaking, the United States still has no national holidays. There are a small number of federal "legal public holidays" designated by the President and Congress, but these apply only to the District of Columbia and to federal employees wherever they may be. Each state designates its own holidays. If New Year's Day, Washington's Birthday, Memorial Day, Independence Day, Labor Day, Veterans' (Armistice) Day, Thanksgiving, and Christmas —which exhaust the list of federal legal public holidays—happen to be observed in each of the states, it is because each of them separately has taken the appropriate legal action. In addition to these holidays on which the decisions of the states have coincided, there are at least fifty other days officially designated as legal or public holidays in one or more states. These serve a wide range of purposes varying (among others) from Arbor Day, Good Friday, Mardi Gras, and Fast Day to Robert E.

Lee's Birthday, Lincoln's Birthday, Texas Independence Day, Bunker Hill Day, Columbus Day, Nathan Bedford Forrest's Birthday, Andrew Jackson's Birthday, Thomas Jefferson's Birthday, Bennington Battle Day, Huey P. Long's Birthday, Pulaski Day, Confederate Memorial Day, Will Rogers Day, General Douglas MacArthur Day, Flag Day, and All Saints' Day. Excepting the purely religious holidays, nearly all these celebrations commemorate events which either did not occur or were not recognized as causes of celebration until after the Civil War.

The Fourth of July, of course, was destined to become the most important and most characteristic American holiday of political significance. But ·this came about only gradually, and the vagaries of the American national spirit are nowhere better illustrated than in the early history of its observance.

American history had been brief. Until at least the third decade of the 19th century, some men's memories ran back to the beginning of the Revolution. George Templeton Strong, the observant young New Yorker, noted this in his diary (November.8, 1854):

> We are so young a people that we feel the want of nationality, and delight in whatever asserts our national "American" existence. We have not, like England and France, centuries of achievements and calamities to look back on; we have no *record* of Americanism and we feel its want. Hence the development, in every state of the Union, of "Historical Societies" that seize on and seal up every worthless reminiscence of our colonial and revolutionary times. We crave a history, instinctively, and being without the eras that belong to older nationalities—Anglo-Saxon, Carolingian, Hohenstauffen, Ghibelline, and so forth—we dwell on the details of our little all of historic life, and venerate every trivial fact about our first settlers and colonial governors and revolutionary heroes. A vivid narrative of the life and manners of New York fifty years ago would be received with enthusiasm here. London would take comparatively little interest in such a picture of the times of Pitt and Fox.

In so new a nation, the occasions of national celebration were likely to be connected somehow with its birth. And thus continued (it had begun in the early 17th century) a distinctive and persistent American preoccupation with "purpose," nourished by the very limitations of the historical raw materials.

When Americans turned to their recent past, a past personally known to their fathers or grandfathers, if not to themselves, they were appealing to the "foundations" of their nation. This was a familiar theme, echoing again and again through the early national decades. "Our origin is within the limits of well-attested history," Chancellor James Kent told the New-York Historical Society in 1828; ". . . we are not permitted, like the nations of ancient Europe, to deduce our lineage from super-human beings, or to clothe the sage and heroic figures who

laid the foundations of our empire, with the exaggeration and lustre
of poetical invention. Nor do we stand in need of such machinery. It is
sufficient honour to be able to appeal to the simple and severe records
of truth." "The springs of American civilization," Francis Parkman
added in the year of Appomattox, "unlike those of the elder world, lie
revealed in the clear light of History. In appearance they are feeble; in
reality, copious and full of force. Acting at the sources of life, instru-
ments otherwise weak become mighty for good and evil and men, lost
elsewhere in the crowd, stand forth as agents of Destiny." The peculiarity of American history could hardly fail to give a special character to
the national rites.

It was impossible to celebrate the nation's identity—its "independence"—without also justifying its separation and proclaiming its mission
to the world. By selecting the enunciation of the reasons for separation
as the crucial act in the birth of the nation, Americans had already begun to express a lasting preoccupation with national purpose and national mission. National celebration and national justification had become one.

The new nation preferred to canonize not an event or an act, but a
statement: a public declaration of legal rights and general principles.
"The glory of the act was overshadowed by the glory of its annuncia-
tion." This was one of the most significant of the gradual, unconscious
choices made by Americans in quest of their nationality. It was a fitting
expression of a nation already characterized by a declamatory literature, a nation whose very motleyness and uncertainties stirred a constant preoccupation with a common national purpose. The American
vagueness made Americans, more than others, feel a need to assert
their nationality and their purpose with hyperbolic clarity.

In the decades before the Civil War, the American nation's holiday,
not surprisingly, expressed a booster spirit toward the past. Americans,
in confused exuberance, compounded their whole national past of
what had really happened, of what probably had happened, and of
what ought to have happened. The Fourth of July was a national jubilee
for retrospective boosters.

What and why was the Fourth of July? Precisely how and why
July 4 happened to become the date of celebration and to be given
its commonly assigned significance is a mystery that may never be
solved.

The resolution that first established American independence was
passed by the Continental Congress on July 2 (not July 4), 1776. For
it was on July 2 that the Congress formally adopted by vote the resolution that had been introduced on June 7 by Richard Henry Lee and
seconded by John Adams, declaring "that these United Colonies are,
and of right ought to be free and independent States, that they are
absolved from all allegiance to the British Crown, and that all political

connection between them and the State of Great Britain is and ought to be totally dissolved." On the very next day (July 3) John Adams wrote to his wife:

> The second day of July, 1776, will be the most memorable epocha in the history of America. I am apt to believe that it will be celebrated by succeeding generations as the great anniversary festival. It ought to be commemorated, as the day of the deliverance, by solemn acts of devotion to God Almighty . . . . with pomp and parade, with shows, games, sports, guns, bells, bonfires, and illuminations, from one end of this continent to the other, from this time forward, forever more . . . . posterity will triumph in that day's transaction . . .

Everything seemed to conspire to deprive Lee (and incidentally John Adams) of a full share of glory. The name of Lee as framer and proposer of the momentous resolution was not then published either in the newspapers or in the records of the Congress. The reasons are obscure. John Adams' own explanation, in his autobiography many years later, was that "Mr. Hancock was President, Mr. Harrison Chairman of the Committee of the Whole House, Mr. Thomson, the Secretary was cousin to Mr. Dickinson, and Mr. R. H. Lee and Mr. John Adams were no favorites of either." But, whatever the public ignorance or uncertainty about the proper distribution of personal glory, there was little uncertainty about the actual date when independence was first declared. As the *Pennsylvania Evening Post* announced on the evening of July 2, "This Day the Continental Congress declared the United Colonies Free and Independent States."

If the Fourth of July was not the date of the first formal declaration of American independence, what then was its claim to distinction? For it was also *not* the date of the signing of Jefferson's Declaration of Independence. A first question, of course, is why, after the decisive action on July 2, any further declaration should have been necessary at all. The answer is simply that, in order to limit debate and save time, the Continental Congress had adopted the general practice of disposing first of the naked proposition. Then it would proceed to agree on a statement of reasons. To prepare such a statement, Jefferson's committee (which included also Benjamin Franklin and John Adams) had actually been appointed some time before the vote on the proposition of independence had been taken. When Lee's resolution was formally adopted, Jefferson's document was thus ready to be discussed in committee of the whole, as it was from July 2 to July 4.

This document was approved by vote of the Continental Congress in Philadelphia on July 4, 1776, and a printed copy (bearing the names *only* of John Hancock, President, and Charles Thomson, Secretary) was made and circulated. In the original vote on July 4, the voting was by states and New York had abstained. Not until July 9 did the Provincial Congress of New York approve. This information reached the Continental Congress on July 15. On July 19, the Continental Congress finally voted that the Declaration "be fairly engrossed on parchment with the title and style of 'The Unanimous Declaration of the Thirteen United States of America.' " But the document was not yet signed by its famous fifty-five names, nor was it unambiguously indicated then or later why these people had to sign it.

One explanation, given by Thomas McKean, a member of Congress from Pennsylvania who had been present on July 4, was that the purpose of the Declaration as finally signed was to provide a kind of public loyalty-oath, a pledge of allegiance to the course already taken. Or (as he put it), "to prevent traitors or spies from worming themselves among us." It seems to have been decided for security's sake that "no person should have a seat in Congress during that year until he should have signed the declaration of independence." If this was the case, the Declaration was as much a loyalty-oath as a declaration of principles. And it was, then, one of the first, and surely the best known and best reputed (as well as most misunderstood) of the long line of Americans' efforts to reassure themselves by public oaths of loyalty.

The whole proceeding was unusually drawn out, if the purpose was simply to express an act of the Continental Congress. Not until August 2 did the journal of the Continental Congress note, "The Declaration of Independence being engrossed and compared at the table was signed by the members." Actually this entry was not quite accurate because not all the signing was done even then. At least one signer, Matthew Thornton of New Hampshire, did not subscribe his name until November (when he first became a member of the Continental Congress); at least five other "signers" (Rush, Clymer, Smith, Taylor, and Ross, all of Pennsylvania) had not even been members of Congress on July 4; at least one (George Read of Delaware) now belatedly became a "signer," though on July 2 he had been present and had refused to vote for independence.

The notion that the Declaration of Independence was signed on July 4 owed its currency to a host of personal mis-recollections and even to some historical post-fabrication. Within a decade of the sacred year 1776, Franklin, John Adams, and Jefferson each independently stated in writing that the Declaration had been signed on July 4. Confusion was compounded by the fact that the Continental Congress itself had not even announced the names of the "signers" during the year 1776, possibly because it was thought prudent to see first how the Declaration would be received by the states. Congress first made public the names of the "signers" on January 19, 1777. Then, when Congress printed its official journal, it actually doctored its own records (going so far as to omit the discordant entries on July 19 and August 2, 1776) to indicate that the Declaration had been signed on July 4. When the truth behind the printed record finally appeared in the *Secret Journals,* which were published by order of the United States Congress in 1821, the myth of the July 4 signing had become so well established that Jefferson himself would not believe the sober facts. By this time, too, the frigidly legalistic title of Jefferson's document had been supplanted by the more appealing title which it was to retain throughout later American history.

The myth of the signing was not the only one that quickly adhered to the date of July 4. There were others more colorful. One concerned the "Liberty Bell," which became almost as prominent in American patriotic iconography as the flag itself. The "Liberty Bell" was part of the legend that the "signing" of the Declaration was universally and immediately celebrated on July 4, 1776. But, in fact, we do not know precisely how or when the news of the vote for independence was generally received. In those days, news was slow to travel. Newspapers waited to copy items from other newspapers. News of Lee's Resolution of July 2 did not appear in New York newspapers until July 8 and in New England newspapers not until July 11. The Continental Congress usually kept its proceedings private, for security and other reasons. On July 6, a copy of Jefferson's Declaration reached the Pennsylvania Committee of Safety, which ordered that it be read and proclaimed at the Statehouse on July 8 at noon. Evidence of the public reception at that time is contradictory. "Three cheers rended the Welkin," reported John Adams. "The Battalions paraded on the common, and gave Us the Feu de Joy, notwithstanding the Scarcity of Powder." But Charles Biddle reported in his autobiography that "there were very few respectable people present. General [name obliterated] spoke against it, and many of the citizens who were good Whigs were much opposed to it; however, they were soon reconciled to it." When the information of the events of early July reached some of the dispersed units of the Continental Army at various times in August, they staged their own celebrations, which were often raucous and alcoholic.

The most popular legend, that the signing of the Declaration of Independence was announced to the world by the pealing of the bell in the steeple of the Philadelphia Statehouse (which from this act was sanctified as the "Liberty Bell") has no foundation in fact. The bell was there, but contemporary historians and the journal of the Congress made no mention of it. Not until the antislavery movement in the 1830's was the bell first given its legendary name. A pamphlet distributed at the Massachusetts Anti-Slavery Fair in Boston in 1839, entitled "The Liberty Bell, by Friends of Freedom," and carrying a picture of the bell, is the earliest such representation that has been found. The same name and the same picture were used in succeeding years. The "Liberty" here referred to was, of course, not the independence of the colonies from Britain but the freedom of the slaves.

A legend was soon invented which qualified the bell historically for its new polemical use. The inventor was George Lippard, a versatile Philadelphia journalist who had abortive careers in the ministry and the law before crowding an astonishing amount of patriotic endeavor into the remainder of the brief thirty-three years of his life. A latter-day Weems, he made his fortune as the author of sensational and sexy novels about monks and slave-catchers. He was also something of a religious crank; he insisted on being married without a clergyman, and even invented his own religion, the Brotherhood of the Union, which he founded in 1850. This sect neatly combined the brotherhood of man with patriotism and a crude proto-Marxism. As head of the sect, he styled himself "Supreme Washington," and traveled about the Union in its behalf; at his death, he left lodges in twenty-three states. His newspaper series ("Legends of the Revolution") in the 1840's was said to be responsible for raising the circulation of the Philadelphia *Saturday Courier* from 30,000 to 70,000, and was widely copied all over the country. He became a popular lecturer. *Godey's Lady's Book* in 1849 called him "unquestionably the most popular writer of the day."

Lippard himself was soon enough forgotten, but he made the Liberty Bell immortal. In his *Washington and His Generals or Legends of the American Revolution* (1847), he earned his place alongside Parson Weems by making up, out of whole cloth, a story destined to become one of the most unforgettable episodes of American "history." And he gave the whole new nation a solemn symbol. The Liberty Bell was to be reproduced endlessly on coins, postage stamps, and government bonds, finally becoming one of the most cherished emblems of American nationality, American purpose, and the American mission. During World War I one of the most effective posters for Liberty bonds showed the Liberty Bell over the motto, "Ring it again!" Without Lippard's fertile if saccharine imagination, this might never have been possible.

Lippard's account of the scene in Philadelphia on July 4, 1776, in *Washington and His Generals,* described "crowds of anxious people" about the Statehouse. In the steeple of Independence Hall was "an old man with white hair and sunburnt face. . . . clad in humble attire," and by his side "a flaxen-haired boy, with laughing eyes of summer blue." Since the lovable old codger could not read, the boy spelled out to him the inscription on the bell: "Proclaim Liberty to all the Land and all the Inhabitants thereof." Impatient to know whether the prophecy of the bell had yet been fulfilled, he sent the blue-eyed boy down to the hall of the Continental Congress.

It needed no second command. The boy with blue eyes and flaxen hair sprang from the old Bell-keeper's arms, and threaded his way down the dark stairs.

The old Bell-keeper was alone. Many minutes passed. Leaning over the railing of the steeple, his face toward Chestnut street, he looked anxiously for that fair-haired boy. Moments passed, yet still he came not. The crowds gathered more darkly along the pavement and over the lawn, yet still the boy came not.

"Ah!" groaned the old man, "he has forgotten me! These old limbs will have to totter down the State House stairs, and climb up again, and all on account of that child—"

As the word was on his lips, a merry, ringing laugh broke on the ear. There, among the crowds on the pavement, stood the blue-eyed boy, clapping his tiny hands, while the breeze blowed his flaxen hair all about his face.

And then swelling his little chest, he raised himself on tip-toe, and shouted a single word—

"Ring!"

Do you see that old man's eye fire? Do you see that arm so suddenly bared to the shoulder, do you see that withered hand, grasping the Iron Tongue of the Bell? The old man is young again; his veins are filled with new life. Backward and forward, with sturdy strokes, he swings the Tongue. The bell speaks out! The crowd in the street hear it, and burst forth in one long shout! Old Delaware hears it, and gives it back in the hurrah of her thousand sailors. The city hears it, and starts up from desk and work-bench, as though an earthquake had spoken.

None of it happened—not the crowds, not the white-haired old codger, not the "flaxen-haired boy, with laughing eyes of summer blue." For none of them is there the least shred of evidence. John Adams did report significantly that the Chimers of Philadelphia's Christ Church (whose rector had continued to pray for the King) chimed away after the reading of the Declaration on July 8, but neither he nor anybody else mentioned the ringing of the bell in the Statehouse steeple.

This Liberty Bell legend was confirmed and perpetuated in the pages of Benjamin J. Lossing's *Pictorial Field Book of the Revolution* (1850–52), a de luxe and not entirely unreliable compendium of drawings and patriotic scenes and objects. Lossing's detailed but toned down version of Lippard's story (accompanied by a drawing of the Bell) firmly established the Liberty Bell as the Holy Grail of the American Revolution.

The central mystery remains why July 4 was chosen for celebration. The early history of the holiday only adds to the confusion. Celebrations of the occasion usually called it vaguely the Anniversary of American Independence although, within five years after 1776, Adams referred to it as the anniversary of the signing, and before another five years had passed both Franklin and Jefferson in writing confirmed the error.

Among the myths connected with this holiday none was more tena-
cious, nor more erroneous, than that from the nation's very beginning
the Fourth of July had been a festival of patriotism and national unity.
During the Revolutionary War, the day was every year celebrated by
festivities in which the Congress participated, but only irregularly had
the holiday been recognized by an official vote. After the end of the
Revolution, Congress had voted Fourth of July celebrations in 1785
and 1786, but not in 1787. The Massachusetts legislature in 1781 voted
the holiday its first official recognition by a state. Boston began municipal celebrations in 1783, when the town meeting voted that the former
celebration of the anniversary of the Boston Massacre (March 5, 1770)
should be regularly displaced by July 4, and that the occasion "shall
be constantly celebrated by the Delivery of a Publick Oration. . . .
In which the Orator shall consider the feelings, manners and principles
which led to this great National Event as well as the important and
happy effects whether general or domestick which already have and
will forever continue to flow from the Auspicious Epoch." But in 1787,
the year in which the Constitutional Convention was convening in
Philadelphia, Congress voted no official celebration. For over three
decades thereafter, celebrations were intensely partisan, with separate
observances by the different political parties. It became notorious
as a day of sharp political dissension, sometimes ending in violence.

Understandably, there was disagreement over the date itself. As late
as 1795 newspapers argued (on the basis of John Adams' letter quoted
above) that the proper date "of American Independence" was not
July 4 but July 2. But by then the Fourth was already too well established. And, beginning in 1788 during the bitter debate between Federalists and Antifederalists over the adoption of the newly proposed
Federal Constitution, it became a popular occasion for airing controversial views over the true nature of patriotism. In New York, Philadelphia, Hartford, and elsewhere, Federalists made party capital by
monopolizing the celebration, by identifying the sacred cause of the
Revolution with the controversial cause of the new Constitution, and by
taking the occasion generally to publicize the Federalist point of view.
Naturally enough, this irritated the Antifederalists. In Providence, for
example, one thousand citizens, headed by a judge of the Superior
Court, made an unsuccessful effort to prevent July 4 from being made
a day for celebrating the ratification (the crucial ninth state, New
Hampshire, had approved on June 21) of the Constitution. Rhode Island
had sent no delegation to the Philadelphia Convention, had been a
scene of intense popular opposition to the new Constitution, and did not
herself ratify until 1790. Citizens argued that the day "ought to be
celebrated by all instead of by a faction."

The Federalists nevertheless tried for years to dominate what might
have been a truly national holiday. The Society of Cincinnati, with

a reputation for being strongly aristocratic and Federalist, fixed their annual state meetings on the Fourth of July, and they too were accused of usurping the occasion. In Boston and Philadelphia, for example, the Federalists so successfully controlled the festivities that these became virtually party rallies. They flaunted the new Constitution, cheered Britain against France, and libelled Jefferson and the Jeffersonians. In the strongholds of Federalism (even at the Antifederalist dinners on the Fourth) Jefferson did not share public credit for his Declaration until he became Adams' Vice-President in 1797. By 1798 partisan feeling was so strong that each of the two parties held its separate processions, dinners, and orations. The spirit of the occasion was expressed in a famous toast offered that year in Boston at the Federalist celebration: "John Adams—may he like Sampson slay thousands of Frenchmen with the jawbone of Jefferson."

During these years, appeals for "unity" were really appeals for party loyalty. In Philadelphia, the Fourth of July celebrations in 1799 were divided between Federalists who were toasting Washington, Adams, Pinckney, and Marshall (but omitting Jefferson), and the Republicans who toasted Jefferson as "the statesman who drew the memorable Declaration of Independence—may his virtue and patriotism live forever in the hearts of the freemen of America." On the Fourth of July, 1800, when it seemed likely that Jefferson would be elected the next president, the Federalists at Philadelphia were already reportedly expressing doubts whether the celebration of the day should be continued at all. They even spread false rumors of Jefferson's death.

The election of Jefferson in 1801 did not so much make the Fourth of July a national holiday as simply transfer to another party (now the Republicans) an opportunity to dominate the occasion. Many Federalist papers, unlike the Republican papers, had not been publishing the Declaration of Independence on the Fourth. In New England the practice of preceding the annual oration by reading the Declaration had been discontinued about 1797. In Philadelphia on July 4, 1800, two schoolmasters walked out of a public celebration when a pupil read Jefferson's subversive document. After 1801 the Republicans were able to exclude Federalists from many official celebrations and to flaunt the Declaration as part of their celebration.

Despite an occasional truce, the two parties generally continued their separate festivities. Federalists now accused the Republicans (who had regularly been excluded from the principal observances) of only belatedly having discovered the Fourth of July, and the Republicans enjoyed the opportunity to retaliate by excluding mention of John Adams from their official accounts and celebrations of the Declaration. Republicans in Boston formed their own Washington Society (1805–22) to insure an appropriately partisan celebration, and the Federalists

then formed a counter-organization. The Boston Fourth of July celebration in 1806 reached its climax in the murder by a Federalist leader
of the son of the presiding officer of the Republican festivities. The
temper of the times was expressed by the Federalist *Columbian Centinel*
(July 17, 1811) which attacked "the advisers of Mr. Jefferson who take
pains annually to beplaister him as the draughtsman of the Declaration
of Independence," and explained that "only a small part of that
memorable instrument, as it passed, was Jefferson's and what was Jefferson's he stole from *Locke's Essays.*" Partisanship was unabated during
the War of 1812, about which New Englanders felt so strongly. It
moderated somewhat under the pacifying influence of President Monroe,
who visited Boston on the Fourth of July, 1817.

Historical uncertainties and partisan bitterness were compounded also
by local rivalries. Where there was any shred of evidence a state, a
town, or a county was glad to claim virtuous priority. Most interesting
and most successful of these efforts was the so-called "Mecklenburg
Declaration of Independence," which attracted attention after the
boasts of Virginia's priority in William Wirt's *Patrick Henry* (1817)
had irritated local patriots outside the state. Counterclaims against
Wirt soon appeared, not only, as we have seen, in Massachusetts, but
elsewhere too, and especially in North Carolina. The "Mecklenburg
Declaration of Independence" (printed in many newspapers in 1819)
was a document supposedly adopted by a meeting of elected representatives at Charlotte in Mecklenburg County, North Carolina, on March
20, 1775. This was an unambiguous Declaration of Independence of
Mecklenburg County from Great Britain, including many phrases which
by 1819 had become famous as the work of Jefferson. If genuine, it
gave the lie to Wirt's claims for Virginia by proving these people of
North Carolina to have been a full year ahead of the Continental Congress and therefore the authentic pioneers of independence. In this
case, too, Jefferson's Declaration was, to put it mildly, a good deal less
original than was generally supposed.

When John Adams first saw the "Mecklenburg Declaration"—"one of
the greatest curiosities and one of the deepest mysteries that ever occurred to me"—in June, 1819, he was shocked and puzzled. He
promptly wrote Jefferson. "How is it possible that this paper should have
been concealed from me to this day? . . . You know, if I had possessed
it, I would have made the hall of Congress echo and reecho with it
fifteen months before your Declaration of Independence. What a poor,
ignorant, malicious, short-sighted, crapulous mass is Tom Paine's
'Common Sense,' in comparison with this paper! . . . The genuine sense
of America at that moment was never expressed so well before, nor
since." He wrote the Rev. William Bentley accusing Jefferson of
plagiarism. "Mr. Jefferson . . . must have seen it, in the time of it, for

he has copied the spirit, the sense, and the expressions of it *verbatim,* into his Declaration of the 4th of July, 1776. . . ."

Jefferson's reply to Adams was that the Mecklenburg document was a hoax, like the "volcano" falsely rumored to have been found in that same part of North Carolina a few years before. North Carolina patriots were not so easily disabused. The North Carolina legislature published an official pamphlet in 1831, reprinting the Mecklenburg Declaration together with documents "proving" it genuine. While the document is sometimes used in textbooks as a classic example, like the Donation of Constantine, of a documentary hoax, some reputable historians still believe it to be genuine. The question of its authenticity is technical and complicated. Whether or not it is genuine outside North Carolina, the Mecklenburg Declaration remains an enacted tradition within the state. There its date, May 20, 1775, remains on the great seal of the state, and May 20 is a legal state holiday celebrating the *first* Declaration of Independence.

In the semicentennial year 1826, the Fourth of July was hallowed by a dramatic coincidence providentially designed to give the anniversary a new national significance. Americans had now survived a second war against Britain and had outlived repeated threats of internal cleavage to complete a full half-century of national life. This was no ordinary Fourth of July and it deserved more than an ordinary celebration. All over the country, newspapers called for festivities that would not be monopolized by "office seekers and demagogues." In the Washington *National Intelligencer,* a writer asked whether the jubilee celebration was to be observed "in the usual way, that is, by frying chickens, firing away damaged powder, or fuddling our noses over tavern wine?" During June, plans were laid all over the country, and the day itself was observed in a variety of ways—by military processions, orations, picnics, private parties, and public dinners.

In Washington, meanwhile, elaborate plans had been made by a committee of thirteen headed by the Mayor, who invited all the surviving signers of the Declaration of Independence and all ex-Presidents. Not Charles Carroll nor John Adams nor Jefferson nor Madison nor Monroe could come, but their eloquent letters of declination were printed in Washington papers. President John Quincy Adams participated in the commemoration, which included a solemn reading of the Declaration, an oration, an appeal for contributions to the fund to pay Jefferson's debts (his plantations had recently suffered from heavy late rains), and "a splendid display of fireworks." The occasion was unmarred by partisanship. Within two days thereafter arrived the news that Jefferson had died at Monticello at midday on the Fourth. Another two days brought word that John Adams too had died at Quincy on the Fourth.

This dual coincidence seemed to Adams' son, President John Quincy

Adams, a "visible and palpable" sign of "Divine favor" to the founders and to the nation. In his double eulogy in the House of Representatives in Washington later that year, William Wirt went still further:

> Hitherto, fellow-citizens, the Fourth of July had been celebrated among us, only as the anniversary of our independence, and its votaries had been merely human beings. But at its last recurrence —the great Jubilee of the nation—the anniversary, it may well be termed, of the liberty of man—Heaven, itself, mingled visibly in the celebration, and hallowed the day anew by a double apotheosis.

In remoter places, far from the sophisticated political animosities of the eastern capitals, a cruder conviviality regularly marked the day. The members of the Lewis and Clark expedition far beyond the Mississippi celebrated with "a sumptuous dinner of fat saddles of venison." Josiah Gregg reported the dawning of the Fourth of July, 1831, as he and his party were encamped at McNees' Creek about two hundred miles northeast of Santa Fe:

> Scarce had gray twilight brushed his dusky brow, when our patriotic camp gave lively demonstrations of that joy which plays around the heart of every American on the anniversary of this triumphant day. The roar of our artillery and rifle platoons resounded from every hill, while the rumbling of the drum and the shrill whistle of the fife, imparted a degree of martial interest to the scene which was well calculated to stir the souls of men. There was no limit to the huzzas and enthusiastic ejaculations of our people; and at every new shout the dales around sent forth a gladsome response. This anniversary is always hailed with heart-felt joy by the wayfarer in the remote desert; for here the strifes and intrigues of party-spirit are unknown: nothing intrudes, in these wild solitudes, to mar that harmony of feeling, and almost pious exultation, which every true-hearted American experiences on this great day.

A dozen years later, John C. Frémont's party on their way to the Pacific Northwest, stopped for their Fourth of July celebration at St. Vrain's Fort in distant Colorado.

In the upstart cities, seeking rituals to bind them together and elevate their community, the Fourth was the time to dedicate a hotel or to open a college.

The Fourth of July Oration soon produced a rhetoric so distinctive that it took the name of the holiday. "Our usual synonyme for bombast and mere rhetorical patriotism is 'a Fourth of July oration,'" observed a supercilious writer on "Holidays" in the *North American Review* (April, 1857), ". . . Pickwickian sentiment, pyrotechnic flashes, torpedos, arrests, bursting cannon, draggled flags, crowded steamboats, the disgust of the educated, and the uproar of the multitude, make up the confused and wearisome details of what should and might be a sacred feast, a pious memory, a hallowed consecration, a 'Sabbath-day of Freedom.' " East, West, North, or South, the Oration was the featured performance on what even a New England writer had to call "our only holiday which can strictly be called national." It was no accident that statesmen and writers often won their first public notice by a particularly eloquent Fourth of July oration. William Tudor's first widely published effort was such an oration in 1809. Daniel Webster's first public oratorical effort, already revealing the style which would bring him fame and fortune, was his Fourth of July Oration, delivered when he was only eighteen to the citizens of Hanover, New Hampshire, and his many later orations on the same anniversary helped keep him in the public eye. John Quincy Adams' first public effort was his Fourth of July Oration, commissioned by the city of Boston when he was not yet 26. George Bancroft's Fourth of July Oration at Springfield in 1826 was his first long prose effort.

Among the more notorious was Artemus Ward's Fourth of July Oration at Weathersfield, Connecticut, in 1859.

Feller Citizens—I hain't got time to notis the growth of Ameriky frum the time when the Mayflowers cum over in the Pilgrim and brawt Plymouth Rock with them, but every skool boy nose our kareer has been tremenjis. You will excuse me if I don't prase the erly settlers of the Kolonies. Peple which hung idiotic old wimin for witches, burnt holes in Quakers' tongues and consined their feller critters to the tredmill and pillery on the slitest provocashun may hav bin very nice folks in their way, but I must confess I don't admire their stile, and will pass them by. I spose they ment well, and so, in the novel and techin langwidge of the nusepapers, "peas to their ashis." Thare was no diskount, however, on them brave men who fit, bled and died in the American Revolushun. We needn't be afraid of setting 'em up too steep. Like my show, they will stand any amount of prase. G. Washington was abowt the best man this world ever sot eyes on. He was a clear-heded, warm-harted, and stiddy goin man. He never slopt over! The prevailin weakness of most public men is to SLOP OVER! [Put them words in large letters—A.W.] They git filled up and slop. They Rush Things. They travel too much on the high presher principle. They git on to the fust poplar hobby-hoss whitch trots along, not carin a sent whether the beest is even going, clear sited and sound or spavined, blind and bawky. Of course they git throwed eventooally, if not sooner. When they see the multitood goin it blind they go Pel Mel with it, instid of exertin their-selves to set it right. They can't see that the crowd which is now bearin them triumfantly on its shoulders will soon diskiver its error and cast them into the hoss pond of Oblivyun, without the slitest hesitashun. Washington never slopt over. That wasn't George's stile. He luved his country dearly. He wasn't after the spiles. He was a human angil in a 3 kornerd hat and knee britches, and we shan't see his like

right away. My frends, we can't all be Washingtons but we kin all
be patrits & behave ourselves in a human and a Christian manner.
When we see a brother goin down hill to Ruin let us not give him
a push, but let us seeze rite hold of his coat-tails and draw him
back to Morality.

*   *   *

Through all these Fourth of July utterances ran at least two motifs:
The Booster Spirit: A National Style with Retrospective Emphasis.
Fourth of July rhetoric expressed for the nation as a whole what booster
language, tall talk, and the language of aspiration expressed for upstart
communities of the Southwest and West. The essentials of the spirit were
the same—the optimism, the enthusiasm, the vagueness of line between
fact and hope, between what had actually happened and what ought to
have happened. Just as the city-booster was undaunted, or even stimulated, by the crudity or non-existence of the community he was praising,
so the nation-booster was undiscouraged by the inchoateness of the
nation he was extolling. The Fourth of July Spirit was a kind of Nationa.
Spiritual Hotel, built prematurely in order to be ready for occupancy
when the nation would appear.

The hazier the outlines of the nation, the more necessary the language
of reassurance. The extravagance of Fourth of July rhetoric was thus a
measure less of the depth than of the uncertainties of national patriotism.
"This anniversary animates, and gladdens, and unites all American
hearts," pollyanna'd Daniel Webster at the capital celebration on July 4,
1851, when the nation was riven by sectional passions. "On other days
of the year we may be party men, indulging in controversies, more or less
important to the public good . . . but today we are Americans all; and
nothing but Americans." The highest praise the imaginative James
Parton could give Andrew Jackson in his popular biography published
just before the outbreak of the Civil War, was to call Jackson "the most
American of Americans—an embodied Declaration of Independence—
the Fourth of July incarnate."

The superlative here was the "first." The nonpareil Declaration of
Independence announced the "beginning" of the nation. It was only one
example of a celebration of "firsts" which continued to mark American
life and to puzzle foreigners. The brevity of American history simply
exaggerated the tendency. Americans measured their priorities with
vernier calipers rather than with a historical yardstick. From the "First
Families of Virginia" to the First Presbyterian Church (as Wesley Frank
Craven remarks), Americans would compete in their boasts of priority.
American history itself seemed a virgin continent, wide open to squatters,
where honor and wealth came to whoever was there first. Absolute
priority was the most indisputable form of superlative.

Celebration as Justification: A Nation "Conceived in Liberty."
Americans had made their nation's holiday a festival of justification. The Day affirmed a national purpose. To read and celebrate the Declaration of Independence was not simply to commemorate the nation's birth; it was to celebrate the *reasons* for the nation's birth, to announce and reaffirm the arguments and purposes of national existence. Thus already Americans betrayed their lasting preoccupation (and uneasiness) about the purposes of their national existence. Americans had begun by assuming that, if there was to be a new nation here, it must be for good reasons and for a good purpose.

The Fourth of July became only one of many American rituals—perhaps they should be called "orgies"—of self-justification. In the United States, national existence and national "purpose" became strangely indistinguishable. The great holiday of the nation was an occasion to affirm, in John Adams' phrase, "the principles and feelings which contributed to produce the Revolution."

Americans, more than other peoples, would continue to be haunted by the question of their "national purpose." Older nations assumed their existence had been ratified by God and History without their needing regularly to produce a Declaration of the reasons for their existence. But the American nation had been born in an act of justification. The Declaration had in the first instance been an utterance to the whole world, and not merely to Americans. The nation had from the beginning set itself the task of continuing to show that it had a world mission, and to justify its mission to the world. By fixing on the Fourth of July, the Americans had chosen the strange course of making their chief patriotic holiday a day of re-explaining their nation's purpose and justifying it to all mankind. This was never better expressed than in Jefferson's letter, written only a few days before his death, regretting his inability to attend the Jubilee celebration in Washington on July 4, 1826, and explaining the meaning of the occasion:

> May it be to the world, what I believe it will be, (to some parts sooner, to others later, but finally to all,) the signal of arousing men to burst the chains, under which monkish ignorance and superstition had persuaded them to bind themselves, and to assume the blessings and security of self-government. The form which we have substituted restores the free right to the unbounded exercise of reason and freedom of opinion. All eyes are opened or opening to the rights of man. The general spread of the light of science has already laid open to every view the palpable truth, that the mass of mankind has not been born with saddles on their backs, nor a favored few, booted and spurred, ready to ride them legitimately, by the grace of God. These are grounds of hope for others; for ourselves, let the annual return of this day forever refresh our recollections of these rights, and an undiminished devotion to them.

PART EIGHT

A SPACIOUS REPUBLIC

> "Confederations are a mongrel kind of government, and the world does not afford a precedent to go by."
>
> ELBRIDGE GERRY

THE United States would be the largest nation long to survive with a republican government, yet would comprise smaller and more numerous and more effective and more competitive independent subdivisions than did any of the republican governments of the Old World. The American political "system" would be a witness both to the novelty of the New World and to the limits of all statesmen's abilities to predict, to project, or to circumscribe political growth. Political parties would be essential—the true centers of power and purpose—yet they would be hardly recognized by law.

Elsewhere the making of a political nation had commonly been the work of a strong province—a Prussia, a Savoy, or an Île-de-France—imposing its will on others; or of an invader—a William the Conqueror or a Napoleon—imposing his administration on a disorganized people. But the United States somehow became a nation spontaneously, strengthened by the very forces of diffusion. Of the many comforting illusions none was to be more seductive than that the American way of government could remain unchanged, or that it could be imprisoned in one generation's conscious purposes.

43

The Imperial Vagueness:
From Sovereignty to Federalism

THE AMERICAN REVOLUTION was a war of secession, and not only in a political sense. It was another way of seceding from European ways of thinking, another dissolving of Old World absolutes. It was, in part, precipitated by the obstinate European insistence that growing, ill-defined institutions should fit obsolete, irrelevant theories.

In Western Europe, modern nations grew through the consolidation of power. In England, for example, in the later middle ages, strong rulers like Henry I and Henry II organized a central administration and used itinerant judges to establish a "common law," while a rising Parliament drew decisions to the center; thus the nation grew through the strengthening of centripetal forces. All over Europe, similarly, centralization was a synonym for the rise of nations.

When the British empire expanded across the Atlantic Ocean in the 17th century, new problems arose. Communities in America had interests more unpredictable and more diverse than those of even the most remote British counties. Obviously, it was wise that their government should be co-ordinated with that of the rest of Britain, yet their remoteness and the irregularity of communication made central control difficult or impossible. Even the most prudent, flexible, far-sighted British administrators could not adapt their programs to colonial conditions if they did not know these conditions or if their information, at best, was months out of date. Of the many circumstances which led to the diffusion of government powers and responsibilities into the different colonial centers, none was more important than the lack of communications. After the middle of the 18th century, communications began to improve, but by then it was too late. A working federalism had already developed. An American political system, the hope and the tribulation of the new United States, had grown slowly out of the conditions of colonial life.

The desultory communications between England and the colonies provide a clue to how the political powers of the colonies grew. Until 1755 there was no regular mail service with England. The Lords of the Committee of Trade and Plantations (after 1696, the Board of Trade)— who were charged with colonial affairs, with instructing the colonial governors, and with uniting the colonies to the empire—had to depend on the haphazard good offices of friendly merchant vessels. While such communication might be frequent enough to preserve ties of kinship, language, literature, and craftsmanship, it was too feeble and irregular to serve as the channel of government.

Colonies whose shores were touched by small coasting ships but by few ocean-going vessels, had no effective direct connection with "home." The Governor of North Carolina, for example, normally received his communications by way of Virginia, which in turn often received its by way of New York. In June, 1745, for example, the Board of Trade in London wrote Governor Johnson complaining that it had received no letter from him for three years. A year later he replied from North Carolina that their letter had only just reached him. Lacking a good ocean port, North Carolina was more isolated than other colonies, but even from the best harbors communications were slow and dilatory. Boston, for example, was usually incommunicado during the whole winter. The letters that a diligent Massachusetts governor wrote in the late fall would normally not be delivered to the Board of Trade in London before April or May. Such delays meant that the Board, which was supposed to give current information to Parliament before the expiration of its session, was actually supplying facts at least a year out of date.

The perils of war also obstructed communications. Between 1689 and the year of the Stamp Act, Britain was in a declared war with at least one European enemy for nearly half the time. Even if all went well and the mail finally reached an English port, delays were not at an end. Sometimes packages of papers addressed to the Board of Trade lay undelivered in the customs house for a year or more. To avoid such delays, letters were frequently passed from person to person, but with the result that confidential communications had become public information long before they were delivered. Since the Board of Trade's letters did not normally have free passage through the mails, the Board tried to cut its postal bill by holding its communications which would be transmitted in large bundles through unofficial channels. Not until 1755 was a regular monthly packet boat scheduled between Falmouth and New York.

By mid-18th century it was already too late for London to tighten the reins on the colonial governments. Distance, irregular communications, and the variety and urgency of local problems had created at least thirteen centers of government in America. This dispersion of powers did not follow anyone's plan; it was not the application of a theory; it did not express the "principles" of any known constitution. It grew fitfully and gradually in the century and a half between the earliest permanent British settlements and the outbreak of the American Revolution. The political machinery of the British Empire thus was anything but neat; without anyone's intending it, a working federalism had grown up in America.

Confusion in England and the inadequacy of the British government for imperial administration had something to do with it too. During the crucial early decades of the 18th century, the Board of Trade was supposed to be governing the colonies, but the Secretary of State for the Southern Department controlled the colonial patronage and appointed the colonial governors, who were sometimes enemies of the Board of Trade and spent their energies intriguing against it. The exigencies of English domestic politics led ministers to use colonial governorships to reward followers who had neither competence nor interest in administration. Nominal governors (in Virginia, for example) often drew their salary as a sinecure, while leaving their powers in the hands of a substitute. All this made for a vagueness and vacillation of British policy, while opening the way for the rise of effective centers of government on the American side. As royal governors became progressively weaker during the 18th century, colonial assemblies filled the vacuum.

These colonial assemblies, using, among others, their power to levy taxes and hence to withhold salaries, gradually dominated. Governors sent out from London, though vocal, tended to become increasingly impotent. Meanwhile, in every one of the thirteen colonies, groups of men acquired the experience and enjoyed the satisfactions of meeting in their own legislatures. In New England and wherever New Englanders carried their institutions, town meetings further enlarged the opportunities for self-government. Thus American federalism grew out of the colonial experience.

By 1760, then, there had grown up a composite empire; it was (in Andrew C. McLaughlin's phrase) "an empirical empire, an opportunistic empire, . . . an empire which the Englishmen . . . did not understand." Inchoate, ill-defined, asymmetrical, and vaguely seen, decades before the Constitutional Convention of 1787 it provided in practice a distribution of powers which would become the American federal system.

The large features of the composite empire were simple enough. A central authority ("The Crown") controlled foreign affairs, administered the army and the navy, declared war and made peace, managed the post office (such as it was), took charge of Indian affairs, and controlled certain lands within the colonies and in the backlands. The Parliament in London did not legislate for the purely internal affairs of the colonies, but primarily to control their trade and navigation, or on such matters as naturalization or currency—matters which plainly touched all the empire. The mercantilist notions of trade and wealth, which aimed at a self-sufficient empire, sometimes intruded into the domestic economy of a colony, yet such intrusions were few. Each colony did most of its own legislating. An inhabitant of Virginia or Massachusetts found his daily life governed primarily, in fact almost exclusively, by laws from his own colonial assembly—although there did loom in the background the extreme possibilities of royal disallowance or of appeal to the Privy Council. Underneath all, of course, lay the English common law, but even this the colonists explicitly modified. As locally applied, by judges increasingly independent of London, the common law was continually being fitted to local needs and local prejudices. With few changes, this would remain, in outline, the American federal arrangement in the 19th and 20th centuries.

Long before these practical arrangements of a British Empire had evolved, the theoretical foundations of the modern state had been accumulating in western Europe—at least since the 15th century. But the imperial arrangements arose with very little regard for (and in many ways inconsistent with) the modern doctrine. A new theory of "sovereignty," for example, had asserted that, essential to the very concept of a state, was a single supreme power, with the sole power to legislate. Feudalism had flourished on various theories of divided and distributed and reciprocal powers, but the modern nation—England or France, for example—became possible only as people accepted the notion that there was in every state a "sovereignty" (supreme power), unitary and indivisible. In France in 1576, Jean Bodin gave classic form to the concept of sovereignty. Every state, he said, possessed one supreme "high and perpetual power," unlimited and unlimitable. Then in England, in the 17th century, Hobbes' *Leviathan* (1651) again insisted that the sovereign power was indivisible. Locke's *Civil Government* (1690), still preoccupied with an indivisible "sovereignty," now located it in the people themselves, in those who had created government. As the modern state grew in Europe, then, the dogma became more and more widespread that the power of government could not be divided. From the early 17th century, while American experience was creating a working federal arrangement, European thinkers were busy asserting that such an arrangement was inconceivable or inconsistent with the very existence of a modern state.

No wonder transatlantic understanding became difficult. The very ideas which had justified and explained the latest development in European government seemed to deny the American experience. Colonial life had produced a working federalism, while European life and thought had produced a dogmatic absolute called "sovereignty." The English state itself (as Maitland was later to point out) was "singularly unicellular." "In sovereignty," Dr. Samuel Johnson asserted in *Taxation no Tyranny* (1774), "there are no gradations." If sovereignty was by definition indivisible, on theoretical, *a priori* grounds, the colonial legislatures (whatever they may actually have been doing) could have no fragment of this sovereign power. From the point of view of the newly dominant ways of European political thought, America was not merely an anachronism; it was an impossibility. This was not the first nor the last time European thought would prove inadequate to American realities.

At the same time, the proverbial British practicality was never less fertile. Many Britons saw no reasonable alternatives for an outlying people between "absolute dependence" and "absolute independence." This theoretic rigidity had long caused trouble for them in Ireland, and now it caused trouble in America. If, they said, Parliament could legislate for the colonies at all, the Parliamentary powers must be unlimited.

American experience had far outrun English (or European) theory. Colonial legislatures, in control of local and internal matters over which faraway London was powerless, were content to leave to London the broad questions of imperial policy, trade, and navigation which required the power of the British navy. Americans had worked out a *modus vivendi* which, with occasional adaptions to the shifting needs of empire, might have continued to function indefinitely. When, in the 1760's, the British government tried to tighten its rein on the American colonies, London was defying the facts of life.

As the conflict sharpened, British writers, hoping to exorcise the mysterious spirit of American rebellion, simply chanted more insistently their beautiful absolutes. The British chorus became a liturgy. The colonies, wrote one Briton in 1769, "must either acknowledge the legislative power of Great Britain in its full extent, or set themselves up as independent states; I say in its full extent, because if there be any reserve in their obedience, which they can legally claim, they must have a power within themselves superior to that of the mother country; for her obedience to the legislature is without limitation." "It is impossible," insisted Governor Hutchinson of Massachusetts in 1773, "there should be two independent Legislatures in the one and the same state." In these loyal phrases, Britons asserted the impossibility of what had long since come into being.

Until nearly the year of Independence, Britons were offering theories against which Americans were posing facts. The British asserted and reasserted the theory of "sovereignty"—pure and incorruptible, one and indivisible and undiffusible—neatly and convincingly supported from the best authorities. Their American antagonists answered not with theories but with facts, not with logic but with experience. Overcome by admiration of their own logic, the British forgot that it was a growing community, now including a large New World, about which they were talking. The British constitution had proved adequate to these expanding needs, but British politicians and political theorists now did not.

This contrast appeared dramatically when Benjamin Franklin, loyal Britisher and salty colonial, at that time Deputy Postmaster-General of North America, testified before the House of Commons in London, February 3–13, 1766. The Stamp Act, passed in the preceding year, had raised a storm and Parliament was debating its repeal. Franklin, recently arrived from Pennsylvania, was questioned at length on the American point of view. On matters of legal theory and imperial doctrine, he was unclear, even confused; he was awkward and ill at ease in the world of neat legalisms. But he was irresistible in the world of fact. He explained how loyally the colonies had borne the heavy burden of Britain's imperial wars. Pennsylvania alone had spent half a million pounds (with only about ten per cent rebated by the crown) on the French and Indian Wars. He reported the scarcity of currency. He described the impossibility of coercing the colonists to pay the stamp tax. In both the weakness of his theories and the strength of his facts, Franklin epitomized the new nation.

Within three weeks after Franklin had told the Commons of the costly consequences of the Stamp Act and had explained why it was unenforceable, they voted (March 4) for its repeal. On the same day (March 18) that the repeal became law, Parliament desperately reassured itself by enacting its theory of absolute sovereignty into a new "Declaratory Act," which proclaimed that Parliament could legislate for the colonists "in all cases whatsoever." Understandably enough, Franklin declared himself "quite sick" of such phrases as "our sovereignty."

From the New World came a stream of theories, none quite convincing, to defend the working composite empire. The American arguments were impressive for their passion and ingenuity but not for their logic. John Dickinson, for example, in his *Letters from a Farmer in Pennsylvania* (1768), testing British claims by what he imagined to be the theory of the British constitution, insisted on a distinction between Parliament's power to regulate trade (which he conceded) and its power to tax (which he denied). John Adams, in his *Novanglus* papers (1775), was learned and eloquent. The heart of the British argument, he said, was that "Parliament is the only supreme, sovereign, absolute and uncontrollable legislative power over all the colonies." But the only proper authority of Parliament over them, Adams retorted, was "to regulate their trade, and this not by any principle of common law, but merely by the consent of the colonies, founded on the obvious necessity." He appealed to the law of God, the law of nature and of nations, the common law of England. Despite the weightiness of his learning and the subtlety of his mind, Adams' argument provided no political theory adequate to the American cause. His most effective assertions were counsels of prudence.

"The law of brickbats and cannon balls," Adams warned the British, ". . . can be answered only by brickbats and cannon balls." He expressed the spirit of his argument when he concluded by reminding Britain's "noblemen and ignoblemen . . . . that Americans understand the laws of politics as well as themselves, and that there are six hundred thousand men in it, between sixteen and sixty years of age; and therefore it will be very difficult to chicane them out of their liberties by 'fictions of law' . . . no matter upon what foundations."

Americans offered all sorts of distinctions—between kinds of legislation, between kinds of jurisdictions, between kinds of taxation, between realms and islands and territories—in all conceivable forms, in speeches and pamphlets and magazines and books and declarations. The great strength of the American position, however, was not in theory. The strongest American arguments finally were historical (like Jefferson's *Summary View* in 1774) or narrowly constitutional (like the specific list of grievances in the Declaration of Independence). *Common Sense* (January, 1776), by Thomas Paine, who had only two years before arrived in America, was an effective, if crude, polemic for independence, but it was hardly a profound or durable theory of government. Paine, anxious to propagandize for revolutionary causes, turned the "sovereignty" absolutes of Tory metaphysicians upside down and proclaimed absolutes of his own which had not much more to do with the case. John Adams, who had a better understanding of the American cause, offered an antidote to Paine's simples and absolutes in his *Thoughts on Government* (1776), where he argued for "mixed" government, and especially for a two-chamber legislature, to be immune from "fits of humor, starts of passion, flights of enthusiasm . . . hasty results and absurd judgments."

Too few Englishmen in high places dared face the full complexity of the unwelcome facts. Too few shared Edmund Burke's vision of the power of history, of the impossibility of erasing the experience of liberty by the logic of "sovereignty." "If that sovereignty and their freedom cannot be reconciled," Burke warned, "which will they take? They will cast your sovereignty in your face, nobody will be argued into slavery." Burke was right.

The Americans and the British were talking at cross purposes: the British were doctrinaire, appealing to the disembodied abstractions for which "revolutionaries" have since become notorious; while the Americans were appealing to history and to experience. In answering Dr. Johnson's dogmatic *Taxation no Tyranny,* an American explained in 1775:

> Now the present dispute is not with respect to this Island alone, which certainly has but one Legislature, but with respect to the British Empire at large, in which there are many Legislatures; or many Assemblies claiming to be so. Here is the fallacy of your position. . . . It is in some degree a new case in legislation, and must be governed therefore more by its own circumstances, and by the genius of our peculiar Constitution, than by abstract notions of Government at large.

However unequal to political theory, Americans had long proved fertile of projects for confederating communities into new and varied combinations. Congregationalism itself was a plan of confederation. From the New England Confederacy (formed in 1643) through Franklin's Albany Plan of Union (1754), the First Continental Congress (1774), the Articles of Confederation (1781), and the Federal Constitution itself, Americans showed a tireless ingenuity in their schemes for affiliating governments—for dividing and diffusing "sovereignty"—in novel ways. The scattered population, the vast and varied continent, the remoteness from "home"—all nourished a federal experimentalism. This experimental spirit, born with the colonies, would flourish with the nation.

44

The Federal Vagueness: Born in Secession

FROM A EUROPEAN point of view, the creation of the United States was topsy-turvy. Its very existence was a paradox. Modern nations of Western Europe, like France or England, had been founded when a power at the center succeeded in dominating the local units. But the United States was born when thirteen separate regional governments asserted their powers against the central authority in London. The nation was a by-product of the assertion of each colony's right to govern itself.

The new nation was relatively free of chauvinism, for there had been no widespread, intense, or calculating national spirit. Perhaps, in some distant past, the national spirit of European nations had also first arisen spontaneously and unselfconsciously; but, at least from the late 18th and early 19th century, nationalism in Europe was, for the most part, self-conscious, elaborately articulated, and passionate. The whole political future of the United States would be shaped by the fact that the nation had not been born in any ecstasy of nationalist passion.

The new nation had the added advantage of unashamed variety, fluidity, and cultural anarchy. American speech remained ungoverned, brash, explosive, and expansive, and Americans were luckily free of the Royal Academies and National Academies that tended to cast cultures in respectable molds. But there were disadvantages too: a weakening of the faculties of controversy and intellectual distinction, a diffuseness and dispersion of cultural resources, a feebleness and uncertainty of political power, and a continuing secessionist tradition.

The United States, then, was not conceived in chauvinistic sin. A price of this virtue was that between the Revolution and the Civil War the national politics was overcast by a federal vagueness. But Americans would not permanently escape the price of chauvinism: the price in hate and blood for the making of nations. With characteristic anachronism, Americans had their nation first and paid the price afterwards. The full price would not be paid until nearly a century after the nation declared its independence.

Before independence, Americans were both British subjects and citizens of Massachusetts, New York, Virginia, or some other colony. After independence, they ceased to be Britons, but had not yet become Americans. There was not yet an American nation to command their loyalty. Still they remained Virginians, or colonists of some other stripe, and their primary and continuing loyalty remained to their own colony, now become a state.

Although Americans lacked the feudal past which plagued European nation-makers in their efforts to unify their countries, there was an American counterpart. Here space played the role of time. If American history had been brief, American geography somehow made up the difference. In the great American emptiness, varied local governments, economies, and traditions were separated from one another by wilderness and rivers and mountains, which speedily created differences elsewhere created by centuries. There were American analogues to the barbarian invasions: in Europe, these had been spread periodically over many centuries; in America, the Indian menace was constant but geographically epidemic. The time-table for political institutions was fantastically accelerated in America as the numerous new states, legislatures, executives, courts, and municipalities were created with unprecedented speed. In Europe the powerful local diversities were, for the most part, the institutional detritus of time. In America they were largely the effects of topography, climate, and physical distance. While European politics was primarily the by-product of history, American politics was primarily a by-product of geography.

The political task of the new nation was quickly to form a government strong enough to hold together the colonial fragments. The ties of language, kinship, myth, history, and tradition required centuries, but the geographic distances and variations that nourished American independence had already created many separate units, jealous of their rights. And the American cause had rested on the belief that these colonial governments could not be created, controlled, or dissolved from afar, that these thirteen separate governments held powers to govern themselves which arose out of the American situation itself. Without the Crown and Empire, where were they to look?

The great symbol of both the strength and the weakness of the American cause was the lack of a single colonial capital. The same sentiments that made any region unwilling to defer to another, that prevented any one of the leading towns from becoming the undisputed political or literary capital of the colonies, had diffused the military defense into every one of the thirteen capitals, and even into the homes and farms of those who cared enough to fight at all. It was as significant for American politics as we have already noted it to be for American military tradition that, during the first four years of the Revolution, every one of the most populous towns (Boston, New York, Philadelphia, and Charleston) had fallen to British troops without decisive effect. If the American colonies seemed a thirteen-headed monster to any colonist who wished them to act in unison, this was also a great advantage against enemies: there was no one head or center where an enemy could deliver a mortal blow. When the new federal government would later require a capital, the solution would be to create a new city as a political headquarters; that city would not in any other sense be the capital of the nation.

The new nation, until the Civil War, was commonly described in the plural, which unwittingly expressed the emotional fact. For John Adams in 1774, Massachusetts Bay was "our country" and the Massachusetts delegation in Congress was "our embassy." For Jefferson, too, until much later, "my country" commonly meant Virginia. Richard Henry Lee's momentous resolution (introduced in the Continental Congress June 7, 1776, seconded by John Adams; adopted July 2, 1776) declared "That *these* United Colonies are, and of right ought to be, free and independent *States*." The provisions of the Lee Resolutions, declaring the intention of the states to form foreign alliances and to confederate among themselves, were familiar enough among a group of independent nations collaborating to wage war. The heading of the final engrossed version of the Declaration of Independence described the document as "The unanimous Declaration of the *thirteen* united States of America." The preamble concluded by referring to "the patient sufferance of *these Colonies*" who were now led to alter "their former Systems of Government" by the injuries and usurpations of the King of Great Britain aiming at "an absolute Tyranny over *these States*." (Italics added) The concluding paragraph proclaimed the (plural) independence of these "Free and Independent States," and affirmed "that as Free and Independent States, they have full Power to levy War, conclude Peace, contract Alliances, establish Commerce, and to do all other Acts and Things which Independent States may of right do." Oddly enough, this national birth certificate nowhere referred to the nation; all references were to the separate states. An unsuspecting historian a thousand years hence might (in the absence of other evidence) assume that the Declaration brought into being thirteen new and separate nations, whose names appeared above those of the delegates signing for them.

This habit of thinking and feeling state-by-state was slow to disappear. "My happiness," Oliver Ellsworth of Connecticut declared in the Federal Convention in 1787, "depends as much on the existence of my State government, as a new-born infant depends upon its mother for nourishment." The "mother-country" had been replaced by mother-states. "What we want," urged the Federalist Fisher Ames in 1792, "is not a change in forms. We have paper enough blotted with theories of government. The habits of thinking are to be reformed. Instead of feeling as a Nation, a State is our country. We look with indifference, often with hatred, fear, and aversion to the other States."

The diversity of the colonies had been frequently noted both by casual travelers and by long residents. In times of stress, London politicians were reassured that the colonies would never unite against the mother-country. "There can be no room for real apprehension of danger of a revolt of the plantations in future ages," the Rev. Hugh Jones noted as early as 1724. "Or if any of them should attempt it, they might very easily be reduced by the others; for all of them will never unite with one another; for although all the plantations agree in this, that they all belong to, and depend entirely upon Great Britain, they have each views different from one another, and as strenuously pursue their separate interests, by various and distinct methods." Experience had already shown, Franklin asserted in 1760, that, except in the "impossible" event of "grievous tyranny and oppression," no effective union among the colonies could be imagined.

> If they could not agree to unite for their defence against the French and Indians, who were perpetually harrassing their settlements, burning their villages, and murdering their people; can it reasonably be supposed there is any danger of their uniting against their own nation, which protects and encourages them, with which they have so many connections and ties of blood, interest and affection, and which 'tis

well known they all love much more than they love one another? In
short, there are so many causes that must operate to prevent it, that
I will venture to say, an union amongst them for such a purpose is not
merely improbable, it is impossible; and if the union of the whole
is impossible, the attempt of a part must be madness: as those colonies,
that did not join the rebellion, would join the mother country in
suppressing it.

Diversity of interests, rooted in a diversity of geography and economy
and in the relatively shallow colonial past, bred a diversity of principles.
This itself helped give the War for Independence its non-ideological
flavor, compared with the historic European rebellions of the 17th, 18th,
and 19th centuries. The Revolution, as John Adams later explained, had
expressed "principles as various as the 13 states that went through it,
and in some sense almost as diversified as the individuals who acted in
it." So local were the sentiments that in Virginia, for example, the
Revolution was sometimes called (1780–81) the "Tobacco War." In
each colony the war was being fought for its local autonomy—for its
right to use its money for its own purposes, to keep its men close to
home, and not to have its treasure drained for anyone's large policies.
Why should colonists who had jealously guarded their autonomy against
the ancient Parliament and Lord Loudoun recklessly give up their autonomy to a novel Continental Congress and George Washington?

The continuity of American history is impressive. It should not be
obscured by any supposed "revolution." To many thoughtful colonists
the War for Independence seemed but a logical sequel to British history
of the previous century and a half. From a British Whig point of view, it
was a second civil war, a fight to extend and localize in America the
principles of the Glorious Revolution of 1689. And it provided the basis
for a secessionist tradition which shook the new nation in the 19th
century. The struggle for a new nation was not to be completed until
1865 or after.

"The colonies," as John Adams remarked, "had grown up under
constitutions of government so different, there was so great a variety of
religions, they were composed of so many different nations, their customs, manners, and habits had so little resemblance, and their intercourse
had been so rare, and their knowledge of each other so imperfect, that to
unite them in the same principles in theory and the same system of
action, was certainly a very difficult enterprise." Insofar as some unity
had been accomplished by 1783, it was largely an unintended by-product
of the War itself. During the War, many shared the suspicion that James
Madison expressed in 1781, writing from the Congress in Philadelphia
to Thomas Jefferson back in Virginia, as a caution (to be communicated
to the House of Burgesses) against Virginia's cession of her western
lands to the precarious new government. "The present Union," Madison

said they should presume, "will but little survive the present War. . . . they ought to be as fully impressed with the necessity of the Union during the war as of its probable dissolution after it."

Independence had created not one nation but thirteen. And if the Articles of Confederation produced a "United States," it was in much the same sense in which the Charter of 1945 created a "United Nations." "Each state retains its sovereignty, freedom and independence," declared the Articles (Art. II) "and every Power, Jurisdiction and right, which is not by the confederation expressly delegated to the United States, in Congress assembled." Each state was represented by "delegates" paid by itself, "annually appointed in such manner as the legislature of each state shall direct, to meet in Congress on the first Monday in November, in every year with a power reserved to each state, to recal its delegates, or any of them, at any time within the year, and to send others in their stead, for the remainder of the Year." (Art. V) Voting on all matters was by states, each state casting a single vote. All central powers were exercised by "the united states in congress assembled" of which nine had to agree to measures of any consequence. (Art. IX) Thus any five states could prevent action either by not sending delegates to the congress, or by refusing to vote for the action. If only nine states happened to be represented at a session, and some states were represented by two delegates, the vote of only one delegate could prevent an affirmative vote of his state and hence obstruct all business. In any event the congress of the Confederation lacked power to raise money by taxation or to regulate trade.

This new central government was even weaker than that of the London government had been while the Empire was still functioning amicably. Some of the powers once exercised by the Crown (for example, appointment of governors and disallowance of local laws) were not exercised by the Continental Congress nor under the Articles of Confederation. But the Articles (proposed 1777; in operation 1781–89) did expressly give to "the united states in congress assembled" certain powers formerly exercised by the Crown (for example: declarations of war and peace; conduct of foreign affairs and Indian relations; control of the alloy and value of coins and of interstate postal service). And before the Articles went into operation, Maryland, a smaller state without western lands, had procured a cession of western lands to Congress as a price of participation. Thus Congress did control the extension of the empire: the Articles of Confederation were thus a product of imperial history, and the new "nation" was an improvised substitute for empire. What is remarkable is not that a strong central government was not immediately organized, but that any appeared at all. Hindsight might mislead one into thinking there must have been something churlish or obtuse in those unwilling to create a powerful central government at one stroke. Actually, they were showing a prudence rare among men who use force to overturn old evils. They were anxious lest their blood and treasures should have been spent merely to exchange one tyrant for another.

45

Quests for Definition: Constitutions of the United States

IN GREAT BRITAIN, the "constitution" was the whole sum of charters, statutes, declarations, traditions, informal understandings, habits, and attitudes by which the government was actually administered. Technically speaking, then, there was no such thing as a British statute being invalid because it was "unconstitutional": any British statute could change the constitution. There was no "constitution" by which a court could test legislation.

And there was thus nothing more definite, nor more uncertain, than the British constitution; it was only another name for the way things really worked. Even at the time of the American Revolution, the primary and most common meaning of "constitution" referred to the general state of health of any organism. To say that a person had a good "constitution" was to say that he actually functioned well; similarly with a government. To have said, then, that a governmental act was "unconstitutional" would have been a contradiction in terms, or meaningless.

"The supposition of law," Sir William Blackstone wrote in 1765, "therefore, is, that neither the king nor either house of parliament, collectively taken, is capable of doing any wrong; since in such cases the law feels itself incapable of furnishing any adequate remedy. For which reason all oppressions which may happen to spring from any branch of the sovereign power, must necessarily be out of the reach of any *stated rule,* or *express legal* provision; but if ever they unfortunately happen, the prudence of the times must provide new remedies upon new emergencies."

This was the state of British thinking when Americans began to make the most intense and prolific efforts of modern times at constitutional definition. They adopted a separate written constitution for each seceding colony, and one for the nation. Before the Civil War, one or more constitutions had been written for each of the twenty-one additional states; an organic law had provided for nearly that many more in the future. Would these prove to be a refuge from political vagueness, and so help avoid another war of secession?

*　　*　　*

It is not clear precisely when the colonies gave up hope of being reunited to the British Empire. Perhaps not until about January, 1776, did they cease to consider themselves "colonies," who were fighting only to force a wiser policy on the home government. By the time of Lee's Resolutions in June, 1776, they were ready to make it plain "That these United *Colonies* are, and of right ought to be, free and independent *States,* that *they* are absolved from all allegiance to the British Crown, and that all political connection between them and the State of Great Britain is, and ought to be, totally dissolved." Meanwhile, from the beginning of the open struggle against the British Government in the 1760's until the formal declaration of independence, the new political arrangements had been expected to last only "during the continuance of the present dispute between Great Britain and the colonies." A reconciliation was still generally expected: the First Continental Congress was originally to do no more than form a loose Continental Association, state grievances, and appeal for relief.

At first it was only gradually and cautiously that the individual colonies refashioned their governments. After all, they were fighting to justify, and not to overturn, the authority of their local representatives. During the early years of ambiguous conflict with Britain, the Americans in each colony, ignoring royal or proprietary governors, informally established provincial congresses or conventions or committees to organize the resistance to the British government. These groups soon proved handy for reshaping the thirteen colonial governments.

Massachusetts led the way. The provincial congress of that colony wrote a momentous letter to the Continental Congress (May 16, 1775) asking for "your most explicit advice respecting the taking up and exercising the powers of civil government, which we think absolutely necessary for the Salvation of our country and we shall readily submit to such a general plan as you may direct for the colonies, or make it our great study to establish such a form of government here, as shall not only most promote our advantage but the union and interest of all America." Congress replied that the people of Massachusetts owed no obedience to the acts of Parliament that purported to alter the Massachusetts charter, nor to the Royal Governor or Lieutenant-Governor who had tried to subvert the charter. Therefore, Congress recommended, "in order to conform, as near as may be, to the spirit and substance of the charter," that the provincial

Convention call for election of an Assembly (which in turn should elect counsellors) to exercise the powers of government "until a Governor, of his Majesty's appointment, will consent to govern the colony according to its charter." When the provincial Conventions of New Hampshire, South Carolina, and Virginia sought similar advice, the Congress also advised them "to call a full and free representation of the people, and that the representatives if they think it necessary, establish such a form of government, as in their judgment, will best produce the happiness of the people, and most effectually secure peace and good order in the province, during the continuance of the present dispute between G[reat] Britain and the colonies." In May, 1776, the Congress made a similar recommendation to all the colonies.

Now approached a crucial test. Again and again political theorists had declared the people to be the source of power, and Americans had adopted the familiar British arguments. Now would Americans practice what they had preached? The people, John Adams said, "must be all consulted, and we must realize the theories of the wisest writers, and invite the people to erect the whole building with their own hands, upon the broadest foundation."

It took some time before the former colonists realized the full novelty of this American experience. At first they did not call special constituent conventions expressly to frame a constitution, and at first the new state constitutions were the work of regular legislatures originally elected for some other purpose. These bodies, therefore, could give their handiwork no more force than that of legislation. Within a few months after the suggestion from the Continental Congress, New Hampshire (January 5, 1776) and South Carolina (March 26) adopted provisional constitutions. These were the work of their regular revolutionary assemblies, not of special constitutional conventions. Similarly, in other colonies, the assemblies which had been charged with temporary government during the Revolution, in 1776 adopted new constitutions: Virginia (June 28), New Jersey (July 2), Delaware (September 20), Maryland (November 9), Pennsylvania (September 28), North Carolina (December 18). Early in 1777, the revolutionary assemblies adopted constitutions in Georgia (February 5) and New York (April 20). Rhode Island and Connecticut simply (with a few changes) confirmed their colonial charters, which remained in effect into the 19th century. Massachusetts, too, until 1780 was governed by her colonial charter, which her assembly had adopted as the frame of a provisional government. None of the constitutions through the year 1777 had yet been made by a constituent convention summoned exclusively for that purpose.

But there were already hints, as R. R. Palmer observes, of a growing belief that a constitution was essentially different from ordinary legislation and could not be framed, adopted, or modified by an ordinary legislative assembly. In New Hampshire, New York, Delaware, Maryland, North Carolina, and Georgia, the revolutionary legislatures did not frame constitutions until after asking that specific authority from the voters. Some sort of popular ratification followed the framing of the constitutions in Maryland and North Carolina. In Pennsylvania under popular pressure (a mass meeting of 4000 in Philadelphia in May 1776) a convention was elected for the express purpose of framing a constitution but its product was not submitted to popular vote.

Not until the Massachusetts Constitution of 1780 was the difference between the source of a constitution and that of ordinary legislation fully and unambiguously illustrated. It is worth recounting the story of that Constitution in some detail, also because it was one of the most influential models for the Federal Constitution of 1787.

The popular motives behind the movement for a new constitution in Massachusetts are confused, but the procedure by which the new constitution was made is plain enough. And the procedure itself gave the constitution its peculiar authority. On May 5, 1777, the two houses of the Massachusetts legislature "recommended" to the towns that they authorize the representatives to be elected later that month to frame a constitution which, if adopted by two-thirds of the adult males, would then become the fundamental law of the state. The towns duly voted this authority, the two houses combined to frame a constitution, and the document was submitted to the towns for their approval in the spring of 1778. This proposed constitution was overwhelmingly rejected (147 towns against; 31 for). It appears to have been too radical for the conservatives and too conservative for the radicals. And it contained no bill of rights.

During 1779 and 1780 the War was going badly, especially in New England, where much of Maine was in British hands; inflation and profiteering were rife. The discontented farmers of Berkshire County, at the extreme western end of the state on the New York border, held a county convention of their own, and actually threatened to secede from Massachusetts. Refusing to recognize the charter held over from British days, they considered themselves to be still in a "state of nature" and reminded the authorities in Boston of "other States, which have Constitutions who Will, we doubt not, bad as we are, gladly receive Us." The Massachusetts General Court, which was being pressed from all sides for a new frame of government, asked selectmen of the towns (February 19, 1779) to put two simple questions to their voters: "*First,* whether they chuse at this Time to have a Constitution or Form of Government made. *Secondly,* Whether they will impower their Representatives for the next Year to vote for the calling of a State Convention, for the sole purpose of forming a new Constitution. . . ." The people voted heavily in favor of both propositions (6612 for; 2639 against). The selectmen then called town meetings to elect the delegates (by a vote of all free adult males). The Convention was to be authorized to put its new constitution into effect if it was accepted by two-thirds of the voters.

Circumstances could hardly have been better suited to dramatize the special authority which the new "frame of government" was intended to have: it was to be no ordinary law. An authority higher than the legislature—the people themselves—was being consulted. The procedures of consultation were not mere formalities, but an effort to let the public speak its mind. When this new Constitutional Convention of Massachusetts met in Cambridge on September 1, 1779, the state was still being governed by the revised version of its royal charter of 1691. After the rejection of the proposals of 1778, some citizens had continued to think the old frame of government, with its patina of antiquity, might be better than any newfangled substitute. By voting down the new frame of government made by the Revolutionary assembly, the people had declared their power to reject as well as to accept a constitution offered them by an existing authority. They insisted that another try be made by a true constituent assembly elected for that sole purpose.

The novel authority of the Convention appeared in another remarkable fact. Property qualifications were in force both for voting and for office-holding under the earlier frames of government and they were also to be enacted in the later constitution. But the initial selection of delegates to the Constitutional Convention and the later ratification (requiring approval by two-thirds of the voters) of the work of the Convention was entrusted to all free adult males.

The Massachusetts Constitutional Convention, which met in Cambridge on September 1, 1779, had thus plainly sought and found the mandate of the people themselves to frame a constitution. This clearly gave a new and wider authority to their deliberations and would make their product a Higher Law in a new and more literal sense. Their new constitution would derive its authority from the explicit consent of a wider suffrage (all adult male citizens) than had authorized ordinary legislation.

The 293 members of the Convention were an extraordinary collection of talent, including John Adams, Samuel Adams, James Bowdoin, George Cabot, John Lowell, Robert Treat Paine, and Theophilus Parsons. On September 4, the Convention appointed a committee of thirty to prepare a draft, and this committee delegated its work to a subcommittee of three, consisting of James Bowdoin (prosperous merchant and Revolutionary leader), John Adams, and Samuel Adams. The subcommittee in turn delegated its work to John Adams, whose draft, with a few changes, was finally adopted.

Adams' remarkable product was accepted by the Convention during sessions which ended March 2, 1780. Attendance had fallen off alarmingly, owing partly to one of the severest winters in memory, partly to apathy and other reasons. In the all-important final sessions, when the document was prepared for submission to the people, there were never more than eighty-two members (less than thirty per cent) present and voting. Still, the meaning of the procedure, which was an effort to find a higher authority than the ordinary legislature and to use that authority to redefine the government, was never in doubt. The preamble of the new constitution, after asserting the right of the people to alter the government, explained:

> The body-politic is formed by a voluntary association of individuals: it is a social compact by which the whole people covenants with each citizen and each citizen with the whole people that all shall be governed by certain laws for the common good. It is the duty of the people, therefore, in framing a constitution of government, to provide for an equitable mode of making laws, as well as for an impartial interpretation and faithful execution of them; that every man may, at all times, find his security in them.
>
> We, therefore, the people of Massachusetts, acknowledging with grateful hearts, the goodness of the great Legislator of the universe, in affording us, in the course of His providence, an opportunity, deliberately and peaceably, without fraud, violence, or surprise, of entering into an original, explicit, and solemn compact with each other, and of forming a new constitution of civil government for ourselves and posterity; and devoutly imploring His direction in so interesting a design, do agree upon, ordain, and establish the following declaration of rights and frame of government as the constitution of the commonwealth of Massachusetts.

The Convention, having revised and adopted Adams' draft, then, for the popular ratification, devised a detailed and elaborate procedure which assured the people of the state the opportunity, not merely to approve or reject the document as a whole, but to discuss each article separately and to state their objections.

A number of facts help explain the Convention's submission of their work to public scrutiny and debate. They had seen the wholesale rejection of the constitution of 1778 (by a five-to-one majority). And they therefore must have welcomed the opportunity to allow the people to separate the more from the less acceptable items, to air grievances, and to face in detail the problem of making something better. Most important, the Massachusetts Convention had ready at hand a network of functioning local assemblies, the town meetings, of which there were about 300. These were a distinctive New England growth which now allowed popular debate of a new frame of government. The Convention recommended: that the proposed new constitution be discussed by the people in their town meetings; that these meetings vote on the constitution clause by clause and state their objections to any article; and that the people again grant authority to their Convention (sending different delegates if they wished) to tabulate the results, to ratify and declare it in force for every part supported by a two-thirds majority, to alter other parts in accordance with the popular will, and finally to ratify it as thus amended. This is precisely what was done.

For fourteen weeks during the spring of 1780, the town meetings of Massachusetts met, discussed, and voted. In some towns, at least, discussion was far from perfunctory, for detailed amendments were listed and voted on. The Convention reconvened on June 7 to receive the returns and, by June 16, proclaimed that the people had accepted the Constitution. They fixed October 25, 1780, as the date for the first election under the new frame of government. There is some evidence that, even after all this elaborate procedure for expression of the popular will, the convention juggled the results in favor of the Constitution. Nevertheless, the tabulation was made in the view of the whole Convention, and every article appears to have received (if not a two-thirds majority, as technically required) at least a bare majority. "Never was a good constitution more needed than at this juncture," Samuel Adams wrote on July 10. In the gloomy days of 1780, with the state at war and drifting toward anarchy, the Convention appears to have preferred the public interest to fractional technicalities.

The meaning of what the people of Massachusetts had done appeared to only a few at the time. In France, when he heard his constitution had been adopted, John Adams saw from that Old World perspective the novelty of the events. The citizens of Massachusetts, he said, were "the first people who have taken so much time to deliberate upon government —that have allowed such universal liberty to all people to reflect upon the subject, and to propose objections and amendments—and that have reserved to themselves at large the right of finally accepting or rejecting the form." "There never was an example of such precautions as are taken by this wise and jealous people in the formation of their government. None was ever made so perfectly upon the principle of the people's rights and equality. It is Locke, Sydney and Rousseau and De Mably reduced to practice, in the first instance." Though not given to easy enthusiasms, John Adams hailed this as "a phenomenon in the political world that is new and singular." Nor was he exaggerating when he proclaimed an "epoch in the history of the progress of society." The Massachusetts achievement has been overshadowed in textbook and tradition by the events of 1787. Yet the Massachusetts Constitution of 1780—in its preparation, discussion, and adoption—was the pioneer.

*   *   *

The first efforts to unite the old colonies under a new central authority were not at all in the nature of a new "frame of government" or a constitution. The thirteen sovereign states, each with a government of its own, sought not a central government but (in the phrase of Governor Cooke of Rhode Island) a "Treaty of Confederation," which was not necessarily a permanent alliance, but primarily (some thought, exclusively) a league to wage the war. There is some reason to believe that there was even less national unity after the adoption of the Articles of Confederation than before it.

In its new constitution, a former colony would declare itself a "Sovereign State." Each of the states actually exercised the sort of powers we associate with an independent government. The South Carolina Constitution, for example, expressly asserted the power of the state to make war, conclude peace, enter into treaties, lay embargoes, and maintain an army and navy. Virginia herself ratified the treaty with France, and was so active in foreign affairs that she had to establish a clerkship of foreign correspondence; Governor Patrick Henry sent William Lee abroad to negotiate a loan with the French government. According to Franklin, three separate states of the American confederation were at one time negotiating with France for war aid. There is evidence that states considered the minister sent abroad by the Congress to be not so much a national emissary as a minister who was acting simultaneously on behalf of each of the states individually. States acted as if, in allowing certain functions to be exercised by the Congress, they had not divested themselves of a power to perform similar functions in their own behalf. Thus they organized their own armies, fitted out their own navies, and directed military movements to serve state interests. In the South, the War was conducted in the beginning without the aid of Congress. Each state regulated its own Indian affairs and postal routes. This sovereignty of the states explained why the vote in the Congress of the Confederation was by states and not by individual delegates. That Congress, according to John Adams, was "not a legislative assembly, nor a representative assembly but only a diplomatic assembly."

The step from a league of states to a federal nation was momentous— not only because it created a new nation, but even more because it created a new kind of nation and a new kind of Higher Law. The Imperial vagueness had left the new states fearful of encroachment and anxious for definition of their powers. Yet the experience of waging a war without a strong central authority, together with the everyday costs of inflation and of petty economic warfare among the states, pointed up the need.

The Annapolis "Convention" of September, 1786, had not been a constitutional convention at all, but an interstate meeting of state delegates on commercial problems. Only five states had been represented there and very little had been accomplished by the twelve delegates present, but the group did propose a meeting in Philadelphia the following May, "to take into consideration the situation of the United States, to devise such further provisions as shall appear to them necessary to render the constitution of the Federal Government adequate to the exigencies of the Union; and to report such an Act for that purpose to the United States in Congress assembled, as when agreed to, by them, and afterwards confirmed by the Legislatures of every state, will effectually provide for the same." The Congress of the Confederation five months later cautiously declared it "expedient" that such a convention of delegates meet "for the sole and express purpose of revising the Articles of Confederation and reporting to Congress and the several legislatures such alterations and provisions."

When the delegates of the states, then, met in convention in Philadelphia in 1787, they did not have the unambiguous popular mandate to devise a new frame of government which their predecessors in Boston had received from the people of Massachusetts nearly a decade before. Delegates at Philadelphia had not been elected directly by the people but had been chosen by the government of each of the separate states (except Rhode Island, which was not represented). Altogether fifty-five delegates attended; an average session was attended by about thirty. Their central problem was how to form a government of governments. No one seriously considered the possibility of a purely national government which would have abolished the separate state governments.

The supposed sovereignty and independence of each of the thirteen states now made it possible to bring into the arena of a single national government many notions before found only in the international sphere. We have often been told that the great significance of the Federal Constitutional Convention was that it showed how separate "sovereign" states could submit themselves to the kind of government formerly found only *within* nations. The Convention, it is said, was a "Great Rehearsal" for the framing of a United Nations. From a 20th-century perspective this comparison may be helpful. But in the late 18th century, much of the significance was precisely the reverse. The working "Federal" government developed by the new nation imported *from the international into the national* sphere novel ideas, which would prove especially useful if self-government was ever to be extended over a large territory.

Relations among sovereign states were traditionally governed by treaties, supposedly enforceable only by the good faith of the parties. The rules governing these treaties were a customary system of unwritten law, sometimes called the Law of Nature and/or the Law of Nations, and often said to be of higher obligation than the will of the particular sovereigns. An extensive learned literature elaborated these rules. The 17th and 18th centuries produced some of the great works of this kind, in the writings of the Dutchman Grotius (1625), the German Pufendorf (1672), the Swiss Burlamaqui (1747) and Vattel (1758), and others. "As it is impossible for the whole race of mankind to be united in one great society," Blackstone explained in 1765, "they must necessarily divide into many, and form separate states, commonwealths and nations entirely independent of each other, and yet liable to a mutual intercourse. Hence arises a third kind of law [in addition to the 'law of nature' and the 'law of revelation'] to regulate this mutual intercourse, called 'the law of nations,' which, as none of these states will acknowledge a superiority in the other, cannot be dictated by any, but depends entirely upon the rules of natural law, or upon mutual compacts, treaties, leagues, and agreements between these several communities: in the construction also of which compacts we have no other rule to resort to, but the law of nature; being the only one to which all the communities are equally subject. . . ."

When the men of 1787 spoke, then, as they often did, of forming a "federal" union, they usually had in mind some way of drawing together sovereign states. This word "federal" was still commonly used in a sense close to its Latin origin (*foedus,* treaty) to describe a relationship resting on good faith (*foedus* in Latin was a cognate of *fides,* faith). "Federal" was used in the Constitutional Convention, and in the debates over the adoption of the constitution, in this technical, and now nearly obsolete, sense. The older spelling—"foederal"—which emphasized the connection to the Latin word *foedus* was in general use. Two days after the first working session of the Philadelphia Convention, Edmund Randolph of Virginia moved, on the suggestion of Gouverneur Morris (as Madison noted):

> 1. that a Union of the States merely federal will not accomplish the objects proposed by the articles of Confederation, namely common defence, security of liberty, & genl. welfare.
> 2. that no treaty or treaties among the whole or part of the States, as individual Sovereignties, would be sufficient.
> 3. that a *national* Government ought to be established consisting of a *supreme* Legislative, Executive & Judiciary. . . .
> Mr. Govr. Morris explained the distinction between a *federal* and *national, supreme,* Govt.; the former being a mere compact resting on the good faith of the parties; the latter having a compleat and *compulsive* operation.

What would be truly remarkable, (in the phrase Joel Barlow used a few days later in his Fourth of July Oration for 1787) would be a "permanent foederal system." Under the new constitution, Madison argued in *The Federalist* (Number 39; 1788), the Senate "will derive its powers from the States, as political and coequal societies; and these will be represented on the principle of equality in the Senate. . . . So far the government is *federal,* not *national.*" A result of this "Federal" Convention and its successors was to make this clearer, older sense of the word obsolete.

While the framers were making something different from a "foederal" compact in the old sense, and were in fact giving a new meaning to that word, they were also wary of using "nation" or "national." It is no accident that neither "nation" nor "national" appears anywhere in the Constitution. The Convention expressly and unanimously voted (June 20), on the motion of Oliver Ellsworth of Connecticut, that the title of the new government "drop the word *national,* and retain the proper title 'the United States.' " "National" was accordingly deleted from other parts of the document, with the resulting repetitive and intentionally ambiguous reference to "the United States."

The government which the Convention actually produced was (in Ellsworth's phrase) "partly national; partly federal." This duality appeared, he explained, in one feature after another. "The proportional representation in the first branch [of the legislature, the House of Representatives] was conformable to the *national* principle & would secure the large States agst. the small. An equality of voices [in the Senate] was conformable to the *federal* principle and was necessary to secure the Small States agst. the large."

The few generalizations that can be safely made about these deliberations of the Philadelphia Convention help explain why it is so hard to make others. First, there was a genuine discussion, during which delegates changed their minds and adapted their positions to the demands of fellow members. Second, there was no general agreement on the underlying theory: the doctrines were nearly as numerous as the delegates themselves; individual members slid from one theoretical base to another. Finally, there was no general agreement on the actual character of the new government they had created. Their product significantly omitted both the words "federal" and "national," which had figured prominently and acrimoniously in the theoretical discussions. Instead, the Constitution simply referred at every point to "the United States." By the end of their deliberations the delegates seem to have recognized their creation as an important new hybrid among political species.

Within only a few decades, "Constitutionalism" itself acquired a new and characteristically American meaning. It was (in Walton H. Hamilton's later phrase) "the name given to the trust which men repose in the power of words engrossed on parchment to keep a government in order." The interpretation of these words required still another distinctively American institution: the power of courts to pass on the constitutionality of laws and to refuse to enforce those they found unconstitutional. This came to be called "judicial review." No such power was specifically described in the Constitution, and it may not have been intended or imagined by the framers. But judicial review kept the constitution alive, giving it a new expansibility and flexibility and vagueness —under the very guise of definition.

46

Unionist Ways from a Secessionist Tradition

THE GENERATION THAT MADE the Federal Constitution was haunted by the suspicion that republican government somehow would not function over a large area. "It is natural for a republic to have only a small territory," Montesquieu had written in his *Spirit of Laws* in 1748, "otherwise it cannot long subsist." And this notion had become a principle of political science. Both John Adams (in his *Defence of the Constitutions of the United States,* 1787), and Alexander Hamilton (in his speech in the Constitutional Convention, June 18, 1787) drew from history the lesson that the vast extent of the United States made it likely that a durable central government would have to verge on monarchy. Patrick Henry, arguing against ratification of the new Federal Constitution in the Virginia Convention (June 9, 1788), offered this difficulty as axiomatic. "One government," he insisted, "cannot reign over so extensive a country as this is, without absolute despotism." "I call for an example of a great extent of country, governed by one government, or Congress, call it what you will."

The story of the American Revolution, it was said, had been only another illustration of this well-known principle. Had not the British proved unable to adapt their representative government to include far-off America?

But some, less pessimistic, began to imagine that the example which all earlier history could not supply might be found in America. James Madison, for example, in the *Federalist* (Number 10) argued hopefully that a great extent of territory, with its great variety of interests, might actually protect the citizens' rights. "Extend the sphere," Madison explained in a familiar passage, "and you take in a greater variety of parties and interests; you make it less probable that a majority of the whole will have a common motive to invade the rights of other citizens; or if such a common motive exists, it will be more difficult for all who feel it to discover their own strength, and to act in unison with each other. . . . the same advantage which a republic has over a democracy, in controlling the effects of faction, is enjoyed by a large over a small republic—is enjoyed by the Union over the States composing it." Thomas Jefferson, after the turbulent presidential election of 1800–1801 when a tie between him and Aaron Burr in the Electoral College had thrown the decision into the House of Representatives and finally elected him on the thirty-sixth ballot, wrote to Joseph Priestley (March 21, 1801), "We can no longer say there is nothing new under the sun. For this whole chapter in the history of man is new. The great extent of our republic is new." "It furnishes a new proof of the falsehood of Montesquieu's doctrine, that a republic can be preserved only in a small territory. The reverse is the truth. Had our territory been even a third only of what it is, we were gone. But while frenzy and delusion like an epidemic, gained certain parts, the residue remained sound and untouched and held on till their brethren could recover from the temporary delusion; and that circumstance has given me great comfort."

There were, nevertheless, some peculiarly American grounds for pessimism: a secessionist tradition was older even than the Revolution. It was as old as the colonial settlements. The discovery of the New World had made secessions and withdrawals feasible on a continental scale, and American life comprised countless efforts to secede. The Pilgrims were the first outspoken American secessionists. As "separatists" they believed what from an Old World point of view was quite shocking, that men who wanted to live by a purer church could of their own accord separate themselves from their old community and form themselves into a new one. The Pilgrims came to Plymouth only after their effort to separate themselves had been unsuccessful in the Netherlands. In the vast American space, the very idea of "Nonconformity" or of "Toleration" was overshadowed by Separatism and Secessionism.

From the early 17th century till the middle of the 19th century, secession was characteristically American. The colonies expanded and acquired their varied character by secessions. Roger Williams and Anne Hutchinson, separatist heretics, were extruded from Massachusetts Bay and seceded into their own Rhode Island. Thomas Hooker, another separatist, seceded to his Connecticut. Lord Baltimore made it possible for a group of Catholics to secede from English life into a community which, for a while at least, was their own. William Penn provided Quakers a separate place of refuge. And so on. Space made all this possible. The Revolution seemed to many at the time to be a triumph of thirteen separate secessionist spirits. In the late 18th and early 19th century, there were westward-moving wagon trains settling new territories and states in a vaguely bounded hinterland, and these too were seceding, after their various secular undogmatic fashions, from the life of the seaboard.

American experience had already shown, then, that the fears of Montesquieu and older political theorists were not without foundation. If a single great republic was to survive here, it would have to find a way of stemming the secessionist tide. Oddly enough, this opportunity was to come through the creation of a new American empire—in Jefferson's phrase, an "Empire for Liberty"—with political arrangements quite similar to those that the American colonists had fought to secede from. The first colonial experience (before the War for Independence) had made an American nation necessary. A second colonial experience (between Independence and the Civil War) would make the nation possible.

The "public domain"—a new American empire controlled now, not from London, but by "the united states in Congress assembled"—became a bond among the states. Without these lands, and the conflicts with foreign powers which they threatened, could a central government have survived between the peace with Britain in 1783 and the convening of the Constitutional Convention in Philadelphia in 1787? What might have happened once the pressure of British attack was removed, once the thirteen separate "Sovereign States" had each started on its own way?

Dreams of this new empire long inspired Jefferson. In 1809, he suggested to President Madison that Napoleon might be willing to let the United States have Cuba. Then, Jefferson went on, by adding Canada, "we should have such an empire for liberty as she has never surveyed since the creation; . . . no constitution was ever before so well calculated as ours for extensive empire and self-government." In the beginning, this new empire was no mere dream, but the very cement of the Union.

Within the next decades, the new central government in America would exercise powers over land and life in a new American empire in which the new colonies were euphemistically called the "public lands" or the "national domain" or the "public domain." This empire was remarkably similar in political structure to that which had driven the earlier American colonies to revolt. The new national government, for example, at first dared to legislate for and to tax this new empire.

In the East, meanwhile, American political institutions would be shaped by this very power and habit of legislating for an ill-defined West. The major measures of the new national government, would, in the vocabulary of an earlier day, have been called measures of imperial control. They were latter-day counterparts of the Proclamation of 1763, the Quebec Act of 1774, and other Acts which disposed of the lives, fortunes, lands, and governments of people far from the central authority in London. Those earlier acts of Parliament were meant to hold an empire together, and bulwark it against foreign enemies. The later acts of the American Congress, such as the Missouri Compromise, the Compromise of 1850, and the Kansas-Nebraska Act of 1854, also imposed decisions from the remote East on people in the West; these decisions were intended to hold together a nation. If the British government had once used Americans as pawns in a world-wide battle for empire, so now the new American government in Washington used Westerners as makeweights between sections of the heavily settled East.

From the point of view of the states already in the Union, the much-debated measures seemed merely domestic "compromises," but they were actually imperial decisions, treating settlers as colonists. The Missouri Compromise (1820), for example, declared that, in the area of the Louisiana Purchase north of 36° 30', slavery should be excluded. The Compromise of 1850 and the Kansas-Nebraska Act (1854) were also firmly based on the assumption that it was within the power of Congress to set the ground rules (e.g. "squatter sovereignty") within which settlers could make decisions about their institutions. The whole federal land policy in the vast public domain (which finally included virtually all the nation except the original thirteen states and Texas) was an assumption by the American central government of the very powers that the colonists had denied to the government in London. The federal government, not the new western states or the operation of the market, fixed the terms on which settlers could acquire their lands. And from the beginning, when the first public-land state (Ohio) was admitted to the Union in 1803, the federal government generally retained title to ungranted lands within the new state boundaries, excepting only the section in each township reserved for educational purposes.

In the forty years before the Civil War, Congress was, in one historian's phrase, little more than a "Union-Saving," or we might say "Empire-Saving," body, spending its energy in "Compromises" that made westerners pawns in the eastern struggle. The other major pieces of federal legislation—the Land Act of 1796, which provided for rectangular survey; the Land Act of 1820, which required cash for land purchases; the Pre-emption Act of 1830, which gave preference to actual settlers at the time; the Distribution–Pre-emption Act of 1841, which permanently authorized settlement before purchase and which distributed a portion of the proceeds of land-sale to the new states; and the Homestead Act of 1862—these too were eastern measures of control over the acquisition of property and the perfection of land titles in the whole West. Control, or efforts at control, from Washington, dominated Western political problems. Congressional rule was not easily abdicated: the slavery issue added still another reason for direct Congressional responsibility. The rush to settle Kansas by both pro- and antislavery factions and the resulting civil war there (November, 1855, to December, 1856), in which about two hundred were killed, were among the many incidents in the western struggle to satisfy the conditions established by Congress. The Union was held precariously together by this new kind of imperial control.

*   *   *

The relation of the western territories (soon to comprise the greater number of the states) to the whole new nation showed characteristics of an American political system with institutions of a strongly unionist tendency which would endure into the 20th century. These were the institutions that were to make possible a spacious republic. Who could have predicted that they would be by-products of a secessionist tradition?

Organic Law: a Legal Substitute for Revolution. The novel American machinery for state-making—the basis for an American colonial system—was given classic form in the Northwest Ordinance, adopted by the Congress of the Confederation in July, 1787. This act described a regular set of stages through which a Territory would pass on its way from complete control by Congress to equality as a new State within the Union.

At first, the sparsely populated Territory was to be governed by Congress through its Congressionally-appointed governor, secretary, and three judges. These officials would put together a legal code, borrowing those laws from the original states which they found "best suited to the circumstances of the district." They had autocratic powers, curbed only by the veto of Congress. The next stage was reached "so soon as there shall be five thousand free male inhabitants of full age in the district," when the inhabitants would, if they wished, begin to have a representative government with a two-chamber legislature: a directly elected house of representatives, and a small "legislative council" of five persons, selected by Congress from a list of ten prepared by that house. The governor had veto on all legislation. The two chambers of the Territorial legislature voting together were to elect a delegate, "who shall have a seat in Congress, with a right of debating but not of voting during this temporary government."

Government during these first two stages resembled that under the old British Empire, with Congress standing in place of the Crown and Parliament, with appointed governors, weak legislatures subject to veto by the national legislature, and non-voting commissioners in the national capital. The third and final stage was reached when the free population numbered sixty thousand, at which time the Territory would be admitted as a State. Within the Northwest Territory there were to be "not less than three nor more than five States," all "on an equal footing with the original States in all respects whatever, and shall be at liberty to form a permanent constitution and State government: *Provided,* the constitution and government so to be formed, shall be republican, and in conformity to the principles contained in these articles."

This American colonial system, unlike the British, provided a normal progress from imperial control to self-government. At the final stage, moreover, the outlying territory was to be thoroughly involved in the government of the whole nation. This procedure for state-making had been enacted in the Northwest Ordinance under the Articles of Confederation; it was re-enacted by the First Congress as part of the new Federal system. Its basic principle—predictable procession from autocratic colonial rule to self-government and involution in the nation—became the American way of national growth.

The United States grew politically, then, by recapitulating its colonial experience. By far the larger area of the United States, as it stood in the later 20th century, had once been governed as a colony from the national capital. The colonial experience, lived in an earlier form by each of the thirteen original states, was now relived in a legally formalized version by nearly all the other states that eventually rounded out the nation. If the earlier version had ended in failure from the point of view of the British government in London, the later version would end in success, from the point of view of a transformed American government in Washington.

A half-century after the adoption of the Ordinance of 1787, this scheme of progressive decolonization had become a glorious fixture among American institutions. "It approaches as nearly to absolute perfection," Judge Timothy Walker of Cincinnati, author of the widely read *Introduction to American Law* (1837), declared, "as anything to be found in the legislation of mankind, for after the experience of fifty years it would perhaps be impossible to alter without marring it . . . . it is one of those matchless specimens of sagacious forecast, which even the reckless spirit of innovation would not venture to assail." A full century after the introduction of the scheme, Lord Bryce, in his *American Commonwealth* (1889), conceded that the American scheme of Territorial government had worked well in practice and gave little ground for discontent even to the inhabitants of the Territories themselves.

The successful application of this notion of a predictable, gradual, step-by-step progress toward self-government and national involvement is one of the marvels of American history. The application of the principles of the Northwest Ordinance was not literal nor uniform, but it was general. For example, Ohio's admission as a state in 1803 and Illinois' in 1818, both occurred before their populations reached the specified sixty thousand; while Dakota in 1880, with a population of more than twice the required number, was not seriously considered for statehood, and Utah when admitted in 1896 had contained more than the required number for over thirty years. Political considerations among the existing states were always important and often decisive. Ohio, the first state created from the Northwest Territory, was admitted by a strongly Jeffersonian Congress just in time to help re-elect Jefferson President in 1804.

Before the Civil War, the slavery issue dominated this, as it did other questions. After the struggle over the admission of Missouri as a slave state in 1821, the balance of forces in the national government in Washington depended on the internal history of the Territories. This reversed the flow of forces under the old British Empire, when government in the colonies had been shaped by the accidents of internal politics in London. The existence of a whole continent from which to make political counterweights in the delicate equilibrium between North and South, Free and Slave States, helped keep sectional issues alive. States were admitted and Territories created in pairs: Free and Slave. Even after the Civil War, the Omnibus Bill of 1889 simultaneously admitted four states (North Dakota, South Dakota, Washington, and Montana) so as not to upset the party balance: two were said to be Democratic, the other two Republican.

What is most remarkable is not that the formation of new states was halting, irregular, and influenced by "mother-country" politics, but rather that it worked as well as it did. Two-thirds of a continent was led from colonial rule to self-government within a century and a half. Threats of secession, like that of the Mormons in Utah in 1857, were rare. The system succeeded in preventing what might have been a series of American Wars for Independence in the West.

After an initial period of experimental adjustment to local conditions (for example to French and Spanish traditions in Louisiana), a remarkably standardized system was developed. And despite involvement with such explosive domestic issues as slavery, land pre-emption, banking, and tariff, new Territories were continually created: Arkansas (1819), Florida (1822), Wisconsin (1836), Iowa (1838), Oregon (1848), Minnesota (1849), Utah and New Mexico (1850), and Kansas and Nebraska (1854). By a characteristic American reversal, the point of view of these "colonies" gradually dominated the politics of the "mother country," which now was the eastern third of central North America.

The system of the Northwest Ordinance of 1787 governed substantially, until the last piece of contiguous continental territory was admitted as the State of Arizona in 1912. But after 1861, when slavery and sectional rivalry no longer dominated domestic politics, the creation of new states became slower; Territorial patronage was too useful to be abandoned by Congress simply to satisfy local ambitions for statehood. Between 1867 and 1889 only a single state (Colorado) was admitted, and in the Territories of Dakota, Montana, Utah, New Mexico, and Washington, a whole generation was raised in quasi-colonialism. But the pace of movement along the clearly defined path to self-government was still swift by Old World standards. The direction (as revealed most recently in Alaska, admitted as a state, January 3, 1959, and in Hawaii, admitted August 21, 1959), remained unchanged.

State-making had been reduced to simple, specified procedures. Over a broad continent, "self-government" was created in place after place with perfunctory simplicity. Just as state constitutions in the West were sometimes slavish replicas of eastern models, so too the Organic Acts themselves, which created new western Territories, followed a pattern.

The Wisconsin Organic Act of 1836, developing out of similar earlier acts, provided the formula repeated in all later Acts. The will to self-government had now been tamed—another evidence that (in R. R. Palmer's phrase) "revolution had already become domesticated in America."

The American colonial-territorial system, with its plain and easy stages for movement from imperial rule to self-government, was another application of know-how. Like the New England system of manufacturing, it was a plan of organization, in this case summarized in the notion of Organic (Government-organizing) Law. And this too would be a substitute for skill. By this way of mass-producing states, a people could be institutionally transformed from a mere territory, a congeries of transient communities and upstart towns, into a fully equipped representative government, even though they had very little political skill of their own. Much as the Territorial judges with the Governor and the Secretary in the first Organic stage, by a system of interchangeable parts put together their code of laws from pieces ready-made in other parts of the Union, so the later constitution-makers of the western states borrowed ready-made pieces from their predecessors.

A Politics of Accretion: New Political Units. The national history of England, France, Germany, or Italy is a story of unification; the national history of the United States is one of accretion. The United States, from the beginning, grew by adding new areas from a vaguely bounded hinterland. While the national politics of Europe consisted of the adjustment of old entities, the national politics of the United States in its first three-quarters of a century consisted of the creation, adjustment, and interrelations of new entities. This distinction was pregnant for American political life.

In 1790, the nation was confined to the eastern side of the Mississippi River, with most of its population east of the Appalachians. It included some nine hundred thousand square miles organized into a national domain (a Northwest Territory and a Southwest Territory) and thirteen states. By 1861, the nation reached to the Rio Grande and the Pacific, and across the continent up to the forty-ninth parallel, a total of some three million square miles, now organized into over a half-dozen territories and thirty-four states. These simple facts of political arithmetic summed up the primary features of American politics. The political time-table was fantastically accelerated: between the Congressional creation of a Territory and its admission as a State, there has never been longer than sixty-two years (New Mexico, 62 years; Hawaii, 61 years; Arizona, 49 years; Alaska, 47 years; Utah, 46 years), and the average span for this process has been only about twenty years. The original thirteen states were the focus of loyalties accumulated over many decades, but the newer states (the twenty-seventh state, Florida, was admitted in 1845) soon outnumbered the old. New states were, for the most part, products of quick-grown transient and upstart communities, which acquired political and constitutional existence by legislative fiat.

A constitution, which for centuries European man had continued to think of "not as a creation but as a growth; not as a national code so much as a national inheritance" was now, in one territory after another, conjured up at will. This new sense of control shaped an American functional attitude toward all government. Nothing was more obvious than that men could create new political entities quickly when they wished. And what men could make, could they not also alter for their convenience?

The geographic peculiarities of the new nation made it possible to add one new "state" after another, without encroaching on a strong neighboring power. In the Old World, addition to one nation could not be achieved without extinction of a nation or subtraction from another. The United States could grow by simple addition. Except for the Atlantic Ocean, the United States had no traditional boundary. Thus the new Union was built by an "Add-a-State" plan, as Americans casually created new political units.

A Politics of Involution: Change Is Normal. Gradually and continually, the government of the metropolitan United States was itself reshaped to incorporate the needs, the voices, and the aspirations of the newly added units. As each new state was added, the whole political frame was slightly altered. This is one reason why there has never been a successful violent political revolution in the United States. Involution has made revolution superfluous. The great exception was, of course, the South, which refused to accept the alterations required by expansion, and tried to make rigid the political arrangements which had survived only by their flexibility.

While it is not clear to what extent the framers of the Constitution of 1787 envisaged this development, there are clues that some of them intended the involution that would distinguish the American empire. The census, for example, showed the expectation that, as new territories and states were added to the Union, the center of political power should shift. It expressed belief that the framework of representation in the Congress should remain fluid, to incorporate the new areas in its activities and involve them in the national business. Population-counts had been taken by European governments for one purpose or another. And there was a rough precedent in the periodic seven-year "census of electors and inhabitants" provided in the first constitution of the State of New York. But the Federal Constitutional provision for a decennial census (Art. I, sec. 2) was in many ways distinctive. The need for it grew out of the great compromise between large and small states, which also provided for two legislatures, in one of which representation was to be by population. Obviously, under the Articles of Confederation, since each state had only one vote in the single-chamber legislature, there was no need for a periodic count for representative purposes. But now both direct taxes and representation in the House of Representatives were to be proportionate to figures based on population, "determined by adding to the whole number of free persons, including those bound to service for a term of years, and excluding Indians not taxed, three fifths of all other persons." The facts for this purpose were to be redefined every ten years. In origin, then, this provision was wholly fiscal and political—to provide a fluid basis for taxation and for the composition of the House of Representatives. Not until 1850 did the census become a substantial source of national statistics for other matters.

The United States Census, for the first time, provided that changing numbers of population (and hence the changing rates of regional growth) should become normal elements in the periodic redistribution of the power of the units in the political system. In England and elsewhere in Europe, parties struggled during the 19th century to make individual changes in the basis of representation, but in America a continual process of change had been incorporated into the original scheme. The census figures would in the normal course of events become public: this, too, was a great change, for, at least until the 19th century (and in some countries into the 20th), statistical data were state secrets. Over there the fears of the tax-farmer and of rival nations dominated, but here the claims of different parts of the country to be represented had to be published to the people.

The effect of the decennial reapportionments was especially dramatic in the first century of national life. In the First Congress, the constituency of a member of the House averaged about 33,000 persons; in 1840 it averaged about 71,000; by 1890 it would average about 176,-000. Instead of redistributing the membership as it existed in 1789, the House allowed itself to grow with the population. This was, of course, only another example of the American penchant for multiplying political units (in this case, congressional districts). Its consequence was not only to alter the apportionment of powers within the House, but substantially to alter the House's character, and its way of doing business. While the House of Representatives in 1789 numbered 65 and in 1790 numbered 106, by 1820 the number had doubled to 213, and by 1860 had increased to 243. The number was finally fixed at 435 in 1910, where it remained until the temporary addition of two more in 1960 after the admission of Alaska and Hawaii.

The committee machinery of the House was gradually elaborated: by 1800 there were still only four standing committees, but by 1850 these had reached thirty-four. As the House and its committees grew, the jurisdiction of the committees widened. Originally the introduction and reference of bills was strictly controlled by the House itself and the committees were left only with problems of detail and draftsmanship. The committees, which at first were mere creatures of the House, by 1825 had begun to assume their modern powers, until they gradually took over its business. By 1885 congressional government had become (in Woodrow Wilson's phrase) "government by the standing committees of Congress."

A Nationalizing Politics: Compromise Parties with Local Roots. "The smaller the society," wrote Madison in a familiar passage in the *Federalist* (Number 10), "the fewer probably will be the distinct parties and interests composing it; the fewer the distinct parties and interests, the more frequently will a majority be found of the same party, and the smaller the compass within which they are placed, the more easily will they concert and execute their plans of oppression." And he went on, as we have noted, to argue that a large country by taking in "a greater variety of parties and interests," would preserve the rights of citizens. It is not surprising that neither Madison nor his fellow framers of the Federal Constitution could imagine the sort of political parties that would arise in the new nation. Party government in the United States, as Lord Bryce observed near the end of the 19th century, "is so unlike what a student of the Federal Government could have expected or foreseen, that it is the thing of all others which any one writing about America ought to try to portray." What arose was the opposite of what the founders had imagined; in identifying "parties" with "interests," they were still taking the point of view of small Old World countries which were not federal. But in the long run, what made feasible Madison's and Jefferson's dream of a spacious republic was the peculiar, and very practical, role of American political parties. The geographical constituency—not an ideological group nor an interest group—was to be the basic unit of American party politics. And the parties, too, were to be "partly national; partly federal."

The tendencies of American political life were centrifugal—expressed in the American Revolution and in the secessionist tradition which long survived the Revolution. As we have seen, the American nation was not the product of any grand national passion, and the Constitution of the United States a precarious and novel arrangement—neither wholly federal nor wholly national. The effective political unifying of the nation was left to the political parties. They focused practical energies and enthusiasms, and they collected local, state, and national efforts, to build a strong nation. They were different from political parties known before, or any that have developed elsewhere since. For they were a by-product of the American vastness and diffuseness, of the multiplicity of independent political units, and of the stark simplicity, novelty, and ambiguity of the Federal Constitution. They supplied the countless living links that would create a political nation; they associated separate political units in all sorts of ways, which could not have been set down in any written laws or constitutions. And they accomplished their unique nationalizing task through certain of their distinctly American characteristics.

First and most important were their local roots. The numerous governments of cities, counties, and states provided a larger number of political offices and opportunities per capita than were found in the centralized Western European nations. The local political party thrived in the countless small puddles of political patronage. As we have already heard a western settler explain, "The conditions were ideal for the organization of a county, inasmuch as there was an office for every man." The American party system could not have grown without the enthusiasm of thousands of party workers, often inspired by hope for a local office.

Before about 1800, each local official generally ran for office on his own. Then the practice developed of combining candidates for offices at different levels, and offering them to the voters on a single "ticket" (an Americanism introduced about this time). The practice of voting orally in the presence of neighbors, which was traditional in the elections in colonial Virginia for the House of Burgesses, was hard to apply to the election of numerous officials; and it was not favorable to a "party ticket." Nor were other early voting laws, like those in Pennsylvania, which as late as 1796, when no printed ballots were supplied by the government, required names to be *handwritten*. One enterprising Republican party candidate covered the state with printed tickets from which voters could conveniently copy the names; and he also asked his Republican friends and their families to write out copies of the party ticket, which voters could then take to the polls and hand in as their ballot.

The very number of officials to be elected (in the Pennsylvania election of 1796, for example, the only way to vote for a President of the United States was to write the names of fifteen electors on your ballot) invited the assistance and organization of political parties. In the New York State elections of 1796, voters could already choose between a "Republican Ticket" and a "Federal Republican Ticket," both of which had been made up at special party meetings. Some Republican party delegates met at Dover, Delaware, "for the purpose of preparing a ticket, to be recommended to the Republican Citizens of Kent County, at the ensuing general election," and they listed candidates both for Congress and for state offices. As candidates for public office at the different levels found it strategic to appear on the same ticket, they joined, too, in stating their political principles and programs. Thus informally, and aided by the organizing activities of effective politicians like Thomas Jefferson, the "party ticket" became normal. Pressures came both from above (as in Virginia) and from below (as in New

Jersey), for politicians to band together their forces on election day. Candidates for county office or the state legislature were glad to be linked with the more widely known candidates for Congress, or with presidential electors supporting a famous man; candidates for Federal office were glad to be joined with local office-seekers who were well known in the neighborhood.

The novel institution of a party ticket at first stirred opposition from political idealists, like the editor of the Philadelphia *General Advertiser,* who in the early 1790's said, "We want no *Ticket Mongers:* let every citizen exercise his own judgment, and we shall have a good representation—intrigue, favoritism, cabal and party will then be at rest." As late as 1800, high-toned Federalists in Connecticut, finding it unseemly that any candidate for public office should tour the state "for the purpose of inducing people to vote for him," attacked the whole "detestable practice of electioneering." But electioneering, meetings for the nominating of candidates, and the other paraphernalia of "party tickets" were too useful for office-seekers, and too entertaining for voters, to be abandoned.

"Ticket-making" became an intriguing public pastime, and the nominating conventions, which were part of the process, stimulated political interest, and stirred party loyalty. Nominating conventions first became important with the widening of the suffrage in the late 1820's. A usual pattern was for the party's state central committee to issue a call for a state convention; township meetings elected delegates to county conventions, which in turn elected their delegates to the state-wide meeting; and if state senators or Congressmen were to be elected, additional delegates were chosen for a district meeting. Such numerous conventions offered a forum to everybody; proceedings were reported in the local press and then often reprinted as pamphlets for party propaganda. When a group of National Republicans in Kentucky in 1830 called a state convention to nominate their idol, Henry Clay, for the presidency they described the reputed virtues of conventions in phrases long since familiar:

> Issuing directly from the people, it will bear and proclaim their genuine sentiments. Essentially popular in its character and composition, it will command respect and secure confidence by its plain straightforward movement, without intrigue, without the corrupt agency of caucus management, without any other motive of origin but the spontaneous impulse of the people themselves.

Conventions not only concentrated party strength on specific candidates and so increased the chance of victory; they aroused enthusiasm, and made citizens glad to work for the party choice. "It is a *glorious* Convention," wrote a supporter of the Anti-Masonic Party of their New York state convention in 1831. "Lobbies, galleries, and all, are over-

flowing. I am proud of Anti-Masonry. What principles beyond all estimation brings honest plain farmers from the extreme bounds of the
State, at the dead of winter." The convention idea, proven effective in
the counties and states, was adopted by national parties. In the election
of 1832, national nominating conventions were for the first time held by
all the major parties that offered candidates for president.

These national nominating conventions drew together the delegates
and candidates from all over the country who found it convenient to
agree on programs and policies and on a single standard-bearer. Individual voters from remote states, in such conventions and in the day-to-
day work of party organization, found a readier opportunity for bargaining than in the official atmosphere of the Congress. Political parties thus
became one of the most effective nationalizing influences in American
life. And the diffuseness of American political life tended to break down
the dogmas and to blur the distinctions which were embittering politics
in the more centralized governments of continental Europe during the
same years.

Even the Electoral College, which the framers of the Federal Constitution devised for electing the President of the United States, served
the same purpose. Although, contrary to the expectations of the framers,
the Electoral College did not actually deliberate to choose a president,
it made the winning of the separate clusters of the electoral votes of
individual states the only way to the presidency. Thus, in the United
States, even the election of the tribune of the people, the one representative of the nation as a whole, was accomplished by weighing the popular
will in separate state units. And our highest official elected at large was
not the president but the governor of a state. This fact gave additional
weight to party organization which, even in the early 19th century, had
become a "connective tissue" of the nation.

"In America," Lord Bryce observed near the end of the 19th century,
"the great moving forces are the parties. The government counts for
less than in Europe, the parties count for more; and the fewer have
become their principles and the fainter their interest in those principles,
the more perfect has become their organization." Such tendencies were
already clear within a half-century after the adoption of the Federal
Constitution. As in many other departments of American life—in
religion, in education, in the very making of new communities—ideology
was displaced by organization. Sharp distinctions of thought and purpose were overshadowed by the need to get together on nearly self-
defining common purposes. So long as problems of American political
life remained compromisable, the political parties were the great arenas
of compromise. When this ceased to be true, the nation itself would be
on the brink of dissolution; and then the political parties, like the
nation itself, would have to be reconstructed.

ACKNOWLEDGMENTS

The University of Chicago for the last twenty years has given me the freedom and the stimulating environment to pursue the research which has gone into this book. To the friendly atmosphere of the Department of History, to my colleagues—and especially to its recent chairman, Walter Johnson and its present chairman William H. McNeill—I owe more than I can say.

To the Relm Foundation of Ann Arbor, Michigan, I am especially indebted for its continuing assistance. The Foundation, and its Secretary, Richard A. Ware, have given me an unrestricted freedom to do my work. Unlike many other foundations, they have shown a faith in the individual scholar which has itself been an inspiration in this collaborative age.

The staff of the University of Chicago Library, and particularly Mr. Robert Rosenthal, Head of the Department of Special Collections, and Miss Katherine M. Hall of the Inter-Library Loan Department have been continually helpful.

A number of my friends and colleagues at the University of Chicago have shared their ideas with me, have given me their suggestions, or have read all or part of the manuscript. For their acute comments, their frankness, and their generosity, it is a pleasure to thank all of them. They include: Walter Blair, Avery O. Craven, John Hope Franklin, William T. Hutchinson, Raven I. McDavid, Jr., Mitford M. Mathews, Roger Shugg, and Richard J. Storr. The stimulus, advice, and criticisms of Richard C. Wade have been invaluable. Others who have offered specific suggestions helpful to the research or who have read all or part of the manuscript are: Professor Allan G. Bogue of the University of Wisconsin, Professor Thomas C. Cochran of the University of Pennsylvania, Professor Richard M. Dorson of Indiana University, Professor William H. Goetzmann of the University of Texas, Professor Thomas Pyles of the University of Florida, Professor George R. Stewart of the University of California, and Professor David D. Van Tassel of the University of Texas. They have all saved me from errors, but I have sometimes differed from them on facts or on interpretations, so that I alone am responsible for the errors which remain.

The spirituals on p. 193 are reprinted by the courtesy of the Hampton Institute Press, from Robert Nathaniel Dett (ed.), *Religious Folk-Songs of the Negro* (1927). Dr. L. H. Butterfield has generously shared with me his unpublished research on John Adams on which I have drawn at pp. 359–62 above.

I have been fortunate in receiving stimulus, suggestions, and criticisms from my former and present students at the University of Chicago. All those who have helped are too numerous to mention; those who particularly come to mind either because they have read parts of the manuscript or have shared their unpublished research with me include: Professor James Chase, now of the University of Texas, Professor Rogers Hollingsworth, now of the University of Wisconsin, and Professor Herbert Klein, now of the University of Chicago.

My research assistants, who worked with me over long periods, helping to gather raw materials, and stirred me with their ideas, have helped make this book possible. Professor Albert U. Romasco of New York University and Professor Harold D. Woodman of the University of Missouri aided me generously while they were graduate students at the University of Chicago; they have shared with me their important unpublished research and have continued to give me the benefit of their advice and criticism. To John T. Juricek, who has been my research assistant during the last two years of the research and writing, I owe a debt which I cannot repay. All these, by their intelligence, industry, imagination, and passion for accuracy have helped make this book a stage in my own education.

The transcription of the manuscript from first draft to the printer's copy has been done by Mrs. Ed Stack of Homewood, Illinois. Her resourcefulness, efficiency, scrupulous care, and unstinting energy have been essential to the completion of the book within a reasonable time.

Secretarial assistance has also come from Miss Margaret Fitzsimmons. David West Boorstin has helped see the manuscript through the press.

To Mrs. Margaret Anderson of London, who has ably prepared the index, I wish to express my thanks.

Mr. Jess Stein, Vice-President of Random House, has had a faith in the conception of *The Americans,* which has encouraged me to carry on the book. The manuscript has immeasurably profited from his ruthless editorial red pencil. Mrs. Leonore C. Hauck has efficiently and patiently dealt with the numerous details of production of this volume.

My greatest debt is to my wife, Ruth F. Boorstin, who has shared this book from the first outlines to the last proof correction. Without her encouragement it could not have been conceived, and without her constant and discriminating editorial advice, its writing would have been impossible. She has been so long and so thoroughly dedicated to this book that it is almost redundant to dedicate the book to her.

Following is a list of works useful for studying the period covered in this volume. It is meant to help the reader who may wish to pursue further some of the topics I discuss, to suggest the kinds of material on which I have relied in my research, and to indicate my heavy debt to other scholars. But it is not a complete bibliography of any aspect of the subject, nor does it include all the works I have used. After a General section, the bibliography is arranged into eight Parts, corresponding with the grouping of topics in my chapters. In each Part, I have begun by mentioning works of general interest and easiest accessibility, and I have then proceeded toward the more "primary" and more esoteric materials. For books on topics which reach back into the colonial period, the reader is also referred to the Bibliographical Notes for *The Americans: The Colonial Experience.*

GENERAL

For American history in the years between the Revolution and the Civil War we have few works that merit a place alongside Bancroft and Parkman. One of these is Henry Adams' *History of the United States during the Administrations of Jefferson and Madison* (9 vols., 1889–91), which opens the grandeur of the subject (the first six chapters, "The United States in 1800," are available in Great Seal Paperback). But Adams—like Bancroft and Parkman—wrote before the rise of an American historical profession (American Historical Association, founded 1884, incorporated, 1889; Mississippi Valley Historical Association, now called the Organization of American Historians, founded 1907). This profession has both raised the level of scholarly competence and sharpened the criticism in monographic literature. But it has also increased the need for the generalizing, dramatizing amateur. More recent scholarly works have too commonly tended to become efforts to arbitrate among other scholars' views [see, for example, Edward Channing's *History of the United States,* (6 vols., 1905–25), or Charles M. Andrews, *The Colonial Period of American History,* (4 vols., 1934–38)], or to illustrate some peculiar historiographic emphasis [see, for example, John Bach McMaster's *History of the People of the United States, from the Revolution to the Civil War,* (8 vols., 1883–1913)].

Biographies still happily remain a refuge of the amateur. These tend to be free from academic jargon and pedantic quibbles, and admit us to the drama and conflict of the age. Among the best are: Albert J. Beveridge's *Life of John Marshall* (4 vols., 1916–19) and his uncompleted *Life of Abraham Lincoln* (2 vols., 1928; coming down only to 1858); Marquis James, *Andrew Jackson* (2 vols., 1933–37); Dumas Malone, *Jefferson and His Time* (4 vols. to date, 1948——); Page Smith, *John Adams* (2 vols., 1962); Samuel Flagg Bemis, *John Quincy Adams* . . . (2 vols., 1949–56); Carleton Mabee, *The American Leonardo . . . Samuel F. B. Morse* (1943); David Donald, *Charles Sumner* (2 vols., 1960——); George Dangerfield, *Chancellor Robert R. Livingston* (1960); Charles G. Sellers, Jr., *James K. Polk, Jacksonian* . . . (1957); Irving Brant, *James Madison* (3 vols., 1941–50); Charles M. Wiltse, *John C. Calhoun* (3 vols., 1944–51).

In our search for the intimate flavor of life in this era, we are lucky to have two copious and vivid diaries. William Bentley (1759–1819), a Boston-born Unitarian clergyman, a fluent linguist, and a man of affairs, kept a diary from April 30, 1784 to December 29, 1819 which lay unexploited in the custody of the American Antiquarian Society until it was published by the Essex Institute (4 vols., 1905–14). It is an invaluable record of daily life in Salem, where Bentley lived from 1783 till his death. The other, by George Templeton Strong (1820–75), a New York City lawyer and aristocrat, (ed. Allan Nevins and Milton H. Thomas, 4 vols., 1952; an enlarged 4th vol., for the Civil War Years, 1964) in a fluent and acid style allows us to share the everyday sights, sounds and smells (and the politics) of the big city.

In a class by itself—a monumental expression of an American genre halfway between history and folklore—is Carl Sandburg's *Abraham Lincoln* (6 vols., 1926–39). Sandburg has awakened popular interest in the American past, and—after the fashion of his predecessor Parson Weems—has made a folk-hero of the author. For an intimate introduction to the changing ways of daily life, one cannot do better than read Conrad Richter's scrupulously researched novels, *The Trees* (1940), *The Fields* (1946), and *The Town* (1950).

One of the last survivors of the great tradition of the amateur, of the historian as a man of letters, was Bernard De Voto (1897–1955). His vivid, if sometimes dyspeptic, books sweep the whole West: *The Course of Empire* (1952), on the exploration of the continent; *Across the Wide Missouri* (1947), on the Rocky Mountain fur trade; *The Year of Decision: 1846* (1943); and *Mark Twain's America* (1932). Never accepted as a "professional" historian, he reached the reading citizen and permanently added to the literature as did few of his more professional contemporaries.

A number of Classic Controversies, established by American historians at the very birth of their profession, have provided a jargon that merits a place alongside that of other social "scientists." In other ways, too, these controversies have helped create a guild; they have tended to center, not around a subject but around personalities in the profession.

A good example is the so-called "Beard" Thesis, supposedly found in the writings of Charles A. Beard (1874–1948)—especially in *An Economic Interpretation of the Constitution* (1913), *Economic Origins of Jeffersonian Democracy* (1915), and *The Rise of American Civilization* (2 vols., 1927). Beard, though academically trained as a political scientist, spent much of his active life outside academic precincts. A man of independent and changing views, he performed the great service, among others, of domesticating Marxian insights into American history. But he has become a stalking horse for a voluminous learned literature, more often incendiary than illuminating. As a result, professional discussion of the Federal Constitution and of the democratizing movements under Jefferson has centered too much around whether and why and how Beard was "wrong" and too little around what really happened.

Another controversy of more recent vintage, which promises to be almost as prolific, originated around Arthur M. Schlesinger Jr.'s *Age of Jackson* (1945; Little, Brown Paperback). This book profited from the New Deal experience to offer some new insights into Andrew Jackson and his age: within twenty years, the "Schlesinger" Thesis had become a popular academic target. By-products of both these controversies have been some important books. For example (on Beard's thesis), Forrest McDonald, *We the People; the Economic Origins of the Constitution* (1958). And (on Schlesinger's thesis): John W. Ward, *Andrew Jackson, Symbol of an Age* (1955); Marvin Meyers, *The Jacksonian Persuasion* (1957); Bray Hammond, *Banks and Politics in America, from the Revolution to the Civil War* (1957); Lee Benson, *Jacksonian Democracy* (1962).

While professional controversies have multiplied and been inflated, many important issues have not received attention proportionate to their importance. For example, while the Civil War has become a popular hobby, and the retracing of its battles a source of family fun, the great question of how and why the war came has had less than its share of attention. Readable and important books— for example, Avery O. Craven's *Coming of the Civil War* (2d ed. 1957), his *Civil War in the Making* (1959), and Roy F. Nichols' *Disruption of American Democracy* (1948)—have chronicled the breakdown of party politics, but no thesis about the coming of the war (not even the hypothesis of an "irrepressible conflict") has quite yet become a classic controversy in the profession. Allan Nevins' *Or-*

deal of the Union (1947) and its successors in his projected twelve-volume series will offer the first full-length social and political history of the war to be written by a professional historian in this century.

It is also curious, and symptomatic of the power of professional orthodoxy, that until lately the so-called "Turner" Thesis, supposedly originating in a paper, "The Significance of the Frontier in American History," read before the American Historical Association in 1893, by Frederick Jackson Turner (1861–1932), has become a dogma to be applied rather than a hypothesis to be tested. It is expressive of Turner's own undogmatic temper that perhaps his principal works on the period of the present volume are collections of essays: *The Frontier in American History* (1920), *The United States, 1830–1850* (1935), and *The Significance of Sections in American History* (ed. Max Farrand, 1950). See also his *Rise of the New West* (1906); and (with Frederick Merk) *References on the History of the West* (1922). The Turner papers, at the Huntington Library, are now being edited by Ray A. Billington.

Turner himself, as much poet as historian, hoped to be a catalyst rather than an indoctrinator. It is doubly ironic, therefore, that the so-called "Turner" thesis, which would make "the frontier" a key to American history and institutions, should have been treated as an article of faith rather than a starting point for investigation. But there have been some helpful efforts to make Turner's writings into the questions he intended them to be, instead of treating them as a sacred text with the answers. These include: Merle Curti, *The Making of an American Community* (1959), an ingenious intensive study of Trempealeau County, Wisconsin, testing the applicability of some of Turner's suggestions concerning community organization; William Appleman Williams, "The Frontier Thesis and American Foreign Policy," *Pacific Historical Review*, XXIV (1955), 379–395 and *The Tragedy of American Diplomacy* (Dell Paperback, 1963); and Richard C. Wade, *The Urban Frontier; the Rise of Western Cities, 1790–1830* (1959; Phoenix Paperback), which queries some of the crucial assumptions about the relation between city and countryside. A promising effort to translate Turner's notions from dogmatic answers into suggestive questions is being made under the imaginative editorship of Ray A. Billington in "Histories of the American Frontier," a multi-volume exploratory series (Holt, Rinehart and Winston, 1963–); see, for example, Rodman W. Paul, *Mining Frontiers of the West, 1848–1880* (1963).

Of the new specialties which have prospered within the last half century, one of the most prolific has been "Intellectual History." This subject has owed much of its impetus in America to the subtle minds of Arthur O. Lovejoy, whose *Great Chain of Being* (1935) illustrated a method followed by others in the *Journal of the History of Ideas* (1940–), of which he was a founder, and of Perry Miller, whose monumental *New England Mind* (2 vols., 1939–53) showed what could be done with American materials. From the beginning this specialty was closely allied to the history of literature, a fact which helped the study quickly become respectable abroad. This also tended to make it a discipline for reworking familiar ground, and hence perhaps less useful than other disciplines for discovering what is distinctive about American culture. The close association with literature began with Vernon L. Parrington, whose engrossing *Main Currents in American Thought* (3 vols., 1927–30) used literary remains in an effort to define what were supposed to be peculiarly American ways of thinking.

The literary emphasis has produced some monumental works of permanent value, like F. O. Matthiessen, *American Renaissance; Art and Expression in the Age of Emerson and Whitman* (1941), and thinner works of popular appeal, like Van Wyck Brooks' series, *The Flowering of New England* (1936), *New England's Indian Summer* (1940), *The World of Washington Irving* (1944), *The Times of Melville and Whitman* (1947), and *The Confident Years* (1952). But even at their best these works tend to be preoccupied with literary influences and counter-influences. By putting American culture in the familiar European belles-lettres tradition, they reassure us that our literature is not so inconsiderable nor so unsubtle as European critics have commonly said it to be. American Intellectual History, then, has been characterized by a heavy emphasis on figures like Cooper, Irving, Poe, Emerson, Hawthorne, Thoreau, Melville, Whitman, and Henry James, (all of whom left accessible and copious literary remains), and by a tendency to subject even minor works to excruciating exegesis. Incidentally, this has confirmed the temptations to treat all American civilization as merely a New World edition of what was essentially a European work. As Bernard De Voto explains in his *Literary Fallacy* (1944), such a belletristic emphasis inclines us to corrupt our aesthetic standards by overvaluing minor essayists and poetasters, and leads us to neglect other more characteristic forms of American expression. One of the most readable of the many efforts to interpret American social history through belles-lettres is Parrington's *Main Currents in American Thought* (see above). He covers the period of the present volume in his volumes I and II. Works which treat literature not as a touchstone of all culture, but rather from the point of view of the professional literary historian, succumb much less to these temptations. We are fortunate to have the admirable *Literary History of the United States,* edited by Robert E. Spiller and others (2 vols., 1948; Vol. 3, Bibliography, 1948), a collaborative work; but it does not entirely supersede many of the individual essays in the *Cambridge History of American Literature,* edited by William P. Trent and others (4 vols., 1931).

In economic history, too, the first half of the 20th century has produced a flood of works which are in a new class both for conceptual sophistication and for exploitation of documentary sources. A whole world separates William B. Weeden's *Economic and Social History of New England, 1620–1789,* 2 vols., 1891 from Edward C. Kirkland's, *Men, Cities and Transportation; a Study in New England History 1820–1900* (2 vols., 1948). A new highway into the subject is provided by "The Economic History of the United States," ed. Henry David and others (Holt, Rinehart and Winston, 9 vols. 1951–), of which Vols. II, III, and IV deal with the years of the present volume: Curtis P. Nettels, *The Emergence of a National Economy, 1775–1815* (1962); Paul W. Gates, *The Farmer's Age: Agriculture, 1815–1860* (1960); George R. Taylor, *The Transportation Revolution, 1815–1860* (1951).

Perhaps because lucre is less honorific than "culture," the writing of economic history has been a great deal less inhibited and more freewheeling than the writing of "intellectual" history, and has tended to move more freely into categories arising out of the American experience. As a result, many of the individual works mentioned below—on railroads, canals, banks, transportation, communications, and business history in general—are among the most useful in helping us discover the American experience.

Two recent developments have transformed the task of learning about American history for the amateur or for the student at some distance from a research library. The first is the rise of the paperback book, especially since World War II: by 1965, paperback titles in print numbered some 30,000, covering all subjects, and including hundreds of items valuable for the period of the present volume. These range from reprints of once scarce items, like the journals and diaries of western travelers (now available, for example, in a paperback series of Yale University Press) to reprints of basic monographs like Albert K. Weinberg, *Manifest Destiny* (1935; Encounter Paperback) and Kenneth Stampp, *The Peculiar Institution* (1956; Vintage-Caravelle Paperback, 1964) and to standard biographies like Henry Steele Commager, *Theodore Parker* (1936; Beacon Paperback). Titles are added to the list so rapidly that I cannot provide up-to-date information on the paperback availability of the items listed in these notes. Up-to-date information can be found in the current issue of *Paperbound Books in Print* (R. R. Bowker Co., New York); students may wish to own the inexpensive annual *Paperbound Book Guide for Colleges.*

Another momentous development is the growth of the multivolume, scrupulously edited, editions of the papers of leading figures of American history. The pioneer work of this kind was the *Papers of Thomas Jefferson,* edited by Julian P. Boyd for the Princeton University Press (1950–), which will run to fifty-odd volumes. These editions differ from their predecessors, not only in the completeness with which they present the writings of their authors, but in the inclusion of a representative selection of the papers received by the author, and in the fullness of their apparatus explaining the social context. While these editions are usually beyond the pocketbook of the amateur or the individual scholar, they are widely available in libraries; they offer an unprecedented opportunity to get the feel of the documentary raw materials. Editions now in preparation include the Adams papers and the papers of Benjamin Franklin, Alexander Hamilton, James Madison, Henry Clay, John C. Calhoun, Daniel Webster, and others.

Useful articles on particular topics will be found in learned journals, such as *The William and Mary Quarterly* (primarily concerned with the colonial period), *The Journal of American History* (until 1964 published under the title, *The Mississippi Valley Historical Review*), *The American Quarterly*, *The New England Quarterly*, *The Journal of Southern History*, *The Journal of Negro History*, *The American West*, *The Pacific Historical Review*, *The American Historical Review*, and others; and in many excellent journals of state and local historical societies whose products are often of much more than regional interest. Some of these are the *Indiana Magazine of History*, *The Pennsylvania Magazine of History and Biography*, *Virginia Magazine of History and Biography*. Other publications of state and local historical societies reprint documents and specialized studies. A rich mine for these years is the Massachusetts Historical Society *Collections* (1792– ; with a general index to publications through 1935).

The voluminousness and variety of printed materials has made impracticable anything like a complete bibliography for the years between Independence and the Civil War. Charles Evans, ed., *American Bibliography: A Chronological Dictionary of all Books, Pamphlets, and Periodical Publications Printed in the United States . . . 1639–1820* (12 vols., 1903–34) reaches into this period. A basic bibliographic tool is Joseph Sabin and others, eds., *Dictionary of Books Relating to America from its Discovery to the Present Time* (29 vols., 1868–92; reprinted 1928–36); but this is less helpful, and less apt to be com-

plete, for the post-Revolutionary years. The multiplication and diffusion of printed matter is itself a major historical phenomenon. For this reason the scholar in search of material on elusive, ephemeral, or unorthodox subjects will do well to use Clarence S. Brigham, comp., *History and Bibliography of American Newspapers, 1690–1820* (2 vols., 1947); Winifred Gregory, comp., *American Newspapers, 1821–1936* (1937); and the first two volumes of Frank Luther Mott, *History of American Magazines* (1930–1957), Vol. I (1741–1850) and Vol. II (1850–1865).

BOOK ONE

COMMUNITY

PART ONE

THE VERSATILES:

New Englanders

A bizarre combination of provincialism and cosmopolitanism has marked recent New England historiography as it has marked much of New England life. Perhaps it is a special product of the sea. To touch this dual spirit in the years between the Revolution and the Civil War, one can do no better than start with Samuel Eliot Morison's *Maritime History of Massachusetts, 1783–1860* (1921; Sentry Paperback). Morison, one of the master American historians of this century, and one of the few American historians whose work on New World subjects has commanded a world-wide audience, has written his most important books either on circumscribed topics in New England history (for example, his history of Harvard College) or on seafaring topics that touch the whole world (for example, his life of Christopher Columbus and his naval history of World War II). That proverbial Bostonian "hub-of-the-universe" frame of mind, which has nevertheless not prevented New Englanders from becoming brilliant cosmopolites, is charmingly expressed in Morison's own account (*Vistas of History*, 1964) of his reactions in Rome on receiving the munificent Balzan Prize in History for 1963, as a recognition of his international stature as a historian. At the splendid ceremonies of presentation of the prizewinners to Pope John XXIII, the Russian laureate brought the Pope greetings from the people of Russia; Morison brought "greetings from Boston."

For a one-volume general account of New England in these years, nothing yet supersedes James Truslow Adams' *New England in the Republic, 1776–1850* (1926). More detailed accounts are: Albert Bushnell Hart, ed., *Commonwealth History of Massachusetts* (5 vols., 1927–30), and William T. Davis, ed., *The New England States* (4 vols., 1897), whose contributors include Henry Cabot Lodge, Edward Everett Hale, and other notable New Englanders with careers and family memories reaching back to the pre-Civil War era. Frederick Jackson Turner gives us a stimulating essay in "Greater New England in the Middle of the Nineteenth Century," American Antiquarian Society, *Proceedings,* n. s., XXIX (1919), 222–41. For bedside reading, Van Wyck Brooks' series (see General section, above) provides a rambling introduction, much by way of gossip and trivia, to the New England literati of this era. Solid works on special topics, which open paths into the general history of the region and the age include: Arthur H. Clark, *The Clipper Ship Era* (1910); Oscar Handlin, *Boston's Immigrants* (rev. ed., 1959) and (with Mary F. Handlin) *Commonwealth: A Study of the Role of Government in the American Economy: Massachusetts, 1774–1861* (1947); Lois K. Mathews, *The Expansion of New England* (1909; 1962).

A useful tool is Appleton P. C. Griffin, *Bibliography of the Historical Publications issued by the New England States* (1895).

A contemporary introduction to New England seafaring life is *Two Years before the Mast,* (pub. anonymously, 1840) by Richard Henry Dana Jr. (1815–82), who left Harvard in 1834 after his sophomore year to become an ordinary seaman on the *Pilgrim*; he sailed from Boston around the Horn to California for hides, and returned in 1836 after a stormy passage. Dana's work, which describes the pastimes and especially the hardships of seamen, was intended as a tract presenting "the light and the dark together." Dana also published *The Seaman's Friend* (1841), explaining to seamen their legal rights and duties, and he championed the cause of fugitive slaves. *Two Years before the Mast,* though designed as a reformist tract, probably affected the genres of writing about the sea more than it did the lives of seamen. No one can read it without increasing his admiration for seafaring New Englanders. See also, James D. Hart, "The Education of Richard Henry Dana, Jr." *N.E.Q.,* IX (1936), 3–25.

Nearly all books about New England in this period somehow touch the meaning of the sea for the life of the region. The New England fisheries, an epic subject, still await their historian. The best general account is Raymond McFarland, *A History of the New England Fisheries* (1911) which is incomplete and lacking in breadth, but which can be supplemented by the copious detail in George Brown Goode, *The Fisheries and Fishery Industries of the United States* (7 vols., 1884–87), and (by Goode and others) "Materials for a History of the Mackerel Fishery," in U.S. Commission of Fish and Fisheries, *Report of the Commissioner for 1881,* pp. 89–531. One must still depend too much on works of local piety, such as *The Fisheries of Gloucester from the First*

Catch by the English in 1623, to the Centennial Year, 1876 (Gloucester, Mass., 1876). Some of the vast possibilities of this subject appear in Harold A. Innis, *The Cod Fisheries: The History of an International Economy* (1940). A classic tale of whale-hunting is Herman Melville's *Moby-Dick, or the White Whale* (1851).

The story of New England seafaring has attracted able historians who have offered a solid factual fare without overlooking the romance. Their works include, in addition to Morison's *Maritime History of Massachusetts* (see above), books on particular kinds of ships, for example, Arthur H. Clark, *The Clipper Ship Era* (1910), Basil Lubbock, *The China Clippers* (4th ed., 1919), and books on the commerce of particular ports, like James Duncan Phillips, *Salem and the Indies* (1947). The adventures of those who went around the Horn to seek gold in California are recounted in: Octavius T. Howe, *Argonauts of '49: History and Adventures of Emigrant Companies from Massachusetts, 1849–1850* (1923), full of well-documented detail; Oscar Lewis, *Sea Routes to the Gold Fields: the Migration by Water to California in 1849–1852* (1949), a readable narrative; and John E. Pomfret, ed., *California Gold Rush Voyages 1848–49: Three Original Narratives* (1954). Of the admirable works by Robert G. Albion, one (with Jennie Barnes Pope), *Sea Lanes in Wartime: The American Experience, 1775–1942* (1942), directly concerns New England; others, for example *Square-Riggers on Schedule, The New York Sailing Packets to England, France and the Cotton Ports* (1938) and his invaluable *Rise of New York Port, 1815–1860* (1939) chronicle some other American adventurers to whom the New Englanders can be compared. A sidelight on other seafaring adventure of the day is found in Jeannette Mirsky's concise and readable account of the pioneer Arctic explorer, *Elisha Kent Kane and the Seafaring Fron-*

tier (1954). For the impingement of world politics, see Gerald S. Graham, *Sea Power and British North America, 1783–1820* (1941), and Eldon Griffin, *Clippers and Consuls* (1938).

The literacy of New England seafarers has left us many of their own narratives, of which a good example is Josiah Quincy, ed., *The Journals of Major Samuel Shaw, the First American Consul at Canton* (1847). The business aspects of seaborne adventure can be sampled in Kenneth W. Porter, *The Jacksons and the Lees* (2 vols., 1937).

While students of intellectual history commonly think of Melville's *Moby-Dick* as New England's great contribution to the literature of the sea, a more characteristic and more influential work is Nathaniel Bowditch, *The New American Practical Navigator* (1802; ten editions before 1837; more than fifty since then), which became the navigator's bible. Bowditch (1773–1838), a self-educated mathematical prodigy of Salem, had traveled the world as ship's clerk, supercargo, and master; besides this work he produced numerous papers on mathematics and astronomy, pioneered in the insurance business, and was active in public affairs. For his extraordinary life see: Robert E. Berry, *Yankee Stargazer: The Life of Nathaniel Bowditch* (1941); Augustus P. Loring, Jr., *Nathaniel Bowditch . . .*, Newcomen Society of London (American Branch, Addresses, V); and the excellent brief article in the *DAB* by Raymond C. Archibald. The other great American sea-scientist of the age was Matthew Fontaine Maury (1806–73), whose *Physical Geography of the Sea* (1855) pioneered modern oceanography; without it the first transatlantic cable might not have been laid. Maury was not a New Englander but a Virginian, and he resigned from the Union navy to serve the Confederacy. His work is now readily available in the John Harvard Library (ed., John Leighly; 1963).

The ice trade and refrigeration, despite their pervasive significance for cuisine, diet, public health, and urban life, have excited little interest among American historians. The best starting point is Richard O. Cummings' valuable little book, *The American Ice Harvests* (1949), which can be supplemented by details in his "American Ice Industry and the Development of Refrigeration, 1790–1860" (Unpublished Ph.D. dissertation, Harvard University). Later chapters of the story are recounted in Oscar E. Anderson Jr.'s standard *Refrigeration in America* (1953). Wider aspects of the subject are explored in Cummings' incomplete but suggestive, *The American and his Food* (1940), and in Edgar W. Martin, *The Standard of Living in 1860* (1942). Frederic Tudor remains one of the great unsung heroes of American business history, and he still awaits his biographer. The contemporary documents about him which have been printed are small in quantity but rich in detail. Most valuable are: Henry G. Pearson, "Frederic Tudor, Ice King," Mass. Hist. Soc., *Proc.*, LXV (Nov., 1933), 169–215, which offers much of his "Ice House Diary"; Frederic Tudor, "Mr. Tudor's Letter on the Ice-Trade," Mass. Hist. Soc., *Proc.*, III (1855–58), 51–60. For a sample of his business letters, see "Frederic Tudor—Ice King," *Bulletin of the Business Historical Society*, VI (Sept., 1932), 1–8, and "Supplementary Material on Frederic Tudor Ice Project," IX (Feb., 1935), 1–6. And see William Tudor, ed., *Deacon Tudor's Diary* (1896). Fugitive facts can be found in contemporary articles like "Ice: And the Ice Trade," *Hunt's Merchants' Magazine and Commercial Review*, XXXIII (Aug., 1855), 169–79, or in local histories like Lucius R. Paige, *History of Cambridge, Massachusetts, 1630–1877* (1877).

The granite industry, too, deserves more attention than historians have given it. The best general work is Arthur W. Brayley, *History of the Granite Industry of New England* (2 vols., 1913), which was published by authority of the National Association of Granite Industries; despite its antiquarianism, its inadequate documentation, and its emphasis on the growth of particular firms, it offers much information on the industry in general, with valuable drawings and photographs illustrating techniques. Solomon Willard (1783–1861), the versatile self-educated architect of Bunker Hill Monument and of many important buildings in Greek revival style, was a pioneer in granite technology, in central heating, and in other areas, and the mentor of the hotel architect Isaiah Rogers (see Part Three, below). He too awaits his biographer. The best now available is a mere sketch: William W. Wheildon, *Memoir of Solomon Willard* (1865). One of the most interesting documents on this subject is Willard's *Plans and Section of the Obelisk on Bunker's Hill, with the Details of Experiments Made in Quarrying the Granite* (1841); the history of the Monument can be followed in the Proceedings of the Bunker Hill Monument Association, dramatizing the interaction of technology, sentiment, patriotism, and business enterprise. An eloquent brief statement of the importance of granite in New England life is in *The Address of Charles Francis Adams Jr., and Proceedings at the Dedication of the Crane Memorial Hall* (1883).

For the significance of the rise of granite-quarrying and cutting for architecture, see: Talbot F. Hamlin's copiously illustrated *Greek Revival Architecture in America* (1944), which describes the history of the movement, region by region; the works of Robert Mills (1781–1855), architect of the Washington Monument at the capital, described in biographies by C. C. Wilson, *Robert Mills, Architect* (1919), H. M. Gallagher, *Robert Mills, Architect of the Washington Monument* (1935), and in the excellent brief sketch in the *DAB* by Fiske Kimball; and William Dunlap, *History of the Rise and Progress of the Arts of Design in the United States* (2 vols., 1834), esp. Vol. II. The relations of architecture to sculpture can be caught in the eloquent writings of Horatio Greenough (1805–52), now handily available as *Form and Function: Remarks on Art, Design, and Architecture* (ed. Harold A. Small; U. of Cal. Press Paperback), or in *The Travels, Observations, and Experience of a Yankee Stonecutter* (1852; Facsimile, intro. Nathalia Wright, 1958). For the larger artistic context see Oliver Larkin's panoramic *Art and Life in America* (rev. ed., 1960).

We still need a readable, up-to-date general history of the origins and development of manufacturing in the United States. A stimulating introduction to some of the distinctively American problems is William Miller, ed., *Men in Business: Essays in the History of Entrepreneurship* (1952), a collection of essays including among others John E. Sawyer, "The Entrepreneur and the Social Order: France and the United States," Robert K. Lamb, "The Entrepreneur and the Community," and Frances W. Gregory and Irene D. Neu, "The American Industrial Elite in the 1870's: Their Social Origins." A readable elementary introduction is Thomas C. Cochran and William Miller, *The Age of Enterprise: A Social History of Industrial America* (1956). For some of the differences between American problems and those elsewhere, see: D. L. Burn, "The Genesis of American Engineering Competition, 1850–1870," *Ec. Hist.*, II (1930–33), 292–311; H. J. Habbakuk, *American and British Technology in the Nineteenth Century* (1962); John E. Sawyer, "Social Structure and Economic Progress: General Propositions and some French Examples," *Am. Ec. Rev.*, XLI (May, 1951), 321–29, and "The Social Basis of the American System of Manufac-

turing," *Journ. Ec. Hist.*, XIV (1954), 361–79; W. Paul Strassman, *Risk and Technological Innovation: American Manufacturing Methods during the Nineteenth Century* (1959); W. Lloyd Warner and J. O. Low, *The Social System of the Modern Factory* (1947). The standard general works are J. Leander Bishop, *A History of American Manufactures* (2 vols., 1864), still a source of much valuable information and Victor S. Clark, *History of Manufactures in the United States* (3 vols., 1916–29), unimaginative but solid.

The history of technology, one of the most dramatic and most relevant chapters of our past, should have a larger audience. Two good starting points are Joseph W. Roe, *English and American Toolbuilders* (1916), full of intriguing detail with wide implications, and John A. Kouwenhoven, *Made in America: The Arts in Modern Civilization* (1948; Anchor Paperback), brilliant essays on the relations of art and technology. The best introductory survey for this period is Roger Burlingame's *March of the Iron Men: A Social History of Union Through Invention* (1949), which can be illuminated by Mitchell A. Wilson's profusely illustrated *American Science and Invention, a Pictorial History* (1954). Standard textbooks are: Abbot P. Usher, *A History of Mechanical Inventions* (1954) and John W. Oliver, *History of American Technology* (1956). Useful on particular topics are: A. Hunter Dupree, *Science in the Federal Government: A History of Policies and Activities to 1940* (1957); Daniel H. Calhoun, *The American Civil Engineer* (1960); the fragmentary Roy T. Bramson, *Highlights in the History of American Mass Production* (1945); Charles H. Fitch, "Report on the Manufactures of Interchangeable Mechanism," *Report on the Manufactures of the United States at the Tenth Census (June 1, 1880)* . . ., U.S. Census Bureau, Tenth Census (1880), II, 611 ff. and in the same volume, Carroll D. Wright, "Report on the Factory System of the United States," II, 527–610; Samuel Rezneck, "The Rise and Early Development of Industrial Consciousness in the United States, 1760–1830," *Journ. Ec. & Bus. Hist.*, IV (1931–32), 784–811; S. C. Gilfillan, "Invention as a Factor in *Economic History*," *The Tasks of Economic History, JEH*, Supplement V (Dec., 1945), 66–85; Courtney R. Hall, *History of American Industrial Science* (1954); Archibald Clow and Nan L. Clow, *The Chemical Revolution . . .* (1952). And on the patent system: U. S. Patent Office, *The Story of the American Patent System* (1940); Gustavus A. Weber, *The Patent Office, Its History, Activities, and Organization* (1924); William B. Bennett, *The American Patent System: An Economic Interpretation* (1943); Floyd L. Vaughan, *The United States Patent System: Legal and Economic Conflicts in American Patent History* (1956).

Because much of the history of technology does not fit conventional academic categories, here, even more than elsewhere, the reader must seek out biographies. The *Dictionary of American Biography* offers many concise and reliable accounts of figures who elude textbooks and conventional surveys. In addition, see, for example: Jeannette Mirsky and Allan Nevins, *The World of Eli Whitney* (1952); Constance McL. Green, *Eli Whitney and the Birth of American Technology* (1956), a delightful brief account; Ferris Greenslet, *The Lowells and their Seven Worlds* (1946); Kenneth W. Porter, *The Jacksons and the Lees* (2 vols., 1937); Carleton Mabee, *American Leonardo . . . Samuel F. B. Morse* (1943).

Especially useful for these chapters are: Nathan Appleton, *Introduction of the Power Loom, and Origin of Lowell* (1858); "Notice of Samuel Appleton," *New England Historical and Genealogical Register*, VIII (1854), 9–17; William P. Blake, "Sketch of Eli Whitney," *Papers of the New Haven Colony Hist. Soc.*, V (1894), 109–31; E. H. Cameron, *Samuel Slater: Father of American Manufactures* (1960); Margaret Clapp, *Forgotten First Citizen: John Bigelow* (1947); M. B. Hammond, ed., "Correspondence of Eli Whitney Relative to the Invention of the Cotton Gin," *AHR*, III (1897–98), 90–127; Denison Olmsted, *Memoir of Eli Whitney* (1846); Jack Rohan, *Yankee Arms Maker: The Incredible Career of Samuel Colt* (1935); Carl P. Russell, *Guns on the Early Frontiers* (1957), which includes accounts of particular manufacturers; George S. White, ed., *Memoir of Samuel Slater, The Father of American Manufactures. . .* (2d ed., 1836); Robert C. Winthrop, *Memoir of the Hon. Nathan Appleton* (1861). Valuable biographies are found in the publications edited by Freeman Hunt (1804–58) in New York: especially in *Hunt's Merchant's Magazine* (under varying titles, 1839–58), and in the several volumes of his *Lives of the Merchants*, collected from his publications.

For the colonial background of manufacturing an indispensable and attractive introduction is Carl Bridenbaugh, *The Colonial Craftsman* (1950; Phoenix Paperback). See also: R. M. Tryon, *Household Manufacturers in the United States, 1640–1860* (1917); Marcus W. Jernegan, "Slavery and the Beginnings of Industrialism in the American Colonies," *AHR*, XXV (1920), 220–40.

For American labor history and some of the peculiarities of the history of labor organizations in this country a readable introduction is Henry Pelling, *American Labor* (1960; Phoenix Paperback), with a selective bibliography. Useful specialized works include: Norman J. Ware, *The Industrial Worker, 1840–1860* (1924); John R. Commons and others, *History of Labour in the United States* (4 vols., 1935–36). The best collection of documents in labor history is John R.

Commons and others, eds., *A Documentary History of American Industrial Society* (10 vols., 1910–11).

Some specifically New England aspects of industrial history can be discovered in two excellent monographs, Oscar and Mary F. Handlin, *Commonwealth; A Study of the Role of Government in the American Economy; Massachusetts, 1774–1861* (1947) and Edward C. Kirkland, *Men, Cities and Transportation: a Study of New England History, 1820–1900* (2 vols., 1948). Useful histories of particular types of manufacturing are: Seth Bryant, *Shoe and Leather Trade of the Last Hundred Years* (1891); A. H. Cole, *The American Wool Manufacture* (2 vols., 1926); B. E. Hazard, *The Organization of the Boot and Shoe Industry in Massachusetts before 1875* (1921); C. B. Kuhlmann, *Development of the Flour Milling Industry in the United States* (1929); Marion N. Rawson, *Handwrought Ancestors: The Story of Early American Shops and those who worked therein* (1936); Caroline F. Ware, *The Early New England Cotton Manufacture* (1931); L. H. Weeks, *A History of Paper Manufacturing in the United States, 1690–1916* (1916); Charles W. Sawyer, *Firearms in American History* (3 vols., 1911). See also, histories of particular companies such as George W. Browne, *The Amoskeag Manufacturing Co.* (1915); or of particular towns such as William P. Blake, *History of the Town of Hamden, Connecticut* (1888), which includes the local history of Eli Whitney's arms manufactory.

* * *

Nothing is more revealing of the peculiar character of the American legal tradition than the lack of a solid body of historical writing about the American legal past. Despite the enormous investment in American law schools within universities, and the unprecedented proliferation of books about American law for practitioners,

American legal history remains a Dark Continent. Except for constitutional history, which has been cultivated mostly outside law schools, and except for the work of a few pioneers —Julius Goebel, George Haskins, Mark de Wolfe Howe, Jr., Willard Hurst, Leonard Levy, Richard B. Morris, Edwin M. Dodd, and some others —the history of American private law has remained unexplored. Some explain this (for the colonial period) by the scarcity of materials, others (for the period covered in the present volume) by the superabundance of materials. Another explanation is the increasing professionalization of American law schools, and (despite their frequently expressed interest in "social sciences" and "interdisciplinary research") their myopic preoccupation with what is in current demand by practitioners. Decades pass, and, while lawyers, judges, and law professors repeat platitudes about their glorious professional past, they find no respectable place for legal history in their extensive curricula. Future historians will marvel that our society could have put the custody of our institutions into the hands of a profession with so little historical perspective.

The best place to begin a study of the development of law in New England in this era is Leonard W. Levy's admirable monograph, *The Law of the Commonwealth and Chief Justice Shaw* (1957). Roscoe Pound's *Formative Era of American Law* (1938) is helpful, but brief and lacking in detail. For the history of the profession the standard work is still Charles Warren, *A History of the American Bar* (1911), which is full of biographical detail, but offers few organizing ideas. On the history of legal education, Alfred Z. Reed's *Training for the Public Profession of the Law . . .* (1921; a report prepared under the auspices of the Carnegie Foundation for the Advancement of Teaching) remains the starting point.

See also: Samuel H. Fisher, *Litch-field Law School, 1774–1833: Biblio-graphical Catalogue of Students* (Yale Law Library, *Pub.* No. 11; 1946); William Draper Lewis, ed., *Great American Lawyers* (8 vols., 1907–9); Joel Parker, *The Law School of Har-vard College* (1871); Josef Redlich, *The Common Law and the Case Method in American University Law Schools* (1914); Charles Warren, *History of the Harvard Law School and of Early Legal Conditions in America* (3 vols., 1908). One can learn much about the requirements for successful judicial service and for prosperous legal practice from biographies: Theophilus Parsons, *Memoir of Theophilus Parsons* (1859); William W. Story, *Life and Letters of Joseph Story* (2 vols., 1851); Benjamin F. Thomas, "Sketch of the Life and Judicial Labors of Chief-Justice Shaw," Mass. Hist. Soc., *Proc.*, X (1867–69), 50–79; Claude M. Fuess, *Daniel Webster* (2 vols., 1930) and *Rufus Choate* (1928).

A pioneer monograph, of wide significance for the legal and social history of the whole period, is Edwin M. Dodd, *American Business Corporations until 1860, with special reference to Massachusetts* (1954). Other useful special studies are: George H. Evans, Jr., *Business Incorporations in the United States, 1800–1943* (1948); William C. Fowler, *Local Law in Massachusetts and Connecticut, Historically Considered* (1872); Shaw Livermore, "Unlimited Liability in Early American Corporations," *Journal of Political Economy*, XLIII (Oct., 1935), 674–87; Walter Nelles, "Commonwealth v. Hunt," *Columbia Law Rev.*, XXXII (Nov., 1932), 1128–69.

On the history of reform the literature is vast, but there is still no general history of American reform movements—even of those in New England. An interesting if unfamiliar pathway into the subject is Harold Schwartz's admirable *Samuel Gridley Howe: Social Reformer, 1801–1876*

(1956), which introduces us to the interrelation of education, reformist projects, national politics, business affairs, and family loyalties. Another readable work which carries the story into the later period is Arthur Mann, *Yankee Reformers in the Urban Age* (1954). Robert H. Bremner, *American Philanthropy* (1960; Phoenix Paperback) puts the New England efforts in context.

The voluminous literature on the antislavery movements can be approached through: Gilbert H. Barnes, *The Antislavery Impulse* (1933), a standard monograph; Dwight L. Dumond, *Antislavery: The Crusade for Freedom* (1961), and the accompanying *Bibliography of Antislavery in America* (1961); Lawrence Lader, *The Bold Brahmins: New England's War against Slavery* (1961); Benjamin P. Thomas, *Theodore Weld, Crusader for Freedom* (1950); and, for the mote in the New Englander's eye, Leon F. Litwack, *North of Slavery: The Negro in the Free States, 1790–1860* (1961).

Other items illuminating the many-sided reforming interests of New Englanders include: John A. Krout, *The Origins of Prohibition* (1925); Jesse H. Shera, *Foundations of the Public Library . . . in New England, 1629–1855* (1949); Carl Bode, *The American Lyceum, Town Meeting of the Mind* (1956); Helen E. Marshall, *Dorothea Dix, Forgotten Samaritan* (1937); Mary Mann, *Life and Works of Horace Mann* (5 vols., 1891); of which the *Life* appeared separately; Merle Curti, *The Social Ideas of American Educators* (1935; Littlefield, Adams Paperback); Louise H. Tharp, *Until Victory: Horace Mann and Mary Peabody* (1953); E. I. F. Williams, *Horace Mann: Educational Statesman* (1937); Rush Welter, *Popular Education and Democratic Thought* (1962). For a vivid contemporary view, see Josiah Quincy, *Remarks on Some of the Provisions of the Laws of Massachusetts, affecting Poverty, Vice and Crime* (1822). Additional material on Samuel Gridley Howe's experiments is found in: Maud Howe Elliot and Florence Howe Hall, *Laura Bridgman, Dr. Howe's Famous Pupil and what He Taught Her* (1903); Laura E. Howe Richards, *Laura Bridgman: The Story of an Opened Door* (1928); Laura E. Howe Richards, ed., *Letters and Journals of Samuel Gridley Howe* (2 vols., 1906–9).

The relation of utopianism and communitarianism to New England reformers can be traced in Alice Tyler, *Freedom's Ferment* (1944; Beacon Paperback) and Arthur Bestor, *Backwoods Utopias* (1950; Beacon Paperback). The relation of immigration to reform and anti-reform movements is discussed in: Oscar Handlin, *Boston's Immigrants* (rev. ed., 1959); Ray A. Billington, *The Protestant Crusade, 1800–1860* (1938; 1952); followed into the later period by John Higham, *Strangers in the Land; Patterns of American Nativism, 1860–1925* (1955), and Barbara Miller Solomon, *Ancestors and Immigrants, a Changing New England Tradition* (1956).

PART TWO

THE TRANSIENTS:

Joiners

Clichés of New England history (e.g., "Yankee Ingenuity") were made, for the most part, by New Englanders, clichés of Southern history (e.g., "Southern Chivalry") by Southerners; or by others reacting against these homemade clichés. Such stereotypes therefore tended to be idealizations by local patriots of their own virtues and vices.

The history of the West, however, generally became an allegory of ideals elsewhere unfulfilled or unattainable. The clichés about Western history coined during the period of the present volume were generally made by writers in the settled centers of culture

and of literature, mostly on or near the east coast. The first instalment of Parkman's *Oregon Trail* (1849) was signed "A Bostonian," and the numerous volumes of his long work on the colonial wars for the West were written in Boston. Similarly, William T. Porter, a Vermonter, published his *Spirit of the Times* from New York City. And in the earlier 20th century, before the age of movies, radio, and television, the most popular notions of westward expansion came from *The Winning of the West* (4 vols., 1889–96) by Theodore Roosevelt, a New Yorker by birth. Roosevelt, like his literary model Parkman, had spent only two years out West; at the time of publication of the final volume of his Western history he was President of the New York City Board of Police Commissioners. Romantic notions were reinforced in the still more popular novels (for example, *The Crossing*, a best-seller in 1904) of the American Winston Churchill (1871–1947); although this Churchill had been born in St. Louis, he was himself an example of the Eastward Movement, since he spent most of his life in New Hampshire. The notion of "The Westward Movement" thus manufactured for the most part in the East, carried overtones of "manifest" destiny, unshakable clear purpose, and "individualism." These, like many of the earlier stereotypes of Davy Crockett and Mike Fink, had been largely fabricated at a great distance from the scenes of Western action.

Romantic clichés gained scholarly respectability when the suggestive poetic statements of the meaning of the West in American history by Frederick Jackson Turner (himself anything but a cliché-monger) were turned by earnest academics into a "Frontier Thesis." Perfunctory disciples made a specialty of documenting the romantic stereotypes. At the same time, some of the best work in Western history was to be done by historians who had been inspired by Turner and stimulated by his ideas to go their own way. See, for example, Avery O. Craven's important monograph, *Soil Exhaustion as a Factor in the Agricultural History of Virginia and Maryland* (1925) and a stimulating collection of his essays, *An Historian and the Civil War* (1964), esp. Ch. XII, "The 'Turner Theories' and the South." Turner, like other important thinkers, has thus become the godfather of some of the best and some of the worst historical writing of this century. It is hard to avoid the suspicion that the magnitude of his influence is itself evidence of the scarcity of large organizing ideas among professional historians.

The best textbook of the subject, in which the student can profitably begin his inquiry into almost any topic, is Ray A. Billington's *Westward Expansion* (2d ed., 1960), with copious bibliographies. For an introduction to many topics, the volumes in *The Economic History of the United States* (10 vols., Holt, Rinehart and Winston, 1951–) are invaluable, especially Vol. II, *The Emergence of a National Economy, 1775–1815* (1962), by Curtis P. Nettels; Vol. III, *The Farmer's Age: Agriculture, 1815–1860* (1960), by Paul W. Gates; and Vol. IV, *The Transportation Revolution: Industry, 1815–1860* (1951), by George Taylor.

For the history of travel there is nothing yet to supplant Seymour Dunbar's *History of Travel in America* (1915; 1937), which is rich in well-indexed detail but poor in generalization; useful material can still be found in Balthasar H. Meyer, ed., *History of Transportation in the United States before 1860* (1917).

Two excellent introductory anthologies including representative selections from travelers in the period of this volume are: W. S. Tryon, ed., *Mirror for Americans* (3 vols., 1959), drawn from Americans; and Oscar Handlin, ed., *This Was America* (1949), drawn from foreigners.

The experience of westward-moving groups can be followed either in the experiences of particular groups, like those chronicled in Bernard De Voto's *Year of Decision, 1846* (1943), in Francis Parkman's familiar *Oregon Trail* (originally entitled, *The California and Oregon Trail;* 1849), or in accounts of particular routes of travel, like the volumes in the readable "American Trails Series" (McGraw Hill, 1962–), for example George R. Stewart, *The California Trail* (1962), Jonathan Daniels, *The Natchez Trace* (1962), or David Lavender, *Westward Vision: The Story of the Oregon Trail* (1963).

Some of the most important travelers' diaries and journals have been reprinted. A good starting point is Josiah Gregg (1805–50), *Commerce of the Prairies* (2 vols., 1844; ed. Max L. Moorhead, 1954), which can be supplemented by Josiah Gregg, *Diary and Letters* (2 vols., ed. Maurice G. Fulton, 1941–44). Invaluable and widely available series are *The Western Frontier Library* and *The American Exploration and Travel Series* (U. of Okla. Press) and the *Yale Western Americana* (Yale U. Press), now in paperback. The student will do best to select a few original accounts and read them from start to finish. Selections tend to emphasize dramatic episodes at the expense of organizational details and daily routine; but the material is so enticing that the reader of selections is not likely to make them a dead end. Among the better anthologies are: Robert W. Howard, *This is the West* (1957); Bayrd Still, ed., *The West* (1961); Robert V. Hine and Edwin R. Bingham, eds., *The Frontier Experience* (1963).

The history of the Mormons, another chapter in the story of westward-moving groups, has been ably chronicled. Of the vast literature, much of it polemical, I have found the following items most useful: Leonard J. Arrington, *Great Basin Kingdom: an Economic History of the Latter-Day Saints, 1830–1900* (1958), a detailed, scholarly survey of Mormon experiments in social and economic organization; Juanita Brooks, *The Mountain Meadows Massacre* (1950), an impressively detached account of one of the most controversial episodes in Mormon history; Richard F. Burton, *The City of the Saints and across the Rocky Mountains to California* (1861; ed. Fawn M. Brodie, 1963), a penetrating, sympathetic view after a brief visit, by the translator of Arabian Nights; Norman F. Furniss, *The Mormon Conflict 1850–1859* (1960), an admirable monograph; LeRoy R. and Ann W. Hafen, *Handcarts to Zion* (1960; Vol. XIV of the fifteen-volume *Far West and Rockies Series,* all by the Hafens) on the dramatic Mormon trek by handcart; Thomas F. O'Dea, *The Mormons* (1957), the best account of the history and practices of the Mormon religion; Ray B. West, *Kingdom of the Saints: the Story of Brigham Young and the Mormons* (1957), a popular history; *The Book of Mormon,* trans. Joseph Smith, Jr. (1830; 1879; 1920).

The westward-travel literature is voluminous and extremely miscellaneous. The best accounts have been competently edited, but the beginner in the subject is sure to be bewildered by their number and to wonder where to begin. An indispensable basic collection is Reuben G. Thwaites, ed., *Early Western Travels, 1748–1846* (32 vols., 1904–7), and a useful bibliography is Henry R. Wagner, *The Plains and the Rockies: A Bibliography of Original Narratives of Travel and Adventure, 1800–1865* (3rd ed., rev. Charles L. Camp, 1953); and, for the earlier period, R. W. G. Vail, ed., *The Voice of the Old Frontier* (1949), a bibliography of North American frontier literature, 1542–1800. See also Lucy L. Hazard, *The Frontier in Literature* (1927), and E. G. Cox,

A Reference Guide to the Literature of Travel (Vol. II covers America, mostly before 1800).

Contemporary accounts (including those of foreign travelers) which I have found most useful include: J. S. Buckingham, *The Eastern and Western States of America* (3 vols., London, 1842); James Hall, *Statistics of the West* (Cincinnati, 1837); Timothy Flint, *Recollections of the Last Ten Years* (1826); Frederick L. Olmsted, *A Journey through Texas* (2 vols., 1857); John Bidwell, *A Journey to California* (1842; 1937) a reprint of his day-by-day journal; Isabella L. Bird Bishop, *A Lady's Life in the Rocky Mountains* (1881; 1960); John Evans Brown, "Memoirs of a Gold Seeker in 'Forty-nine," *J. of Am. Hist.,* II (Jan.–March, 1908), 129–54; Richard F. Burton, *The City of the Saints and across the Rocky Mountains to California* (1861; ed. Fawn M. Brodie, 1963), also available in University of Nebraska Press Paperback (1963) under the title, *The Look of the West, 1860;* Chauncey de Leon Canfield, ed., *Jackson's Diary of a Forty-Niner, and Guide* (1947); Bennett C. Clark, *Diary of a Journey from Missouri to California in 1849,* reprinted from *Missouri Hist. Rev.,* XXIII (Oct., 1928), ed. Ralph P. Bieber; Alonzo Delano, *Across the Plains and Among the Diggings* (1853; 1936); David DeWolf, "Diary of the Overland Trail and Letters of Captain David Dewolf," Ill. State Hist. Soc., *Trans.,* (1925) pp. 183–222; Ulla Staley Fawkes, ed., *The Journal of Walter Griffitn Pigman* (1942), the first printing of a journal of a trip to California in 1850–51; Lodisa Frizzell (Victor H. Paltsits, ed.) *Across the Plains to California in 1852;* Kate L. Gregg, ed., *The Road to Santa Fe* (1952), reprinting the journal and diaries of George Champlin Sibley and others, 1825–27; Overton Johnson and William H. Winter, *Route Across the Rocky Mountains* (1846; ed. Carl L. Cannon, 1932); William

G. Johnson, *Overland to California* (1892; 1948); Dale L. Morgan, ed., *The Overland Diary of James A. Pritchard from Kentucky to California in 1849* (1959); Irene D. Paden, ed., *The Journal of Madison Berryman Moorman, 1850–1851* (1949); Sarah Royce, *A Frontier Lady: Recollections of the Gold Rush and Early California* (ed. Ralph H. Gabriel, 1932), a reflective and poetic record by the mother of the philosopher, Josiah Royce; David M. Potter, ed., *Trail to California, The Overland Journal of Vincent Geiger and Wakeman Bryarly* (1945), reprinting a diary kept in 1849; Lorenzo Sawyer (Edward Eberstadt, ed.), *Way Sketches, Containing Incidents of Travel Across the Plains . . . in 1850* (1926); C. W. Smith, (R. W. Vail, ed.) *Journal of a Trip to California* (1920); John Steele (Joseph Schafer, ed.), *Across the Plains in 1850* (1930); Joseph Williams, *Narrative of a Tour From the State of Indiana to the Oregon Territory in the Years 1841–2* (1843; 1921).

The guide-books bought by westward travelers are among our most intimate sources for their fears and hopes. Among the more important and more available are: Andrew Child, *Overland Route to California* (1852; 1946); Lansford W. Hastings, *The Emigrants' Guide to Oregon and California* (1845; ed. Charles H. Carey, 1932); Randolph B. Marcy, *The Prairie Traveler, a Hand-Book for Overland Expeditions* (1859 under auspices of the War Department, and many times reprinted); Joseph E. Ware, *The Emigrants' Guide to California* (1849; ed. John Caughey, 1932).

In a special class, too, are the accounts by notable eastern journalists who often showed detachment and a feeling for the vivid and characteristic episode, if sometimes embellished for "human interest": J. H. Beadle, *The Underdeveloped West* (1873); Horace Greeley, *An Overland Journey from New York to San Francisco in the Summer of 1859* (1860; 1964); Albert R. Richardson, *Beyond the Mississippi* (1866), a vastly popular and lively work by the pioneer war correspondent who reported the Civil War for the New York *Daily Tribune*.

Readable specialized studies, monographs, and articles which I have found especially informative or suggestive include: Thomas Perkins Abernethy, *From Frontier to Plantation in Tennessee* (1932); Robert G. Athearn, *High Country Empire: The High Plains and the Rockies* (1960); R. Carlyle Buley, *The Old Northwest: Pioneer Period, 1815–1840* (2 vols., 1951), invaluable for details of daily life; D. Douglas Branch, *Westward: The Romance of the American Frontier* (1930) and *The Hunting of the Buffalo* (1929; ed. J. Frank Dobie, Bison Paperback, 1962), works of a literary prodigy which deserve wider notice; Thomas D. Clark, *Frontier America: The Story of the Westward Movement* (1959); Everett Dick *The Sod-House Frontier, 1854–1890* (1954), indispensable for the social history of the northern plains; Octavius T. Howe, *Argonauts of '49* (1923), describing the adventures of New Englanders going west round the Horn; Rockwell D. Hunt, *John Bidwell, Prince of California Pioneers* (1942); Henry Inman, *The Old Santa Fe Trail* (1898); W. Turrentine Jackson, *Wagon Roads West* (1952); Lois K. Mathews, "The Mayflower Compact and its Descendants," MVHA, *Proc.*, VI (1912–13), 79–106, on the formation of *ad hoc* organizations with examples from the emigrant companies; Jay Monaghan, *The Overland Trail* (1947); Arthur K. Moore, *The Frontier Mind* (1957), bold in upsetting stereotypes about those who moved westward from Virginia and elsewhere into Kentucky; Irene D. Paden, *The Wake of the Prairie Schooner* (1943), an account enriched by the author's retracing of the pioneer trails; Elizabeth Page,

Wagons West, A Story of the Oregon Trail (1930); George W. Pierson, "The M-Factor in American History," *Am. Q.*, XIV (Summer, 1962), 275–89, an essay on the wider significance of American vagrancy; Andrew F. Rolle, *California: A History* (1963); Paul F. Sharp, *Whoop-Up Country: The Canadian–American West, 1865–1885* (1955); John Walton, *John Filson of Kentucke* (1956), a life of the pioneer cartographer (c. 1747–88) whose *Discovery, Settlement, and Present State of Kentucky* (1784) was the first history of the state and the origin of legendary accounts of the career of Daniel Boone; George R. Stewart, *Donner Pass* (1960); P. A. M. Taylor, "Emigrants' Problems in Crossing the West, 1830–1870," *University of Birmingham* [England] *Historical Journal*, V (1955), 83–102; Walter Prescott Webb, *The Great Plains* (1931), a classic study of the interrelations of climate, economy, and society; Louis Wright, *Culture on the Moving Frontier* (1948); William F. Hooker, *The Prairie Schooner* (1918), a study of the vehicle; Madeline S. Waggoner, *The Long Haul West: The Great Canal Era, 1817–1850* (1958); Sidney Warren, *Farthest Frontier: The Pacific Northwest* (1950).

For the early settlements in Ohio, the Old Northwest and neighboring territory, I have found especially valuable: Beverley W. Bond, Jr., *The Foundations of Ohio* (1941), which is Vol. I of Carl Wittke, ed., *The History of the State of Ohio* (6 vols.); and Henry Howe, ed., *Historical Collections of Ohio* (1847; 1889). General works which touch usefully on these topics are: Ralph H. Brown, *Historical Geography of the United States* (1948) esp. Ch. 21; Harlan H. Hatcher, *The Western Reserve: The Story of the New Connecticut in Ohio* (1949); Walter Havighurst, *Wilderness for Sale: The Story of the First Western Land Rush* (1956); Dale Van Every, *Ark of Empire: The American Frontier, 1784–1803* (1963). For

some of the prominent figures in the early settlement of Ohio, the *DAB* remains the best secondary source.

The history of the fur trade has commanded some of the best talent among New World historians. A classic work, too little read, and still the best starting point is Hiram M. Chittenden, *The American Fur Trade of the Far West* (3 vols., 1902; 2 vols., 1954). Chittenden (1858–1917), a West Point graduate, whose career was the army, is in the Parkman–De Voto tradition of the great amateurs. His interest in the history and topography of the West was awakened while he was serving as a lieutenant in the army engineers on road construction in Yellowstone National Park (1891–93), out of which experience came his book *The Yellowstone National Park* (1895 and later editions); he also helped organize Yosemite National Park. His writings, which show vast industry, a passion for accuracy, and a feeling for the dramatic, include *The History of Early Steamboat Navigation on the Missouri River* (1903) and (with Alfred T. Richardson) *The Life, Letters and Travels of Father Pierre Jean de Smet* (1905). A more up-to-date, but less readable treatise is Paul C. Phillips, *The Fur Trade* (2 vols., 1961). The most vivid account of the trade is Bernard De Voto's *Across the Wide Missouri* (1947), which tells the story of the crucial years 1833–38 as a commentary on the early 19-century paintings and drawings of the scenes by Alfred Jacob Miller, Charles Bodmer, and George Catlin, many of which are reproduced in De Voto's volume.

Especially useful works on the British, French, and Canadian background include: Harold A. Innis, *The Fur Trade in Canada* (1930), a brilliant monograph; Douglas MacKay, *The Honourable Company: A History of the Hudson's Bay Company* (1936), now largely superseded by Edwin Ernest Rich, *Hudson's Bay Company* (3 vols., 1960); Grace Lee Nute,

Caesars of the Wilderness ... (1943), on the French pioneers; Frederick Merk, ed., *Fur Trader and Empire: George Simpson's Journal* (1931), with a valuable introduction pointing out many of the important distinctions between the British and the American fur traders.

Of peculiar interest is the "Autobiography" of Gideon Lincecum (1793–1874), the backwoods physician and naturalist, who was himself an Indian trader in the Choctaw country of central Mississippi where he learned several Indian languages: Frank L. Riley, ed., "Autobiography of Gideon Lincecum," Miss. Hist. Soc., *Pub.*, VIII (1904), 443–519. Other useful items are: Cecil J. Alter, *James Bridger* (1925); William Blackmore, *The Hunting Grounds of the Great West* (1877); Agnes C. Laut, *The Fur Trade of America* (1921); Kenneth W. Porter, *John Jacob Astor: Business Man* (2 vols., 1931); Milo Quaife, ed., *Kit Carson's Autobiography* (1935); Edwin L. Sabin, *Kit Carson's Days* (1935); Wayne E. Stevens, *The Northwest Fur Trade: 1763–1800* (1926); John E. Sunder, *Bill Sublette, Mountain Man* (1959); Frederick Jackson Turner, "The Character and Influence of the Indian Trade in Wisconsin," J.H.U. *Studies in Hist. & Pol. Sci.*, IX (1891), 547–615.

A good starting point for discovering the place of western lands in American history is Roy M. Robbins, *Our Landed Heritage: The Public Domain 1776–1936* (1942; 1950); it should be supplemented by the collection, Vernon Carstensen, ed., *The Public Lands: Studies in the History of the Public Domain* (1963), which makes available many standard articles otherwise inaccessible. For the earlier period, see Thomas Perkins Abernethy, *Western Lands and the American Revolution* (1937; 1959); and for the later period, Paul W. Gates, *Fifty Million Acres, 1854–1890* (1954).

For the agricultural aspects of land sale, see: Percy W. Bidwell and John I. Falconer, *History of Agriculture in the Northern United States* (1941); Allan G. Bogue, *From Prairie to Corn Belt: Farming on the Illinois and Iowa Prairies in the Nineteenth Century* (1963) and "Farming in the Prairie Peninsula, 1830–1890," *JEH*, XXIII (March, 1963), 3–29; Paul W. Gates, *The Farmer's Age: Agriculture, 1815–1860* (1960), Vol. III. in *The Economic History of the United States* (Holt, Rinehart and Winston); Benjamin H. Hibbard, "The History of Agriculture in Dane County Wisconsin," U. of Wis., *Bull.*, Ec. and Pol. Sci. Ser., I (Sept., 1904), 67–214.

On claim clubs and related topics, see: Allan G. Bogue, "The Iowa Claim Clubs: Symbol and Substance," and other items in Carstensen, *The Public Lands* (above); Thomas LeDuc, "Public Policy, Private Investment, and Land Use in American Agriculture, 1825–1875," *Agric. Hist.* XXXVII (1963), 3–9; Allan G. Bogue, *Money at Interest* (1955); Seth K. Humphrey, *Following the Prairie Frontier* (1931); Howard R. Lamar, *Dakota Territory, 1861–1889* (1956), a pioneer study of great interest for its suggestions on the development of political institutions and their relations to growing social needs; Thomas A. McNeal, *When Kansas was Young* (1934); Charles J. Ritchey, "Claim Associations and Pioneer Democracy in Early Minnesota," *Minn. Hist.*, IX (June, 1928), 85–95; Benjamin F. Shambaugh, *Constitution and Records of the Claim Association of Johnson County, Iowa* (1894) and "Frontier Land Clubs or Claim Associations," Am. Hist. Assn., *Ann. Report* (1900), I, 69–84; Hawkins Taylor, "Squatters and Speculators at the First Land Sales," *Annals of Iowa*, VIII (July, 1870), 269–74; Western Historical Company, *The History of Jefferson County, Iowa*, (1879); Paul W. Gates, "Frontier Estate Builders and Farm Laborers," in Walker D. Wyman and

Clifton B. Kroeber, eds., *The Frontier in Perspective* (1957) 143–63.

Especially valuable contemporary accounts include: Erastus F. Beadle, *To Nebraska in '57* (1923), a diary; Alfred Brunson, *A Western Pioneer* (2 vols., 1879); Fannie E. Cole, "Pioneer Life in Kansas," Kans. State Hist. Soc., *Coll.*, XII (1912), 353–58; Michael Frank, "Early History of Kenosha," State Hist. Soc. Wisc., *Coll.*, III (1856), 370–94; Alexander F. Pratt, "Reminiscences of Wisconsin," State Hist. Soc. Wisc., *Coll.*, I (1854), 127–45.

In a class by themselves are the books of Mrs. Caroline Stansbury Kirkland (1801–1864), the New York City–born wife of a minister who was one of the first settlers of Pinckney, Michigan. In *A New Home—Who'll Follow?* (1839) written under the pseudonym of Mrs. Mary Clavers (reissued as *Our New Home in the West*, 1874, ed. John Nerber, as *A New Home*, 1953), she recorded much that was grim and amusing, and little that was flattering about her neighbors and their way of life. This volume, which made her reputation on the eastern seaboard and left her *persona non grata* in the West, remains one of the most vivid and intimate records of the new farming communities. After her return to New York City in 1843, her writing continued to be popular, but became less original. See also her *Forest Life* (1842) and *Western Clearings* (1845). She gives contemporary witness to some of the 20-century interpretations of Conrad Richter in *The Trees* (1940) and *The Fields* (1946).

A useful tool is E. E. Edwards (ed.), *Bibliography of the History of Agriculture in the United States* (1930).

* * *

For the relation of peculiarly American conditions to the development of the law, pioneer work has been done by Willard Hurst: *The Growth of American Law: the Law Makers* (1950), *Law and the Conditions of Freedom in the Nineteenth-Century United States* (1956), and *Law and Economic Growth: The Legal History of the Lumber Industry in Wisconsin, 1836–1915* (1964), a monumental study of how legal institutions were shaped by local circumstances.

The popular imagination, stirred by works like Walter Van Tilburg Clark's *Ox-Bow Incident* (1940) and by movies made from them, and horrified by the lynching of innocent Negroes in the South, is too ready to assume that Western vigilantism was nothing more than lynch law. While some of the evils of Western vigilantism were similar to those of Southern lynch law, the roots of the two practices were different. Western vigilantism expressed a search for law where established government was new, weak, or sometimes even nonexistent; its ostensible technicality (entirely lacking from Southern lynch law) expressed a desperate desire to have the benefits of an established system, but before circumstances had brought a technical legal system into existence. Southern lynch law, on the contrary, expresses a spirit of lawlessness masquerading in the guise of law, although often (as in the Ku Klux Klan and the White Citizens' Councils) it does not even make the pretence; it is a violent and organized refusal to use the technical apparatus of the established courts where they actually exist. The one expresses a quest for law; the other a defiance of it. The difference can be understood only by seeing them both in context. For a different view see John Caughey, *Their Majesties, the Mob* (1960).

One way to begin to see Western vigilantism in context is in the pages of Josiah Royce's *California, from the Conquest in 1846 to the Second Vigilance Committee in San Francisco: A Study of American Character* (1888; ed. R. G. Cleland, 1948). Royce (1855–1916), born in Grass Valley, California, of parents who had made a perilous and nearly fatal crossing of the continent to California in the Gold Rush of '49, became famous as a philosopher and a teacher of philosophy at Harvard (1882–1916), where he had been brought by William James. Royce's voluminous writings (for example, *The Philosophy of Loyalty*, 1908) explored the meaning of community for the problems of knowledge, truth, ethics, and consciousness; this preoccupation appears to have been rooted in his early family experiences and in the California age of "community before government." See, also, the diary of Josiah Royce's mother, Sarah (Bayliss) Royce, *A Frontier Lady: Recollections of the Gold Rush and Early California* (ed. R. H. Gabriel, 1932), and the admirable brief sketch of Royce in the *DAB*, by Ralph Barton Perry.

Another writer who should be better known among readers of American history is Charles Howard Shinn (1852–1924), who as a historian is in the Parkman–Chittenden–De Voto tradition of the great amateurs. Trained as a political scientist, he became, like Chittenden and De Voto, a leading conservationist. No one interested in the West or in the origins of American attitudes to law should fail to read his *Mining Camps: A Study in American Frontier Government* (1885; reprinted in 1948 with an admirable introduction and biography of the author by Joseph Henry Jackson). Shinn's other relevant works are: "Land Laws of Mining Districts," JHU, *Studies in Hist. & Pol. Sci.*, II (1884), 551–615; "Cooperation on the Pacific Coast," ibid., VI (1888), 447–81; *The Story of the Mine* (1897); *Graphic Description of Pacific Coast Outlaws* (1958).

The papers of the San Francisco Vigilance Committee have been preserved and competently edited: Porter Garnett, ed., "Papers on the San Francisco Committee of Vigilance of 1851," Acad. of Pac. Coast Hist., *Pub.*, I (1910), 285–353, and II (1911),

121–39; Mary Floyd Williams, ed., *Papers of the San Francisco Committee of Vigilance of 1851*, Pac. Coast Hist. *Pub.*, Vol. IV (1919). The history of the committee is chronicled in Mary Floyd Williams, *History of the San Francisco Committee of Vigilance of 1851* (1921). A recent interpretation is George R. Stewart, *The San Francisco Committee of Vigilance* (1964).

For the atmosphere of the West and its meaning for vigilantism, there is no more accessible source than the well-selected and handsomely reprinted volumes in the *Western Frontier Library* (U. of Okla. Press), for example: John Xavier Beidler, *X. Beidler: Vigilante* (ed., Helen F. Sanders and William H. Bertsche, Jr., 1957); Edward Bonney, *The Banditti of the Prairies, or The Murderer's Doom!!* (1963); General D. J. Cook, *Hands Up* (1958), reminiscences by the Superintendent of the Rocky Mountain Detective Association; Thomas J. Dimsdale, *The Vigilantes of Montana* (1953); Pat F. Garrett, *The Authentic Life of Billy, The Kid* (1954); Charles L. Martin, *A Sketch of Sam Bass, the Bandit* (1956); A. S. Mercer, *The Banditti of the Plains* (1954); John Rollin Ridge, *The Life and Adventures of Joaquin Murieta* (1955).

A valuable general account of Western vigilantism, but one which must be used with caution, is Hubert Howe Bancroft, *Popular Tribunals* (2 vols., 1887), a product of the notorious "history factory." Other useful items are: James Truslow Adams, "Our Lawless Heritage," *Atlantic Monthly*, CXLII (1928), 732–40, an illustration of the traditional view; John W. Caughey, *H. H. Bancroft* (1946) and *California* (1940); Stanton A. Coblentz, *Villains and Vigilantes* (1936), on James King of William and on pioneer justice in California; William H. Ellison, *Self Governing Dominion: California, 1849–1860* (1950); Wayne Gard,

Frontier Justice (1949); Alan Valentine, *Vigilante Justice* (1956).

For the mining background of the vigilante tradition, a readable, up-to-date introduction is Rodman W. Paul, *Mining Frontiers of the Far West, 1849–1880* (1963) and accompanying bibliographies. Other especially useful items besides those mentioned above are: Chauncy L. Canfield, ed., *The Diary of a Forty–Niner* (1920); *Contributions to the Historical Society of Montana*, II (1896), III (1900), VII (1910); Georgia W. Read and Ruth Gaines, eds., *Gold Rush; the Journals, Drawings, and other Papers of J. Goldsborough Bruff* (2 vols., 1944); Thomas A. Rickard, *The History of American Mining* (1932); Helen Fitzgerald Sanders, *A History of Montana*, Vol. I (1913), a basic book; William J. Trimble, "The Mining Advance into the Inland Empire," U. of Wis., *Bull.*, III (1912–14), 137–390.

Ghost towns remain a subject to reward future historians. There are numerous picture-books, mostly on standing ghost mining towns of the Far West, and also some popular or antiquarian general works such as: Fessenden S. Blanchard, *Ghost Towns of New England* (1960); John T. Faris, *The Romance of Forgotten Towns* (1924); Robert W. Howard, *The Race West: Boom Town to Ghost Town* (1963). But these books hardly begin to suggest the vast significance of the subject. On the other hand, there is a wealth of valuable detail in the publications of state and local historical associations, and in more obscure publications, for example: Peter Vanden Berge, "A Paper Village," *Mich. Mag. Hist.*, XXI (Summer–Aut., 1937), 264–66; Dudley S. Brainard, "Nininger, a Boom Town of the Fifties," *Minn. Hist.*, XIII (June, 1932), 127–51; S. B. Evans, "The Blotting out of an Iowa Town," *Annals of Iowa*, 3d ser., VIII (April, 1907), 57–59; Alan W. Farley, "Annals of Quindaro: A Kansas Ghost Town," *Kans. Hist. Q.*, XXII (Win., 1956), 305–20; Robert J. Forrest, "Mythical Cities of Southwestern Minnesota," *Minn. Hist.*, XIV (Sept., 1933) 243–62; A. T. Glaze, *Incidents and Anecdotes of Early Days . . . in . . . Fond du Lac . . .* (Fond du Lac; 1905); Mildred Holsapple, "The Disappearance of New London," *Ind. Mag. Hist.*, XXXI (March, 1935), 10–13; John F. Hume, "Are We a Nation of Rascals?" *North Am. Rev.*, CXXXIX (Aug., 1884), with an account of a Kansas community which became a ghost town when its inhabitants moved away to escape a heavy debt; Charles C. Jones, *The Dead Towns of Georgia* (1878); Kate J. Kimball, "Bath—A Town that Was," *Granite Monthly*, LIV (Dec., 1922), 453–61; Theodore H. Scheffer, "The Old Ghost Town of Lindsey in the Solomon Valley," *Kans. Hist. Q.*, XXI (Aut., 1955), 552–59; James McManus, "The Tragedy of Richland City," *Wis. Mag. Hist.*, VII (1923–24), 63–80; George W. Martin, ed., "Some of the Lost Towns of Kansas," Kans. State Hist. Soc., *Coll.*, XII (1912), 426–90; Ralph C. Meima, "A Forgotten City," *Mich. Mag. Hist.*, V (July, 1921), 397–409, an account of Port Sheldon, Mich.; Ib. Melchior, "East Coast's only Ghost Town," *Travel*, CIV (July, 1955), 54–56, an account of Allaire, N.J., one of the few standing ghost towns in the East; Roy W. Meyer, "The Story of Forest Mills, A Midwest Milling Community," *Minn. Hist.*, XXXV (March, 1956), 11–21; Howard Mitcham, "Old Rodney; a Mississippi Ghost Town," *Journ. Miss. Hist.*, XV (Oct., 1953), 245–51; David C. Mott, "Abandoned Towns, Villages and Post Offices of Iowa," *Annals of Iowa*, 3d ser., XVII (Oct., 1930) 435–65, (Jan., 1931) 513–43, (April, 1931) 579–99, and XVIII (July, 1931) 42–69, (Oct., 1931) 117–48, and "Index to Abandoned Towns of Iowa," *Annals of Iowa*, 3d ser., XVIII (Jan., 1932), 189–220, an alphabetical listing of

2807 abandoned sites, 2205 of which are properly ghost towns; Mrs. W. F. Pett, "A Forgotten Village," *Wis. Mag. Hist.*, XII (Sept., 1928), 3–18, an account of La Pointe, Wis.; E. O. Randall, "Location of Site of Ohio Capital," *Ohio Archaeological and Hist. Pub.*, XXV (April, 1916), 210–34; L. Benjamin Reber, "Vanished Villages of Berrien County," *Mich. Mag. Hist.*, XII (April, 1928), 322–26; Walter Ridgway, "Ghost Towns and Centenarian Communities of Central Missouri," *Mo. Hist. Rev.*, XXV (April, 1931), 421–24; John L. Roll, "Sangamo Town," *Ill. State Hist. Soc., Journ.*, XIX (July, 1926), 153–60; William R. Sandham, "A Lost Stark County Town," *Ill. State Hist. Soc. Journ.*, XIII (April, 1920), 109–12; Sue I. Silliman, "Paper Villages of St. Joseph County," *Mich. Mag. Hist.*, IV (July, 1920), 588–95; F. Bernice Stoddard, "Ghost Town of Assyria Township in Barry County," *Mich. Hist.*, XLII (1958), 324–30; Elbert Waller, "Some Half-Forgotten Towns in Illinois," *Ill. State Hist. Soc., Trans.* (1927), 65–82.

For the history of the modes of Western travel and for the experience of travelers, see books listed near the beginning of the present section. An obvious and amusing beginning is *Life on the Mississippi* (1883) by Mark Twain, whose very pseudonym was a phrase from riverboat piloting. For travel by water, see, for example: Leland D. Baldwin, *The Keelboat Age on Eastern Waters* (1941), valuable for detail; Hiram Chittenden, *The History of Early Steamboat Navigation on the Missouri River* (1903); Walter Havighurst, *The River: The Story of the Mississippi Waterways* (1964), a popular study; Madeline S. Waggoner, *The Long Haul West: The Great Canal Era, 1817–1850* (1958); John H. Morrison, *History of American Steam Navigation* (1903); Louis C. Hunter, *Steamboats on the Western Rivers* (1949), the standard monograph. And see Leroy R. and Ann W. Hafen, *Handcarts to Zion* (1960) for the remarkable story of the Mormon trek with pushcarts.

The literature of railroad history is vast; much of it is for the buff. But the subject has commanded some of the best scholarly talent. A handy one-volume introduction is John F. Stover, *American Railroads* (1961; Phoenix Paperback), with bibliographies. The items I list are the barest selection among works I have found most valuable. On the construction of particular lines and "colonization" by railroad companies, see: Carlton J. Corliss, *Main Line of Mid-America* (1950); Paul W. Gates, *The Illinois Central Railroad and its Colonization Work* (1934); Richard C. Overton, *Burlington West: A Colonization History of the Burlington Railroad* (1941); Grenville M. Dodge, *How We Built the Union Pacific Railway*, U. S. Sen. Docs., 61st Cong., 2d Sess., Doc. No. 447 (1910). And on other topics: Ira G. Clark, *Then Came the Railroads: The Century from Steam to Diesel in the Southwest* (1958); Thomas C. Cochran, *Railroad Leaders 1845–1890: The Business Mind in Action* (1953); Carter Goodrich, *Government Promotion of American Canals and Railroads, 1800–1890* (1960); George R. Taylor and Irene D. Neu, *The American Railroad Network, 1861–1890* (1956), an important monograph with valuable accompanying maps showing the numerous differences of gauge, which are too often omitted from students' maps; Henry M. Flint, *The Railroads of the United States* (1868).

For the history of railroad construction techniques and of locomotive and passenger car design, see: E. P. Alexander, *Iron Horses* (1941), a handsomely illustrated guide to famous early locomotives; Charles Barnard, "English and American Locomotives," *Harper's New Monthly Magazine*, XVIII (March 1879), 555–59; William H. Brown, *The History of the First Locomotive in America* (1871); Roger Burlingame, *March of the Iron*

Men (1949); Lyon Sprague de Camp, *The Heroic Age of American Invention* (1961); H. J. Habakkuk, *American and British Technology in the Nineteenth Century* (1962); John A. Kouwenhoven, *Made in America* (1948), stimulating essays full of suggestive detail; August Mencken, *The Railroad Passenger Car* (1957), especially valuable for its illustrations and as a guide to observations by 19th-century travelers; Glenn Chesney Quiett, *They Built the West* (1934); Edward W. Watkin, *A Trip to the United States and Canada* (1852), observations by a British expert. On accidents and railroad safety, see: Charles Francis Adams, Jr., *Notes on Railroad Accidents* (1879); Robert B. Shaw, *Down Brakes* (1961); L. T. C. Rolt, *Red for Danger* (1955) and H. Raynar Wilson, *The Safety of British Railways* (1909), on the British side. For the history of "Standard Time" see: Carlton J. Corliss, *The Day of Two Noons* (Assn. of Am. Railroads; 9th ed., 1959). For further references on railroads, especially on government aid to their construction, see Bibliographical Notes to Book Two, Part Five (below).

A history of haste in the United States, which focused on relevant aspects of the land rush, the gold rush, and the many implications of haste for diet, cuisine, reading matter, entertainment, friendship, nomenclature, and family relations would show us some of the neglected causes and consequences of American democracy.

PART THREE

THE UPSTARTS:

Boosters

The history of the city—not to mention that of the small town—has not had its due from professional American historians. One of the reasons for this is the overwhelming appeal of the romantic stereotypes—the fur trapper, the backwoodsman, the heroic lonely settler, and the Indian fighter—all from the pages of Roosevelt's *Winning of the West* or other books of the same school. Such romanticism attained academic status through the appeal of the writings of Frederick Jackson Turner. Since the 1920's, when American historical scholarship has flourished as never before, some of our most potent literary figures have directed their irony against the small town. Not only Sinclair Lewis, but Sherwood Anderson, in *Winesburg, Ohio* (1919), Edgar Lee Masters in *Spoon River Anthology* (1915) and other writings, and many other writers have documented the sterility and pettiness of the small town; while Stephen Crane's *Maggie: A Girl of the Streets* (1893), Upton Sinclair's *The Jungle* (1906), Theodore Dreiser's *Sister Carrie* (1900; 1912), *The Financier* (1912), *The Titan* (1914), and later John Dos Passos' *Manhattan Transfer* (1925) and *U.S.A.* (1930–36) described the cruelty and meaninglessness of life in the big city.

Behind all this was a traditional antipathy of intellectuals to the city, described by Morton and Lucia White in *The Intellectual versus The City: From Thomas Jefferson to Frank Lloyd Wright* (1962). In addition, an anticapitalist bias led many historians to oversimplify the small town into a place of exploitation by small businessmen and the big city into a place of exploitation by big businessmen. Bertrand de Jouvenel's brilliant essay, "The Treatment of Capitalism by Continental Intellectuals," in Friedrich Hayek, ed., *Capitalism and the Historians* (1954; Phoenix Paperback) helps us understand some of the deeper reasons for these biases. Meanwhile, Gustavus Myers' *History of Great American Fortunes* (1909), whose point of view was popularized by Matthew Josephson in *The Robber Barons* (1934), persuaded many readers of American history to see the city as the headquarters for the rifling of a continent and the destruction of the democratic ideal.

The upshot was to leave a mythical "frontier" as the scene where the heroic and creative deeds of Democratic America were accomplished. Otherwise competent chroniclers made merry over the philistinism and follies of the small-town Babbitt-warrens, and hurled epithets at the carnivorous rich of the metropolitan jungles. There were many earlier histories of American cities, but not until the last thirty years or so has there been anything like an American urban history; only recently have urban historians developed large organizing ideas comparable to those that gave form to our political and rural history.

A leader has been Professor Arthur M. Schlesinger, Sr., of Harvard University, who pioneered in *New Viewpoints in American History* (1922) and *The Rise of the City* (1933) and who has stimulated many important works. Others who have helped us discover the urban world, which had long remained hidden, include: Carl Bridenbaugh, in his pioneer works in the colonial period, *Cities in the Wilderness. . . . 1625–1742* (1938) and *Cities in Revolt . . . 1743–1776* (1955); Lewis Atherton, *Main Street on the Middle Border* (1954), a study of the country towns of the Midwest; Constance McL. Green, *American Cities in the Growth of the Nation* (1957); Jean Gottmann, *Virginia at Mid-Century* (1955) and *Megalopolis* (1962); Blake McKelvey, *Urban America* (1964); Bessie L. Pierce, *A History of Chicago* (3 vols., 1937–57; and a 4th vol. to come); Richard C. Wade, *The Urban Frontier: The Rise of Western Cities, 1790–1830* (1959; Phoenix Paperback) and *Slavery in the Cities* (1964), and others. Essays pointing the way to some of these new possibilities are found in Werner Z. Hirsch, ed., *Urban Life and Form . . .* (1963); a useful collection of documents is Charles N. Glaab, *The American City: A Documentary History* (1963).

Old-style city histories were compendia of biographies of leading citizens, statistics of local commerce, and data proving the nonpareil promise of the particular metropolis being chronicled. Still, these works contained much solid information, hard to gather at a later date, and they remain useful: Alfred T. Andreas, *History of Chicago* (3 vols., 1884–86); Theodore S. Case, *History of Kansas City, Missouri* (1888); Charles T. Greve, *Centennial History of Cincinnati* (2 vols., 1904); John Hogan, *Thoughts about the City of St. Louis* (1854); L. U. Reavis, *St. Louis: the Future Great City of the World* (1876); J. Thomas Scharf, *History of Baltimore City and County* (1881) and *History of Saint Louis City and County* (2 vols., 1883).

Recent city histories include works by some of the ablest professional historians; they differ from their predecessors in their selectivity of data, in their critical and comparative approach to the history and promise of the city chronicled, and in their care in organizing detail. A common weakness is a lack of large organizing ideas and a failure to put the subject within the context of American civilization as a whole, or to describe the subject as part of the growth of the modern cosmopolitan urban environment. Some of the best of the new city histories, so well done that they can be considered definitive for some time to come, include: A. Theodore Brown, *Frontier Community, Kansas City,* (1964); Constance McL. Green, *Washington: Village and Capital, 1800–1878* (1962), and a second volume following (1964); Blake McKelvey, *Rochester* (4 vols., 1945–61); Bessie L. Pierce, *A History of Chicago* (3 vols., 1937–57; and a fourth volume to come), the pioneer full-length study by a professional historian; Bayrd Still, *Milwaukee* (1948). Popular histories of particular cities which are useful to the historian include:

Clara L. De Chambrun, *Cincinnati: Story of the Queen City* (1939); Alvin F. Harlow, *The Serene Cincinnatians* (1950); Shields McIlwaine, *Memphis Down in Dixie* (1948).

For a glimpse of the ways in which English cities were growing during the period of this volume, see Asa Briggs' *Victorian Cities* (1963) and accompanying bibliography; and for the world perspective, see the writings of Lewis Mumford, especially *The City in History* (1961).

Among the specialized urban studies that I have found valuable are: Wyatt W. Belcher, *The Economic Rivalry Between St. Louis and Chicago, 1850–1880,* (1947); Nelson M. Blake, *Water for the Cities* (1956), a history of the urban water supply problem in the United States; R. Carlyle Buley, *The Old Northwest: Pioneer Period, 1815–1840* (2 vols., 1950); Gerald Carson, *The Old Country Store* (1954); Robert Cromie, *The Great Chicago Fire* (1958); Charles N. Glaab, *Kansas City and the Railroads* (1962), an important monograph on urban rivalry and community support of transportation; James C. Malin, *Grassland Historical Studies* (one vol. to date, Lawrence, Kans., 1950); Bessie L. Pierce, ed., *As Others See Chicago* (1933); George Rosen, *A History of Public Health* (1958); Wilson Smith, ed., *Cities of Our Past and Present* (1964); Bayrd Still, "Patterns of Mid-Nineteenth Century Urbanization in the Middle West," *MVHR,* XXVIII (1941–42), 187–206; Kenneth Sturges, *American Chambers of Commerce* (1915); Thornton Wilder, "The American Loneliness," *Atlantic Monthly,* CXC (July–Dec., 1952), 65–69; R. Richard Wohl and A. Theodore Brown, "The Usable Past: A Study of Historical Traditions in Kansas City," *Huntington Lib. Q.,* XXIII (May, 1960), 237–59.

For real-estate aspects of urban history see Pearl J. Davies, *Real Estate in American History* (1958); Homer Hoyt, *One Hundred Years of Land Values in Chicago* (1933); Frank A. Randall, *History of the Development of Building Construction in Chicago* (1949); Martin Ridge, *Ignatius Donnelly: The Portrait of a Politician* (1962); Roy M. Robbins, *Our Landed Heritage* (1950); A. M. Sakolski, *The Great American Land Bubble* (1932); Karl Scholz, ed., "Real Estate Problems," Am. Acad. Pol. & Soc. Sci., *Annals,* CXLVIII (March, 1930), 1–244.

The history of the businessman can best be approached through biographies of individuals, for which the *DAB* is invaluable. General books, like Miriam Beard, *The History of the Business Man* (1938), tend to homogenize the business men of all times and places, and therefore neglect the symbiosis of the business man and the upstart city (or some other particular environment) which is my special concern. Useful studies are: John Chamberlain, *The Enterprising Americans: A Business History of the United States* (1963); Thomas C. Cochran, *Basic History of American Business* (1959; Anvil Paperback) and *Railroad Leaders, 1845–1890: The Business Mind in Action* (1953); Irvin G. Wyllie, *The Self-Made Man in America: The Myth of Rags to Riches* (1954). The valuable volumes in the Harvard Studies in Business History deal, for the most part, with nationally famous figures such as John Jacob Astor, Jay Cooke, or with large firms such as Macy's or the House of Baring, but they do include some volumes relevant to the emergent businessman in the upstart city. A useful tool is Henrietta M. Larson's *Guide to Business History* (1948).

Material on the figures I have selected for my examples is found in: Isaac N. Arnold, *William B. Ogden: and Early Days in Chicago* (1882); Beverley W. Bond, Jr., ed., "Dr. Daniel Drake's Memoir of the Miami Country, 1779–1794," Hist. and Phil. Soc. of Ohio, *Q. Pub.,* XVIII (April–Sept., 1923), 39–93; Daniel Drake, *An In-*

augural Discourse on Medical Education, delivered in Cincinnati, Nov. 11, 1820 (ed. Emmet F. Horine, 1951), *Discourse on the History, Character, and Prospects of the West* (1834; Scholars' Facsimiles and Reprints, 1955), *Natural and Statistical View, or Picture of Cincinnati and the Miami Country* (1815), "Notices Concerning Cincinnati," reprinted in Hist. and Phil. Soc. of Ohio, *Q. Pub.,* III (Jan.–June, 1908), 1–60, *Pioneer Life in Kentucky* (1870), reminiscing letters to his children, *Remarks on the Importance of Promoting Literary and Social Concert, in the Valley of the Mississippi as a Means of Elevating its Character, and Perpetuating the Union* (Louisville, Ky., 1833); Alice M. Ruggles, "Unpublished Letters of Dr. Daniel Drake," *Ohio State Arch. and Hist. Q.,* XLIX (1940), 191–212; James T. Flexner, *Doctors on Horseback* (1938), with a valuable chapter on Drake; Emmet F. Horine, *Daniel Drake (1785–1852), Pioneer Physician of the Midwest* (1961); Otto Juettner, *Daniel Drake and His Followers* (1909); Edward D. Mansfield, *Memoirs of the Life and Services of Daniel Drake* (1855); Herman S. Davis, ed., *Reminiscences of General William Larimer and of his son William H. H. Larimer* (1918); Henry Marie Brackenridge, *Journal of a Voyage up the River Missouri* (1816; in Thwaites, *Early Western Travels,* Vol. VI, 1904), *Recollections of Persons and Places in the West* (1834; 1868); William F. Keller, *The Nation's Advocate* (1956), a life of H. M. Brackenridge; Claude M. Newlin, *The Life and Writings of Hugh Henry Brackenridge* (1932); James Fenimore Cooper, ed., *A Guide in the Wilderness or the History of the First Settlements in the Western Counties of New York with Useful Instructions to Future Settlers* (1810; 1897), letters from Judge Cooper of Cooperstown to a New York City lawyer.

Histories of journalism tend to focus on the big-city newspapers, es-pecially those of the eastern seaboard: they have the longest histories, have played the most continuous role in national politics, and often have well-kept archives. The best general works are by Frank Luther Mott: *American Journalism* (rev. ed., 1950), an excellent textbook survey; *The News in America* (1952), topical essays; a *History of American Magazines* (4 vols., 1930–57). Other useful surveys are: Frederic Hudson, *Journalism in the United States* (1873); Sidney Kobre, *Foundations of American Journalism* (1958); James Melvin Lee, *History of American Journalism* (1917); R. A. Peddie, ed., *Printing: A Short History of the Art* (1927); Isaiah Thomas, *History of Printing in America* (2 vols., 1873–74); Bernard A. Weisberger, *The American Newspaperman* (1962).

My heaviest debt here is to the indefatigable Douglas C. McMurtrie, whose most relevant works are: *Early Printing in Milwaukee* (1930), *Early Printing in Wisconsin* (1931), *Pioneer Printing in Minnesota* (1932), *Pioneer Printing in Nebraska* (1932), *The Printing Press Moves Westward* (1934), *The Need of a Printer in Indiana Territory* (1936), *The Contributions of the Pioneer Printers to Illinois History* (1939), *Early Printing in Wyoming and the Black Hills* (1943). Among other useful specialized studies are: C. B. Galbreath, "The First Newspaper of the Northwest Territory," *Ohio Arch. and Hist. Q.,* XIII (July, 1904), 332–49; Milton W. Hamilton, *The Country Printer: New York State, 1785–1830* (1936); Henry King, "The Story of Kansas and Kansas Newspapers," Board of Dir. of Kans. State Hist. Soc., *Twentieth Biennial Report,* (1916), 3–320, vivid detail and sharp insights from a leading Kansas newspaperman; William H. Perrin, *The Pioneer Press of Kentucky* (Filson Club Pub. No. 3; 1888); Reuben G. Thwaites, "The Ohio Valley Press before the War of 1812–15," Am. Antiq. Soc., *Proc.,* n.s., XIX (April, 1908–April, 1909).

* * *

The hotel, perhaps because it is so characteristic and so commonplace an American institution, has not had adequate treatment from historians. A pioneer essay is Doris E. King, "The First-Class Hotel and the Age of the Common Man," *JSH*, XXIII (May, 1957), 173–88; see also her "Early Hotel Entrepreneurs and Promoters, 1793–1860," *Explorations in Entrepreneurial Hist.* VIII (Feb., 1956), 148–60 and "The Community Hotel: A Salute to Hotel Fredonia, Nacogdoches [Texas]," *The SFA Economist*, IV (Spr., 1960), 3–15, (pub. Dept. Bus. Adm. of Stephen F. Austin State College, Texas). A general work with much valuable detail is Jefferson Williamson, *The American Hotel* (1930). The story of the hotel must still be pieced together from casual remarks of travelers, who, then as now, attached undue significance to the facilities for transients as a touchstone of a whole civilization, but who nevertheless noticed many features too obvious for Americans to observe. See, for example, the comments in Francis J. Grund, *Aristocracy in America . . . Sketch-Book of a German Nobleman* (2 vols., 1839) and Alexander Mackay, *The Western World: or, Travels in the United States in 1846–47* (2d. ed., 2 vols., 1849). One of the most valuable contemporary sources is William Havard Eliot, *A Description of the Tremont House, with Architectural Illustrations* (Boston, 1830), which had wide circulation and great influence. Other works which touch on the hotel are: R. C. Buley, *The Old Northwest: Pioneer Period, 1815–1840* (2 vols., 1950); Arthur W. Calhoun, *A Social History of the American Family* (3 vols., Barnes and Noble Paperback), esp. Vols. II and III; Harry E. Cole, *Stage-Coach and Tavern Tales of the Old Northwest* (1930); J. Winston Coleman, Jr., *Stage-Coach Days in the Bluegrass* (1935); B. D., "Cincin-

nati," *Western Monthly Mag.*, V. (March, 1836), 152–57; Talbot F. Hamlin, *Greek Revival Architecture in America* (1944); Robert B. Ludy, *Historic Hotels of the World* (1927); Helen F. Randolph, *Mammoth Cave and the Cave Region of Kentucky* (1924).

The balloon-frame house has nearly escaped historians who have dealt at length with other phenomena less widespread, less permanent, and less influential. The invention was anonymous; the subject falls between conventional topics; it does not concern monumental structures like churches and government buildings; and it has therefore seemed almost too commonplace to be noted. Apparently the first description of balloon-framing was in Gervase Wheeler, *Homes for the People* (1855; several times reprinted). See also George F. Woodward, *Woodward's Country Homes* (1865) and Catharine E. Beecher and Harriet Beecher Stowe, *The American Woman's Home* (1869), a description, with floor-plans and illustrations, of movable walls, prefabricated units, and other domestic conveniences, together with one of the first suggestions of the value of an open plan. The best brief introduction is in John Kouwenhoven's brilliant *Made in America* (1948), Ch. 3; an excellent summary is found in Carl Condit's indispensable *American Building Art: The Nineteenth Century* (1960), at pp. 22–25, and in his *Chicago School of Architecture* (1964), fig. 1.

Specialized studies which illuminate the subject are: Turpin C. Bannister, "Architectural Development of the Northeastern States," *Arch. Rec.*, LXXXIX (June, 1941), 61–80; Alfred Bruce and Harold Sandbank, *A History of Prefabrication* (1944); Walker Field, "A Re-examination into the Invention of the Balloon Frame," *Journ. Am. Soc. Arch. Hist.*, II (Oct., 1942), 3–29, the most detailed treatment of the problem of origins; Sigfried

Giedion, *Space, Time and Architecture* (1949), esp. pp. 280–89; James C. Malin, "Housing Experiments in the Lawrence Community, 1855," *Kans. Hist. Q.*, XXI (Summer, 1954), 95–121, showing how the urgent need for housing stimulated experiments; Charles E. Peterson, "Early American Prefabrication," *Gazette des Beaux-Arts*, 6th ser. XXXIII (Jan., 1948), 37–46, an important article; "Prefabs for the Prairies," *Journ. Am. Soc. Arch. Hist.*, XI (March 1952), 28–30.

The balloon-frame is mentioned in some of the general histories: John Burchard and Albert Bush-Brown, *The Architecture of America* (1961); John Maas, *The Gingerbread Age . . . Victorian America* (1957), at p. 140. There is no better illustration of the domination of American historical writing by the categories of European culture (belles-lettres and beaux-arts) than that this revolutionary American innovation is barely touched on in the standard books. Even Horatio Greenough (1805–1852) who purported to plead for a new American spirit in architecture neglected the balloon-frame; see his *Form and Function: Remarks on Art, Design, and Architecture* (ed. Harold A. Small, 1957).

The best introduction to the history of American higher education is Richard Hofstadter and Wilson Smith, *American Higher Education: A Documentary History* (2 vols., 1961), supplemented by Richard Hofstadter and Walter P. Metzger, *The Development of Academic Freedom in the United States* (1955). Other valuable general histories are Frederick Rudolph, *The American College and University* (1962) and George P. Schmidt, *The Old Time College President* (1930) and *The Liberal Arts College* (1957). An indispensable monograph is Donald G. Tewksbury, *The Founding of American Colleges and Universities before the Civil War* (1932); see also Theodore R. Crane, ed., *The Colleges and the Public, 1787–1862* (1963). For particular colleges, the most accessible sources are biographical works, like Julian M. Sturtevant, Jr., ed., *Julian M. Sturtevant: An Autobiography* (1896) or entries in *DAB;* and college histories, such as Arthur O. Beach, *A Pioneer College: The Story of Marietta* (1935); *The John P. Branch Historical Papers of Randolph-Macon College*, Vol. III (1909–1912); Delavan L. Leonard, *The History of Carleton College* (1904); John S. Nollen, *Grinnell College* (1953); Lucy L. Notestein, *Wooster of the Middle West* (1937); David B. Skillman, *The Biography of . . . Lafayette College* (2 vols., 1932). An especially valuable contemporary document is William S. Tyler, *Colleges: Their Place Among American Institutions* (New York, 1857), an address delivered (Nov. 12, 1856) by this Amherst professor before the Society for the Promotion of Collegiate and Theological Education at the West in Bridgeport, Conn. For some later implications of the collegiate developments of this period, see Thorstein Veblen, *The Higher Learning in America* (1918).

The county-seat wars would make a dramatic subject for a broad narrative survey by an imaginative historian. They must now be pieced together mostly from works of local history, for example: Owen C. Coy, *California County Boundaries* (1923); Randolph C. Downes, "Evolution of Ohio County Boundaries, *Ohio Arch. and Hist. Q.*, XXXVI (July, 1927), 340–477; S. A. Gilpin, "The Minor Political Divisions of the United States," in Francis A. Walker, comp., *Statistical Atlas of the United States* (1874); J. N. Gridley, "The County Seat Battles of Cass County, Illinois," Ill. State Hist. Soc., *Journ.* VII (Oct., 1914), 166–94; R. D. Holt, "Texas has Hot County Elections," West Texas Hist. Assn., *Year Book*, XXIV (Oct., 1948), 3–26; T. A. NcNeal, *When Kansas was Young* (1934); Henry F. Mason, "County Seat Controversies in Southwestern Kansas,"

Kans. Hist. Q., (Feb., 1933), 45–65; William D. Miller, "The Removal of the County Seat from Tower Hill to Little Rest, 1752," Rh. I. Hist. Soc., *Coll.*, XVIII (1926), 11–15, 46–48; Alfred Paschall, "Selecting the County Seat," Bucks County Hist. Soc., *Papers*, IV (1917), 174–80; Ernest V. Shockley, "County Seats and County Seat Wars in Indiana," *Ind. Mag. Hist.*, X (March, 1914), 1–46; Jacob A. Swisher, "The Location of County Seats in Iowa," *Iowa Journ. Hist. & Pol.*, XXII (1924), 89–128, 217–94, 323–62. Works of political science, like Arthur W. Bromage, *American County Government* (1933) and Kirk H. Porter, *County and Township Government in the United States* (1922), while thin in history, help us understand why so little progress has been made against the largely obsolete county system.

PART FOUR

THE ROOTED AND THE UPROOTED:

Southerners, White and Black

The South, however it fared on the battlefields of history, until very recently at least, was winning on the battlefields of historiography. Southerners and the pre-Civil War Southern point of view have dominated the writing of the history of the South; loyal Southerners and their partisans have, with a few conspicuous exceptions, remained firmly in control of the citadels of historical writing. In the 20th century, the dominant figure in the interpretation of Southern history has been the Georgia-born, and mostly Georgia-educated, Ulrich B. Phillips (1877–1934), whose point of view differed only in detail from that of the Southern champions of slavery and secession in the late 1850's. In his most widely read work, *Life and Labor in the Old South* (which won the Little, Brown & Co. prize for the best unpublished work in history in 1929), Phillips begins his chapter on "The

Peculiar Institution" by an analogy between the status of a slave and the status of a divorced man who must pay alimony; his chapter on "Life in Thraldom," while not omitting the darker side, emphasizes how life in Africa had prepared Negroes for slavery on the plantation, "the master taking the place of the accustomed chief," and he organizes his account around these notions: "The plantation force was a conscript army. . . . The plantation was of course a factory . . . The plantation was a school. . . . The civilizing of the Negroes was not merely a consequence of definite schooling but a fruit of plantation life itself. . . . The plantation was a parish, or perhaps a chapel of ease. . . . The plantation was a pageant and a variety show in alternation. . . . The plantation was a matrimonial bureau, something of a harem perhaps, a copious nursery, and a divorce court. . . . The home of a planter or of a well-to-do townsman was likely to be a 'magnificent negro boarding-house'. . . ." The prevailing note is benevolence: a society whose faults were probably no worse than those of others—where, on the whole, the ruling class lived up to the duties of its noblesse, and where the working class (who happened to be slaves) learned while it worked, and enjoyed it a good deal, too.

The best professional historians writing after Phillips on the whole did not dissent from his emphasis. But they talked less about the uplifting influence of slavery on the Negro, and more about the tragedy of the Southern whites, caught in a system they did not invent, pushed to secession and violence by self-righteous Northerners who saw nothing but the evil in the Peculiar Institution. Some of the best volumes in the monumental *History of the South* (ed. Wendell H. Stephenson and E. Merton Coulter, 10 vols., 1948–)—for example, Charles S. Sydnor's *Development of Southern Sectionalism 1819–1848*

(1948) and Avery O. Craven's *Growth of Southern Nationalism, 1848–1861* (1953)—describe the tensions among the Southern white leaders; but in their accounts the Negro (except as someone about whom the white statesmen and thinkers debated) had almost disappeared. "Life in Thraldom," which interested U. B. Phillips, however much he romanticized it, was displaced by life in the state and national capitals, and occasionally in the manor house.

Of course the whites made up the bulk of the population in the South; yet for nearly the whole of the 19th century before the Civil War, Negroes amounted to roughly one-third of the populace. It was the whites who made the public decisions, who wrote the record, and finally sifted the chronicle. But the Negroes were there too. The more recent "revision" of the Phillips emphasis has required not so much a harshening of the portrait of slavery as a simple restoration of the Negro to the historical picture. Important in this shift of focus was Frederic Bancroft (1860–1945), an Illinois-born historian educated at Amherst and Columbia, whose *Slave-Trading in the Old South* (1931) emphasized the experience of the Negroes themselves. It was followed by a number of important works by others who also asked new questions about slavery, who used the fragmentary and elusive evidence to construct a more realistic view of Negro life in the ante-bellum South, and who explored the significance of all this for Southern life and for American civilization as a whole.

These works restored the American Negro to his historical rights, treating him not as the negligible or invisible third of the Southern population, but as a person worth discovering and chronicling. Some landmarks in this new historiography are: W. E. B. DuBois, *Black Reconstruction* (1935); E. Franklin Frazier, *The Negro Family in the United States* (1939) and *The Negro in the United States* (1947;

1959); John Hope Franklin, *From Slavery to Freedom: A History of American Negroes* (1947; 1964), the pioneer critical survey of American Negro history by a professional historian; Oscar and Mary F. Handlin, "Origins of the Southern Labor System," *Wm. & Mary Q.*, 3d ser., VII (April, 1950), 199–222; V. O. Key, *Southern Politics in State and Nation* (1949; Vintage Paperback); Benjamin E. Mays and Joseph W. Nicholson, *The Negro's Church* (1933); Gunnar Myrdal and others, *An American Dilemma: The Negro Problem and Modern Democracy* (2 vols., 1944); Roger Shugg, *Origins of Class Struggle in Louisiana* (1939); Kenneth M. Stampp, *The Peculiar Institution: Slavery in the Ante-Bellum South* (1956); Richard C. Wade, *Slavery in the Cities* (1964); Carter G. Woodson (founder of the *Journal of Negro History* 1916–), *The Education of the Negro prior to 1861* (1915) and *The History of the Negro Church* (1921).

These and other historians, and the events of the mid-20th century, are confirming the truism that the basic facts in the history of the South are slavery and the difficulties of Southerners (white and Negro) in casting off the attitudes that came with it. The writing of the history of the South continued to be pervaded by a latter-day defense of slavery.

The literature of Southern history is so vast that the following list must be even more selective than that for earlier parts; it is especially focused on the particular questions I have tried to ask. Useful general works, in addition to *The History of the South* (ed. Wendell H. Stephenson and E. Merton Coulter, 10 vols., 1948–) mentioned above, are: Hodding Carter, *Southern Legacy* (1950); Avery O. Craven, *The Coming of the Civil War* (2d. ed., 1957) and *Civil War in the Making 1815–1860* (1959); William E. Dodd, *The Cotton Kingdom* (1919); Clement Eaton, *A History of the Old South* (1949) and *The Growth* of *Southern Civilization, 1790–1860* (1961); William B. Hesseltine and David L. Smiley, *The South in American History* (2d ed., 1960); Robert W. Howard, ed., *This is the South* (1959), an anthology; Ulrich B. Phillips, *American Negro Slavery* (1918), *The Course of the South to Secession* (1939), "The Central Theme of Southern History," *AHR*, XXXIV (Oct., 1928), 30–43; Frank L. Owsley, *Plain Folk of the Old South* (1949); Rupert B. Vance, *Human Geography of the South* (1935).

The colonial background can be discovered in the first four volumes of *The History of the South* (see above), and in: John R. Alden, *The First South* (1961); Carl Bridenbaugh, *Myths and Realities: Societies of the Colonial South* (1952); Verner W. Crane, *The Southern Frontier, 1670–1732* (1921; Ann Arbor Paperback); Charles S. Sydnor, *Gentlemen Freeholders* (1952); Thomas J. Wertenbaker, *The Shaping of Colonial Virginia* (1958).

Especially valuable for intellectual history and for the growth of Southern attitudes are: W. J. Cash, *The Mind of the South* (1941; Vintage Paperback); Richard Beale Davis, *Intellectual Life in Jefferson's Virginia (1790–1830)* (1964); Clement Eaton, *Freedom of Thought in the Old South* (1940), *The Growth of Southern Civilization, 1790–1860* (1961); W. S. Jenkins, *Pro-Slavery Thought in the Old South* (1935; 1960); Arthur W. Lloyd, *The Slavery Controversy, 1831–1860* (1939); R. G. Osterweis, *Romanticism and Nationalism in the Old South* (1949); Joseph C. Robert, *The Road from Monticello . . . the Virginia Slavery Debate of 1832* (1941); Louis Rubin (intro.), *I'll Take My Stand: The South and the Agrarian Tradition, by Twelve Southerners* (1930; Harper Paperback), personal manifestos of Southern agrarians; William R. Stanton, *The Leopard's Spots: Scientific Attitudes toward Race . . . 1815–1859* (1960); William R. Taylor, *Cavalier and Yankee: The Old South and American National Character* (1961); C. Vann Woodward, *The Burden of Southern History* (1960).

On agriculture, the basic work remains Lewis C. Gray, *History of Agriculture in the Southern United States to 1860* (2 vols., 1933); a valuable collection of documents is found in Vols. I and II (ed. Ulrich B. Phillips) of the *Documentary History of American Industrial Society* (ed. John R. Commons and others; 10 Vols., 1910–11). For material on the history of the cotton factor, I am deeply indebted to Harold D. Woodman, and especially to his "Marketing and Financing the Cotton Crop in the Ante-Bellum South," unpublished M.A. thesis, and "King Cotton and His Retainers: A Study of Cotton Marketing in the South," unpublished Ph.D. dissertation (Dept. of History, U. of Chicago; 1959, 1964). On economic history, J. D. B. DeBow's *Industrial Resources . . . of the Southern and Western States* (3 vols., 1853), collected from *DeBow's Review*, is in a class by itself among contemporary sources.

Other works I have found especially useful on agriculture, the plantation, marketing, and the southern economy are: Thomas P. Abernethy, *From Frontier to Plantation in Tennessee* (1932); Lewis Atherton, *The Southern Country Store, 1800–1860* (1949); James C. Ballagh, *A History of Slavery in Virginia* (1902), and (ed.) *Southern Economic History, 1607–1865* (Vol. V in *The South in the Building of the Nation;* 1909); John A. Caruso, *The Southern Frontier* (1963); Avery O. Craven, *Edmund Ruffin, Southerner* (1932), *A Historian and the Civil War* (1964); Horace Kephart, *Our Southern Highlanders* (1913); Hugh T. Lefler and Albert R. Newsome, *North Carolina* (1963); Edward Ingle, *Southern Sidelights . . . Social and Economic Life in the South a Generation before the*

War (1896); John S. Bassett, "The Relation between the Virginia Planter and the London Merchant," AHA, *Ann. Report*, I (1901), 553–75 and *The Southern Plantation Overseer* (1925); N. F. Cabell, "Early History of Agriculture in Virginia," *DeBow's Review*, XXIX (1858), 280–84, 411–21, 542–49; Cornelius O. Cathey, "Agricultural Implements in North Carolina, 1783–1860," *Agric. Hist.*, XXV (1951), 128–35; Ezekiel J. Donnell, *Chronological and Statistical History of Cotton* (1872); Francis P. Gaines, *The Southern Plantation* (1924); Hugh F. Grant, *Planter Management and Capitalism in Ante-Bellum Georgia: The Journal of Hugh Fraser Grant, Ricegrower* (ed. Albert V. House, 1954); Matthew Brown Hammond, *The Cotton Industry* (1897); Ralph W. Haskins, "Planter and Cotton Factor in the Old South: Some Areas of Friction," *Agric. Hist.*, XXIX (Jan., 1955), 1–14; Broadus Mitchell, *Frederick Law Olmsted* (1924) and *The Rise of Cotton Mills in the South* (1921); Ulrich B. Phillips, *The Economics of the Plantation* (1903); Joseph C. Robert, *The Tobacco Kingdom: Plantation, Market, and Factory in Virginia and North Carolina, 1800–1860* (1938), the best monograph on tobacco planting, and *The Story of Tobacco in America* (1949), a popular account; Robert R. Russel, *Economic Aspects of Southern Sectionalism, 1840–1861* (1924; 1960); J. Carlyle Sitterson, "Financing and Marketing the Sugar Crop of the Old South," *JSH*, X (1944), 188–199; Wendell H. Stephenson, "Ante-Bellum New Orleans in an Agricultural Focus," *Agric. Hist.*, XV (Oct., 1941), 161–74; Alfred H. Stone, "The Cotton Factorage System of the Southern States," *AHR*, XX (April, 1915), 557–65; Harold D. Woodman, "The Profitability of Slavery: A Historical Perennial," *JSH*, XXIX (Aug., 1963), 303–25.

Although there is no comprehensive history of ante-bellum efforts at Southern diversification, guidance can be found in Broadus Mitchell, *The Rise of Cotton Mills in the South* (1921) and (with George S. Mitchell), *The Industrial Revolution in the South* (1930), and in several useful works on leaders in the sporadic movement. On J. D. B. DeBow the best starting point is his own works, mentioned above, and also: Robert F. Durden, "J. D. B. DeBow: Convolutions of a Slavery Expansionist," *JSH*, XVII (Nov., 1951), 441–61; Ottis C. Skipper, *J. D. B. DeBow, Magazinist of the Old South* (1958). On William Gregg, the basic work is his own *Essays on Domestic Industry* (1845; 1941), and the best monograph is Broadus Mitchell, *William Gregg: Factory Master of the Old South* (1928). See also Thomas B. Martin, ed., "The Advent of William Gregg and the Graniteville Company," *JSH*, XI (Aug., 1945) 389–423. For other aspects of the problem of diversification, see: John Hope Franklin, *The Free Negro in North Carolina, 1790–1860* (1943); Richard C. Wade, *Slavery in the Cities* (1964) *passim*, on the employment of slaves in commerce and industry; Herbert Weaver, "Foreigners in Ante-Bellum Towns of the Lower South," *JSH*, XIII (Feb., 1947), 62–73.

An indispensable guide to the travelers' accounts, and through them to all aspects of Southern life, is Thomas D. Clark, ed., *Travels in the Old South, a Bibliography* (3 vols., 1956) Vol. I (1527–1783), Vol. II (1750–1825), Vol. III (1825–1860); for the later period, see E. Merton Coulter, ed., *Travels in the Confederate States* (1947). These are models of their kind, without parallel for other comparably extensive areas of American history. They offer précis of all the principal travel accounts, together with brief biographies and critical appraisals of the authors, with bibliographical details, and an excellent index. Travelers' accounts, if among the most vivid historical sources, are also among the most treacherous; almost any generalization or attitude can be documented from somebody or other's "original" observation, printed to confirm the prejudices of the writer or his audience. Nowhere is this more true than in travels to the ante-bellum South, where most travelers, whether from the United States or abroad, seem to have come with ready-made conclusions. These accounts must then be studied along with the biographies of their authors.

Among the travelers' and other personal accounts I have found most useful are: J. S. Buckingham, *The Slave States of America* (2 vols., 1842); G. W. Featherstonhaugh, *Excursion through the Slave States* (2 vols., 1844); D. R. Hundley, *Social Relations in Our Southern States* (1860), a sprightly and perceptive interpretation of Southern folkways from a sympathetic observer; Joseph H. Ingraham, *The South-West* (2 vols., 1835); James K. Paulding, *Letters from the South* (2 vols., 1835); Ada Sterling, ed., *A Belle of the Fifties: Memoirs of Mrs. Clay of Alabama* (1905); James Stirling, *Letters from the Slave States* (1857); sharp observations and some original ideas from an anti-Southern Scotsman.

Peculiarly valuable are the writings of the versatile New York landscape architect, Frederick Law Olmsted (1822–1903), whose works included Central Park and Riverside Park in New York City, Prospect Park in Brooklyn, South Park in Chicago, the Boston Park System, the capitol grounds in Washington and in Albany, the campuses of the University of California and Stanford University, and the Chicago World's Fair of 1893, and who more than any other one man created the American institution of public parks; he was also active in conserving natural beauties for public purposes, especially at Yosemite and Niagara Falls. Olmsted's literary fame rests on his full-bodied travel books, which are judicious without being dull, colorful without being lurid; they restore the reader's faith in the human capacity for precise and reliable observation, when few others seemed capable of it. His first Southern trip, incited by a discussion with the fire-eating abolitionist William Lloyd Garrison, was commissioned by Henry J. Raymond of the New York *Times* who wanted to have the facts. The result was: *A Journey in the Seaboard Slave States* (1856), *A Journey Through Texas* (1857), *A Journey in the Back Country* (1860); condensed together as *The Cotton Kingdom* (2 vols., 1861; ed. Arthur M. Schlesinger, 1953). There is no better introduction to Southern life on the brink of the War, and there are few comparable travel books in all American history. See also: Broadus Mitchell, *Frederick Law Olmsted* (1924); Frederick L. Olmsted, Jr., and Theodore Kimball, eds., *Frederick Law Olmsted, Landscape Architect, 1822–1903* (2 vols., 1922, 1928); and the admirable brief essay by Theodore Kimball in the *DAB*.

* * *

The history of law in the antebellum South is an enticing subject for a broad work which would interrelate many aspects of society, but only fragments have been written. The interested student must piece together most of the story for himself from statutes, reported cases, and legal treatises, all of which, for reasons explained in the text, are extremely unreliable guides to the actual practice. A useful collection is Helen T. Catterall, ed., *Judicial Cases concerning American Slavery and the Negro* (5 vols., 1926); much legal material will also be found in Ulrich B. Phillips, ed., *Plantation and Frontier* (2 vols., 1910), which comprise Vols. I and II in the *Documentary History of American Industrial Society* (ed. John R. Commons and others, 10 vols., 1910–11).

Some contemporary writings which

throw light on legal ideals and legal practices are: Thomas R. R. Cobb, *An Inquiry into the Law of Negro Slavery in the United States* (1858); William Goodell, *The American Slave Code in Theory and Practice* (1853) and *Slavery and Anti-Slavery* (1855); John C. Hurd, *The Law of Freedom and Bondage in the United States* (2 vols., 1858); John B. O'Neall, *The Negro Law of South Carolina* (1848), "Slave Laws of the South," in J.D.B. De Bow, ed., *Industrial Resources . . . of the Southern and Western States* (3 vols., 1853), at II, 269–92, *The Biographical Sketches of the Bench and Bar of South Carolina* (2 vols., 1859), and *The Annals of Newberry, Historical, Biographical, Anecdotal* (1859), observations of a many-sided South Carolina judge who became a leader in the state and national temperance movement, and promoted railroads, Sunday Schools, and agricultural reforms; George M. Stroud, *Sketch of the Laws Relating to Slavery in the Several States of the United States* (1827); Jacob D. Wheeler, *A Political Treatise on the Law of Slavery* (1837).

The whole proslavery and antislavery literature is, of course, largely concerned one way or another with the legal status (real or supposed) of the Negro. Defences of slavery which rest heavily on interpretations of the spirit and practice—rather than the letter—of the law include: Thomas R. Dew, *Review of the Debate in the Virginia Legislature of 1831 and 1832* (1832; better known under the title, *The Pro-Slavery Argument*, 1852; 1853), *An Essay on Slavery* (2d ed., 1849), and *Digest of the Laws, Customs, Manners, and Institutions of the Ancient and Modern Nations* (1853), an attempt to put slavery in its social context; George Fitzhugh, *Sociology for the South* (1854), *Cannibals All! or, Slaves without Masters* (1857; ed. C. Vann Woodward, 1960). And see Eric L. McKitrick, ed., *Slavery Defended: The Views of the Old South*

(1963), an anthology. On the other side, see Hinton R. Helper, *The Impending Crisis of the South* (1857), where an anti-Negro North Carolinian attacks slavery because of its effect on Southern whites; see also the extreme abolitionist view of Southern law in [Theodore D. Weld], *American Slavery as It Is* (1839), an anthology of atrocities.

The literature on the slave insurrections, real or imaginary, is full of controversy. There has been a lamentable tendency to believe that the Negro must somehow be "justified" by proving that he did rebel on every possible occasion. In the case of most of the supposed slave plots, rumors and traditions have been inextricably mixed with facts. Of special interest is *The Confessions of Nat Turner, the Leader of the Late Insurrection in Southampton, Va.* (Richmond, 1832) by Thomas R. Gray, who was the lawyer appointed by the court to defend Turner. This twenty-four-page pamphlet reveals a great deal not only about Turner, who seems to have given a substantially true report of himself, but also about Gray and others of the white citizenry. A recent important article on the Vesey "plot" is: Richard C. Wade, "The Vesey Plot: A Reconsideration," *JSH*, XXX (May, 1964), 143–61. Other relevant works are: Herbert Aptheker, *American Negro Slave Revolts* (1943), a defensive, Marxist interpretation; Joseph C. Carroll, *Slave Insurrections in the United States, 1800–1865* (1938); John Hope Franklin, *From Slavery to Freedom* (1952), esp. Ch. XIII; P. Slaughter, *The Virginian History of African Colonization* (Richmond, 1855), an insight into contemporary attitudes, illustrated by the motto of the book, "Africa gave to Virginia a Savage and a Slave; Virginia gives back to Africa a Citizen and a Christian"; Kenneth M. Stampp, *The Peculiar Institution* (1956; Vintage Paperback), esp. Chs. III and IV.

Other items which throw light on

the theory and practice of the law of slavery are: J. Winston Coleman, Jr., *Slavery Times in Kentucky* (1940); James Elbert Cutler, *Lynch-Law* (1905); Clement Eaton, "Mob Violence in the Old South," *MVHR*, XXIX (Dec., 1942), 351–70; Stanley M. Elkins, *Slavery: A Problem in American Institutional and Intellectual Life* (1959); Ralph B. Flanders, *Plantation Slavery in Georgia* (1933); John Hope Franklin, *The Militant South* (1956); H. M. Henry, *The Police Control of the Slave in South Carolina* (1914); Oscar and Mary F. Handlin, "Origins of the Southern Labor System," *Wm. & M. Q.*, 3d ser. VII (April, 1950), 199–222; John A. Krout, *The Origins of Prohibition* (1925); Herbert S. Klein, "Slavery in Cuba and Virginia, a Comparative History of the First Hundred Years," unpublished M.A. thesis (Dept. of History, U. of Chicago, 1959); Almon W. Lauber, *Indian Slavery in Colonial Times within the Present Limits of the United States* (1913), still the best work on the subject; Leon Litwack, *North of Slavery: the Negro in the Free States (1790–1860)* (1961); Albert Matthews, "Origin of the Term Lynch Law," *Col. Soc. Mass., Pub., Trans.*, XXVII (Dec., 1926), 256–71; Ulrich B. Phillips, *American Negro Slavery* (1940), esp. Chs. 14, 22, 23; N. S. Shaler, "The Peculiarities of the South," *North Am. Rev.*, CLI (Oct., 1890), 477–88; Kenneth M. Stampp, *The Peculiar Institution* (1956; Vintage Paperback), esp. Chs. IV and V; Charles S. Sydnor, "The Southerner and the Laws," *JSH*, VI (Feb–Nov., 1940), 3–23, especially suggestive; Frank Tannenbaum, *Slave and Citizen: The Negro in the Americas* (1947), a useful comparison of slavery in Anglo-America and in Latin America; Jack K. Williams, *Vogues in Villainy: Crime and Retribution in Ante-Bellum South Carolina* (1959).

Duelling is an institution much **more** important than has been sug-**gested** in the literature; it is com-monly treated as only a curiosity. One volume that puts the practice in context is John Hope Franklin, *The Militant South, 1800–1861* (1956). I have found invaluable the index to the *DAB*. Many travelers' accounts and other personal observations of Southern life describe or reveal the ruling concepts of honor. Some of the contemporary sources I have found most valuable are: Timothy Dwight, *A Sermon on Duelling* (1805); D. R. Hundley, *Social Relations in Our Southern States* (1860); Augustus B. Longstreet, *Georgia Scenes* (1835; Sagamore Paperback); Lorenzo Sabine, *Notes on Duels and Duelling* (1856); William H. Sparks, *The Memories of Fifty Years* (1882); John Lyde Wilson, *The Code of Honor, or Rules for the Government of Principals and Seconds in Duelling* (1858); Mrs. G. Wright, *A Southern Girl in '61* (1905).

Readily accessible biographies with detailed accounts of duels are: Marquis James, *Andrew Jackson* (1937) Ch. VIII and *passim;* the final chapter in John C. Miller, *Alexander Hamilton* (1959); Carl Schurz, *Life of Henry Clay* (2 vols., 1886); Bernard Mayo, *Henry Clay* (1937); and G. G. Van Deusen, *Life of Henry Clay* (1937). Other relevant items are: Philip A. Bruce, *History of the University of Virginia, 1819–1919* (5 vols., 1920–22), for origins of the honor system of examination; J. Winston Coleman, Jr., *Famous Kentucky Duels* (1953); Heloise H. Cruzat, "When Knighthood was in Flower," *La. Hist. Q.*, I (April, 1918), 367–71; Dixon Ryan Fox, "Culture in Knapsacks," N.Y. State Hist. Assn., *Q. Jnl.*, XI (Jan., 1930), 31–52, an account of the importation of the duelling custom by military men during the American Revolution; Harnett T. Kane, *Gentlemen, Swords, and Pistols* (1951); John S. Kendall, "The Humors of the Duello," *La. Hist. Q.*, XXIII (April, 1940), 445–70, and "Pistols for Two, Coffee for One,"

XXIV (July, 1941), 756–82; Grace King, *New Orleans, the Place and the People* (1896); Rollin G. Osterweis, *Romanticism and Nationalism in the Old South* (1949); Don C. Seitz, *Famous American Duels* (1929); Myra L. Spaulding, "Duelling in the District of Columbia," Columbia Hist. Soc. *Records*, XXIX–XXX (1928), 117–210; William O. Stevens, *Pistols at Ten Paces* (1940); Charles S. Sydnor, *A Gentleman of the Old Natchez Region: Benjamin L. C. Wailes* (1938).

Some of the peculiar tribulations of Southern editors, and the relation of the code of honor to freedom of expression can be followed in: Dwight L. Dumond, *Southern Editorials on Secession* (1931); Clement Eaton, *Freedom of Thought in the Old South* (1940) and "A Dangerous Pamphlet in the Old South," *JSH*, II (1936), 323–34; William W. Holden, *Address on the History of Journalism in North Carolina* (2d ed., 1881); Frederic Hudson, *Journalism in the United States, from 1690–1872* (1873), esp. Ch. LV, "The Duels of Editors," mostly southern; Lillian A. Kibler, *Benjamin F. Perry: South Carolina Unionist* (1946); Benjamin F. Perry, *Reminiscences of Public Men* (1883); Joseph C. Robert, *The Road from Monticello: A Study of the Virginia Slavery Debate of 1832* (1941), esp. Ch. V; W. Sherman Savage, *The Controversy over the Distribution of Abolition Literature, 1830–1860* (1938).

On the origins of the peculiarities of Southern politics, there is no better starting point than V. O. Key, *Southern Politics* (1949; Vintage Paperback), a brilliant study of contemporary politics, which reminds us of some of the things that still call for historical explanation. Since most historical writing on the South is sharply oriented to politics, the following list is only the barest selection from the items I have found especially useful: Gilbert H. Barnes, *The Antislavery Impulse* (1933); Jesse T. Carpenter, *The South as a Conscious Minority, 1789–1861* (1930); Arthur C. Cole, *The Whig Party in the South* (1913); Webb S. Fiser, "The Political Theory of the American Pro-Slavery Argument," unpublished M.A. thesis (Dept. of Pol. Sci., U. of Chicago, 1947); Edwin A. Miles, *Jacksonian Democracy in Mississippi* (1960); William R. Taylor, *Cavalier and Yankee* (1961); William S. Willis, "Divide and Rule: Red, White, and Black in the Southeast," *JNH*, XLVIII (July, 1963), 157–76; Charles G. Sellers, Jr., "Who were the Southern Whigs?" *AHR*, LIX (Jan., 1954), 335–46.

Southern political and social theory written before the Civil War (though heavily preoccupied with defending slavery and the cause of the South, and though astonishingly doctrinaire) is of surprising subtlety and brilliance. Its very irrelevance to the then pressing problems of the South is, paradoxically, one of the qualities that has helped it to a long life. The leading political theorists are John Taylor of Caroline (1753–1824) and John C. Calhoun (1782–1850). Taylor's principal works are: *Arator* (1813), a series of agricultural essays; *An Inquiry into the Principles and Policy of the Government of the United States* (1814; 1956); *Construction Construed and Constitutions Vindicated* (1820); *Tyranny Unmasked* (1822); and *New Views of the Constitution* (1823). Calhoun's most important political theory was published posthumously: *A Disquisition on Government and a Discourse on the Constitution and Government of the United States* (ed. Richard K. Crallé, 1851). These can be found in his *Works* (6 vols., 1861–64), Vol. I; a new edition of Calhoun is in preparation.

Francis Lieber (1800–72), who spent much of his life teaching at the University of South Carolina (1835–1857), had not come from his native

Germany until he was twenty-seven; he finished his career at Columbia University in New York City, where he supported the Union cause. His metaphysical and ponderous writings, sometimes called the first systematic works on political science to appear in the United States, though not focused on Southern problems, were actually written in the South: *Manual of Political Ethics* (2 vols., 1838–39); *Legal and Political Hermeneutics* (1839); *On Civil Liberty and Self-Government* (2 vols., 1853). See also the excellent biography by Frank Freidel, *Francis Lieber, Nineteenth-Century Liberal* (1947). The most brilliant and perverse of the Southern extremists was George Fitzhugh (1806–81), who is still very much worth reading to help us break up some of our clichés. His defense of slavery often took the form of searing attacks (many of which are still relevant) on the hypocrisies and injustices of free society. His principal works are: *Sociology for the South; or, the Failure of Free Society* (1854) and *Cannibals All! or, Slaves without Masters* (1857; ed. C. Vann Woodward, 1960). See also the biography by Harvey Wish, *George Fitzhugh, Propagandist of the Old South* (1943).

* * *

To write the history of the Southern Negro, who was the inarticulate (or at least the unliterary) third of the population, offers the difficulties characteristic of all efforts to transcend literary remains. With the best will in the world, we find it hard to say much that can be "documented" about what the Negro was thinking and feeling. Slavery made him fill his life with illegal, or at least extra-legal, institutions and practices, which left no archives. Therefore it requires extraordinary ingenuity to penetrate into the features of Negro life that are analogous to those that white citizens freely recorded, chronicled, and embellished for future generations.

While the early history of white Americans is distinguished by the great extent of our knowledge, and in this sense the very beginnings of the American nation (in Parkman's phrase) "stand forth in the bright light of history," the early history of Negro Americans is obscure. Even the origins of many of the Negroes imported as slaves are only vaguely known. The most tantalizing questions of the early American institutional history of the Negroes strangely resemble those of Western European nations. Where did they come from? What institutional baggage did they bring with them? Here the mists of time are replaced by the mists of space and by the shroud of slavery, which conceals the identity of its victims. Such writings as Bradford's *History of Plymouth* and the Winthrop *Papers* reveal the origins of the early settlers, what they left behind and what they brought with them; and the diaries of countless later immigrants add to the story. But for comparable facts about Negro immigrants we must sift the discrete clues of folk dance, folk song, and word origins—much as students of European prehistory sift Indo-Aryan linguistics and Homeric songs.

The history of Negro religion in America also illustrates this contrast. The Negro, through religion and his church, sought and found a kind of community, even under slavery. In the cities he did, as Professor Richard C. Wade has shown, find, in the grocery store and the grog shops, communities which can be traced in documents; and there he had organized and identifiable churches. But in the countryside slavery made his church from the beginning (in Frazier's words) an "invisible institution": its origins and significance must be discovered mostly indirectly and through circumstantial evidence. Melville Herskovits, in his fascinating but widely controverted *Myth of the Negro Past* (1941; Beacon Paperback), argues that the Negro's Christian churches were a domestication and partial transformation of attitudes and institutions developed in Africa. Here, he says, American and Christian notions were "reintegrated," but into an essentially African pattern, by "the cultural processes . . . of addition and synthesis to achieve congruence with older forms, rather than of subtraction and substitution, with their resulting fragmentation."

Long before Herskovits, and with much less anthropological equipment, W. E. B. DuBois (ed., *The Negro Church,* 1903) had declared the Negro Church to be "the only social institution among the Negroes which started in the African forest and survived slavery." On the other hand, E. Franklin Frazier argues persuasively (for example, in *The Negro Church in America,* 1963) that the Negro church was nothing of the sort, but simply filled a cultural vacuum: coming to America in slavery broke the Negro's connection with his African background, and Christianity provided an entirely new basis of social cohesion, with a quite new orientation toward existence. Since little is known of the actual religious practices of slaves in the ante-bellum South, all these theses depend largely on conjecture; I find the arguments for African survivals only partly convincing.

This controversy, which, of course, has the widest implications for the relations (past, present, and future) of the American Negro to Africa, has lately been focused on one topic: Negro music, and especially Negro song. Here is a kind of evidence, however elusive and kaleidoscopic, which survives, despite the lack of printed records. The Negro "spiritual" has been prominent in the distinctively American musical repertoire. But how "spiritual" were the spirituals? Did Negro spirituals develop out of white spirituals? Were they primarily worksongs, religious anthems, or perhaps even directions for fugitive slaves to follow the underground railroad? Were they in melody, rhythm, structure, and motif, mainly American

inventions or African survivals? While these questions call for specialized knowledge, they are by no means esoteric, and around them an engrossing literature has recently grown up.

Some of the more interesting works on this subject are: Lily Y. Cohen, *Lost Spirituals* (1928); Harold Courlander, *Negro Folk Music, U.S.A.* (1963), a sensible and eclectic book with the thesis that, though Negro folk music is "preeminently 'American,'" yet "many characteristics of African musical styles persist to this day"; Robert Nathaniel Dett, *Religious Folk-Songs of the Negro* (1927); Miles Mark Fisher, *Negro Slave Songs in the United States* (1953) and "The Evolution of Slave Songs of the United States," unpublished Ph.D. dissertation (Divinity School, U. of Chicago, 1948), interpreting spirituals as historical documents which chronicle and react to the problems of everyday life in slavery; George P. Jackson, *White and Negro Spirituals: Their Life Span and Kinship* (1943); Henry E. Krehbiel, *Afro-American Folksongs* (1914); Dorothy Scarborough, *On the Trail of Negro Folk-Songs* (1963); Irwin Silber, *Songs of the Civil War* (1960), esp. pp. 267–300, showing how Negro songs served as detailed instructions for escape from slavery; Howard Thurman, *The Negro Spiritual Speaks of Life and Death* (1947); John W. Work, *American Negro Songs and Spirituals* (1940), which emphasizes African origins. For more light on this question see: Lorenzo D. Turner, *Africanisms in the Gullah Dialect* (1949), a study of linguistic survivals in the dialect of a large number of Negroes of coastal South Carolina and Georgia; Richard Dorson, *American Folklore* (1959; Phoenix Paperback), on the problem of discovering nationally distinctive folk motifs.

Other especially useful items from the growing literature on the Negro church and on Negro religion are: George F. Bragg, Jr., *History of the Afro-American Group of the Episco-*

pal Church (1922); Richard B. Cook, *The Story of the Baptists in All Ages and Countries* (1887), with a chapter on "the colored Baptists"; Joseph B. Earnest, *The Religious Development of the Negro in Virginia* (1914); John T. Gillard, *The Catholic Church and the American Negro* (1929); L. M. Hapgood, *The Colored Man in the Methodist Episcopal Church* (1890); Ruby F. Johnson, *The Development of Negro Religion* (1954); Charles C. Jones, *Negro Myths from the Georgia Coast* (1925); Samuel M. Lawton, "The Religious Life of South Carolina Coastal and Sea Island Negroes," George Peabody College, *Abstract . . . No. 242* (1939); William H. Pipes, *Say Amen, Brother!* (1951); Walter B. Posey, "The Baptists and Slavery in the Lower Mississippi Valley," *JNH*, XLI (April, 1956), 117–30, and "Influence of Slavery upon the Methodist Church in the Early South and Southwest," *MVHR*, XVII (1931), 530–42, especially valuable on the relations of Negroes to whites within the churches; William R. Rigell, "Negro Religious Leadership on the Southern Seaboard —Maryland, Virginia, North Carolina, South Carolina, and Georgia, 1830– 1861," unpublished M.A. thesis (Dept. of Church History, U. of Chicago, 1916); George A. Singleton, "The Effect of Slavery upon the Religion of the Negro," unpublished Bachelor's thesis (Dept. of Church History, U. of Chicago, 1930). A particularly valuable contemporary work is Charles C. Jones, *Religious Instruction of the Negroes in the United States* (1842); see also, *Proceedings of the Meeting Charleston, S. C., May 13–15, 1845, on ·the Religious Instruction of the Negroes* (1845).

For obvious reasons, writings by Southern Negroes of this period are not copious. A useful selection is Carter G. Woodson, ed., *The Mind of the Negro as Reflected in Letters Written During the Crisis 1800–1860* (1926). Some of the more accessible books by Negroes include: Lewis Garrard Clarke, *Narrative of the Sufferings of Lewis and Milton Clarke* (1846); Frederick Douglass, *Narrative of the Life of Frederick Douglass* (1845: rev. ed., 1892; ed. Benjamin Quarles, 1960); Moses Grandy, *Narrative of the Life of Moses Grandy* (1844); Josiah Henson, *Truth Stranger than Fiction: Father Henson's Story of His Own Life* (1849; rev. ed., 1858); Lunsford Lane, *The Narrative of Lunsford Lane* (2d ed., 1842); Solomon Northrup, *Twelve Years a Slave* (1854); Austin Steward, *Twenty-Two Years a Slave, and Forty Years a Freeman* (1851).

BOOK TWO

NATIONALITY

PART FIVE

THE VAGUENESS OF THE LAND

Nothing is more difficult than to drive out of our mind, even momentarily, knowledge that has become commonplace; this is a form of what Coleridge called "the willing suspension of disbelief which is poetic faith." The historian trying to recover the past is like the mythical alchemist whose formula for making base metals into gold would work only if he was *not* thinking of a white elephant. How can we recapture ignorance? Yet this is precisely what we must do if we are to imagine ourselves back into the frame of mind of the Americans of the early 19th century.

It is worth exerting all our imaginative energy to recapture the vagueness and the false certainties which encompassed the geography of their age; without those, we will misunderstand their plans and hopes. Unwittingly we commit the anachronism of imagining their events taking place on our maps and not on theirs. Until recently, historians have not helped us much. The history of geographic knowledge, the first necessity for placing the men of the past where they actually thought themselves to be, has, oddly enough, remained a branch of historical esoterica. A clue to the importance of this subject is Edmundo O'Gorman's brilliant essay, *The Invention of America* (1961) which explores neglected ambiguities in our notion of "discovery"; see also Wilcomb E. Washburn, "The Meaning of 'Discovery' in the Fifteenth and Sixteenth Centuries," *AHR*, LXVIII (Oct., 1962), 1–21.

Ralph H. Brown's *Historical Geography of the United States* (1948), with accompanying bibliographies, is the best general introduction. Seventeenth- and eighteenth-century notions of American geography are described in Howard Mumford Jones's lively *O Strange New World* (1964). For the state of geographic knowledge in the early 19th century a starting point is Ralph H. Brown's ingenious and readable *Mirror for Americans: Likeness of the Eastern Seaboard, 1810* (1943), drawn from the writings of early 19th-century geographers. Our most vivid view of their picture of the continent comes, of course, from their maps; reproductions are found in Charles O. Paullin, *Atlas of the Historical Geography of the United States* (1932), plates 8–32, with accompanying interpretation, pp. 7–15. For more detail we must examine contemporary geographies, for example those by Jedidiah Morse (1761–1826), "father of American geography": *Geography Made Easy,* the first geography published in the United States (1784; twenty–seven editions before 1826); *The American Geography* (1789), in later editions known as *The American Universal Geography;* these and other Morse works dominated the subject during the author's lifetime. Travel books and accounts by explorers, which often contain maps, are also helpful; see those mentioned in General section and Book I, above.

Carl I. Wheat, a practicing lawyer, and a historian in the tradition of the great amateurs, has provided the in-dispensable work on the history of the cartography of the American West; I am deeply indebted to him. See his magnificent *Mapping the Transmississippi West, 1540–1861* (4 vols. to date, of five projected; 1957–), summarized in his more accessible "Mapping the American West, 1540–1857," Am. Antiq. Soc., *Proc.,* LXIV (April, 1954), 19–194. Obliquely valuable for cartographic history are: Percy G. Adams, *Travelers and Travel Liars, 1660–1800* (1962), a scholarly and amusing study of the relation of literary conventions to the distortion of geographic information; John N. L. Baker, *A History of Geographic Discovery and Exploration* (1937); John Bakeless, *The Eyes of Discovery: America as seen by the First Explorers* (Dover Paperback, 1960); Richard Beale Davis, *Intellectual Life in Jefferson's Virginia, 1790–1830* (1964), pp. 196–204; Bernard De Voto, *The Course of Empire* (1952); Ellen C. Semple, *American History and its Geographic Conditions* (1903); Henry Nash Smith, *Virgin Land: the American West as Symbol and Myth* (1950; Vintage Paperback), a delightful dramatic essay.

The long search for a westward sea passage to the Orient is one of the most ironic and pathetic chapters in the unveiling of the New World. The best introduction to that story in this period is Gloria G. Cline's admirable monograph, *Exploring the Great Basin* (1963), to which I am much indebted; the standard work on the larger story is Lawrence J. Burpee, *The Search for the Western Sea* (rev. ed., 2 vols., 1936). Other useful items are: John L. Bakeless, *Lewis and Clark, Partners in Discovery* (1947; Apollo Paperback), C. Gregory Crampton and Gloria G. Cline, "The San Buenaventura, Mythical River of the West," *Pac. Hist. Rev.,* XXV (May, 1956), 163–71; Dale L. Morgan, *Jedediah Smith and the Opening of the West* (1953); Allan Nevins, *Frémont, the West's Greatest Adventurer* (2 vols., 1928); Charles Preuss, *Exploring with Frémont* (1958); Henry R. Wagner, "Some Imaginary California Geography," Am. Antiq. Soc., *Proc.,* XXXVI (April, 1926), 83–129.

Especially valuable contemporary accounts touching this topic are: Timothy Flint, *Recollections of the Last Ten Years* (1826); John C. Frémont, *Narratives of Exploration and Adventure* (ed. Allan Nevins, 1956); Washington Irving, *A Tour on the Prairies* (1835), *Astoria* (1836), and *The Adventures of Captain Bonneville,* (1843), all many times reprinted; Edwin James, *Account of an Expedition from Pittsburgh to the Rocky Mountains . . . in . . . 1819 and 1820 . . . under . . . Major Stephen H. Long* (2 vols., 1823); Meriwether Lewis and William Clark, *Original Journals of the Lewis and Clark Expedition, 1804–1806* (ed. R. G. Thwaites, 8 vols., 1904–5), the journals of the leaders themselves, also more concisely available in 2 vols., ed., James K. Hosmer (1902), and as selected and edited by Bernard De Voto (1953); see also *Letters of the Lewis and Clark Expedition with Related Documents, 1783–1854* (ed. Donald D. Jackson, 1962), with much valuable new material; Howard Stansbury, *An Expedition to the Valley of the Great Salt Lake of Utah* (1852).

On the role of the Federal government and the army in mapping and surveying the West, two basic works are William H. Goetzmann, *Army Exploration in the American West, 1803–1863.* (1959), an extraordinarily broad and suggestive work, and Richard A. Bartlett, *Great Surveys of the American West* (1962), on both of which I have leaned heavily. See also: Dwight L. Agnew, "The Government Land Surveyor as a Pioneer," *MVHR,* XXVIII (Dec., 1941), 369–82; A. Hunter Dupree, *Science in the Federal Government* (1957); Francis P. Prucha, *Broadax and Bayonet: the Role of the United States Army in the Development of the Northwest, 1815–1860* (1953).

For the origins and history of the system of rectangular survey, see Bibliographical Notes to Bk. I, Pt. 2, above, and also see: William D. Pattison, *Beginnings of the American Rectangular Land Survey System, 1784–1800* (pub. of Dept. of Geography, U. of Chicago, 1957), an indispensable monograph to which I am much indebted, and "The Survey of the Seven Ranges," *Ohio Hist. Q.,* LXVIII (April, 1959), 115–40; "The History of Surveying in the United States (A Panel Discussion)," *Surveying and Mapping,* XVIII (April–June, 1958), 179–219. On the long-term consequences of the rectangular survey, an essential work is John Wesley Powell, *Report on the Lands of the Arid Regions of the United States* (2d ed., 1879; ed. Wallace Stegner, 1962); and see Wallace Stegner's readable *Beyond the Hundredth Meridian: John Wesley Powell and the Second Opening of the West* (intro. Bernard De Voto, 1954; Sentinel Paperback). The exciting account of Powell's pioneering boat trip is found in his *Exploration of the Colorado River* (1875; rev. 1895; ed. Wallace Stegner, 1957, which contains an abridgment of the 1875 ed. of Powell's *Report*). See also: Walter Prescott Webb, *The Great Plains* (1931); Carl F. Kraenzel, *The Great Plains in Transition* (1955). On the "Great American Desert" and some counter-myths see: Ralph C. Morris, "The Notion of a Great American Desert East of the Rockies," *MVHR,* XIII (Sept., 1926), 190–200; Francis P. Prucha, "Indian Removal and the Great American Desert," *Indiana Mag. Hist.,* LIX (Dec., 1963), 299–322; Henry Nash Smith, "Rain Follows the Plow: The Notion of Increased Rainfall for the Great Plains, 1844–1880," *Huntington Lib. Q.,* X (Feb., 1947), 169–93.

The flamboyant William Gilpin (1813–94), first territorial governor of Colorado, and without peer as an author of booster geography, still awaits his biographer. H. H. Bancroft's *History of the Life of William Gilpin* does not meet the challenge and, like

Bancroft's other books, must be used with caution. The best brief account is Charles N. Glaab, "Visions of Metropolis: William Gilpin and Theories of City Growth in the American West," *Wis. Mag. Hist.*, XLV (Aut., 1961), 21–31; see also Ch. I, "Prophets of Railroad Destiny," in his *Kansas City and The Railroads* (1962). Gilpin's works are almost too good to be true, and no one interested in the power of man's will to believe should neglect them: *The Central Gold Region* (1860), *Notes on Colorado* (1870); *Mission of the North American People, Geographical, Social and Political* (1873; 1874), and *The Cosmopolitan Railway* (1890). Some other examples of booster geography are by Logan U. Reavis, *A Change of National Empire: or, Arguments in Favor of the Removal of the National Capital from Washington City to the Mississippi Valley* (St. Louis, 1879), *St. Louis: The Future Great City of the World* (1876), *The Nation and its Capital* (1881), and *The Continental Supremacy of the Constitution* (1882); for some broader implications, see Josiah Strong, *Our Country* (1885), esp. Chs. II and III.

On the Great Diamond Hoax, see: Richard E. Bartlett, *Great Surveys of the American West* (1962), Ch. IX, and accompanying bibliographical references; Asbury Harpending, *The Great Diamond Hoax and Other Stirring Incidents in the Life of Asbury Harpending* (ed. James H. Wilkins, 1915; in *Western Frontier Library*, intro. Glen Dawson, 1958), unreliable but all the more interesting because the author was supposedly a promoter of the hoax; and, for a more recent popular account, A. J. Liebling, "The American Golconda," *New Yorker*, XVI (Nov. 16, 1940), 40–48.

The relation of western experience to the development of a distinctively American art can be best approached through James T. Flexner's admirable, *That Wilder Image: The Painting of America's Native School from Thomas Cole to Winslow Homer* (1962), with bibliographies and illustrations. The definitive work on Banvard and his fellow panoramists is John F. McDermott, *The Lost Panoramas of the Mississippi* (1958), an entertaining treatment of an elusive subject. Every student of this period should spend some time with George Catlin, *Letters and Notes on the Manners, Customs, and Condition of the North American Indians* (2 vols., 1841, and later editions) or one of his other numerous illustrated volumes. The monographic literature on individual engravers and painters of the West is large; much of it tends to be antiquarian or precious. Some works I have found helpful on the relation of Western conditions, knowledge, and ignorance to the graphic arts are: Bernard De Voto, *Across the Wide Missouri* (1947), which includes an account of the discovery of the Alfred Jacob Miller collection by Mae R. Porter, and which uses the paintings of Miller (supplemented by the works of Bodmer and Catlin) as a framework for a vivid account of the Rocky Mountain fur trade; Hans Huth, *Nature and the American: Three Centuries of Changing Attitudes* (1957), which explores the relation between the works of artists and writers and the American attitudes toward the outdoors, and toward conservation. For John James Audubon, see: Audubon's *Journals* (ed. Elliott Coues; 2 vols., 1897), and a selection under the title, *Delineations of American Scenery and Character* (1926); F. H. Herrick, *Audubon the Naturalist* (2 vols., 1917); Constance Rourke, *Audubon* (1936).

The role, expected and actual, of governments in improving land and developing transportation can be approached through Carter Goodrich's definitive *Government Promotion of American Canals and Railroads* (1960), on which I have drawn heavily; and see also his "Public Spirit and American Improvements," *Am. Phil. Soc., Proc.*, XCII (1948), 305–9, "The Revulsion against Internal Improvements," *Journ. Ec. Hist.*, X (1950),

145–69, "Local Government Planning of Internal Improvements," *Pol. Sci. Q.*, LXVI (1951), 411–45, "American Development Policy: The Case of Internal Improvements," *Journ. Ec. Hist.*, XVI (1956), 449–60. Other especially useful items are: Wylie J. Daniels, "The Village at the End of the Road," Indiana Hist. Soc., *Pub.*, XIII (1941), 3–112; Leland H. Jenks, "Railroads as an Economic Force in American Development," in Joseph T. Lambie and Richard V. Clemence, eds., *Economic Change in America* (1954), pp. 52–68; Edward C. Kirkland, *Men, Cities and Transportation, a Study in New England History, 1820–1900* (2 vols., 1948); Reginald C. McGrane, *The Panic of 1837* (1924); George R. Taylor, *The Transportation Revolution, 1815–1860* (Vol. IV in *The Economic History of the United States*, 1951); Henry Varnum Poor, *Influence of the Railroads of the United States in the Creation of its Commerce and Wealth* (1869) and *History of the Railroads and Canals of the United States . . . their Progress, Cost, Revenues, Expenditures, and Present Condition* (Vol. I of an incompleted work; 1860), by the founder of *Poor's Manual of Railroads*, the dominant railway authority of his day. Valuable pioneer monographs show the relation of local circumstances to activities of state governments: Oscar and Mary F. Handlin, *Commonwealth: A Study of the Role of Government in the American Economy: Massachusetts, 1774–1861* (1947); Louis Hartz, *Economic Policy and Democratic Thought: Pennsylvania, 1776–1860* (1948); James N. Primm, *Economic Policy in the Development of a Western State: Missouri, 1820–1860* (1954). An especially interesting contemporary item is Jared Sparks, "Internal Improvements of North Carolina," *North Am. Rev.*, XII (Jan., 1821), 16–37. For a theoretical exploration of some problems in the history of the growth of railroads which go beyond

the scope of the present chapter, see Robert W. Fogel, *The Union Pacific Railroad: A Case in Premature Enterprise* (1960), "A Provisional View of the 'New Economic History,' " *American Economic Review: Supplement*, LIV (May, 1964), 377–89, and *Railroads and American Economic Growth: Essays in Econometric History* (1964). For further references on railroads, see Bibliographical Notes to Book One, Part Two (above).

On the relation of Indians to the establishment of land titles by Europeans the best starting point is William C. MacLeod, *The American Indian Frontier* (1928), a brilliant and suggestive book, which should be better known. General works which touch on the subject include: Harold E. Driver, *Indians of North America* (1961); William T. Hagan, *American Indians* (1961), the best concise treatment of a large subject; A. L. Kroeber, *Cultural and Natural Areas of Native North America* (1939); D'Arcy McNickle, *They Came Here First: the Epic of the American Indian* (1949); James C. Malin, *Indian Policy and Westward Expansion* (1921); Roy H. Pearce, *The Savages of America* (1953), a history of attitudes toward the Indian in American literature; Ruth M. Underhill, *Red Man's America* (1953). Relevant specialized studies include: Annie H. Abel, "The History of Events Resulting in Indian Consolidation West of the Mississippi River," Am. Hist. Assn., *Annual Report* (1906), I, 235–412, and "Proposals for an Indian State, 1778–1878," *Annual Report* (1907), I, 89–102; Bernard De Voto, *The Year of Decision: 1846* (1943); Henry E. Fritz, *The Movement for Indian Assimilation, 1860–1890* (1963); William T. Hagan, *The Sac and Fox Indians* (1953); A. Irving Hallowell, "The Backwash of the Frontier: the Impact of the Indian on American Culture," the best short treatment of a neglected subject, in Walker D. Wyman and Clifton B. Kroeber, eds.,

The Frontier in Perspective (1957), 229–57; M. A. Hanna, *Trade of the Delaware before the Revolution* (Smith Coll. Studies in Hist., 1907); W. J. Hoffman, "The Menomini Indians," and J. Mooney, "The Ghost-Dance Relation," in J. W. Powell, *Fourteenth Annual Report of the U.S. Bureau of American Ethnology to the Secretary of the Smithsonian Institution, 1892–93*, Part I; George E. Hyde, *Indians of the High Plains* (1959) and *Indians of the Woodlands* (1962); Wilbur Jacobs, *Diplomacy and Indian Gifts* (1950); Karl N. Llewellyn and E. Adamson Hoebel, *The Cheyenne Way: Conflict and Case Law in Primitive Jurisprudence* (1941); Bernard Mishkin, *Rank and Warfare among the Plains Indians* (1940); Francis P. Prucha, *American Indian Policy in the Formative Years: the Indian Trade and Intercourse Acts, 1780–1834* (1962). Easily accessible collections of documents are: Jack D. Forbes, ed., *The Indian in America's Past* (1964) and Wilcomb E. Washburn, *The Indian and the White Man* (Anchor Paperback, 1964).

Especially valuable contemporary accounts of the Indian in different periods before the Civil War include: George Catlin, *Letters and Notes on the Manners, Customs, and Condition of the North American Indians* (above); Samuel G. Drake, ed., *Tragedies of the Wilderness* (1839), a standard collection of early narratives of Indian captivities; Albert Gallatin, "A Synopsis of the Indian Tribes of North America," Am. Antiq. Soc., *Trans. and Coll.*, II (1836), 9–423; Daniel Gookin, "An Historical Account of the Doings and Sufferings of the Christian Indians of New England," Am. Antiq. Soc., *Trans. and Coll.*, II (1836), 423–535; Lee Nelson, *Three Years among the Comanches* (in *Western Frontier Library*, 1957), a narrative by the Texas Ranger; Lewis Henry Morgan, *The Indian Journals, 1859–62* (1959). An indispensable tool is George P. Murdock, *Ethnographic*

Bibliography of North America (3d ed., 1960).

The Louisiana Purchase, the story of its negotiation, the ambiguity of its extent, and the attendant constitutional problems, can be first approached through Henry Adams' dramatic chapters in *History of the United States in the Administrations of Jefferson and Madison* (9 vols., 1889–91; 1921), Vol. II. A readable and scholarly account of the Purchase is found in George Dangerfield, *Chancellor Robert R. Livingston* (1960). Other useful items are: Everett S. Brown, *The Constitutional History of the Louisiana Purchase* (1920); George Dangerfield, *The Era of Good Feelings* (1952); Louis Houck, *The Boundaries of the Louisiana Purchase* (1901); Charles McKnight, *Our Western Border* (1876); Thomas M. Marshall, *A History of the Western Boundary of the Louisiana Purchase* (1914); Edward S. Wallace, *The Great Reconnaissance* (1955).

No subject in American history is more plagued by clichés than "Manifest Destiny." The best corrective, and a good starting point, is Frederick Merk, *Manifest Destiny and Mission in American History: a Reinterpretation* (1963), which can be supplemented by his *Albert Gallatin and the Oregon Problem* (1950) and "The Genesis of the Oregon Question," *MVHR*, XXXVI (March, 1950), 583–612. The standard history of justifications for American expansionism is Albert K. Weinberg, *Manifest Destiny: A Study of Nationalist Expansionism in American History* (1935; Encounter Paperback), a useful compendium of the shifting arguments. See also, Dexter Perkins' standard *History of the Monroe Doctrine* (rev. ed., 1955).

PART SIX

AMERICAN WAYS OF TALKING

While a few familiar "classics" of American literature—and especially the writings of Thoreau, Emerson, Hawthorne, Melville, and Whitman—are researched to death, the American language itself is left out of the mainstream of the study of American civilization. This is doubly strange because there are now many books on the subject that are both readable and scholarly. (See Bibliographical Notes to *The Americans: The Colonial Experience*, Part Ten.)

The history of the American language between Independence and the Civil War presents many of the same problems found in the colonial period. The continued absence of any adequate and widely used contemporary system of phonetics for recording the actual sounds as spoken, leaves much of the history of spoken usage open for speculation. But, since this later period sees the introduction of many new words, and the innovations tend to be more radical and more obvious, they begin to attract more attention among contemporaries. And in these years, for the first time, the American language becomes the subject of numerous and extensive specialized works. The history of pronunciation and of other features of the spoken language remains largely conjectural, but innovations of vocabulary, usage, and spoken style begin to be expertly noted.

The basic work, too little known outside professional linguistic circles, is Richard H. Thornton, *An American Glossary: Being an Attempt to Illustrate Certain Americanisms Upon Historical Principles* (2 vols., 1912; plus a third volume published posthumously in *Dialect Notes*, Vol. VI (1931–39); republished as 3 vol. set, 1962). Thornton (1845–1925), an English-born lawyer who was nearly thirty when he came to the United States, became the first dean of the Oregon Law School (1884–1903), and then practiced in Philadelphia. He too is thus in the great tradition of the amateurs. The two volumes published in his lifetime collected some 14,000 dated quotations, illustrating about 4000 terms from scattered sources. Evidence of his genius was his discovery of a use for all the countless words uttered in Congress: he drew copiously on the *Congressional Globe* (1837–72) and the *Congressional Record* (1872——) for authentic examples of expressions on every conceivable topic by speakers from all over the country. These examples had the advantage of being precisely dated and the place of origin of their users was easily ascertained. Thornton's quotations are an incomparable kaleidoscope of American thought and expression, encompassing in print the range, variety, and novelty of the life of the new nation.

To place this era in the whole story of the growth of an American language we must return to H. L. Mencken's magnificent *American Language* (3 vols., Vol. 1, 4th ed., 1937; Supplement I, 1952; Supplement II, 1956), now conveniently abridged into one volume and updated, with new material, by Raven I. McDavid, Jr. (1963). Mencken's work, which gives no sign of being displaced by any other of comparable scope, is both an example and a history of the peculiar vitality of the American language. Brief interpretations which the beginner may find more digestible are: Thomas Pyles, *Words and Ways of American English* (1952) and Albert Marckwardt, *American English* (1958; Galaxy Paperback). An important earlier work, more academic in approach and useful on special topics, is George P. Krapp, *The English Language in America* (2 vols., 1925; 1960); see also the application of a developmental approach to language in Donald J. Lloyd and Harry R. Warfel, *American English in its Cultural Setting* (1956), a college textbook. To place American developments in the Anglo-American context, see Thomas Pyles' readable *The Origins and Development of the English Language* (1964), esp. Ch. IX, which argues for "the essential oneness of all English."

The basic tools for the history of particular words and phrases remain: the monumental *Oxford English Dictionary . . . On Historical Principles* (ed. James A. H. Murray and others; 12 vols. and one supp. to date, 1933), supplemented by *A Dictionary of American English on Historical Principles* (ed. Sir William A. Craigie and James R. Hulbert; 4 vols. 1938) and *A Dictionary of Americanisms on Historical Principles* (ed. Mitford M. Mathews; 2 vols., 1951; one vol. ed., 1960).

There is no better introduction to the peculiar colloquialism of the American language—and to the public reluctance to recognize its existence—than the entertaining paperback *Dictionaries and* THAT *Dictionary: A Casebook on the Aims of Lexicographers and the Targets of Reviewers* (ed. James Sledd and Wilma R. Ebbitt, 1962), which collects reviews (for and against; few are neutral) of *Webster's Third New International Dictionary* (1961), and reprints many inaccessible items on the changing aims of dictionary-makers and the shifting criteria of linguistic propriety. The newcomer to this subject will quickly discover that the *odium theologicum* is nothing compared to the *odium linguisticum*. From there he can turn to two handy anthologies, both of which include material from the period of the present volume: Mitford M. Mathews, ed., *Beginnings of American English* (1931; Phoenix Paperback) and C. Merton Babcock, *The Ordeal of American English* (Houghton Mifflin Research Series Paperback No. 9; 1961).

The first half of the 19th century was the pioneer period of American linguistics and lexicography, as it was the formative era of the American language and the great age of word immigration. Noah Webster (1758–1843) is, of course, the dominant figure in the popular lexicography of the age. Every student should savor Webster's writings, for example: *A Grammatical Institute of the English Language* (1783–85, of which the first part became the fantastically successful *Spelling Book,* which had sold some sixty million copies by 1890; it was in the course of his efforts to secure an enforceable copyright for this book that Webster became a firm Federalist); *Dissertations on the English Language* (1789; facsimile, intro. Harry R. Warfel, 1951); *Compendious Dictionary of the English Language* (1806), and, finally, *An American Dictionary of the English Language* (2 vols., 1828), the introduction to which summarizes his linguistic theories. Webster's career can be followed in his *Letters* (ed. Harry R. Warfel, 1953), and in Harry R. Warfel, *Noah Webster, Schoolmaster to America* (1936) or Ervin C. Shoemaker, *Noah Webster, Pioneer of Learning* (1936).

In this period, too, appeared the first considerable collections of "Americanisms," a word which in its linguistic sense appears to have been invented by John Witherspoon in 1781. The first volume to collect Americanisms, real or supposed, was John Pickering's *Vocabulary or Collection of Words and Phrases which have been supposed to be peculiar to the United States of America* (1816), which excited a reply from Noah Webster, his *Letter to . . . Pickering on the Subject of His Vocabulary* (1817). The most important contemporary collection was the *Dictionary of Americanisms: A Glossary of Words and Phrases usually Regarded as Peculiar to the United States* (1848; 4th ed., 1877) by the versatile John Russell Bartlett. Other especially valuable items by authors who had personal knowledge of the language of the period include: Charles Astor Bristed, "The English Language in America," in *Cambridge Essays, Contributed by Members of the University* (1855), pp. 57–78, a brilliant pioneer essay; Maximilian Schele De Vere, *Americanisms: The English of the New World* (1872); Alfred L. Elwyn, *Glossary of Supposed Americanisms* (1859); John S. Farmer, *Americanisms Old and New* (1889); William C. Fowler, *The English Language . . . with a History of its Origin and Development* (1857); Robley Dunglison's glossary of Americanisms, originally in *Virginia Literary Museum (1829–30)*, reprinted in *Dialect Notes*, Vol. V, Pt. X (1927); Henry James, *The Question of our Speech* (1905); Samuel L. Knapp, *Lectures on American Literature* (1829); George P. Marsh, *The Origin and History of the English Language* (2d ed., 1863) and *Lectures on the English Language* (4th ed. 1874); Thomas L. Nichols, *Forty Years of American Life, 1821–61* (1864; 1937); Charles L. Norton, *Political Americanisms . . . Terms and Phrases Current at Different Periods in American Politics* (1890); "The Restorator: Columbian Language," *The Port Folio*, 1st ser., I (Oct. 10, 1801), 325–26; Mark Twain, *A Tramp Abroad* (1880); Walt Whitman, *An American Primer* (1904).

Elijah H. Criswell's *Lewis and Clark: Linguistic Pioneers* (1940) is in a class by itself as an intensive study of the vocabulary and usage of non-literary material of this period. Other valuable scholarly works which throw light on this subject include: Harold W. Bentley, *A Dictionary of Spanish Terms in English* (1952); Lester V. Berrey and Belvin Van den Bark, *The American Thesaurus of Slang* (1942); Sir William A. Craigie, *The Growth of American English* (2 vols., 1940); Elrick B. Davis, "John Mason and the American Language," *American Speech*, II (1926–27), 21–33, which compares the vocabulary of Peck's gazeteer of Illinois (1837) with items in the *OED;* Charles C. Fries, *American English Grammar* (1940) and *The Structure of English* (1952); Eric Partridge, *Origins: A Short Etymological Dictionary of Modern English* (1958), *Slang To-Day and Yesterday* (3rd ed., 1930), and *A Dictionary of Slang and Unconventional English* (5th ed., 1961); Archer Taylor and Bartlett J. Whiting, *A Dictionary of American Proverbs and Proverbial Phrases, 1820–1880* (1958); W. H. Venable, *Beginnings of Literary Culture in the Ohio Valley* (1891); Harold Wentworth and Stuart B. Flexner, *Dictionary of American Slang* (1960), with important discursive appendices.

On tall talk there is no general book. I have found Thornton's *Glossary* (above) indispensable. The best general discussions of American humor are several scholarly and readable books by Walter Blair: *Horse Sense in American Humor* (1942); *Native American Humor (1800–1900)* (1937; Chandler Paperback), a basic anthology with commentary; *Tall Tale America* (1944). Other useful items include Dorothy Dandore, "Big Talk! —The Flyting, the Gabe, and the Frontier Boast," *American Speech*, VI (Oct., 1930), 45–55; Bernard De Voto, *Mark Twain's America* (1932); Franklin J. Meine, ed., *Tall Tales of the Southwest* (1930); Constance M. Rourke, *American Humor: A Study of the National Character* (1931; Anchor Paperback), a cryptic and allusive study, considered by some the classic treatment of the subject: Jennette Tandy, *Crackerbox Philosophers in American Humor and Satire* (1925). See also the literature of folklore, discussed in the opening section of Bibliographical Notes to Book II, Part Seven, below.

The indispensable general book on place names is George R. Stewart's readable and scholarly *Names on the Land: A Historical Account of Place-Naming in the United States* (rev. ed., 1958), to which I am heavily indebted. Additional valuable facts and bibliography are scattered through Mencken's volumes (above), especially in *The American Language* (4th ed., 1937), pp. 525–44, in *Supp. II* (1956), pp. 525–75, and in the one-volume ed. by Raven I. McDavid, Jr., pp.

642–66; the notes to these volumes are an excellent guide to the periodical and other literature. *American Speech* (1925——) is rich in articles on special topics. The basic bibliographic tool is R. B. Sealock and P. A. Seely, *Bibliography of Place Name Literature: United States, Canada, Alaska, and Newfoundland* (1948). Especially suggestive is *Places: Studies in Geographical and Topographical Nomenclature* (1888), by Josiah Dwight Whitney (1819–96), a pioneer geologist and surveyor in California and other parts of the West. Relevant material is found in the most miscellaneous places, from travel books like Morris Birkbeck, *Notes on a Journey in America* (2d. ed., 1818) to Horatio Greenough, *Form and Function: Remarks on Art* (ed. Harold A. Small, 1947).

* * *

The best introduction to the development of a distinctive "Declamatory Literature" is through the history of institutions that helped bring this literature into being. These institutions, though not given their due in general histories of American civilization, have been ably chronicled. A good starting point is Carl Bode, *The American Lyceum, Town Meeting of the Mind* (1956), *The Anatomy of American Popular Culture, 1840–1861* (1959), and "The Sound of American Literature a Century Ago," *Journ. of Gen. Ed.* XV (April, 1963), 1–17; supplemented by William Charvat, *Literary Publishing in America, 1790–1850* (1959), "A Chronological List of Emerson's American Lecture Engagements," N.Y. Pub. Lib., *Bull.* LXIV (1960–61), 492–507, 551–59, 606–10, 657–63, and "Melville and the Common Reader," Bibl. Soc. U. of Va., *Papers*, XII (1959), 41–57; Alan Heimert, "Moby-Dick and American Political Symbolism," *Am. Q.*, XV (Win., 1963), 398–534; see also David Potter, *Debating in the Colonial Chartered Colleges: An Historical Survey, 1742 to 1800* (1944). Walter Harding,

"A Check List of Thoreau's Lectures," N.Y. Pub. Lib., *Bull.*, LII (Feb., 1948), 78–87. A useful illustrative selection is Joseph L. Blau, ed., *American Philosophic Addresses, 1700–1900* (1946). For a survey see William N. Brigance, ed., *A History and Criticism of American Public Address* (2 vols., 1943).

Collections of "great orations," which more often served as furniture than as reading material, are myriad. Valuable early collections are: Ebenezer B. Williston, comp., *Eloquence of the United States* (5 vols., 1827); James S. Loring, *The Hundred Boston Orators Appointed by the Municipal Authorities . . .* (1852), biographies and brief selections; Thomas Hart Benton's *Thirty Years' View: or, a History of the Working of the American Government . . . from 1820 to 1850 . . .* (2 vols., 1854–1856), which, in fifteen hundred double-column pages, chronicles the political history of the age largely through its forensics; and, on a larger scale, Benton's *Abridgement of the Debates of Congress from 1789 to 1856* (16 vols., 1857–61). For Edward Everett, see his *Orations and Speeches on Various Occasions* (4 vols., 1836; 1850–68) and Paul R. Frothingham, *Edward Everett, Orator and Statesman* (1925). See also: Thomas Wentworth Higginson, *American Orators and Oratory* (1901); William Matthews, *Orators and Oratory* (1883); Edward G. Parker, *The Golden Age of American Oratory* (1857). Of special interest is John Quincy Adams' *Lectures on Oratory and Rhetoric* (2 vols., 1810), which he delivered as the first Boylston Professor of Rhetoric and Oratory at Harvard, and which long remained the standard American work on the subject.

In schoolbooks, and especially in the most popular school readers, one can see the prominence of declamatory matter. The most accessible first-hand view is in the McGuffey Readers, for example *The Fifth Eclectic Reader* (1844; 1879 ed. reprinted, intro.

Henry Steele Commager, Signet Paperback, 1962), which are ably interpreted by Richard D. Mosier, *Making the American Mind: Social and Moral Ideas in the McGuffey Readers* (1947). See also: Harvey C. Minnich, *William Holmes McGuffey and his Readers* (1936); Henry H. Vail, *A History of the McGuffey Readers* (1911). More generally, see: Charles Carpenter, *History of American Schoolbooks* (1963); J. Merton England, "England and America in the Schoolbooks of the Republic, 1783–1861," *U. of Birmingham* [Eng.] *Hist. Journ.,* IX (1963), 92–111; James D. Hart, *The Popular Book: A History of America's Literary Taste* (1950); D. H. Lawrence, *Studies in Classic American Literature* (Anchor Paperback, 1953), an irritating and suggestive essay; Frank L. Mott, *Golden Multitudes: the Story of Best Sellers in the United States* (1947); A. S. W. Rosenbach, *Early American Children's Books* (1933); Constance M. Rourke, *Trumpets of Jubilee* (1927); Elmer E. Stoll, "The Downfall of Oratory: Our Undemocratic Arts," *Journ. Hist. Ideas,* VII (1946), 3–34.

The forensic aspect of American religious history is best approached through: *Lectures on Revivals of Religion* (ed. William G. McLoughlin, 1960), the practical handbook by Charles Grandison Finney (1792–1875), a master of the techniques of declamatory religion; or *The Autobiography* (1857; ed. Charles L. Wallis, 1956) of Peter Cartwright (1785–1872), one of the most successful backwoods practitioners. A readable and scholarly survey of the revivalists is Bernard A. Weisberger, *They Gathered at the River* (1958), and an excellent institutional study is Charles A. Johnson, *The Frontier Camp Meetings* (1955).

For guidance into the voluminous but fugitive writings of the horse-sense humorists, see: Walter Blair, *Native American Humor* (1800–1900)

(1937; Chandler Paperback) and *Horse Sense in American Humor* (1942). Of special interest for this section are: Seba Smith (pseud. Major Jack Downing), *Jack Downing's Letters* (1845) and *My Thirty Years out of the Senate* (1859); Charles Farrar Browne (pseud. Artemus Ward), *The Complete Works of Artemus Ward* (1862; rev. ed., 1898).

The literature on the platform techniques and writings of Abraham Lincoln and of Mark Twain is considerable, and can be found through the bibliographies of their writings, for example in Robert E. Spiller and others (eds.) *Literary History of the United States* (3 vols., 1948), Vol. III. From Daniel Drake, the Cincinnati-booster, we have a prophetic essay on the American literary destiny, *Discourse on the History, Character, and Prospects of the West* (1834; facsimile, 1955). The writings of Mrs. Caroline Matilda Kirkland (in Bibliographical Notes to Bk. I, Pt. 2, above) help us to understand the literary needs of people in upstart towns.

PART SEVEN

SEARCH FOR SYMBOLS

The United States had the advantage, of course, of inheriting Old World heroes; but those it made after its own fashion cannot readily be fitted into Old World categories. Therefore, a book like Dixon Wecter's readable *Hero in America* (1941; Ann Arbor Paperback), which tells us how the careers of Great Americans tend to fit into traditional Western European national types, leaves a great deal out of the story.

To assess the literature of American heroism and to discover its peculiarities, we must see how in America the compression of time and the extension of space transformed the whole problem. To consider this question, then, we are forced to become cosmopolites, transcending modern

European culture and its stereotypes. I have found especially suggestive: H. Munro Chadwick and N. Kershaw Chadwick, *The Growth of Literature* (3 vols., 1932–40) esp. on "The Heroic Age" (see also their *Heroic Age*, 1912), a search for the common characteristics of all literature; Lord Raglan's brilliant and perverse *The Hero: A Study in Tradition, Myth, and Drama* (1936; Vintage Paperback); Joseph Campbell, *The Hero with a Thousand Faces* (1949; Meridian Paperback).

The "comic" is of course no less elusive nor less culturally conditioned than the heroic; some of these peculiar problems of cultural provincialism are revealed unwittingly in George Meredith's *Idea of Comedy and the Uses of the Comic Spirit* (1877; 1897) and in Henri Bergson's *Laughter* (1900) which are now conveniently available in a single volume (ed. Wylie Sypher, *Comedy*, Anchor Paperback, 1956). Therefore the description and interpretation of American idols of the subliterature, who somehow combined what superficially looks like the heroic and the comic, is doubly difficult. A conscientious effort to find Americans to fit Thomas Carlyle's solemn prescriptions for hero-worship will not help us much.

An admirable guide to the history of American folklore and its vast uneven literature is Richard M. Dorson, *American Folklore* (1959; Phoenix Paperback), with an accompanying bibliography. The subject is extremely miscellaneous and plagued by addicts of the quaint and the cute; much that has been published on the subject is "fakelore" (to borrow Dorson's phrase) about folklore, expressing an adult's notion of what ought to appeal to children. But there are also many scholarly and valuable volumes. Defining the subject is not as simple as it might seem. An initial question, which sophisticated scholars will not evade, is whether a useful purpose is served by restricting "folklore" to "the spoken or sung tradition." Richard M. Dorson, for example, urges this distinction as a way of helping the scholar sift from the contrived and the self-consciously literary what is authentically oral and traditional; at the same time he urges the distinctiveness of the role of American folklore. Walter Blair, on the other hand, is less "purist" by professional folklorists' standards; he is wary of any distinction that might exclude the non-oral as an authentic source of folk tradition. These and other subtle students of the subject, like students of the history of the spoken language, are on the most difficult of historical quests: the search for the ways of feeling, thought, and expression of the inarticulate people. In a sense, all surviving evidence is only circumstantial. To explore some of these problems, see Richard M. Dorson, "A Theory for American Folklore," with accompanying comments by folklorists, anthropologists, and others, *Journal of American Folklore*, LXXII (July, 1959), 197–242.

For Crockett, the best starting point is his own "autobiography" which appeared in many different forms, and from many different authors (1833——). Since very likely none of these was from Crockett's own hand, they must be treated as variations on a theme rather than as deviations from an authentic text. A usable reprint of one of them is available in a Signet Paperback (1955). The principal contemporary writings ostensibly by Crockett are itemized in the text above. The Crockett almanacs, despite their great significance, have not been widely reprinted, but individual items are found in anthologies. Extensive selections, together with reproductions of the original crude illustrations, which are essential to their flavor, are found in: Richard M. Dorson, ed., *Davy Crockett, American Comic Legend* (1939), with almanac references given in "The Sources of *Davy Crockett, American Comic Legend*,"

Midwest Folklore, VIII (1958), 143–49; Franklin J. Meine, ed., *The Crockett Almanacs, Nashville Series, 1835–1838* (1955). For one popular dramatization of Crockett, see James Kirke Paulding, *The Lion of the West* (ed. James N. Tidwell, 1954). I have found especially useful Richard M. Dorson's important though brief article, "Davy Crockett and the Heroic Age," *Southern Folklore Quarterly*, VI (June, 1942), 95–102. A scholarly and detailed biography of the real Crockett is James A. Shackford, *David Crockett: the Man and the Legend* (1956), which aims to defend his character against the misrepresentations of the subliterature. Mike Fink is best discovered in: Walter Blair and Franklin J. Meine, eds., *Mike Fink, King of Mississippi Keelboatmen* (1933), with bibliography, a composite narrative drawn from the literature, and *Half Horse Half Alligator: The Growth of the Mike Fink Legend* (1956). Two important and easily accessible contemporary collections are: A. B. Longstreet *Georgia Scenes* (1835; Sagamore Paperback), and Joseph G. Baldwin, *The Flush Times of Alabama and Mississippi* (1853; Sagamore Paperback).

The "Big Bear" School of American humor is too little known. Every student of American culture should read the unforgettable story which gave the school its name: "The Big Bear of Arkansas," by T. B. Thorpe (1815–78), which first appeared in Porter's *Spirit of the Times* in 1841, and is reprinted by Blair, *Native American Humor*, pp. 337–48. Epochal collections by William T. Porter, ed., are: *The Big Bear of Arkansas, and Other Sketches* (Phila., 1843) and *A Quarter Race in Kentucky, and Other Sketches, Illustrative of Scenes, Characters, and Incidents, throughout 'The Universal Yankee Nation'* (Phila., 1854). The essential book on Porter is Norris W. Yates, *William T. Porter and the Spirit of the Times* (1957).

On almanacs and the almanac tradition, see: George Lyman Kittredge,

The Old Farmer and his Almanack (1904), for predecessors of the Crockett almanacs; Clarence S. Brigham, "An Account of American Almanacs and Their Value for Historical Study," Am. Antiq. Soc., *Proc.*, n.s., XXXV (1924), 1–25, 194–209; Chester N. Greenough, "New England Almanacs, 1766–1775, and the American Revolution," Am. Antiq. Soc., *Proc.*, n.s., XLV (1935), 288–316; Hugh A. Morrison, *Preliminary Check List of American Almanacs, 1639–1800* (1907); Douglas C. McMurtrie, "A Check-List of Kentucky Almanacs, 1789–1830," Ky. State Hist. Soc., *Register* (July, 1932), pp. 237–59. And for the chapbooks, the pamphlet miscellanies which were first cousins to the almanacs, see Harry B. Weiss, *American Chapbooks, 1722–1842* (1945).

Other items, especially relevant to Book II, Part Seven, are: Mody C. Boatright, *Folk Laughter on the American Frontier* (1949); V. L. O. Chittick, "Ring-Tailed Roarers," *The Frontier*, XIII (May, 1933), 257–63, 340–41 and *Ring-Tailed Roarers* (1941); Thomas D. Clark, *The Rampaging Frontier* (1939), using tales of the Old Southwest to illustrate social history; Samuel L. Clemens, *Mark Twain's Speeches* (1910); Merle Curti, "Dime Novels and the American Tradition," *Yale Rev.*, XXVI (June, 1937), 761–78; Richard M. Dorson, *America Rebels: Narratives of the Patriots* (1953), *Buying the Wind: Regional Folklore in the United States* (1963), "The Identification of Folklore in American Literature," and "Standards for Collecting and Publishing American Folktales," *Journ. Am. Folklore*, LXX (Jan.–March, 1957), 1–8, 53–57, "Folklore and Cultural History," in *Research Opportunities in American Cultural History* (1961), 102–23, "The Yankee on the Stage—a Folk Hero of American Drama," *N.E.Q.*, XIII (1940), 467–93, "Mose the Far-Famed and World-Renowned," *Am. Lit.*, XV (Nov., 1943), 288–300; Max

Eastman, *The Sense of Humor* (1922); Clifton J. Furness, *Walt Whitman's Workshop* (1928); George Washington Harris (pseud. Sut Lovingood), *The Lovingood Papers* (ed. Ben H. McClary, 2 vols., to date, 1962——); D. H. Lawrence, *Studies in Classic American Literature* (Anchor Paperback, 1953); Dorothy Lee, "Freedom, Spontaneity and Limit in American Linguistic Usage," *Explorations*, IV (Feb., 1955), 6–14; James G. Leyburn, *Frontier Folkways* (1935), a comparison of "frontiers" in different parts of the world; Kenneth S. Lynn, *Mark Twain and Southwestern Humor* (1960); James C. Malin, *John Brown and the Legend of Fifty-Six* (1942); Franklin J. Meine, ed., *Tall Tales of the Southwest* (1930); Arthur K. Moore, *The Frontier Mind: A Cultural Analysis of the Kentucky Frontiersman*, a vigorous and original study, which breaks many stereotypes; Edmund Pearson, *Queer Books* (1929), Ch. I, "Making the Eagle Scream"; Constance Rourke, *American Humor* (1931; Anchor Paperback); John Walton, *John Filson of Kentucke* (1956), which should be studied, along with Filson's own *Discovery, Settlement and Present State of Kentucke* (1784), for clues to why Daniel Boone never acquired Crockett's comic features.

* * *

The iconography of George Washington has gone through at least three overlapping stages. First, the mythologizing or idealizing stage, expressed popularly by Parson Mason Locke Weems's *Washington* (1800 and later eds.; ed. Marcus Cunliffe, 1962) and learnedly by John Marshall's *Washington* (5 vols., 1804–7) and Jared Sparks's *Life* (1837) and *Writings* (12 vols., 1834–37). Second, the debunking stage, expressed by William E. Woodward's *George Washington—the Image and the Man* (1926) and Rupert Hughes's *George Washington* (3 vols., 1926–30). And finally, the historical stage, marked by John C. Fitzpatrick's editions of Washington's

Diaries (4 vols., 1925) and his *Writings* (39 vols., 1931–44) and by Douglas Southall Freeman's *George Washington* (6 vols., 1948–54; 7th vol. by John A. Carroll and Mary W. Ashworth, 1957). The best brief summary of the present state of our knowledge of Washington is Marcus Cunliffe's lively *George Washington: Man and Monument* (1958). The Washington literature is enormous; much is of little use to any but the student of iconolatry. Some notion of its extent and variety can be secured from: W. S. Baker, *Bibliotheca Washingtoniana: A Descriptive List of the Biographies and Biographical Sketches of George Washington* (1889) and from the bibliographies in Freeman's *Washington*.

The literary history of the Washington legend can be surveyed in William A. Bryan's *George Washington in American Literature, 1775–1865* (1952). The best introduction to Weems's work is Marcus Cunliffe's introduction to Weems's *Washington* (John Harvard Library, 1962). Weems (1759–1825) is an enticing subject, still to be exploited as a touchstone for the history of publishing, politics, religion, and salesmanship. Among useful items are: William A. Bryan, "The Genesis of Weems' 'Life of Washington,'" *Americana*, XXXVI (April, 1942), 147–65, with the detailed and amusing story of Weems's relation to his publishers; Wesley Frank Craven, *The Legend of the Founding Fathers* (1956); Evert A. and George L. Duyckinck, *Cyclopaedia of American Literature* (2 vols., 1856); Edward Everett, *Orations and Speeches on Various Occasions* (4 vols., 1868), containing his often-delivered "The Character of Washington," at IV, 3–51; Bernard Faÿ, *The Two Franklins* (1933), for the slanders by Benjamin Bache and others during Washington's last years; Sidney Fisher, "The Legendary and Myth-Making Process in Histories of the American Revolution," *Am. Philos. Soc., Proc.*, LI

(April, 1912) 53–75, a brilliant essay by one of the most neglected American historians of this century; Paul L. Ford and Emily E. Skeel, *Mason Locke Weems, His Works and Ways* (3 vols., 1928–29), with bibliographies; Thomas W. Gilmer, "An Address Delivered before the Virginia Historical and Philosophical Society," *Southern Literary Messenger*, III (Feb., 1837), 97–102; James D. Hart, *The Popular Book: A History of America's Popular Taste* (1950); Harold Kellock, *Parson Weems of the Cherry Tree* (1928), a popular account; Frank L. Mott, *Golden Multitudes: The Story of Best Sellers in the United States* (1947); Bernard Mayo, *Myths and Men* (1959); Theodore Parker, *Historic Americans* (ed. Samuel A. Eliot, 1908); David D. Van Tassel, "The Legend Maker," *American Heritage*, Feb., 1962, pp. 58–59, 89–94; Dixon Wecter, *The Hero in America* (1941; Ann Arbor Paperback).

The indispensable work on Jared Sparks is Herbert Baxter Adams, *The Life and Writings of Jared Sparks* (2 vols., 1893), which is especially interesting because Adams (1850–1901), a founder of the American Historical Association (1884), was himself a leading American exponent of the German "scientific" method in history. At Johns Hopkins University, he introduced the seminar technique for training professional historians, and must bear much of the responsibility for the definition of the American Ph.D. Though a champion of the most "rigorous" techniques of historical criticism in his own day (and a teacher of Woodrow Wilson, Frederick J. Turner, and others nearly as eminent), Adams was surprisingly sympathetic to Sparks's vagaries. For some different expert views of Sparks, see John S. Bassett, *The Middle Group of American Historians* (1917) and J. Franklin Jameson, *The History of Historical Writing in America* (1891; 1961). Sparks's quarrel with Lord Mahon can be followed in: John Gorham Palfrey, "Lord Mahon's *History of England*," *North American Review*, LXXV (July, 1852), 125–208; Jared Sparks, *Letter to Lord Mahon, being an Answer to His Letter Addressed to the Editor of Washington's Writings* (Boston, 1852), and *A Reply to the Strictures of Lord Mahon and Others, on the Mode of Editing the Writings of Washington* (Cambridge, Eng.; 1852); William B. Reed, *Reprint of the Original Letters from Washington to Joseph Reed, during the American Revolution* (1852), correcting certain items in his controversial earlier *Life and Correspondence of Joseph Reed* (2 vols., 1847), which had been one of the prime causes of the trouble.

The standard works on artists' images of Washington are: Gustavus A. Eisen, *Portraits of Washington* (3 vols., 1932), indispensable for the Gilbert Stuarts; and Frances D. Whittemore, *George Washington in Sculpture* (1933). For the history of Washington's birthday, see: Charles Warren, "How Politics Intruded into the Washington Centenary of 1832," *Mass. Hist. Soc., Proc.*, LXV (Dec., 1932) 37–62, especially valuable; Albert Mathews, "Celebrations of Washington's Birthday," Col. Soc. of Mass., *Pub.*, X (Feb., 1906), 252–58; Robert H. Schauffler, ed., *Washington's Birthday* (in *Our American Holidays* series, 1925), a popular account. For Washington as a place name, and in relation to the Capital, see: George R. Stewart, *Names on the Land* (rev. ed., 1958), *passim*, and the map found at pp. 256–57, "States and Counties named for Washington"; and Constance McL. Green, *Washington, Village and Capital, 1800–1878* (1962).

The best scholarly life of Patrick Henry is Robert D. Meade, *Patrick Henry: Patriot in the Making* (1957); see also W. W. Henry, *Patrick Henry: Life, Correspondence and Speeches* (3 vols., 1891). William Wirt's

Sketches of the Life and Character of Patrick Henry (1817) immortalized its hero without itself becoming immortal. A significant contemporary review was "Mr. Wirt's Life of Patrick Henry," *North Am. Rev.*, VI (March, 1818), 293–324. A valuable survey of the period is John P. Kennedy, *Memoirs of the Life of William Wirt* (2 vols., 1849; rev. ed., 1850). See also: William R. Taylor, "William Wirt and the Legend of the Old South," *Wm. & M. Q.*, 3d ser., XIV (Oct., 1957), 473–93, and *Cavalier and Yankee* (1961), esp. Ch. II. Since James Otis tried to destroy all his papers before his death, and since he seems to have corresponded very little anyway, the biographical materials are scanty; but see John Adams' "Diary" and his letters to Tudor about Otis, in Adams' *Works* (ed. Charles F. Adams, 10 vols., 1850–56), Vols. II (1850) and X (1856), and Governor Thomas Hutchinson's comments in his *History of the Colony and Province of Massachusetts Bay* (3 vols., 1828; ed. Lawrence Shaw, 1936), Vol. III; see also Francis Bowen, "Life of James Otis," in *Library of American Biography* (ed. Jared Sparks, 2d ser., Vol. II, 1846).

For biography generally see: Edward H. O'Neill, *A History of American Biography, 1800–1935* (1935); Marshall W. Fishwick, *A Bibliography of the American Hero* (1950). An interesting contemporary view is found in "Biography," *North Am. Rev.*, LXXXIV (April, 1857), 406–25. For a hint of the extent and subtlety of the problem of chronicling our hero-worship see, for example: Paul L. Ford, *Franklin Bibliography* (1889); Merrill D. Peterson, *The Jefferson Image in the American Mind* (1960; Galaxy Paperback), and accompanying bibliography.

On the relation of local history to the growth of a national historiography, the indispensable book is David D. Van Tassel, *Recording America's Past: An Interpretation of the Development of Historical Studies in America, 1607–1884* (1960), with a valuable appendix and selective bibliography. Walter Muir Whitehill's *Independent Historical Societies* (1962) is a delightful book, not only a sprightly guide to what might seem an unpromising subject, but an avenue into many colorful and unexpectedly interesting bypaths of social and intellectual history. See also: Herman E. Ludewig, *The Literature of American Local History: A Bibliographical Essay* (1846); Julian P. Boyd, "State and Local Historical Societies in the United States," *AHR*, XL (Oct., 1934), 10–37; Stephen T. Riley, *The Massachusetts Historical Society, 1791–1959* (1959). More general works touching this period are: J. Franklin Jameson, *The History of Historical Writing in America* (1891; 1961) and John S. Bassett *The Middle Group of American Historians* (1917). Recent standard monographs include Michael Kraus, *A History of American History* (1937) and *The Writing of American History* (1953), and Harvey Wish, *The American Historian* (1960). James C. Malin offers some stimulating suggestions by his treatment of two examples in *John Brown and the Legend of Fifty-Six* (1942) and "Notes on the Writing of General Histories of Kansas," *Kans. Hist. Q.*, XXI (1955), 331–78, 407–44.

The best starting point for the historiography of the American Revolution is Wesley Frank Craven, *The Legend of the Founding Fathers* (1956), which throws much light on political history, on holidays, and on many other subjects. See also Sidney Fisher, "The Legendary and Myth-Making Process in Histories of the American Revolution," Am. Philos. Soc., *Proc.*, LI (April, 1912), 53–75.

George Bancroft is today probably the most unread of the great American "literary" historians of the 19th century. The best introduction to him is his own works, not only his *History of the United States* (1834–1882; "The Author's Last Revision," 6 vols., 1883–1885), but his *Literary and Historical Miscellanies* (1855). A valuable monograph is Russel B. Nye, *George Bancroft, Brahmin Rebel* (1944). The main source of information about him is M. A. DeWolfe Howe, ed., *The Life and Letters of George Bancroft* (2 vols., 1908). Bancroft needs a more extensive biography. See also David Levin's suggestive comparative study, *History as Romantic Art: Bancroft, Prescott, Motley, and Parkman* (1959). A stimulating discussion of Bancroft, Hildreth, and their relation to contemporary politics is found in Arthur M. Schlesinger, Jr., *The Age of Jackson* (1945: Little, Brown Paperback). See also the relevant chapters in Jameson and in Bassett (above).

On the flag, the essential book is Milo M. Quaife, Melvin J. Weig, and Roy E. Appleman, *The History of the United States Flag* (1961). And on the anthem, see: Oscar Sonneck, *Report on "The Star-Spangled Banner," "Hail Columbia," "America," "Yankee Doodle"* (1909), and *"The Star-Spangled Banner"* (1914); John A. Kouwenhoven and Lawton M. Patten, "New Light on 'The Star-Spangled Banner,'" *Musical Quarterly*, XXIII (April, 1937), 198–200. For some suggestive comparisons, see Donald R. Wakeling, "National Anthems," in *Grove's Dictionary of Music and Musicians* (5th ed., ed. Eric Blom, 10 vols., 1954), VI, 14–29, and Martin Shaw and Henry Coleman (eds.), *National Anthems of the World* (1960).

There is no satisfactory general history of American holidays. A model of the scholarly monograph that would be valuable on other holidays is William De Loss Love, *The Fast and Thanskgiving Days of New England* (1895). The story of the Fourth of July must be pieced together from miscellaneous sources. A helpful general guide is Wesley Frank Craven's *Legend of the Founding Fathers* (1956). Also helpful are histories of American patriotism and national sentiment, for example: Merle Curti, *The Roots of American Loyalty* (1946); Wallace Evan Davies, *Patriotism on Parade: The Story of Veterans' and Hereditary Organizations in America, 1783–1900* (1955); Ralph H. Gabriel, *The Course of American Democratic Thought* (2d ed., 1956); Paul C. Nagel, *One Nation Indivisible: the Union in American Thought 1776–1861* (1964); Edwin C. Rozwenc, *Ideology and Power in the Age of Jackson* (1964); Benjamin T. Spencer, *The Quest for Nationality: An American Literary Campaign* (1957). I have found especially useful: Charles Warren, "Fourth of July Myths," *Wm. & M. Q.*, 3d ser., II (July, 1945), 237–72, and Lyman H. Butterfield, "The Jubilee of Independence: July 4, 1826," *Va. Mag. of Hist. & Biog.*, LXI (April, 1953), 119–40.

On the complicated question of the precise purpose of the Declaration of Independence and the date of the signings, see: Mellen Chamberlain, *John Adams, the Statesman of the American Revolution, with other Essays* (1898), esp., "The Authentication of the Declaration of Independence," and the article by Charles Warren (above). Because of the destruction of evidence, the question of the "authenticity" of the Mecklenburg Declaration of Independence is not likely to become any more settled than it now is. For a sampling of the literature on this heated subject see: William H. Hoyt, *The Mecklenburg Declaration of Independence* (1907), an attack, and long considered the standard monograph; Archibald Henderson, *Cradle of Liberty* (Charlotte, N.C.; 1955) and V. V. McNitt, *Chain of Error and the Mecklenburg Declaration of Independence* (Palmer, Mass., 1960), ingenious and nearly convincing defenses. And see the review of McNitt by Henry S. Stroupe in *No.*

Car. Hist. Rev., XXXIX (1962), 93–94. Especially relevant are the letters from John Adams, to Hezekiah Niles (Feb., 13, 1818) at X, 282–89, to Jefferson (June 22, 1819) X, 380 f., and the letter from Thomas McKean to Adams (Jan., 1814), X, 87–89, all in Adams' *Works* (10 vols., ed. C. F. Adams, 1850–56).

Some other items especially useful for sidelights on the holiday, its observances, its myths, and its mythmakers, are: Charles Farrar Browne (pseud., Artemus Ward), "Fourth of July Oration," at *Complete Works of Artemus Ward* (1862; rev. ed., 1898), pp. 176 ff.; Alexander Davidson, "How Benson J. Lossing wrote his 'Field Books'. . . ," Bibl. Soc. Am., *Papers*, XXXII (1938), 57–64; Henry J. Ford, "The Liberty Bell," *American Mercury*, III (Nov., 1924), 279–84; "Holidays," *North American Review*, LXXXIV (April, 1857), 334–63; James S. Loring, *The Hundred Boston Orators* (1852); Albert Mathews, "Brother Jonathan," Col. Soc. of Mass., *Pub.*, VII (Jan., 1901), 94–125, "Uncle Sam," Am. Antiq. Soc., *Proc.*, n.s., XIX (April, 1908), 21–65 and "Centennial Celebrations," Col. Soc. of Mass., *Pub.*, XXVI (April, 1926), 402–26; James K. Paulding, *The Bulls and the Jonathans* (ed. William I. Paulding, 1867); Alice W. Spieseke, *The First Textbooks in American History and their Compiler John M'Culloch* (1938); David D. Van Tassel, "Benson J. Lossing: Pen and Pencil Historian," *Am. Q.*, VI (Spr., 1954), 32–44; Charles Warren, *Odd Byways in American History* (1942), for the celebration of July 4, 1800, and the false rumors of Jefferson's death; William Wirt, "A Discourse on the Lives and Characters of Thomas Jefferson and John Adams," in E. B. Williston, comp., *Eloquence of the United States* (5 vols., 1827), at V, 454–503.

PART EIGHT

A SPACIOUS REPUBLIC

One of the most significant facts about American political thinking in the mid-20th century is the decline of a broad scholarly interest in American constitutional history. Law schools, though they have cooperated in preparing a full-scale history of the Supreme Court (under the able editorship of Professor Paul Freund, and partly financed from the estate of Justice Oliver Wendell Holmes, Jr.), still pursue constitutional law mainly for its professional uses; historians have increasingly focused their constitutional interests on the economic conditions affecting the making, adoption, and growth of the Federal Constitution or on the history of public opinion about the Federal Constitution; political scientists have devoted themselves more and more to recent and contemporary constitutional issues.

Is it not odd that in an age when we have allowed many crucial public issues to turn on constitutional interpretation, we have been content to provide so little historical depth for our understanding? One explanation is the practical bias of our law schools, which still claim a virtual monopoly of competence on legal subjects. Another possibility is that—despite widespread reverence for the Federal Constitution—there has been a growing popular and scholarly suspicion that constitutional law itself is somehow less real than other forms of law. This attitude seems to date from the early 1930's, when constitutional law, more than at any earlier time since the Civil War, became entangled in everyday politics. The then retrograde view of many members of the Supreme Court, and the cynical or purely instrumental attitude toward law on the part of many government lawyers, inspired a general exasperation with the subject among sensible people. Students and scholars turned to political, social, economic, or intellectual history as subjects with more continuity and substance.

The best introduction remains Andrew C. McLaughlin, *A Constitutional History of the United States* (1935), which gains stature with the years. A good up-to-date textbook is Alfred H. Kelley and Winfred A. Harbison, *The American Constitution* (3d ed., 1963). The literature on the causes and consequences of the American Revolution, on the framing of the Constitution, and on the growth of an American system of government is vast. The following list, therefore, must be even more selective and less comprehensive than for the earlier Parts. (See also the Bibliographical Notes to *The Americans: The Colonial Experience,* Part Thirteen.)

For the imperial background of the American Revolution, a good starting point is Oliver M. Dickerson, *American Colonial Government, 1696–1765: A Study of the British Board of Trade in its Relation to the American Colonies* . . . (1912; 1962). Some other items I have found especially useful on the history of the administrative and theoretical decline of "Sovereignty" in the era of the American Revolution are: Charles M. Andrews, *The Colonial Background of the American Revolution* (1931); George L. Beer, *British Colonial Policy, 1754–1765* (1907) and *The Old Colonial System, 1660–1754* (1933); A. V. Dicey, *Introduction to the Study of the Law of the Constitution* (8th ed., 1915), a classic study of British constitutionalism; Oliver M. Dickerson, *The Navigation Acts and the American Revolution* (1951); Otto Von Gierke, *Natural Law and the Theory of Society* (trans. and intro. Ernest Barker; 2 vols., 1930); James K. Hosmer, *The Life of Thomas Hutchinson* (1896); Sydney George Fisher, *The Struggle for American Independence* (2 vols., 1908); Leonard W. Labaree,

Royal Government in America (1933), and *Royal Instructions to British Colonial Governors* (2 vols., 1935); J. G. A. Pocock, *The Ancient Constitution and the Feudal Law* (1957); Carl Van Doren, *Benjamin Franklin* (1938); Claude H. Van Tyne, "Sovereignty in the American Revolution, an Historical Study," *AHR,* XII (April, 1907), 529–45.

Contemporary items of special relevance include: Sir William Blackstone, *Commentaries on the Laws of England* (4 vols., 1765–69); David Hume, *Essays Moral, Political, and Literary* (2 vols., 1741–42; 1882); Thomas Hutchinson, *History of the Colony of Massachusetts Bay, from its First Settlement in the year 1628 to the year 1750* (2 vols., 1764; 3d vol., 1828; ed. Lawrence S. Mayo, 3 vols., 1936); Samuel Johnson, *Taxation No Tyranny: An Answer to the Resolutions and Address of the American Congress* (1775); Hugh Jones, *The Present State of Virginia* (1724; ed. Richard L. Morton, 1956). The first convincing technical argument justifying the American Revolution by the subtleties of British constitutional law of the Revolutionary age appeared 150 years after the event: Charles H. McIlwain's tightly reasoned *American Revolution: A Constitutional Interpretation* (1923); but even he carried his point only by the aid of far-fetched analogies to the Channel Islands and Ireland.

For new light on the relation of British domestic politics to imperial problems, see Sir Lewis Namier, *The Structure of Politics at the Accession of George III* (1929; Macmillan Paperback); *England in the Age of the American Revolution* (1930; Macmillan Paperback) *Charles Townshend* . . . (1959); and (with John Brooke) *The House of Commons 1754–1790* (3 vols., 1964). And see Professor Herbert Butterfield's *George III, Lord North, and the People* (1949) and his suggestive critiques: *The Whig Interpretation of History*

(1931), and *George III and the Historians (1957)*.

On the emergence of American federalism before, during, and immediately after the Revolution, a good starting point is Randolph G. Adams, *Political Ideas of the American Revolution* (3d ed., 1958). Especially valuable is Andrew C. McLaughlin, "The Background of American Federalism," *Am. Pol. Sci. Rev.*, XII (1918), 215–40. Relevant also are: John R. Alden, *The American Revolution, 1775–83* (1954); Carl Becker, *The Declaration of Independence* (1933; Vintage Paperback) and *The Eve of the Revolution* (1918); Daniel J. Boorstin, *The Genius of American Politics* (1953; Phoenix Paperback); Julian P. Boyd, *Anglo-American Union: Joseph Galloway's Plans to preserve the British Empire, 1774–1781* (1941); and Edmund C. Burnett, *The Continental Congress* (1941) and, ed., *Letters of Members of the Continental Congress* (8 vols., 1921–36); Philip G. Davidson, *Propaganda and the American Revolution, 1763–1783* (1941); Sydney George Fisher, *The Struggle for American Independence* (2 vols., 1908); J. Franklin Jameson, *The American Revolution Considered as a Social Movement* (1940; Beacon Paperback), and Frederick B. Tolles, "The American Revolution Considered as a Social Movement: A Re-evaluation," *AHR*, LX (1954), 1–12; Merrill Jensen, *The Articles of Confederation* (1940) and *The New Nation: A History of the United States During the Confederation, 1781–1789* (1950); Bernhard Knollenberg, *Origin of the American Revolution: 1759–1766* (1960); Leonard W. Labaree, *Conservatism in Early American History* (1948); Andrew C. McLaughlin, *The Confederation and the Constitution* (1905); John C. Miller, *Origins of the American Revolution* (1943); Lynn Montross, *The Reluctant Rebels: The Story of the Continental Congress, 1774–1789* (1950); Edmund S. Morgan,

The Birth of the Republic, 1763–1789 (1956; Phoenix Paperback), the best brief narrative, and (with Helen M. Morgan), *The Stamp Act Crisis* (1953); Curtis P. Nettels, *George Washington and American Independence* (1951); Eric Robson, *The American Revolution in its Political and Military Aspects* (1955); Clinton Rossiter, *Seedtime of the Republic* (1953); Arthur M. Schlesinger, *The Colonial Merchants and the American Revolution* (1918; 1957) and *Prelude to Independence; the Newspaper War on Britain, 1764–1776* (1958); James Allen Smith, *The Growth and Decadence of Constitutional Government* (1930), and *The Spirit of American Government* (1907); George Otto Trevelyan, *The American Revolution* (new ed., 4 vols., 1926–29; one vol. abridgment by Richard B. Morris, 1964); Moses Coit Tyler, *The Literary History of the American Revolution, 1763–1783* (2 vols., 1957); Carl Van Doren, *The Great Rehearsal* (1948); U. S.. Lib. Cong., Leg. Ref. Service, *Documents Illustrative of the Formation of the Union* (1927).

The history of the secessionist tradition would make an interesting volume. The following suggest the sort of material that might be included: James Truslow Adams, *America's Tragedy* (1934); Henry Adams, ed., *Documents Relating to New-England Federalism* (1877); Thomas P. Abernethy, *The Burr Conspiracy* (1954); Leonard J. Arrington, *Great Basin Kingdom: an Economic History of the Latter-Day Saints, 1830–1900* (1958); Arthur E. Bestor, *Backwoods Utopias . . . 1663–1829* (1950); Lewis B. Bramkamp, "Secession in New England, 1803–1809," unpublished M. A. thesis (Dept. of History, U. of Chicago, 1930); Avery O. Craven, *The Coming of the Civil War* (2nd ed., 1957); Norman F. Furniss, *The Mormon Conflict, 1850–1859* (1960); Lois K. Mathews, "The Mayflower Compact and its Descendants," *MVHA, Proc.*, VI (1912–13), 79–106, on the formation of *ad hoc* organizations (in the Mayflower Compact tradition) by withdrawing communities; Perry Miller, *Orthodoxy in Massachusetts* (1933); Edmund S. Morgan, *Visible Saints* (1963); Paul C. Nagel, *One Nation Indivisible: The Union in American Thought, 1776–1861* (1964); Alice F. Tyler, *Freedom's Ferment* (1944); Laura A. White, *Robert Barnwell Rhett: Father of Secession* (1931); Samuel C. Williams, *History of the Lost State of Franklin* (1924).

* * *

Despite the federal character of our government, "constitutionalism" in the United States nowadays is popularly identified almost exclusively with the Federal Constitution. Few students or scholars have read the constitution of their state; and the history of state constitutions is relegated to antiquarians or local historians. Yet these state constitutions preceded the Federal Constitution and they are no less distinctive of our government. We badly need a general interpretative history of the state constitutions. The numerousness of our state constitutions and the meagerness of interpretive scholarship about them tempts us to approach "constitutionalism" through miasmic generalities, instead of by way of those specifics that have given our American constitutions vitality.

Perhaps the best starting point, which avoids this mistake, is Breckenridge Long, *Genesis of the Constitution of the United States of America* (1926), especially its appendix, which annotates the provisions of the Federal Constitution with the precedents in state or colonial constitutions or charters, and so reveals the derivative character of the Federal Constitution. Two admirable monographs, which open up the subject, are: Fletcher M. Green, *Constitutional Development in the South Atlantic States, 1776–1860* (1930); Elisha P. Douglass, *Rebels and Democrats: The Struggle for Equal Political Rights and Majority Rule during the American Revolution* (1955). The definitive work on state constitution-making, which every student should peruse, is *The Constitutional Convention: Its History, Powers, and Modes of Proceeding* (1867) by John Alexander Jameson (1824–90), a Vermont-born lawyer who came to Chicago in 1853. Jameson was impelled to produce this work, as he explains in his Preface, because, "In 1862, certain influential members of the Illinois Constitutional Convention, then in session, set up for that body, in debate, a claim of inherent powers amounting almost to absolute sovereignty." They claimed, for example, that they did not have to submit their work to the people; and there were rumors that "a secret organization supposed to be disloyal to the Union, called the 'Knights of the Golden Circle,'" aimed at control. See also his "Fourth Edition" (1887) under the title, *A Treatise on Constitutional Conventions,* which reveals how American federalism continued to dissolve Old World dogmas of "sovereignty."

Useful collections of documents include: Benjamin P. Poore, ed., *The Federal and State Constitutions, Colonial Charters, and Other Organic Laws of the United States* (2 vols., 1877); Francis N. Thorpe, comp., *The Federal and State Constitutions, Colonial Charters, and Other Organic Laws of the States, Territories, and Colonies Now or Heretofore Forming the United States of America* (7 vols., 1909); Charles Kettleborough, ed., *The State Constitutions and the Federal Constitution and Organic Laws of the Territories and Other Colonial Dependencies of the United States of America* (1918). On the Massachusetts Constitution of 1780, see: Robert E. Brown, *Middle-Class Democracy and the Revolution in Massachusetts, 1791–1780* (1955); Elisha P. Douglass, *Rebels and Democrats* (1955), esp. Chs. IX–XI; Samuel Eliot Morison, "The Vote of Massachusetts on Summoning a Constitutional Convention, 1776–1916," Mass. Hist. Soc., *Proc.*, L (April, 1917), 241–49 and "The Struggle over the Adoption of the Constitution of Massachusetts, 1780," *ibid.*, L (May, 1917), 353–411.

On the state constitutions see: William C. Bruce, *John Randolph of Roanoke* (2 vols., 1922); Richard Buel, "Democracy and the American Revolution: A Frame of Reference," *Wm. & M. Q.*, 3d ser., XXI (April, 1964), 165–90, an original and stimulating article; Frank L. Esterquest, "State Adjustments to the Federal Constitution," unpublished Ph.D. dissertation (Dept. of History, U. of Chicago, 1940); Roger S. Hoar, *Constitutional Conventions* (1917); J. Franklin Jameson, "Early Political Uses of the Word Convention," Am. Antiq. Soc., *Proc.*, n.s., XII (Oct., 1897), 183–96; Andrew C. McLaughlin, *The Background of American Federalism* (1918) and *The Foundations of American Constitutionalism* (1961); John M. Matzen, *State Constitutional Provisions for Education* (1931); Conrad H. Moehlman, comp., *The American Constitutions and Religion* (1938); Allan Nevins, *The American States During and After the Revolution, 1775–89* (1924); Robert A. Rutland, *The Birth of the Bill of Rights* (1955); Carl B. Swisher, *Motivation and Political Technique in the California Constitutional Convention, 1878–79* (1930). For John Adams' part, see: Page Smith, *John Adams* (2 vols., 1962); Correa Moylan Walsh, *The Political Science of John Adams* (1915). There is need for an up-to-date history of state constitution-making with a collected comparative edition of the state constitutions.

A cosmopolitan introduction to some of the distinctive features of the Federal Constitution and American constitutionalism is Robert R. Palmer, *The Age of the Democratic Revolution: a Political History of Europe and America, 1760–1800*, Vol. I., *The Challenge* (1959), esp. pp. 44–55 and Chs. VI–IX, and appendices III–V;

see also his Vol. II, *The Struggle* (1964). General works on constitutionalism which throw light on the American Federal Constitution include: C. K. Allen, *Law in the Making* (6th ed., 1958); Walter Bagehot, *The English Constitution* (rev. ed., 1927); Charles Borgeaud, *Adoption and Amendment of Constitutions in Europe and America* (trans. Charles D. Hazen, 1895); A. V. Dicey, *The Law of the Constitution* (8th ed., 1927); Charles H. McIlwain, *Constitutionalism, Ancient and Modern* (rev. ed., 1958) and *The High Court of Parliament and its Supremacy* (1910); Sir Henry Maine, *Ancient Law* (1861; 1931).

A handbook of facts about the framing of the Federal Constitution is Broadus and Louise P. Mitchell, *A Biography of the Constitution of the United States* (1964; Galaxy Paperback). Charles Warren's *The Making of the Constitution* (1937) still has not been superseded as a guide to the interrelations of the happenings in the Philadelphia convention and the public reactions outside. Other useful items which illustrate the range of scholarship and of points of view are: Charles A. Beard, *An Economic Interpretation of the Constitution of the United States* (1913); W. W. Crosskey, *Politics and the Constitution in the History of the United States* (2 vols., 1953), a perverse and devious, but ingenious, argument that the Founding Fathers envisaged a government similar to that of the New Deal of President Franklin D. Roosevelt; Max Farrand, "Compromises of the Constitution," *AHR*, IX (April, 1904), 479–89 and *The Framing of the Constitution* (1913); Sydney George Fisher, *The Evolution of the Constitution of the United States* (1897); Walton Hamilton and Douglass Adair, *The Power to Govern* (1937); James Hart, *The American Presidency in Action, 1789* (1948); Forrest McDonald, *We the People: the Economic Origins of the Constitu-*

tion (1958), an invaluable guide to economic life in the era of the framing; Conyers Read, ed., *The Constitution Reconsidered* (1938), a collection of suggestive essays; Charles Page Smith, *James Wilson, Founding Father* (1956); Carl Van Doren, *The Great Rehearsal* (1948),

On the development of judicial review and the changing interpretations of the Federal Constitution, see: Charles A. Beard, *The Supreme Court and the Constitution* (1922); Albert J. Beveridge, *The Life of John Marshall* (4 vols., 1916–19); Louis Boudin, *Government by Judiciary* (2 vols., 1932), a Marxist interpretation; Edward S. Corwin, *The Doctrine of Judicial Review and Other Essays* (1914) and *The "Higher Law" Background of American Constitutional Law* (1929; Great Seal Paperback); C. G. Haines, *The American Doctrine of Judicial Supremacy* (1932); Homer C. Hockett, *The Constitutional History of the United States* (2 vols., Vol. I, 1776–1826, Vol. II, 1826–1876; 1939); Robert G. McCloskey, *The American Supreme Court* (1959); James S. Smith, *Freedom's Fetters: the Alien and Sedition Laws and American Civil Liberties* (1956); James B. Thayer, "The Origin and Scope of the American Doctrine of Constitutional Law," in *Legal Essays* (1908); Charles Warren, *The Supreme Court in United States History* (2 vols., rev. ed., 1937), on the relation of the Court's work to the currents of opinion in American society, and *Congress, the Constitution, and the Supreme Court* (1930).

Essential contemporary documents will be found in: Jonathan Elliot, ed., *The Debates in the Several State Conventions on the Adoption of the Federal Constitution* (4 vols., 1843–45; 2d ed., 5 vols., 1861); Max Farrand, ed., *The Records of the Federal Convention of 1787* (rev. ed., 4 vols., 1937); Peter Force, comp., *American Archives* (9 vols., 1837–53); Alexander Hamilton, James Madison, and

John Jay, *The Federalist* (ed. Benjamin F. Wright, 1961, and numerous other editions); U. S. Lib. of Cong., Leg. Ref. Service, *The Constitution of the United States (Annotated)* (1938, and later eds.).

On the constitutional problems of expansion, especially in relation to land policy, see Bibliographical Notes for Book II, Part Five, above. Items not mentioned there, or which are peculiarly relevant to the problems of an expansive federalism and constitution-making for new territories are: T. P. Abernethy, *Western Lands and the American Revolution* (1937); Charles Abrams, *Revolution in Land* (1939); Douglass Adair, "'That Politics May be Reduced to a Science': David Hume, James Madison, and the Tenth Federalist," *Huntington Lib. Q.*, XX (Aug., 1957), 343–60; Beverley W. Bond, Jr., "Some Political Ideals of the Colonial Period as They Were Realized in the Old Northwest," in *Essays in Colonial History Presented to Charles McLean Andrews* . . . (1931), pp. 299–325; Vernon Carstensen, ed., *The Public Lands* (1963); Max Farrand, *The Legislation of Congress for the Government of the Organized Territories of the United States, 1789–1895* (1896); Amelia C. Ford, *Colonial Precedents of Our National Land System as it Existed in 1800* (1910); John D. Hicks, "The Constitutions of the Northwest States," Univ. Neb., *Univ. Studies*, XXIII (Jan.–April, 1923), 1–162; William T. Hutchinson, "Unite to Divide; Divide to Unite: The Shaping of American Federalism," *MVHR*, XLVI (June, 1959), 3–18, a seminal article to which I am much indebted; Merrill Jensen, "The Creation of the National Domain, 1781–1784," *MVHR*, XXVI (Dec., 1939), 323–42; Jesse Macy, "Institutional Beginnings in a Western State [Iowa]," J.H.U., *Studies in Hist. & Pol. Sci.*, II (July, 1884), 53–8; William D. Pattison, *Beginnings of the American Rectangular Land Survey System, 1784–1800* (Dept. of Geography, U. of Chicago, 1947); Francis S. Philbrick, ed., *The Laws of Indiana Territory, 1801–1809* (Vol. XXI of Ill. State Hist. Lib., *Pub.*; 1930) and *The Laws of Illinois Territory, 1809–1818* (Vol. XXV, 1950), with valuable introductions; Earl S. Pomeroy, *The Territories and the United States, 1861–1890* (1947); Report on a bill "providing for the admission of the State of Dakota . . . and for the organization of the Territory of North Dakota," U. S., 49th Cong., 1st sess., *Senate Reports,* No. 15; Roy M. Robbins, *Our Landed Heritage: The Public Domain, 1776–1936* (1942); Aaron M. Sakolski, *The Great American Land Bubble* (1932); Charles W. Spencer, "The Land System of Colonial New York," N.Y. Soc. of Hist., *Proc.,* XVI (1917); Payson J. Treat, *The National Land System: 1785–1820* (1910); Donald F. Warner, *The Idea of Continental Union* (1960); Raynor G. Wellington, *The Political and Sectional Influence of the Public Lands, 1828–42* (1914). The basic collection of documents is Clarence E. Carter, ed., *The Territorial Papers of the United States* (26 vols., to date; 1934——).

The literature on the development of American political parties is vast. There is no better introduction to their peculiar role in the national history than Herbert Agar, *The Price of Union* (1950); a useful survey of the parties themselves is W. E. Binkley, *American Political Parties: Their Natural History* (1943). Other items of special interest include: Charles A. Beard, *Economic Origins of Jeffersonian Democracy* (1943); William B. Brown, *The People's Choice: The Presidential Image in the Campaign Biography* (1960); Joseph Charles, *The Origins of the American Party System* (1956), a brilliant brief essay with the thesis that early American parties emerged primarily from disagreements on foreign policy; James S. Chase, "The Emergence of the National Nominating Convention," un-published Ph.D. dissertation (Dept. of History, U. of Chicago, 1962), and "Jacksonian Democracy and the Rise of the Nominating Convention," *Mid-America,* XLV, 229–249; James Fenimore Cooper, *The American Democrat* (1838; intro. H. L. Mencken, 1931), a hostile critique; Noble E. Cunningham, *The Jeffersonian Republicans* (1957) and *The Jeffersonian Republicans in Power* (1963), throwing new light on the varying relation between local and national party organizations, to which I am especially indebted; Peter F. Drucker, "A Key to American Politics: Calhoun's Pluralism," *Rev. of Pol.,* X (Oct., 1948), 412–26; Henry Jones Ford, *The Rise and Growth of American Politics* (1898); Robert G. Gunderson, *The Log-Cabin Campaign* (1957), full of vivid detail on the emergence of modern campaigning techniques in the presidential election of 1840; George D. Luetscher, *Early Political Machinery in the United States* (1903); George A. Lipsky, *John Quincy Adams: His Theory and Ideas* (1950); Marvin Meyers, *The Jacksonian Persuasion: Politics and Belief* (1957; Vintage Paperback); Arthur M. Schlesinger, Jr., *The Age of Jackson* (1945; Little Brown Paperback); Glyndon G. Van Deusen, *The Jacksonian Era, 1828–1848* (1959); Charles M. Wiltse, *The Jeffersonian Tradition in American Democracy* (1960).

Items especially illustrative of the flexibility of institutions under the Constitution are: Felix Gilbert, *To the Farewell Address: Ideas of Early American Foreign Policy* (1961); George B. Galloway, *History of the House of Representatives* (1961); George Y. Haynes, *The Senate of the United States: Its History and Practice* (2 vols., 1938); Leonard D. White, *The Federalists* (1948), *The Jeffersonians* (1951), and *The Jacksonians* (1954), pioneer studies in administrative history.

INDEX

Daniel J. Boorstin is the Librarian of Congress. He has been senior historian of the Smithsonian Institution, Washington, D.C., director of The National Museum of History and Technology and Preston and Sterling Morton Distinguished Service Professor of American History at the University of Chicago where he taught for twenty-five years.

Dr. Boorstin has spent a good deal of his life viewing America from the outside, first in England where he was a Rhodes Scholar at Balliol College, Oxford, winning a coveted "double-first." More recently he has been visiting professor of American History at the University of Rome and at Kyoto University, consultant to the Social Science Research Center at the University of Puerto Rico, the first incumbent of the chair of American History at the Sorbonne, and Pitt Professor of American History and Institutions and a Fellow of Trinity College, Cambridge University, which awarded him its Litt.D. degree.